The Palgrave Handbook of Critical Human Resource Development

Joshua C. Collins · Jamie L. Callahan
Editors

The Palgrave Handbook of Critical Human Resource Development

Editors
Joshua C. Collins
University of Minnesota-Twin Cities
Minneapolis, MN, USA

Jamie L. Callahan
Durham University Business School
Millhill Lane, Durham, UK

ISBN 978-3-031-10452-7   ISBN 978-3-031-10453-4   (eBook)
https://doi.org/10.1007/978-3-031-10453-4

Cover credit: smartboy10/Getty Images

This Palgrave Macmillan imprint is published by the registered company Springer Nature Switzerland AG
The registered company address is: Gewerbestrasse 11, 6330 Cham, Switzerland

CONTENTS

Notes on Contributors

Eniola A. Aderibigbe is an SHRM Senior Certified Professional and Ph.D. candidate in the Human Resource Development program in the Department of Organizational Leadership, Policy, and Development at the University of Minnesota. Originally from Lagos, Nigeria, she earned her bachelor's degree in Industrial Relations and Personnel Management at the University of Lagos, Nigeria, and her master's degree in Human Resource Management and Industrial Relations at the Carlson School of Management at the University of Minnesota. She previously held several HR roles providing strategic HR support to different organizations internationally. Her research interest areas include learning and development; diversity, equity, and inclusion in HRD; leadership; critical HRD, and National HRD.

Kenneth R. Bartlett, Ph.D. is Professor of Human Resource Development and Chair of the Department of Organizational Leadership, Policy, and Development at the University of Minnesota. Originally from Christchurch, New Zealand he previously worked in a variety of management positions in the public sector and tourism industry in both New Zealand and the United States. He holds a Bachelor of Parks and Recreation Management from Lincoln University in New Zealand, M.Sc. in Leisure Studies, and Ph.D. in human resource development from the University of Illinois at Urbana-Champaign. Prior to his academic career, he worked in a variety of recreation management and outdoor education positions. His research agenda is focused on the process and outcomes of human resource development and leadership development. He has considerable international experience as a consultant and adviser with organizations across the United States as well as with educational institutions, not-for-profits, and government agencies in over 40 counties.

Lisa Baumgartner is Professor of Adult Education. Her research interests include learning and development in marginalized populations including those living with chronic illnesses, women, and older adults. She won the

Cyril O. Houle Award for Outstanding Literature in Adult Education for her co-authored text Learning in Adulthood: A Comprehensive Guide (3rd and 4th editions) with Jossey-Bass.

Judith D. Bernier, Ed.D. is an associate teaching professor and director of the Center for Labor Studies and Research at Florida International University. Her publications include topics on critical race theory, career mobility, and critical issues of equity and social justice within and outside organizations.

Laura L. Bierema is Professor and Program Coordinator of the Adult Learning, Leadership, and Organization Development program at the University of Georgia where she is the Founder and Co-director of the Graduate Certificate in Organization Coaching. Her research focuses on applying critical, feminist lenses to leadership, women's learning and career development, organization development, and developmental relationships. She is the author of 9 books, over 100 chapters and articles, and the recipient of multiple awards for her scholarship and contributions.

Jeremy Bohonos Texas State University, San Marcos, Texas, USA is an Assistant Professor of Adult Education, Assistant Editor for New Horizons in Adult Education and Human Resource Development, and Chair of the Academy of Human Resource Development Critical HRD & Social Justice Perspectives Special Interest Group. His research focuses on organizational (in)justice with a special emphasis on race and racism in the workforce. He has published in journals including Adult Education Quarterly Advances in Developing Human Resources, Adult Learning, and New Horizons in Adult Education and HRD.

Joseph C. Brenes-Dawsey holds a Ph.D. in Learning, Leadership, and Organization Development from the University of Georgia. His research interests include emotions and the management of emotions, particularly emotion work and emotional labor, in higher education and other organizational settings. He is currently a librarian at Piedmont University in Demorest, Georgia.

Dr. Deborah N. Brewis is Senior Lecturer in Management, Strategy, and Organisation at the University of Bath. Her research focuses on critical diversity studies, creative methodologies for management research and learning, and digital labor.

Jamie L. Callahan, Ed.D., Ph.D. is Professor of Organisation and Ethics at Durham University Business School, UK. She is the former Editor of *Human Resource Development Review* and current Co-Editor of *International Journal of Management Reviews*, She has earned numerous research awards, including the inaugural Laura Bierema Excellence in Critical HRD Award, Scholar of the Year Award, and Outstanding Book of the Year Award. Her research addresses issues of power and privilege in organized contexts, leading her to explore marginalized groups' experiences of leadership, learning, and organizational transformation. Her particular passion is championing gender equity.

Joshua C. Collins, Ed.D. is Associate Professor of HRD in the Department of Organizational Leadership, Policy, and Development at the University of Minnesota-Twin Cities. His research seeks to interrogate learning, development, and change in organizational settings with a focus on the experiences of racial, ethnic, gender, and sexual minorities. He has won several awards for his research including the Academy of HRD's Early Career Scholar and Laura Bierema Excellence in Critical HRD awards.

Oliver S. Crocco is Assistant Professor of Leadership and Human Resource Development at Louisiana State University. He holds graduate degrees in Human and Organizational Learning from George Washington University and Human Development and Psychology from Harvard University. After living in Thailand for four years beginning in 2009, he has remained active throughout the region conducting research, teaching, and giving presentations. His research focuses on HRD in Southeast Asia, a global mindset in university and work contexts, adult development, and learning experience design.

Maria Cseh is Associate Professor in Human and Organizational Learning (HOL), and Director of the HOL Doctoral Program at The George Washington University. She holds graduate degrees in electronics engineering, and business administration with a focus on international management, a certificate in global policy studies, and a Ph.D. in adult education with a specialization in global human resource development. Her research interests include informal learning, organizational development and change, global leadership, and the development of a global mindset and cultural competence that will help leaders and change agents address the increasingly complex issues facing our world.

Dr. Carole J. Elliott is Professor of Organisation Studies, and Associate Dean for Equality, Diversity, Inclusion, and Development at Sheffield University Management School, UK. She is a former editor-in-chief of Human Resource Development International, and is currently Associate Editor of *Gender, Work and Organization*. In 2021 Carole was the recipient of the Laura Bierema Excellence in Critical HRD Award, and she was elected to the British Academy of Management's College of Fellows. In 2022 she became a Fellow of the Royal Society of Arts. Her research interests are interdisciplinary and broadly lie in the field of Critical HRD, and management and leadership learning.

Dr. Tomika W. Greer is Assistant Professor and Undergraduate Program Coordinator of Human Resource Development at the University of Houston in Houston, Texas. Previously, Dr. Greer worked as a management consultant and training & development professional in several organizations. She conducts and publishes research related to career development, including (1) education/training, (2) career transitions, and (3) work–life integration for women and marginalized groups. Her research is published in peer-reviewed journals, including *Human Resource Development Review, New Horizons in Adult Education and Human Resource Development, Advances in Developing*

Human Resources, and *New Directions in Adult and Continuing Education*. Dr. Greer earned a bachelor's degree in Chemical Engineering, a master's degree in Instructional Technology, and a Ph.D. in Human Resource Development. She has won awards for excellence in her research, teaching, and service to women.

Dr. Robin S. Grenier is Professor of Adult Learning in the Neag School of Education at the University of Connecticut. Her research focuses on informal and experiential learning, learning in cultural institutions, and qualitative inquiry. She was a 2-term Board Member for the Academy of Human Resource Development and in 2014 was awarded a Fulbright to teach and conduct research at the University of Iceland.

Weixin He is a Ph.D. student in Learning, Leadership, and Organization Development at the University of Georgia. Her research interests include human resource development, women studies, life-long learning, and leadership. She holds a bachelor's degree from Nanchang University in China and a master's degree from the University of Sydney, Australia.

Sherman T. Henry, M.S. is a program manager at Morehouse College, Advancing Black Strategists Initiative. His publications include topics on critical race theory, labor studies, and inclusive issues of equity in organizational culture and leadership.

Jessica Hinshaw is a Doctoral Student of Human and Organizational Learning at the George Washington University. She also holds a Master of Public Health degree from Vanderbilt University. Before starting her doctoral studies, Jessica worked for years as a participatory evaluator of community-based and maternal health initiatives in Nicaragua and the United States. Jessica's research interests include community engagement through participatory action research and learning within sustainable development and climate resilience initiatives.

E. Paulette Isaac-Savage is a professor of adult education at the University of MO-St. Louis. She served as co-editor of *Adult Learning* and is on the editorial review board for Education and Urban Society, *Adult Learning*, *Adult Education Quarterly*, and *New Horizons in Adult and Human Resource Development*. She is president-elect of the American Association for Adult and Continuing Education and a member of the International Adult and Continuing Education Hall of Fame.

Kristi Kaeppel, Ph.D. is a learning designer at Brown University in Providence, Rhode Island. Kristi's work focuses on designing, delivering, and investigating inclusive, transformative learning experiences. Her research interests include teaching and learning methods in higher education, critical thinking, metacognition, and women's friendships in the workplace.

Dr. Amir Keshtiban is the Head of Program, Business at York St John University London Campus. He has his Ph.D. in Management Studies from the University of Essex. His research is focused on alternative forms of organization, critical leadership studies, social movement studies, and prefigurative politics. Prior to joining York St John, Amir was a senior lecturer at Northumbria University; he taught at Essex Business School for four years while pursuing his Master of Research and Ph.D.

Chang-kyu Kwon, Ph.D. is an assistant professor of Human Resource Development in the Department of Education Policy, Organization, and Leadership at the University of Illinois at Urbana-Champaign. His scholarship focuses on diversity and inclusion with particular emphasis on disability. Specifically, his work addresses ableism as it intersects with other power structures in various educational and work settings so that people with disabilities are provided with conditions where they can fully demonstrate what they are capable of and thrive in the world of work. He is the recipient of the Academy of Human Resource Development's 2022 Richard A. Swanson Research Excellence Award and the 2019 Cutting Edge Award.

Chelesea Lewellen, Southern Illinois University, Carbondale, Illinois, USA is a Ph.D. student in Educational Administration and Higher Education at Southern Illinois University. Her research interests focus on Black Feminist Thought, Critical Race Theory, and Intersectionality. Chelesea is passionate about diversity, inclusion, engagement, equity, and social justice. She deeply believes in the value of student-centered education, continued education and collaboration, and the transformative power of mentoring.

Ciarán McFadden is a lecturer in Human Resource Management and Organizational Behavior at the Business School at Edinburgh Napier University. He researches and teaches equality, diversity and inclusion, human resource development, and labor relations. His work focuses on the careers and workplace experiences of LGBTQ+ employees, hiring/labor market discrimination, and diversity and inclusion initiatives in the workplace.

Robert C. Mizzi is the Canada Research Chair in Queer, Community and Diversity Education and Associate Professor in the Faculty of Education at the University of Manitoba, Canada. He has over 200 publications and presentations, including articles published in the *Journal of Homosexuality* and the *Journal of Studies in International Education*. He has also published five books, including *The Handbook of Adult and Continuing Education* in 2020. He is President Emeritus of the Canadian Association of Adult Education and is Editor Emeritus of the Canadian Journal for the Study of Adult Education.

Catherine H. Monaghan is Associate Professor Emeritus at Cleveland State University in the graduate program of Adult Learning and Development. In retirement, she continues to teach online classes and mentor students at both the masters and doctoral level. She continues to present and publish in the field in areas related to human resource development, diversity, inclusion, and equity, communities of practice, and leadership.

Aliki Nicolaides, Ed.D. is Associate Professor of Adult Learning and Leadership at the University of Georgia in the program of Learning, Leadership & Organization Development. She seeks to optimize vital developmental conditions for self and society to learn and evolve. Dr. Nicolaides is a founding steward and current Director of the International Transformative Learning Association.

Dr. Rose Opengart serves as Adjunct Faculty at Texas A&M University, and has taught both HRM and HRD classes at several universities. Her research has focused primarily on career development/elements of career success, emotions, and women in the workplace. Dr. Opengart holds professional certification in Human Resource Management and is a Career Coach.

Dr. April L. Peters is Associate Professor of Professional K-12 Leadership and Associate Department Chair at the University of Houston in Houston, Texas. Dr. Peters has worked in the K-12 context as a middle school teacher, a school social worker, Dean of students, and high school principal. In addition, Dr. Peters served four years as a consultant in the Atlanta Public Schools, providing professional learning and support to small school reform leaders. Dr. Peters is passionate about equity and social justice for the most vulnerable populations of students. Her research interests include: (a) women in school leadership; (b) mentoring and support for early career administrators; (c) urban schooling; and (d) leadership and small school reform. She has published in *Teachers' College Record*, *The Journal of School Leadership*, *International Journal of Qualitative Studies in Education*, *Educational Administration Quarterly*, and others.

Esther Pippins Texas State University, San Marcos, Texas, USA is a Ph.D. student in Adult, Professional, and Community Education at Texas State University. Her research interests focus on Intergenerational Learning, Dialogic Learning, Critical Reflection, and Transformative Learning situated in Critical Race Theory, and Black Feminist Thought. As a researcher, she hopes to add to scholarship that highlights Black women's ways of knowing, family literacies, and the experiential learning of nontraditional students. As a practitioner, she values instructional approaches that provide adult learners with challenging, engaging, empowering, and equitable educational experiences.

Greg Procknow is a first-year Ph.D. student in Critical Disability Studies who has published two books and articles in top journals in human resource development, adult education, and qualitative methods. His work focuses on mad studies, cultural pedagogy, and recruitment and training.

Tonette S. Rocco is a professor in adult education and human resource development at Florida International University in Miami, Florida. She co-edited the 2020 *Handbook of Adult and Continuing Education* (Rocco,

Smith, Mizzi, Merriweather & Hawley, 2020), and *The Handbook of HRD* (Chalofsky, Rocco, and Morris 2014). She is the Editor-in-Chief of *New Horizons in Adult Education and Human Resource Development*.

Eunbi Sim is a Ph.D. student of Learning, Leadership, and Organization Development (LLOD) at the University of Georgia. Her research interests include critical human resource development, intersectionality, and data mining. Her research focuses on intersectional, transnational feminist intervention in workplaces and higher education and the prediction of employee oppression and discrimination.

Matthew Sinnicks is an Associate Professor of Human Resource Management and Organisational Behaviour at University of Southampton. He received his Ph.D. in philosophy from the University of Hertfordshire. His research interests include flourishing and alienation in the workplace, the ethical quality of market society, virtue ethics in business and organizations, and the work of Alasdair MacIntyre. His work has appeared in journals such as *Business Ethics Quarterly*, *Journal of Business Ethics, and Business & Society*.

Stephanie Sisco, Ph.D. is an assistant professor at the University of Minnesota–Twin Cities in the Department of Organizational Leadership, Policy, and Development. Her areas of interest include diversity management, social and participatory learning, and race-conscious equity and social justice. Dr. Sisco explores these topics through qualitative methods to identify and examine business practices and organizational cultures that negatively influence the employability, experience, and advancement of racial minorities. Dr. Sisco also teaches courses and develops curricula for Business & Marketing Education, Human Resource Development, and Adult Education programs at the University of Minnesota–Twin Cities.

Dr. Karen E. Watkins is Professor of Learning, Leadership, and Organizational Development in the College of Education at The University of Georgia. Karen's scholarly interests include organizational learning assessment, informal and incidental learning, action research, and action science. She is currently on the Board of Trustees of the Geneva Learning Foundation in Switzerland.

Dr. Emily Yarrow is a senior lecturer in Management and Organisations, in the Leadership, Work and Organisation Subject Group at Newcastle University Business School. She is also Fellow of the Higher Education Academy. Emily's scholarly work focuses on and contributes to contemporary understandings of gendered organizational behavior, women's experiences of organizational life, and the future of work. Her research interests broadly include organizational theory, gender and inequality regimes, impact, and governance in higher education. She has contributed to leading journals including *Gender, Work and Organization; Work, Employment and Society; The British Educational Research Journal*, and *Academy of Management Learning and Education*. Emily is an

Editorial Review Board Member of *Gender, Work and Organization*; *Work Employment and Society*; and *Group & Organization Management*.

Jill Zarestky is an associate professor in the Adult Education and Training program at the Colorado State University School of Education. Her research interests include informal, nonformal, and community-based education, particularly in international and STEM-based contexts, with funding from the National Science Foundation and the U.S. Department of Agriculture. Zarestky was the 2019 recipient of the CPAE Early Career Award and the 2020 recipient of the University Council for Workforce and Human Resource Education Assistant Professor Award. She served as Secretary of AAACE from 2014 to 2018 and currently serves as an assistant editor for the journal New Horizons in Adult Education and Human Resource Development.

The Kintsugi Collective is a collective of people working in business schools in the UK, Denmark, and France. The members who have authorship of this chapter include (our members are always listed randomly): Tali Padan, Copenhagen Business School; Tony Wall, Liverpool Business School; Jamie Callahan, Durham University Business School; Sarah Robinson, Rennes School of Business; Maribel Blasco, Copenhagen Business School; Carole Elliott, Sheffield University Management School; and Annemette Kjaergaard, Copenhagen Business School. As a collective, we want to embrace the spirit of kintsugi in work—"ultimately to guide shadows to beauty's ends."

LIST OF FIGURES

LIST OF TABLES

PART I

Introduction

CHAPTER 1

Critical and Social Justice Perspectives in HRD

Joshua C. Collins and Jamie L. Callahan

Over the last two decades, we have witnessed a significantly increased interest in critical and social justice perspectives among students, scholars, and practitioners of Human Resource Development (HRD). We believe that this increased interest has been fueled by a multitude of factors including but not limited to a shift in generational dynamics, movements for social change such as Black Lives Matter and the rights of transgender people, response to the rise of oppressive populist political leaders around the world, and wider recognition of the ways in which the personal and the professional are often interconnected and inseparable.

With this recognition have come many changes in the field of HRD. Most literature addressing critical and social justice perspectives in HRD emerged after Fenwick (2004) challenged the field to be more critical in an issue of *Adult Education Quarterly*. Additional early works were primarily been published in either *Human Resource Development International* (e.g., Callahan, 2007; Fenwick, 2005; Lawless et al., 2012) or the *Journal of European Industrial Training* (e.g., Holden & Griggs, 2010; Trehan & Rigg, 2011). In 2014, an issue of *Advances in Developing Human Resources* (Gedro,

J. C. Collins (✉)
University of Minnesota-Twin Cities, Minneapolis, MN, USA
e-mail: collinsj@umn.edu

J. L. Callahan
Durham University Business School, Durham, UK
e-mail: jamie.callahan@durham.ac.uk

Collins, & Rocco) was dedicated to exploring critical perspectives in the field. This issue has gained great traction since being published, logging hundreds of citations and joining Rigg, Stewart, and Trehan (2007) as a comprehensive foundational critical HRD (CHRD) text.

In 2015, the field ushered in the inaugural granting of the Laura Bierema Excellence in Critical HRD Award given by the Academy of HRD on an annual basis, further increasing the profile of critical perspectives in HRD. In 2020, after the murder of George Floyd in Minneapolis, Minnesota, USA, sparked global protest against the forces of anti-Blackness and white supremacy, the Academy of HRD took further steps to establish a permanent Antiracism Committee, complete with a policy stipulating ongoing represen- tation on the Board of Directors. Still, there is often a lack of understanding regarding what it "means" to be a CHRD scholar or to maintain a concern for/with social justice in the field of HRD. Byrd (2018) defined social injustice as "the repression of a person's individual and civil rights which in the process could hinder their capacity to achieve full potential to learn and perform (Byrd 2014a)" (p. 3). Byrd added: "A social injustice can be either an overt or covert act or behaviour that is intended to demean or degrade by calling attention to the person's social identity, or to emphasize and remind the person of their marginalized location in society" (2018, p. 3). Finally, Byrd (2018) defined social justice as "a democratic, participatory, inclusive process and vision" (pp. 7–8) which demands diversity, equity, and inclusion of all. This hand- book fills a need in the discipline of HRD for an expansive text introducing, explaining, and advancing CHRD with an eye toward social justice. This hand- book is distinguished by its perspective on HRD that does not prioritize the neoliberal focus primarily on productivity and performance. Instead, CHRD seeks to critique dominant paradigms related to what the field can and should be doing to advance human development.

Critical Human Resource Development aims to challenge the normative structures, practices, policies, definitions, and approaches that have historically dominated the field of HRD. As an approach to HRD, CHRD raises awareness of social systems, organizational policies and practices, and research paradigms that silence new ways of knowing and understanding, while advancing under- represented and emerging approaches. Through an analysis of power and privilege, morality and ethics, and ideology and context, CHRD situates diver- sity, equity, inclusion, social justice, and resistance as a path forward in a rapidly-changing global society. The purpose of this first-ever *Handbook of Critical Human Resource Development* is to provide an expansive exploration of critical theory, critical perspectives, critical praxis, and the impact on the research, theory, and practice of HRD. To help set the stage in this opening chapter, we begin with the question: *"In whose interest should HRD serve?"* (Callahan, 2007).

In Whose Interest Should HRD Serve?

Within CHRD, stakeholders are generally understood to include "customers, employees, suppliers, and citizens" who actively participate and are affected by "policy development and oversight" within or as a result of an organization (Bierema, 2009, p. 76). Stakeholders may be any person or group of people who will be impacted by an organization's decisions, actions, vision, or mission. The stakeholder orientation implies the capacity of HRD to impact individuals, organizations, and communities, and it is foundational to advancing critical and social justice perspectives in the field. Whether the impact is planned, unplanned, reactionary, positive, neutral, or negative hinges on an organization's view of their relationship to and with society. In addition, the stakeholder orientation recognizes HRD's position as an intermediary between management and employees, but instead of merely favoring the objectives of management, an inclusive stakeholder approach is ideally capable of balancing the desires of multiple stakeholders while also tending to the needs of the most vulnerable. Pursuant to this understanding, the stakeholder orientation stands in direct opposition to the more traditional and dominant "stockholder orientation that is performative, placing value on economics and performance, only considering social responsibility when it is profitable or required by law" (Bierema, 2009, p. 75).

The stockholder orientation draws its strength by depending on capitalistic conceptions of power. These conceptions of power as a zero-sum game can be plainly seen in the prevalence of hierarchical organizational structures, in politics, and even in pop culture. The boss has the final say, one President moves out while another moves in, and the rise of a talented new artist must surely mean the demise or irrelevance of another. And yet, power may also be consolidated. Sometimes, the consolidation of power can lead to more equitable and just outcomes for the collective, such as through labor unions or employee resource groups, and other times, it can lead to furthered entrenchment within exploitative systems, such as through certain mergers and acquisitions which can leave workers displaced, under-supported, or even unemployed.

Han et al. (2017) discussed the historical evolution of HRD in three waves. In the first wave, "defining HRD centered around the distinction of HRD focus on learning or performance" (p. 297). The impacts of this first wave can still be seen in the contemporary study and practice of HRD, through the propagation of such popular concepts as employee engagement. Depending on the perspective a person chooses to take, employee engagement can be about individual learning, development, and growth and how systems either support or discourage that growth and the individual's well-being, or it can be about maximizing systems and resources to improve and encourage performance to the benefit of the organization. In the second wave, "HRD shifted its primary focus from individuals to the organization" (Han et al, 2017, p. 297). This wave is evidenced by the prominence of and continued interest in such aspects of HRD as strategic HRD, the idea of the learning organization, and organization development and change, all of which tend to emphasize the importance of the organizational mission, vision, and values over that of the individual. Finally, in the third wave, HRD has seen "the expansion of the postmodern identity, covering human development, ethics, and corporate social responsibility" (Han et al, 2017, p. 298). It is in this wave when critical perspectives became more prominent within HRD, primarily through the introduction of research which explicitly highlighted the importance of individual social identities, as well as individual values, in understanding the experience of work and organizations. To more fully understand the contributions of each of these waves to our overall understanding of HRD as it is now, it is also important to discuss the ways in which the relationship between HRD and organizations has been framed.

Sambrook (2000) described a typology of three types of relationships between HRD and organizations: tell (training and development) in which "organizational strategy is determined by senior managers, following a linear model, and then told, or communicated to other employees" (p. 168), sell (component HRD) in which "the focus is on a component and efficient approach to learning interventions at a tactical level within the organization" which may or may not be "explicitly linked to corporate needs and future requirements" (p. 169), and gel (strategic HRD) in which "the HRD function is concerned with nurturing learning within work activities, encouraging greater individual responsibility and the sharing of learning, and helping line managers create a learning climate, culture or environment" (p. 170). While some may view HRD, with its focus on human development, performance, and learning, as a more naturally critical discipline, traditionally HRD functions as an intermediary between organizations and employees. While HRD processes may seek to develop employees on an individual basis, it is usually in order to serve organizational objectives such as productivity, profitability, and efficiency. Collins and Chlup (2014) stated:

> Given that workplaces exist for organizational objectives, such as creating shareholder value and maximizing profits, we recognize that for HRD practitioners there may be a disconnect between supporting and implementing such objectives while also maintaining a social justice [or critical] perspective. (p. 483)

Obviously, HRD's position as an intermediary between organizations and employees can complicate the work of those who view HRD in a more critical manner. Critical HRD responds to traditions and histories within HRD by emphasizing the importance of treating all organizational stakeholders as fundamental building blocks to organizational success, while also promoting a "whole person" approach that allows for individual development which may or may not directly impact the organization but enhances the overall wellbeing of the employee. It is therefore the responsibility of HRD to serve the interests of everyone who is impacted by what an organization does, or what is done in a space of organizing, while tending to the needs of the most vulnerable and underrepresented first. Because of this, and as is discussed in many chapters throughout this handbook, many critical theories and perspectives emphasize individual narratives and storytelling as useful tools for disseminating knowledge that challenges or critiques the status quo.

EDITORS' NARRATIVES: WHY ARE WE CRITICAL?

We signed the contract to edit this handbook and invited authors in March 2020. Crafting the first-ever expansive resource for the study of Critical HRD at a time that exactly coincided with a pandemic, challenges with caregiving and schooling, wide-scale economic hardship, contentious political elections, attempts to usurp democratic governmental processes, overt public racial injustices, mass shootings, and the cascading social, physical, emotional, and psychological effects presented many challenges. We lost authors and chapters along the way due to the crushing weight of it all. But we gained other authors and co-authors as we leaned on each other to continue getting the work done. We wish all who were, at any time, involved with this project a heartfelt thank you for your continued dedication to advancing CHRD. Relationships and relational skills got this handbook across the finish line despite challenges. As the editors, we are in awe of the ways we have witnessed the power of individual experience and narrative to shape the context of our work over these last two years. In the next section, we present our narratives, as editors, focusing on the principal question: *Why are we critical?*

Joshua's Narrative: Self-Discovery, Validation, and Liberation Through Critical HRD

I entered the field of HRD at a particularly vulnerable moment in my own development and self-discovery. As I was completing my undergraduate studies at Texas A&M University, I had a very loose idea of what I wanted to do. I knew that I had skill sets in verbal and written communication. I had been working as a graphic designer for nearly five years, and I also knew that I did not want to continue with that work but that I was often most engaged with my work when I had the ability to be creative. I had always been interested in corporate life and how business is conducted, particularly how people communicate or cooperate—or do not—across differences in the workplace. These factors drew me to apply to the master's program in HRD at Texas A&M.

As I was leaving my previous job as a graphic designer to begin graduate school, a member of executive leadership asked me to go to lunch as a thank you for my years of service. Of course, I agreed. While at this lunch, among many other topics of conversation, the executive leader expressed to me that he had been surprised I succeeded in the organization for as long as I did because I was "fru fru." This took me completely off guard for a number of reasons. First, I felt immediately that it was inappropriate for anybody to say such a thing in any context at any time, let alone at work. Second, the statement clearly alluded to a perception that this executive leader held about my sexual orientation. While the perception was ultimately correct, I was not yet out as gay—not even to myself. This experience shaped the spirit with which I entered my graduate studies in HRD. In entering the field, I hoped I would find ways to help create organizational cultures where no one else would have this kind of experience, and I also sensed that it was time for me to learn more about myself and to find ways to live my truth.

From the beginning of my time in the field, I did not see studying organizational systems and individual experiences as separate areas of interest. My vantage point allowed me to clearly see many of the ways in which systems matter and that individuals interact with systems in particular ways based on who they are. In one of my earliest graduate courses in HRD, the professor (who happens to be my co-editor for this handbook) came into class one evening fired up about an article that had been recently published in one of the HRD journals. The article in question had discussed sex work(ers) in an international context in a manner that the professor and several of her colleagues felt was exploitative and lacked a feminist analysis (Storberg-Walker et al., 2010). She had printed the article out for us to read and to reflect on its implications as it related to the topic of the course (training and development). As I flipped through the article, I was honestly shocked. This was the first moment when I began to see the many ways in which the field of HRD lacked critical voices. My assumption had been that HRD would be a field that would be leading in the space of diversity, equity, inclusion, and treating people with dignity and respect. What I saw at this moment was how much work remained to be done.

As I began to read the work of the few critical scholars at that time—people such as Laura Bierema, Tonette Rocco, and many of the other scholars whose work appears or is cited in this handbook—I started to realize that this was where I could make a difference, at first primarily around lesbian, gay, bisexual, transgender, and queer (LGBTQ+) issues which were vastly understudied in the field. I began taking graduate courses in women's and gender studies as well, to better inform my perspectives and my learning. Today, I would say I am critical because once my eyes were opened to injustices faced by those who do not hold the same privileges that I do, I could not unsee those injustices and would not wish to. Seeing the deep unfairness that seemed to seep from society, to communities, and into organizations did not sit well with me, but I was still simultaneously working through my own development.

One summer, I had the opportunity to take a course about women in education with Mary Alfred. I believe there were about 20 students in the course. At the time, I was the only student who identified as a man. The course felt like a safe space to use academic research and theory as a way to interrogate my own identity in a way that eventually led me to come out as gay a couple months later. The course offered me the opportunity, in a safe environment, to intellectualize being gay. I became comfortable with being gay, as a concept, through theory. Reading about the LGBTQ+ community and the experiences of other gay men and lesbians helped me to see myself more clearly. It was validating. I was able to say the words to myself for the first time, and once I did that, coming out came naturally. Coming out and being out became a reality of my life that had been derived directly from my academic experience in HRD and which liberated me from my conservative Christian roots which told me—nearly every single day growing up—that I would never be happy. As I moved through my doctoral studies at Florida International University, my first faculty position at the University of Arkansas, promotion and tenure at the University of Minnesota, and as I presently navigate being a mid-career academic with influence in the field, these foundational experiences have stayed with me and informed the ways that I approach my work, my research, mentorship, and leadership. As a cisgender white gay man, I know that my privileges have been as influential over my experiences as the marginality I have faced. I have always hoped that HRD can become a field that can encourage and sustain human flourishing, both inside and outside of organizations, no matter what differences we may have. I believe CHRD is a body of research and practice which can help us to achieve this objective.

Jamie's Narrative: Moving from Disrupted to Disrupter Through Critical HRD

I was introduced to the field of HRD through my military service when I got involved with Total Quality Air Force, back in the day of Total Quality Management (TQM). They needed somebody to teach about TQM in the context of the Air Force, so I got involved in training and eventually became a certified Air Force instructor. Being an instructor gave me the opportunity to share and engage in a way that I really enjoyed. I started to think about what it meant to learn and develop at work, so when I had the opportunity to exit the Air Force and work toward a doctorate and what I assumed would be a career in consulting, I took it.

At George Washington University, my introduction to the field of HRD was, at the time, rather performative in nature. Of course, the performance paradigm aligned well with my military background and views at the time. My initial understandings of learning, development, and performance assumed that everyone had the same opportunities for growth and advancement and that those who did not were simply making a choice. I had a professor early on in adult learning who helped to challenge this viewpoint by highlighting the ways in which societal inequities and injustices are designed and sustained in such a way that can make it difficult for those without access and resources. My professor told me about some of her research in the Appalachian mountains, talking to women who shared experiences such as being forced to leave school in the sixth grade because that was simply when girls left school, being sexually assaulted by family members, and being kept from reading or watching television. Many of the women my professor had talked to in her research had no idea that there was a world out there or that there were additional opportunities because they were never exposed to it.

This experience disrupted many of the values and viewpoints I had taken for granted up to that point. I saw plainly how influential the availability of resources and opportunities are to a person's ability to learn and develop. It stuck with me. Nevertheless, at the time I went through graduate school, the field of HRD was still almost exclusively dominated by the performance paradigm. It was not until I went to Texas A&M University as a faculty member that I started working with Jenny Sandlin and Ralf St Clair, who asked me to write a chapter in their *New Directions in Adult and Continuing Education* monograph focused on how critical perspectives are very frequently not enacted into praxis. They asked me to write about emotion in the class-room because they saw me teaching in critical ways. I had not yet made that connection for myself because I had not heard the language. I had never read Paulo Friere's *Pedagogy of the Oppressed*. Jenny and Ralf introduced me to these ideas by asking me to write the chapter, which shifted the way that I thought about critical perspectives and their applications in HRD.

From there, I realized that my critical perspective had always been present. As I learned and developed the language to better articulate this perspective, I had many opportunities to become a leader and voice within the movement toward CHRD. Reflecting on how far the field has come, I know that there is still a long way to go. I now believe that we are at a very important juncture as we determine the future of the field. Peoples' voices are getting louder, and I think that people are less and less willing to be complicit with the powers that reinforce oppressive and exploitative structures that we live and work in. We are developing greater understandings of power, equity, equality, and diversity, so I have to be hopeful—the alternative is unthinkable.

A Framework for Understanding the Scope of Critical HRD

Like many in HRD, our initial introduction to and training in the field oriented us to understand the scope and outcomes of HRD research and practice primarily across three "pillars" or areas of focus: organization develop-ment (OD), training and development (TD), and career development (CD). As we have developed our identities as CHRD scholars, these pillars have become less accurate to fully encompass a more equitable and justice-oriented vision of the field. We also explicitly acknowledge the long history of Adult Education's contributions to HRD's capacity to advance critical and social justice perspectives. The relationship between Adult Education and HRD is an issue that continues to be a part of conversations in both fields. Cunningham (2004) and Hatcher and Bowles (2013, 2014) suggested that critical and social justice perspectives may be the bridge the two fields need to encourage greater collaboration and understanding. In this handbook, we have encouraged authors—who identify as scholars of management, Adult Education, HRD, and other disciplines—to adopt a more critical and cross-disciplinary vantage point that classifies the scope and outcomes of HRD across five domains identified by CHRD scholars as key to understanding the nature and work of the field— organizing, relating, learning, changing (Bierema & Callahan, 2014), and advocating (Collins et al., 2015). Drawing from these perspectives, this handbook explores each of these five domains as follows:

- We seek to "explore the space of *organizing*," (Bierema & Callahan, 2014, p. 440) shifting focus away from organizations in the traditional sense toward a more inclusive perspective that more fully encompasses all the spaces, places, and contexts where HRD does or could occur.
- We seek to explore the ways in which *relating* communicates how "HRD is grounded in relationships between people," (Bierema & Callahan, 2014, p. 437) and we believe this grounding to be central to effectively encouraging and facilitating the development of people and greater social and organizational justice.
- We seek to explore the "different types of *learning*, different places of learning, different philosophies of learning, [and] different purposes of learning" (Bierema & Callahan, 2014, p. 438) which inform, influence, and shape development and performance in spaces of organizing.
- We seek to explore *changing* in spaces of organizing, including "the ethical implications of implementing [change]" (Bierema & Callahan, 2014, p. 439), while drawing a distinction between inclusive change and change which creates and perpetuates exclusion.
- We seek to explore *advocating*, or "relating, learning, changing, and organizing on behalf of others," (Collins et al., 2015, p. 218) as a core conviction and skillset of those who engage or wish to engage in CHRD research and practice.

Organization of the *Handbook of Critical HRD*

To guide our exploration of these five domains, this handbook is structured across three sections: Recontextualizing, Reconceptualizing, and Reconnecting. The chapters in the section focused on Recontextualizing lay a foundation of critical theory and practice which aid in understanding how critical perspectives both align with and diverge from traditional approaches in the field. In this section, a group of international authors explores the contexts, principles, spaces, agreements, collaborations, and understandings that situate the importance of viewing the scholarship and practice of HRD from alternative viewpoints. This section is intended to help even a novice to the field better understand and see themselves or their experiences through the lens of critical and social justice perspectives.

The chapters in the section focused on Reconceptualizing further this important work by reimagining commonly understood components of HRD theory and practice in a more critical manner. In this section, the authors work to reimagine an HRD that integrates critical thinking and critical perspectives throughout its operations, to place human thriving at the center of HRD's agenda, and to present alternative ways of thinking about concepts such as leadership, mentorship, inclusion, and learning in the field.

Finally, the chapters in the section focused on Reconnecting aim to remind us of CHRD's roots in theories and concepts which were derived to provide a better understanding of identity, intersectionality, and the interplay between individuals, communities, organizations, and society. In this section, authors explore HRD through the vantage point of individual identity, while centering that conversation first and foremost on what the field can and should do for those from more vulnerable and underrepresented groups in spaces of organizing. This section argues in favor of a responsible and socially just HRD and offers suggestions for a future where this vision can be achieved.

REFERENCES

Bierema, L. L. (2009). Critiquing human resource development's dominant masculine rationality and evaluating its impact. *Human Resource Development Review, 8*(1), 68–96.

Bierema, L., & Callahan, J. L. (2014). Transforming HRD: A framework for critical HRD practice. *Advances in Developing Human Resources, 16*(4), 429–444.

Byrd, M. Y. (2018). Does HRD have a moral duty to respond to matters of social injustice? *Human Resource Development International, 21*(1), 3–11.

Callahan, J. L. (2007). Gazing into the crystal ball: Critical HRD as a future of research in the field. *Human Resource Development International, 10*(1), 77–82.

Collins, J. C., & Chlup, D. T. (2014). Criticality in practice: The cyclical development process of social justice allies at work. *Advances in Developing Human Resources, 16*(4), 481–498.

Collins, J. C., McFadden, C., Rocco, T. S., & Mathis, M. K. (2015). The problem of transgender marginalization and exclusion: Critical actions for human resource development. *Human Resource Development Review, 14*(2), 205–226.

Cunningham, P. M. (2004). Critical pedagogy and implications for human resource development. *Advances in Developing Human Resources, 6*(2), 226–240.

Fenwick, T. J. (2004). Toward a critical HRD in theory and practice. *Adult Education Quarterly, 54*(3), 193–209.

Fenwick, T. (2005). Conceptions of critical HRD: Dilemmas for theory and practice. *Human Resource Development International, 8*(2), 225–238.

Gedro, J., Collins, J. C., & Rocco, T. S. (Eds.). (2014). Critical perspectives and the advancement of HRD. *Advances in Developing Human Resources, 16*(4), 407–535.

Han, S. H., Chae, C., Han, S. J., & Yoon, S. W. (2017). Conceptual organization and identity of HRD: Analyses of evolving definitions, influence, and connections. *Human Resource Development Review, 16*(3), 294–319.

Hatcher, T., & Bowles, T. (2013). Bridging the gap between human resource development and adult education: Part one, assumptions, definitions, and critiques. *New Horizons in Adult Education and Human Resource Development, 25*(4), 12–28.

Hatcher, T., & Bowles, T. (2014). Bridging the gap between human resource development and adult education: Part two, the critical turn. *New Horizons in Adult Education & Human Resource Development, 26*(1), 1–12.

Holden, R., & Griggs, V. (2010). Innovative practice in the teaching and learning of human resource development. *Journal of European Industrial Training, 34*(8–9), 705–709.

Lawless, A., Sambrook, S., & Stewart, J. (2012). Critical human resource development: Enabling alternative subject positions within a master of arts in human resource development educational programme. *Human Resource Development International, 15*(3), 321–336.

Rigg, C., Stewart, J. & Trehan, K. (Eds.). (2007). *Critical human resource development: Beyond orthodoxy*. Pearson Education.

Sambrook, S. (2000). Talking of HRD. *Human Resource Development International, 3*(2), 159–178.

Storberg-Walker, J., Johnson-Bailey, J., Bierema, L., Callahan, J. L., Chapman, D., & Gedro, J. (2010). Five HRD women professors discuss Wilson's Thai bar girls. In *Proceedings of the 2010 Academy of Human Resource Development International Research Conference in the Americas*.

Trehan, K., & Rigg, C. (2011). Theorising critical HRD: A paradox of intricacy and discrepancy. *Journal of European Industrial Training, 35*(3), 276–290.

PART II

Recontextualizing

Speaking Up in a Brave New World: Recontextualizing HRD in Postemotional Society

Jamie L. Callahan

INTRODUCTION

In the preface to Brave New World, Aldous Huxley wrote, "The greatest triumphs of propaganda have been accomplished, not by doing something, but by refraining from doing. Great is truth, but still greater, from a practical point of view, is silence about truth" (1932/1965, p. xix). Huxley wrote Brave New World in 1932 as a cautionary tale of the implications of totalitarianism, technology, capitalism, and mass media. He describes a future state in which society is genetically engineered to be pre-disposed for contentment and happiness, regardless of the meaninglessness of their work lives; in which citizens are controlled by the only class of people who have been genetically engineered to think critically; in which citizens are numbed by subliminal propaganda messages so that they engage in rampant impulse gratification and drug themselves to happy bliss when gratification is not immediately available; and in which consumption is the main goal of all human activity. As managerialist forces continue to reshape the context of organizations, employees find themselves slipping ever closer to the brave new world Huxley imagined nearly a century ago. Mirroring Huxley's predictions, one of the hallmarks of contemporary society is a world awash in manufactured emotion and devoid of authentic emotion; Meštrović (1997) calls this postemotionalism.

J. L. Callahan (✉)
Durham University Business School, Durham, UK
e-mail: Jamie.callahan@durham.ac.uk

J. C. Collins and J. L. Callahan (eds.), *The Palgrave Handbook of Critical Human Resource Development*, https://doi.org/10.1007/978-3-031-10453-4_2

Kanai and Gill (2021) highlight that "good" neoliberal workers learn not only correct behavior, but also correct emotion; they are socialized into a form of neoliberal feeling rules (Kanai, 2019). This becomes particularly important in a culture of overwork in which large segments of the population in Western society are desperately unhappy at work (Bunting, 2004). To survive this, workers turn to "playing the game" at work to manage complex scripts of manufactured emotions (Alvesson & Spicer, 2016) and seeking to numb their unhappiness through consumption (Bunting, 2004) and "feel good" media discourses (Kanai & Gill, 2021).

Alvesson and Spicer (2016) suggest it is the "defeatist acceptance of neoliberal ideas" (p. 42) that continues to drive the way work is transformed into a "game" workers are compelled to play. The more employees comply with the rules of the game, the stronger the game becomes. This renders workers complicit in the loss of their autonomy, subjugation to technology, and manipulation by managerial powers. Human resource development can, and should, play a role to remediate this.

Bierema (2002) notes that the history of the field is embedded in an ethos of humanism and care. Sorenson (1971) contended more than fifty years ago as the field was emerging that the task of HRD professionals was "nothing less than that of training revolutionaries" (p. 8, as cited in Lippitt, This, & Bidwell, 1971). The manipulation of emotion recontextualizes HRD to return to our roots and resist postemotionalism by reintroducing genuine emotions of care and well-being, and speaking out against workplace injustices.

Inspired by Huxley's prescient dystopian fiction, this chapter recontextualizes CHRD within a postemotional society. In this chapter, I first set the stage by reviewing what a "critical" HRD is and how emotion appears within CHRD. I follow with an overview of Meštrović's theory of the postemotional society. I then provide an overview of Huxley's classic novel, *Brave New World*, as the backdrop for using dystopian fiction as an analytic lens (Gatto & Callahan, 2021) before exploring how postemotionalism manifests in organizations. I conclude with implications for CHRD professionals.

CRITICAL HRD

What differentiates critical HRD from traditional understandings of HRD is the focus of inquiry and action within each approach to the field. Critical HRD is concerned with structures of power and control and seeks to challenge assumptions that guide HRD research and practice (Trehan et al., 2006). As a field of practice, in particular in the U.S., HRD "pays significant attention to the U.S. corporate context, skews loyalties toward management, and lauds performance improvement above other results" (Bierema, 2002, p. 245). This bias in action has led to a number of critiques of the field. Fenwick (2004) notes that HRD has been challenged for commodifying human development and subjugating human interests to exploitative organizational interests and for engaging various technologies to observe and regulate worker behavior, to classify and normalize worker tasks, and to engineer cultural diversity within the organization.

In general, critical theorists seek to empower the oppressed in order to redress the inequalities and injustices of social systems (McLaren, 1994). One of the distinctions of critical theory is that it focuses heavily on reason as a means to distance itself from accusations of irrationality (Brookfield, 2001) as it challenges the dominant discourse. Despite this emphasis on reason in critical theorizing, I have argued that critical theory is inherently emotional (Callahan, 2004); emotions infuse the systems and structures that inform our daily lives, leading CHRD professionals to ask "In whose interest does this serve?" To counter this rationality, Meštrović (1997) proposed exploring representations of emotion from a critical perspective as a more effective means of understanding social phenomena today. This alternative perspective is postemotionalism.

POSTEMOTIONAL SOCIETY

In contemporary society, Meštrović (1997) argued, emotions are exploited and transformed, lacking authenticity. Postemotionalism has three primary components—other-directedness, mechanization of emotion, and voyeuristic inaction (Meštrović, 1997).

First, Meštrović suggests that Western society externalizes emotion in such a way that emotions are no longer private spaces of reflection moving one toward action. Instead, emotions are directed outward toward others as vehicles to communicate a perceived "correct" expression of positive emotions. Negative emotions of hate, sorrow, suffering, and the like are not part of the other-directed culture of postemotionalism. This is drawn from David Reisman's conceptions of other-directedness in *The Lonely Crowd* and resonates with Arlie Russell Hochschild's conceptions of emotion management.

Second, Western society suffers from a mechanization, or commodification, of emotion (Meštrović, 1997) in which emotions pass through a cognitive filter in order for individuals to achieve instrumental gains. This mechanization of emotion is, in part, the result of the overuse of emotionally-laden language used to "sell" concepts and goods. This inundation of emotional messages has numbed the masses to genuine emotion.

Finally, this other-directedness and mechanization of emotion has created a culture of voyeuristic inaction. Because our other-directed culture of niceness disavows negative emotions, the culture media transmits images such as pain, suffering, tragedy, and anger to create an outlet for these emotions. Witnessing this suffering through simulations (i.e., television and movies) has numbed society to genuine suffering that exists all around us.

THE *BRAVE NEW WORLD*

The term "brave new world" is often bandied about as a positive herald of a new time. The essence of Huxley's novel, however, is not to praise the new society but to warn of the consequences of phenomena such as technology, medicine, and popular culture. For those not familiar with the novel, this section provides a brief plot overview.

In this brave new world Huxley creates, totalitarianis keeps the world free from disease, hunger, poverty, war, and hatred. To maintain this utopian state, a small group of individuals, called Controllers, eliminate most individual freedoms and redefine traditional Western values. For example, marriage is rendered taboo, free sex is required, and pregnancy is forbidden. Human beings are part of the production process in which individuals are genetically engineered in Petri dishes to happily fulfill tasks in society in one of five caste levels. These five castes range from the most intelligent Alphas, who perform the leadership roles in the society, to the least intelligent Epsilons, who perform the most menial of tasks. Children are raised in collectives under strict conditioning, both while awake and while asleep, to ensure that they never question their role in society. As adults, individuals unquestioningly assume their appointed roles, operate with efficiency in those roles, participate as expected in mindless leisure activities, and consume a drug called "soma" to ensure that they are always happy. The core values of society are consumption, standardization, and progress.

When Bernard, an Alpha from London who appears to be the "victim" of faulty programming, begins to question the values of his society, he is branded an outcast and threatened with banishment to Iceland. However, during a trip to the savage reservation (a portion of the world untouched by modern technological progress), he discovers Linda and John. Linda is a Beta who had traveled to the reservation twenty years earlier with Bernard's supervisor, she became lost in the reservation and discovered that she was pregnant while she was lost. She was never rescued and raised her son, John, among the savages. Bernard decided to return to London with Linda and John in a bid to regain his stature in society. Linda is unable to cope with her assimilation back into society. Having lost her prized youth and becoming addicted to alcohol while on the reservation, she longs for the days when she was pretty and happy and content with her life. Seeking comfort, she gradually overdoses on soma and eventually dies. John, whose education has been based on reading a book of Shakespeare's works, is baffled and horrified by the supposedly civilized society. He also is unable to cope with assimilation into society; he rejects the lack of individuality, compassion, and challenge. Forced to choose between conformity or death, John chooses to hang himself rather than lose his individuality and personal values.

A BRAVE NEW WORLD OF POSTEMOTIONALISM FOR CHRD

This section ties together the lens provided by dystopian fiction with the postemotionalism that confronts HRD professionals in organizations today. Manifestations of neoliberalism are threaded through the novel—the commodification of human beings, the erosion of autonomy, the quest for ultimate efficiency, the veneer of emotion, and the pursuit of consumption. These can be linked to the postemotionalism of other-directedness, mechanization of emotion, and voyeuristic inaction that Meštrović (1997) describes.

Other-Directedness

Other-directedness can be seen in the repeated references to the ultimate pursuit of happiness programmed into citizens of the brave new world. Controllers in the brave new world seek to maintain a state of stable positivity, "...that is the secret of happiness and virtue—liking what you've *got* to do. All conditioning aims at that: making people like their unescapable social destiny" (Huxley, 1932/1965, p. 10). Further, the cultivation of impulse gratification begins at an early age because "impulse arrested spills over, and the flood is feeling, the flood is passion, the flood is even madness: it depends on the strength of the barrier. The unchecked stream flows smoothly down its appointed channels into a calm well-being" (p. 32). Therefore, everyone is programmed to gratify all impulses as a means to control emotion.

This outward veneer of managed emotion to meet societal expectations manifests in a variety of ways within organizations. For HRD professionals, the ubiquitous smile sheets as evaluation mechanisms for training are other-directed symptoms. Kirkpatrick's level one evaluation is the most common form of evaluation of training events; this level is often referred to as a smile sheet because it really does nothing more than provide plausible assurance the participant was happy with the training experience (Holton, 1996).

Another example of how emotions are controlled for external appearances can be traced to the metrification of tasks to measure productivity. This effort at controlling outcomes shifts work from "workmanship of risk," which is based on expert judgment by the worker, to "workmanship of certainty," which is based on creating systems of conformity (Pye, 1968). Such a shift has long been considered detrimental to worker well-being and happiness at work, but could be mitigated through entertaining diversions such as training (c.f., Adam Smith, [1776] 1993, as cited in Grugulis, 2007). These measurements of productivity are also co-opted for proxies of "excellence" that extend into public management and the professions. The third sector has been hollowed out by fictitious commodification that quantifies what constitutes social value (Roy & Teasdale, 2021). Referencing academics, Lock and Martin (2011) commiserate, "In our brave new world, it seems that a final criterion of value is recognized: a quantitative, economic criterion. All else is no more than a means. And there is a single method for ensuring that this criterion is satisfied: quantified control" (p. 1).

Finally, there is perhaps a no better example of the pressure of other-directedness in organizations today than the relentless calls for "civility." Andersson and Pearson's (1999) article introducing workplace incivility introduced the ultimate of control mechanisms by characterizing as uncivil those employees who did not express their emotions in accordance with established affective norms. Their "inappropriate" behavior made them subject to zero tolerance policies, blacklisting from future job opportunities, remedial training, and more (Pearson et al., 2000). However, in a work context in which autonomy has been stripped from employees within a societal culture that calls for suppression of negative emotion (Meštrović, 1997; Stearns, 2008), incidents of incivility may well be cries for help (Callahan, 2011).

Mechanization of Emotion

The mechanization of emotion occurs first through biogenetic engineering of embryos, "We also predestine and condition. We decant our babies as socialized human beings, … as future sewage workers or future … World controllers" (Huxley, 1932/1965, p. 9). Then through hypnotic messages delivered while children are sleeping, "Till at last the child's mind *is* these suggestions" (p. 20). This programming is continued by cultural messages regarding leisure activities and work roles. And, finally, when threats to the programming occur, citizens indulge in a happiness inducing drug called "soma."

This element of postemotionalism is about manipulating the emotions of others for instrumental gain, prescribing how emotions should be deployed to be most conducive to the organization's goals. The search for the next best way to make training more effective and less expensive (Callahan et al., 2006) frequently results in sound bite messages that are designed to create loyalists for the organization (Carden & Callahan, 2007). Socialization programs are designed to assimilate individuals into the culture of the organization (Reio, 2000).

The communication medium of email is another space of mechanization of emotion. Employees are conditioned to balance pleasantry and efficiency, using template signature blocks that save time and present a veneer of niceness to appeal to readers. This reinforces and reproduces the underlying masculinist culture of contemporary organizations and serves to nullify genuine feelings of individuals (The Kintsugi Collective, 2021). A template removes the mindfulness of the feeling for the writer but offers manufactured friendliness to the recipient.

Digital emotion manipulation also occurs in social media platforms such as Twitter, Facebook, LinkedIn, and Instagram. As employee presence on social media became more widespread, employers began to capitalize on using the platform to surveille employee behavior (Ghoshray, 2013). This surveillance has only intensified. Whereas a conversation about frustrations with an employee's company among a group of friends over dinner would have been unlikely to result in termination, getting fired over Facebook posts has become a real phenomenon (Long, 2015). Increasingly, institutional policies incorporate the right to terminate employees whom they deem have tarnished the reputation of the organization by posts on their private social media accounts (Stohl et al., 2017). This reaches the long arm of emotion manipulation to "sell" the company even in private spaces that have the potential for public reach.

Voyeuristic Inaction

In the novel, voyeuristic inaction can be seen in the programming to blandly accept emotional events, such as death, and also in the rampant self-interest manifested in most citizens. For example, children are programmed to accept death and expressions of grief associated with death are unconscionable. When a character sobs uncontrollably at the death of his mother in front of future workers in the hospital, the head nurse struggles, "Should she ... try to bring him back to a sense of decency? Remind him ... of what fatal mischief he might do to these poor innocents? Undoing all their wholesome death-conditioning with this disgusting outcry—as though death were something terrible..." (Huxley, 1932/1965, p. 158).

The veneer of niceness makes it challenging for people to confront hard or negative emotions. Voyeuristic inaction is about becoming frozen in the face of negative emotional experiences because the employee does not know what to do or say, or feels powerless to make a difference.

Awareness of pending layoffs and subsequently surviving those layoffs is purported to cause a type of survivor guilt (Worrall et al., 2000). Upset that their colleagues were terminated and beset with increased workloads, employees can become hyper-focused on work tasks and fail to confront the implications of their loss. This leads to reduced morale and motivation and the development of automaton employees.

Mass shootings in places of work, school, worship, and daily life in the US are so frequent that many Americans are simply numb and anesthetized from taking action. Rather than be genuinely horrified at the carnage of mass shootings, the mantra "thoughts and prayers" has gained traction under such conditions. Employees are exposed to training videos on what to do should an active shooter enter the premises (Ford & Frei, 2016). Indeed, although I now live in a country with stringent firearms restrictions, the first thing I do when I enter a room or get a new office is to take note of where exits are located and what the best hiding place is. Gun violence plays out on television so frequently that people come to see it as banal. This is the essence of Mestrovic's concept of watching the carnage from a distance and not feeling compelled to act out of fear or anger.

Experiences of the marginalized are another space in which voyeuristic inaction occurs. Line managers can be quick to write off the experiences of BIPOC (Black, Indigenous, People of Color), transgender, women, disabled, and other groups that lack privilege by suggesting that the latest indignity they have suffered is a "one-off" coincidence. However, while felt deeply and immediately by the targets, patterns of microaggressions emerge over time to bystanders who are observant. But such patterns, especially of racial microaggressions, have been infrequently studied (Pitcan et al., 2018). Furthermore, when efforts to address such racial discrimination are proposed or implemented, they are not well received (Sisco et al., 2022). Increasing awareness of one's complicity in inequity and inequality can lead to dominant groups withdrawing out of shame, anger, or fear (Callahan, 2004); in so doing, the opportunity to dialogue, learn, and change is short-circuited.

IMPLICATIONS FOR HRD

While postemotionalism offers an explanation of our current society and shows how the brave new world is manifested in our society, the brave new world also offers glimpses of how such a society is created. In this creation, we see how a cadre of citizens is engaged to train others for their roles in society. We can relate this to the role that HRD professionals take within organizations to engage in activities that often include elements of training or learning. There are a number of lessons HRD professionals might take from the realization that we may be operating within a brave new world. As HRD professionals take a critical turn in their work, they can resist the postemotional work-place by enacting resistance to the managerialism through relating, organizing, learning, changing (Bierema & Callahan, 2014), and advocating (Collins et al., 2015). This section offers an example for each of the CHRD framework components proposed by Bierema and Callahan (2014) and extended by Collins and colleagues (2015). These actions to counter the postemotional brave new world offer HRD professionals new ways to contextualize what a Critical HRD could be.

Relating

Building relationships is challenging in an environment of mechanized and inauthentic emotion. One way to counter the way that our context drives cold and impersonal computer-mediated communication is to infuse it with the thoughtfulness of caring or "love" (The Kintsugi Collective, 2021). By consciously and explicitly typing out an email closure (e.g., with kind regards), employees are able to keep the emotion in mind (Kiriakos & Tienari, 2018) and, therefore, at heart. In so doing, this intentional act of relationality reframes the writer and holds the promise of reframing the recipient.

Organizing

Workers can organize to resist the social media surveillance by turning obser-vational digital technologies back on the observer (Taylor & Dobbins, 2021). Called "sousveillance," this strategy can be a collective effort to problema-tize oppressive policies and power relations. Rogue alternative government accounts on Twitter during the Trump presidency are an example of such sousveillance (https://www.core77.com/posts/60230/Heres-a-List-of-All-the-US-Govts-Rogue-Twitter-Accounts-Fighting-Trumps-Crackdown-on-Sci ence). These sites reported on government policy by exposing the ugly under-belly of what was really happening within their agencies. Various institutions are known to have underground blogs or social media accounts to document contested managerial actions or scandals. For example, @DurhamScandal asks its followers, "Has Durham had a scandal today?". Friending and then excluding managers from private discussion groups on social media facilitates observing their posts to turn the tables on them for their own surveillance (Taylor & Dobbins, 2021).

Learning

Instead of viewing incivility as a dysfunction to be eliminated or as an opportunity to censure or punish workers, HRD professionals can view such behavior as an opportunity to learn. Acts of incivility can be an early warning system that can be used to diagnose emergent problems in the systems and structures of the organization, much like canaries were once used to detect hidden methane in coal mines (Callahan, 2011). One way of uncovering the underlying causes of the symptom of incivility is to use action learning conversations (Marsick & O'Neil, 1999). For example, this technique has been used to uncover the source of bullying in school settings—revealing that misperceptions and biases resulted in accusations of incivility against innocent students (Ghosh et al., 2020).

Changing

Instead of "playing the game" (Alvesson & Spicer, 2016), change the nature of the game. One way this can be done is by asking questions when emotionally triggered. Such a strategy can help reveal and resist the type of gaslighting organizations engage in when trying to emotionally manipulate workers to perform in preferred ways (Sweet, 2019). Industrial action responses to unreasonable demands by employers can include strategies to change the game, such as action short of strike (ASOS) and finding ways to "game the system" or engage in malicious compliance are ways to do one's job.

Advocating

Confronting emotions in difficult conversations can be an effective advocating tool. It is well-documented that the marginalized often carry the burden of fighting for equity and equality (Ahmed, 2012). Consciousness raising is an important technique to create the conditions under which allies can form (Sisco et al., 2022). Bierema (2010) calls for using interventions such as "verbal jujitsu" to have allies from the dominant group stand in support of marginalized and minoritized individuals. One of the ways this is done is by intervening in conversations when microaggressions occur.

Conclusion

Ultimately, we should not blindly accept the word of management. HRD professionals should always question the status quo and the logic behind any intervention we are asked to design, deliver, or implement. HRD professionals should also cultivate self-awareness to reveal our own motives for choosing to either act or not to act; coupled with self-awareness is the awareness of the injustices and suffering experienced by others. Perhaps most importantly, HRD professionals should resist efforts that result in deskilling (Kincheloe, 1999) workers within organizations. To do this, our HRD efforts must cultivate holistic understanding through broadening interventions, such as cross-training. We must refuse to create narrowly focused experts who no longer have the skills to be marketable and are, therefore, dependent upon the "controllers" of the organization. We must be creative to be critical.

Do we live in a brave new world? Perhaps, perhaps not; we certainly have many manifestations of the brave new world in our society today. But what HRD professionals must bear in mind is that it takes action to break the silence that may unconsciously propel them toward being unwitting collaborators in the creation, or maintenance, of the brave new world. By speaking up to challenge the other-directedness of controlled emotion, the mechanization and commodification of emotion, and the bystander voyeurism of negative emotions, a CHRD can recontextualize what the field can mean in a neoliberal, postemotional society and regenerate more authentic emotion.

References

Ahmed, S. (2012). *On being included: racism and diversity in institutional life*. Duke University Press.

Alvesson, M., & Spicer, A. (2016). (Un)conditional surrender? Why do professionals willingly comply with managerialism. *Journal of Organizational Change Management, 29*(1), 29–45.

Andersson, L. M., & Pearson, C. M. (1999). Tit for tat? The spiraling effect of incivility in the workplace. *Academy of Management Review, 24*(3), 452–471.

Bierema, L. L. (2002). A feminist approach to HRD research. *Human Resource Development Review, 1*(2), 244–268.

Bierema, L. L. (2010). *Implementing a critical approach to organization development*. Krieger.

Bierema, L. L., & Callahan, J. L. (2014). A framework for Critical HRD practice: Transforming HRD. *Advances in Developing Human Resources, 16*(4), 429–444.

Brookfield, S. (2001). Repositioning ideology critique in a critical theory of adult education. *Adult Education Quarterly, 52*(1), 7–22.

Bunting, M. (2004). *Willing Slaves: How the overwork culture is ruling our lives*. HarperCollins.

Callahan, J. L. (2004, Summer). Breaking the cult of rationality: Mindful awareness of emotion in the critical theory classroom. In R. StClair & J. Sandlin (Eds.), *New directions in adult and continuing education* (Vol. 102, pp. 75–83).

Callahan, J. L. (2011). Incivility as an instrument of oppression: Exploring the role of power in constructions of civility. *Advances in Developing Human Resources, 13*(1), 10–21.

Callahan, J. L., & Dunne de Davila, T. (2004). An impressionistic framework for theorizing about human resource development. *Human Resource Development Review, 3*(1), 75–95.

Callahan, J. L., & Elliott, C. (2020). Fantasy spaces and emotional derailment: Reflections on failure in academic activism. *Organization, 27*(3), 506–514.

Callahan, J. L., Whitener, J. K., Mathis, R. S., & Carden, L. L. (2006). Messages to the profession: A discursive content analysis of *Training & Development* tables of contents. Paper presented at the Academy of Human Resource Development, Columbus, OH.

Carden, L., & Callahan, J. L. (2007). Creating leaders or loyalists: Conflicting identities in a leadership development programme. *Human Resource Development International, 10*(2), 169–186.

Collins, J. C., McFadden, C., Rocco, T. S., & Mathis, M. K. (2015). The problem of transgender marginalization and exclusion: Critical actions for human resource development. *Human Resource Development Review, 14*(2), 205–226.

Fenwick, T. J. (2004). Toward a critical HRD in theory and practice. *Adult Education Quarterly, 54*(3), 193–209.

Ford, J. L., & Frei, S. S. (2016). Training for the unthinkable: Examining message characteristics on motivations to engage in an active-shooter response video. *Communication Studies, 67*(4), 438–454.

Gatto, M., & Callahan, J. L. (2021). Exposing interpellation with dystopian fiction: A critical discourse analysis technique to disrupt hegemonic masculinity. In S. Mavin, C. Elliott, & V. Stead (Eds.), *Handbook of research methods in gender and management*. Edward Elgar Publishing.

Ghosh, R., Callahan, J. L., & Hammrich, P. (2020). Supporting teachers who witness student bullying: (Re)shaping perceptions through peer coaching in action learning. *International Journal of Mentoring and Coaching in Education, 9*(1), 87–102.

Ghoshray, S. (2013). Employer surveillance versus employee privacy: The new reality of social media and workplace privacy. *Northern Kentucky Law Review, 40*, 593–626.

Grugulis, I. (2007). *Skills, training and human resource development: A critical text.* Palgrave Macmillan.

Holton, E. F., III. (1996). The flawed four-level evaluation model. *Human Resource Development Quarterly, 7*(1), 5–21.

Huxley, A. (1932/1965). *Brave new world & brave new world revisited.* Harper & Row Publishers, Inc.

Kanai, A. (2019). On not taking the self seriously: Resilience, relatability and humour in young women's Tumblr blogs. *European Journal of Cultural Studies, 22*(1), 60–77.

Kanai, A., & Gill, R. (2021). Woke? Affect, neoliberalism, marginalised identities and consumer culture. *New Formations: A Journal of Culture/theory/politics, 102*, 10–27.

Kincheloe, J. L. (1999). *How do we tell the workers? The socioeconomic foundations of work and vocational education.* Westview Press.

Kiriakos, C., & Tienari, J. (2018). Academic writing as love. *Management Learning, 49*(3), 263–277.

Lock, G., & Martins, H. (2011). Quantified control and the mass production of "psychotic citizens." *EspacesTemps.net [En ligne]*, Laboratoire. https://www.esp ecestempts.net/articles/quantified-control-and-the-mass-production-of-ldquospyc hotic-citizensrdquo.

Long, J. (2015). #Fired: The National Labor Relations Act and employee outbursts in the age of social media. *Boston College Law Review, 56*(3), 1217–1248.

McLaren, P. (1994). *Life in schools: An introduction to critical pedagogy in the foundations of education.* Longman.

Marsick, V. J., & O'Neil, J. (1999). The many faces of action learning. *Management Learning, 30*(2), 159–176.

Meštrović, S. (1997). *Postemotional society.* Sage.

Pearson, C. M., Andersson, L. M., & Porath, C. L. (2000). Assessing and attacking workplace incivility. *Organizational Dynamics, 29*(2), 123–137.

Pitcan, M., Park-Taylor, J., & Hayslett, J. (2018). Black men and racial microaggressions at work. *The Career Development Quarterly, 66,* 300–314.

Pye, D. (1968). *The nature and art of workmanship.* Cambridge University Press.

Reio, T. G. (2000). Field investigation of the relationship among adult curiosity, workplace learning, and job performance. *Human Resource Development Quarterly, 11*(1), 3–30.

Roy, M. J., & Teasdale, S. (2021). Monetising social impact: A critique of the 'financialisation' of social value. In R. Hazenberg & C. Paterson-Young (Eds.), *Social impact measurement for a sustainable future.* Palgrave Macmillan.

Sisco, S., Hart-Mrema, T. S., & Aderibigbe, E. (2022). Engaging in race-conscious research and applying racial equity in human resource development: A collective autoethnography. *Human Resource Development International, 25*(1), 59–75.

Sorenson, T. (1971). The revolutions of our time and their implications for training and development. In G. L. Lippitt, L. E. This, & R. G. Bidwell (Eds.), *Optimizing human resources: Readings in individual and organization development* (pp. 2–9). Addison-Wesley Publishing Company.

Stearns, P. N. (2008). History of emotions: Issues of change and impact. In M. Lewis, J. M. Haviland-Jones, & L. Feldman Barrett (Eds.), *Handbook of emotions* (3rd ed., , pp. 17–31). The Guilford Press.

Stohl, C., Etter, M., Banghart, S., & Woo, D. J. (2017). Social media policies: Implications for notions of corporate social responsibility. *Journal of Business Ethics, 142*(3), 413–436.

Sweet, P. (2019). The sociology of gaslighting. *American Sociological Review, 84*(5), 851–875.

Taylor, C., & Dobbins, T. (2021). Social media: A (new) contested terrain between sousveillance and surveillance in the digital workplace. *New Technology, Work, and Employment, 36*(3), 263–284.

The Kintsugi Collective. (2021). Micro-activism and wellbeing in organisational life: 1,000s of snowflakes and the potential avalanche. In T. Wall, C. Cooper, & P. Brough (Eds.), *The SAGE handbook of organisational wellbeing.* Sage.

Trehan, K., Rigg, C., & Stewart, J. (2006). Critical human resource development. *International Journal of Training and Development, 10*(1), 2–3.

Turnbull, S. (2002). The planned and unintended emotions generated by a corporate change program. *Advances in Developing Human Resources, 4*(1), 22–38.

Worrall, L., Campbell, F., & Cooper, C. (2000). Surviving redundancy: The perceptions of UK managers. *Journal of Managerial Psychology, 15*(5), 460–476.

CHAPTER 3

The Ideological, Theoretical, and Socio-Economic Context of Critical HRD: A Foundational Introduction

Emily Yarrow

INTRODUCTION

The various chapters of this text are situated to 'challenge the predominately performative and learning outcome focus of the HRD field' (Elliot & Turnbull, 2003, p. 971), exploring the ways in which various contemporary contextual factors, may shape the five key domains of organizing, relating, learning, changing Bierema and Callahan (2014) and advocating (Collins et al., 2015). Further, this chapter will set out the critical ideologies for challenging truth in the contemporary context; a critical overview of ideology and relations to theory; theoretical dilemmas and tensions of CHRD including problematizing performativity, dominant masculine rationality in HRD, and the commodified worker in the neoliberal context; the tensions, quandaries, and opportunities concerning critical compromise and radical change are discussed. Finally, the role of CHRD in organizational equality, diversity, and inclusion is explored, setting the scene for later chapters of this handbook.

It would be remiss to underestimate the role of the global [socio-political, economic, environmental, and technological] context (Johns, 2006) on CHRD scholarship, practitioners, and praxis. This will aid the development of not only sustainable and social businesses (Hoque, 2007), but also inclusive and contextually sensitized pedagogies and theorizations of (C)HRD practice. We must be attuned to contextual changes, patterns, trends, and social

E. Yarrow (✉)
Newcastle University Business School, Newcastle upon Tyne, UK
e-mail: Emily.Yarrow2@newcastle.ac.uk

J. C. Collins and J. L. Callahan (eds.), *The Palgrave Handbook of Critical Human Resource Development*, https://doi.org/10.1007/978-3-031-10453-4_3

justice requirements that effectively challenge performative biases, thereby critiquing and questioning the status quo to contribute to dynamic, contemporary, sustainable, and inclusive HRD. Such awareness, agility, and the ability to drive change, as well as willingness to embrace change is imperative to foster the transformation of hierarchical and masculine business practices (Helgesen, 1990; Wheatley, 1992).

Global Political Shifts

In many parts of the world there is a worrying shift to the right in politics (Abou-Chadi et al., 2020), characterized in the US by the post 9/11 conservative shift (Nail & McGregor, 2009), Brexit in the UK, and a more general pan-European shift toward increasingly conservative politics (Liebhart, 2020), as well as the emergence of 'Conservative political movements, right-wing governments and populism in the democratic states of the Asia-Pacific' (Chacko & Jayasuriya, 2018, p. 529). Worryingly, such globally widespread political shifts have also been found to casually affect mainstream parties' positions (Abou-Chadi & Krause, 2020). As we find ourselves in an epoch where the protection of critical thought in scholarship is ever more important, so is the deliberation of the future direction of the CHRD discipline. This Conservative shift also further entrenches and exacerbates existing societal inequalities and tensions, such as gender inequality, racism, ableism, and class divisions which are all still rampant and deeply engrained around the world today. Ultimately, there is an epochal shift toward right-leaning world capitalism; the 'underlying structural dynamic that drives social, political, economic, and cultural processes around the world' (Robinson & Robinson, 2008, p. 1).

The related focus on a free-market economy and the rhetoric of institutionalized individualization (Beck & Beck-Gernsheim, 2002) whereby the onus is placed on individual success, rather than the collective in numerous contexts. Such socio-economic, socio-political, and rhetorical shifts also shape CHRD practices, processes and theory making particularly in a volatile, uncertain, complex, and ambiguous (VUCA) socio-political climate. Moreover, it is of significant value and intellectual importance to consider social, political, and economic contextual factors as interrelated, bounded by masculine rationality, and as factors which are played out through performative and actual commodification. This drives the need for further developments, and indeed awareness of critical theory (Bierema, 2009; Elliott & Turnbull, 2003; Fenwick, 2004, 2005; Sambrook, 2003) and critical perspectives of HRD, and by implication CHRD, as well as education as activism (Contu, 2009), particularly in the neoliberal Business School.

Ideology and Its Relations to Theory

The following section provides a critical overview of ideology and relations to theory in order not only to help situate other chapters in this text, but also to further explore how ideology operates in contemporary organizations. It is important to situate Human Resource Development early on as a 'system saturated with sexism, racism, and managerialism' Bierema (2009, p. 68), and in doing so, the aim is to reinstate a focus on the inclusive, egalitarian, and humanistic roots of HRD. When we think and write critically about the world, we are also communicating a certain direction of interpellation (Althusser, 1971), allowing, and enabling ideologies to permeate, influence, and shape our thinking. In considering Althusser's theory of interpellation, individuals are positioned as ideological subjects, whereby in the everyday reality of inequality—that is [intersectionally] gendered, racialized, and classed—the ideological function of CHRD' importance is further increased as an opportunity for contributing to the enactment of Critical ideologies for challenging '*truth*'. In turn, three core theoretical tensions in the CHRD corpus; performativity, the dominant masculine rationality in HRD, and resisting worker commodification, are inextricably linked to not only equality, diversity, and inclusion, but the ideological function of CHRD.

Critical Ideologies for Challenging 'Truth'

The notion of challenging truth has deep ontological and epistemological ties to the pragmatic theory of truth (De Waal, 1999), as well as the notion of settled beliefs. To return to the work of Bierema (2009), and the proposition that HRD is 'co-opted into hegemonic practices of management' (2006, pp. 68–69), as well as societal and socio-economic inequalities, it is evident that there is an ongoing and ever-increasing need for critical ideologies for challenging 'truth' and indeed, the status quo of performative ideas and practices. This need is further amplified if we consider the notion of HRD as a hologram (McGoldrick et al., 2001; Ruona, 2016) whereby HRD mirrors social reality and, in turn, issues of social justice and opportunities for positive social change. It is also noteworthy that McGoldrick et al., argue that the metaphor of the hologram '*depicts "social reality" as multi-dimensional, multi-causal, mutually dependent and constantly changing*' (2001, p.351) which is particularly apt in the context of uncertainty and change in the global marketplace. When social reality is positioned as a non-fixity, theorizations and practice will also, by implication, become further flexible and potentially, more inclusive.

In exploring critical ideologies, the reader is called upon to reflect upon their own experiences, conceptualization, theorizations, and writings of HRD in preparation also for later chapters of this text. One of the tasks facing readers of this text, is the deliberation of how current ideologies of organization shape lived experiences of organizations, training and development and policy making within them. Scholars and practitioners alike need to consider what ideological remains of HRD can and should be retained, and how these elements can be reconstructed to pay heed to the [ever-changing] character of modern societies and organizations (Thompson, 1990), not least in the [globalized and neoliberal] post-covid-19 context, globally.

The Globalized, Neoliberal Context

In the context of globalization, neoliberalism, technology development, big data, artificial intelligence, and the rise of the machine learning revolution (Harrison et al., 2020), and to move beyond current orthodoxy (Rigg et al., 2007), critical human resource development faces many contemporary opportunities and challenges. Furthermore, drawing on the work of Torraco and Lundgren (2020) there is a strong case for transforming HRD through closer alignment between HRD and organizational strategy, but this must also be approached critically and be based on humanistic and egalitarian practices and processes, rather than the capitalist rhetoric of profit maximization and efficiency gains.

Drawing on Bierema and Callahan's (2014) framework of CHRD, and ideologies of HRD more broadly, it becomes ever clearer that a shift away from the 'the field's own "Holy Trinity" of practices and research foci' (2014, p. 431) with a renewed focus on critical ideologies for challenging 'truth' and by implication, the status quo. In a capitalist, managerial context, forms of 'truth' and reality, are driven by shareholder requirements and market forces, which are predominantly controlled and inflicted by white, cis-gender, able-bodied, heteronormative, male power, through the practices and policies of the organization/s (Acker, 1990, 2006). Bierema (2009) contends that HRD requires 'unsettling' (2009, p. 70) and it is this unsettling which holds the potential to act a catalyst for challenging 'truth'. By implication, such 'unsettling' needs to be founded on critical ideologies of organizing, mobilizing, and theorizing, as well as being enacted by practitioners.

Discourse Domination

In ruminating critical ideologies, it is also of the utmost importance to remain aware of and try to counter the dominance of voices from the global north and critique of the 'colonial boundaries of how HRD is theorized and practiced' (Syed & Metcalfe, 2017, p.403), as well as striving for scholarship that reflects contextual, political contestations, cultural and social complexities, and differences (Syed & Metcalfe, 2017, p. 403), positioned here as *'contemporary recontextualizing'*. Currently, it may be argued that HRD more broadly focusses on neoliberal and capitalist ideologies, ideologies which are played out through international organizations priorities and strategies (Kay, 2008; Syed, 2010; Syed & Metcalfe, 2017) and it is here where CHRD plays a central role in informing critical change and a shift away from the [neoliberal] status quo that underemphasizes and underplays the 'heterogeneous and plural formations of economies, cultures, and identities' (Syed & Metcalfe, 2017, p. 405) as well as currently being under developed in terms of its acknowledgment of the [problematic] role of global capitalism for example. Further, it is also important to develop the discourse around the critique of corporations in the globalized context and drive a theory and practitioner shift which encompasses deeper and more critical deliberations of what it means to be a part of a global corporation (Short & Callahan, 2005).

Theoretical Dilemmas of CHRD

The extant body of CHRD literature encompasses several not only theoretical dilemmas, but also a range of tensions, which in and of themselves require deliberation and exploration within scholarly works, as well as ongoing, contemporary insight from praxis. However, there are two foundational commitments which shape the direction of CHRD, in that *'CHRD generally promotes critical analysis of power relations in work organizations'* (Fenwick, 2014, p. 113) and *'tends to be oriented towards action that aims to address unfair inequities and improve life and wellbeing in work organizations'* (Fenwick, 2014, p. 113). However, it is also important to consider what is deemed critical and by whom, and how, in turn, this influences not only the CHRD discourse, but also how this may shape perceptions of organizations the power herein, and subsequent theorizations and discursive practices. However, what is a consistent theme, as well as an oft-discussed source of tension is the ongoing jostling between notions of critical compromise and radical change, pragmatic orientation, and critical integrity in the field. This is an area which not only needs disentangling within the scholarly field, but where epistemological and ontological tensions and differences can be harnessed to create synergies between pragmatic orientation and critical integrity, particularly the post-covid-19 context which presents opportunities for bold research and change (Bierema, 2020). The contemporary post-pandemic world presents both new and different challenges and opportunities for CHRD, a calibrated recontextualizing, which need to be considered, harnessed, and explored by both scholars and practitioners alike, most notably around the impact of home, remote, and online working, as well as the role of organizations in employee wellbeing, as well as overall increases in complexity of the labor market. CHRD, now more than ever, needs to further emphasize and embody a humanistic approach, while championing critical integrity, as a future scholarly avenue for change, and the further promotion of humanitarian business models (Hoque, 2007). For example, Davies (2021) argues that in the post-covid-19 era that 'HRD Practices are being severely disrupted and established theoretical models are being tested' (2021, p. 7) which serves to underpin the importance of not only the existing theoretical tensions of HRD and CHRD, but also the contemporary theoretical and practical challenges coming to the fore in the post-covid-19 context, and the resultant implications for practice, as well as how CHRD as a discipline should respond. In turn, this chapter explores performativity and the patriarchy, the dominant masculine rationality in HRD, and the rise of the commodified gig worker in the neoliberal context, as well as the importance of bridging the research-practice gap for both critical compromise, radical change, and critical integrity, all of which are increasingly shaped by contextual changes. However, to situate these challenges further we must consider the current theoretical tensions of CHRD that shape scholarly understandings of direction in, and of the field in the context of contemporary recontextualizing.

Theoretical Tensions of CHRD

There are clear linkages between the three main theoretical tensions of CHRD and the wider [patriarchal] socio-economic context. We know that performativity privileges patriarchy's power and control in organizations (Bierema & Callahan, 2014, p. 433), as well driving the commodification of workers and their labor—one of the most pressing, and indeed ever increasing, contemporary labor market issues globally.

In the context of globalization, worker rights are often seen and treated as tradeable commodities in what is a deeply flawed, problematic, and deeply unequal marketplace. Globalization and global capitalism is built on and predicated on the exploitation of [geographic] labor market differences for economic gain and being heavily influenced by 'the folly of ignoring the distributional consequences of economic forces just because they may lead to growth' (Stiglitz, 2017, p. 129). Global capitalism is oftentimes characterized by incongruous relationships between organizational profit maximization, and ultimately, the abuse of human rights and the exploitation of socio-economic power differences. CHRD Theorizations need to remain not contextually sensitive, but also cognizant of the inextricable nature of patriarchal capitalist rhetoric, which provides the domain for performativity and in turn, the commodification of workers and subsequent inequalities to flourish.

Furthermore, in the post covid-19 context, it is becoming increasingly clear that global and local inequities and other inequalities are set to worsen. Indeed, the global pandemic is already being framed within aspects of the social reproduction theory literature as: 'a crisis of social reproduction for both capital and labor' (Rao, 2021, as cited in Mezzadri et al., 2021, p. 2).

Problematizing Performativity

Performativity is becoming increasingly engrained in our day to day and working lives, and notionally it needs to be more rigorously critiqued and explored in order not only better understand facets of organizational life, but also the effects of performativity on individuals. While there are of course a range of conceptualizations of performativity, ranging from Austin's (1962) speech act theory and seminal text: '*how to do things with words*' to Butler's Classic work *Gender Performativity* (1988), and Derrida (1988), introducing the notion of linkage between performativity and historical events for example. While this chapter seeks not to explore the intricacies of the tensions between different theorization of performativity, it is nonetheless important to problematize performativity within organizations, as well as also performativity within CHRD and the scholars who write within this space. We must look inwards, as well as outwards to better understand the ideological, theoretical, and socio-economic context of CHRD and the role that performativity plays within this, both within our writing, and within organizational lives more broadly. It is here where we can draw on the various works of Lyotard, but *The Postmodern Condition* in particular (1984) and the notion of the metanarrative of meaning and indeed, knowledge.

Performativity and the Patriarchy

In reflecting on and critiquing current stances in Critical Human Resource Development, we can begin to critically explore how the role of performativity may shape future directions of scholarly writing in the field, exploring and developing *petit récits* [localized narratives] (Lyotard, 1979) within subfields and a range of organizational contexts in order to further set the scene for a diversity and plurality of theoretical standpoints, in order to '*not only challenge the performative bias of the organization but also help its members achieve success on their own terms*'. (Bierema, 2009, p. 91), as well as representing a more inclusive and diverse social and economic world which also emphasizes disciplinary transformation. Petit Récits is a helpful concept to mobilize in developing theorizations and deeper understandings of imagining and so setting the stage for a more critical form of mainstream HRD, to destabilize and question the status quo and *old grand narratives* of organization and praxis, that are infiltrated with the [hegemonic] masculine, productivist, capitalist ethos.

In challenging performativity, it is important to situate the debate within the context of patriarchy, [gendered] power, and control in that these are all factors which stymie not only HRD but also equality and diversity more broadly, as well as contributing inequitable distribution of wealth, access to power and control, characterized by gendered, racialized, and classed organizational inequality regimes (Acker, 2006). Critically, Hanscome and Cervero (2003) for example also found that men and women HRD managers' experiences are not only vastly and profoundly different, but that this also shapes [gendered] organizational culture (Hanscome and Cervero, 2003, p. 522) and the realms of possibility for sustainable, inclusive, and meaningful change.

Patriarchy is alive and well, and strongly linked to performativity, and idealized notions of for example, the unencumbered worker. Patriarchy as a concept has essentially highlighted the ways in which political, and social agendas are embedded in society and social structure (Cockburn, 1991) which in turn ensures a fruitful arena for dominant masculinity to flourish in contemporary organizational contexts; characterized as the homosocial reproduction of gender inequality. However, it is also important to deliberate not only that patriarchy highlights the toxic masculinity in relation to many more [intersectional] inequalities (Crenshaw, 1991) but that this also is an everyday feature in the contemporary academy and wider world, where networks, nepotism, and gendered micropolitics are deeply entrenched (Yarrow, 2021). Vis-à-vis it is imperative to not only consider patriarchal structures as a stand-alone concept, but rather as a politicized, gendered, racialized, classed notion which serves a select minority, and further needs to be understood and situated in the context of post-colonialism, European imperialism, and neoliberal globalization (Patil, 2013).

Dominant Masculine Rationality in HRD

Dominant masculine rationality in HRD is deliberated as a site where performativity in scholarly writing comes to the fore, and where there is a need for change, pragmatic orientation, and critical integrity. In turn, there are opportunities for the shaping of policy and practice for social justice. Tensions between shareholder supremacy and stakeholder theory and its implications for CHRD and sustainable business are integral within these debates and discussed later in the chapter. It is also important to deliberate and indeed theorize the nature of tensions between the business case for CHRD, social justice, and Corporate Social Responsibility in the context of organizational strategy making. The future of the CHRD discipline is set to be shaped by wider societal challenges, whereby social, political, and economic ideologies influence policy, practice, and experience.

Evidently HRD has become vastly influenced and informed by not only the neoliberal and capitalist ideologies, homogenous and hegemonic management practices but is also shaped by dominant masculine rationality (Bierema & Callahan, 2014); 'in which masculine characteristics of assertiveness, objectivity, control, and performance are privileged without question, resulting in inequitable practices and social systems such as sexism, racism, and capitalism' (Bierema & Callahan, 2014, p. 429). It is here where the various chapters of this text provide a broad and deep exploration of critical theory and its increasingly important role within HRD research, practice, and theory, as well as experience. Dominant masculine rationality is central to and shapes every aspect of business, management, and HRD, serving to undermine and exclude a wide range of people that do not fit the dominant, status quo of [white] hetero masculinity (Gedro & Mizzi, 2014), and in this chapter, as well as through this handbook. How this can be contested, interrogated, and challenged through the mobilization of CHRD and the problematization of performativity, proletarianization, questioning, and dismantling shareholder supremacy is also explored. This may also serve to further raise awareness for action in scholarly writings and critical pedagogy.

Furthermore, there is a latent need for a text of this nature to inform and stimulate curiosity among future HRD practitioners and scholars and set strong foundations for ongoing disciplinary transformation. We need, and need to advocate for, a shift toward more inclusive theory building, organizational development and ultimately, more egalitarian experiences of organizational life and human resource management, albeit an awareness of the attenuation of employee rights (Grey, 2009). This places the onus of change and control on or indeed over, the individual (Bierema & Callahan, 2014, p. 431), thereby creating a false and problematic sense of autonomy, control and most problematically, normalization in the dominant discourses. In a world that is marred by dominant masculine rationality, organizational life is deeply gendered and inequitable. Vertical gender segregation, whereby women remain underrepresented in the upper echelons of organizations, is the status quo in most organizations around the world, with notions of gendered power (Bradley, 1999, 2016) deeply entwined with organizational power.

The Commodified [Gig] Worker in the Neoliberal Context

Globally, there has been a shift in many sectors toward employing 'gig workers' who are typically not employed on standard contracts of employment or in many cases afforded the same rights and protection as other workers. The rise of the 'gig economy' has been exponential, with estimates of the size of the 'gig' labor force varying due to the difficulty of measuring non-standard work and associated employment patterns. However, the Gig Economy Data Hub run by Cornell University and The Aspen Institute, estimate drawing on existing surveys of the US labor market, that: ' between 25 and 35 percent of workers had engaged in non-standard or gig work on a supplementary or primary basis in the preceding month' (Gig Economy Data Hub, 2021) demonstrating that gig workers make up a substantial part of the labor force, not only in the United States but increasingly in other contexts around the world, and so must be factored into CHRD scholarship and theorizations as a core influence. Current data suggests that there are currently around 57.3 m gig workers in the US alone (Statista, 2021) and research from the UK government in 2018 found that '4.4 per cent of the population in Great Britain had worked in the gig economy in the last 12 months' equating to around 2.8 million people (Department for Business, Energy, and Industrial Strategy, 2018). Thus, employment in the gig economy is contended to be one of the most significant market forces impacting and effecting contemporary HRD policy, practice, and scholarship, but also one of the potentially most detrimental modes of employment in terms of worker protection and labor rights. Given the growth of the gig economy, it is imperative to deliberate the ways in which its rise influences not only the CHRD field, but also the way in which HRD professionals do their work in the globalized context of both large corporations and SMEs (Nolan & Garavan, 2016), and the third sector.

The rise of the gig economy and precarious working is also driving pragmatic orientation in the field, particularly regarding how HRD professionals do their work, and the context within which they operate. The amorphous and fluid nature of the gig economy presents a wide range of new and different challenges for HRD as a field (Yerby & Tickell, 2020), as well as for HRD scholars and practitioners alike, in that the localities of power [and power-lessness] are destabilized, disrupted and fluctuating, presenting both new and different challenges and opportunities. Nevertheless, it is also imperative to note that 'differential treatment and outcomes for women and marginalized groups working in the gig economy' (Hunt & Samman, 2019, as cited in Yerby & Tickell, 2020) are not only deeply engrained, but also characteristic of the gig-economy. The gig economy is also shifting the way in which HRD professionals do their work, with Torraco and Lundgren (2020) for example arguing that HRD professionals will need to further develop transformative capabilities both within the discipline and for organizations, given that the gig economy is also changing notions of where, how, and by whom learning and development in organizations occurs. Algorithmic control of gig workers (Wood et al., 2019) is also leading to a 'shifting of economic risks and respon-sibility for skill development on to workers, as firms are no longer willing to provide security and training for their workforces' (Wood et al., 2019, p. 59). This in turn drives precarity and destabilizes conditions and employment terms for the workforce.

The rapid rise of the gig economy and precarious working is also driving pragmatic orientation in the HRD field, thus in itself presenting the need for reflection on the way gig economy in particular shifts the way HRD professionals do their work for example. The clearest example surrounds changing notions of where, how, and with whom learning development activi-ties occur in organizations engaged in platform work, such as Uber, Deliveroo, and TaskRabbit for example. Technology is driving what may appear on the surface to be new and different income opportunities for people, but there are many human rights, labor rights, and questions surrounding equality that arise; all of which shape the wider landscape and context in which CHRD operates, and indeed to meaningfully contribute to the critical turn in manage-ment studies. Indeed, if we are to embrace the development of workers and the development of the organization in the contemporary context, which is characterized by free-market capitalism, productivity and profitability, further meaningful resistance to the masculine, capitalist rationality must underpin both critical compromise and radical change. This needs to be paired with an ongoing problematization and critical questioning of 'HRD's ongoing pursuit of becoming a strategic partner' Bierema and Callahan (2014, p. 433) and deeper consideration of how labor market forces and changes affect understandings and theorizations of HRD, practice, and also critically orga-nizational learning and development, which does not function in an economic vacuum, but rather is predisposed to respond to market changes, which becomes further problematic when capitalist rhetoric is deliberated and how this further deepens the tensions between critical compromise and radical change; pragmatic orientation and critical integrity.

Even in more 'traditional' organizations, learning and development is increasingly being outsourced or moved online with very real implications for virtual HRD (Bennett, 2010), and this may particularly be the case in the post-covid-19 era (Nachmias & Hubschmid-Vierheilig, 2021) which in itself drives new and different ways of learning and development, but also implications for CHRD and equality and diversity, with Bierema (2020) arguing that now is the time for 'bold, critical, research'.

Bridging the Research-Practice Gap
In the scholarly domain, it is also noteworthy, drawing on the work of Ross et al. (2020) which explored the role of HRD in bridging the research-practice gap (Merriam & Bierema, 2013; Ross et al., 2020), subsequently and identified learning and development as a key path to impact (Ross et al., 2020, p. 108) and thus demarcates the importance of learning and development as a site for change. It is also notable that the academy itself is also deeply gendered, and there are gendered implications of research evaluation (Davies et al., 2020; Yarrow, 2018, 2021), as well as the sector being marked by persistent vertical gender segregation. The context within which management research more broadly and CHRD research is conducted cannot be ignored, in the sense that scholars are under increasing managerial pressure from evaluation mechanisms such as the Research Excellence Framework (REF) in the UK; Excellence in Research in Australia (ERA); Performance Based Research Fund (PBRF) in New Zealand; The National Higher Education Assessment System (SINAES) in Brazil, among many others around the globe. There is a worldwide trend toward measuring and evaluating research, for the purposes of research funding distribution. As an example, Davies et al. (2020) found that in the UK context of research evaluation and research impact case studies, which serve to document the change that research has made, that women are vastly underrepresented in the writing of impact case studies, which record the impact of research on wider society, representing only around a quarter of impact case studies submitted to REF2014, which is a notable concern, as well as being indicative of the permeation of the patriarchal nature of scholarship, as a part of the wider neoliberal, commodified academic context, in turn also creating further dilemmas for theory and practice and what scholarly work is seen to be 'impactful'.

A notable and deeply problematic example of commodification and marketization is within the academy itself, which has become increasingly neoliberal. In several contexts around the world, this is characterized by rankings, evaluations, and increases in student fees and the marketization of the student experience overall. However, educational neoliberalism is also flourishing globally (Gray et al., 2018). Furthermore, it is notable that the adoption of journal rankings is not only problematic and entangled with various value-based judgments but shaping scholarship and what work is conducted and indeed valued in the neoliberal, marketized academy. The ever-increasing use of journal ranking lists such as the CABS (Chartered Association of Business Schools) and the Financial Times 50 list, in both management studies more broadly as well as in the HRD field, is seen as a source of both 'power and powerlessness' (Anderson et al., 2020). This is also known to result in a loss of 'opportunities to engage in knowledge generation processes characterized by imagination, creativity, and vision' (Anderson et al., 2020, p. 38) for academic practitioners. All of which again drive the need for further [critical] theorizations in the field, that serve to counter sources of power and powerlessness, and in turn, also counter the deepening of divisions and existing hierarchies. In the academy, the use of journal ranking lists and their effects on scholarly activity are an expression of the commodification of knowledge, with scholars vying for places in the most respected journals, and there being evidence that this is also shaping the nature of work that some scholars carry out, and indeed the changing identity of the HRD field (Ghosh et al., 2014). It is also important to highlight that, increasingly, critical scholarly work, is also attracting criticism, particularly in the neoliberal Business School, characterized by redundancies of critical management scholars in different contexts around the world. There have been numerous, sustained attacks on critical management studies as an area of scholarship, both by university management in some institutions, as well as by other scholars. The most current and notable example being the redundancy of 16 critical management and Political Economy colleagues at Leicester University, in the UK in 2021 (ULSB16, 2021). The [neoliberal] Business School around the world is deeply gendered, racialized, shaped by dominant masculine hegemony, in many respects is a microcosm of the wider business world. The dominant masculine rationality in HRD as a byproduct of neo-liberalization will be deliberated, serving to highlight and position the role of CHRD in the wider discourse and context.

Tensions, Quandaries, and Opportunities Concerning Critical Compromise and Radical Change; Pragmatic Orientation and Critical Integrity, a Dichotomy?

The previous section explored the commodification of labor and how the gig economy, as a contemporary expression of the commodification of labor, is contributing to shifts in how HRD professionals do their work. Notably, as identified previously, this is also shaping the coeval discourse around HRD, and CHRD, as well as *how* CHRD research is carried out (Callahan & Connor, 2015), as well as the adoption and mobilization of both quantitative and qualitative) methods that work to 'expose power differences and create a more equitable evaluation within a learning environment' (Callahan & Connor, 2015, p. 314). Indeed, adopting a Freirean stance of critical pedagogy, it is clear that epistemological pluralism, rather than purism holds the potential to be more fruitful in contributing to radical change, both within critical theorizations and praxis. Notably, Callahan and Connor (2015) posit that 'scholars' purist conformism impairs the act of engaging in the praxis of critical theory (Callahan & Connor, 2015, p. 323), an important assertion in a scholarly context where we are oft confronted with epistemological and ontological binarism, and shift beyond orthodoxy (Rigg et al., 2007).

Particularly in a world characterized by volatility, uncertainty, complexity, and ambiguity (the VUCA context), critical ideologies and critical pedagogies, as well as a suite of methods for data collection, are imperative not only for radical change, but also challenging truth, as well as the status quo. There are of course subtle distinctions between the neoliberal, capitalist critiques from Bierema (2009) and the global divide, postcolonial work of Syed and Metcalfe (2017), but it is clear that CHRD plays a central role in future intersectional theorizations of critical ideologies for challenging truth and problematizing the entrenched status quo, both at the macro-economic and institutional level, and within scholarship itself, which is also being distorted by neoliberal ideologies of ranking, and the commodification of scholarship.

Further, drawing on the work of Pleasant (2017), it is also important to remember that we cannot disentangle socio-political issues from scholarly work, as well as from educational and professional spaces, but rather that awareness of and critical engagement with pressing socio-political, socio-cultural, and socio-economic challenges, can serve as a fruitful critical opportunity for more meaningful HRD, organizational diversity and inclusion, as well as wider stakeholder engagement in order to drive a shift away from shareholder supremacy.

However, one of the main barriers to the integration of [critical] pragmatic orientation and critical integrity is the consistent gap between theorizations of HRD and organizations, and pragmatic orientation. It is contended here that, drawing on the philosophy of *praxis*, and some of the philosophy of education literature, that to shift away from dialectical opposition between pragmatic orientation and critical integrity, we must as a field begin to reconcile differences, straddling the existing dichotomies to rather develop 'dialectical synthesis of theory and practice' Scatamburlo-D'Annibale et al. (2018, p. 549) and bolster pragmatic orientation.

This is also a pertinent point to return to the foundational work of Bierema and Callahan (2014) and their framework for critical HRD practice, in particular because of the fluid, flexible, contextually driven theorization of understanding and practicing HRD, which also constructs contemporary liminal spaces of (C)HRD Action (Bierema & Callahan, 2014, p. 440). It is within these liminal spaces that consideration of how and where critical compromise may be made lies. To drive radical change and contribute to the humanistic origins of HRD, while maintaining critical integrity, a renewed pragmatic orientation is required, and it is here where future scholarly opportunities for change lie. Indeed, this is one of the, if not the most pressing challenges of contemporary CHRD, which is also quintessentially bound up in the ongoing shareholder vs. stakeholder debate, but ultimately it is about transforming HRD and indeed, critical HRD practice more broadly. Further, it is clear that HRD has commitment to shareholders that overrides other stakeholders (Bierema & Callahan, 2014) which is not only short-termist, but also bounded in ethical issues, equality and diversity issues, the fragmentation of ethics and morality in leadership and is at odds with the humanistic origins of HRD. Moreover, shareholder supremacy undermines servant leadership, corporate social responsibility, and the reasons why it is enacted in that in organizations that exercise shareholder supremacy, although contested, only engage in CSR when it is legally required, profitable or demanded by core customer bases, hence again being linked to shareholder satisficing and, in turn, profit. Fenwick and Bierema (2008) identify the still latent need for further research into how HRD more broadly can engage in CSR (Fenwick & Bierema, 2008, p. 34) and critically, also that there is an ongoing disconnect between HRD units in organizations and CSR initiatives in many organizations. For organizations to truly embed CSR in their strategy, it also needs to be embedded and integrated in HRD practices and policies, as well as in organizational culture.

It is also important to explore and problematize HRD in SMEs (Nolan & Garavan, 2016), given that this area makes up a significant part of HRD scholarship, and where there is scope for better and more diverse understandings of the complexity of HRD in SMEs and the evolution of HRD over time (Nolan & Garavan, 2016, p. 101). Furthermore, in the post-pandemic world, SMEs are experiencing unique challenges, as well as unprecedented state involvement in ensuring not only the liquidity and survival of SMEs, but also their longer-term recovery (OECD, 2021), which, in turn, will also have a long-term effect on strategy making, decision making, and human resource development. This serves as a highly contemporary and clear example of the ways in which social, political, and economic factors, as expressions of economic ideologies shape policy, practice and indeed, experience. However, there is a large body of extant literature and data which makes it patently clear that in the longer-term organizations need to further engage with a wider range of stakeholders, not only to foster sustainable long-term competitive advantage, but also long-term survival. It is here where we must also deliberate and problematize the notion and effects thereof of profit maximization and the relationships between organizations, their various stakeholders, and whom the discipline of HRD and indeed CHRD, serves to benefit most fruitfully and inclusively.

Tensions Between Profit Maximization, Stakeholders, and (C)HRD

To return to the Framework for Critical HRD Practice (Bierema & Callahan, 2014), and link this to the tensions between profit maximization and stakeholders and HRD, it is important to bring back to the fore the central question both for HRD and CHRD scholars and practitioners, of *'Whom do we serve?'* (Bierema & Callahan, 2014, p. 437). The notion of service, servant leadership and reflecting on who is served by organizations is an important and powerful one; it is not asked nearly enough yet holds the power to create a renewed starting point for the critical thinking and action in human resource development, as will be explored in other chapters of this text. Further, when returning to the central question of '*whom do we serve*' we also stimulate debates and research that may help bridge the existing dichotomy between pragmatic orientation and critical integrity, which is at the heart of the tensions between not only HRD, Virtual Human Resource Development (VHRD), National Human Resource Development (NHRD), and CHRD, but also between the existing tensions, quandaries, and by implication opportunities concerning critical compromise and radical change in [critical] human resource development.

As well as the inextricable and important relationship between education, scholarship, practice, and maintaining the critical discourse in the neoliberal academy which is also increasingly devaluing critical thought and scholarship and the proletarianization of academic labor (Wilson, 1991). Furthermore, drawing on the work of Collins et al. (2017) it is also crucial to further deliberate how consideration of NHRD, HRD, and CHRD, to drive emancipation in HRD research and practice, and an integrated model of NHRD and CHRD, which in turn holds the potential to 'incorporate issues of both social and economic justice in all contexts, from a single workplace to national workforce development initiatives' (Collins et al., 2017, p. 249). The context and [re]-contextualization of policy and practice is also an integral part in creating, critiquing, and developing policy and practice that is contextually [re] situated to transform hierarchical and masculinized business practices, as well as to challenge the dominant masculine rationality which has permeated and continues to influence HRD.

It is here where the notion of critical compromise and radical change must also be discussed in that, oftentimes compromise is interpreted and presented as a limitation, however it is contended that in contemporary CHRD and HRD, compromise and further theorization in liminal spaces holds the potential for positive change through opening new spaces and directions for 'practitioners' critical questioning of key organizational practices and discourses that influence their own and others' thinking, identities, and behaviors' (Fenwick, 2014, p. 4), in order to create opportunities for the problematization of existing modes of practice and policy. In the following section shaping policy, practice, and experience for social justice, and the role of CHRD in organizational equality, diversity and inclusion is discussed.

Shaping Policy, Practice, and Experience for Social Justice. The Role of CHRD in Organizational Equality, Diversity, and Inclusion

There has never been a more important time for CHRD in driving and influencing organizational equality, diversity, and inclusion, in turn shaping policy, practice, and experience for social justice due to the vast changes which have occurred globally, even in the last five years. There have been triumphs, such as the collapse of the Trump administration, the creation of a covid-19 vaccine, and the election of Kamala Harris, the US' first Black and Indian American female Vice President, yet the world has also seen much suffering and disaster, all of which further drive the need for the further interpellation of the CHRD discourse in organizational strategy making, policy, and practice. Indeed, the ideological fractures between pragmatic orientation and critical integrity may be bridged by CHRD, contributing to a shift away from the dominant masculine rationality (Bierema & Callahan, 2014). Furthermore, in a world where corporate social responsibility is increasingly socially, strategically, and politically important for organizations, further deliberation of what this means from, and for, a CHRD perspective is important (Jang & Ardichvili, 2020), albeit not in the sense of how to improve organizational effectiveness and by implication profitability, but rather in terms of how CHRD may harness opportunities for critical reflective praxis, and further mobilize alternative conceptualizations of HRD, to 'help provide clearer operational definitions to assist practitioners enact and evaluate critical approaches to HRD' (Sambrook, 2009, p. 61).

Given that one of the facets of CHRD work is to address, problematize, and critique inequities and inequitable working practices and policies, mention must also be made of the United Nations Sustainable Development Goals (United Nations, 2021) in that they characterize the world's most urgent human, economic, and environmental issues. The UN SDGs have been posited as a powerful framework for 'embedding ethics, CSR, and sustainability in management education' (Setó-Pamies & Papaoikonomou, 2020) and this is set to become an even further influential framework and driver for change, and in turn also theorizations and praxis in the future. While an ecosystems approach to CHRD is currently somewhat underdeveloped, Garavan et al. (2019) have explored and conceptualized the notion of ecosystems within IHRD. They highlight the importance of multi-level theorizations and research that demonstrate and explore 'the interactive and dynamic nature of IHRD processes' (2019, p. 275). The ecosystems argumentation and conceptualization can and indeed should be further mobilized in contemporary CHRD research, particularly when the shift beyond orthodoxy (Rigg et al., 2007) and a [required] shift away from purist conformism (Callahan & Connor, 2015) are considered within the context of an increasingly volatile, uncertain, complex, and ambiguous world (VUCA), at the macro, meso, and micro level.

One of the most pressing contemporary challenges to face organizations that is explored in this text pertains to the deeply engrained tensions and frictions between shareholders and stakeholders, long-term HRD sustainability and effectiveness, both of which interact to shape not only peoples' lived experiences of organizational life; equality, diversity, and inclusion; HRD policy and practice; but also set the scene for new and different opportunities for CHRD, and the action that is taken on critiquing and problematizing the status quo.

The role of CHRD in organizational equality, diversity, and inclusion is central, not only because of the critical importance of developing further opportunities for [intersectional] inclusion in organizations (Healy, et al.,

2011), but also to create further meaningful space for the creation and development of 'strategies that address gender and equity issues' (Fenwick, 2014, p. 115) and for the embedding of such strategies into practice, to further bridge the policy-practice gap. That said, it is also critical to remain aware of the complexity of how this may occur in the context of global capitalism and in a context where profit maximization and shareholder supremacy reign supreme; the notion of 'sustaining radical purpose amidst managerialism' (Fenwick, 2014, p. 119) is imperative. Reconciling autonomy and community must also play a central role in Elliott and Turnbull (2003) 'to encourage a deeper engagement with social, existential and philosophical questions that lie at the heart of organizational life' (Elliott & Turnbull, 2003, p. 457), serving as a modus for stimulating renewed pragmatic orientation while maintaining critical [inclusive] integrity in the field. This also requires further bolstering by HRD practitioners communicating 'the distinctive contribution they can make in formulating and implementing organizational change programmes' Hamlin, (2016, p. 10), as well as the wider adoption of humanitarian business models (Hoque, 2007), both as a vehicle for change and for advocacy of the marginalized (Jacobson et al., 2015).

Chapter Summary

This chapter has explored and problematized the contemporary ideological, theoretical, and socio-economic context of CHRD, situating not only critical HRD in the extant literature and the neoliberal, globalized context but also setting the scene for subsequent chapters and the broader exploration of critical human resource development, and how this shapes the five key domains of organizing, relating, learning, changing (Bierema & Callahan, 2014), and advocating (Collins et al., 2015). The tensions, quandaries, and opportunities concerning critical compromise and radical change have been explored, to not only situate other chapters in this text, but most importantly to situate the imperative need for further critical HRD opportunities for change; change that contributes pragmatically to more egalitarian, inclusive, and diverse, and critically aware management, training, and development in organizations. Indeed, an organizational socio-cultural turn in conscientization through both critical scholarly work, refection, and action is required, and as critical scholars there are a number of questions which we must ask not only ourselves but aim to build into scholarship and practice in order to ensure an ongoing and robust cognizance of the most pressing issues in the field and the tumultuous context within which we find ourselves. Further, keeping such questions at the forefront of our minds, scholarly endeavors and practice holds the potential to contribute in the longer term to a renewed pragmatic orientation while maintaining critical [inclusive] integrity in the field.

- *'Whom do we serve' as a discipline and how can we ensure that equality, diversity and inclusion both scholarship and practice are championed?*

- *How can we develop and integrate further discussion of opportunities for change and positive, inclusive, and critical development in organizations?*
- *What can I do both as an individual and as a scholar as part of a scholarly community or as a practitioner to contribute [meaningfully] to more egalitarian experiences of organizational life?*
- *How can we actively resist and critique the masculine, capitalist rationality, particularly in the post-covid 19 era, in the context of the labor market inequality and the rise of the gig economy?*

The integral role of CHRD in organizational equality, diversity, and inclusion has been discussed as an area which needs to be further integrated into mainstream HRD discussion, policy, and practice, to counter the masculine rationality which is played out through performativity and commodification in the contemporary neoliberal context. CHRD serves as an important scholarly field which is needed more now than ever before, not only to critique dominant masculine rationality, shareholder supremacy, problematize marketization and performativity, but also to maintain and develop fora that center critical ideologies for challenging truth and oppression in the contemporary, neoliberal, and globalized context. Critical understanding of the ways in which social, political, and economic ideologies shape policy, practice, and experience are central to the further development of the discipline of CHRD, as well as needing to be central to our own awareness and sensitivity of the challenges and opportunities we face as scholars and inclusive citizens. Returning briefly to the notion of interpellation (Althusser, 1971), in allowing, and enabling ideologies to permeate, influence, and shape our thinking, the ideological function of CHRD' importance is further increased as an opportunity for contributing to the enactment of critical ideologies for challenging '*truth*'.

References

Abou-Chadi, T., & Krause, W. (2020). The causal effect of radical right success on mainstream parties' policy positions: A regression discontinuity approach. *British Journal of Political Science, 50*(3), 829–847.

Acker, J. (1990). Hierarchies, jobs, bodies: A theory of gendered organizations. *Gender and Society, 4*(2), 139–158.

Acker, J. (2006). Inequality regimes. Gender, class, and race in organizations. *Gender and Society, 20*(4), 441–464.

Althusser, L. (1971). *Lenin and Philosophy*. Monthly Review.

Anderson, V., Elliott, C., & Callahan, J. (2020). Power, powerlessness, and journal ranking lists: The marginalization of fields of practice. *Academy of Management Learning & Education.* https://doi.org/10.5465/amle.2019.0037

Austin, J. L. (1975/1962). How to do things with words. *The William James Lectures delivered at Harvard University in 1955.*

Beck, U., & Beck-Gernsheim, E. (2002). *Individualization: Institutionalized individualism and its social and political consequences.* Sage.

Beigi, M., Callahan, J., & Michaelson, C. (2019). A critical plot twist: Changing characters and foreshadowing the future of organizational storytelling. *International Journal of Management Reviews, 21*(4), 447–465.

Bennett, E. E. (2010). The coming paradigm shift: Synthesis and future directions for virtual HRD. *Advances in Developing Human Resources, 12*(6), 728–741.

Bierema, L. L. (2020). HRD research and practice after 'The Great COVID-19 Pause': the time is now for bold, critical, research. *Human Resource Development International*, 1–14.

Bierema, L. L. (2009). Critiquing human resource development's dominant masculine rationality and evaluating its impact. *Human Resource Development Review, 8*, 68–96.

Bierema, L., & Callahan, J. L. (2014). Transforming HRD: A framework for critical HRD practice. *Advances in Developing Human Resources, 16*(4), 429–444.

Bradley, H. (2016). *Fractured identities: Changing patterns of inequality* (4th ed.). Polity Press.

Bradley, H. (1999). *Gender and power in the workplace: Analysing the impact of economic change*. Macmillan.

Chacko, P., & Jayasuriya, K. (2018). Asia's conservative moment: Understanding the rise of the right. *Journal of Contemporary Asia, 48*(4), 529–540.

Butler, J. (1988). Performative acts and gender constitution: An essay in phenomenology and feminist theory. *Theatre Journal, 40*(4), 519–531.

Callahan, J., & Connor, G. (2015). The competing interests of paradigm and praxis in critical HRD research: Incorporating quantitative methods to enact critical practice. In M. Saunders & P. Tosey (Eds.), *Handbook of research methods on human resource development* (pp. 311–324). Edward Elgar. https://doi.org/10.4337/978178100 9246

Cockburn, C. (1991). *In the way of women: Men's resistance to sex equality in organizations* (Vol. 18). Cornell University Press.

Collins, J. C., McFadden, C., Rocco, T. S., & Mathis, M. K. (2015). The problem of transgender marginalization and exclusion: Critical actions for human resource development. *Human Resource Development Review, 14*(2), 205–226.

Collins, J. C., Zarestky, J., & Tkachenko, O. (2017). An integrated model of national HRD and critical HRD: Considering new possibilities for human resource development. *Human Resource Development International, 20*(3), 236–252.

Contu, A. (2009). Critical management education. In M. Alvesson, T. Bridgman, & H. Willmott (Eds.), *The Oxford handbook of critical management studies*. https://doi.org/10.1093/oxfordhb/9780199595686.013.0027

Crenshaw, K. (1991). Mapping the margins: Intersectionality, identity politics, and violence against women of color. *Stanford Law Review, 43*(6), 1241–1299.

Davies, J. (2021). Implications for HRD practice and impact in the COVID-19 era. *Human Resource Development Review, 20*(1), 3–8.

Davies, J., Yarrow, E., & Syed, J. (2020). The curious under-representation of women impact case leaders: Can we dis-engender inequality regimes? *Gender, Work & Organization, 27*(2), 129–148.

Department for Business, Energy, and Industrial Strategy. (2018). *The characteristics of those in the gig economy-final report*. Source: https://assets.publishing.service.gov.uk/government/uploads/system/uploads/attachment_data/file/687553/The_cha racteristics_of_those_in_the_gig_economy.pdf. Retrieved 5 March 2021.

Derrida, J. (1988). Limited Inc. Northwestern University Press.

De Waal, C. (1999). Eleven challenges to the pragmatic theory of truth. *Transactions of the Charles S. Peirce Society, 35*(4), 748–766. Retrieved 4 June 2020, from www.jstor.org/stable/40320796

Elliott, C., & Turnbull, S. (2003). Reconciling autonomy and community: The paradoxical role of HRD. *Human Resource Development International, 6,* 457–474.

Elliott, C., & Turnbull, S. (Eds.). (2004). *Critical thinking in human resource development* (Vol. 12). Routledge.

Fenwick, T. J. (2004). Toward a critical HRD in theory and practice. *Adult Education Quarterly, 54*(3), 193–209.

Fenwick, T. J. (2005). Conceptions of critical HRD: Dilemmas for theory and practice. *Human Resource Development International, 8*(2), 225–238.

Fenwick, T., & Bierema, L. (2008). Corporate social responsibility: Issues for human resource development professionals. *International Journal of Training and Development, 12*(1), 24–35.

Fenwick, T. (2014). Conceptualizing critical HRD (CHRD): Tensions, dilemmas, and possibilities. In R. F. Poell, T. S. Rocco, & G. L. Roth (Eds.), *The Routledge companion to human resource development* (pp. 113–123). Routledge.

Garavan, T. N., McCarthy, A., & Carbery, R. (2019). An Ecosystems perspective on international human resource development: A meta-synthesis of the literature. *Human Resource Development Review, 18*(2), 248–288. https://doi.org/10.1177/1534484319828865

Gedro, J., & Mizzi, R. C. (2014). Feminist theory and queer theory: Implications for HRD research and practice. *Advances in Developing Human Resources, 16*(4), 445–456.

Ghosh, R., Kim, M., Kim, S., & Callahan, J. L. (2014). Examining the dominant, emerging, and waning themes featured in select HRD publications: Is it time to redefine HRD? *European Journal of Training and Development, 38*(4), 302–322. https://doi.org/10.1108/EJTD-02-2013-0012

Gig Economy Data Hub. (2021). *How many gig workers are there?* Source: https://www.gigeconomydata.org/basics/how-many-gig-workers-are-there. Retrieved 12 October 2021.

Gray, J., O'Regan, J. P., & Wallace, C. (2018). Education and the discourse of global neoliberalism. *Language and Intercultural Communication, 18*(5), 471–477. https://doi.org/10.1080/14708477.2018.1501842

Grey, C. (2009). *A very short, fairly interesting and reasonably cheap book about studying organizations* (2nd ed.). SAGE.

Hamlin, B. (2016). HRD and organizational change: Evidence-based practice. *International Journal of HRD Practice, Policy and Research, 1*(1), 7–20.

Hanscome, L., & Cervero, R. M. (2003). The impact of gendered power relations in HRD. *Human Resource Development International, 6,* 509–525.

Harrison P., Nichol L., & Gold J. (2020) Redefining HRD roles and practice in the machine learning revolution. In M. Loon, J. Stewart, & S. Nachmias (Eds.), *The future of HRD* (Vol. I). Palgrave Macmillan. https://doi.org/10.1007/978-3-030-52410-4_6

Healy, G., Bradley, H., & Forson, C. (2011). Intersectional sensibilities in analysing inequality regimes in public sector organizations. *Gender, Work and Organization, 18*(5), 467–487.

Helgesen, S. (1990). *The female advantage: Women's ways of leadership.* Doubleday.

Hoque, F. (2007). Corporate social responsibility: Using a humanitarian business model. *Corporate Responsibility Officer, 2*(6), 45–46.

Jacobson, S. A., Callahan, J. L., & Ghosh, R. (2015). A place at the window: Theorizing organizational change for advocacy of the marginalized. *Human Resource Development Review, 14*(4), 462–485.

Jang, S., & Ardichvili, A. (2020). Examining the link between corporate social responsibility and human resources: Implications for HRD research and practice. *Human Resource Development Review,* 1534484320912044.

Johns, G. (2006). The essential impact of context on organizational behavior. *Academy of Management Review, 31*(2), 386–408.

Kay, C. (2008). Reflections on Latin American rural studies in the neoliberal globalization period: A new rurality? *Development and Change, 39*(6), 915–943.

Liebhart, K. (2020). 25 years later–Austria's shift to the populist right: National characteristics of a pan-European trend. *Politics in Central Europe, 16*(2), 399–417.

Lyotard, J. F. (1984/1979). *The postmodern condition: A report on knowledge* (G. Bennington & B. Massumi, Trans.). University of Minnesota Press.

McGoldrick, J., Stewart, J., & Watson, S. (2001). Theorizing human resource development. *Human Resource Development International, 4*, 343–356. https://doi.org/10.1080/13678860126443

Merriam, S. B., & Bierema, L. L. (2013). *Adult learning: Bridging theory and practice.* Jossey-Bass.

Mezzadri, A., Newman, S., & Stevano, S. (2021). Feminist global political economies of work and social reproduction. *Review of International Political Economy,* 1–21. https://doi.org/10.1080/09692290.2021.1957977

Nachmias, S., & Hubschmid-Vierheilig, E. (2021). We need to learn how to love digital learning 'again': European SMEs response to COVID-19 digital learning needs. *Human Resource Development International, 24*(2), 123–132. https://doi.org/10.1080/13678868.2021.1893503

Nail, P. R., & McGregor, I. (2009). Conservative shift among liberals and conservatives following 9/11/01. *Social Justice Research, 22*, 231–240. https://doi.org/10.1007/s11211-009-0098-z

Nolan, C. T., & Garavan, T. N. (2016). Problematizing HRD in SMEs: A "critical" exploration of context, informality, and empirical realities. *Human Resource Development Quarterly, 27*(3), 407–442.

OECD. (2021, April 8). *OECD Policy Responses to Coronavirus (COVID-19) One year of SME and entrepreneurship policy responses to COVID-19: Lessons learned to "build back better".* Source: https://www.oecd.org/coronavirus/policy-responses/one-year-of-sme-and-entrepreneurship-policy-responses-to-covid-19-lessons-learned-to-build-back-better-9a230220/. Retrieved 4 October 2021.

Patil, V. (2013). From patriarchy to intersectionality: A transnational feminist assessment of how far we've really come. *Signs, 38*(4), 847–867. https://doi.org/10.1086/669560

Pleasant, S. (2017). Crossing the boundaries of employee engagement and workplace diversity and inclusion: Moving HRD forward in a complicated socio-political climate. *New Horizons in Adult Education and Human Resource Development, 29*(3), 38–44.

Rigg, C., Stewart, J., & Trehan, K. (2007). *Critical human resource development: Beyond orthodoxy.* Financial Times/Prentice Hall.

Robinson, W. I., & Robinson, W. I. (2008). *Latin America and global capitalism: A critical globalization perspective*. Johns Hopkins University Press.

Ross, C., Nichol, L., Elliott, C., Sambrook, S., & Stewart, J. (2020). The role of HRD in bridging the research-practice gap: The case of learning and development. *Human Resource Development International, 23*(2), 108–124.

Ruona, W. E. (2016). Evolving human resource development. *Advances in Developing Human Resources, 18*(4), 551–565.

Sambrook, S. (2003, July 7 – 9). *A critical time for HRD?* Paper presented to the Critical Management Studies Conference, University of Lancaster.

Sambrook, S. (2009). Critical HRD: A concept analysis. *Personnel Review, 38*(1), 61–73. https://doi.org/10.1108/00483480910920714

Scatamburlo-D'Annibale, V., Brown, B. A., & McLaren P. (2018) Marx and the philosophy of praxis. In P. Smeyers (Ed.), *International handbook of philosophy of education*. Springer International Handbooks of Education. Springer. https://doi.org/10.1007/978-3-319-72761-5_44

Setó-Pamies, D., & Papaoikonomou, E. (2020). Sustainable development goals: A powerful framework for embedding ethics, CSR, and sustainability in management education. *Sustainability, 12*(5). https://doi.org/10.3390/su12051762

Short, D. C., & Callahan, J. L. (2005). 'Would I work for a global corporation?' And other ethical questions for HRD. *Human Resource Development International, 8*(1), 121–125.

Statista. (2021). *Gig economy in the U.S.—Statistics & Facts*. Statista Research Department. Source: https://www.statista.com/topics/4891/gig-economy-in-the-us/. Retrieved 5 March 2021.

Stiglitz, J. E. (2017). The overselling of globalization. *Business Economics, 52*(3), 129–137. https://doi.org/10.1057/s11369-017-0047-z

Syed, J. (2010). Reconstructing gender empowerment. *Women's Studies International Forum, 33*(3), 283–294.

Syed, J., & Metcalfe, B. D. (2017). Under western eyes: A transnational and postcolonial perspective of gender and HRD. *Human Resource Development International, 20*(5), 403–414.

Thompson, J. B. (1990). *Ideology and modern culture: Critical social theory in the era of mass communication*. Wiley.

Torraco, R. J., & Lundgren, H. (2020). What HRD is doing—What HRD should be doing: The case for transforming HRD. *Human Resource Development Review, 19*(1), 39–65.

ULSB. (2021). *A campaign against the attack on academic freedom and the targeting of CMS/PE*. Briefing to Colleagues. Source: https://ulsb.uculeicester.org.uk/briefing-to-colleagues/. Retrieved 11 October 2021.

United Nations. (2021). *The 17 goals*. Source: https://sdgs.un.org/goals. Retrieved 11 October 2021.

Wheatley, M. (1992). *Leadership and the new science: Learning about organization from an orderly universe*. Berrett-Koehler.

Wilson, T. (1991). The proletarianisation of academic labour. *Industrial Relations Journal, 22*(4), 250–262.

Wood, A. J., Graham, M., Lehdonvirta, V., & Hjorth, I. (2019). Good gig, bad gig: Autonomy and algorithmic control in the global gig economy. *Work, Employment and Society, 33*(1), 56–75.

Yarrow, E. (2018). Gender and the research excellence framework. In J. Robertson, A. Williams, D. Jones, & D. Loads (Eds.), *EqualBITE: Gender equality in higher education* (pp. 63–68). Brill Sense. https://doi.org/10.1163/9789463511438

Yarrow, E. (2021). Knowledge hustlers: Gendered micro-politics and networking in UK universities. *British Educational Research Journal, 47*(3), 579–598. https://doi.org/10.1002/berj.3671

Yerby, E., & Tickell, R. P. (2020). Talent disrupted: Opportunities and threats for human resource development (HRD) Strategy and practice in the gig economy through the critical HRD lens. In *The Future of HRD, Volume I* (pp. 93–114). Palgrave Macmillan.

CHAPTER 4

Morality, Ethics, and Critical HRD

Matthew Sinnicks

This chapter aims to explore some of the ethical contours of CHRD. To do so, it introduces the theoretical bases which inform a critical understanding of ethics, and of the ways in which morality can be leveraged to the advantage of some and the disadvantage of others. The discussion that follows will comprise three subsections. Firstly, the section "What is morality and ethics?" draws on the work of Williams and MacIntyre to outline a distinction between these related concepts. Secondly, "What is a human resource?" outlines the implicit morality of standard approaches to HRD and explores their limitations. Finally, "What is a human?: Toward an Ethics of CHRD" moves beyond the limitations of standard approaches to HRD and outlines some of the positive bases for an ethics of CHRD.

While HRD resists easy definition (Lee, 2001), and must be understood in broad terms (Fenwick, 2004), it is closely associated with HRM (Harrison et al., 2021; Sambrook, 2004), a field notable for its "remarkable ethics deficit" (Alzola, 2018, p. 835). In practice, CHRD is perhaps best regarded as the wing of HRM concerned with employee development, understood in terms of training, education, and learning, but theoretically, it has a far broader scope. Given that the concept of development connotes growth, evolution, and maturation, ethics is central to HRD (Swanson, 1999), and such concepts

M. Sinnicks (✉)
Southampton Business School, University of Southampton, Southampton, UK
e-mail: m.sinnicks@soton.ac.uk

© The Author(s), under exclusive license to Springer Nature Switzerland AG 2023
J. C. Collins and J. L. Callahan (eds.), *The Palgrave Handbook of Critical Human Resource Development*, https://doi.org/10.1007/978-3-031-10453-4_4

clearly extend well beyond the narrow purview of HRM. However, Shirmo-hammadi et al.'s literature review found that "[s]urprisingly, ethics did not show up as a cluster or even as an item in a cluster for HRD" (2021, p. 219). Because of this, "[i]f ethics is truly going to be a part of HRD… scholars need to be doing more research and writing about this concept" (Shirmohammadi et al., 2021, p. 219). The present chapter marks an attempt to contribute to this aim.

If ethics is central to HRD, then it seems likely to be even more important to CHRD, given that the critical project is unavoidably concerned with human emancipation. Indeed, if we allow that the concept of development implies a concern with ethics, then ethics in turn implies a degree of criticality.

WHAT IS MORALITY AND ETHICS?

While the concepts of morality and ethics are often used interchangeably, and indeed have a common etymology—'*moralis*' is a Latin translation of the Greek "*ethikos*"—it is possible to distinguish between them in a way that captures an important tension in our normative thinking. This tension is between morality as a system of social control that relies on rules and prin-ciples and has connotations of severity and proscription, and ethics as a set of value-laden commitments that aims to promote human flourishing.

This distinction has roots in the work of a variety of figures in the history of ethical thought. Hegel (1991) distinguishes between individualistic and narrow "morality" ("Moralitat") and a community-focused "ethical life" ('Sit-tlichkeit') which relates to all aspects of human conduct. Nietzsche (1998) contrasts a slavish "good/evil" conception of ethics, in which evil has logical priority and goodness is seen as its negation, and a more life-affirming "good/bad" conception, in which goodness has priority and badness is its negation.

Other thinkers have rejected morality and yet retained an irreducibly ethical focus. Kierkegaard can be read as calling for a "teleological suspension of the ethical" (2003, p. 83), and yet this suspension can be understood as a way of encouraging an appreciation of the importance of grace (Lippitt, 2003; Mulhall, 2001). Marx and Engels claimed that "Communists do not preach morality at all" (1970, p. 104), and yet Marxism is animated by a set of ethical concerns, which are clearly implicit in Marx's discussion of alienated labor and his remarks on good work (see Sinnicks, 2021). Freud offers a psychoana-lytic critique of morality (Freud, 2002), which he associates with a culture's restrictions on sexual behavior and with religious belief, and yet it is undeni-able that the psychoanalytic project has an ethical and emancipatory *telos* (see Lear, 2015, ch.7). A similar position is occupied by Foucault, whose employ-ment of concepts such as "regime" and "power" coupled with an apparent rejection of normativity led to the charge of "cryptonormativity" (Habermas, 1987), and yet is perhaps better read as a rejection of one *kind* of normativity, alongside an implicit acceptance of another in his later work on the care of the self (Foucault, 1988). Adorno suggests that ours is a "wrong life" that "cannot be lived rightly" (2005, p. 39), and yet even if a positive ethics is impossible an ethic of resistance remains possible (Adorno, 2000, p. 168), including within contemporary work (Reeves & Sinnicks, 2021). MacKinnon claims that her work on patriarchy "is not about right and wrong or what I think is good or bad to think or do" (1989, p. xii) and even that pornography is not a moral issue (1984). Nevertheless, this seems to be an attempt to distance feminism from mere moralizing, as an implicit ethics of resistance emerges from MacKinnon's work.

Despite the historical precedent, the distinction between morality and ethics has perhaps been most explicitly elaborated by more recent figures such as Williams (1985) and MacIntyre (2016), both of whom reject morality—the "morality system" for Williams, capital "M" "Morality" for MacIntyre—as being antagonistic to ethics, properly understood. For Williams, this morality system is a "peculiar institution" (1985, p. 174) for which "blame is the characteristic reaction" (1985, p. 177). It is unable to properly account for a variety of human goods—happiness, talent, love, (Williams, 1985, p. 195) and so on—which are clearly part of the domain of ethics as a result of its requirement for the utmost purity. It is fundamentally concerned with abstract rights and duties and sees moral agency as compartmentalized from our broader commitments and concerns. For Williams, it expresses "a deeply rooted and still powerful misconception of life" (1985, p. 196).

While this system presents itself as being universal, for MacIntyre it is,

> peculiar to and characteristic of early and late capitalist modernity. Morality, has flourished and still flourishes in Western and Central Europe, in North America, and in other parts of the earth that their inhabitants have colonized from the early eighteenth to the twenty-first century. (2016, pp. 114–115)

This conception is fundamentally individualistic, and thus underplays the importance of both our embeddedness within communities, and relationships between people (for a discussion of the importance of relationships in HRD see Armitage, 2018). It is a conception that depends upon an illusion of self-sufficiency and casts morality as a private matter for independent agents understood as the "unencumbered abstract rational self of liberal political and moral theories" (Held, 2006, p. 14). It takes a special kind of myopia to imagine human beings in this way. No real person is so unencumbered, though those most able to imagine themselves in this way can only do so in the relative absence of poverty, illness, discrimination, and other such realities which make our dependence on others sometimes painfully clear.

If Williams and MacIntyre are right, it is easy to see how morality can be used as a tool to punish perceived deviance, and thus to the advantage of some and the disadvantage of others. When wielded in this way, Morality is not simply a misconception, but becomes a tool of social control or of unjust social domination.

When Fenwick says her aim "is to offer a more diffuse and perhaps less morally strident orientation in CHRD" (2014, p. 113), something like this distinction between morality and ethics seems to be tacitly assumed. The stridency characteristic of morality fails to do justice to the contours of many real human lives. Ethics, in the sense employed here, aims to avoid this shortcoming. Ethics in this sense is inherently critical: tacitly critical of morality, and of institutions and social structures which impede human flourishing. Thus, in the remainder of this chapter, I will reserve the term "ethics" for this broader and more critical conception, and "morality" for the morality system critiqued by Williams and MacIntyre.

This is not the only way to distinguish between ethics and morality, nor is it the only way to make sense of the place of human values within the critical project. The critique of CSR, for instance, is framed in terms of broader values rather than restrictive moral duties, and thus pertains to ethics. Insofar as "ethics" is a form of practice business organizations can engage in, it is susceptible to being subordinated to business ends, and thus to "CSR programmes," featuring statements of values, codes of conduct, ethics training, compliance officers, and so on. Such CSR initiatives are at the service of perception management, managerial control, the justification of self-regulation, and various other ends that ultimately converge in being, or appearing to be, conducive to profitability. Critics of CSR have been keen to highlight the ideological nature of businesses' attempts to manage ethics. Fleming and Jones suggest that CSR has always been a matter of manipulating public perception, and suggest that genuine CSR "never really began" (2013, p. 1). Fleming argues, "CSR has emerged as a key ideological weapon" (2015, p. 137) used to legitimize business, rather than a genuine ethical movement. Cederström and Marinetto argue that the ideology of CSR seeks to "render invisible those contradictions that exist between, for instance, profit-seeking business activities and a notion of the social good" (2013, p. 417).

However, within CSR ethical initiatives there is a reductive aspect at odds with the breadth of ethics as I have outlined it which again aligns it with morality. The underlying assumption seems to be that as pursuing profit—the maximization of owner value—is the essence of corporate activity, all ethical initiatives themselves are justifiable only insofar as they contribute to this aim, and therefore any initiatives which challenge it or are in tension with it are necessarily illegitimate. As such, the questions of CSR are bracketed-off from a broader understanding of ethics and ethical enquiry, and indeed our everyday conception of ethics. Again, there is a separation from other concerns—Williams' happiness, talent, and love noted above.

Nevertheless, it is worth noting that there is not a single ethical position underpinning CHRD. Rather, there are a variety of critical approaches. Marxism, Frankfurt School Critical Theory, Critical Realism, Feminism, Postmodernism, and so on, are all varieties of critical social theory, and have distinctive ethical commitments. However, they all share a commitment to human emancipation. They all share the suspicion that the dominant conception of the self, presupposed by morality (i.e., the abstract, unencumbered individual chooser best understood atomistically) is woefully inadequate and unable to capture the realities of human experience and agency. Thus, there is unity in the diversity of ethics, and this chapter uses this concept to contrast CHRD, a fundamentally ethical concept, with standard approaches to HRD.

What Is a Human Resource?

This section focuses on the implicit morality of standard approaches to HRD, and thus aims to outline some of the ethically salient problems with such approaches which provide an essential part of the rationale for adopting a critical approach. It focuses in particular on the model of the self that links standard approaches to HRD and the conception of morality outlined in the preceding section.

The understanding of the self in play in standard HRD discussions is ostensibly neutral: the human as resource is just that, something that can be put to use in any number of ways. Indeed, what seems to be neutral or reasonable is often reflective of unstated value judgments, and particular non-neutral frameworks. Sometimes the aimed at neutrality is reflective of a laudable desire to be inclusive, for example when an institution like marriage becomes less wedded to a particular conception of the relationship marriage names and thus closer to "neutrality" between incompatible views. However, apparently neutral presentations may also be reflective of values and presuppositions, and the claim of ostensible neutrality may in fact discourage a proper examination of these, as is often the case when we dutifully and uncritically accept role demands in the workplace.

Furthermore, it is a mistake to hold "that metaphysical neutrality is possible and desirable", as any substantive doctrine "will presuppose metaphysical commitments" (Reeves, 2016, p. 218). We do not, of course, want every ethical claim to rest or fall with the acceptance of some highly particular metaphysical theory—basic ethical truths, relating for instance to the prima facie goodness of kindness and love, are compatible with a wide range of metaphysical conceptions of humanity, just as they are compatible with a wide range of expressly ethical theories. Nevertheless, Reeves' insight allows us to understand why the apparently neutral, thin conception of the self has long been the subject of critique, particularly in the context of ethics and political philosophy. This critique has been raised in the context of Nozick's (1974) libertarianism by Taylor (1979), and Rawls' (1971) liberalism by Sandel (1984). This line of thought is also implicit in much of care ethics (see Held, 1983, Gilligan, 1993, as well as MacIntyre, 1999a) which encourages us to be wary of moral theories which take autonomous and atomistic individuals as their central protagonists. Nevertheless, this conception retains a powerful place in contemporary society (Zuboff, 2019). By understanding the limitations, or rather, the inadequacies, of this conception we will be better placed to understand the ethics of CHRD outlined in the following sections.

Bierema and Cseh note that "HRD focuses little on issues of social justice in the workplace or larger social context" (2003, p. 23), reflective of the compartmentalization characteristic of Morality. Elliot and Turnbull note the predominantly performative focus of the HRD field (2003). Poell and van der Krogt suggest that "[d]eveloping employees is often regarded as an instrument to improve the internal labor market and support organizational change" (2017, p. 180). This conception of HRD as asocial, performative, and instrumental implies a set of normative commitments—a morality—that inevitably undermine and may even exclude those whose lives, commitments, and ethical orientations are ill-suited to such narrow strictures, a category which includes both HRD professionals themselves and those whom such professionals aim to serve. Indeed, it seems to favor just those relatively unburdened individuals, whose agency can be compartmentalized from a broader set of relationships and community-focused concerns, identified as the subjects of morality above.

Bierema highlights five shortcomings of standard approaches to HRD: "(a) a performative philosophy; (b) the commodification of employees; (c) the allegiance to shareholders; (d) the ignoring of power relations; and (e) the lack of alternative models and theories for HRD practice" (2009, p. 72). This conception maps onto the presuppositions of morality, and frames the human resource as a rational chooser, understandable without reference to a wider community, relationships, or dependencies. The allegiance to shareholders reflects a certain conception of legitimate power which necessarily goes unquestioned as power relations are ignored, a coupling which prevents ameliorative challenges that might empower the powerless. The lack of alternative models frames the status quo as the only viable option, attempting to undermine the scope of our imagination, and thus serving as a tool of control that prevents us from appreciating the breadth of possibilities open to us, possibilities that might allow us to realize better workplaces and indeed better, more just, and more humane societies. Performative philosophy and commodification of employees casts the self as inherently fungible, divorced from any sense of intrinsic value. As such, humans are resources, to be mastered, manipulated, and controlled just like any other resource. Such a way of thinking tends to presuppose managerial superiority and is dismissive of the capacities of ordinary employees (see Munro & Thanem, 2018). As MacIntyre puts it, "those who arrogate to themselves an exclusive, professionalised authority of a certain kind by that very act of arrogation discredit their own claims to legitimate authority" (2006, p. 51).

If the self is regarded as being essentially separate from wider commitments and memberships of different communities, then it is more readily imaginable that it can be molded to enhance organizational performance, to prioritize organizational aims, entirely separately from a broader set of identities or a broader life narrative. Again, this is the compartmentalized self which is presupposed by morality. This self is available to fill the employment role demanded of it without recourse to wider commitments, commitments which may be in tension with those role demands.

This tension is precisely why integrity is so central to ethics. However, the concept of integrity has a bizarre double life. On the one hand, it connotes a wholeness at odds with the narrowly proscribed role expectations one often finds in the context of employment, and on the other, it is a favorite term of the corporate statement of values—Audi refers to it as "that favorite omnibus virtue" in business (2012, p. 286)— used to imply a general commitment to upstanding behavior even as such organizations often render proper integrity unavailable.

Again, Williams and MacIntyre are instructive here. Williams (1973) provides a fictional example in which "George" is deciding whether to take a job at a bio-chemical weapons company. Without the job, George's family is in danger of poverty, and his reservations about the role make it likely that, if he refuses to take the job, the person who does in fact take it will likely do more harm than George (by working more diligently and efficiently). However, what such considerations ignore is that it matters to George whether it is he who develops the weapons. To focus merely on the function—to see oneself as a "human resource"—is to ignore the importance of integrity.

Integrity "cannot be specified at all except with reference to the whole-ness of a human life" (MacIntyre, 2007, p. 203), and so is at odds with the bracketing-off of ethics from role expectations as the performative model requires. As MacIntyre says, "To have integrity is… to have set inflexible limits to one's adaptability to the roles that one may be called upon to play (1999b, p. 317). In this view integrity is a condition of the avoidance of irresolvable role conflict, and thus a prerequisite of effective moral agency. Our moral agency will be compromised if we are unable to adjudicate between competing ethical demands.

And yet, our social world generates considerable pressure toward adaptive role-identification, wherein people identify with their employer, employment role, or working conditions, or at least formulate their dissatisfaction and demands in thin and minimal terms that object to the extremes while implicitly accepting the essentials of their predicament. Many sorts of jobs create pres-sures on people to adapt to their situation, by identifying with their employers and/or their employment role (Musílek et al., 2020).

Many of the trappings of HRD appear to have humanistic ends, in the positive sense of affirming the value of human beings. However, these are often illusory, and merely serve to conceal a focus on performance entirely at odds with this humanistic veneer. After all, it would be remarkable if the goal of human development always coincided with enhanced organizational performance and increased profitability, regardless of the organization and its aims. Nevertheless, it is worth acknowledging the humanistic impulse behind HRD, which seeks to develop meaning and purpose (Chalofsky & Cavallaro, 2013). According to Chalofsky, there are rival conceptions of human beings within debates in HRD: "One has the emphasis more on human resources as commodities, and the other, and the one I like better, has the emphasis more on developing the human – developing inner resources of human beings to help them reach their potential." (Chalofsky, cited in Callahan & Ward, 2001, p. 239).

In some ways we can understand CHRD as attempting to deliver on these humanistic ethical aspirations of HRD. CHRD goes further, and seeks to manifest the developmental impulse in a way that standard—one hesitates to use the term "uncritical"—approaches cannot. This is in part because what makes CHRD *critical* is a recognition of the deeply embedded nature of the barriers to this fulfillment of potential, and thus of the radical approach required to overcome sources of frustration to human development and well-being. Being able to transcend the narrowly proscribed role morality of the contemporary workplace is essential to human flourishing, and thus an examination of the model of the human that becomes available when we no longer place such a heavy emphasis on the *resource* aspect is the task of the following section.

What Is a Human?: Toward an Ethics of CHRD

This section focuses on ethics as a basis of CHRD. In order to move beyond the assumptions of standard approaches to HRD, we need a clearer understanding of that which is to be developed—the *human* element rather than the *resource*. This section, therefore, addresses the positive bases of an ethics of CHRD. The concept of development implies some desired and desirable transformation of the self.

It would be misleading to claim that CHRD presupposes a single, homogeneous model of the self—indeed, for CHRD identity is "wonderfully heterogeneous" (Gedro et al., 2014, p. 533). In any case, this is not the place to attempt to provide a comprehensive treatise on human nature. Nevertheless, it is possible to attempt to articulate, perhaps only *via negativa*, some aspects that the "human resource" approach necessarily neglects. There are unifying values and commitments in CHRD that suggest an overlapping consensus regarding the broad shape of a flourishing human life and of flourishing human communities. These include equality and empowerment, as well as a recognition of the importance of vulnerability and dependence which are also central features of the human experience but are often unduly ignored in accounts of ethics (MacIntyre, 1999a) as well as the HRD literature (Collins, 2019). The result is a more holistic concept that is available to standard approaches to HRD (Bierema & Callahan, 2014) and in particular emphasizes our social nature, something which, as noted above, standard approaches to HRD fail to appreciate.

CHRD is partially rooted in radical accounts of adult education, which emphasizes the importance of self-education, rather than conceiving of people as mere recipients of training. More broadly, this background also suggests that the vision of "liberal education"—in the sense that implies lifelong learning and freedom of mind—is able to shed light on the implicit conception of the human. The well-trained employee is not always the well-educated or enlightened person, and indeed sometimes these separate goals are in tension. According to this vision, there are capacities that we all share which can be developed through education, and which can empower us and make our lives more meaningful, and yet which are not only underdeveloped by the typical workplace, but are in fact systematically marginalized by capitalist society, and by the typical workplace. This means that in order to understand human beings adequately, and thus to begin to develop an adequate conception of ethics, is necessary to depart from the presuppositions of Morality. Education and human development, properly conceived, are, given the realities of the culture we inhabit, counter-cultural processes.

However, appeals for emancipation, liberation, and social justice can at times obscure the object of enquiry by appearing to encourage a radical refusal of practice. However, this radical refusal is less available to HRD practitioners than to scholars (Callahan, 2007), and is not always well-suited to persuading the uninitiated of the worth of a critical orientation. Indeed, no matter how pessimistic we are about the possibility of achieving genuinely good practice under current conditions, the belief in human potential, implicit in the Critical project, inevitably shapes our conception of ethics. Thus, as practically inert as they may seem, such critical approaches can help us to best understand the shortcomings of the standard self-understanding of management and of the nature of the contemporary workplace. As Adorno puts it, human beings "have yet to become themselves. By the concept of the self we should properly mean their potential, and this potential stands in polemical opposition to the reality of the self" (1973, p. 278) as it exists under present circumstances. What seems to be needed is a balance between a recognition of the severity of the ethical deficits of contemporary organizational life, and a recognition that, "[w]e must own our institutions or they will surely own us" (Railton, 2015, p. 148).

This recognition calls to mind the notion that "HRD professionals face a reality of serving two masters," (Callahan, 2007, p. 78): the dominant structures, such as organizations and institutions, and individuals within those. We need to be mindful of the inevitable conflict to which this can give rise to (MacKenzie et al., 2012). CHRD's rejection of the shortcomings of standard approaches, suggested by Bierema (2009) and noted above, itself has positive implications for ethics based on the implicit conception of the self. In place of a performative philosophy, we ought to recognize human creativity and intelligence, which may be stifled by a relentless emphasis on performance measurement. In place of the commodification of employees, we ought to recognize the dignity and the intrinsic value of human beings. In place of a monomaniacal allegiance to shareholders, we ought to recognize the embeddedness of the self within communities and relationships, to which our work may be a valuable contribution. Such aims can only be achieved if we recognize the importance of power within the workplace. To ignore institutions and organizations would leave us unable to attend to those individuals we wish to serve, to develop, and to see flourish. In this way, we come to see organizations and institutions are a part of our world that deserve our care and attention. This point reinforces the notion that CHRD requires a holistic conception of the self and society, and one that necessarily addresses Bierema's fifth challenge to standard approaches to HRD: that of developing a wider theoretical basis for understanding HRD.

Ethics, in the sense used in this chapter, is not something bolted on to CHRD; CHRD is a fundamentally ethical endeavor. According to Lawless et al. (2012), CHRD is inherently concerned with human emancipation, a goal clearly committed to the value of human flourishing, and only intelligible if we recognize the ethical deficits of a pre-emancipated state. According to Collins et al. CHRD involves "questioning whose interests HRD interventions truly serve," (2017, p. 240), and aims to combat "racism, homophobia, and sexism in organizations, communities, and society" (2017, p. 242). This set of commitments can be seen in CHRD work on topics such as gender and sexual orientation (Worst & O'Shea, 2020) and social movements (Callahan, 2013; Sisco et al., 2019). Again, these goals reflect a set of ethical commitments: a rejection of oppressive power structures, and a rejection of the injustice embodied in various forms of discrimination.

In light of this ethical orientation, it is unsurprising that one of the central challenges facing CHRD is ethical in nature: that of addressing the apparently inegalitarian nature of development and emancipation. Alvesson and Deetz argue that "the irony of an advocate of greater equality pronouncing on what others should want or how they should perceive the world 'better' is not lost on either dominant or dominated groups" (2000, p. 195). Fenwick (2005) also notes that emancipation is an inherently hierarchical concept. Thus, there is an imperative for CHRD as a field of academic enquiry to provide an account of how we can avoid some of the pitfalls that result from asymmetric power relations. Even if we are alive to the importance of the understanding of knowledge and learning as co-created, we cannot make sense of the notions of education or development, let alone emancipation, without some conception of what it is to pass from ignorance to knowledge, or from a less well-developed state to a more well-developed one. As such, the ethical challenge for CHRD is to account for this asymmetry without unwittingly providing a defense of the power inequalities which are all too capable of undermining relationships within organizations (Sinnicks, 2020).

While there is no panacea, one key facet of any credible approach to this problem is epistemic humility: a virtue that must be exhibited and role-modeled if the deleterious effects of hierarchy and power asymmetries are to be avoided. Epistemic humility can be manifested in many ways, but it requires that we remember that any claim to knowledge is likely to be provisional, that we are liable to be mistaken, and that we all possess a number of limitations that pertain to our claims to know more or better than others. As de Bruin puts it, "epistemic humility makes you acknowledge that you may in reality fail to know what you believe you know, and that when you are of a different opinion than others, they might be right and you may be wrong" (2013, p. 592).

Given that CHRD is partially rooted in education studies, we may regard self-education as an ideal as noted in the previous section. However, there are occasions where experience or specialist knowledge is required, and so asymmetries are liable to persist. Indeed, this is a challenge for any educational setting, and we might regard Larvor's comment on teachers as apt here:

> Teachers expect students to leave their comfort zones and run the risk of making errors in public. The teacher can gain moral authority by running the same risk. The teacher must not bluff or bluster, and must take seriously the thought that a student may have an insight first. If the teacher makes an error, he or she should acknowledge it... Such intellectual honesty is the difference between 'authoritative' and 'authoritarian'. (2010, p. 82)

This pursuit of intellectual openness and honesty, as well as attempts to attain epistemic humility, point us in the direction of an egalitarian ethos. We must recognize the contingency of any claim we might have to a position of authority, and remain open to correction by others. This is also a prerequisite of being able to persuade both "masters"—institutions and individuals—of the legitimacy of a Critical approach to HRD. A conviction of our own superiority is likely to alienate both groups, and a commitment to facilitating the development and deliberation of others is key.

Furthermore, such honesty, openness, and humility can enable us to see how the position of authoritative—but not authoritarian—educator depends upon human relationships and a wider community. Only in light of those relationships can we remember what we owe to others, how we have been shaped by these relationships, and continue to be shaped by them. With this in mind, we can more clearly perceive the necessity of the broader, more holistic focus that is a central ethical advantage of CHRD. Its breadth enables us to see opportunities for development beyond the traditional, formal routes central to standard approaches to HRD, for instance, book groups (Grenier et al., 2021), trade unions qua communities of practice (Smith, 2021), and even good work itself (Sinnicks, 2019).

Market societies "make it difficult for working- and middle-class people to engage in the kind of shared reflection and deliberation which are necessary" for their flourishing (MacIntyre, 2016, p. 123), and the ethical nature of CHRD makes it one small, but important, part of our attempt to overcome this.

References

Adorno, T. W. (1973). *Negative dialectics*. Continuum.
Adorno, T. W. (2000). *Problems of moral philosophy*. Polity Press.

Adorno, T. W. (2005). *Minima moralia: Reflections on a damaged life*. Verso.

Alvesson, M., & Deetz, S. (2000). *Doing critical management research*. Sage.

Alzola, M. (2018). Decent work: The moral status of labor in human resource management. *Journal of Business Ethics, 147*(4), 835–853.

Armitage, A. (2018). Is HRD in need of an ethics of care? *Human Resource Development International, 21*(3), 212–231.

Audi, R. (2012). Virtue ethics as a resource in business. *Business Ethics Quarterly, 22*(2), 273–291.

Bierema, L. L. (2009). Critiquing human resource development's dominant masculine rationality and evaluating its impact. *Human Resource Development Review, 8*(1), 68–96.

Bierema, L. L., & Callahan, J. L. (2014). Transforming HRD: A framework for critical HRD practice. *Advances in Developing Human Resources, 16*(4), 429–444.

Bierema, L. L., & Cseh, M. (2003). Evaluating AHRD research using a feminist research framework. *Human Resource Development Quarterly, 14*(1), 5–26.

Callahan, J. L. (2007). Gazing into the crystal ball: Critical HRD as a future of research in the field. *Human Resource Development International, 10*(1), 77–82.

Callahan, J. L. (2013). 'Space, the final frontier'? Social movements as organizing spaces for applying HRD. *Human Resource Development International, 16*(3), 298–312.

Callahan, J. L., & Ward, D. B. (2001). A search for meaning: Revitalizing the 'human' in human resource development. *Human Resource Development International, 4*(2), 235–242.

Cederström, C., & Marinetto, M. (2013). Corporate social responsibility á la the liberal communist. *Organization, 20*(3), 416–432.

Chalofsky, N., & Cavallaro, L. (2013). A good living versus a good life: Meaning, purpose, and HRD. *Advances in Developing Human Resources, 15*(4), 331–340.

Collins, J. C. (2019). A more radical human resource development: The time is now. *Human Resource Development International, 22*(4), 405–411.

Collins, J. C., Zarestky, J., & Tkachenko, O. (2017). An integrated model of national HRD and critical HRD: Considering new possibilities for human resource development. *Human Resource Development International, 20*(3), 236–252.

de Bruin, B. (2013). Epistemic virtues in business. *Journal of Business Ethics, 113*(4), 583–595.

Elliott, C., & Turnbull, S. (2003). Reconciling autonomy and community: The paradoxical role of HRD. *Human Resource Development International, 6*(4), 457–474.

Fenwick, T. J. (2004). Toward a critical HRD in theory and practice. *Adult Education Quarterly, 54*(3), 193–209.

Fenwick, T. (2005). Ethical dilemmas of critical management education: Within classrooms and beyond. *Management Learning, 36*(1), 31–48.

Fenwick, T. (2014). Conceptualising critical human resource development: Tensions, dilemmas, and possibilities. In R. Poell, T. Rocco, & G. Roth (Eds.), *Routledge companion to human resource development* (pp. 113–123). Routledge.

Fleming, P. (2015). *The mythology of work: How capitalism persists despite itself*. Pluto Press.

Fleming, P., & Jones, M. T. (2013). *The end of corporate social responsibility: Crisis and critique*. Sage.

Foucault, M. (1988). *The care of the self*. Vintage.

Freud, S. (2002). *Civilisation and its discontents*. Penguin.

Gedro, J., Collins, J. C., & Rocco, T. S. (2014). The "critical" turn: An important imperative for human resource development. *Advances in Developing Human Resources, 16*(4), 529–535.

Gilligan, C. (1993). *In a different voice: Psychological theory and women's development*. Harvard University Press.

Grenier, R. S., Callahan, J. L., Kaeppel, K., & Elliott, C. (2021). Advancing book clubs as non-formal learning to facilitate critical public pedagogy in organizations. *Management Learning*. https://doi.org/10.1177/13505076211029823

Habermas, J. (1987). *The philosophical discourse of modernity*. MIT Press.

Harrison, P., Tosey, P., Anderson, V., & Elliott, C. (2021). HRD professional education provision in the UK: Past, present and future. *Human Resource Development International, 24*(2), 200–218.

Hegel, G. W. F. (1991). *The philosophy of right* (A. Wood, Ed.). Cambridge University Press.

Held, V. (1983). *Rights and goods: Justifying social action*. University of Chicago Press.

Held, V. (2006). *The ethics of care: Personal, political and global*. Oxford University Press.

Kierkegaard, S. (2003). *Fear and trembling*. Penguin.

Larvor, B. (2010). Authoritarian versus authoritative teaching: Polya and Lakatos. In G. Hanna, H. Niels Jahnke, & H. Pulte (Eds.), *Explanation and proof in mathematics* (pp. 71–83). Springer.

Lawless, A., Sambrook, S., & Stewart, J. (2012). Critical human resource development: Enabling alternative subject positions within a master of arts in human resource development educational programme. *Human Resource Development International, 15*(3), 321–336.

Lear, J. (2015). *Freud* (2nd ed.). Routledge.

Lee, M. (2001). A refusal to define HRD. *Human Resource Development International, 4*(3), 327–341.

Lippitt, J. (2003). *The Routledge philosophy guidebook to Kierkegaard and fear and trembling*. Routledge.

MacIntyre, A. (1999a). *Dependent rational animals: Why human beings need the virtues*. Open Court.

MacIntyre, A. (1999b). Social structures and their threats to moral agency. *Philosophy, 74*(3), 311–329.

MacIntyre, A. (2007). *After virtue: 3rd Edition*. Duckworth.

MacIntyre, A. (2016). *Ethics in the conflicts of modernity*. Cambridge University Press.

MacKenzie, C., Garavan, T., & Carbery, R. (2012). Through the looking glass: Challenges for human resource development (HRD) post the global financial crisis—Business as usual? *Human Resource Development International, 15*(3), 353–364.

MacKinnon, C. A. (1984). Not a moral issue. *Yale Law & Policy Review, 2*(2), 321–345.

MacKinnon, C. A. (1989). *Toward a feminist theory of the state*. Harvard University Press.

Marx, K., & Engels, F. (1970). *The German ideology* (C. J. Arthur, Ed.). International.

Mulhall, S. (2001). *Inheritance and originality: Wittgenstein, Heidegger*. Clarendon Press.

Munro, I., & Thanem, T. (2018). The ethics of affective leadership: Organizing good encounters without leaders. *Business Ethics Quarterly, 28*(1), 51–69.

Musílek, K., Jamie, K., & McKie, L. (2020). Cold winds and warm attachments: Interrogating the personal attachment to neoliberal work and economy. *Work, Employment and Society, 34*(3), 514–525.

Nietzsche, F. (1998). *On the genealogy of morals*. Oxford World Classics.

Nozick, R. (1974). *Anarchy, state, and Utopia*. Basic Books.

Poell, R. F., & Van Der Krogt, F. (2017). Why is organizing human resource development so problematic? *The Learning Organization, 24*(3), 180–193.

Railton, P. (2015). Innocent abroad: Rupture, liberation, and solidarity. *Proceedings and Addresses of the American Philosophical Association, 89*, 138–158.

Rawls, J. (1971). *A theory of justice*., MA: Harvard University Press.

Reeves, C. (2016). Beyond the postmetaphysical turn: Ethics and metaphysics in critical theory. *Journal of Critical Realism, 15*(3), 217–244.

Reeves, C., & Sinnicks, M. (2021). Business ethics from the standpoint of redemption: Adorno on the possibility of good work. *Business Ethics Quarterly, 31*(4), 500–523.

Sambrook, S. (2004). A "critical" time for HRD? *Journal of European Industrial Training, 28*(8/9), 611–624.

Sandel, M. J. (1984). The procedural republic and the unencumbered self. *Political Theory, 12*(1), 81–96.

Shirmohammadi, M., Hedayati Mehdiabadi, A., Beigi, M., & McLean, G. N. (2021). Mapping human resource development: Visualizing the past, bridging the gaps, and moving toward the future. *Human Resource Development Quarterly, 32*(2), 197–224.

Sinnicks, M. (2019). Moral education at work. *Journal of Business Ethics, 159*(1), 105–118.

Sinnicks, M. (2020). The just world fallacy as a challenge to the business-as-community thesis. *Business & Society, 59*(6), 1269–1292.

Sinnicks, M. (2021). "We ought to eat in order to work, not vice versa": MacIntyre, practices, and the best work for humankind. *Journal of Business Ethics, 174*(2), 263–274.

Sisco, S., Valesano, M., & Collins, J. C. (2019). Social movement learning and human resource development: An agenda for a radical future. *Advances in Developing Human Resources, 21*(2), 175–192.

Smith, H. (2022). The 'indie unions' and the UK labour movement: Towards a community of practice. *Economic and Industrial Democracy*. https://doi.org/10.1177/0143831X211009956

Swanson, R. A. (1999). HRD theory, real or imagined? *Human Resource Development International, 2*(1), 2–5.

Taylor, C. (1979). Atomism. In A. Kontos (Ed.), *Powers, possessions and freedom: Essays in honour of C. B. Macpherson* (pp. 39–62). University of Toronto Press.

Worst, S., & O'Shea, S. C. (2020). From chess to Queergaming: 'Play'ing with and disrupting heteronormative assumptions in the performance of gender and sexual orientation. *Human Resource Development International, 23*(5), 519–541.

Williams, B. (1973). 'A critique of utilitarianism' in *Utilitarianism: For and against*, with J. J. C. Smart. Cambridge University Press.

Williams, B. (1985). *Ethics and the limits of philosophy*. Fontana Press.

Zuboff, S. (2019). *The age of surveillance capitalism: The fight for a human future at the new frontier of power*. Profile Books.

CHAPTER 5

Emotional Labor and Resistance: Implications for Critical HRD

Joseph C. Brenes-Dawsey and Karen E. Watkins

INTRODUCTION

Interest in emotional labor has continued to grow since Hochschild (1983) first introduced the concept in her groundbreaking study of flight attendants in the late 1970s and early 1980s. Succeeding studies have explored emotional labor as a type of emotion management in various workplace (e.g., Bellas, 1999; Bierema, 2008; Bolton & Boyd, 2003; Brotheridge & Grandey, 2002; Brotheridge & Lee, 2003; Callahan, 2000, 2002, 2004; Callahan & McCollum, 2002a, 2002b; Fineman & Sturdy, 1999; Grandey, 2003; Grandey & Gabriel, 2015; Kahn, 1990, 1992; Rafaeli & Sutton, 1987; Sutton & Rafaeli, 1988; Tolich, 1993; Tracy, 2000, 2005, 2008; Turnbull, 1999, 2002) and educational settings (e.g., Hargreaves, 1998a, 1998b, 2000; Isenbarger & Zembylas, 2006; Zembylas, 2005a, 2005b). While interest in the concept of emotional labor has grown along with broader acceptance and development of the concept (Grandey & Gabriel, 2015), there has remained a certain amount of confusion (Callahan, 2000) and, to some extent, frustration (Bolton & Boyd, 2003) over how emotional labor informs one's

J. C. Brenes-Dawsey (✉)
Piedmont University, Demorest, GA, USA
e-mail: jdawsey@piedmont.edu

K. E. Watkins
Department of Lifelong Education, Administration, and Policy, Mary Frances Early College of Education, University of Georgia, Athens, GA, USA
e-mail: kwatkins@uga.edu

J. C. Collins and J. L. Callahan (eds.), *The Palgrave Handbook of Critical Human Resource Development*, https://doi.org/10.1007/978-3-031-10453-4_5

understanding of emotions in the workplace. Part of the challenge in studying emotional labor lies with the subtle distinctions that distinguish emotion work from emotional labor (Callahan, 2000; Callahan & McCollum, 2002b). Additionally, Hochschild's (1983) Marxist framing of emotional labor implies an oppressive relationship between frontline workers and the organization, a type of oppression that ultimately restricts authentic emotional displays and associated feelings within the organizational structure (McQuarie & Spaulding, 1989). In this chapter, we use Callahan and McCollum's (2002b) framework for emotion management to further explore the differences between emotion work and emotional labor. We also consider the implications of power and, in particular, resistance within the context of the emotion management framework.

Literature Review

One issue that has remained problematic for studies of emotional labor is the distinction between emotion work and emotional labor (Callahan, 2000, 2002, 2004; Callahan & McCollum, 2002b; Tolich, 1993). Hochschild (1983) defines emotional labor as a type of emotion work conducted publicly in an organizational setting for an exchange-value. Private emotion work is conducted individually for a value characterized as a "use" value (Hochschild, 1979). In each instance, both emotion work and emotional labor reflect the application of similar emotion management strategies not easily distinguished except by a better understanding of contextual demands beyond public and private emotion management. As Callahan and McCollum (2002b) observe, "we manage our emotions in the workplace both to benefit ourselves and to benefit the organization" (p. 220). Callahan and McCollum also observe the following about emotional labor and emotion work: (1) "emotion work is appropriate for situations in which individuals are personally choosing to manage their emotion for their own noncompensated benefit" (p. 221); (2) emotional labor "is appropriate only when emotion work is exchanged for something such as a wage or some other type of valued compensation" (p. 221); and, (3) emotion management "describes the general control of emotions in either form of use-value or exchange-value" (p. 222).

To better articulate the difference between emotion work and emotional labor, Callahan and McCollum (2002b) developed a matrix framework of four emotion management strategies that incorporates the dichotomies created by the intersection of issues related to exchange and locus of control. The four forms of emotion management strategies include emotion work, emotional labor, autonomous emotional labor, and indirect emotional labor. In keeping with Hochschild's (1979, 1983) definition, emotion work is internally controlled and performed for a use-value. Also, in keeping with Hochschild's (1983) definition, emotional labor is externally controlled and performed for an exchange-value. With autonomous emotional labor, "the employee manages emotions to conform to her own standards not only because she feels it is right, but also because she chooses to" (Callahan & McCollum, 2002b, p. 224). And finally, in performing indirect emotional labor, the individual may retain a perceived sense of use-value while simultaneously responding to external requirements (p. 224).

A discussion of power is inherently complex and riddled with difficulties. Hochschild's (1983) Marxist framing of emotional labor both helps and inhibits the discussion of power within the organizational structure (e.g., Bryant & Cox, 2014; Tracy, 2000, 2008). Her definition of emotional labor places the individual worker within a highly oppressive top-down structure. The assumption is that once private emotional gestures or signals no longer entirely belong to the worker through a process of transmutation, they are commodified and transformed into a product designed to meet organizational goals.

Organizational power, then, lies with the ability to compel top-down compliance with organizational display expectations. Goffman (1969/2021) defined control moves in terms of the strategic and intentional manipulation of emotional expressions to influence the behavior of others. Collectively, at the organizational level, these control moves project uniform emotional fronts (Sutton & Rafaeli, 1988) intended to influence the behavior of those who come into contact with the organization, regardless of their status as internal employees or external constituents. Hochschild's (1983) use of display rules as a key requirement for the performance of emotional labor is characteristic of a type of control move intended to influence or manipulate the emotion work performed in the workplace. Additionally, control moves reinforce the top-down structural power inherent in Hochschild's Marxist framing of emotional labor. Control moves are codified within the bureaucratic organizational structures in the form of policies and procedures (Hargreaves, 1998a) that carry both implicit and explicit performance expectations. The power associated with this sort of control move is often achieved through training and other materials produced by the organization. Some researchers have argued that this conceptualization of power is limited and does not capture the full complexity of the relationship between power and organizational attempts to influence workers' feelings and emotional displays (Bryant & Cox, 2006, 2014; Callahan, 2000; Tracy, 2000, 2005, 2008). We turn to Callahan and McCollum's (2002a) description of emergent power to better understand this complexity. This view of power echoes Foucault's (e.g., 1994/1997) description of power as contingent and relational. Any discussion of power that evokes post structural critique is fraught with myriad difficulties and endless debates, debates that Fineman (2000, 2008) noted produce constant epistemological heat. It is not our intent to wade into these debates here. Given that Hochschild's work is situated within a feminist critique of modern labor practices, we reference the post structural critique of power as a means of enhancing and extending the discussion of power within organizational settings. Emergent power then, much like Foucault's use of power, is a type of power that is contingent and only present when observed.

Resistance, in the organizational development (OD) and human resource development (HRD) literature, has frequently been described in terms of resistance to change, often in terms of a single unidimensional construct studied in isolation (García-Cabrera & Hernandez, 2014; Smollan, 2011). At the same time, a lack of agreement about what is meant by resistance to organizational change has produced a wide array of conceptualizations and definitions (Smollan, 2011). Smollan (2011) notes that the literature on resistance to change runs along two lines of inquiry with the first being those studies focusing on resistance as an inherent quality of organizational life, and the second being those studies focusing on resistance as a characteristic of employees' desire for autonomy. The desire for autonomy is the juncture where emotional labor and resistance overlap. Tolich (1993) characterized the dichotomy of emotion management as regulated emotion management and autonomous emotion management. Callahan and McCollum (2002b) later extended this to include four types of emotion management strategies that retained dichotomies between the internal and external regulations of emotions and the use- and exchange-values of emotion management interactions. Resistance as a form of encroachment against autonomy is a common theme throughout the OD and HRD literature and is expressed in various ways, including resistance to loss of control and resistance through consent (e.g., Ashcraft, 2005). In keeping with Hochschild's (1983) definition of emotional labor, emotional resistance in the workplace can be thought of as resistance to an influence tactic that interferes with a worker's autonomous control of emotions (e.g., Callahan & McCollum, 2002b; Tolich, 1993). In this sense, resistance is something more than resistance to a change initiative. Rather, it is resistance to the loss of something of value to the worker (Burke, 2014). Piderit (2000) called for reconsideration of the concept of resistance to include the nuanced complexities that are not always reflected in resistance to change. Building on this reconsideration, we expand the discussion of resistance to include resistance to an organization's efforts to influence the emotional displays of its employees. Agency and autonomy are at the heart of many of the critiques of emotional labor (e.g., Bolton & Boyd, 2003; Callahan, 2000; Tolich, 1993; Tracy, 2000, 2008). Bolton and Boyd (2003) assert that Hochschild's use of the public/commercial dichotomy is oversimplified and that for "Hochschild's cabin crew there is no distinction between emotion work as part of the capitalist labour process, emotion work due to professional norms of conduct, or emotion work during normal social interaction in the workplace" (p. 293). Callahan (2000) and Grandey (2000) have also observed difficulties distinguishing between emotion work and emotional labor. Bolton and Boyd (2003) also argue that the commoditization of and comparison of emotional labor and physical labor is problematic in that airline workers retain control over their ability to choose when and how to manage their emotions and, in doing so, create spaces of resistance. It is here in these spaces where resistance is inflected that we turn for further exploration of emotion work and emotional labor in an organizational setting. We use Kahn's

(1990, 1992) conceptualization of personal engagement to explore the extent of the calibration of self (Hochschild, 1983) to in-role performance. This, combined with Turnbull's (2002) extension of emotional labor performance into middle management, provides a framework to explore further Callahan and McCollum's (2002b) four types of emotion management.

Method

For this study, we utilized Flanagan's (1954) critical incident technique (CIT) as a means of collecting data with the critical incident serving as the unit of analysis. CIT is recognized as a useful approach during the initial stages of exploring a particular phenomenon (Kain, 2004). Semi-structured interviews were conducted with eight participants who serve as faculty members and administrators in a teacher training program that prepares working professionals in science, technology, engineering, and math (STEM) fields to become public school teachers in areas with disadvantaged or underserved populations. We incorporated Ellinger and Watkins' (1998) contextual approach to CIT to capture participants' perceptions of managing feelings in a teaching and organizational setting.

A single site implementation of the program was selected for this study. At the time of the study, participants had one to two years of experience teaching in the program; however, all of the participants had several years of combined experience in a wide array of educational settings, including public schools, corporate training, and adult and higher education. Six of the participants were female, and two were male. The ages of participants ranged from 31–40 and 51 or older.

Following a naturalistic design (Lincoln & Guba, 1985, 1986), we conducted in-depth semi-structured interviews with each participant over a six-month period. In keeping with Ellinger and Watkins' (1998) adaptation of Flanagan's (1954) CIT, we asked participants to think about a time when they used or suppressed emotion in their role as faculty members within the program. We maintained fidelity with Hochschild's (1979, 1983) interpretation of emotional labor as an extension of Goffman's (1959) approach to symbolic interactionism and dramaturgy. The raw transcript data were analyzed for the presence of critical incidents. Critical incident data were culled and configured using narrative (Ollerenshaw & Creswell, 2002) and poetic (Butler-Kisber, 2002; Poindexter, 2002) inquiry approaches, resulting in the construction of 71 narrative critical incidents and 1 poetic critical incident. Using Katz's (1983, 2001) process of analytic induction and following Hochschild's (1983) definition of emotional labor, we created analytic assertions for each critical incident. We used these assertions to identify the critical incident narratives that best informed the emotional labor process. After reviewing the initial set of incident narratives, we selected a sample of 31 total incidents for analysis that included 30 narrative incidents and 1 poetic incident. Examples from this set of 31 critical incidents are presented in this chapter. We utilized member checking to establish the credibility of the data (Butterfield et al., 2005; Lincoln & Guba, 1985; Merriam, 2009). Critical incident narratives and corresponding analytical assertions were shared with participants for feedback and suggestions. Following revisions, participants were given an additional opportunity to review the critical incidents and analytical assertions for accuracy.

Findings and Discussion

Initial findings indicate resistance to emotional labor expectations occurs in different types of interactions across the organization, including interactions with students, colleagues, and administrators, as well as interactions external to the organization. Faculty members in this study operated from a somewhat unique position in that they performed roles that blended different layers of organizational responsibility, including those typically associated with managers and frontline workers. Emotion work performance is multidirectional and consists of constant negotiations or calibrations (Kahn, 1990, 1992) of self to personal, professional, and organizational roles and emotional labor requirements. Associated costs include the personal costs of compliant and non-compliant behaviors and those associated with the organization, such as recruitment, retention, and reputation. Also, resistance functions as a type of advocacy when emotional labor expectations are resisted to benefit relationships with student teachers in the program. Emotional impacts include conflict and uncertainty associated with role performance. In the following sections, we present and discuss selected critical incidents from a larger study on emotional labor (Brenes-Dawsey, 2018) illustrative of Callahan and McCollum's (2002b) four types of emotion management. The words of study participants are italicized throughout.

Emotion Work

Callahan and McCollum (2002b) describe the management of emotions associated with emotion work as "the social lubricant of our everyday lives" (p. 223). Emotion work is what is performed daily, sustaining the ebb and flow of routine interactions. On the surface, these interactions are seemingly mundane, but even mundane interactions carry a certain amount of risk. The incidents in this study most closely linked to Hochschild's (1979, 1983) definition of emotion work are illustrative of the difficulties encountered when attempting to capture the subtle nuances distinguishing emotion work from emotional labor, especially in a setting where such work is multidirectional. Emotion work is largely interpersonal in nature and is performed with little, if any, influence on the part of the organization. However, as Hochschild (1983) notes, the social apparatus of personal emotion work undergoes a transmutation into a different form within the organizational setting. The incidents presented below are illustrative of this transmutation in the sense that each offers a glimpse into the move from and through the personal expression of emotion work to the public expression of the organizational emotion work that becomes emotional labor.

We take as our starting point the ebb and flow of emotions in the classroom and the daily interactions between teacher and student. Stephanie, a faculty member in the program, applied her training as a marriage and family therapist to a situation that evolved in her classroom. While this training was not related to any provided by the institution or the program, she adapted it to meet her needs as a faculty member, especially in instances where she wanted to encourage student teachers to challenge their own learning: *...I find myself very often knowing how to use words and tones to trigger things, and I think probably I do it more to get people to go deeper.* She cautions that *I do that fairly often, but I'm careful to know that that trust level is already established before I push somebody to that point.* For her, developing a trusting relationship is an important part of managing emotions in adult learning and organizational settings. In this case, a student teacher demonstrated a regular lack of confidence in her own work, and Stephanie used her emotional reaction to challenge the student teacher's thinking:

One time, I was just tired of it. I had just handed back a set of papers, and I don't know if sarcasm is an emotion, but it's certainly what I used. She made some comment to indicate that she had struggled with the assignment and I just said, 'Could you turn to the back of your paper and read aloud my feedback?' And of course, it said, 'This is the best.' I tried to process with her, 'What is it that you don't see there?' It was kind of risky and probably put her on the spot more than she wanted to be on the spot. But that's a time that I can remember saying, 'I'm not going to let this go,' and use whatever to break this down. I did see a little bit of a change in her after that. It was kind of passive aggressive on my part too. If I think back strongly enough, I probably set it up so that whatever her comment was led to that [interaction].

While the institution may benefit from Stephanie's interaction with this student, there is no evidence of reliance on institutional guidelines for her approach. Overall, this exchange remains at a personal level, and as such retains a use-value that is internally controlled without evidence of external influences or control moves (Callahan & McCollum, 2002b; Goffman, 1969/2021). The emotional negotiation that takes place is between the faculty member and the student and is outside the formal role expectations associated with leading full classroom instruction.

Barbara's poetic critical incident narrative catches a glimpse of her struggles with attempting to understand the treatment by others of a colleague also teaching in the program (see the Appendix for the complete text of this critical incident). She struggles with the question: *How is it?* She suppresses frustration and disappointment while attempting to understand how others can be *so negative toward* her colleague. She questions whether to intercede but also recognizes that her colleague would not want her *to be the white knight.* The incident remains unresolved, but we are left with a strong emotional reaction that questions: *How is it that other people get beat on so much?* This incident is indicative of the intense pressure that occurs during what Hochschild (1983) describes as the transmutation of the private self into the public self of the workplace, the area where emotion work and emotional labor begin to commingle. The deeply personal nature of this exchange retains a use-value associated with concern for a colleague. Once again though, the difficulty of the transmutation of personal emotion management into the public arena is fully, if painfully, exposed. Even at the most personal level, emotion work is never performed with complete autonomy from organizational influence. Speaking up for her colleague might be considered acting in bad faith on the part of the organization while acting in good faith on the part of her colleague (Rafaeli & Sutton, 1987). The doubly articulated suppression of emotions serves as a point of resistance and resignation. In not speaking up for her friend, she gives the impression of compliance with what the organization might expect in this situation, namely silence, but the fact that she remains concerned for her colleague indicates resistance to the pull of emotional labor compliance, a pull indicative of the emotional dissonance experienced when the self-control of emotions is relinquished. Her resistance to the pull of organizational expectations further highlights the intensity and complexity of the negotiation between the individual and the organizational selves that are co-constructed within the dissonant tension of the emotional experience.

Autonomous Emotional Labor

With autonomous emotional labor, the need to comply with organizational expectations aligns with individual expectations in the sense that one "manages emotions to conform to her own standards not only because she feels it is right, but also because she chooses to" (Callahan & McCollum, 2002b). The authenticity of day-to-day private interactions intermingle with the role demands of the workplace, but in the case of autonomous emotional labor, the boundaries of authenticity are not completely blurred. The worker retains a sense of autonomy in making decisions for both personal and organizational reasons, similar to Tracy's (2005) description of emotional labor as a type of strategic interaction. However, the difficulty in maintaining a balanced sense of autonomy is greatly accentuated in the performance of autonomous emotional labor, especially when protecting the self from the pull of multidirectional demands and expectations (Turnbull, 1999, 2002).

Sandra, a faculty member in the program, described an incident where she felt that one of her student teachers was lacking in his demonstration of professionalism, even though he was in a *phenomenal placement* with a host teacher. The student teacher did not seem to be paying attention and did not seem to grasp the importance of attending to the related activities of becoming a teacher: *I was frustrated and irritated with him and concerned about how his behavior was going to reflect on us—almost just out of respect for his host teacher.* Sandra began to experience everything within the context of the student teacher's unprofessional behavior. Irritation and frustration heightened her awareness of his behaviors, so much so that the entire experience of the incident came to be felt like a sort of unprofessionalism. What potentially began as irritation escalated into the sustained suppression of frustration while still attempting to support the relationship with this student teacher. Everything seems to have reached a tipping point when the student teacher requested the day off for his birthday during the middle of parent-teacher conferences. Sandra described how she had to learn to try to *disengage* and remain *unemotional* while working with this student teacher:

> *Some of the frustration that I've had with this one student, I've had to keep in check and make sure that I'm focused on specific behaviors* [and] *specific outcomes instead of just saying, 'Get your act together.' I disengage* [while] *trying to remain unemotional and trying to focus on the situation at hand. That's been in the face of feeling really frustrated or irritated—those times where you feel like you've had a conversation five times and you have to have it another time....*

By focusing on certain behaviors (both hers and the student teachers), she attempted to disengage and suppress her feelings of irritation. The hesitation with trying to remain unemotional suggests a buffer potentially shielding her from organizational and student–teacher expectations. Disengagement implies something of an emotional silence (experienced in association with the student teacher's unprofessionalism) that disrupts the relationship with the student teacher in a way that prevents Sandra from being fully engaged with her role as a faculty member (Kahn, 1990, 1992). In some ways, the effort of disengagement only intensifies the feelings of irritation associated with the event. She remained aware of the need to sustain a positive image for the institution and the program. In a sense, she emotionally disengaged from the immediate situation while remaining emotionally engaged with the program expectations. The difficulty of achieving this balance cannot be understated. To accomplish this, Sandra had to learn to withhold certain aspects of her own personal concern for the student teacher while maintaining a display of organizational professionalism—something of an inversion of the professional relationship with the student teacher. The way that Sandra struggles with this is reminiscent of the emphasis placed on traditional masculine behaviors in many organizations, as Turnbull (2002) notes, "there is evidence that many traditional organizations still like their managers to be strong, in control, leave their personal problems at home and stay cool under pressure" (p. 127). Sandra's resistance manifests in her concern for both the student teacher and the organization. Disengagement serves as a personal buffer shielding her from the stress of needing to remain calm and in control under pressure.

In another incident, Amy emphasized the need to manage simultaneous emotional labor efforts stemming from the same event. In this instance, a student teacher in the program was caught sleeping during a staff development training session by a host school administrator. Personally, Amy empathized with the student teacher and wanted to tell him that it happens to everyone:

> *With this* [student teacher], *what wanted to come out of my mouth when he told me what happened was, 'It's okay, everybody does it.' I wanted to tell him the story of us as teachers on our cell phones, or us laughing, or us in a faculty meeting—because I understood that.*

However, she realized that she also needed to attend to the relationship between the host school and the program. Amy suppressed her frustration and presented a firm demeanor to better help the student teacher work through the process on his own:

> *But realizing the nature of the relationship I had with him and that at that point what I needed to present to him was much more firm than I normally have to be. I almost wanted to reach out and say, 'It's okay, it's okay.' Because he'd been crying. I tried to be very adult—I really had to almost be a parent—and very supportive of him but facilitating his working through it and dealing with it. I wasn't going to pick up the pieces for him.*

Amy next turned her attention to the relationship with the host school.

> *And my thoughts were, 'We have a good relationship with this school.' One of our lab facilitators was a host teacher last year. And this* [student teacher] *and another one are in their clinical experiences there.*

The level of anger she was suppressing is immediately evident. Also evident is the range and scope of emotion management efforts she felt responsible for:

> *I'm like, 'Oh, you know this relationship is important to us, to me.' I'm* [from the county]. *I'm proud of my personal relationship with* [the school], *but also our* [program] *and* [our College's] *relationship with* [the school]. *His actions were not just a reflection—it was a reflection of him—but it also had a potential to tarnish the way the other* [student teachers] *were perceived if the assistant principal said, at the county office, 'This is a* [student teacher from this program].' *It took us so long to get into* [this school district], *so I was disappointed. I was angry.*

As with earlier examples, this incident further highlights the complexities associated with emerging distinctions between emotion work and emotional labor. Personally, Amy again focused her attention on demonstrating empathy and providing a supportive but firm environment. While shielding him from some of the friction generated by his falling asleep during staff development, Amy also encouraged the student teacher to take responsibility for his actions. She elected to manage her emotions in a way that was mutually beneficial to herself and the organization (Callahan & McCollum, 2002b; Tracy, 2005). It is also possible that Amy's initial anger stemmed from the dissonance of having to suppress her nurturing instinct to cope with organizational expectations. In other words, she suppressed or resisted her natural tendencies in order to satisfy what the organization expected of her while also negotiating her relationship with the student teacher.

Emotional Labor

The requirement to "induce or suppress feeling" is at the heart of Hochschild's (1983) definition of emotional labor. However, as some have argued (e.g., Turnbull, 2002), this requirement is not isolated to just one level of interaction within an organization. In the following incident, Amy highlights the complexity of sustaining separate emotion management acts as she struggles with the process of dismissing a student teacher from the program:

> *...I kind of watched across the table from me while we were trying to share these things that were happening, that were reality, that she agreed with, you know, it was almost these pleading eyes looking at me, 'Help me, help me.' And I'm trying to get her to embrace this, which she did on some level, 'I get that, but, but, but....' And that was difficult.*

This came into direct conflict with the reactions of her colleagues as they assembled for the final meeting with the student teacher:

> *...I became really uncomfortable when we met downtown at* [the foundation representative's local office], *where he flies into.* [The program director] *and I drove down and* [the foundation representative] *met us there, and* [the student teacher] *was in the room. He was really savvy in his conversation with her explaining what was happening, what was going on, that this wasn't a good fit. But then after she left there was some, almost laughter and making fun of her in some ways that disturbed me, not that it would have changed the outcome....*

Amy focuses her emotional effort on providing support for the student teacher, to try to provide some level of comfort when the student teacher's eyes are pleading with her from across the table. She struggles to maintain a vestige of her nurturing self. Amy's emotions are authentic and genuinely felt, and in an effort of personal emotion work and sympathy, she attempts to share these feelings with the student teacher while also guarding against her feelings about the scene as it unfolds during the meeting, a scene resonates with the overtones of masculine staging indicative of the authority of the funding organization. The setting is a conference room in the middle of a large metropolitan area several miles away from the student teacher's home campus. Acting as the masculine voice of reason, the foundation representative arrives to deliver the final judgment in a ceremonial severing of ties. The only expectation of Amy is one of silence, a complete suppression of her authentic self as a nurturer (Jansz & Timmers, 2002), a silence indicative of the sort of powerlessness experienced when the act of caring is marginalized (Hargreaves, 1998a) and participation in decision-making neutralized (Bryant & Cox, 2006). Resistance is impossible at this point for Amy, as her silence is the only currency of value. The foundation representative and the program director successfully executed what at first appears to be a coolly delivered performance of surface acting. Yet the performance rings hollow once the student teacher leaves the room, and Amy notes laughter and disparaging remarks that made her uncomfortable. Hochschild (1983) describes surface acting where one deceives others but not oneself. Amy's colleagues displayed a lack of concern that betrays a distancing from both organizational and individual feeling expectations—potentially a double feign where they fool themselves as well as the student teacher, thus creating a dissonance that resonates both personally and professionally. Which begs the question: Did the emotional labor performance continue once the student left the room? In some ways, it did:

> It's something [the program director] and I have talked about several times. It haunts both of us. 'What could we have done differently? Should we have seen this before she was admitted? Was there anything that informed the way we looked at the current cohort of [student teachers]?'

If emotional labor involves preparing the body for an "imaginary action," as Hochschild (1983) suggests, then this implies the remnants of an emotional dissonance that has lingered since the dismissal of the student teacher, a dissonance that occurred at both the individual and organizational levels (p. 230). An organizational dissonance occurred when the organizational expectation of maintaining an environment of student success failed to follow through at the end of the meeting. This organizational level of dissonance extended to the host teacher as well:

> [I] was very sensitive to that particular host teacher's [feelings], she felt responsible too.

For the host teacher, this dissonance resolved with the placement of a new student teacher. For Amy, this dissonance caused her to adjust how she approaches her supervision work in the field:

> I was more intentional about record keeping, more intentional about the work that I did in the triads... I think I tried to be more facilitative in my role as site coordinator. I am now more aware of it.

The resolution of the organizational dissonance remains unclear.

It is also possible that Amy's overt compliance contained its own bit of deception. In maintaining an active concern for the student teacher, Amy disengaged from certain aspects of the dismissal process (Kahn, 1990, 1992). Fleming and Sewell (2002) refer to this type of disengagement as compliance without conformity. She can do this because, in some ways, the entire scene plays out at the organizational level. The dismissal process calls for the organizational performance of emotional labor delivered with a unified voice. The hollow performance delivered by Amy's colleagues punctuates her cynicism about the role of the unfolding organizational performance (Tracy, 2000). At the individual level, however, Amy continues to advocate for the student teacher. Amy's overt compliance serves as a point of covert resistance that lacks full compliance, or what Ashcraft (2005) referred to as resistance through consent.

Indirect Emotional Labor

Callahan and McCollum (2002b) describe indirect emotional labor as "other actions in the workplace [that] can have a perceived use-value to the individual but are directed by external requirements" (p. 224). Workplace retreats and team-building workshops are examples of activities that might be included as examples of indirect emotional labor. These activities, while guided by the organization, are not typically directly related to a worker's job responsibilities. An example of this type of indirect emotional labor was reported by Stephanie when she described her reaction to building planes as a team-building activity for student teachers in the program. A considerable amount of emotional effort went into developing the support structure for this activity to happen, not unlike the emphasis placed on developing trusting and supporting relationships with student teachers described in other incidents. In this instance, though, the activity's success, the fact that one of the planes flew, acted as a point of release and relief, as though Stephanie had been holding her breath waiting not only for the plane to fly but for the program to fly as well. At that moment, the small plane taking off to the cheers of a small group of graduate students became symbolic of the success of the program and the release of a sustained emotion work effort:

> I actually started crying on this one. The first one finally flew. Not many of them got up, but it wasn't the fact that the airplane flew, it was looking up at them, and their arms were in the air. I've got a picture of it. They were like, 'Yes!' For me, it was like, 'Wow! This is powerful, and we created this opportunity for them.'

At the same time, Stephanie recognized the importance of expressing positive emotions as a means of nurturing emotional trust and support:

> [It was powerful] to see professional people engage in what I would call play. It required a lot of academic knowledge to build these things. The launching of them was child's play. It was so joyful and uninhibited—like licking icing or something. You don't get that much in academia. We do a lot of that in [this program]. We do a lot where things that don't normally happen in learning environments get to happen. It was [significant] because it was so emotional. It was like you gave somebody a present that they really liked. You were just so overwhelmed with how

much it meant to them, and it wouldn't have happened if we hadn't done it. I
think that goes back to the familial environment that surrounds the learning.

In a sense, the incident was so emotional for her because it reflected
the culmination of a collective emotion work effort, an effort comprised
of multiple emotion work experiences over time, resulting in a delayed,
yet genuinely felt, sense of joy (e.g., Lois, 2006). The effort or work
associated with emotion management techniques faded effortlessly into the
background—an integrative transduction of technique allowing the genuine
feeling of experiencing experience to emerge. As Stephanie engages with the
experience her perceptions of role associations also fade.

Emotional Labor Enactments

As suggested in the preceding analysis using Callahan and McCollum's
(2002b) model of emotion management, emotional labor is most evident
in those moments where external influences converge in an organization's
attempted influence over certain aspects of emotion work performed in the
workplace. Emotional labor can be thought of as the effort needed to
respond to such organizational influences, the goal of which is compliance
with the organizational performance expectations (whether implicit or explicit)
associated with in-role responsibilities and workplace interactions.

Callahan (2000) noted the difficulties of distinguishing emotion work from
emotional labor, at one point remarking that there would be little need
for the concept of emotional labor if all emotion work were commoditized
(Callahan & McCollum, 2002b). Control moves (Goffman, 1969/2021)
establish the structural parameters that shape the emotional life of the organization. The subtle shift to performance compliance changes the nature of
both the interaction and the emotion work performed during the interaction.
To this end, emotional labor is a type of emotion work, but it is not the
same as emotion work performed during in-role interactions. When successful,
emotional labor can result in the presentation of organizationally sanctioned
and carefully scripted aspects of in-role interactions.

To illustrate this point, it is perhaps helpful to think of emotional labor
as a three-stage process (see Fig. 5.1) consisting of pre-enactment, enactment, and post-enactment performance activities similar to those described
by Goffman (1959). Emotional labor is used to demonstrate compliance
with pre-enactment and post-enactment performance expectations. In other
words, emotional labor is used to demonstrate compliance with the expected
script to be performed during a performance enactment. If successful, pre-
enactment compliance influences or shapes the performance during enactment
to meet the desired outcome (smiling in a particular way or at a specific
moment, for example). Emotional labor can also be observed during the
post-enactment debriefing period. The emotional labor exerted during pre-
enactment and enactment reinforces compliance or moves toward complete

Fig. 5.1 Three-stage process of emotional labor enactment

conformity (potentially leading over time to the sense of separation from self and role that Hochschild (1983) characterized as alienation).

Pre-enactment activities set the stage for performance interactions. In the case of Hochschild's (1983) flight attendants, these activities centered around the training necessary to gain compliance with the scripted aspects of pre-enactment performance expectations. Here, Hochschild's use of acting metaphors is especially helpful. Deep and surface acting techniques help individuals respond to scripted demands of "getting into" character. Emotional labor, then, is the conditioned response to similarly scripted aspects of in-role performance interactions. Much of the work or labor associated with emotional labor is performed before and after the enacted part of the interaction occurs.

Take, for example, the critical incident from the preceding analysis depicting a student teacher's dismissal from the program. The pre-enactment stage was set as faculty members, and others gathered beforehand to prepare for the meeting with the student. The formal nature and location of the meeting implied something of the gravitas of the proceedings. At the same time, the faculty member recounted how taken aback she was by the general atmosphere and attitudes displayed by the others who were present. The faculty member struggled to contain and push down her feelings for the student, while her colleagues appeared to display little to no emotions at all. The decision to dismiss had already been made. It becomes clear that the only expectation of this meeting is a compliant performance aligned with the organizational expectations, the procedural script if you will, associated with the dismissal process. During the enactment phase, the faculty member continued to struggle with her feelings for the student but maintained compliance through modified emotion work and remained "in character" throughout the meeting. Post-enactment, she continued to perform emotional labor as she sought to reconcile her lingering feelings for the student with the need to move past the incident personally and professionally.

Additionally, separating the performance of role enactment from the conditions that set the stage for performance further informs Hochschild's (1983) use of a Marxist framing for the concept of emotional labor. Given a Marxist critique, it is typically the frontline or lowest level worker that experiences the effects of power, oppression, alienation, etc. However, other researchers (e.g., Turnbull, 1999, 2002) have noted the presence of emotional labor throughout various organizational layers. When viewed in terms of pre- and post-enactment, all workers, regardless of role association, occupy a similar position. In other words, all workers are frontline performers, and the product of their labor is the same, emotional compliance with performance expectations. Emotional labor is oppressive in that it conditions a worker to calibrate in a particular way to in-role enactment requirements. Over time, the worker gradually cedes control of personal emotions and displays (emotion work) to the organization. Hochschild's use of surface and deep acting implies a need to respond to something, in this case, an organization's attempt to influence in-role performance enactments. The initial response to this calibration may or may not be felt strongly. Still, the need to respond is always present, ultimately resulting in alienation that represents a separation from both a sense of self and the enacted self. Engagement (Kahn, 1990, 1992) with the work role and the enactment of the professional persona associated with the role are equally disrupted, resulting in dissonances felt both professionally and personally.

Power, Resistance, and Emotional Labor

The implementation of a new program is representative of a change initiative for any organization, and quite often, the management of associated emotions is an integral part of the change process. The structural management of emotions for organizational success lies at the heart of Hochschild's (1983) conceptualization of emotional labor. However, as Callahan and McCollum (2002a) observed, the structural management of emotions "minimizes the human power of emotion as a force for development both individually and collectively" (p. 10). When considered an emergent force, the power inherent in the relationships observed between faculty and student teachers is productive, authentic, and indicative of the individual growth and change necessary for the program's overall success. Hargreaves (1998a) characterized the emotional bounding of such relationships as a type of discretionary commitment related to a positive sense of engagement. The dominant structural power of the control moves (Goffman, 1969/2021; Sutton & Rafaeli, 1988) of emotional labor can potentially disrupt or inhibit the productive power and commitment associated with these relationships, even while ultimately meeting the needs and expectations of the organization. Resistance, as performed by faculty members in this study, frequently resembled a protective posture intended to shield student teachers from encountering the structural manipulation of emotion work inherent in the performance of emotional labor, as well as shielding faculty members from the potential loss of the relationship. This was especially noticeable in incidents related to autonomous emotional labor where emotional labor was performed voluntarily for the benefit of all associated parties.

Resistance to the control moves intended to manipulate the performance of emotion work draws further attention to the nature of the structural elements distributing power throughout the organization. In the case of Hochschild's (1983) observations, the enacted emotional fronts were portrayed at an intersection where frontline services workers interact with customers, thus creating a narrowly defined scope for highly prescribed display enactments. In educational settings, similar frontline interactions are less well defined, often governed by professional norms not specifically regulated by the organization. In higher education, the structural elements governing organizational norms reside with external accreditors and regulators. These external pressures influence the performance parameters of policies, procedures, etc. developed within the organization. Program success is a performance intended for an external observer that retains considerable control over the organization through ongoing accreditation status or funding. This is perhaps the reason that the faculty members in this study did not perceive the presence of emotional labor in their day-to-day interactions with student teachers. In fact, when emotional labor was detected, students were also faced with their own performance expectations, implying that they were not the ultimate target of the observed control moves. If considered at the level of the organization, then, emotional labor is deployed in support of the institutional emotional fronts enacted for external accreditors and regulators. In turn, these emotional fronts shape the emotional contexts or metaphors (e.g., Katz, 1990) that influence how emotions are socialized within the organization. Emotion work, influenced by professional norms and expectations, sustains the ebb and flow of daily organizational life as institutions navigate the emotional fronts associated with enactments of ongoing compliance. To Callahan and McCollum's (2002a) point, the "power of emotion as a force for development" (p. 10) is potentially diminished in this dance of compliance as faculty members attempt to shield student teachers from the effects by resisting the pressures of emotional labor enactments.

CONCLUSION

As a mechanism of compliance, emotional labor accentuates the inherent power structures that might be observed within any organization. These structures position workers within the organizational hierarchy where emotion management expectations govern the limits of cultivation of self within the confines of organizational roles. For the participants in this study, the cultivation of personal and professional selves is easily entangled in the relational bond between the faculty member and student teacher. A dominant theme that underpins emotion management performance across this study is the desire of faculty members to cultivate nurturing and trusting relationships with their student teachers. At the same time, such relationships are challenging when student teachers possess high levels of subject expertise, often exceeding those of faculty members.

To better understand power as an emergent force (Callahan & McCollum, 2002a), we used Callahan and McCollum's (2002b) four types of emotion management strategies to look for the subtle moments of interplay between resistance and compliance that characterize the balancing of emotional forces that coalesce into performances of emotion work and emotional labor. It immediately became evident that emotion work and emotional labor were not unidirectional phenomena, as initially suggested by Hochschild's (1983) Marxist framing of the concept (Turnbull, 1999, 2002). The presence of organizational influence or control moves (Goffman, 1969/2021) was observed across all critical incidents, including the more personal incidents associated with emotion work. Evidence of this presence was noted in how and to what degree faculty members made themselves available to perform either emotion work or emotional labor (Kahn, 1990, 1992). Critical incidents related to the performance of emotion work, autonomous emotional labor, emotional labor, and indirect emotional labor within the organizational setting revealed that the negotiation between private and public displays of emotion management is ever-present. Distinctions between use-value and exchange-value and internal and external control (Callahan & McCollum, 2002b) proved helpful in determining the presence of both emotion work and emotional labor. At the heart of the negotiation between emotion work and emotional labor in this study was the relationship between the faculty members and their student teachers and the overarching concern that faculty members had for sustaining nurturing and trusting relationships with them. This was evident in incidents where faculty members suppressed or buffered organizational display and feeling expectations to benefit their relationships with their student teachers. This also provided evidence that faculty members function in a capacity similar to that of middle managers and supports the findings of Turnbull (1999, 2002), indicating the multidirectional nature of emotion management performance within the organization. Additionally, the presence of the negotiation between private and public displays also lends support to Callahan and McCollum's (2002a) argument that power is emergent and relational.

Implications for HRD and Future Research

Teaching has long been recognized as one of many caring professions (Palmer, 2007). Issues surrounding the recent pandemic are changing how we view the feelings of stress and burnout often associated with these professions, especially in the area of health care (e.g., Dzau et al., 2020; Shanafelt et al., 2020). One of the concerns with terms such as stress, burnout, or compassion fatigue, is the implication that something is inherently wrong with someone who cannot "cope" with a stressful situation on their own (Bonsall, 2020). In a similar vein, resistance has also been portrayed negatively in the OD and HRD literature as something to be overcome from within the individual during organizational change initiatives (e.g., García-Cabrera & Hernandez, 2014; Smollan, 2011). Resistance, however, as indicated by the findings of this study, is much more fluid and nuanced. In the case of emotion management, resistance often seems to function as a buffer that is part of a larger multidirectional coping strategy. Faculty members in this study described resisting feeling and display expectations from one direction while focusing emotion management efforts on another. They also described various coping strategies often learned through experience and adaptation. One implication for HRD and future research is the need to understand better how organizations might provide support for a broader array of emotion management approaches, including emotion work, autonomous emotional labor, emotional labor, and indirect emotional labor.

Stress and burnout, recognized early on by Hochschild (1983), have remained among the leading consequences of emotional labor. In the case of health care workers, Shanafelt et al. (2020) suggest providing "psychologic first aid" training to help workers cope with stress, anxiety, and other issues. Several of the incidents in this study included descriptions of stress and anxiety, often associated with a prevailing sense of vulnerability at moments when personal and professional expectations intersect with the influences of organizational control moves aimed at regulating emotions. At the level of the organization in higher education, this sense of anxiety is reflected in concerns with rankings, reputation (e.g., Espeland & Sauder, 2015), retention, and long-term student success (such as the return-on-investment project at the Georgetown University Center on Education and the Workforce). At a more personal level, practitioner publications, such as *The Chronicle of Higher Education*, are filled with accounts of the effects of the pandemic on faculty and students, including stress, burnout, and a prevailing sense of disengagement personally, professionally, and in the classroom. The addition of masking mandates and pandemic protocols only served to impose further opportunities for disrupting the relationships between faculty and students. Given the emphasis on the importance of such relationships by some scholars (e.g., Felten & Lambert, 2020; Hargreaves, 1998b), another implication for future research might be the continued exploration of the emotional vulnerabilities associated with the structural management of emotions through organizational control moves. Wherever future research goes, it is clear from this study that Callahan and McCollum's (2002b) expansion of the concept of emotional labor enhances the capture of the dynamic richness and complexity associated with the performance of and resistance to emotional labor enactments.

APPENDIX

Poetic Critical Incident: How is it?

How is it?

One of the
Most exciting
Experiences

How is it?

Extraordinarily
Good listener
A math teacher

How is it?

Training people
To go into
High needs schools

How is it?

Only person of color
So negative towards her
Should do something

How is it?

She would not
Want me
To be the white knight

How is it?

Irritated me
Didn't know what to do
Contained a lot of feeling

How is it
That other people
Get beat on so much?

REFERENCES

Ashcraft, K. L. (2005). Resistance through consent? Occupational identity, organizational form, and the maintenance of Masculinity among commercial airline pilots. *Management Communication Quarterly, 19*(1), 67–90. https://doi.org/10.1177/0893318905276560

Bellas, M. L. (1999). Emotional labor in academia: The case for professors. *Annals of the American Academy of Political and Social Science, 561*, 96–110. https://www.jstor.org/stable/1049284

Bierema, L. L. (2008). Adult learning in the workplace: Emotion work or emotion learning? *New Directions for Adult and Continuing Education, 120*, 55–63.

Bolton, S. C., & Boyd, C. (2003). Trolley dolly or skilled emotion manager? Moving on from Hochschild's managed heart. *Work Employment Society, 17*(2), 289–308. https://www.jstor.org/stable/23749407

Bonsall, L. (2020, December 11). *Beyond burnout—The moral injury of health care today.* NursingCenter Blog. https://www.nursingcenter.com/ncblog/december-2020/moral-injury

Brenes-Dawsey, J. C. (2018). *Exploring the teaching heart: A critical incident study of the emotional labor experiences of adult educators* (Publication No. 9949332799802959) [Doctoral dissertation, University of Georgia]. ScholarWorksUGA. http://getd.libs.uga.edu/pdfs/brenes-dawsey_joseph_c_201805_phd.pdf

Brotheridge, C., & Grandey, A. (2002). Emotional labor and burnout: Comparing two perspectives of "people work." *Journal of Vocational Behavior, 60*(1), 17–39. https://doi.org/10.1006/jvbe.2001.1815

Brotheridge, C. M., & Lee, R. T. (2003). Development and validation of the emotional labour scale. *Journal of Occupational and Organizational Psychology, 76*(3), 365–379. https://psycnet.apa.org/doi/10.1348/096317903769647229

Bryant, M., & Cox, J. W. (2006). The expression of suppression: Loss and emotional labour in change narratives of organizational change. *Journal of Management & Organization, 12*(2), 116–130.

Bryant, M., & Cox, J. W. (2014). Beyond authenticity? Humanism, posthumanism and new organization development. *British Journal of Management, 25*, 706–723. https://doi.org/10.1111/1467-8551.12005

Burke, W. W. (2014). *Organization change: Theory and practice* (4th ed.). Sage.

Butler-Kisber, L. (2002). Artful portrayals in qualitative inquiry: The road to found poetry and beyond. *The Alberta Journal of Educational Research, 48*(3), 229–239.

Butterfield, L. D., Borgen, W. A., Amundson, N. E., & Maglio, A. (2005). Fifty years of the critical incident technique: 1954–2004 and beyond. *Qualitative Research, 5*(4), 475–497. https://doi.org/10.1177/1468794105056924

Callahan, J. L. (2000). Emotion management and organizational functions: A case study of patterns in a not-for-profit organization. *Human Resource Development Quarterly, 11*(3), 245–267. https://doi.org/10.1002/1532-1096(200023)11:3%3C245::AID-HRDQ4%3E3.0.CO;2-J

Callahan, J. L. (2002). Masking the need for cultural change: The effects of emotion structuration. *Organization Studies, 23*(2), 281–297. https://doi.org/10.1177/0170840602232005

Callahan, J. L. (2004). Reversing a conspicuous absence: Mindful inclusion of emotion in structuration theory. *Human Relations, 57*(11), 1427–1448. https://doi.org/10.1177/0018726704049416

Callahan, J. L., & McCollum, E. E. (2002a). Conceptualizations of emotion research in organizational contexts. *Advances in Developing Human Resources 4*(1), 4–21. https://doi.org/10.1177/1523422302004001002

Callahan, J. L., & McCollum, E. E. (2002b). Obscured variability: The distinction between emotion work and emotional labor. In N. M. Ashkanasy, W. J. Zerbe, & C. E. J. Hartel (Eds.), *Managing emotions in the workplace* (pp. 219–231). Routledge.

Dzau, V. J., Kirch, D. K., & Nasca, T. (2020). Preventing a parallel pandemic - A national strategy to protect clinicians' well-being. *New England Journal of Medicine, 383*, 513–515. https://doi.org/10.17226/25521

Ellinger, A. D., & Watkins, K. E. (1998). Updating the critical incident technique after forty years, In, R. Torraco (Ed.), *Proceedings of the academy of human resource development* (pp. 285–292). Academy of Human Resource Development.

Espeland, W. N., & Sauder, M. (2015). *Engines of anxiety: Academic rankings, reputation, and accountability*. Russell Sage.

Felten, P., & Lambert, L. M. (2020). *Relationship-rich education: How human connections drive success in college*. Johns Hopkins University Press.

Fineman, S. (2000). Emotional arenas revisited. In S. Fineman (Ed.), *Emotion in organizations* (2nd ed., pp. 1–24). Sage.

Fineman, S. (2008). Introducing the emotional organization. In S. Fineman (Ed.), *The emotional organization: Passions and power* (pp. 1–11). Blackwell.

Fineman, S., & Sturdy, A. (1999). The emotions of control: A qualitative exploration of environmental regulation. *Human Relations, 52*(5), 631–663. https://doi.org/10.1177/001872679905200504

Flanagan, J. C. (1954). The critical incident technique. *Psychological Bulletin, 51*(4), 327–358). https://psycnet.apa.org/doi/10.1037/h0061470

Fleming, P., & Sewell, G. (2002). *Looking for the good soldier, Švejk: Alternative modalities of resistance in the contemporary workplace*. https://doi.org/10.1177/003803850203600404

Foucault, M. (1997). Michel Foucault: An interview with Stephen Riggins (S. Riggins, Trans.). In P. Rabinow (Ed.), *Ethics: Subjectivity and truth* (pp. 121–133). The New Press (Original work published 1994).

García-Cabrera, A. M., & Hernandez, F. G. B. (2014). Differentiating the three components of resistance to change: The moderating effects of organization-based self-esteem on the employee involvement-resistance relation. *Human Resource Development Quarterly, 25*(4), 441–469. https://doi.org/10.1002/hrdq.21193

Goffman, E. (1959). *The presentation of self in everyday life*. Random House.

Goffman, E. (2021). *Strategic interaction* [eBook edition]. University of Pennsylvania Press (Original work published 1969). https://www.amazon.com/Strategic-Interaction-Erving-Goffman-ebook/dp/B092MTG9HC/ref=tmm_kin_swatch_0?_encoding=UTF8&qid=1648741853&sr=8-1

Grandey, A. A. (2000). Emotion regulation in the workplace: A new way to conceptualize emotional labor. *Journal of Occupational Health Psychology, 5*(1), 95–110. https://doi.org/10.1037/1076-8998.5.1.95

Grandey, A. A. (2003). When "the show must go on": Surface acting and deep acting as determinants of emotional exhaustion and peer-rated service delivery. *The Academy of Management Journal, 46*(1), 86–96. https://doi.org/10.5465/30040678

Grandey, A. A., & Gabriel, A. S. (2015). Emotional labor at a crossroads: Where do we go from here? *Annual Review of Organizational Psychology and Organizational Behavior, 2*, 323–349. https://doi.org/10.1146/annurev-orgpsych-032414-111400

Hargreaves, A. (1998a). The emotional politics of teaching and teacher development: With implications for educational leadership. *International Journal of Leadership in Education, 1*(4), 315–336. https://doi.org/10.1080/1360312980010401

Hargreaves, A. (1998b). The emotional practice of teaching. *Teaching and Teacher Education, 14*(8), 835–854. https://psycnet.apa.org/doi/10.1016/S0742-051X(98)00025-0

Hargreaves, A. (2000). Mixed emotions: Teachers' perceptions of their interactions with students. *Teaching and Teacher Education, 16*(8), 811–826. https://doi.org/10.1016/S0742-051X(00)00028-7

Hochschild, A. R. (1979). Emotion work, feeling rules, and social structure. *American Journal of Sociology, 85*(3), 551–575. https://doi.org/10.1086/227049

Hochschild, A. R. (1983). *The managed heart: Commercialization of human feeling.* University of California Press.

Isenbarger, L., & Zembylas, M. (2006). The emotional labour of caring in teaching. *Teaching and Teacher Education, 22*(1), 120–134. https://doi.org/10.1016/j.tate.2005.07.002

Jansz, J., & Timmers, M. (2002). Emotional dissonance: When the experience of an emotion jeopardizes an individual's identity. *Theory & Psychology, 12*(1), 79–95. https://doi.org/10.1177/0959354302121005

Kahn, W. A. (1990). Psychological conditions of personal engagement at work. *Academy of Management Journal, 33*(4), 692–724. https://doi.org/10.5465/256287

Kahn, W. A. (1992). To be fully there: Psychological presence at work. *Human Relations, 45*(4), 321–349. https://doi.org/10.1177/001872679204500402

Kain, D. L. (2004). Owning significance: The critical incident technique in research. In K. deMarrais & S. D. Lapan (Eds.), *Foundations for research: Methods of inquiry in education and social sciences.* Lawrence Erlbaum Associates.

Katz, J. (1983). A theory of qualitative methodology: The social system of analytic field work. In R. M. Emerson (Ed.), *Contemporary field research: A collection of readings* (pp. 127–148). Little, Brown, and Company.

Katz, J. (2001). Analytic induction revisited. In R. M. Emerson (Ed.), *Contemporary field research: Perspectives and formulations* (2nd ed., pp. 331–334). Waveland Press Inc.

Katz, P. (1990). Emotional metaphors, socialization, and roles of drill sergeants. *Ethos, 18*(4), 457–480. https://www.jstor.org/stable/640315

Lincoln, Y. S., & Guba, E. G. (1985). *Naturalistic inquiry.* Sage.

Lincoln, Y. S., & Guba, E. G. (1986). But is it rigorous? Trustworthiness and authenticity in naturalistic evaluation. In D. D. Willians (Ed.), *New directions for program evaluation, no. 30* (73–84). Jossey-Bass.

Lois, J. (2006). Role strain, emotion management, and burnout: Homeschooling mothers' adjustment to the teacher role. *Symbolic Interaction, 29*(4), 507–530. https://www.jstor.org/stable/10.1525/si.2006.29.4.507

McQuarie, D., & Spaulding, M. (1989). The concept of power in Marxist theory: A critique and reformulation. *Critical Sociology, 16*(1), 3–26. https://doi.org/10.1177/089692058901600101

Merriam, S. B. (2009). *Qualitative research: A guide to design and implementation.* Jossey-Bass.

Ollerenshaw, J. A., & Creswell, J. W. (2002). Narrative research: A comparison of two restorying data analysis approaches. *Qualitative Inquiry, 8*(3), 329–347. https://doi.org/10.1177/10778004008003008

Palmer, P. J. (2007). *The courage to teach: Exploring the inner landscape of a teacher's life.* Jossey-Bass.

Piderit, S. K. (2000). Rethinking resistance and recognizing ambivalence: A multi-dimensional view of attitudes toward an organizational change. *Academy of*

Management Review, 25(4), 783–794. https://doi.org/10.5465/amr.2000.370 7722

Poindexter, C. C. (2002). Research as poetry: A couple experiences HIV. *Qualitative Inquiry, 8*(6), 707–714. https://doi.org/10.1177/1077800402238075

Rafaeli, A., & Sutton, R. I. (1987). Expression of emotion as part of the work role. *Academy of Management Journal, 12*(1), 23–37. https://doi.org/10.5465/amr.1987.4306444

Shanafelt, T., Ripp, J., & Trockel, M. (2020). Understanding and addressing sources of anxiety among health care professionals during the COVID-19 pandemic. *JAMA, 323*(21), 2133–2134. http://jamanetwork.com/article.aspx?doi=10.1001/jama.2020.5893

Smollan, R. K. (2011). The multi-dimensional nature of resistance to change. *Journal of Management & Organization, 17*(6), 828–849. https://doi.org/10.5172/jmo.2011.828

Sutton, R. I., & Rafaeli, A. (1988). Untangling the relationship between displayed emotions and organizational sales: The case of convenience stores. *The Academy of Management Journal, 31*(3), 461–487. https://doi.org/10.5465/256456

Tolich, M. B. (1993). Alienating and liberating emotions at work: Supermarket clerks' performance of customer service. *Journal of Contemporary Ethnography, 22*(3), 361–281. https://doi.org/10.1177/089124193022003004

Tracy, S. J. (2000). Becoming a character for commerce: Emotion labor, self-subordination, and discursive construction of identity in a total institution. *Management Communication Quarterly, 14*(1), 90–128. https://doi.org/10.1177/0893318900141004

Tracy, S. J. (2005). Locking up emotion: Moving beyond dissonance for understanding emotion labor discomfort. *Communication Monographs, 72*(3), 261–283. https://doi.org/10.1080/03637750500206474

Tracy, S. J. (2008). The prison: Power, paradox, social support, and prestige: A critical approach to addressing correctional officer burnout. In S. Fineman (Ed.), *The emotional organization: Passions and power* (pp. 27–43). Blackwell.

Turnbull, S. (1999). Emotional labour in corporate change programmes: The effects of organizational feeling rules on middle managers. *Human Resource Development International, 2*(2), 125–146. https://doi.org/10.1080/13678869900000014

Turnbull, S. (2002). The planned and unintended emotions generated by a corporate change program. *Advances in Developing Human Resources, 4*(1), 22–38. https://doi.org/10.1177/1523422302041003

Zembylas, M. (2005a). Discursive practices, genealogies, and emotional rules: A poststructuralist view on emotion and identity in teaching. *Teaching and Teacher Education, 21*(8), 935–948. https://doi.org/10.1016/j.tate.2005.06.005

Zembylas, M. (2005b). *Teaching with emotion: A postmodern enactment*. Information Age Publishing.

CHAPTER 6

Prefigurative Spaces: Building Community and Collective Record of Resistance to Create Change in Spaces of Organizing

Amir Keshtiban

INTRODUCTION

There are emerging calls for the field of Human Resource Development (HRD) to move away from its existing mainstream approaches on performativity toward more inclusive and participative approaches. The main criticism of mainstream approaches of HRD is their tendency to rely on tick boxing activities as associated with Training & Development, Career Development, and Organization Development that stealthily strip away employee rights. Moving toward more inclusive approaches of Critical Human Resource Development (CHRD) that challenge the historically dominant normative structures, practices, policies, and definitions will enable practitioners and scholars to examine new possibilities and potentialities.

Focusing on current debates regarding the CHRD, in this chapter, I will discuss spaces of organizing for inclusive change, considering the Occupy London (OL) movement as a case study. I will analyze the nature of the prefigurative space of the OL movement by looking at the repertoires of protest, decentralized structure, and leaderlessness that characterized the movement. I will argue the importance of such spaces with regard to HRD, which provide a safe and nurturing space to the members of an organization to identify new opportunities, recruit new participants, develop new identities, and form and discuss multiple perspectives. This will enable the stakeholders to challenge the

A. Keshtiban (✉)
York St John University, London Campus, London, UK
e-mail: a.keshtiban@yorksj.ac.uk

J. C. Collins and J. L. Callahan (eds.), *The Palgrave Handbook of Critical Human Resource Development*, https://doi.org/10.1007/978-3-031-10453-4_6

dominant discourses, which in turn will extend our knowledge of creating an alternative, nested framework of understanding and practicing HRD.

One of the important parts of the social movements that emerged in 2011 (the Arab Spring, the 15 M in Spain, and the Occupy Movements across the world) was their tendency to advocate for an alternative form of organizing. Their approach to organizing promoted a decentralized, leaderless organizational form without any formal hierarchy in place (Gerbaudo, 2012) and advocated open spaces for discussions that foster real, direct, and participatory democracy (Sitrin, 2011). This organizing strategy is built upon the concept of prefigurative politics. Boggs (1977) defines the 'prefigurative' as a critique to bureaucratic domination, which promotes horizontal organizational structures embodying 'within the ongoing political practice of a movement, of those forms of social relations, decision-making, culture, and human experience that are the ultimate goal' (p. 100). This new alternative form of organizing not only criticizes hierarchy and authority but creates new relationships that foster other ways of being and relating. Prefigurative politics have been implemented mostly in social movements and have only recently captured the attention of those attempting to apply its key concepts into traditional organizational settings.

Despite this recent attention, social movements and organization studies are 'like twins separated at birth' (Davis et al., 2005, p. 10). Although Callahan (2013) used the Occupy Wall Street movement to illustrate how HRD can learn from social movements as an alternative form of organization, Grenier (2019) noted that Human Resource Development (HRD) scholars have not started to properly look at social movements as organizations. This is problematic, she argues, because 'social movements have the potential to make visible and ignite discussions in HRD around the notions of politics, society, culture, globalization, justice, and education, as well as the role of organizations in contributing and responding to social movements' (p. 145).

Grenier's special issue of *Advances in Developing Human Resources* remains one of the few spaces in which HRD scholars have attempted to bring SMOs into HRD's literature. Kwon and Nicolaides (2019) argue for a need to reconceptualize social movement learning in HRD. Emphasizing on the new forms of collective bargaining, Germain et al. (2019) argue that the grassroot activism has taken over the traditional and hierarchical trade unions. Their work suggests that social movements are applicable to the field of HRD by revealing how facilitating change has shifted from change agents to employees' empowerment. In this chapter, I further this argument by introducing the social movement concept of prefigurative politics and prefigurative spaces, arguing the importance of such spaces with regard to HRD, which HRD professionals can use to facilitate inclusive change in organizations.

This chapter begins with a brief discussion of prefigurative politics and the recent social movements that employed it as their alternative form of organizing. Using the London Occupy Movement as an exemplar case, I discuss how prefiguration manifests in practice. This will then lead to a discussion of how spaces of social movement organizing can be used in HRD to open up new possibilities for changing (Bierema & Callahan, 2014; Collins et al., 2015) and the lessons learned to meet the changing environment of the future. The chapter concludes with some suggestions for future research.

PREFIGURATIVE POLITICS

Although the term 'Prefigurative politics' was coined by Boggs (1977) in the 1970s, it can be argued that the ideology on which it was based was an important part of social movement organizations (SMOs) from the 1960s onwards. The term is linked with the New Left and its associated movements, such as the student and youth, peace, women's, LGBT, environmental, and animal rights movements (cf. Hetland & Goodwin, 2013; Melucci, 1980), which are known as the 'New Social Movements' (NSM). Contrary to the Old Social Movements that focused on class as the central issue in politics, the NSMs have worked outside formal institutional channels, emphasizing concerns about lifestyle, ethics, and identity rather than narrow economic goals (Calhoun, 1993).

A key point of reference of the NSM that employed the prefigurative politics was their criticism of the states/status quo and their available alternative, Marxism and socialist revolution, at the same time. Carl Boggs (1977) argues that the persistent issue is not because of the Stalinism and revisionism, but because of the deep-seated problem of Marxism to spell out the process of transition. This shortcoming was clear in the Marxist states, where they reinvented the wheel of bureaucracy. Under Leninism, organization/party members were downgraded to technicians who stress the organizational ends while downplaying the means. Under this agenda, the suppression of values institutionalized, which justified the hierarchical structures, centralization, and alienated labor. This process reproduced what the leftists' critics dubbed as 'state capitalism' (Howard & King, 2001).

This persistence problem led to the emergence of the New Left and its prefigurative nature. The key point of reference for the prefigurative politics of the NSM was the emphasis put on the concept of community that attempted to create and sustain relationships and political forms within the live practice of the movements to resemble their desired society (Boggs, 1977; Breines, 1980). The prefigurative politics as an alternative form of organizing not only criticizes hierarchy and authority but attempts to promote horizontal organizational structures within the ongoing political practice of a movement, in which achieving that prefiguration is through emphasizing on the means such as social relations, decision-making, culture, and human experience as ultimate goal (Boggs, 1977). In other words, the prefigurative politics brings all aspects of our social life to the fore, whether it is political analysis, our broader practices, language, ideas and assumptions, physical spaces, food, or social relationships (Rowbotham et al., 2013).

However, the NSM movements and their prefigurative politics have been criticized for their decentralized, spontaneous, and activist nature, where most of their members energies were consumed by direct action, demonstration, sit-ins, etc., initiated at the local level. These characteristics led the scholars to dub the New Left and its associated movements as utopian, anti-organizational, even antipolitical movements which, for these very reasons, were bound to fail (Breines, 1980, p. 420). Moreover, the so-called lack of strategy (as defined by conventional theories) due to its decentralized structure, its multiplicity of the goals and its members spontaneity have received huge criticism. Responding to these criticisms, Maeckelbergh (2011) argues that the prefigurative nature of these movements itself becomes a precise strategy that emphasizes on the practices of the movements in their 'here and now' and illustrates how the utopian society could be exercised now rather than in the future. As she puts it, prefiguration 'is thought to be cultural, unorganized, and without any goal beyond the enactment of new cultural relations in the here and now among movement actors' (p. 6). We have seen this in famous slogan of the feminist movements, one of the prominent movements associated with the New Left, 'the personal is political' that became an important part of prefigurative critiques highlighting hierarchies, inequalities, and exploitation that go beyond the reach of formal rules and laws (Raekstad & Gradin, 2020).

One aspect that has not been considered properly is the very fact that these failures are measured against the modernist, hierarchical, party organization's standards that seek to see success as an achievement of power not against the prefigurative politics, which seeks to focus not only on goal(s) but also more importantly on the means and ways those goal(s) are achieved. As Breines (1980) puts it, 'The process, the means, the participation and the dialogue were as important as the goal' (p. 422). These movements have a clear political agenda in their own terms that does not focus on the party politics, dismantling state power, or achieving the power, but on participatory democracy and direct action as ways to showcase its alternative way of perceiving the organization/world and political structure. These alternative organizational structures and processes enable those movements to avoid co-optation by bringing politics to all spheres of social life and all structure of domination to their 'here and now'. As Maeckelbergh (2011) argues, by citing Sub comandante Marcos, these movements do not want to conquer the world, they seek instead to build the world anew (p. 2). Emphasizing on the processes and practices, Lebowitz (2012) argues that through practice, 'people are able to develop their capacities and make themselves fit to create a new world' (Lebowitz, 2012, p. 188). In other words, these movements wanted to literally remain as a movement in its processual sense rather than committing themselves to structure, strategy (in its mainstream conceptualization) and consequently any goal(s).

Now that we have considered the concept of prefigurative politics and its responses to the criticisms on structure/organization and strategy, we move to discuss the spaces that the prefigurative politics create for its members to exercise their intended utopian society in their 'here and now'.

Prefigurative Space

So far, I discussed the importance of means over the ends and how the means have consequences and affect the overall ends. I have also discussed the emphasis that the prefigurative politics put on practice and process rather than strategy (in its mainstream conceptualization) and how this alternative form of organizing could create a viable option to Michels (1968) 'Iron Law of Oligarchy'. Although it is very promising, however, this exercise needs to be done within nurturing spaces that advocate and promote such activities. It is worth noting that throughout the history of social movements, physical spaces have played major role in getting the movements organized. Evans and Boyte (1992) call these public places 'free spaces' in the community, which are 'the environments in which people are able to learn a new self-respect, a deeper and more assertive group identity, public skills, and values of cooperation and civic virtue. Put simply, free spaces are settings between private lives and large-scale institutions where ordinary citizens can act with dignity, independence and vision' (p. 17). There are different reasons why these spaces called 'free spaces' such as their ability to provide a freedom from the authorities' surveillance, but according to Polletta (1999), the term 'free' associated to these spaces as they offer people a chance to preserve and build upon a collective record of resistance. In other words, these spaces enable people to envision their alternative society by supplying the activist networks, skills, and solidarity, which in turn enable people to experience a schooling in citizenship and learn a vision of common good in the course of struggling for change (Evans & Boyte, 1992; Polletta, 1999). Haug (2013) argues that these free spaces fulfill two functions for the movements. First, they provide 'a structural integration by connecting groups with each other, collecting resources, preparing protest activities, and doing public relations. Second, they aim at a cultural integration of the various groups and networks in developing a common frame of meaning (p. 708). One of the well-known examples of creating network and solidarity through these free spaces is the radical feminist movement's consciousness-raising group in the late 1960s, which were facilitated by non-hierarchical, loosely structured, face-to-face settings isolated from those in power (Hirsch, 1990).

These free spaces facilitate within movements the spread of identities, frames, and tactics from one movement to another. Movements' members do not necessarily create free spaces, but they do enable existing spaces to become free spaces. For instance, churches, played a critical role in mobilizing and organizing the US civil rights movement (Goodwin & Jasper, 2015). Schools, student lounges, bars, or even military sites such as the Greenham Common Women's Peace Camp (Feigenbaum et al., 2013) have also functioned as free spaces. These instances demonstrate how protesters leveraged existing spaces to their advantage to further their agendas. These spaces could be expanded to organizational settings, where members of organizations transform current settings into a free space to advocate for inclusive and positive changes. For instance, Kellogg (2009) reports on the importance of the 'free spaces' as small-scale settings that allowed for interaction among reformers outside their daily work in the process of organizational change in teaching hospitals. Kellogg refers to these free spaces as 'relational spaces'. Others have discussed these free spaces with different names, such as 'discursive space' (Hardy & Maguire, 2010) or 'experimental space' (Bucher & Langley, 2016; Cartel et al., 2019). Courpasson et al. (2017) call these spaces 'resisting places' and argue that how specific places within organizations are used creatively to resist the status quo and efficiency targets that have been put up by senior managers. Toilets or backstage rooms in Shortt's (2015) study on hairdressers working in hair salons and the meaning of 'liminal spaces' used by hairdressers in their everyday lives or Kellogg's work on operating room and Iedema et al. (2010) hospital corridors are examples of those resisting places. The prefigurative spaces contribute to this literature by attempting to transform those free spaces into nurturing and reproductive spaces that do not merely oppose or resist the status quo or advocate mainstream changes, as was the case with the preceding literature, but rather propose and live the positive and inclusive change that they desire within their here and now.

Prefigurative spaces are the 'autonomous zones' in which actors attempt to 'prefigure the society that the movement is seeking to build by modeling relationships that differ from those characterizing mainstream society' (Polletta, 1999: 11). These settings, Polletta argues, provides people with the network intersection that enable people to have access not only to physical, financial, and communicative resources, but also to people whose only weak ties and consequent social distance and status enable them to challenge existing relations of deference. This is crucial in organizational contexts because employees may empower one another via practice by constructing and enacting within these prefigurative spaces, allowing them to enhance their abilities in the here and now. To illustrate this capacity of prefigurative spaces and connect it to the organizational settings, I will explore the prefigurative nature of Occupy London and how they have leveraged the prefigurative space in their SMO. The next part will go through the methods used to collect the data.

Methodology

Data gathering for the original study began some ten months after the Occupy London movement at St Paul's steps. This included interviews carried out with protesters all of whom had participated in the occupation of the St Paul's site. The data gathered also included the analysis of photographs and other visual material relating to the encampment. Some of this material was gathered from online sources (Occupy blogs websites and Twitter feeds). The original study also drew on a variety of press and media sources that reported on the development of the protests from its inception in October 2011 to the eviction of the protesters in February 2012. A total of 7 semi structured interviews and 22 conversational interviews with participants were conducted between early December 2012 and June 2013. Initial attempts to secure interviews with protesters met with refusals from potential respondents. This was due to the fact that there was a strong sense on the part of protesters that action at St Paul's had been misrepresented by established news media. Over the course of four months, I engaged with programs and meetings, such as general assemblies, workshops, and different subgroups taking opportunities to contribute to the discussions. This engagement presented opportunities for informal interviews that allowed qualitative data to be gathered incrementally. This recalls Spradley (1980) argument that 'conversational' interview material can be elicited from unstructured and open ended encounters (Douglas, 1985; Fontana & Prokos, 2007). While the 'outsider' status of the researcher presented difficulties at the outset, close engagement with the movement provided important insights and meaningful data was garnered from a variety of situations.

The Occupy London

The Occupy London (OL) was initiated on October 15, 2011, when a small group of anti-austerity protestors gathered outside St Paul's cathedral. Following a number of failed attempts to occupy the buildings of the London Stock Exchange (Occupy LSX) the protesters occupied the steps that surround the cathedral. Up to 3000 protestors were involved in these actions. The OL emergence was in solidarity with the Occupy Wall Street (OWS) that emerged on 17 September 2011. The OWS emergence was linked to the Adbusters magazine call that asked people to flood into lower Manhattan, set up tents, kitchens, peaceful barricades, and occupy Wall Street for a few months. It can be argued that the OWS in turn was influenced by the Arab Spring in the Middle East and 15M movement in Spain. Although these movements had slightly different motives, the Arab Spring movement's motive was to protest against dictatorship and corruption whereas the Western movement in 2011 was protesting against the austerity measures and unfair distribution of wealth in those countries, they all have the same repertoire of protest, or the range of tactics (Goodwin & Jasper, 2015; Tilly, 1978) such as decentralized and horizontal structure with no assigned leader(s). Because of the similarity of their repertoires of protest, the Time Magazine chose the 'Protester' as Person of the Year, arguing that whether marching against dictatorships in Tunisia, Egypt, Yemen and Libya, or protesting against neoliberal capitalism and austerity measures in Western countries, people have complained about the failure of traditional leadership and the fecklessness of institutions (Time Magazine).

Although the Occupiers did not use St Paul's steps, 'free space', as discussed above, in a sense to recruit people from the Cathedral community at first, however, they used it to showcase their own prefigurative space to the world. They achieved this in two mediums. First, St Paul's cathedral is a major UK tourist attraction and one of the world's largest religious buildings, so it is always on the radar of news agencies and the public sphere. Second, St Paul's occupies a site adjacent to the medieval City whose walls define the present-day footprint of London's financial district, so by occupying the steps, the Occupiers challenged the taken-for-granted rules and beliefs of the society. According to Milkman and her colleagues, the capacity for securing symbolic and/or physical control of urban spaces, (particularly those close to prominent centers of political or financial power) is a central feature of social movements (Milkman et al., 2013). Positioning the encampment on the cathedral steps provided the protesters with an opportunity for politically inspired remoralization of what had become an officially sanctioned tourist destination. Following the early discussion on 'prefigurative spaces', the St Paul's encampment camp can be understood as a site of ongoing social interaction (Elden, 2004).

The Prefigurative Space of the Occupy London

The Occupiers tried to live the future in present by creating the utopian city in their 'here and now'. In doing so, they built first aid tents, a recycling area for their rubbish, a cinema tent, a university tent, a library tent, a food donation counter, kitchen, and used their tents as offices and homes in their occupied physical space, all free for everyone to adhere to their alternative society. In other words, they used the occupied space to 'prefigure the society that the movement is seeking to build by modelling relationships that differ from those characterizing mainstream society' (Polletta, 1999, p. 11).

Interviews with protesters communicated vividly the lived experience of the encampment as a participatory space that offered mutuality and support, identity, and a conduit for symbolic communication with the outside world.

> The identity we gained from occupying St Paul's was enormous. There was a clear space that brought us together, and suddenly it wasn't there anymore, and Occupy isn't fine. (Linda)

Members of the movement had a kind of prejudice about St Paul's steps, and the feeling of belongingness that physical space had on them in terms of support and collaboration:

> When I am talking about the space, I talk about the physical space. I think that was really the change; because we have had activism online, but it was bringing people that were acting online to one physical space, because that brings in not only, you know, getting to know each other as well, but, like, collaboration and support, emotional support, physical support, which you don't have in the same way online. (Nick)

The encampment worked as a participatory community in which protesters could gain access to free education, health services, or communal kitchens.

Some participants spoke about the sense of ownership that pervaded the site. This was apparent even among those who did not sleep overnight in the camp.

> When we had St Paul's steps, that was my home, even if I didn't sleep there overnight because I needed to wash myself, and also my daughter who is only six. So, I was there every day; it was my real home. (Christine)

Others talked about the power of the space and how the space brought them together.

> I think we didn't realize how powerful it actually was to have a fixed space, because first of all, it became our home for days, you know! We started building tents, and we started using it in different ways, but then people always knew that we were there, so they could always come back. (Sally)

Another participant also spoke about the importance of the physical space in terms of convergence, which helped them significantly to get back together, communicate more easily and quickly, and broaden their radius of acquaintances:

> When we had the occupation in St Paul's, what was very useful about the occupation of this area was everybody was together. It is not happening this much now. It enables the different groups to report back to general assembly more easily. The occupation of an area actually facilitates, makes easier the interconnection of the groups, of the general assembly. (James)

It can be argued that by occupying the physical space and making that space their home by erecting tents, they created a social space. This social space acted as a source of identity and a symbol of the movement, where people knew where to go and find each other. In other words, the occupied physical space became a convergence spot for new recruits and a collective identity for the movement. Apart from identity building through the aid of space and gaining support and convergence from the physical space, the occupied space also played a role as a representational space for the Occupiers, representing the society they aspired to build, in contrast to the existing dysfunctional capitalist system. In other words, the protesters appropriated a politically and historically significant public space, transforming it into a political commons and establishing a prefigurative free space.

The importance of building an alternative society was underlined on another occasion by a group of three Occupiers, when asked what St Paul's steps meant to them now, after the eviction. One replied that it had everything they needed to live in a civilized way. Indeed, he called it a 'small village'. He also expressed his sadness that there was no longer any physical space:

> Within a few days, there was this entire village, hundreds of people, black and white, pink and blue, old and young, and children and hippies and suits,

scholars. We had some people who came and gave us lectures from the academic community day after day. It was amazing. Many of us are still sad, you know, that we have no camp anymore. (Paul)

Another member of that particular group also commented on the importance of physical space in terms of decision-making, as they used to hold general assemblies in that space:

We used to have general assemblies every single day. After the eviction, we had chaos for a while. (Rob)

This indicates the importance of the space not only for convergence, but also for organizing the movement and, more importantly, its existence. The physical space became a decision-making arena for the Occupy members, who exercised real, direct, and participatory democracy in their general assemblies by building their community while at St Paul's steps within their 'here and now'.

DISCUSSION

The Occupiers converted a public space (empty space) into a political common that functioned as a site for open discussion and debate (Harvey, 2012). The occupied space can be seen as a prefigurative free space (Polletta, 1999) in which the Occupiers attempted to build and exercise their own desired society. The occupied space enabled them to act with dignity, independence, and vision (Evans and Boyte 1986). Participants in the research consistently talked about the encampment and St Paul's steps as their utopia, a place that made many things possible for them, such as friendship, unity, and mutual support. The protesters felt empowered by the sense of unity that occupation of the physical space had given them. The occupied space provided an opportunity to show how participative democracy could develop around alternative social forms at the very heart of London's financial district.

As I discussed earlier, the location of the Occupy London movement, St Paul's steps, and the subsequent eviction from the steps of St Paul's raised real and significant consequences, leading many to question the legitimacy of the civic and religious authorities who were nominally in control of the site. In other words, the Occupy movement managed to create a 'crack' (Holloway, 2010) in the capitalist system. As Breines argues, Citing Piven and Cloward's (1977) work on the analysis of poor people's movement in America, protest and mass insurgency are the only alternatives open to poor people seeking redress of their grievances. In other words, due to resources available to poor people in terms of organization, disruption becomes their only political alternative that has been proven successful throughout history. Experiences show that they have achieved more this way than through building their own ultimately bureaucratic organizations. This was the case for the Occupy London movement, as the occupiers managed to disrupt the major UK tourist attraction and one of the world's largest religious buildings as the symbol of status quo at the very heart of London's financial district. They even managed to create a 'crack' within the management of the Cathedral in terms of how to respond to the occupation of the St Paul's steps. The London Evening Standard reported on Monday 31 October that the Dean of St Paul's the reverent Graeme Knowles (who was believed to be 'with the protesters'), had resigned. Church authorities within St Paul's were said to be 'in crisis' after the Dean had 'sensationally resigned over his handling of the "tent city" protest' (Harper et al., 2011).

Similar to other movements that adopted the prefigurative politics, the Occupy movements have been criticized for not having an assigned goal, which eventually led to the demise (eviction) of the movement. Similar criticism was discussed earlier regarding the NSMs. We have discussed earlier that not following the established rules of the game in terms of having an assigned goals and strategies to achieve those goals, was at the heart of these movements and it was their chosen structure by choice to avoid the co-optation attempts. These movements tried to disrupt the system and create a crack in the neoliberal capitalism. As Graeber (2002) argues, 'It's one thing to say, "Another world is possible". It's another to experience it, however momentarily' (p. 72). The Occupy London have shown that another world is possible and attracted several people from various backgrounds to engage in this discussion and gave them the chance to live it in their 'here and now' within the live practice of the movement rather than awaiting it in the future. As Cornell (2011) argues, the prefigurative actions 'propose' alternatives to the status quo.

Prefigurative Politics and CHRD

Emphasizing on the needs of embracing alternative forms of organizing, Callahan (2013) argues that the HRD field needs to loosen its 'definitions of what constitutes an 'organization' that is relevant for the study and practice of HRD in order to meet the changing environment of the future' (p. 299). This is where the prefigurative politics come to the fore, as an alternative setting that enables people to free themselves from pre-defined, fixed roles and rules within a structured organization toward a new alternative organizational setting. In other words, the prefigurative politics is a shift from mainstream, already defined roles and structures toward a new fluid and unstructured alternative forms of organization.

The findings from the OL illustrate that the combined use of virtual and physical spaces enabled the Occupiers to showcase their prefigurative movement, by resisting the capitalist state, while proposing an alternative. This could be a lesson for the organizational members to learn from the OL movement and how to embed prefigurative nature in their change process that not only opposes the status quo, but also proposes new practices. Employees should perceive this prefigurative space as their own property, which they may manage, preserve, and oversee among themselves. This will empower them to personalize it, transform it, or even keep it as it is; the key fact is that it is employees' space, and within that space they can begin to not just challenge the status quo but also to implement their inclusive change. This will enable individuals to make sense of their environment, which will encompass both their personal lives and large-scale institutions in which they may act with dignity, freedom, and vision. In order to elaborate this discussion in terms of organizational settings in more detail, I discuss the prefigurative space in a recent event at Google, The Google Walk Out.

On November 1, 2018, thousands of Google employees across the world walked out at 11 am in their local time zone to protest Google's decision to pay millions of dollars in departure packages to male executives accused of misconduct while remaining silent about the offenses (*The New York Times*). Within three days the walkout organizers managed to organize this huge walk out across Google's branches that attracted 20,000 Google employees. They used various online platforms to inform the employees and the world about their walkout and on November 1, 2018 Google workers around the world stopped working and poured out of their offices into the streets to protest. A significant point of reference here is their clever use of the Google walkout hashtag to include all stakeholders in their campaign, as well as their enormous engagement with mainstream and social media while protesting on the streets of Google buildings, similar to what happened in OL case, discussed earlier. Google employees used these physical and virtual spaces to showcase their protest to the public, recruit new participants and create agendas for discussion in their here and now. As with the OL movement, which was eventually evicted, the Google walk out organizers' demands were not met at the start of their process, however, this gave those involved in the process integrity with oneself and others, dignity, and pride of being part of the change process while trying to maintain hope even though the mainstream current is extremely strong (Noelliste, 2013). This also offered support, knowledge, and inspiration to other giant tech companies' employees as a new era for tech companies being challenged by their own employees (Bhuiyan, 2019). The prefigurative space that brought the Google employees together (streets of Google's buildings) that enabled bottom-up change initiation by disrupting the system. The prefigurative space, gave them identity, dignity, and being empowered as they took the matter in their hand by promoting and enacting grassroot activism rather than considering traditional and hierarchical methods such as trade unions. The prefigurative space gave the employees the power of showcasing their protest as well as the ability to identify new opportunities, recruit new participants, develop new identities, form and discuss multiple perspectives to create their inclusive future and fight against inequality in their workplace.

Criticizing the current state of Human Resource Development (HRD), Bierema and Callahan (2014) argue that the field is dominated by masculine characteristics of assertiveness, objectivity, control, and performance.

What is needed is not another tick boxing activity to equalize the inequalities by balancing the numbers without a comprehensive understanding of the inclusivity and equality issues (Collins et al., 2015), or focusing on big multinational companies and ignoring the small and medium-sized enterprises (SMEs) (Nolan & Garavan, 2016) but for workers and stakeholders to get involved in big decision-making processes and make real differences. For doing so, we need to emphasize on the role of prefigurative spaces that facilitate bottom-up change in organizations as safe and nurturing spaces to the members of organization that enable them to identify new opportunities, recruit new participants, develop new identities, form and discuss multiple perspectives (Polletta, 1999, p. 8). This will allow stakeholders to build a shared frame of meaning by integrating the cultures of diverse groups and networks to challenge dominant discourses, therefore expanding our knowledge of developing an alternative, integrated framework for understanding and practicing HRD. This is only possible if employees believe in themselves and begin to create the necessary prefigurative space, both physical and virtual, which in turn initiates the dialogue that allows them to not only ask but also provide answers to challenging questions as was the case for the Google Walkout. It will be a rough road, but as the OL case illustrated it can create a 'crack' within the established system. The key point of reference is that the means, the participation, and the dialogue within this process is as important as the goal (Breines, 1980). As Callahan and Elliott (2020) argue, resisting managerialist doctrine will be worthwhile regardless of the consequences.

The prefigurative politics create a safe and inclusive space for everyone with different mindset to join and express their opinions, which was missing from mainstream HRD discourse (Bierema & Callahan, 2014; Collins et al., 2015). This inclusivity of the prefigurative politics creates a prefigurative space that brings diverse opinions from multiple stakeholders to the change process. The emphasis on means rather than ends makes the prefigurative politics an ethical process, in which the strategic ends will not justify any means to achieve them. This is because the change agents are not working toward a planned change to make their future workplace a better place to work but enacting their proposed practices for that better workplace in their 'here and now'. As they will be emphasizing on the means such as social relations, decision-making, culture, and human experience as ultimate goal (Boggs, 1977).

This is in line with Bierema and Callahan's (2014) conceptualization of Critical Human Resource Development (CHRD), where their focus is on the inclusive processes and practices rather than rigid planned developments that in reality just enhance organizational aims. They borrowed Lee's (2001) account on HRD as a becoming process rather than a thing of being, which enables HRD to be continuously recreated into renewed becoming. This is consistent with the prefigurative politics' processual nature that emphasizes on the processes and practices that enable people to 'develop their capacities and make themselves fit to create a new world' (Lebowitz, 2012, p. 188). According to Cotter (2014), there is an impasse in moving forward for HRD practitioners when it comes to power structures in their organizations. This impasse is the result of an apparent means–end discrepancy between CHRD and practitioner aims. However, these prefigurative spaces, combined with critical reflexivity, would allow practitioners to challenge and change structures that are frequently assumed to be dominant (Cotter, 2014; Sambrook, 2009).

It is worth noting that although the prefigurative politics is an ideal approach for an organization's members to create their prefigurative space within their 'here and now', this may not be the case for all organizations on every occasion. What the prefigurative spaces would help to achieve, though, is a creation of safe and nurturing space to discuss and engage with progressive and inclusive ideas and discussions, while resisting the non-prefigurative, performative approaches. We need to bear in mind that prefigurative politics is an incremental process for social change that illustrates such a utopian society is possible and can be enacted in our 'here and now'. Therefore, what is needed is a consistent emphasis and safeguarding on these prefigurative spaces that enable us to create a necessary force to become powerful change agents in the organizations by showcasing the new cultural relations in the here and now among actors. Employees as change agents can treat these prefigurative spaces as theirs, open to use and personalization, where they can be in control and be present in an embodied way (Kociatkiewicz et al., 2020). As discussed earlier, these spaces will try to create a 'crack' (Holloway, 2010) in the system by 'proposing' alternatives to the status quo while 'opposing' to the current way of doing things (Cornell, 2011).

CONCLUSION

I started off this chapter arguing of the need for HRD to seek new ideas by taking on alternative forms of organizing to embrace more inclusive approaches that challenge the historically dominated normative structures, practices, policies, definitions, and approaches. In this chapter, I discussed how the HRD practitioner could incorporate 'prefigurative spaces' to start an inclusive conversation and enact the social change that they want in their 'here and now'.

As I outlined in my case study, the Occupiers used the prefigurative space not only to gather in a particular space, but also as a space that gave them collective identity in a sense of being acknowledged as members of a group. The prefigurative space also provided them with a sense of belongingness. This sense of belongingness is created by the safe and nurturing space that was available for them to use. The space allowed them to establish a welcoming environment in which any idea could be shared and explored. They were able to re-connect, interact more simply and swiftly, and extend their circle of acquaintances as a result of this convergent space. It also enabled people not just to discuss those ideas, the majority of which were about creating a better future, but also to put them into action.

The examples from organizational settings and the different terms that they have used for the free spaces such as 'relational spaces', 'discursive spaces', 'liminal spaces', or 'resisting spaces' illustrated that practitioners have also started to create spaces similar to prefigurative spaces, which gave them independence and vision that enabled them to learn a new self-respect, develop a deeper and more assertive group identity, share new skills, and create new values of cooperation. However, as this chapter illustrated, the prefigurative space moves one step further from those spaces in which it enables diverse range of stakeholders to enact their proposed changes in their 'here and now' even though that those changes are the limited ones. The prefigurative spaces serve as identity-shaping resources for practitioners, allowing them to challenge the status quo and live an alternative that they co-created. Critical HRD's main task thus is to ensure that these spaces are valued and produced in the process of becoming. As the OL and the Google Walk Out example illustrated, the improvements offered by these spaces will not result in a fast shift, as with management restructuring changes, but in a negotiated space that will allow its members to act with dignity, independence, and vision (Evans and Boyte 1986). These prefigurative spaces serve as a foundation for members to build their discursive content and cultural aspirations. These spaces promote political, cultural, economic, and ecological encounters with common interests as a 'participatory way of practi[c]ing effective politics' (Routledge, 2003, p. 345), which in turn will enable them 'to develop their own micro-political skills and to ask questions about power and powerlessness' (Trehan & Rigg, 2011, p. 286). The prefigurative spaces therefore will be employed as a shapeshifting alternative that 'negotiate their own boundaries vis-à-vis the status quo' (Parker et al., 2014, p. 361) that moves away from critical reflection ideas in CHRD that place too much emphasis on making practitioners critical rather than engaging with them in critically reflective ways (Cotter, 2014). This is in line with what Callahan (2013) argues that such spaces encourages creative risk-taking which enables the practitioners to challenge and potentially shape their identity.

Future research could look at these prefigurative spaces in different organizational contexts to examine HRD practitioners' experiences in developing and sustaining these spaces while resisting the status quo as well as normative modes of change. This will expand our understanding of the roles of SMOs and prefigurative spaces as an inclusive alternative to resist organizational settings and normative modes of change from various levels of analysis.

References

Bhuiyan, J. (2019). How the Google walkout transformed tech workers into activists. *The Los Angeles Times*.

Bierema, L., & Callahan, J. L. (2014). Transforming HRD: A framework for critical HRD practice. *Advances in Developing Human Resources, 16*(4), 429–444.

Boggs, C. (1977). Marxism, prefigurative communism, and the problem of workers' control. *Radical America, 11*(6), 99–122.

Breines, W. (1980). Community and organization: The new left and Michels' "Iron Law". *Social Problems, 27*(4), 419–429. https://doi.org/10.2307/800170

Bucher, S., & Langley, A. (2016). The interplay of reflective and experimental spaces in interrupting and reorienting routine dynamics. *Organization Science, 27*(3), 594–613. https://doi.org/10.1287/orsc.2015.1041

Calhoun, C. (1993). "New social movements" of the early nineteenth century. *Social Science History, 17*(03), 385–427.

Callahan, J. L. (2013). 'Space, the final frontier'? Social movements as organizing spaces for applying HRD. *Human Resource Development International, 16*(3), 298–312. https://doi.org/10.1080/13678868.2013.782945

Callahan, J. L., & Elliott, C. (2020). Fantasy spaces and emotional derailment: Reflections on failure in academic activism. *Organization, 27*(3), 506–514. https://doi.org/10.1177/1350508419831925

Cartel, M., Boxenbaum, E., & Aggeri, F. (2019). Just for fun! How experimental spaces stimulate innovation in institutionalized fields. *Organization Studies, 40*(1), 65–92. https://doi.org/10.1177/0170840617736937

Collins, J. C., McFadden, C., Rocco, T. S., & Mathis, M. K. (2015). The problem of transgender marginalization and exclusion: Critical actions for human resource development. *Human Resource Development Review, 14*(2), 205–226.

Cornell, A. (2011). *Oppose and propose: Lessons from movement for a new society* (Vol. 2). AK Press Distribution.

Cotter, R. J. (2014). Reflexive spaces of appearance: Rethinking critical reflection in the workplace. *Human Resource Development International, 17*(4), 459–474. https://doi.org/10.1080/13678868.2014.932090

Courpasson, D., Dany, F., & Delbridge, R. (2017). Politics of place: The meaningfulness of resisting places. *Human Relations, 70*(2), 237–259. https://doi.org/10.1177/0018726716641748

Davis, G. F., McAdam, D., & Scott, W. R. et al. (2005). *Social movements and organization theory*. Cambridge University Press.

Douglas, J. D. (1985). *Creative interviewing*. Sage. https://books.google.co.uk/books?id=nq2lPwAACAAJ

Elden, S. (2004). *Understanding Henri Lefebvre*. Bloomsbury Academic. http://books.google.co.uk/books?id=0r3GuXoz77UC

Evans, S. M., & Boyte, H. C. (1986). *Free spaces: The sources of democratic change in America*. Harper & Row.

Evans, S. M., & Boyte, H. C. (1992). *Free spaces: The sources of democratic change in America*. University of Chicago Press. https://books.google.co.uk/books?id=M3Ui_j2RwNsC

Feigenbaum, A., Frenzel, F., & McCurdy, P. (2013). Protest camps. *Zed Books*.

Fontana, A., & Prokos, A. H. (2007). *The interview: From formal to postmodern*. Left Coast Press. https://books.google.co.uk/books?id=rpExgChKB4wC

Gerbaudo, P. (2012). *Tweets and the streets: Social media and contemporary activism*. Pluto Press. http://books.google.co.uk/books?id=sjb_ygAACAAJ

Germain, M.-L., Robertson, P., & Minnis, S. (2019). Protests, rallies, marches, and social movements as organizational change agents. *Advances in Developing Human Resources, 21*(2), 150–174. https://doi.org/10.1177/1523422319827903

Goodwin, J., & Jasper, J. M. (2015). *The social movements reader: Cases and concepts* (3rd ed.). Wiley. https://books.google.co.uk/books?id=jTbcBAAAQBAJ

Graeber, D. (2002). The new anarchists. *New Left Review, 13*(6), 61–73.

Grenier, R. S. (2019). Speaking truth to power through social movements and learning. *Advances in Developing Human Resources, 21*(2), 143–149. https://doi.org/10.1177/1523422319827902

Hardy, C., & Maguire, S. (2010). Discourse, field-configuring events, and change in organizations and institutional fields: Narratives of DDT and the Stockholm Convention. *Academy of Management Journal, 53*(6), 1365–1392.

Harper, T., Bryant, M., & Dominiczak, P. (2011, October 31). *Dean who shut St Paul's resigns: second cleric quits over 'tent city' protest.* The Evening Standard. https://www.standard.co.uk/news/dean-who-shut-st-pauls-res igns-second-cleric-quits-over-tent-city-protest-6362916.html. Accessed 7 January 2018.

Harvey, D. (2012). *Rebel cities: From the right to the city to the urban revolution.* Verso. http://books.google.co.uk/books?id=s4s5f7NnaZAC

Haug, C. (2013). Organizing spaces: Meeting arenas as a social movement infrastructure between organization, network, and institution. *Organization Studies, 34*(5–6), 705–732. https://doi.org/10.1177/0170840613479232

Hetland, G., & Goodwin, J. (2013). The strange disappearance of capitalism from social movement studies. *Marxism and Social Movements, 46*, 86–98.

Hirsch, E. L. (1990). Sacrifice for the cause: Group processes, recruitment, and commitment in a student social movement. *American Sociological Review*, 243–254.

Holloway, J. (2010). *Crack capitalism.* Pluto Press.

Howard, M., & King, J. E. (2001). 'State capitalism' in the Soviet Union. *History of Economics Review, 34*(1), 110–126.

Iedema, R., Long, D., & Carroll, K. (2010). Corridor communication, spatial design and patient safety: Enacting and managing complexities. *Organizational spaces: Rematerializing the workaday world*, 41–57.

Kellogg, K. C. (2009). Operating room: Relational spaces and microinstitutional change in Surgery. *American Journal of Sociology*, 115, 657–711.

Kociatkiewicz, J., Kostera, M., & Parker, M. (2020). The possibility of disalienated work: Being at home in alternative organizations. *Human Relations.* https://doi.org/10.1177/0018726720916762

Kwon, C.-K., & Nicolaides, A. (2019). Reconceptualizing social movement learning in HRD: An evolutionary perspective. *Advances in Developing Human Resources, 21*(2), 267–279.

Lebowitz, M. A. (2012). *The contradictions of "real socialism": The conductor and the conducted.* Monthly Review Press. https://books.google.co.uk/books?id=NfknAA AAQBAJ

Lee, M. (2001). A refusal to define HRD. *Human Resource Development International, 4*(3), 327–341. https://doi.org/10.1080/13678860110059348

Maeckelbergh, M. (2011). Doing is believing: Prefiguration as strategic practice in the alterglobalization movement. *Social Movement Studies, 10*(1), 1–20.

Melucci, A. (1980). The new social movements: A theoretical approach. *Information (International Social Science Council), 19*(2), 199–226.

Michels, R. (1968). *Political parties: A sociological study of the oligarchical tendencies of modern democracy.* Free Press. https://books.google.co.uk/books?id=1GwcBd QwIZYC

Milkman, R., Lewis, P., & Luce, S. (2013). The Genie's out of the Bottle: Insiders' perspectives on occupy Wall Street. *The Sociological Quarterly, 54*(2), 194–198.

Noelliste, M. (2013). Integrity: An intrapersonal perspective. *Human Resource Development Review, 12*(4), 474–499. https://doi.org/10.1177/153448431349 2333

Nolan, C. T., & Garavan, T. N. (2016). Problematizing HRD in SMEs: A "critical" exploration of context, informality, and empirical realities. *Human Resource Development Quarterly, 27*(3), 407–442. https://doi.org/10.1002/hrdq.21261

Parker, M., Cheney, G., Fournier, V., Land, C., Parker, M., Cheney, G., Fournier, V., & Land, C. (2014). Advanced capitalism: Its promise and failings. *The Routledge companion to alternative organization,* 3–17.

Piven, F. F., & Cloward, R. A., (1979). *Poor people's movements: Why they succeed, how they fail.* Vintage.

Polletta, F. (1999). "Free spaces" in collective action. *Theory and Society, 28*(1), 1–38. https://doi.org/10.1023/A:1006941408302

Raekstad, P., & Gradin, S. S. (2020). *Prefigurative politics: Building tomorrow today.* Wiley. https://books.google.co.uk/books?id=k31wxAEACAAJ

Routledge, P. (2003). Convergence space: Process geographies of grassroots globalization networks. *Transactions of the Institute of British Geographers, 28*(3), 333–349. https://doi.org/10.1111/1475-5661.00096

Rowbotham, S., Segal, L., & Wainwright, H. (2013). *Beyond the fragments: Feminism and the making of socialism.* Merlin Press.

Sambrook, S. (2009). Critical pedagogy in a health service management development programme. *Journal of Health Organization and Management, 23*(6), 656–671. https://doi.org/10.1108/14777260911001662

Shortt, H. (2015). Liminality, space and the importance of 'transitory dwelling places' at work. *Human Relations, 68*(4), 633–658. https://doi.org/10.1177/001872671 4536938

Sitrin, M. (2011). Horizontalism: From Argentina to Wall Street. *NACLA Report on the Americas, 44*(6), 8–11. https://doi.org/10.1080/10714839.2011.11722131

Spradley, J. P. (1980). *Participant observation.* Holt, Rinehart and Winston. http://books.google.co.uk/books?id=sQClDJXc5vkC

Tilly, C. (1978). *From mobilization to revolution.* McGraw-Hill.

Trehan, K., & Rigg, C. (2011). Theorising critical HRD: A paradox of intricacy and discrepancy. *Journal of European Industrial Training, 35*(3), 276–290. https://doi.org/10.1108/03090591111120421

Reflecting Upon the Rise, Fall, and Re-emergence of Unions: Critical Approaches to the Organization of Labor

Judith D. Bernier and Sherman T. Henry

The concept of worker advocacy has a long history in unions. Unions are known for coalition building and mobilization. These practices have been historically embedded in unions' operational DNA through well-crafted rhetoric, persuasion techniques, and collective bargaining. Unions have a formal and legally sanctioned role to organize. Unions are non-profit organizations that represent workers in the political economy. They are constructed out of the social movements from a need for workers to advocate and organize. Unions are also "goal-oriented" and facilitate a sense of mission in industries to bargain terms of employment with specific employers after employees establish legal recognition of an exclusive relationship with employers as a bargaining agent (Bierema, 2015; Callahan, 2013). They also operate in a traditional organizational structure within the legal process and manage entities and personnel such as board of directors, staff, offices, payroll, etc.

In addition to operating in a traditional organizational structure, unions are also governed by specific organizational constitutions that describe the power of officers, leadership, and financial responsibilities. The National Labor Relations (NLRA) Act, 1935, known as the Wagner Act, and secondly, the

J. D. Bernier (✉)
Florida International University, Miami, FL, USA
e-mail: jbernier@fiu.edu

S. T. Henry
Morehouse College, Atlanta, GA, USA
e-mail: sherman.henry@morehouse.edu

© The Author(s), under exclusive license to Springer Nature Switzerland AG 2023
J. C. Collins and J. L. Callahan (eds.), *The Palgrave Handbook of Critical Human Resource Development*, https://doi.org/10.1007/978-3-031-10453-4_7

Taft Hartley Act, 1947, outlines unions' existence to operate and register for licensing. The NLRA also made it possible for many private-sector workers to organize in the United States. The union's mission, organizational foundation, and notions of the labor movement are that labor and fair wages, along with benefits, family, and community, are to improve living standards for workers who produce goods and provide services through unionization. Unions are formal organizations that helped deliver workers significant economic settlements through collective bargaining. Unions operationalize their core beliefs, norms, and culture in terms of advocacy, negotiation, organizing, training, and collective action that help improve living standards, equity, and justice to workers in various industries (McAlevey, 2015; Oswalt & Marzán, 2018; Windham, 2017).

Like unions, most of HRD practices occur within the context of an organization. HRD's core mission is to connect people, work, learning, and activities within organizations and communities. However, the practices of advocacy, coalition building, mobilization, or negotiation are not embedded in HRD's operational DNA. The primary practices that are embedded in HRD's DNA are relating, learning, changing, and organizing. The first practice, relating, forms the membrane for which the other three practices are cultivated and become critical actions in HRD. According to Bierema and Callahan (2014), "relating forms the context for learning, changing, and organizing, and has tremendous leverage in our ability to facilitate effective HRD when relationships between people are nurtured and developed in a positive direction" (p. 437). Learning, by questioning or seeking information, is therefore possible when relationships are valued, and where inclusion exists. Change is possible through knowledge acquisition. Organizing, in a sense, operationalizes the forementioned practices for HRD practitioners and scholars, laying out what their concerns should be and what their actions should look like. Critical actions can manifest as engaging in "critical organization development, highlighting storytelling and sense-making, critiquing the power and politics of organized spaces, elevating corporate social responsibility and sustainability, and problematizing strategic HRD" (p. 440). However, some argue that one key practice that is missing from HRD's arsenal practices is advocating (Collins et al., 2015). The authors contend that the forementioned four practices should be defined within the context of advocacy, stating that "we define advocating as relating, learning, changing, and organizing on the behalf of others" (p. 218).

Advocating on behalf of others may cause some level of cognitive dissonance for HRD because of the double-consciousness needed to serve both the organization's mission and human resources needs simultaneously. What if we rethink the boundaries of HRD? Not merely extending its size and scope, but reimagining HRD's boundaries and spaces in which its practice occurs? Imagine a space where HRD change agents protect liberties, equalize wages, negotiate and bargain benefits, and promote training, not primarily to serve the organization's needs, but to sustain employees' core competences, safety, and well-being. According to Callahan (2013), such a space can and should exist, if we challenge our notion of what constitutes HRD and what space it should occupy. Callahan (2013) argues that HRD practitioners need to loosen their definition of an organization to meet our contemporary societal needs and effective study and practice HRD. The author proposes a space that is not steeped in dominant masculinity, utilizes critical HRD principles, and engages our humane sensibilities (Callahan, 2013).

The purpose of this chapter is to provide a critical exploration of the historical advocacy powers of unions and to envision a way forward in contemporary spaces of relating, learning, changing, and organizing on behalf of others. This vision includes acquiring a core conviction and skillset of those who engage or wish to engage in critical HRD work. This chapter will also provide an overview of what it means to be an advocate and various aspects of advocacy. After an overview of advocacy practices in unions, the chapter will discuss various applications to the field of HRD, specifically to Critical HRD research and practice to assess its usefulness in creating contemporary spaces of relating, learning, changing, and organizing. We will conclude with a discussion of emerging and intersecting advocacy practices in HRD, unions, and social movements. This chapter draws on CHRD and union literature to define/describe effective workers' advocacy practices in terms of relating, learning, changing, and organizing on behalf of others (Bierema, 2015; Callahan, 2013).

In this chapter, we argue that a broader view of worker advocacy and practice are needed to create new sources of worker power in the twenty-first-century economy. While we argue that many of these practices are embedded features of both CHRD and labor unions, these practices are not necessarily the same or enacted in the same way. For example, in CHRD, the advocacy potential of these practices is limited by the structure of the contemporary spaces of organizing that systematically disadvantage workers, and in particular workers in marginalized communities. On the other hand, in unions, the advocacy potential of these practices fortifies the structure of the contemporary spaces of organizing for disadvantaged workers, and in particular workers in marginalized communities. We also argue that effective practices need to be de-coupled from their existing roles and distributed to actors across the political economy—and—new practices are required to successfully respond to the challenges facing workers and their needs in the twenty-first-century economy. We will look to existing and emerging practices in CHRD, unions, and social movements to envision several possible scenarios for the future of worker advocacy in twenty-first-century economy.

DEFINING AND PRACTICING ADVOCACY

Advocacy involves more than acts of goodwill that people do on behalf of others. Advocacy may be used to shape decisions that affect the well-being or interests of individuals or a group, enable people to get the information they need, enhance understanding of their rights and make their own choices, and foster social equity (Martin, 2015). Advocacy has long been a tool used by community groups, unions, and policymakers, to confront the series of cascading issues that poor and marginalized communities have and continue to face. Confrontation may occur on three levels (i.e., individual, administrative, or policy) to coordinate short-term and long-term strategies. The individual level may involve acting or speaking on behalf of another or others to help with a specific issue. The administrative level may include working with coalitions or organizations to clarify, monitor, and dismantle regulations and administrative procedures that cause barriers and prevent change. The policy level may include working with coalitions or organizations to propose legislations (Barsky, 2017).

The way organizations, institutions, or people advocate is contingent on their orientation or views about what influences people and how they can bring about social institutional change (Barsky, 2017). The author contends that for organizations with a system orientation, change occurs by modifying the transaction between people. Alternatively, critical theorists coming from a critical race perspective might advocate by raising awareness of the impact of racism in all facets of life. Whereas union leaders and community organizers, with an activist orientation, might advocate by building a coalition and mobilizing people to work or act together for a common cause (Rubin, 2018). HRD practitioners and theorists might advocate by examining workplace inclusion and diversity from a critical theory perspective, mainly among marginalized groups (Brooks & Edwards, 2009; Collin, 2012; Collins et al., 2015; Henry, 2021; Rocco et al., 2014). Hence, illuminating the value of an inclusive work environment. Human and equal rights organizations or activists might advocate for social change through organized protests and voting and policy changes.

The practice of advocacy can take many forms based on the orientation of the advocate. However, Schatzki's (2002) practice theory provides a cautionary tale and argues that people engage in action that makes sense to them. Not only should actions make sense, but the theory also implies that the incentives and rationales to act is more important than the practice itself. That is, actual activities and enacted performances and the situations are also much more important than the actors or advocates themselves. One of the criticisms directed at the Black Lives Matter (BLM) movement was the absence of visible leaders, although present, they were not leading the marches or the movement. Applying a practice-based approach, everything is not about the actors, it is about the practice. The basic units of analysis for understanding organizational phenomena are practices, not practitioners (Nicolini, 2012). He argues that practices come first because of the set of practices (i.e., organizing, marching, protesting, voting, etc.) that are involved in a scene of action. Therefore, it is only when we can appreciate the set of practices that we can ask what sort of agency and actor-ship is made by these specific conditions. Nicolini's (2012) stance echoes the premise of Schatzki's (2002) practice theory, that is, practice is not about the individual. Furthermore, the advent of social media has created virtual spaces for faceless or bodyless leaders to operate incognito while leading social movements and advocating. Hence, making the practices or actions of advocates more visible than practitioners or actors.

CRITICAL THEORY FRAMEWORK

A critical perspective in HRD is not new. This perspective has been used to contest the perfunctory representation of marginalized peoples' issues and experiences. Nevertheless, this perspective represents a meager fraction of the overall HRD's literature and lacks clear application for critical action and advocacy. What if there was a navigable path to critical action? According to Merriam and Bierema (2013), there is such a path through the lens of critical theory, and by incorporating critical thinking, and critical action. Bierema's (2009) earlier five critiques of HRD's role and focus provide a backdrop for her later propositions for the application of critical theory. First, the critiques focused on HRD's role and functions relating to (a) performativity, (b) commodification, (c) shareholders, (d) power, and (e) limited exploration of alternative models and theories that provide an explanation for the arrested development of critical action within HRD. These five critiques form the theoretical foundation for understanding the current state of HRD's limitations and how these restrictions can create new boundaries in contemporary spaces where social action occurs and create (Bierema, 2009). Later, she offers three propositions on how to move forward. The author proposes that the first step, using critical theory, is to challenge the truth that is commonly advanced by dominant groups. The next step is critical thinking with the purpose to actively connect individual experiences to broader social conditions. The final step, and the step that is least taken or intentionally overlooked, is the critical action (Bierema, 2015). These propositions, especially the need for critical action, will underpin the discussions in this chapter.

ADVOCACY PRACTICES IN UNIONS: THE HIGHS AND THE LOWS

Unions' advocacy practices are often well known or synonymous with critical actions such as collective bargaining, organizing, mobilizing, policy setting, and training. Collective bargaining critical actions may manifest as bargaining for pay equity, group healthcare, or for the common good for teachers, law enforcement, and various unionized trades and professions. Organizing critical actions may entail the mobilization of employees across pay equity, social issues, the right to work, "at will employment," "just cause employment separation," employment safety, and the protection for temporary, contractual, independent, and full-time employees. Public policy setting includes setting working standards, such as minimum wage law, FMLA, health and safety, title VII of the 1964 Civil Rights Act. In terms of critical training actions, unions conduct local trainings for stewards to help them develop advocacy skills to enforce contract terms of the collective bargaining agreement. Labor centers, in universities, offer certificate programs in conflict resolution, and collective bargaining to assist union members with knowledge development. Learning may be online or in-person at unions' offices or facilities. Unions are now effectively using Zoom technology to connect with rank-and-file members and conducting more learner activities on the state of worker's rights in the United States.

Union advocacy practices past and present are not without challenges. Despite unions' history of advocacy, advocacy is potentially constrained by the systematic dismantling of labor regulation that has provided its formal sources of power (Fisk & Rutter, 2015; Garden, 2016; Le & Hersh, 2019). The National Labor Relations Act (NLRA) of 1935 and amendments govern private-sector unions and collective bargaining. While states generally have no jurisdiction over private-sector unions, the NLRA Act 1935, as amended, does allow states to enact specific laws that govern fees paid by workers in unionized private workplaces. Hence, the NLRA Act 1935, excluded jobs that were heavily occupied by women, African Americans, and other people of color (Windham, 2017). NLRA restrains certain activities from union against employers like secondary boycotts and limits on picketing the employer. Recently, the National Labor Relations Board (NLRB) ruling limited some classification from unionization. In the *Merck, Sharp & Dohme Corp.*, 367 NLRB No. 122 (May 7, 2019) case, the NLRB clarified and reaffirmed that for the most part, employers are free to treat union and nonunion workforces differently if the employer does not have an improper anti-union motive in doing so. The company was allowed to provide additional time-off to nonunion employees while denying union members the same benefit. The NLRB decision promoting an anti-union sentiment among the company is legitimate, as long as the company doesn't acknowledge union animus as the motivation for the new benefit. This example is repeated in several other legal cases that companies are now using as a strategy against unions in the workplace.

The workers' right to organize pickets in an exercise of free speech to bring attention to the employer's behavior. Workers join picket lines to demonstrate solidarity to form a belief and make sense of the contract bargaining issues in a public space to generate knowledge. The U.S. Supreme Court has issued several decisions that adversely impacted labor union's dues collections and worker's speech like the case of Knox et al. v. Service Employees International Union, Local 1000. The Wisconsin ACT 10 dismantles union ability to bargain overcompensation, collect dues, and required new reauthorization by workers. Unions play a role in the efforts to defeat the Wisconsin Act 10 and after its passage help fund the recall efforts of then Governor Scott Walker. The union pays for campaign ads and mobilizes volunteers in most electoral policies and endorses candidates.

The Supreme Court rationale was First Amendment rights of speech and workers in agency fees for dues collection. Associate Justice Samuel Alito signaled that the time had come to revisit the precedent set in Abood v. Detroit Board of Education. This 1977 case judged fair-share fees to be constitutional. In Harris v. Quinn (2014), Alito authored an opinion that brought the reversal of Abood agency dues collection based on the First Amendment. There was momentous reversal of due collections in the case of Friedrichs v. California Teachers Association. In this case, the plaintiffs argued that being forced to pay fair-share fees to the union that bargained on their behalf infringed on their rights to free speech. Unions are involved in most court cases through filing amicus curiae and sometimes finding citizens with legal standings to file lawsuits in cases that adversely impact workers.

The Supreme Court Janus case highlights formidable change to the public-sector law "right to work" and increased employer protection of collective bargaining laws (Le & Hersh, 2019). The Janus ruling disrupted decades of labor union "fair-share" dues collection. Unions relied on the sustained legal rights to collect "agency" or "fair-share" fees from the non-members they are required to represent in collective bargaining and grievance procedures from the precedent set in Abood v. Detroit Board of Education. This 1977 case judged fair-share fees to be constitutional and allowed the union to collect dues without ever speaking with the worker under these contracts. The fair-share employee was not a union member, nor could they voice their views at a union membership meeting to establish policy, bargaining goals, or vote on union political endorsements. The Janus case has multiple consequences for public-sector unions: (1) union organizers will need to develop interpersonal skills, (2) empower shop stewards and member leaders as organizers in the workplace, (3) find common ground with workers who have historically opposed union politics, and (4) organize against the opt-out campaign by employer groups.

Since the 1970s, urban labor markets in North America have undergone profound restructuring. Immigration, de-industrialization, and the expansion of service sector employment have significantly altered the urban landscape. The rise of contingent work, or precarious employment, challenges traditional forms of trade unionism, and has opened the way for new initiatives, including community unionism (Black, 2005). The core objectives of community unionism initiative are to: (1) change character, skills, and knowledge associated with social roles of community and labor union integration; and (2) the skill and knowledge involved in the formalization of these new roles in alternative policies and practices of new organizational forms. Together these elements underpin the core context of any community unionism initiatives and may help move community unionism from a largely descriptive to a more analytical endeavor, which leverages concrete data to make more far-reaching policy gains.

ADVOCACY AS RELATING, LEARNING, ORGANIZING, AND CHANGING IN HRD

There is no doubt the nature of work is changing, and workers are seeking new ways to perform work. This work evolution urges organizations and the field of HRD to be more intentional about what influences people and how they can bring about social institutional change. The actions of relating, learning, organizing, and changing are not foreign to HRD. In this section, we discuss how HRD can re-imagine the practices of relating, learning, organizing, and changing to elevate its role as an advocate or change agent for social change.

Relating as Advocacy

Relating fosters new relationships that can produce novel and enduring outcomes. HRD professionals' relationships are often centered on key stakeholders, such as investors, employees, customers, and suppliers. At the core of these relationships is organizational performance improvement or effectiveness. Within the past decade, we have witnessed an increased interest in corporate social responsibility (CSR) to create win–win outcomes for employees, the organization, and society. Often, this social awareness is not always an innate response, but a forced response to social pressure. Whereas unions build relationships and empower workers before the law makes it a mandate, such as in the case of pay equity, safe working conditions, and the right to unionize, acts of corporate social responsibility tend to be reactionary and merely bounded in diversity and inclusion, and training and development initiatives. In addition to being reactionary, some may describe some organizational CSR initiatives as performative. Beyond philanthropy and tackling environmental emissions and waste, relating, within HRD, could look like collective bargaining, negotiating, and organizing for the common good, deepening organizations' relatability and sensibilities to issues that impact their employees within and outside the organization, including human rights (i.e., religious, sexual, ethnic, gender, and socio-economic victimization and oppression), environmental issues (i.e., water crisis in Flint, Michigan, pipeline access and protest in Dakota), and epidemic and pandemic issues (i.e., opioid, mental health issues, and COVID-19 pandemic). A social justice and critical approach to advocacy asks that we understand individual social identity and experiences in relation to the social, political, and environmental structures that perpetuate advantages and disadvantages. In a research study exploring issues of HRD involvement in organizational CSR initiatives, Fenwick and Bierema (2008) concluded the following: (a) HRD professionals' familiarity with the principles and possibilities of CSR is necessary to assess their roles in furthering CSR objectives; (b) HRD professionals' ability to distinguish the levels of stakeholders can assist the organization focus and prioritize its CSR activity, (c) HRD professionals ability to examine and communicate possible links among learning, organizational development, and CSR can play an integral part of the success of CSR.

Learning as Advocacy

The process of learning knows no bounds. Learning can occur anywhere as an individual or collective process and with or outside a social movement. A social movement refers to any collective movement with a goal to address the oppression and liberation of marginalized groups. Within this movement, learning is collective, that is, cocreation of knowledge and meaning by group members or advocates. Collective learning involves multidirectional and critical dialogue about core assumptions and lived experiences. It also involves envisioning a different society and reflecting critically on issues and making changes, and mobilizing, sustaining, and maintaining the movement (Sandlin & Walther, 2009). Learning is a process of self-transformation and knows no bounds. Beyond merely producing practice-specific participatory competences or outcomes, learning itself can transform what is learned (Hager et al., 2012). Hence, illuminating the situational nature of learning, that is, considering the authentic contexts and activities that promote learning based on real-life experiences. Within a community of practice, learning and social membership are co-dependent; it is a relationship where learning appears as a precondition of and form of social membership (Lave & Wenger, 1991; Wenger, 1998). The act of learning then becomes the scene of action for advocacy, agency, and actor-ship to manifest. This perspective supports Nicolini (2012) and Schatzki's (2002) stance that "practice" is the heart of advocacy practices, not practitioners. Bennett and McWhorter (2019) contend that social movement learning (SML), and social innovation are integral to produce outcomes that resolve unmet social needs. The authors examined social movement as an underlying learning process with implications for HRD. These implications include embedding empathy and design thinking when partnering with corporate affiliates and social organizations. Hence, allowing a greater understanding of organizational learning processes and activities within social movements or social justice advocacy practices. On the other hand, some contend that an artistic expression is also a powerful framework to assist learners to engage in SML and a meaningful approach that HRD practitioners can employ (Bohonos et al., 2019). Whereas others believe a radical change is necessary for social movements future, that is, more support and less direction, and more understanding from HRD, who is well equipped to provide training and development to advocate for change (Sisco et al., 2019). Organizations' interest in social movement should be genuine to the cause and desired outcomes, not merely a public relations opportunity to gain social capital.

Organizing as Advocacy

Organizing can take many forms. Organizing can manifest as marches, rallies, sit-ins, walk-outs, protests, strikes, and picketing all of which are critical and an integral part of social movements actions. This collective show of discontent often represents a form of political participation and resistance against the status quo (Germain et al., 2019). With the wavering support of unions as the champions of employees, in the United States, HRD scholars and professionals can fill this vacuum by assisting organizations to align their mission and vision to support issues of pay equity, diversity and inclusion, and social issues that plague marginalized employees within and outside the organization. HRD can become a movement within social movements, that is, constantly scanning the work environment for issues that mirror larger social issues. Hence, striking alliances with civil society groups and organizations. This position would preempt the need to write meaningful or meaningless corporate statements about standing, supporting, or aligning with contemporary social movements' agendas or actions for restorative justice. Callahan (2013) argues that organization development, training and development, and career development may prove useful for social movements. Within this context, organization development activities would include identity, integration, adaption, and achievement (Callahan & Dunne de Davila, 2004). Therefore, making each activity a critical and actionable advocacy practice. The authors believe that the critical action of creating identity can be a role that HRD professionals can assume to help social movements engage advocates to create space for strategic discourse that facilitates institutionalization of the process enacted in the movement. Integration, as critical action, would include acts of establishing dissemination and diffusion mechanism to bring awareness and build inter-relatedness to all members in the organization, concerning decision-making process, action items, learning experiences. Adaptation as a critical action would involve scanning the environment for opportunities of strategic planning to realize collective goals.

Changing as Advocacy

Change is evitable and constant. The COVID-19 pandemic and Great Resignation forced many organizations to come face-to-face with the cascading impact of a changing labor force. Some of these changes included massive lockdowns, shutdowns of services due to COVID-19 guidelines and regulations, unprecedent layouts, in a short period of time, adjusting to remote work, and managing teams that were, in some cases, displaced locally, nationally, or globally. Home life and work life emerged, and organizations had to determine how to delicately traverse the blurry lines that remote work created and continues to create. Change is hard and uncomfortable; it unsettles us to say the least. However, change creates opportunities to advocate for new resources that align with current realities and experiences. It is time for full-scale organizational transformation around learning, training, developing, and employees' wellness and work flexibility.

Some scholars have identified several challenges for HRD professionals and organizations against the backdrop of the COVID-19 pandemic. Since COVID-19, not only the lines between work and home but the lines between formal and informal learning too have blurred. Yeo and Li (2022) argue that the pandemic has blurred and transcended formal and informal learning. They attributed these phenomena to the availability of online content and open-source materials and learning from home. Hence, redefining the setting, location, and process in which formal and informal learning occurred and still occurring. This uniquely transcendent learning space must be reimagined by HRD professionals, presumably into the future, in terms of how practitioners design, develop, and facilitate training and learning.

EMERGING ADVOCACY PRACTICES IN UNIONS AND HRD

In this section, we discuss emerging and intersecting advocacy practices in HRD, unions, and social movements. First, we discuss the nature and benefits of collective bargaining for the common good, an all-inclusive perspective that includes all, not select workers. Next, we discuss the rewards and risks of organizing within the political economy of organizations and industries, concluding with a discussion on coalition building and moving beyond trans-actional focused actions and outcomes to more transformative experiences and spaces.

Collective Bargaining for the Common Good

Collective bargaining is shaped by using and leveraging power relations. Power relations can take many forms. McAlevey (2015) offers two models as case studies to examine how unions develop a top-down organizing model "corporate campaigns," which is a small group of national union leaders and staff making decisions without involvement from workers. The second model centers on workers' participation in organizing practice; decision-making strategies are known as the "bottom-up," organizing model. The organizing methodology is an important critical factor for reviewing organizing, training, and organizational culture.

By analyzing collective bargaining in social and power relation context, this approach illuminates outcomes and consequences of collective action. It is essential to understand union member's share of the labor market in the United States. In 1983, the first year for which comparable union data are available, the union membership rate was 20.1%, and there were 17.7 million union workers (BLS, 2019). McAlevey notes that in 1995, a decade and a half later, after the AFL-CIO new labor organizing emphasis, union ranks continued to plummet to 6.7% in the private sector and11.3% overall. More than two decades and a half later in 2019, the percent of workers who are members of unions represent 10.3%, down by 0.2 percentage points from 2018, the U.S. Bureau of Labor Statistics reported. The number of wage and salary workers belonging to unions, at 14.6 million in 2019, had little changed from 2018. According to the BLS report, African Americans are most likely to join unions. Among full-time wage and salary workers, union members had median weekly earnings of $1,095 in 2019, while those who were not union members had median weekly earnings of $892. In addition to coverage by a collective bargaining agreement, these earnings differences reflect a variety of influences, including variations in the distributions of union members and nonunion employees by occupation, industry, seniority, age, gender, firm size, or geographic region.

This perspective of collective action shows not only the role of unions to garner fair wages, but how the legal paradigm shift from "fair-share" dues collection to the public-sector "right to work" and the ominous threat to political-economic inequities for wages and other benefits can be. To sustain the collective bargaining power of union and common good outcomes, from an HRD perspective, we can look to Fenwick's (2005) propositions for guidance. These propositions include four dimensions in which critical HRD can strive as a place for study and practice, while bargaining for the common good. The author suggests: (a) acknowledging the traditional legal rights and role of unions' interest in collective bargaining social and economic justice, (b) accepting training as change agents, (c) empowering social justice and economic advocates and efficacy, and (d) organizing for workers' empowerment. Using similar strategies, McCartin (2016) provides evidence in his work where AFL and CIO locals, churches, and civic groups were able to unite to form unions and communities to lay the groundwork for labor's economic and social movement rise. One of the key principles of collective bargaining is echoed in Brussel's (2015) book, *Fighting for Total Person Unionism: Harold Gibbons, Ernest Calloway, and Working-Class Citizenship*. He discussed the community grievance lens for intersecting through organized meetings and problem-solving.

Organizing Within the Political Economy of Organizations and Industries

Organizations are simultaneously economic and political entities, existing in a state of power—dependent on other driving forces that comprise a broader social system (Yorks, 2004). Unions have a formal, legally sanctioned role to organize and represent workers in the political economy of organizations and industries (McAlevey, 2015; Oswalt & Marzán, 2018; Windham, 2017). Both entities share a common stakeholder, the worker, and must remain cognizant of workers' needs and interests within various social, political, and economic contexts.

In 1995, the biggest shake-up in the U.S. labor movement in more than fifty years took place when a new generation of unionists forced the first contested election in the history of the AFL-CIO (McAlevey, 2015). The victors, dominated by the service workers' unions and often referred to as "New Labor" dominant hegemonic leadership, promised revitalization through aggressive new organizing strategies as change agents. One lens for this analysis is the multi-employer, and multiple geographic places a national union may have a membership. In HRD scholar's recognition, often, there is "No One Shoe Fit All." Thus, unionists are exploring different ways to utilize the voluntary collective momentums of members committed to mutually constructed gains and laboring for social justice (McAlevey, 2015; McCartin, 2016). The CIO's organizing methods were deeply embedded in, and reliant on, an understanding of workers in relation to the communities in which they lived.

The cost of living is directly related to bargaining compensation ranges for workers' pay scales and defining classification job descriptions with management. For example, salary contract negotiation for schoolteachers starts with a standard of living of a reasonable expectation for pay equity, considering the education levels and professional development for skills needed to teach diverse students. The local organizing for contract bargaining campaigns consists of membership action teams in the schools and teacher forums with Parent Teacher Association (PTA). McAlevey (2015) identified organizing as an essential practice of the labor movement and not defined by one traditional space. Organizing and training are the sense-making influence foundation of the union's activities, growth, power, and human resources set of endeavors. Union leaders must know their audience to relate and perform a power analysis and develop recruitment strategies. Windham (2017) found textile workers had a certain culture and organization norms shaped by the industry. The employer needed to comply with various Occupational Safety and Health Administration (OSHA) laws. The union would help file complaints against a company in violation of OSHA standards to win workers' trust. Another example is women working on the shipyard required to work and denied benefits outlined in the Family Medical Leave Act (FMLA), a law which the union lobbied and provided input in the legislation. So, union organization play an essential role in advocating in the legislative process to enact laws favorable to worker's needs. Windham (2017) pointed out the voluminous cases that some unions have intervened in work discrimination lawsuits and in advocating for women and African Americans in dominant white work locations.

Oswalt and Marzán (2018) contend that more collaborative activities are needed to promote public policy that improves worker's living standards. These new coalitions could promote new rights for workers through co- or tri-party negotiations and relationships, deemed "social bargaining." The authors believe that much of these collaborations or new labor laws are premised on developments by "alt-labor" groups like the "Fight for $15" and worker centers. Workers centers have formal office space, but the work is on the streets of cities and marching for justice to generate public support and organize town hall meetings to educate the public. Unions often work with community activists that advocate for employment rights absent traditional collective bargaining relationships. The new advocacy role is union support for lobbying state and local officials to initiate increased minimum wages far above the federal level and provided masses of workers with paid sick time, "fair scheduling" rules, and better "wage theft" protections. The consequences for unions are advocating for nonunion workers to gain pay raises and benefits through legislative action and not direct bargaining with employers.

Coalition Building: Moving from Transactional to Transformational Spaces

The labor movement's approach to its role also embodies many of the features of effective worker advocacy practice needed today (Grayson, 2011; Hlatshwayo, 2018; McCartin, 2016). McCartin (2016) contends that two examples linked to labor and community programs to organize working interest groups. The Minneapolis People's Congress alignment of community and labor organizations, and interests, organizationally went well beyond the merely transactional forms of coalition-making that HRD professionals often seek between learners and allied organizations, establishing a collective vision for social, racial, and economic justice. The coffee shop meetings and planning strategies are unique to HRD practice. They are nonconforming meeting spaces for strategic planning. For many, in this case, unions enlist community groups to support their contract campaigns in various ways; instead, unions and their allies build a joint plan from the ground up in different settings to recruit members for participation. Second, convening conferences to develop phenomenon: unions and community partners collaborating to challenge twenty-first-century capitalism, reviving democracy, and advocating government intervention in the process. McCartin (2016) asserts that the content of "Bargaining for the Common Good" strategy with unions engaged in community training and learning to influence organizational effectiveness in informal and formal networks. Furthermore, unions use community allies to advance collective political actions.

Since the rise of structured collective bargaining laws, in the private sector in the 1930s through the1950s and in the public sector in the 1960s and 1980s, collective bargaining has come to mean more than just economic benefits but advocating and collaboration for human dignity on and off the job, organizing to get out the vote politically to change the law and public policy. The labor movement and civil rights movement converged in the 1968 Memphis sanitation strike of 1600 black workers. Theoretically, social justice, the nonviolent philosophy, was included in the union's organizing training that built on diversity, picketing, and peaceful protest. The Memphis strike organizing propelled public-sector organizing in the southern United States and racial inequities. Unions are a tool and resource center where workers learn to develop skills, message for unity, endorse political candi-dates, form coalitions, lobby government officials, and mobilize stakeholders to improve living conditions (Grayson, 2011; Hlatshwayo, 2018; McAlevey, 2015). Some community-based organizations are natural allies for worker's rights like NAACP, Job with Justice for the leftist social movement, etc. The multiple voices of the "rights" movement intersect with unionization against the backdrop of historical right-wing movements like white supremacy group's influence and racial inequities in capitalism practice.

DISCUSSION

One of the most contentious spaces is the proverbial organizational shop floor where interests and needs tend to collide. These collusions occur for several reasons including, class struggle against the ruling class, top-down manage-ment, labor law violations, opposition to any forms of oppression, particularly ageism, sexism, and racism. The COVID-19 pandemic has underscored the role, function, and importance of unions in giving essential and nonessential workers a collective voice in the workplace and the urgent need to reform U.S. labor laws to halt the erosion of workers' rights. During the pandemic, unions were able to secure enhanced safety measures, premium pay, paid sick time, and negotiate terms of furloughs or workshare arrangements to help save a job or minimize job loss. These critical actions of advocacy are notice-able because the pandemic unearthed America's weak system of labor practices and protections, resulting in disproportionately women and workers of color, particularly low-wage workers bearing brunt of the costs of the pandemic. Furthermore, while providing their essential services, many workers performed their duties without protective gear, no access to sick leave, and were silenced or fired if they spoke up about health and safety conditions or concerns. The pandemic workplace has created an even more contentious work environment. The pandemic has also given rise to self-organized groups confronting big business and toppling political regimes. As mentioned earlier, unions have and continue to play pivotal roles in our society. Unions were instrumental in the efforts to defeat the Wisconsin Act 10 and after its passage helped to fund the recall efforts of then Governor Scott Walker. Union paid for campaign ads and mobilized volunteers in most electoral policies and endorse candi-dates. Union advocates are fighting to unionize Amazon workers with varying degrees of success. Although these collective efforts of organizing strategies are far removed from decades old tactics, the goals and visions of pay equity and social justice remain the same for all workers.

REFERENCES

Barsky, A. E. (2017). *Conflict resolution for the helping professions: Negotiation, mediation, advocacy, facilitation, and restorative justice.* Oxford University Press.

Bennett, E. E., & McWhorter, R. R. (2019). Social movement learning and social innovation: Empathy, agency, and the design of solutions to unmet social needs. *Advances in Developing Human Resources, 21*(2), 224–249.

Bierema, L. L. (2009). Critiquing human resource development's dominant masculine rationality and evaluating it impact. *Human Resource Development Review, 11*(1), 68–96.

Bierema, L. L. (2015). Critical human development to enhance reflexivity, change discourse, and adopt a call-to-action. *Human Resource Development Review, 14*(2), 119–124. https://doi.org/10.1177/1534484315585206

Bierema, L., & Callahan, J. L. (2014). Transforming HRD: A framework for critical HRD practice. *Advances in Developing Human Resources, 16*(4), 429–444. https://doi.org/10.1177/1523422314543818

Black, S. J. (2005). Community unionism: A strategy for organizing in the new economy. *New Labor Forum, 14*(3), 24–32.

Bohonos, J. W., Otchere, K. D., & Pak, Y. (2019). Using artistic expression as a teaching strategy for social justice: Examining music from the civil rights and black lives matter movements. *Advances in Developing Human Resources, 21*(2), 250–266.

Brooks, A. K., & Edwards, K. (2009). Allies in the workplace: Including LGBT in HRD. *Advances in Developing Human Resources, 11*(1), 136–149. https://doi.org/10.1177/1523422308328500

Brussel, R. (2015). *Fighting for the total person unionism: Harold Gibbons, Ernest Calloway, and working-class citizenship*. University of Illinois Press.

Bureau of Labor Statistics. (2022, January 20). Economic New Release: Union Members 2021. Occupational Employment Statistics. U.S. Department of Labor. Retrieved August 28, 2022 from https://www.bls.gov/news.release/union2.nr0.htm

Callahan, J. L. (2013). 'Space, the final frontier'? Social movements as organizing spaces for applying HRD. *Human Resource Development International, 16*(3), 298–312. https://doi.org/10.1080/13678868.2013.782945

Callahan, J. L., & Dunne de Davila, T. (2004). An impressionistic framework for theorizing about human resource development. *Human Resource Development Review, 3*(1), 75–95.

Collins, J. C. (2012). Identity matters: Critical exploration of lesbian, gay, and bisexual identity, and leadership in HRD. *Human Resource Development Review, 11*(3), 349–379.

Collins, J. C., McFadden, C., Rocco, T. S., & Mathis, M. H. (2015). The problem of transgender marginalization and exclusion: Critical actions for human resource development. *Human Resource Development Review, 14*(2), 205–226.

Fenwick, T. (2005). Conceptions of critical HRD: Dilemmas for theory and practice. *Human Resource Development International, 8*(2), 225–238. https://doi.org/10.1080/13678860500100541

Fenwick, T., & Bierema, L. (2008). Corporate social responsibility: Issues for human resource development professionals. *International Journal of Training and Development, 12*(1), 24–35.

Fisk, C., & Rutter, J. (2015). Labor protest under the new first amendment. *Berkeley Journal of Employment and Labor Law, 36*(2), 277–329. https://doi.org/10.15779/Z384S04

Garden, C. (2016). The deregulatory first amendment at work. *Harvard Civil Rights-Civil Liberties Law Review, 51*, 323.

Germain, M.-L., Robertson, P., & Minnis, S. (2019). Protests, rallies, marches, and social movements as organizational change agents. *Advances in Developing Human Resources, 21*(2), 150–174.

Grayson, J. (2011). Organising, educating, and training: Varieties of activist learning in left social movements in Sheffield (UK). *Studies in the Education of Adults, 43*(2), 197–215. https://doi.org/10.1080/02660830.2011.11661613

Hager, P., Lee, A., & Reich, A. (2012). Problematising practice, reconceptualising learning and imagining change. In P. Hager, A. Lee, & A. Reich (Eds.), *Practice, learning, and change* (pp. 1–14). Springer.

Henry, S. (2021). Critical engagement: Lessons learned and implications for HRD about black male faculty leadership in higher education. *Advances in Developing Human Resources, 8*, 300–318.

Hlatshwayo, M. (2018). Building workers' education in the context of the struggle against racial capitalism: The role of labour support organisations. *Education as Change, 22*(2). https://doi.org/10.25159/1947-9417/3806

Lave, J., & Wenger, E. (1991). *Situated learning: Legitimate peripheral participation.* Cambridge University Press.

Le, T., & Hersh, R. (2019). *The Post-Janus v. AFSCME world for teachers' unions* (Unpublished Master's thesis). Yale University.

Martin, M. E. (2015). *Advocacy for social justice: A global perspective.* Pearson.

McAlevey, J. (2015). The crisis of new labor and Alinsky's legacy: Revisiting the role of the organic grassroots leaders in building powerful organizations and movements. *Politics & Society, 43*(3), 415–441. https://doi.org/10.1177/0032329215584767

McCartin, J. A. (2016). Bargaining for the common good. *Dissent, 63*(2), 128–135. https://muse.jhu.edu/article/616491

Merriam, S. B., & Bierema, L. L. (2013). *Adult learning: Bridging theory and practice.* Jossey-Bass.

Nicolini, D. (2012). *Practice theory, work, and organization: An organization.* Oxford University Press.

Oswalt, M. M., & Marzán, C. F. R. (2018). Organizing the state: The "new labor law" seen from the bottom-up. *Berkeley Journal of Employment & Labor Law, 39*(2), 415. https://doi.org/10.15779/Z381G0HV4j

Rocco, T. S., Bernier, J. D., & Bowman, L. (2014). Critical race theory and HRD: Moving race front and center. *Advances in Developing Human Resources, 16*(4), 457–470. https://doi.org/10.1177/1523422314544294

Rubin, H. J. (2018). *Advocacy for social change.* Routledge.

Sandlin, J., & Walther, C. (2009). Complicates simplicity: Moral identity formation and social movement learning in the voluntary simplicity. *Adult Education Quarterly, 59*(4), 298–317.

Schatzki, T. R. (2002). *The site of the social: A philosophical account of the constitution of social life and change.* Penn State University Press.

Sisco, S., Valesano, M., & Collins, J. (2019). Social movement learning and human resource developing: An agenda for a radical future. *Advances in Developing Human Resources, 21*(2), 175–192.

Wenger, E. (1998). *Communities of practice: Learning, meaning, and identity.* Cambridge University Press.

Windham, L. (2017). *Knocking on labor's door: Union organizing in the 1970s and the roots of a new economic divide.* UNC Press Books.

Yeo, R., & Li, J. (2022). Breaking the silence of psychological impact while working from home during COVID: Implications for workplace learning. *Human Resource Development International*, 25(2), 114–144. https://doi.org/10.1080/13678868.2022.2047149

Yorks, L. (2004). Toward a political economy model for comparative analysis of the role of strategic human resource development leadership. *Human Resource Development Review*, 3(3), 189–208. https://doi.org/10.1177/1534484304266260

Recontextualizing Learning in Work and Leisure

Kenneth R. Bartlett and Eniola A. Aderibigbe

Research in human resource development (HRD) has continued to expand the boundaries that frame definitional perspectives, as well as the range of disciplines and theories that inform scholarship and professional practice (Garavan et al., 2004; Hamlin & Stewart, 2011; Kuchinke, 2000; Lee, 2007). During this process, and somewhat concurrent with efforts to extend the traditional scope of HRD, several authors have focused attention on the existence of false dichotomies (such as learning vs. performance) that have constrained the field (Bierema et al., 2014; Rocco et al., 2014). The purpose of this chapter is to challenge dominant paradigms related to the dichotomy between work and leisure, and to (re)-conceptualize a broader approach to theorizing learning that includes and is inclusive of leisure-related learning. To achieve this purpose requires critique of traditional representations of differentiated values associated with learning in non-work contexts compared to workplace learning within organizations. The limitations and constraints of the work/leisure dichotomy in HRD theory and practice are considered with proposition made for inclusion of the potential role of learning in, and from, leisure. A broader view, reflective of boundary-spanning learning experiences

K. R. Bartlett (✉) · E. A. Aderibigbe
University of Minnesota, Minneapolis, MN, USA
e-mail: bartlett@umn.edu

E. A. Aderibigbe
e-mail: aderi005@umn.edu

J. C. Collins and J. L. Callahan (eds.), *The Palgrave Handbook of Critical Human Resource Development*, https://doi.org/10.1007/978-3-031-10453-4_8

in work and leisure is presented as a more inclusive, representative, and expansive recognition of learning across multiple life domains to potential benefit individuals, organizations, and society.

Learning has always been viewed as a primary goal of HRD (Bates et al., 2001), but the HRD field has traditionally separated learning at work and/or learning for work, from learning in other domains of life, such as leisure. This separation has in effect given power, privilege, and prioritized work-related learning as higher value to the individual and organization than learning that occurs outside of work. The artificial divide of work and leisure as separate and unrelated domains of life has diminished recognition from HRD scholars and practitioners of learning that may occur outside of work, such as during leisure time. As such, leisure-related learning is treated as a marginal activity at best, and perhaps trivialized as incompatible with the contemporary definition and study of HRD. Further, consideration of learning in non-work life domains must acknowledge that unequal access exists to both work-related and leisure-related learning. Consequently, efforts to broaden conceptualizations of learning align with efforts to address diversity, equity, and inclusion within HRD research and practice with acknowledgment of the need for awareness and action related to support all people in work and non-work contexts.

This chapter begins with a summary of conceptualizations of leisure, drawing from the broad multi-disciplinary literature in leisure studies. Work and leisure are considered from perspectives descriptive of independence and conflict then compatibility and interdependence to draw attention to the limitations of the view that separates learning into false dichotomies when this activity spans multiple life domains. Learning as a core feature of HRD is briefly reviewed, firstly from the work perspective, before literature focused on learning in leisure, and learning as a leisure activity, is reviewed. The relationship between work-focused and leisure-related learning in the context of HRD research and practice is presented with critique of dominant narratives that have historically separated work and leisure with work-related learning privileged. Alternative perspectives to the work/leisure dichotomy are discussed with alternative non-binary conceptualizations of learning in work and leisure presented to encourage future consideration, theory development, and research for HRD.

CONCEPTUALIZATIONS OF LEISURE

Leisure is a common human phenomenon, yet there is no agreed upon definition as the concept is socially constructed with its meaning dependent on specific historical and cultural contexts (Bammel & Burrus-Bammel, 1996; Leitner & Leitner, 2012). The academic study of leisure is a well-established branch of social science with a focus on theoretical based analysis of a diverse range of complex individual, familial, societal, and cultural phenomena related to leisure. The highly interdisciplinary approach to the study of leisure has produced a deep body of literature that continues to expand and produce theory and research.

Reflective of the evolution of the academic study of leisure is the diversity and plurality of definitional approaches. The definition of leisure has evolved over time, and continues to develop, with the proliferation of perspectives indicative of both the wide breadth of approaches to conceptualization and the multiplicity of meaning applied to the construct. As Hunnicutt (2006) explained, the origins of leisure are usually traced in the West to Classical Greece and Rome, with a rich historiography of significant philosophical writing from this time period. Additional important contributions to foundational aspects to the study and understanding of leisure were then made during the medieval period, Reformation, Industrial Revolution, and up to the current day. While the majority of core theory and writing on leisure has relied on European, and more recently North American and other western societies for contributions, others have explored non-western traditions of leisure (Bhattacharya, 2006) as well as diverse cultural and linguistic origins of the meanings of leisure (Liu et al., 2008).

An early influential definition, provided in 1899 by the noted sociologist Thorstein Veblen, saw leisure as "nonproductive consumption of time" (1899, p. 46). Since that period, leisure theorists have adopted a variety of approaches to defining leisure, often in comparison and contrast to the definition of work. For example, Kelly (1972) stated that generally,

> work is understood to be remunerative, required by social norms, and necessary for the maintenance of the self and family. Leisure is "nonwork." That is, leisure is not remunerative, not required by social expectations, and not necessary for status or survival. (p. 50)

In understanding the history and development of definitional approaches to leisure, Kelly (2012) identified three common approaches used to define the construct based on: leisure as time, leisure as activity, and leisure as experience.

First, the time approach to define leisure is bound by the 24-hour day, or some other standard unit measure. An example of a definition that focused on leisure as time was given by Brightbill (1960), who described leisure as:

> time beyond that which is required for existence, the things which we must do, biologically, to stay alive....and substance, the things we must do to make a living...It is discretionary time, the time to be used according to our judgement or choice. (p. 4)

This definition focused on two elements of time; first, residual time left after obligations, and second, time that is "free" in that individuals have the choice of what to do. It is however important to mention that free time does not necessarily mean leisure. As DeGrazia (1964, p. 5) elaborated, "Leisure and free-time live in two different worlds.... Anybody can have free time.

Not everybody can have leisure." While there is a relationship between leisure and time (Zuzanek, 2006) there is also an awareness of inequalities with respect to the amount of time people have for leisure. An example from Codina and Pestana (2019) found strong gender differences in leisure time and corresponding inequalities manifested in the experiences derived from leisure. However, the time perspective continues in common language usage as well as a frequent element to conceptualize, define, and explore leisure behavior.

Second, the activity approach to the conceptualization and definition of leisure is most often associated to the work of French sociologist Joffre Dumazedier. In his widely cited publication, Dumazedier (1967) stated that leisure is activity "apart from the obligation of work, family, and society – to which the individual turns at will, for either relaxation, diversion, or broadening his (sic) knowledge and his spontaneous social participation, the free exercise of his creative capacity" (pp. 16–17). Dumazedier's often cited definition or description of leisure, as noted above, was originally published in his native French, with Veal (2019) recently reconsidering the transcription and meaning. Identifying an earlier description written by Dumazedier in 1960, Veal's updated translation presented four aspects of activity that define leisure:

> Leisure consists of a number of occupations in which the individual may indulge of his (sic) own free will – either (1) *to rest*, (2) *to amuse himself*, (3) *to add to his knowledge or improve his skills disinterestedly*, or (4) *to increase his voluntary participation in the life of the community* after discharging his professional, family and social duties. (Dumazedier, 1960, p. 527, italics and numbers added in Veal, 2019, p. 189)

Veal's translation of Dumazedier's core ideals of leisure reflects a strong connection of leisure functions to HRD activity with conceptual acknowledgment that leisure can include knowledge acquisition, skill improvement, or community participation. The potential for leisure activity to be related to learning or experiences in work was not specifically addressed by Dumazedier, although as noted in the following section, the work and leisure connection has attracted significant attention in the literature.

Third, the experiential approach to define leisure was an important contribution originally made by Pieper (1963) who defined leisure as "an attitude of the mind, a condition of the soul" (p. 40). Pieper was a noted German philosopher who in 1948 authored "Leisure: The basis of culture" (translated 1963) as a call to center leisure, not work, as the core activity for individual and cultural growth. Foreshadowing recognition and interest in the topics of burnout, well-being, and workplace spirituality, Pieper advocated for leisure to temporarily relinquish the affairs of everyday mundane reality for appreciation of the gift of life (Kleiber et al., 2011). The experiential approach views leisure as an important aspect of human life noted for positive contributions to both personal welfare and benefits to society

(Kelly, 1990; Tinsley & Eldredge, 1995). Researchers have sought to identify common elements of leisure experiences with factors including emotion and mood; cognitions; arousal, activation, and relaxation; time duration; focus of attention, concentration, and absorption; differentiated involvement leading to self-consciousness, self-awareness, and ego-loss; sense of competence; sense of freedom; and sense of interpersonal relatedness (Kleiber et al., 2011). The diversity and plurality of leisure experiences help give individual meaning, whether these are positive or negative, that in turn, influence intrinsic and extrinsic leisure motivation. This was reflected in the description of leisure as freely chosen behavior accompanied by a sense of enjoyment and intrinsic motivation (Kleiber, 1999).

However, not every person has equal access to experience leisure. A more recent development in the definition of leisure is understanding the role of constraints on leisure time, activity, and/or experience. Jackson et al. (1993) identified that constraints on leisure vary in intensity and impact. Researchers have categorized barriers or leisure constraints into intrapersonal, interpersonal, and structural constraints, as well as their interactions, that limit or influence leisure participation and experiences (Kleiber et al., 2011). Examination of individual efforts to increase leisure participation and enhance leisure experiences found people cultivate affordances and negotiate or adjust to constraints (Crawford, Jackson, & Godbey, 1991). The literature on leisure constraints-negotiations highlighted the role that individuals and leisure-service organizations, such as city park and recreation departments, can have to assist people learn to optimize leisure (Raymore, 2002).

WORK AND LEISURE

Research shows that kindergarten-aged children are able to describe the difference between work and play (Goodhall & Atkinson, 2019). For much of the adult years, work and non-work are different but important defining aspects of life. The unique aspects of work, leisure, and the work–leisure relationship as a core aspect of the intersection of major life domains has produced a broad and expanding body of literature. Research centered on work as a source of tension or conflict with other life roles has drawn attention to dynamics across the life span to examine how people spend their time, create and maintain their identities and roles, and make meaning of their experiences. Studies on work–family (Greenhaus & Beutell, 1985) and work–leisure conflict (Zuzanek & Mannell, 1983) have matured beyond simple unidirectional models that place employment as the source of undesirable impacts (Tsaur et al., 2012). There is also acceptance that the work/leisure dichotomy has tended to oversimplify employment as a physical and emotional draining activity whereas, leisure is restorative.

One of the first major contributions to the study of work and leisure was made by Parker (1971). Parker was employed as a civil servant for a central government agency in Britain when he published what is still regarded as one of the most influential treatises to examine the work and leisure inter-section. In this, and subsequent publications, Parker (1971, 1975) broadened the scope to consider historical, philosophical, psychological, and sociolog-ical perspectives on the relationship between work and leisure, the future of that relationship, and how policymakers could influence for the betterment of people. A subsequent major development was made by Haworth and Smith (1975) who published their seminal book titled "Work and Leisure" which was noted for playing an instrumental role in framing scholarly discourse on work and leisure. As other scholars have noted, this text shaped the future trajec-tory of research and theorizing on work and leisure, encouraging acceptance of the "complexity of the field of study, due in part to the multifaceted nature of the concepts involved" (Haworth & Veal, 2004, p. 1). Researchers sought to expand beyond descriptions of work and leisure interactions to develop models to explain how work impacts leisure. As such, Snir and Harpaz (2002) described three basic models: spillover, compensation, and segmentation. They elaborated on each noting:

> The spillover model states that the nature of one's work experiences will carry over into the non-work domain and affect attitudes and behaviors there (Wilensky, 1960). According to the compensation model, workers who experi-ence a sense of deprivation at work will compensate in their choice of non-work activities (Wilensky, 1960). In contrast to these two models, Dubin's (1958, 1973) segmentation model claims that no relation exists between one's work and one's non-work domains; the two are lived out independently. (p. 179)

A major shift in the study of the work and leisure relationship occurred with the move from the topic being a dominant theme of sociologists to an increasingly studied phenomena from management scholars interested in the analysis of the harsh dichotomy between the two terms. For example, Beatty and Torbert (2003) challenged the false duality of work and leisure to suggest reconsideration as potentially complementary concepts. To further explore the positive connections, researchers selected occupations where the boundary between work and leisure is blurred or overlapping to examine if a mutually beneficial relationship exists. For example, Boon (2006) studied hotel workers in a mountain resort area who regularly engaged in skiing as a leisure time activity. The findings from this study showed positive impacts on career development as well as work and career identity reflective of positive interdependencies between work and leisure. Others have considered outdoor recreation occupations, such as rafting guides, as examples illustrative of the positive aspects of an integrated leisure and work lifestyle (Filho, 2010). Berg et al. (2010) explored how people connect job crafting, a strategy to reshape and improve work conditions, and leisure when they are unable to work in occupations that answer their calling. More recent research has examined crafting strategies used by employees in different life domains to obtain desired outcomes and how these relate to work engagement (Petrou et al., 2017).

These studies suggest that work and leisure can have compensatory benefits across life domains. This encourages consideration of compensatory benefits across life domains from learning, both in work and non-work contexts.

An alternative perspective on work and leisure interactions research was presented by Buchholz (1976) to contrast the prevailing dominant orientation toward studies of work–leisure conflict. Buchholz regarded work as a means to personal fulfillment primarily through its provision of the means to pursue leisure activities. He proposed a leisure ethic in which:

> Work has no meaning in itself, but only finds meaning in leisure. Jobs cannot be made meaningful or fulfilling, but work is a human necessity to produce goods and services and enable one to earn the money to buy them. Human fulfillment is found in leisure activities where one has a choice regarding the use of his (sic) time and can find pleasure in pursuing activities of interest to him (sic) personally. This is where a person can be creative and involved. Thus the less hour's one can spend working and the more leisure time he (sic) has available the better. (p. 1180)

A summary review of research related to the leisure ethic was conducted by Furnham (2003) who found greater value ascribed to leisure by high-status workers, younger workers, and those from select nationalities (e.g., more highly valued in the United States than the United Kingdom). The leisure ethic was proposed as the positive opposite of the Protestant Work Ethic (Dose, 1997). In connecting the leisure ethic to workplace spirituality, Furnham paraphrased Buchholz to state "it is in leisure rather than in work that one recreates, refreshes, and renews oneself. Thus, the more work approaches the idea of leisure, the better" (p. 208).

Benefits of leisure emerged as a sub-theme of literature on the work and leisure intersection. Part of this specific body of literature has considered how leisure may benefit work, specifically work for paid employment in the workplace. An especially influential text on this topic was published by Driver et al. (1991). They considered the word "benefit" as an advantageous change viewed by an individual or group to have valued consequences related to one or more outcomes from leisure considered from a psychological, sociological, health environmental, and economic perspective. Much of the writing related to the benefits of leisure has taken a social-psychological approach to incorporate both the social context of roles that change through the life course and the development of identities in and through those roles. Leisure has been found to be influentially beneficial in adulthood at work, in the family, in the community, and for personal physical and mental health.

Before focus is directed to the benefits of leisure in the context of work, an important distinction on changing patterns of work and leisure across the lifespan is highlighted. Kelly (1990) described the connections between the life course of employment and leisure. He noted, that throughout a career, an individual transitions from school to job, job to job, and then job to retirement. In family careers, the transitions are related to the selection of a partner, marriage or committed relationship, parenthood, separation of children from the home, and widowhood. In a similar way, he observed that leisure also follows a life course with distinct stages engaged in an effort to find and establish a leisure identity (Solan, 1984). Newman et al. (2014) found that leisure activity was a significant identity-shaping force within people's lives. Moreover, leisure was just as capable as work for the potential to guide an individual's understanding of who they are, what matters to them, and the meaning of their life. Further, a leisure career or leisure life course contains transitions that can be traced with patterns of non-work interest and activities at various stages of life (Featherstone, 1985). As the leisure life course evolves through various transitions there are identified benefits of leisure to work that also occur.

A dimension of the literature on benefits of leisure specific to work has focused on well-being. Increasingly, leisure, or the lack of leisure, features as core aspect of the study of well-being (Mansfield et al., 2020). As Haworth and Lewis (2005) stated, "both work and leisure are essential for well-being" (p. 67). Yet, as they noted, "despite a very substantial literature on work/family (or more recently, work/life) balance or integration and well-being, there has been relatively little explicit focus on the work and leisure interface" (p. 67). This is important for HRD research and practice with greater attention on expanding the HRD role to improve employee well-being (Gilbreath & Montesino, 2006).

Participation in leisure activities and satisfaction with leisure have been found to increase individuals' well-being (Brajša-Žganec et al., 2011; Cho, 2021). Studies on work and leisure impacts on well-being are numerous and research has found the work–leisure interface has both important individual and organizational outcomes (Kuykendall et al., 2015; Wiese et al., 2018). The positive relationship between engagement with leisure and well-being has included measures such as life satisfaction (Becchetti et al., 2012), happiness (Lu et al., 2005; Wang et al., 2011), and quality of life (Iwasaki, 2007). Leisure participation, and satisfaction with leisure, have positive relationships in the workplace with reduced turnover intention, increased job satisfaction, organizational commitment, employee engagement, and favorable perceptions of work-life balance and subjective well-being (Cho, 2021). Haworth et al. (1997) studied women in full-time employment and found that enjoyment in both leisure and work was equally important for well-being. More recent research has moved toward the development of a benefits theory of leisure well-being (Sirgy et al., 2017). These authors proposed that leisure participation enhances life satisfaction by the achievement of basic needs and growth needs with the impact amplified when benefits are aligned with individual goals and personality. A conclusion drawn from the benefits of leisure literature would suggest that as organizational leaders prioritize well-being for their workforce, more so in light of the COVID-19 pandemic (George et al., 2021), a greater need exists for awareness of non-work activities and their relationship to well-being at work.

An important, though often neglected, dimension in the literature on the benefits of leisure is the critical perspective to challenge the notion of universal positive access and outcomes to leisure participation. As Kleiber (1999) observed; age, gender, ethnicity, socioeconomic status, and other individual differences "can determine when and where leisure is a problem and when and how it can be a solution" (p. xv). He goes on appropriately to question the conventional claims for a consistent positive influence of leisure on well-being as this fails to consider exactly who the intended beneficiaries might be and in what ways leisure might work for some but not for others. Research supports both historic and persistent patterns of inequality for leisure quantity and quality in the United States (Sevilla et al., 2012), unequal leisure constraints for women (Deem, 1982; Henderson & Allen, 1991), and additional barriers across a wide range of cultural and socioeconomic variables (Jackson & Henderson, 1995). Given these important differences in access and participation in leisure, it is possible that inequities also impact the perceived and actual benefits from learning in and from leisure in work and non-work settings.

Learning in Work and Learning in Leisure

Learning in the broadest sense, can be thought of as a process that involves acquiring knowledge and skill which can occur in any place and at any time. There are a variety of ways humans learn which may include formal and informal learning. The phenomena of learning is an important part of human existence and therefore, the study of learning cuts across many academic fields and disciplines. Consequently, learning as a human activity occurs in all stages and areas of life, not just those directly connected to schooling and then work. However, in the academic and professional field of HRD, learning and development tends to be viewed as core to the discipline, but mostly learning as it relates to adults, the workplace, and career (Sleezer, 2004). Learning from non-work life domains is under-valued or neglected at best, or worse, dismissed as irrelevant or beyond the scope of concern for HRD research and practice.

As the HRD field continues to develop so has the conceptualization of learning and development as well as appropriate approaches, modes, and methods to support learning. Traditionally, HRD scholars and practitioners have focused on formal learning with less attention to informal learning. Specifically, attention has been given to learning that happens within an organized environment (e.g., school and work) with activities such as training, mentoring, and coaching. Hence, work and the workplace have received ample attention with regards to learning, and this has perhaps shaped underlying philosophical views on the centrality of work by HRD scholars. Kuchinke

(2013), noted that "Work can be experienced as opportunity for development and growth, as affirmation of self, and as grace, but also as tedium, toil, and exploitation" (p. 203). Ardichvili and Kuchinke (2009) described work as "central to human existence, providing the necessities for life, sources of identity, opportunities for achievement, and determining standing within the larger community" (p. 155). Notwithstanding the core and central role of work, HRD scholars seem less inclined to consider leisure as opportunity for development and growth, as affirmation of self, and as grace, as well as sources of identity, opportunities for achievement, and determining standing within the larger community. Inclusion of the full range of experiences from non-work life domains may be equally important for future theorizing in HRD.

Although work and learning are an integral part of HRD, and have been historically integrated to promote workplace development, the conceptualization of work and learning has evolved. Factors such as globalization, technology, the COVID-19 pandemic, and shifting employee attitudes and values have impacted the definition, process, and experience of work. Likewise, the process of learning is no longer constrained to schools, the workplace, or other formal settings. The acceptance, development of theory, and identification of practices to foster informal learning at work as vital aspects of HRD (Watkins et al., 1992) was an important contribution. However, as recognition of the amount, type, and value of learning that occurs outside of formal education, training, and development in non-work settings increases, a corresponding need exists for greater examination of the process and outcomes of non-work-related learning.

Important contributions have been made in the HRD literature by Holden and colleagues in response to managerial, organizational, and professional association acceptance of employee-led training program that embrace a lifelong learning philosophy. For example, Holden and Hamblett (1998) interrogated unexamined, but prevailing orthodoxy that non-work learning benefits individual employees and their employers. They rightly observed, "one of the difficulties associated with any learning activity is the assessment and attribution of outcomes" (p. 246). Yet, further examination of learning as a leisure activity as well as learning that occurs in leisure time is warranted before consideration of potential benefits to work.

Henderson (2007) explained that "the connection between leisure and education includes ideas such as 'education for leisure,' 'education to leisure,' 'education through leisure,' 'education as leisure,' 'education during leisure,' and 'education about leisure'" (2007, p. 90). Leisure education is defined as a process though which individuals develop "an understanding of leisure, of self in relation to leisure, and of the relationship among leisure, their own lifestyle, and society" (Mundy, 1998, p. 5). John Dewey (1921) saw a clear responsibility for education in preparation for the role of leisure in life with his statement that "education has no more serious responsibility than making adequate provision for enjoyment of recreative leisure; not only for the sake of immediate health, but still more if possible for the sake of its lasting effect upon habits of mind" (p. 241). As Thoidis and Pnevmatikos (2014) suggested, the learning which takes place within the context of leisure time can be considered as "a type of 'leisure education' and more specifically as 'education during leisure time'" (p. 660). They stated, leisure education would benefit from a definition to reflect a much broader term, which includes: (a) Education for leisure (how leisure time can be spent productively, enjoyably, and how available leisure activities are), (b) Education during leisure time (dedicating non-working time to the pursuit of both formal and non-formal education programs), and (c) Education as a leisure activity (education which adheres to the basic principles of leisure time) (Kleiber, 2012; Ruskin & Sivan, 1995).

Learning, both as leisure and in leisure, is a commonly reported activity in research of how people chose to allocate time and resources across life domains (Roberson, 2005; Verduin & McEwen, 1984). Learning as a leisure activity or learning during leisure time is well documented in adult education (Jarvis, 1995). Kleiber (1999) considered personal development as an important function of leisure. Packer and Ballantyne (2004) listed many leisure settings that offer an educational component; these include: "art, history and natural history museums, botanical gardens, nature centers, national parks, science centers, zoos, aquaria, historic houses, historic reconstructions, heritage and archaeological sites" (p. 54). While not all visitors to these sites seek learning, instead perhaps favoring entertainment, the free-choice educational aspect of leisure at these, and many other places or locations selected to spend leisure time, is established as a form of lifelong learning (Rennie & Johnston, 2004). As Sargant (1996) stated, the boundaries between leisure and learning are virtually invisible for some people with leisure activities being a bridge into active learning. "On the other hand, many people learn from their leisure activities without realizing the knowledge or skills they are gaining" (p. 198). And as Sargant further noted, "alternatively, there are people who chose actively to construct their learning as leisure, often providing a different perspective to the rest of their lives" (p. 198).

There is considerable research interest in the study of reading as a leisure activity and source of learning (Moyer, 2007). Also, tourism and travel experiences have received attention as opportunities for learning (Falk et al., 2012; Mitchell, 1998). The changing patterns of leisure behavior in the twenty-first century have seen an increased number of people who view tourism as an opportunity to expand their understanding of themselves and their world (Falk, 2011; Freysinger & Kelly, 2004). Educational tourism has been identified as a major trend in the travel industry (Gibson, 1998; Williams, 2010) and an important context for adult learning (Pitman et al., 2010). A literature review of the educational benefits of travel experiences found personal growth, increased life skills, and enhanced knowledge resulted from international travel (Stone & Petrick, 2013). Although, in the case of tourism, the extent to which this learning is applied for developmental purposes both within work and non-work contexts remains largely elusive to definitive research conclusions (Ryan, 1998).

Employers have long expressed frustration at formal education providers for the failure to provide learning experiences to students (future employees) to enhance interpersonal skills and capacities (Doh, 2003; Gosling & Mintzberg, 2004). There is research evidence to indicate that leisure experiences during international travel improves employability (Jones, 2013) and positively influences key, highly valued workplace skills related to communication, independence, open-mindedness, and feeling comfortable around all kinds of people (Scarinci & Pearce, 2012). Much focus on specific attributes of learning beneficial to work and career from travel and tourism are found in literature grounded in theories of transformative education (Mezirow, 1991, 2000; Morgan, 2010; Nada et al., 2018; O'Sullivan, 1999) and experiential learning (Kolb, 1984; Ng et al., 2009). Research on learning from leisure related to travel and tourism has an advantage of being a popular activity subject to clearly bound definitional and measurement parameters. However, learning that may occur in many other leisure experiences is confronted by significant measurement challenges related to the highly individualized and contextualized situations of leisure participation.

In response to challenges with understanding activity and outcomes, leisure theorists identified and have studied in considerable detail the concept of serious leisure (Jones et al., 2001). Serious leisure is defined as: "The systematic pursuit of an amateur, hobbyist, or volunteer activity that participants find so substantial and interesting that, in the typical case, they launch themselves on a career centered on acquiring and expressing its special skills, knowledge, and experience" (Stebbins, 1992, p. 3). Jones and Symon (2001) proposed that lifelong learning be viewed as an example of serious leisure. Further, they argued that government policy toward lifelong learning would be better pursued from a serious leisure rather than vocationally or occupationally oriented philosophy. Research has demonstrated that extended participation in serious leisure brings positive benefits to work careers (McQuarrie, 1999). The findings of this research found that the benefits of serious leisure participants were "portable in that they produced skills desirable and useful in the workplace, but which are not associated with or specific to a particular job" (McQuarrie, p. 133).

RECONTEXTUALIZING LEARNING IN WORK AND LEISURE FOR HRD THEORIZING AND PRACTICE

Although strides have been made in the HRD field to broaden conceptualization and theory building related to learning, there is more work to be done. One area that the field is yet to fully conceptualized and examine is learning in non-work contexts, specifically, learning that occurs in leisure. Learning in leisure is a common activity and a prominent theme in leisure theory and applied leisure-related research (Roberson, 2005). Indeed, the origins of learning as a leisure activity are ancient. For example, in Plato's teaching and philosophy of learning, leisure was seen primarily as time free for self-development (Hunnicutt, 1990). For Aristotle, leisure was the contrast to work "done for its own sake and for the sake of the development of character" (Kelly, 1990, p. 105). By contrast, today there are very few HRD scholars and writers on workplace learning who consider leisure-related contexts. HRD literature makes scant mention of leisure as a context or site for learning. Moreover, HRD appears to have failed to consider the possibility of learning and leisure having outcomes beneficial to HRD and the workplace. Reconsideration and recontextualization of learning as a core HRD-related activity in both work and non-work contexts would connect the philosophy and practice of lifelong learning across permeable life domain boundaries. Thoidis and Pnevmatikos (2014) noted that "traditionally theories of lifelong education have focused on three separate theoretical strands (profession, personality and leisure)" (p. 657). Yet, the theory and research focus on workplace HRD has mostly considered learning linked to profession and personality with the strand related to leisure largely overlooked.

The combination of "leisure" and "human resource development" as keywords in the literature search produced a single paper (Isopahkala-Bouret, 2008) published in *Human Resource Development International*. This study examined why many professionals engage in work-related learning after formal working hours. Adopting a critical HRD perspective, the author conducted a series of qualitative life story interviews and focus groups to examine how leisure intertwines with HRD and how it is positioned discursively in relation to work-related learning. Grounded in the spillover model of leisure (Kando & Summers, 1971) leisure was found in this study to act as a resource for work-related learning. Learning at leisure was discussed by study participants in similar ways to learning at work although, importantly, leisure and work were not positioned as opposite but rather they were indifferent regarding the development of competency. This is an important finding that could suggest that established aspects of work and leisure may operate in different ways when the focus is placed on learning from a HRD perspective within the interactions of work–leisure relationships.

The only other prominent references to leisure in HRD literature is the use of the outdoor environment for learning activities (Hamilton & Cooper, 2001; Irvine & Wilson, 1994; McEvoy & Buller, 1997). However, comparatively little of the literature on outdoor development activities, especially for managers and organizational leaders for individual and group-level learning, considers if these programs and constitute activities are viewed as work or leisure by participants. Regardless, if outdoor leisure is initiated by individual motivation or employer sponsorship, there are established connections to learning outcomes that include workplace benefits (Hattie et al., 1997). There is an increasing number of agencies, centers, and programs that have emerged to cater to the demand for structured learning events connected to leisure pursuits conducted in outdoor environments. While the evidence of this HRD practice shows continued growth and the literature base continues to expand, it is noted (Hattie et al., 1997) that many scholarly papers on outdoor learning programs read more like program advertisements than research. Other authors in HRD have critiqued the general lack of rigorous empirical research exploring both the outcomes and the mechanisms perhaps unique to outdoor management development (Walton, 2014). More focus on the learning and outcomes from increasingly popular organizational sponsored off-site training and development activities that include leisure as a core feature, such as outdoor ropes courses (Haras et al., 2005), improvisation theater training (Vera & Crossan, 2005), and escape rooms (Guckian et al., 2020) is needed.

CONCLUSION

The boundaries that define the study and shape the professional practice of HRD have traditionally ignored or minimized contexts, life roles, and experiences outside of work. Leisure is one such area that has received very little attention from HRD researchers. The dichotomy of work versus leisure has meant that the former construct is considered core and receives much research attention, while the latter is ignored or considered beyond the scope of HRD. This chapter has reviewed literature to present an argument that the work and leisure boundary can, and should be, challenged in efforts to extend exploration and understanding of theory and phenomena related to learning in HRD. Falk (2011) suggested that as "we continue to transition into the 21st century, the boundaries between leisure and learning will become increasingly blurred" (p. 229). Consequently, he proposed that:

> More and more people will be seeking to spend more of their time engaging in leisure experiences that afford opportunities to both better understand the world and better understand themselves. (p. 229)

The complexity of conceptualizations of leisure, work, and their relationship demands a thorough investigation of the potential for these constructs to advance HRD theory and practice. Further, such efforts require local, national, and international perspectives that take into account the defining characteristics and impacts from culture, economic and political systems, gender roles, diverse identities, and other structural processes that influence life and work roles. The experience and indeed, our being, at work is likely driven or guided by activities, ascribed meanings, and identities brought from and across other domains of life, including leisure. So too, our experience of HRD and learning at work is likely guided by learning experiences in other domains of life such as leisure.

The failure of HRD research to seriously examine learning in non-work contexts has limited knowledge production of roles for HRD to develop human potential, performance, and processes for effective and beneficial change. Future theory building and research are needed to address these complex issues. Consideration of work and leisure as multifaceted and inter-acting constructs extends the HRD field beyond the false dichotomy that has permeated much of the theorizing to date. As such, a recontextualization of learning in both work and leisure presents an opportunity to disrupt traditional discipline boundaries and unleash the potential in HRD.

REFERENCES

Ardichvili, A., & Kuchinke, K. P. (2009). International perspectives on the meanings of work and working: Current research and theory. *Advances in Developing Human Resources, 11*(2), 155–167. https://doi.org/10.1177/1523422309333494

Bammel, G., & Burrus-Bammel, L. (1996). *Leisure and human behavior*. Brown and Benchmark.

Bates, R. A., Hatcher, T., Holton III, E. F., & Chalofsky, N. (2001). Redefining human resource development: An integration of the learning, performance, and spirituality of work perspectives. In O. A. Aliaga (Ed.), *Academy of human resource development 2001 conference proceedings* (pp. 205–212). Tulsa, OK: Academy of Human Resource Development. ERIC Document Reproduction Service No. ED453416.

Beatty, J. E., & Torbert, W. R. (2003). The false duality of work and leisure. *Journal of Management Inquiry, 12*(3), 239–252.

Becchetti, L., Ricca, E. G., & Pelloni, A. (2012). The relationship between social leisure and life satisfaction: Causality and policy implications. *Social Indicators Research, 108*(3), 453–490.

Berg, J. M., Grant, A. M., & Johnson, V. (2010). When callings are calling: Crafting work and leisure in pursuit of unanswered occupational callings. *Organization Science, 21*(5), 973–994.

Bhattacharya, K. (2006). Non-western traditions: Leisure in India. In C. Rojek, S. M. Shaw, & A. J. Veal (Eds.), *A handbook of leisure studies* (pp. 75–89). Palgrave Macmillan.

Bierema, L., & Callahan, J. L. (2014). Transforming HRD: A framework for critical HRD practice. *Advances in Developing Human Resources, 16*(4), 429–444.

Boon, B. (2006). When leisure and work are allies: The case of skiers and tourist resort hotels. *Career Development International, 11*(7), 594–608.

Brajša-Žganec, A., Merkaš, M., & Šverko, I. (2011). Quality of life and leisure activi-ties: How do leisure activities contribute to subjective well-being? *Social Indicators Research, 102*(1), 81–91.

Brightbill, C. (1960). *The challenge of leisure*. Prentice-Hall.

Buchholz, R. (1976). Measurement of beliefs. *Human Relations, 29*(12), 1177–1198.

Cho, H. (2021). The impacts of leisure nostalgia on well-being and turnover inten-tion: The mediating roles of leisure satisfaction and work commitment. *Leisure Sciences*, 1–21. https://doi.org/10.1080/01490400.2021.2016521

Codina, N., & Pestana, J. V. (2019). Time matters differently in leisure experience for men and women: Leisure dedication and time perspective. *International Journal of Environmental Research and Public Health, 16*(14), 2513–2514. https://doi.org/10.3390/ijerph16142513

Crawford, D. W., Jackson, E. L., & Godbey, G. (1991). A hierarchical model of leisure constraints. *Leisure Sciences, 13*(4), 309–320.

Deem, R. (1982). Women, leisure and inequality. *Leisure Studies, 1*(1), 29–46.

deGrazia, S. (1964). *Of time, work, and leisure.* Doubleday.

Dewey, J. (1921). *Democracy and education: An introduction to the philosophy of education.* Macmillan.

Doh, J. P. (2003). Can leadership be taught? Perspectives from management educators. *Academy of Management Learning & Education, 2*(1), 54–67.

Dose, J. J. (1997). Work values: An integrative framework and illustrative application to organizational socialization. *Journal of Occupational and Organizational Psychology, 70*(3), 219–240.

Driver, B. L., Brown, P. J., & Peterson, G. L. (1991). *Benefits of leisure.* Venture Publishing.

Dubin, R. (1958). *The world of work: Industrial society and human relations.* Prentice-Hall.

Dubin, R. (1973). Work and non-work: Institutional perspectives. In M. D. Dunnette (Ed.), *Work and non-work in the year 2001.* Brooks/Cole.

Dumazedier, J. (1960). Current problems in the sociology of leisure. *International Social Science Journal, 12*(4), 522–533.

Dumazedier, J. (1967). *Toward a sociology of leisure.* Free Press.

Falk, J. H. (2011). The learning tourist: The role of identity-related visit motivations. *Tourism in Marine Environments, 7*(3–4), 223–232.

Falk, J. H., Ballantyne, R., Packer, J., & Benckendorff, P. (2012). Travel and learning: A neglected tourism research area. *Annals of Tourism Research, 39*(2), 908–927.

Featherstone, M. (1985). Leisure, symbolic power and the life course. *The Sociological Review, 33*(S1), 113–138.

Filho, S. C. (2010). Rafting guides: Leisure, work and lifestyle. *Annals of Leisure Research, 13*(1–2), 282–297.

Freysinger, V. J., & Kelly, J. R. (2004). *21st century leisure: Current issues.* Venture Publishing.

Furnham, A. (2003). Ethics at work: Money, spirituality and happiness. In R. Giacolone & C. Jurkiewicz (Eds.), *Handbook of workplace spirituality and organizational performance* (pp. 257–276). M.E. Sharp.

Gilbreath, B., & Montesino, M. U. (2006). Expanding the HRD role: Improving employee well-being and organizational performance. *Human Resource Development International, 9*(4), 563–571.

Garavan, T. N., McGuire, D., & O'Donnell, D. (2004). Exploring human resource development: A levels of analysis approach. *Human Resource Development Review, 3*(4), 417–441.

George, T. J., Atwater, L. E., Maneethai, D., & Madera, J. M. (2021). Supporting the productivity and wellbeing of remote workers: Lessons from COVID-19. *Organizational Dynamics.* https://doi.org/10.1016/j.orgdyn.2021.100869

Gibson, H. (1998). The educational tourist. *The Journal of Physical Education, Recreation and Dance, 69*(4), 6–9.

Goodhall, N., & Atkinson, C. (2019). How do children distinguish between 'play' and 'work'? Conclusions from the literature. *Early Child Development and Care, 189*(10), 1695–1708.

Gosling, J., & Mintzberg, H. (2004). The education of practicing managers. *MIT Sloan Management Review, 45*(4), 19–22.

Greenhaus, J., & Beutell, N. (1985). Sources of conflict between work and family roles. *The Academy of Management Review, 10,* 76–88.

Guckian, J., Eveson, L., & May, H. (2020). The great escape? The rise of the escape room in medical education. *Future Healthcare Journal, 7*(2), 112–115. https://doi.org/10.7861/fhj.2020-0032

Hamilton, T. A., & Cooper, C. (2001). The impact of outdoor management development (OMD) programmes. *Leadership and Organization Development Journal, 22*, 330–340. https://doi.org/10.1108/EUM0000000006163

Hamlin, R. G., & Stewart, J. (2011). What is HRD? A definitional review and synthesis of the HRD domain. *Journal of European Industrial Training, 35*(3), 199–220.

Haras, K., Bunting, C. J., & Witt, P. A. (2005). Linking outcomes with ropes course program design and delivery. *Journal of Park & Recreation Administration, 23*(2), 36–63.

Hattie, J., Marsh, H. W., Neill, J. T., & Richards, G. E. (1997). Adventure education and outward bound: Out-of-class experiences that make a lasting difference. *Review of Educational Research, 67*(1), 43–87.

Haworth, J. T., Jarman, M., & Lee, S. (1997). Positive psychological states in the daily life of a sample of working women. *Journal of Applied Social Psychology, 27*, 345–370.

Haworth, J. T., & Lewis, S. (2005). Work, leisure, and well-being. *British Journal of Guidance and Counselling, 33*(1), 67–79.

Haworth, J. T., & Smith, M. A. (1975). *Work and leisure: An interdisciplinary study in theory, education and planning.* Princeton Book Publishing.

Haworth, J. T., & Veal, A. J. (2004). Work and leisure: Themes and issues. In J. T. Haworth & A. J. Veal (Eds.), *Work and leisure* (pp. 213–230). Routledge.

Henderson, K. A. (2007). Quality of life and leisure education: Implications for tourism economies. *World Leisure, 49*(2), 88–93.

Henderson, K. A., & Allen, K. R. (1991). The ethic of care: Leisure possibilities and constraints for women. *Loisir et Societe/Society and Leisure, 14*(1), 97–113.

Holden, R. J., & Hamblett, J. (1998). Learning lessons from non-work related learning. *Journal of Workplace Learning, 10*(5), 241–250.

Hunnicutt, B. K. (1990). Leisure and play in Plato's teaching and philosophy of learning. *Leisure Sciences, 12*(2), 211–227.

Hunnicutt, B. K. (2006). The history of western leisure. In C. Rojek, S. M. Shaw, & A. J. Veal (Eds.), *A handbook of leisure studies* (pp. 55–74). Palgrave Macmillan.

Irvine, D., & Wilson, J. P. (1994). Outdoor management development—Reality or illusion. *The Journal of Management Development, 13*(5), 25–37.

Isopahkala-Bouret, U. (2008). Developmental leisure: Why work-related learning takes place outside of working hours. *Human Resource Development International, 11*(5), 479–491.

Iwasaki, Y. (2007). Leisure and quality of life in an international and multicultural context: What are major pathways linking leisure to quality of life? *Social Indicators Research, 82*(2), 233–264.

Jackson, E. L., Crawford, D. W., & Godbey, G. (1993). Negotiation of leisure constraints. *Leisure Sciences, 15*, 1–11.

Jackson, E. L., & Henderson, K. A. (1995). Gender-based analysis of leisure constraints. *Leisure Sciences, 17*(1), 31–51.

Jarvis, P. (1995). *Adult and continuing education: Theory and practice* (2nd ed.). Routledge.

Jones, E. (2013). Internationalization and employability: The role of intercultural experiences in the development of transferable skills. *Public Money & Management*, *33*(2), 95–104.

Jones, I., & Symon, G. (2001). Lifelong learning as serious leisure: Policy, practice and potential. *Leisure Studies*, *20*(4), 269–283.

Kando, T. M., & Summers, W. C. (1971). The impact of work on leisure: Toward a paradigm and research strategy. *Pacific Sociological Review*, *14*(3), 310–327.

Kelly, J. R. (1972). Work and leisure: A simplified paradigm. *Journal of Leisure Research*, *4*(1), 50–62.

Kelly, J. R. (1990). *Leisure* (2nd ed.). Prentice Hall.

Kelly, J. R. (2012). *Leisure* (4th ed.). Sagamore.

Kleiber, D. A. (1999). *Leisure experience and human development: A dialectical interpretation*. Basic Books.

Kleiber, D. A. (2012). Taking leisure seriously: New and older considerations about leisure education. *World Leisure Journal*, *54*, 5–15.

Kleiber, D. A., Walker, G. J., & Mannell, R. C. (2011). *A social psychology of leisure* (2nd ed.). Venture Publishing.

Kolb, D. A. (1984). *Experiential learning: Experience as the source of learning and development*. Prentice Hall.

Kuchinke, K. P. (2000). Debates over the nature of HRD: An institutional theory perspective. *Human Resource Development International*, *3*(3), 279–283.

Kuchinke, K. P. (2013). Education for work: A review essay of historical, cross-cultural, and disciplinary perspectives on vocational education. *Educational Theory*, *63*(2), 203–220.

Kuykendall, L., Tay, L., & Ng, V. (2015). Leisure engagement and subjective well-being: A meta-analysis. *Psychological Bulletin*, *141*(2), 364.

Lee, M. (2007). Human resource development from a holistic perspective. *Advances in Developing Human Resources*, *9*(1), 97–110.

Leitner, M., & Leitner, S. (2012). *Leisure enhancement*. Sagamore Publishing.

Liu, H., Yeh, C. K., Chick, G. E., & Zinn, H. C. (2008). An exploration of meanings of leisure: A Chinese perspective. *Leisure Sciences*, *30*(5), 482–488.

Lu, L., & Hu, C. H. (2005). Personality, leisure experiences and happiness. *Journal of Happiness Studies*, *6*(3), 325–342.

Mansfield, L., Daykin, N., & Kay, T. (2020). Leisure and wellbeing. *Leisure Studies*, *39*(1), 1–10.

McEvoy, G. M., & Buller, P. F. (1997). The power of outdoor management development. *Journal of Management Development*, *16*(3), 208–217.

McQuarrie, F. A. (1999). Work careers and serious leisure: The effects of non-work commitment on career commitment. *Leisure/loisir*, *24*(1–2), 115–138.

Mezirow, J. (1991). *Transformative dimensions of adult learning*. Jossey-Bass.

Mezirow, J. (2000). *Learning as transformation: Critical perspectives on a theory in progress*. Jossey Bass.

Mitchell, R. D. (1998). Learning through play and pleasure travel: Using play literature to enhance research into touristic learning. *Current Issues in Tourism*, *1*(2), 176–188.

Morgan, A. D. (2010). Journeys into transformation: Travel to an "other" place as a vehicle for transformative learning. *Journal of Transformative Education*, *8*(4), 246–268.

Moyer, J. E. (2007). Learning from leisure reading: A study of adult public library patrons. *Reference and User Services Quarterly, 46*(6), 66–79.

Mundy, J. (1998). *Leisure education: Theory and practice* (2nd ed.). Sagamore.

Nada, C. I., Montgomery, C., & Araújo, H. C. (2018). 'You went to Europe and returned different': Transformative learning experiences of international students in Portugal. *European Educational Research Journal.* https://doi.org/10.1177/147 4904118765334

Newman, D. B., Tay, L., & Diener, E. (2014). Leisure and subjective well-being: A model of psychological mechanisms as mediating factors. *Journal of Happiness Studies, 15*(3), 555–578.

Ng, K. Y., Van Dyne, L., & Ang, S. (2009). From experience to experiential learning: Cultural intelligence as a learning capability for global leader development. *Academy of Management Learning & Education, 8*(4), 511–526.

O'Sullivan, E. (1999). *Transformative learning: Educational vision for the 21st century.* University of Toronto Press Inc.

Packer, J., & Ballantyne, R. (2004). Is educational leisure a contradiction in terms? Exploring the synergy of education and entertainment. *Annals of Leisure Research, 7*(1), 54–71.

Parker, S. R. (1971). *Future of work and leisure.* MacGibbon and Key.

Parker, S. R. (1975). The sociology of leisure: Progress and problems. *The British Journal of Sociology, 26*(1), 91–101.

Petrou, P., Bakker, A. B., & den Heuvel, M. (2017). Weekly job crafting and leisure crafting: Implications for meaning-making and work engagement. *Journal of Occupational and Organizational Psychology, 90*(2), 129–152.

Pieper, J. (1963). *Leisure: The basis of culture.* Random House.

Pitman, T., Broomhall, S., McEwan, J., & Majocha, E. (2010). Adult learning in educational tourism. *Australian Journal of Adult Learning, 50*(2), 219.

Raymore, L. A. (2002). Facilitators to leisure. *Journal of Leisure Research, 34*(1), 37–51.

Rennie, L. J., & Johnston, D. J. (2004). The nature of learning and its implications for research on learning from museums. *Science Education, 88*(S1), S4–S16.

Roberson, D. N., Jr. (2005). Leisure and learning: An investigation of older adults and self-directed learning. *Leisure/Loisir, 29*(2), 203–237. https://doi.org/10.1080/14927713.2005.9651330

Rocco, T. S., Bernier, J. D., & Bowman, L. (2014). Critical race theory and human resource development (HRD): Moving race front and center. *Advances in Developing Human Resources, 16*(4), 457–470.

Ruskin, H., & Sivan, A. (Eds.). (1995). *Leisure education towards the 21st century.* Brigham Young University.

Ryan, C. (1998). Playful tourists: Constructs of learning—A commentary on Mitchell's 'Learning through play and pleasure travel: Using play literature to enhance research into touristic learning'. *Current Issues in Tourism, 1*(2), 189–194.

Sargant, N. (1996). Learning and leisure. In R. Edwards, A. Hanson, & P. Raggatt (Eds.), *Adult learners, education and training: Boundaries of adult learning* (pp. 196–210). The Open University.

Scarinci, J., & Pearce, P. (2012). The perceived influence of travel experiences on learning generic skills. *Tourism Management, 33*(2), 380–386.

Sevilla, A., Gimenez-Nadal, J. I., & Gershuny, J. (2012). Leisure inequality in the United States: 1965–2003. *Demography, 49*(3), 939–964.

Sirgy, M. J., Uysal, M., & Kruger, S. (2017). Towards a benefits theory of leisure well-being. *Applied Research in Quality of Life, 12*(1), 205–228.

Sleezer, C. M. (2004). The contribution of adult learning theory to human resource development (HRD). *Advances in Developing Human Resources, 6*(2), 125–128.

Snir, R., & Harpaz, I. (2002). Work-leisure relations: Leisure orientation and the meaning of work. *Journal of Leisure Research, 34*(2), 178–203.

Solan, D. S. (1984). Leisure identities and interactions. *Journal of Leisure Research, 16*(3), 258.

Stebbins, R. A. (1992). *Amateurs, professionals, and serious leisure.* McGill-Queen's University Press.

Stone, M. J., & Petrick, J. F. (2013). The educational benefits of travel experiences: A literature review. *Journal of Travel Research, 52*(6), 731–744.

Thoidis, I., & Pnevmatikos, D. (2014). Non-formal education in free time: Leisure- or work-orientated activity? *International Journal of Lifelong Education, 33*(5), 657–673. https://doi.org/10.1080/02601370.2014.918197

Tinsley, H. E., & Eldredge, B. D. (1995). Psychological benefits of leisure participation: A taxonomy of leisure activities based on their need-gratifying properties. *Journal of Counseling Psychology, 42*(2), 123–132.

Tsaur, S. H., Liang, Y., & Hsu, H. (2012). A multidimensional measure of work-leisure conflict. *Leisure Sciences, 34*, 395–416.

Veal, A. J. (2019). Joffre Dumazedier and the definition of leisure. *Loisir et Société/Society and Leisure, 42*(2), 187–200. https://doi.org/10.1080/07053436.2019.1625533

Veblen, T. (1899). *The theory of the leisure class.* Macmillan.

Vera, D., & Crossan, M. (2005). Improvisation and innovative performance in teams. *Organization Science, 16*(3), 203–224.

Verduin, J. R., Jr., & McEwen, D. N. (1984). *Adults and their leisure: The need for lifelong learning.* Thomas.

Walton, J. (2014). A critique of outdoor team development. In J. Walton & C. Valentin (Eds.), *Human resource development: Practices and orthodoxies* (pp. 272–304). Palgrave Macmillan.

Wang, M., & Sunny Wong, M. C. (2011). Leisure and happiness in the United States: Evidence from survey data. *Applied Economics Letters, 18*(18), 1813–1816.

Watkins, K. E., & Marsick, V. J. (1992). Towards a theory of informal and incidental learning in organizations. *International Journal of Lifelong Education, 11*(4), 287–300.

Wiese, C. W., Kuykendall, L., & Tay, L. (2018). Get active? A meta-analysis of leisure-time physical activity and subjective well-being. *The Journal of Positive Psychology, 13*(1), 57–66.

Wilensky, H. L. (1960). Work, careers and social integration. *International Social Science Journal, 12*, 543–560.

Williams, P. (2010). Educational tourism: Understanding the concept, recognising the value. *Tourism Insights.* http://www.insights.org.uk/articleitem.aspx?title=Educational+Tourism%3A+Understanding+the+Concept%2C+Recognising+the+Value

Zuzanek, J. (2006). Leisure and time. In C. Rojek, S. M. Shaw, & A. J. Veal (Eds.), *A handbook of leisure studies* (pp. 185–202). Palgrave Macmillan.

Zuzanek, J., & Mannell, R. (1983). Work-leisure relationships from a sociological and social psychological perspective. *Leisure Studies, 2*(3), 327–344.

PART III

Reconceptualizing

A New Organizational Space for Inclusion Through the Evolutionary Wholeness Praxis

Chang-kyu Kwon and Aliki Nicolaides

Almost 20 years have passed since critical HRD was first introduced in the early 2000s. Initially, scholars Bierema and Cseh (2003) analyzed over 600 conference proceedings from the Academy of Human Resource Development (AHRD), published between 1996 and 2000, and found that less than 1% were concerned with issues of diversity, power, racism, sexism, and social justice, calling for more research using critical feminist lenses. Later, Callahan (2007) challenged HRD professionals to continue to reflect on whose interest HRD efforts truly serve, and ambitiously envisioned critical HRD as a central inquiry in HRD scholarship. More recently, Collins (2019) insisted on the need for a move toward more radical HRD research that explicitly covers the experiences of women, people of color, and LGBTQIA people, so that their increasing presence in the workplace can be better understood by organizations. Thus far critical HRD scholars have done much to shape the field, moving away from an excessive focus on performance and becoming more social justice-oriented.

Notably, the recent assumption of the AHRD's presidential roles by early critical HRD scholars, such as Julie Gedro and Laura Bierema, signals the

C. Kwon (✉)
University of Illinois at Urbana-Champaign, Champaign, IL, USA
e-mail: kwonc@illinois.edu

A. Nicolaides
University of Georgia, Athens, GA, USA
e-mail: alikin@uga.edu

149

J. C. Collins and J. L. Callahan (eds.), *The Palgrave Handbook of Critical Human Resource Development*, https://doi.org/10.1007/978-3-031-10453-4_9

enhanced status of critical HRD in the larger HRD community. These role changes are creating more substantial opportunities in the academy to raise awareness of the problems associated with social inequality prevailing in the world and organizations: it is now relatively more common than before to find scholars working from and articles published with critical traditions. Bierema (2020) reported that she found about a 5% increase in the number of published articles in four AHRD-sponsored journals between 2002 and 2018. Although there is much work ahead, it is important to recognize these accomplishments in order to envision the future of HRD, and the role that critical HRD can play in that developmental process.

Recent sociopolitical milieus characterized by the wide spread of the COVID-19 pandemic and antiracist movements sparked by the killings of many innocent Black people and Asian women make critical approaches even more timely. It has become apparent that the traditional ways of living, working, leading, and learning no longer meet the unprecedented and complex challenges facing humans and organizations. Pernicious racism and xenophobia have only been aggravated in these times of uncertainty as the effects of the pandemic unravel upon global issues of health inequality, economic collapse, and political instability. In responding to these moments of disruption, Bierema (2020) called for HRD scholars to reimagine organizations and to engage in research that boldly addresses topics that humanity across the globe is concerned with—such as diversity, inclusion, social justice, organizational health, human sustainability, and transforming systems of inequality. She asserted that HRD, which finds its identity in changing systems through learning and development, is in a good position to be at the forefront of this global transformation.

We, as the authors of this chapter, agree with and welcome Bierema's invitation to reframe the current turbulent reality as an opportunity to grow, develop, and make transformative changes. We have been grappling with these issues even before the outbreak of the pandemic and, through our research, proposing ways to bring about transformations at organizational, societal, and disciplinary levels (Kwon & Nicolaides, 2017, 2019; Nicolaides & Kwon, in preparation). This chapter is thus a continuation of our ongoing inquiry that we want to share with and make explicit for the critical HRD community and beyond; those who aspire to find new ways of leading, organizing, and including diversity. Our current inquiries are: what will the future of work look like and what organizing principles will guide us differently? How, if at all, will diversity and inclusion permeate such a future? In this chapter, we focus our attention on inquiring which new organizing principles will lead to a new paradigm of work, where diversity and inclusion are not separate from an organization's ontology. However, before moving on, we think it necessary to offer two observations that have been made in relation to the discourse of critical HRD, which will help us contextualize our perspective and message. We will later revisit these points as we conclude this chapter.

First, the claims of critical HRD scholars have remained largely theoretical. Fenwick (2005) discussed the dilemma that critical HRD faces in putting critical ideas into practice. She stated that "this dilemma is voiced in debate between those advocating the development of a practical critical agenda and those worried that such engagement dilutes the critical project" (Fenwick, 2005, p. 229). One presumptive reason for difficulties in enacting the mission of critical HRD is its tendency to view the world and organizations dichotomously. For example, critical HRD's radical privileging of social justice over performance has made those in power resistant to openly participating in dialogue and change efforts. The implication is that breaking free of this dichotomy would allow better challenge and would transform existing systems of power. In practice, this means that the perspectives of all stakeholders, including those who have been advantaged for their earned or unearned privileges, must be genuinely acknowledged and embraced. Otherwise, the efforts of critical HRD will always remain at the margins and result in the exclusion of certain individuals or groups in organizations. Plaut et al.'s (2011) study has shown that whites and other people from high-status groups tend to perceive exclusion (more than inclusion) by pro-diversity organizational practices. Therefore, critical HRD scholars need to start researching ways to create spaces in which everyone can be involved in collectively envisioning and co-constructing a more just and equitable organizational reality for all.

Second, the increased visibility of critical HRD has relied upon the active but separate voices of scholars who identify more with certain demographic groups. For example, the work of Bierema (2009) is widely known for its commitment to gender equality, but not necessarily the inclusion of people with disabilities. We also see that racial and ethnic discourse in HRD is primarily led by and focused on the lived experiences of Black people, and not Hispanic or Asian people (Byrd, 2009). Most organizations promote diversity by taking a similar approach. Despite growing interest, organizations are constrained in their capacity to become inclusive of all forms of diversity. As a result, implementing policies, programs, and procedures targeted for one group may not always lead to the desirable outcomes that are not exclusionary—ostracizing, for example, those who have intersecting identities or do not belong to "mainstream" diversity. A qualitative study conducted by Solebello et al. (2016) serves as good evidence. Their analysis of data gathered from 23 leaders of professional and trade associations in the United States showed that attempts to increase the association inclusive often competed with the desire to keep the association exclusive. The polarity of inclusion/exclusion demands a different approach that includes the awareness that critique raises, which is an evolution toward new organizing principles. To this end, our thinking takes us to a more radical direction of thinking beyond current systems of organizing, and to consider what might happen if organizations are genuinely oriented toward all who participate: so that everyone can thrive and succeed as who they are. Such thinking demands the disruption and transformation of existing organizing principles.

Based on the preceding two observations, our specific intent in this chapter is to present an alternative organizational space for inclusion where not few or many, but *all* are engaged. We will accomplish this goal by drawing upon Frederic Laloux's theory and practice of teal organization. His evolutionary perspective on organizational development provides insights into how organizations can be fundamentally reorganized to cultivate a new form of inclusion that is healthier and more sustainable for all. We believe that, without discussion of what it means to organize, critical HRD's long-held aspiration of transforming taken-for-granted organizational practices and making just and equitable workplaces may be hard to achieve. We call for shifting the playing field of critical HRD—the space from which critical HRD takes place. This is perhaps the most ambitious but practical mission that critical HRD scholars can engage with as we map the next evolution of the field. This chapter is comprised as follows: first, we provide our analysis of the current paradigm of diversity and inclusion. Next, we discuss how the new organizing principles of Frederic Laloux's teal organization may distinctively advance the practice of diversity and inclusion. Finally, we conclude by articulating how this chapter contributes to the evolving literature of critical HRD. We hope that this chapter is instrumental in urging critical HRD scholars to continue to expand their ways of knowing, doing, and being, in order to create a future of organizations that is just, inclusive, and productive for all.

WHAT WE KNOW: ANALYZING THE CURRENT PARADIGM OF DIVERSITY AND INCLUSION

Critical HRD scholars have been liberal with the critique of practices related to performative ambitions shared across various organizational contexts; but less so regarding diversity and inclusion practices specifically, largely due to organizations' publicized values for equality and social justice. However, diversity and inclusion practices are stereotypically masculine, oppressive, and exploitative, just like other domains of organizational practice, and even have direct influences on less privileged employee groups in organizations.

Closely looking at how organizations promote diversity from an outside vantage point, the sincerity of their commitment to creating an inclusive workplace is questionable. For example, Marques' (2010) analysis of three U.S. corporations—Abercrombie & Fitch, Coca-Cola, and Walmart—showed that their diversity-related efforts were merely reactions to massive discrimination lawsuits that brought into sharper relief the significant gap that existed as to how inclusion was stated and performed. Kuznetsova's (2016) study on two large Norwegian corporations similarly revealed that their intent to include people with disabilities was neither fully shared nor internalized among employees. These examples point to the superficial aspects of diversity initiatives and provide evidence for why it is necessary to conduct a more critical analysis of how organizational systems for inclusion are understood and practiced today. Below we present three propositions as they relate to the current paradigm of diversity and inclusion. To do so, we borrow Bierema and Callahan's (2014) framework for critiquing the overall philosophy, orientation, and values of HRD.

Proposition 1: The Current Paradigm of Diversity and Inclusion Privileges Performativity

Like most other organizational initiatives, diversity and inclusion often begins with the motivation to fulfill an organization's needs. Thomas and Ely (1996) explained the historical development of diversity and inclusion in organizations as follows. In the 1960s, when the rights of minority people started to be formally incorporated into legislation alongside the civil rights movement, the primary interest of organizations was to include diversity for the purpose of complying with laws or avoiding potential discrimination lawsuits. In the 1990s, a new understanding of diversity as organizational strategy emerged, as business leaders recognized the expansion of the global market and the need for adapting to such a change. This is what is widely known today as diversity management or a business case approach to inclusion, the rationale of which is to enhance the competitive advantage of organizations by internally reflecting the diversity of the customers that they serve (Cox & Blake, 1991). Diversity management is a remarkable evolution that has fundamentally transformed how diversity is viewed in organizations and connected it with business outcomes such as creativity and innovation. Despite this, the inclusion of diversity is still driven by masculine organizational performativity, which penalizes and oppresses the characteristics perceived as feminine such as being warm, kind, supportive, or compassionate.

Proposition 2: The Current Paradigm of Diversity and Inclusion Commodifies Workers

As a result of including diversity to maximize organizational gain, those who are hired for such a purpose may be reduced to instruments of organizations. The point here is not to blindly criticize successful business cases where the dignity of the individual is ensured while pursuing organizations' strategic objectives. The point we make is to raise awareness of the fallacy of business cases where efforts for diversity and inclusion can at any time be reduced or eliminated when forces (i.e., economic, social, political) cause struggles that interfere with performance goals. That is, the current business case approach keeps in place the commitments to performance and inclusion as a binary that can be halted at the first sign of trouble. Minority employees are included not because of who they are, but because of the monetary value that they bring to organizations, thus viewed by organizations as easily replaceable (Noon, 2007). In doing so, diversity initiatives, programs, and policies become hollow, paying no more than lip service (Hoobler, 2005). Such a transactional view of human relations is not without costs: it creates an unhealthy organizational culture and impedes authentic self-expression, disconnecting individuals from one another, as well as disengaging them from full participation in organizations. The prevalence of expressing controlled selves (Alvesson & Willmott, 2002), more seriously, hampers the sustainable development of organizations that effectively incorporate the diverse backgrounds, perspectives, and experiences of all. For example, the COVID-19 pandemic has created an unintended experiment in widescale remote work, revealing that many employees who work at home become more efficient, productive, and happier; while others struggle and miss structured office life (Neeley, 2021). This has complicated the way organizations rethink how people work, when they work, why they work, and what it means to feel safe and cared for at work. Under the current and usual commodified workplace structures, the failure of organizations to acknowledge waning senses of meaning as well as a lack of emotional support for and care of employees (needed to thrive in times of great uncertainty) have tipped the scales.

Proposition 3: The Current Paradigm of Diversity and Inclusion Reproduces Power Relations

The dominant assumption in HRD literature returns to the undeniable pretext that in including diversity, the main interest of organizations is to reinforce their governing status rather than to reshape internal power relations. For example, a critical discourse study of Zanoni and Janssens (2004) that analyzed 25 human resource managers' discussions about their diverse employees found a discursive pattern that confirmed the prevalence of managerial practices and underlying power relations. Mik-Meyer's (2016) analysis of 19 managers and 43 non-disabled employees in 13 organizations showed that outwardly inclusive comments about coworkers with disabilities were actually creating results that led to their othering. We use "othering" here as a term that provides a clarifying frame that reveals a set of common processes which propagate group-based inequality and marginality (Gülerce, 2014). Unequal distribution of power continues to engender a variety of disadvantaged experiences for some, while others enjoy the benefit of privilege. Issues of racism, sexism, ableism, and more that derive from human diversity are hardly brought up and engaged with at a deeper level, resulting in persisting taken-for-granted assumptions and beliefs within organizations. Managers' unawareness of and biases toward power differentials often inadvertently inhibits minority employees from getting buy-in from power holders and from creating momentum for equitable change. In sum, under the current paradigm of diversity and inclusion, asymmetrical power relations are reproduced and maintained rather than being challenged or transformed.

The three propositions outlined above are largely grounded in a stream of research called critical diversity studies, the goal of which is to challenge essentialist and utilitarian understandings of diversity. Ahonen et al. (2014) problematized approaches that reduce complex and fluid individual identities as if they are fixed, stable, objectifiable, and measurable for managerial purposes. While distinguishing critical from non-critical diversity studies, Janssens and Zanoni (2014) further pointed out that dominant diversity and inclusion practices, such as diversity-focused hiring, training, and mentoring, are aimed at mitigating individual biases and rarely address structural factors that perpetuate various forms of inequality. Their assertion rightly reflects our perspective that the authentic inclusion of diverse people in organizations is contingent on whether or to what extent there is a fundamental power shift in the way individuals relate to each other; and as a result, how the meaning of individual or group differences are constructed. If people are structurally regulated to open up and bring all of who they are to organizations as a person and a professional, inclusion may be effective in reinforcing managerial agendas but would be far from individually freeing. To summarize, the development of mainstream diversity research and practice has until now heavily relied on a positivist, social psychological lens that represents the functionalist perspectives of organizations. As such, critical diversity scholars have recently begun to argue for the need to search for new, emancipating forms of organizing investigating how diversity is conceptualized, experienced, and processed in such a context (Zanoni et al., 2010).

WHERE WE GO: ENVISIONING AN EVOLVING PARADIGM OF DIVERSITY AND INCLUSION

Developing organizations into more liberating and inclusive spaces for all demands a paradigm shift. We intentionally call this a paradigm shift because the subject of inclusion is expanded to everyone, not just those of minoritized status (Kwon & Nicolaides, 2017). In practice, the leading discourse of inclusion is now shifting from welcoming traditionally marginalized individuals to engaging *every* individual. Jennifer Brown, a global diversity and inclusion consultant, describes in her recent book that a truly inclusive organization is one where everyone can be accepted and thrive by being comfortable expressing their distinct identities (Brown, 2016). Her central idea is that current hierarchical and siloed organizational systems make it hard for people to actively share their perspectives and have them heard by others, which is exacerbated for those already experiencing discrimination and subordination on a daily basis. She further maintains that restoration of humanity in the workplace ultimately requires a transformation toward conscious capitalism, where organizations are driven by larger purposes beyond simply making monetary rewards for their own sake. Conscious capitalism may sound like an abstract concept, however, there is extensive research on this already in play, with global systems paying attention to new forms of economic models that respect the dignity of all persons (Brennan et al., 2015; Scharmer & Kaufer, 2013). Put simply, when the structures that hold an organization to its mission are reorganized to serve all of its stakeholders—including diverse employees—success is redefined as inclusion (Boulding, 1990; Musho-Hamilton, 2013).

Importantly, the shift in the conception of inclusion is motivated by and reflects the changing demographic trend in the labor market. According to an October 2019 report from the U.S. Bureau of Labor Statistics, millennials make up 29.3% of the population and are 35% of the workforce. Given this rise of individuals in the workplace who prefer their jobs to be flexible, meaningful, and engaging, it seems that finding ways to accommodate the diverse needs and desires of all employees is not an option but a necessity for organizations to remain competitive, as well as to become more inclusive in today's complex business environment. The outbreak of the COVID-19 pandemic has presented many critical questions to organizational leaders and managers about which employees have been found to be impacted most by the virus, and therefore how to pay special care and attention to such individuals—for example, caregivers; those with a lack of privacy or online access at home; those with underlying medical conditions; or other able-bodied people who cannot navigate new mandates for health and safety outside their home environments. That is, the global pandemic has provided a catalyst for a transformation in how dignity is expressed, acknowledging that anxiety, fear, and concerns for our loved ones unite us across our diversity. It is no longer easy to ignore the pain and suffering of people who are different, and organizations cannot turn their gaze away from a workforce that deserves their attention: because each of us is experiencing unprecedented challenges in some way. This shared complexity is paradoxically a ripe context for transformation. A radical reshaping of organizational culture, structure, and procedures has already begun to ensure greater empathy, patience, and support toward each other, and is calling for linking issues of inclusion more broadly with employee engagement, in order to move beyond the idea of inclusion being only helping employees with traditionally categorized marginal identities.

Frederic Laloux's theory and practice of teal organization provide a useful lens through which organizations can reimagine what it means to organize and transform into ecologies that consciously include everyone. In his 2014 book entitled *Reinventing Organizations*, Laloux offers three ground-breaking findings regarding the organizing principles of future organizations—self-management, wholeness, and evolving purpose—and calls for rethinking what management can and should be in evolving society. Drawing from evolutionary and developmental psychology, Laloux uses a color scheme first devised by Don Beck and Chris Cowan (1996) and later refined by Ken Wilber (2000) to illustrate how organizations have culturally and historically developed over time to meet the environmental demands placed on them. Just like human beings go through their own developmental stages—from being a prerational newborn baby to a mature adult with the capacity to hold complex systems of thinking and feeling in mind—so do organizational systems evolve. Table 9.1 shows Laloux's conception of organizational evolution.

As organizations evolve from red to teal (evolutionary, inclusive of individual and collective unfolding, and inner rightness as wholeness), they utilize more complex ways of organizing. More complex ways of organizing

Table 9.1 Laloux's color scheme conception of organizational evolution

Characteristic	Impulsive (Red)	Conformist (Amber)	Achievement (Orange)	Pluralistic (Green)	Evolutionary (Teal)
Organizing principle	Power and ego, fear-base, short-term focus	Rules and regulations, hierarchy, top-down authority	Profit and growth, competition, management by objectives	Fairness and equality, harmony, consensus	?
Example	Mafia, street gangs	Catholic church, government agencies	Most business organizations	Culture-driven organizations	?
Metaphor	Wolf pack	Army	Machine	Family	?

transcend (but include) the organizing principles of previous management paradigms; thus, organizations operating in later management paradigms have access to a wider range of organizing principles that they can act upon (Beck & Cowan, 1996; Fisher et al., 2003; Kegan, 1994; Wilber, 2000). In effect, as an organization evolves, it becomes an ecology of change where more complex ways of organizing emerge, making new pathways for all ways of knowing, doing, and being to serve a shared purpose with true acceptance and dignity.

Most contemporary organizations fall under the productivity-driven orange paradigm, and in some evolved cases, the egalitarian green paradigm. As discussed earlier, it is more obvious that the forces that influence the orange paradigm privilege achievement and materialistic success, where diversity and inclusion are marginalized and treated as a token of an organization's mission that is aspirational; whereas the egalitarianism of the green paradigm reaches beyond tokenism to address issues of power differential and inequitable organizational practices deriving from them. However, confronting power here paradoxically comes from both one's righteousness as well as a humble awareness of post-modern relativism that allows for anything to be valid, and therefore is made aware of yet not critically engaged (Erfan, 2021; Erfan & Torbert, 2015). Another dark side of the green paradigm is that by focusing on resolving various inequities caused by the pursuit of materialistic values, it denies and thus loses the growth capacity that the orange paradigm has built to be productive. Yet, the teal paradigm, in a sense, simultaneously embraces the orange and green paradigms in order to be both democratic and social justice-oriented as well as effective and profitable (Kwon & Nicolaides, 2019). Working in the teal paradigm also enables an organization to more generatively engage with the polarities, differences, and incongruities that different people bring, and allows an organization to become somewhat less attached to specific outcomes of its diversity and inclusion initiatives, and allows them to work within "the mystery of what is unfolding" as a whole (Erfan, 2021, p. 10). After all, Laloux suggests that it is important to continue to challenge our way of leading and participating in organizations and potentially look toward the teal paradigm, given the increasing complexity of the issues that organizations are facing, such as diversity and inclusion. Below we discuss three organizing principles of teal organizations and how they may distinctively contribute to the issues of diversity and inclusion we identified above.

The Principle of Whole Self

Above all, teal organizations encourage employees to bring their full selves to work. In traditional organizations characterized by politics and competition, identities are drafted to keep the whole self behind the protection of the superego—that is, the ego determines which identity is safe to bring forward in an organizational culture that lacks trust (Kwon et al., 2020; Nicolaides & Poell, 2020). People tend to cover up deep thoughts and feelings, showing partial selves and creating identities that fit the culture of the organization that may not include all dimensions of their diverse ways of knowing, doing, and being. Pfeffer (2018) pointed out the toxicity of many modern management practices—such as long working hours, work-family conflict, and economic insecurity to name a few—that disengage and harm employees both physically and mentally. His decades of research on power and politics in organizations have led him to insist that in reality, the nature of organizational life often reinforces individuals enacting political behaviors and learning ways to effectively navigate such work contexts, making them agile enforcers of well-engrained organizational politics to achieve personal goals.

In teal organizations, however, the expectation to know the politics of a system is replaced and guided by the principle of being true to oneself. Being true to oneself means pursuing the integration of partial identities that are forged out of the fear and anxiety bred by systems of power and oppression (Kegan & Lahey, 2016). It also means embracing vulnerability as a radical practice of disclosing one's internal thoughts and feelings against inequities that otherwise would have been silenced in order to generate a culture of acceptance, where differences and similarities may interact in ways that are mutually respectful. Brown (2018) defined vulnerability as the emotion that we experience during times of uncertainty, risk, and emotional exposure. Therefore, according to this definition, embracing vulnerability enables the courage to speak up and engage with tough conversations that are unlikely to be controlled; whereas the whole purpose of engaging in political behaviors is to be in control. We recognize that there is also a vulnerability that comes from manipulation and which may cause trauma, which having multiple identities serve as a mechanism for protection in orange and green organizational systems; however, here we take up the view of Brown who presents vulnerability as the capacity to bring one's authentic self to a system with trust and dignity.

Our recent research, conducted both in educational (Nicolaides & Kwon, in preparation) and workplace settings (Kwon, 2021), has shown that relational vulnerability is a catalyst for greater compassion toward the differences arising from authentic sharing. This finding has a particular implication for members of marginalized groups in organizations, who have been socialized to hide or manage their unaccepted identities in order to fit themselves into a dominant organizational culture. Brown (2016) stated that "part of the work of inclusion is helping those already in the workforce to feel safe bringing more of themselves to work, versus what they have done historically, such as downplaying parts of themselves for purposes of assimilation" (p. 25). Ferdman and Roberts (2014) similarly noted that "the ways in which we as individuals combine, manage, and express our multiple identities—in short, how we show up and express our full selves at work—is a key part of the dynamic process of inclusion" (p. 95). Thus, as each and every organizational member consciously practices seeing and understanding one another from within, there is a real potential for reviving human value and dignity in organizations. Specifically, embodying radical openness leading to mutual trust and vulnerability would enable a qualitatively different, new form of organizational participation, which can potentially liberate instrumental relationships that have constructed minority employees as a means for organizational gain.

The Principle of Self-Management

Self-management, another characteristic of teal organizations, is concerned with the way in which power is held and practiced in organizations. Distinct from traditional organizations where power is centered at the top and owned by a few, self-management is a formal and systematic way in which power is radically decentralized throughout the organization (Lee & Edmondson, 2017). In this evolved form of organizational space, the removal of a hierarchical relationship between manager and subordinate allows individuals to freely exchange their ideas and collaborate, and as a result, helps organizations become more flexible, adaptive, and innovative. The full power, freedom, and autonomy made available to all employees through shared rules and agreements differs from the management rhetoric of employee empowerment in that the authority delegated from managers through such a technique can be taken back at any point when control seems necessary.

An interesting part of self-management is that it has a natural power to balance outwardly contradictory individual and organizational needs, and ultimately contribute to the growth of the organization. Scharmer and Kaufer (2013) explained such a phenomenon through the notion of ecosystem awareness, which is defined as "an internalization of the views and concerns of other stake-holders in one's system" (p. 57). That is, people in self-managing organizations have the capacity (or at least the willingness) to see problems beyond their own interests and engage with the whole. From Torbert's (1991) point of view, the quality of relationships cultivated in such a mature way can be described as mutual. In discussing various forms of power, Torbert (1991) defined mutually transforming power as the power that allows for the individuals involved in relationships to not only be open to, but actively seek differences, challenges, and even contradictions.

These accounts of how individuals relate to each other give us meaningful insights into how to engage with challenging and often polarized issues like diversity and inclusion. By structurally enabling people to search for ways to be connected with the perspectives of others, self-management serves as a generative space in which any related party can come together without pre-determined or fixed agendas, for the purpose of benefiting the whole system in which everyone is part of (Bohm, 1996). In other words, the overall culture of self-managing organizations is co-created rather than being dominated by a few individuals or groups in power; therefore, there would exist more room for minority employees to voice themselves based on their unique identities, perspectives, and experiences. Equally as important, through the radical disruption and transformation of the conventional power structure, asymmetrical power relations would be less likely to be reproduced, but would always be open for reconfigurations as all employees, including those in power, deliberately engage in mutual relational learning processes.

The Principle of Evolving Purpose

Finally, evolving purpose represents teal organizations' ongoing efforts to search for a vision that serves all stakeholders—in the whole system as well as outside the organization. While traditional organizations are led through mechanisms of prediction and control for maximizing profits, in teal organizations finding a higher organizational purpose becomes a driving force for authentic employee engagement and productivity. Such an organizational purpose does not come from leaders but is co-created by all employees. There is trust that organizations have their own sense of rhythm and energy, and therefore the role of employees is to collectively sense a deeper meaning as to why they as an organization exist: to serve a larger purpose that they are part of through their products and services. Laloux (2014) described the view of teal organizations on profit as "Profit is like the air we breathe. We need air to live, but we don't live to breathe" (p. 197). Once the directionality of the organization is determined, employees are free to organically work together to reach those goals; yet, those goals are constantly revisited to better align them with larger organizational intentions.

The purpose-driven way of leading organizations, as exemplified by teal organizations, holds the promise of embracing diversity and inclusion as part of an organization's ontology. Seeking a variety of voices and addressing the desires of all employees as a vital condition for co-constructing a shared future of the organization would transcend a business case approach to inclusion that evaluates the merits of diversity and inclusion solely from a profit standpoint. Although it may feel risky and vulnerable to take such an initiative, disrupting a unilateral power approach that leaders often rely on to meet the demands of profitability would paradoxically create a space for collective responses that are in turn more creative, inclusive, and mission-driven. In short, building organizational muscle by living with and learning from diversity and inclusion is likely to be accomplished by growing a more conscious space for new ways of expressing and enacting performance.

In conclusion, the preponderance of control (profitability and effectiveness measured by bottom line numbers) as the sole force of organizing is limiting the potential for reimaging organizations that are truly diverse and inclusive; where differences and similarities are forces that produce greater outcomes such as dignity, right livelihood, sustainability, and societal evolution. However, the three organizing principles of teal organizations as discussed above help us imagine how organizations can be reorganized in ways that innovatively meet the persistent demands produced by the current paradigm of diversity and inclusion. Specifically, issues of commodification, dehumanization, and marginalization of human resources can be transformed by inviting employees' whole selves to work. Issues of power imbalance and reproduction can be transformed by the distribution of leadership throughout the organization in ways that are emergent and authentic. Issues of performativity can be transformed by the cultivation of a mission-driven approach that is organizational and societal at the same time.

We argue that the theme that cuts across these three organizing principles is, as Thakadipuram (2010) described, "never losing the awareness that we are all connected to each other, and that we live for the universe through our choices and actions" (p. 464), whether such an awareness is practiced at an intrapersonal (whole self), interpersonal (self-management), or interorganizational (evolving purpose) levels. Thakadipuram (2010) further stated that "To be whole means to envision the reality of individuals, organizations, society, and nature as interconnected phenomena designed for the purpose of common well-being, progress, and maximum happiness" (p. 464). Though it may seem paradoxical that our argument hinges on accepting all human differences and similarities to reimagine organizations: we strongly adhere to the evolutionary power of trust and to the organic distribution of roles and responsibilities that self-organize. Such principles generate systems where profit and people, planet and purpose are held together effortlessly. This makes for systems where diversity and inclusion are not separate; they are the system itself.

Conclusion

Li and Lin (2011) stated that "a critical factor constantly prohibiting organizational transformation is not the problems themselves or how the problems are framed; rather it is how we collectively relate ourselves to the problems we confront" (p. 108). The authors further stated that "when we transcend from the bondage and boundaries of problems, we would see the alternative path leading away from the problem maze which confines our vision of a truly sustainable and co-existing world for all" (p. 129). In this chapter, we have attempted to show, through the wholeness praxis of teal organizations, how an organizational space can be reconceptualized in a way that allows for our inner and outer selves (the relationships we form individually and collectively inside and outside the organization) to be recognized as part of an inseparable whole, and thus naturally create conditions for diversity and inclusion. As organizational leaders, members of the organization, and whole systems develop their ways of thinking and action and begin to see the potential of and embrace the new way of leading and participating in organizations as we described in this chapter, the generative power of such an organizational evolution will guide us to a new pathway for inclusion and make it as part of the DNA of any organization—that is, creating an ecology of wholeness that evolves organizational purpose in synergy with those who serve and are served by its mission. Such an organization embraces mutual forms of power that have an orientation toward integrity, generosity, reciprocity, and the whole, which is well-aligned with diversity and inclusion and the aspiration of critical HRD to deconstruct the dominant power structures that prevail in organizations.

Returning to the two observations that we offered earlier in this chapter, the contributions that this chapter makes to critical HRD are as follows. First, this chapter opens up a scholarly conversation around which new organizing principles may serve as an alternative to strengthen the critique that critical HRD has been making against current work systems, and how we may move into a collective responsibility for actions that close its theory–practice gap. Second, these new organizing principles create a new form of unity between groups, finding a third way beyond the bifurcation of those with power and those othered to galvanize a new ecology of inclusion that respectfully generates conditions for the growth and flourishing of the whole. In this sense, we believe that this chapter compliments and extends our current understanding of how inclusion should be conceived of and practiced; by consciously engaging multiple expressions of wholeness that are generatively invited to enact the always emerging and evolving dimensions of individual, organizational, and societal harmony.

References

Ahonen, P., Tienari, J., Meriläinen, S., & Pullen, A. (2014). Hidden contexts and invisible power relations: A Foucauldian reading of diversity research. *Human Relations, 67*(3), 263–286. https://doi.org/10.1177/0018726713491772

Alvesson, M., & Willmott, H. (2002). Identity regulation as organizational control: Producing the appropriate individual. *Journal of Management Studies, 39*(1), 619–644. https://doi.org/10.1111/1467-6486.00305

Beck, D. E., & Cowan, C. C. (1996). *Spiral dynamics: Mastering values, leadership, and change.* Blackwell.

Bierema, L. L. (2009). Critiquing human resource development's dominant masculine rationality and evaluating its impact. *Human Resource Development Review, 8*(1), 68–96. https://doi.org/10.1177/1534484308330020

Bierema, L. L. (2020). HRD research and practice after 'The Great COVID-19 Pause': The time is now for bold, critical, research. *Human Resource Development International, 23*(4), 347–360. https://doi.org/10.1080/13678868.2020.1779912

Bierema, L. L., & Callahan, J. L. (2014). Transforming HRD: A framework for critical HRD practice. *Advances in Developing Human Resources, 16*(4), 429–444. https://doi.org/10.1177/1523422314543818

Bierema, L. L., & Cseh, M. (2003). Evaluating AHRD research using a feminist research framework. *Human Resource Development Quarterly, 14*(1), 5–26. https://doi.org/10.1002/hrdq.1047

Bohm, D. (1996). *On dialogue*. Routledge.

Boulding, K. (1990). *The three faces of power*. Sage.

Brennan, G., Tennant, M., & Blomsma, F. (2015). Business and production solutions: Closing loops and the circular economy. In H. Kopnina, & E. Shoreman-Ouimet (Eds.), *Sustainability: Key issues* (pp. 219–239). Routledge. https://doi.org/10.4324/9780203109496-11

Brown, B. (2018). *Dare to lead: Brave work, tough conversations, whole hearts*. Random House.

Brown, J. (2016). *Inclusion: Diversity, the new workplace & the will to change*. Publish Your Purpose Press.

Byrd, M. Y. (2009). Telling our stories of leadership: If we don't tell them they won't be told. *Advances in Developing Human Resources, 11*(5), 582–605. https://doi.org/10.1177/1523422309351514

Callahan, J. L. (2007). Gazing into the crystal ball: Critical HRD as a future of research in the field. *Human Resource Development International, 10*(1), 77–82. https://doi.org/10.1080/13678860601170344

Collins, J. C. (2019). A more radical human resource development: The time is now. *Human Resource Development International, 22*(4), 405–411. https://doi.org/10.1080/13678868.2018.1506649

Cox, T., & Blake, S. (1991). Managing cultural diversity: Implications for organizational competitiveness. *The Executive, 5*(3), 45–56. https://doi.org/10.5465/ame.1991.4274465

Erfan, A. (2021). The many faces of JEDI: A developmental exploration. *Integral Review, 17*(1). Advance online publication.

Erfan, A., & Torbert, B. (2015). Collaborative developmental action inquiry. In H. Bradbury (Ed.), *The SAGE handbook of action research* (pp. 64–75). Sage. https://doi.org/10.4135/9781473921290.n7

Fenwick, T. (2005). Conceptions of critical HRD: Dilemmas for theory and practice. *Human Resource Development International, 8*(2), 225–238. https://doi.org/10.1080/13678860500100541

Ferdman, B. M., & Roberts, L. M. (2014). Creating inclusion for oneself: Knowing, accepting, and expressing one's whole self at work. In B. M. Ferdman & B. R. Deane (Eds.), *The professional practice series. Diversity at work: The practice of inclusion* (p. 93–127). Jossey-Bass/Wiley. https://doi.org/10.1002/9781118764282.ch3

Fisher, D., Rooke, D., & Torbert, W. R. (2003). *Personal and organizational transformations: Through action inquiry*. Edge\Work Press.

Gülerce, A. (2014). Selfing as, with, and without othering: Dialogical (im)possibilities with Dialogical Self Theory. *Culture & Psychology, 20*(2), 244–255. https://doi.org/10.1177/1354067X14526897

Hoobler, J. M. (2005). Lip service to multiculturalism: Docile bodies of the modern organization. *Journal of Management Inquiry, 14*(1), 49–56. https://doi.org/10.1177/1056492604270798

Janssens, M., & Zanoni, P. (2014). Alternative diversity management: Organizational practices fostering ethnic equality at work. *Scandinavian Journal of Management, 30*(3), 317–331. https://doi.org/10.1016/j.scaman.2013.12.006

Kegan, R. (1994). *In over our heads: The mental demands of modern life.* Harvard University Press.

Kegan, R., & Lahey, L. L. (2016). *An everyone culture: Becoming a deliberately developmental organization.* Harvard Business Press.

Kuznetsova, Y. (2016). An inclusive corporate culture: Examining the visible and invisible levels of disability inclusiveness in two large enterprises. *Scandinavian Journal of Disability Research, 18*(3), 179–190. https://doi.org/10.1080/15017419.2015.1063541

Kwon, C. (2021). Resisting ableism in deliberately developmental organizations: A discursive analysis of the identity work of employees with disabilities. *Human Resource Development Quarterly, 32*(2), 179–196. https://doi.org/10.1002/hrdq.21412

Kwon, C., Han, S., & Nicolaides, A. (2020). The impact of psychological safety on transformative learning in the workplace: A quantitative study. *Journal of Workplace Learning, 32*(7), 533–547. https://doi.org/10.1108/JWL-04-2020-0057

Kwon, C., & Nicolaides, A. (2017). Managing diversity through triple-loop learning: A call for paradigm shift. *Human Resource Development Review, 16*(1), 85–99. https://doi.org/10.1177/1534484317690053

Kwon, C., & Nicolaides, A. (2019). Reconceptualizing social movement learning in HRD: An evolutionary perspective. *Advances in Developing Human Resources, 21*(2), 267–279. https://doi.org/10.1177/1523422319827948

Laloux, F. (2014). *Reinventing organizations: A guide to creating organizations inspired by the next stage of human consciousness.* Nelson Parker.

Lee, M. Y., & Edmondson, A. C. (2017). Self-managing organizations: Exploring the limits of less-hierarchical organizing. *Research in Organizational Behavior, 37*(1), 35–58. https://doi.org/10.1016/j.riob.2017.10.002

Li, M. F., & Lin, K. K. (2011). A new paradigm of organizational transformation: Enacting wholeness praxis in the oneness of problem and possibility. *Systemic Practice and Action Research, 24*(1), 107–132. https://doi.org/10.1007/s11213-010-9179-z

Marques, J. F. (2010). Colorful window dressing: A critical review on workplace diversity in three major American corporations. *Human Resource Development Quarterly, 21*(1), 435–446. https://doi.org/10.1002/hrdq.20045

Mik-Meyer, N. (2016). Othering, ableism and disability: A discursive analysis of co-workers' construction of colleagues with visible impairments. *Human Relations, 69*(6), 1341–1363. https://doi.org/10.1177/0018726715618454

Musho-Hamilton, D. (2013). *Everything is workable: A Zen approach to conflict resolutions.* Shambala Publications.

Neeley, T. (2021). *Remote work revolution: Succeeding from anywhere.* Harper-Collins.

Nicolaides, A., & Kwon, C. (in preparation). *A generative ecology of knowing, doing, and being.*

Nicolaides, A., & Poell, R. F. (2020). "The only option is failure": Growing safe to fail workplaces for critical reflection. *Advances in Developing Human Resources, 22*(3), 264–277. https://doi.org/10.1177/1523422320927296

Noon, M. (2007). The fatal flaws of diversity and the business case for ethnic minorities. *Work, Employment and Society, 21*(4), 773–784. https://doi.org/10.1177/095 0017007082886

Pfeffer, J. (2018). *Dying for a paycheck: How modern management harms employee health and company performance—And what we can do about it.* Harper Business.

Plaut, V. C., Garnett, F. G., Buffardi, L. E., & Sanchez-Burks, J. (2011). "What about me?" Perceptions of exclusion and Whites' reactions to multiculturalism. *Journal of Personality and Social Psychology, 101*(2), 337–353. https://doi.org/10.1037/a00 22832

Scharmer, O., & Kaufer, L. (2013). *Leading from the emerging future: From ego-system to eco-system economies.* Berrett-Koehler Publishers.

Solebello, N., Tschirhart, M., & Leiter, J. (2016). The paradox of inclusion and exclusion in membership associations. *Human Relations, 69*(2), 439–460. https://doi.org/10.1177/0018726715590166

Thakadipuram, T. (2010). Leadership wholeness: A human resource development model. *Human Resource Development International, 13*(4), 463–475. https://doi.org/10.1080/13678868.2010.501993

Thomas, D. A., & Ely, R. (1996). Making differences matter: A new paradigm for managing diversity. *Harvard Business Review, 74*(5), 79–90. https://hbr.org/1996/09/making-differences-matter-a-new-paradigm-for-managing-diversity

Torbert, W. R. (1991). *The power of balance: Transforming self, society, and scientific inquiry.* Sage.

Wilber, K. (2000). *Integral psychology: Consciousness, spirit, psychology, therapy.* Shambhala Publications.

Zanoni, P., & Janssens, M. (2004). Deconstructing difference: The rhetoric of human resource managers' diversity discourses. *Organization Studies, 25*(1), 55–74. https://doi.org/10.1177/0170840604038180

Zanoni, P., Janssens, M., Benschop, Y., & Nkomo, S. (2010). Guest editorial: Unpacking diversity, grasping inequality: Rethinking difference through critical perspectives. *Organization, 17*(1), 9–29. https://doi.org/10.1177/135050840935 0344

Learning, Knowing, and Resisting Through Critical Approaches in Spaces of Organizing

Jill Zarestky and Lisa Baumgartner

To enact change, it may be necessary to learn in preparation for or in tandem with action. Such learning may center on navigating the resources, systems, or processes for change, such as legal systems or grant funding, or the deeply personal work required of effective social justice action and reform. Our primary concern is the latter, which may be pursued by individuals or groups, and self-directed or assisted by a facilitator.

The purpose of this chapter is to provide an overview of select adult learning theories, their applications, and their potential for explaining learning, knowing, and resisting from a critical and social justice perspective within spaces of organizing. We begin by presenting select philosophical foundations that inform the purpose and goals of adult learning. We then describe theoretical frames of relevant adult learning theories, including the related processes and contextualized examples of such learning. Since this chapter focuses on knowing and resisting, we investigate how theories that focus on marginalized positionalities can help people learn about themselves and others through these lenses. Specifically, critical race theory, feminist theory, and queer theory

J. Zarestky (✉)
School of Education, Colorado State University, Fort Collins, CO, USA
e-mail: Jill.Zarestky@colostate.edu

L. Baumgartner
Texas State University, San Marcos, TX, USA
e-mail: Lbaumgartner@txstate.edu

© The Author(s), under exclusive license to Springer Nature
Switzerland AG 2023
J. C. Collins and J. L. Callahan (eds.), *The Palgrave Handbook of Critical Human Resource Development*, https://doi.org/10.1007/978-3-031-10453-4_10

are theories that resist the dominant hegemony of the White, male, hetero-sexual lens. These theories help learners know and understand their worlds from different perspectives and can foster transformative learning.

PHILOSOPHIES OF ADULT LEARNING THAT FRAME THEORY

Adult learning theory draws from various philosophical perspectives (Elias & Merriam, 2005). The philosophies presented here help us respond to the questions "What do we hope to accomplish through adult learning?" and "What can adult learning do for us?" and frame some of the historical context and evolution of adult education as a social justice endeavor. Therefore, we summarize the underlying purpose of learning as drawn from four select philosophies: progressive, humanist, radical, and critical. We picked these four because of their influence and foundational role in the development of adult education as a field of study and practice, and the ways in which they build upon one another to inform common, current conceptions of adult education. In subsequent sections, each theory leverages elements of one or more of these philosophies.

Before we describe the four select philosophies, let us first present behaviorism, as the early learning theory that functions as a foil for the bulk of adult learning theory. Behaviorists (in the discipline of psychology) were certain that (a) only children learned, (b) learning only occurred in formal settings, and (c) the outcome of learning is an observable behavior or action. This perspective neglects the continued learning that occurs in adulthood and out-of-school settings, and cannot account for the cognitive, emotional, and identity processes associated with all kinds of learning.

One of the first perspectives to counter behaviorism, the *progressive* philosophy is at the origination of adult education and advocates for social change through a broadened view of education (i.e., out-of-school, lifelong). Education is experiential and problem- or situation-centered (e.g., Dewey, 1938; Lindeman, 1926). The very *idea* that learning is lifelong was a progressive idea in contrast to behaviorism. In its day, the progressive philosophy (Dewey, 1938; Lindeman, 1926) was critical of the status quo ideas and assumptions about education and subsequently advocated for increased opportunity and support for learners of all ages and a focus on process rather than content (Ross-Gordon et al., 2017).

Another reaction against behaviorism, the *humanist* philosophy emphasizes learners' dignity, freedom, autonomy, individuality, and self-directedness, with a responsibility for the self and for others. Such responsibility arguably leads to a reformed and better society (e.g., Maslow, 1970). Because humanism emphasizes freedom and individual potential, it necessarily suggests reform, although perhaps tempered (Elias & Merriam, 2005).

Aiming to overhaul systems of oppression, the *radical* and *critical* philosophies (including Queer, Critical Race Theory, and some Feminist perspectives) do not aim for tempered change. These philosophies challenge the systems and structures of the societal and educational status quo and seek to emancipate (e.g., Freire, 2018; hooks, 1994; Collins, 2000; Sedgwick, 2008; Thurer, 2005; Tong & Botts, 2018).

The radical and critical approaches to learning and knowing as these philosophies lend themselves to resistance. Individuals need to understand that they are oppressed which may require a change in world view which is why we focus on two ways of conceptualizing transformative learning. As this chapter concerns theorizing knowing and resisting, in the second part of the chapter we discuss critical theories centered on race, gender, and sexual orientation. These theories serve as ways to know the world differently resist the status quo, and may foster transformative learning as students come to know the world through these lenses.

TRANSFORMATIVE LEARNING

All learning theories share some qualities of advocacy for change of some kind. However, transformative learning is associated with profound, seismic changes in worldview that can lead people to action. Conceptualized as a "metatheory," transformative learning "refers to processes that result in significant and irreversible changes in the way a person experiences, conceptualizes, and interacts with the world" (Hoggan, 2016, pp. 70–71). These changes occur in one's "worldview, self, [or] epistemology" (p. 71). A social-emancipatory approach pushes learners to consider the larger social context in which learning occurs. Learners are encouraged to critically examine the world around them. They comprehend societal inequities and work toward self-emancipation and community problem-solving (Freire, 2018). Mezirow's (2000) psycho-critical approach focuses on individuals engaging in "premise reflection" which causes them to deeply reflect on the reasons for valuing a particular way of life, resulting in personal perspective transformation.

Social-Emancipatory Approach to Transformative Learning

Freire's (2018) theory contains concepts that apply to teaching and learning from a critical justice perspective. He distinguishes between "banking education" (p. 73) and "problem-posing education" (p. 83). Banking education is teacher-centered, learners are passive receptacles of knowledge, and creativity and critical thought are discouraged (Freire, 2018). In problem-posing education the teacher and student co-create knowledge through dialogue and critical thought (Freire, 2018). Problem-posing education emboldens individuals to view themselves as social change agents who are in the constant "process of becoming" (p. 84). Liberation is central to problem-posing education.

The process of "becoming" includes an awareness of the oppressive forces in one's life (Freire, 2018). In Freire's process of conscientization, learners discuss their daily concerns. Workers discussing their wages might learn the words "taxes" or "government." These dialogues help workers understand how the larger socio-political context affects wage inequities. The level of conscientization can range from learners being silent and believing things are externally controlled, to beginning to gradually see social inequities, to learners having the agency and confidence to question the status quo. Ultimately, learners recognize that they have agency to construct a better reality in an unjust world.

Freire's (2018) change process, includes "praxis" or "reflection and action which truly transform reality" (p. 109). Other learning theories also cite reflection and action although in Freire's conceptualization, social transformation a goal. Mezirow (2000) mentions critical reflection and action as part of an individual's transformative learning process. Kolb's (1984) experiential learning model cycle includes reflective observation (watching) and active experimentation (doing) (Kolb, 1984). Likewise, Schön (1987) talks about reflection-in-action when an instructor is surprised and must reflect and react in the moment.

Ultimately, education for emancipation requires applying the principles of mutual respect humility, openness, trust, cooperation, commitment, vigilance, honesty, truth, and passion to support the following aims (Allman, 2010, pp. 167–169):

- Critical, creative, and hopeful thinking
- Transformation of self and social relations of learning and teaching
- Democratization
- Embracing and internalizing the principles
- Unquenchable thirst for understanding, or genuine critical curiosity
- Solidarity and commitment to self and social transformation and the project of humanization

Highlander Folk School (now Highlander Research and Education Center (HREC), founded by Myles Horton, Jim Dombrowski, and others, has used these principles prior to their popularization by Friere. Highlander was founded in 1932 to organize groups and advance causes (88 Years of Fighting for Justice, n.d.). Community members came together to discuss labor issues and train union organizers in the 1930s and 1940s (88 Years of Fighting for Justice, n.d. para 10). Training community leaders to fight for civil rights for African Americans through the creation of Citizenship Schools, was a focus of the HREC lead in the 1950s and 1960s. Applchian people's struggles regarding including environmental issues and "globalization issues" (paragraph 12) and current concerns regarding "leadership development among Latino immigrants" (paragraph 13). Each cause involved organizing individuals, discussing citizens' concerns, and engaging in praxis.

Social-emancipatory approaches have been applied and researched in additional contexts. A Brazilian community used concepts such as praxis, dialogue, generative themes, and conscientization to explore "collective learning processes focused on advancing sustainable practices" (Souza et al., 2019, p. 1606). In another study, researchers explored the pedagogy used when implementing an active citizenship curriculum in high schools and found praxis, conscientization, and generative themes especially helpful "when developing pedagogical approaches for critical and transformative forms of active citizenship" (Wood et al., 2018, p. 260). Dialogue between the students and teachers and action and reflection or deep knowledge helped students produce quality community projects. Larri and Whitehouse (2019) used Freirean concepts to frame the social justice learning for older adult women (the "Knitting Nannas against Gas and Greed") who use non-violent approaches such as "knit-ins" to protest fracking. Last, Formosa (2012) critiqued Universities of the Third Age (U3As) through a Freirean lens. He urged U3As, learning groups in which older adults share their knowledge, skills, and interests, to use a "critical geragogical practice" (p. 211) to enlighten learners on the social inequities and apply Freire's "problem posing" strategies.

Psycho-Critical Approach

While the social-critical approach, as exemplified by Freire's work, strives to transform society on a group level, and community action is key, Mezirow's psycho-critical approach to transformation, concentrates on the individual. Aspects of his theory promote individual learning and resisting from a critical and social justice perspective. Transformations occur in beliefs or attitudes (meaning schemes) or perspectives (habits of mind) (Mezirow, 2012). These changes can occur suddenly or over time. The 10 phases include: "(1) a disorienting dilemma, (2) self-examination, (3) a critical assessment of assumptions (4) recognition of a connection between one's discontent and the process of transformation (5) exploration of options for a new roles, relationships, and action, (6) planning a course of action (7) acquiring knowledge and skills for implementing one's plan (8) provisional trying of new roles (9) building competence and self-confidence in new roles and relationships (10) a reintegration into one's life on the basis of conditions dictated by one new perspective" (Mezirow, 2009, p. 19).

Common Themes in Transformative Learning

We have described two ways of looking at transformative learning. In this section we discuss some common themes and compare and contrast the two approaches (social emancipatory and psycho-critical). There are several concepts common to transformative learning including the role of experience and critical reflection (Merriam & Baumgartner, 2020). How we interpret present experiences can be informed by our past experiences, our culture, and our age during an historical event, as this informs how we make sense of the event (Merriam & Baumgartner, 2020). In Freire's version of transformative learning, individuals live in their social worlds and make sense of their experiences. Mezirow's 10 steps imply that *individuals* have a "disorienting dilemma" due to an experience which starts the process of transformative learning.

As previously mentioned, reflection is at the heart of many types of learning (Kolb, 1984; Schön, 1987). Reflection and critical reflection are part of Freire's praxis (reflection and action) aspects of his theory whereas critical reflection occurs during the process of conscientization as learners begin to become aware of and critically reflect on the systemic inequalities that affect their lives (Freire, 2018). In Mezirow's (2009) theory, reflection occurs during the period of self-examination in the second phase and critical reflection on an individual's assumptions about the world occurs in the third phase.

The type of critical reflection that most readily prompts changes in world-view is reflection on one's premises about the world. *Why?* is the question asked in these scenarios. When traumatic events happen people often ask why they happened and they re-arrange their priorities. Kroth and Cranton (2014) present stories of transformative learning that respond to loss and trauma, and advocate for social change, contextualizing the experiences that launch and result from transformative learning. These stories share the common theme of new perspectives on the world after distressing or disappointing experiences, many of which take a negative event and transform it into a positive action.

Coyer et al. (2019) used the psycho-critical approach to foster "global learning outcomes" through community-based service learning (p. 162). Undergraduate students worked at a university-sponsored community-kitchen engaged in critical reflection about "the community's diversity and limited resources" (p. 162). As a result, they formed relationships with community members and got involved in other community events because of their experiences at the community kitchen (Coyer et al., 2019). Such activities helped the learners build and enact a new worldview in which they are valuable members of their communities.

POSITIONALITIES THROUGH A CRITICAL LENS: CRITICAL RACE, FEMINIST, AND QUEER THEORIES

The theories we discuss in this section put a particular positionality at the center. Exposure to these theories may foster transformative learning in that they may create a "disorienting dilemma" (Mezirow, 2009, p. 19) for individuals. The theories make visible marginalized populations and counter the dominant White, male, heterosexual ideologies prevalent in many learning environments. These theories center the "Other" and may foster critical reflection in learners, enabling a previously unarticulated knowing to surface. Grounded in the previously described philosophies, the learning theories in this section delve into changes in worldview or challenges to the status quo for individuals and society. We place emphasis on the critical nature of these theories as distinct from more mainstream or traditional theories which may also associate with the philosophies. In the following sections we briefly delineate the tenets and critiques of each theory, supported by examples from the literature that use these frameworks.

Feminist Theory

Feminist theory places women at the center of the analysis. Lorber (2012) classifies the various theories in three categories: reformist, resistant, and rebellious. Reform feminisms such as liberal, Marxist, socialist, and transnational feminisms argue that gender inequality "are structural and not the outcome of personal attributes, individual choices or unequal interpersonal relationships" (p. 10). They work toward equality through advocating for equal numbers of men and women in various areas or "gender balancing" and ensuring that "all policies and organizational arrangements consider women" (p. 10).

For example, Clover et al. (2017) discuss how feminism "influences leadership and adult education" (p. 22). Feminism illuminates how the patriarchy has oppressed women. Feminist adult educators can address this discrimination and take leadership roles to change policies. Women can also examine their internalized oppression to understand how this may affect their interactions at work (Clover et al., 2017). The focus for feminist leadership is not on what leadership is but instead "the nature of change" that leadership brings (p. 26). Feminist leadership principles include working with allies and valuing a group's skills (Clover et al., 2017). So, although feminist leaders value the communal nature of leadership on one hand, there is also the idea that "feminist leader is a title that is earned" and is equivalent to "a knowledge authority" (p. 27). Feminist leadership has no single definition but is characterized by adapting to change, strategizing, and collaboration. Clover et al. (2017) add, "When we begin with the question of the *nature of change leadership is seeking to bring about,* we can understand feminist leadership not as a naturalized gender attribute of women but as a means to advance agendas to dismantle oppressions of all kinds" (p. 29).

Resistant feminisms include the radical, lesbian, psychoanalytic, and standpoint types (Lorber, 2012). These types of feminisms say there is a "gender ideology" as gender inequality is legitimized through religion, science, and the legal system (Lorber, 2012). These types of feminism discuss "gender inequality in the exploitation of women's bodies, sexuality, and emotions" (p. 11). They favor women-only spaces "for refuge, recreation, religious workshop and cultural production" (p. 12).

Gender-rebellion feminisms include "social construction, multiracial/multiethnic, feminist studies of men, postmodern, and third wave" (p. 12). They examine the social construction of gender, how it is performed, and they critique the binary male/female designation saying that gender can be performed in many ways. They continue to examine how "multiple inequalities" based on race, ethnicity, and social class" (p.12). They "question the stability and necessity of the whole gendered social order" (p. 203).

Scholars use race and feminism to analyze their experiences of the Women's March on Washington, DC. Specifically, they discuss their experiences with the Women's March through the lens of "white feminists/white feminism" as well as the heteronormativity characteristic of white feminism to explore the "tensions inherent within the present sociopolitical environment" (Zarestky et al., 2019, p. 4). The march was critiqued "for appropriating the title of prior Black protests," was viewed as "reactionary" and for only paying "superficial lip service to diversity and inclusion" (p. 8). Opportunities for more research and scholarship that explicitly link adult education and politics and recommendations for practice are needed (Zarestky et al., 2019). For example, educators can call out racism or tell their stories about privilege, and should familiarize themselves with "black feminist blogs and websites" (Zarestky et al., 2019, p. 13) as well as encouraging service-learning for students.

Scholars used critical race feminist theory to frame a study concerning student participation in a class concerning "the historical and contemporary experiences of Women of Color" (Vaccaro, 2017, p. 31). Six Women of Color and four White women participated in focus groups to discuss their participation during the class. Although students spoke about course content, they were hesitant to tell their "experiences with privilege and oppression" (p. 35). Since course materials presented stories of overt oppression for women of color, some of the women of color in the course did not share their stories because they experienced racial microaggressions or did not find their stories "worthy" (p. 36). The complications of intersectionality of race and class differences also led to their silence concerning personal stories. White women did not share their stories of race and they felt their race was only mentioned when White privilege was discussed when in fact, some of them were marginalized by other positionalities such as being immigrants.

Recent scholarship that focuses on feminism in adult learning includes English and Irving's (2015) *Feminism in Community,* that includes topics such as feminist organizations and women's leadership, women-centered health learning, social transformative learning and women, and power, resistance, and informal learning. They note, "Our focus... is on how feminists have negotiated identity and learning in international contexts or multisector environments; struggled to lead, learn, and participate in nonprofit organizations; and enacted a feminist pedagogy through arts processes, Internet fora, and in the community" (p. 1). English (2020) calls for more research and scholarship on adult learning through a critical feminist lens and urges educators to look to Mary Parker Follett's work to "re-infuse adult education with a critical feminist framework" (p. 100). Follett worked in community organizations in the late nineteenth and early twentieth century in Boston, Massachusetts and is known for her concept of having "power with" as opposed to "power over" people (Follett, 1941 as cited English, 2020, p. 102). She valued community members engaging in dialogue to find solutions to their issues and thought individuals' power could be developed (English, 2020). Her ideas of power centered on "collective resistance and change" (p. 103) and were akin to "feminism's struggle to create equality and to have democratic principles at the core" (p. 103). Parker's work can inform feminism and those who seek education for change (English, 2020).

Critical Race Theory

Critical race theory (CRT) developed from discussions in the legal profession. Individuals wanted to address more insidious forms of racism that continued to occur after the passage of the Civil Rights Act of 1964 (Delgado & Stephancic, 2017). Education applies the following CRT concepts, namely, CRT

- argues that racial inequality in education is the logical outcome of a system of achievement premised on competition,
- examines the role of education policy and educational practices in the construction of racial inequality and the perpetuation of normative whiteness
- rejects the dominant narrative about the inherent inferiority of people of color and the normative superiority of white people
- rejects ahistoricism and examines the historical linkages between contemporary educational inequality and historical patterns of racial oppression
- engages in intersectional analysis that recognize the ways that race is mediated by and interacts with other identity markers (e.g., gender, class, sexuality, linguistic background, and citizenship status,
- agitates and advocates for meaningful outcomes that redress racial inequality (p. 122).

For example, Lee et al. (2020) described teaching an Introduction to Critical Race Theory course to incarcerated students. To engage in counter-storytelling, a way used in CRT to center the experiences of people of color, students described their educational experiences through a Critical Race Theory lens. Participants refuted the stereotype that only vocational education is fitting for felons. They stated that Black and Brown felons can think critically. One student, Harrell stated, "Vocational classes possess the potential to pigeonhole you into a narrow field, while the humanities has the potential to broaden your perspective" (p. 6). Another student, Villareal, understood how his background as a child of migrant workers as well as his race affected his school experiences. Telling his educational journey through the lens of CRT helped him begin "a transformative journey from victim to survivor" (p. 8). A White student learned how being raised in an all-White town shaped his worldview and during the course he recognized the history of institutional racism in the United States.

CRT also frames studies in higher education. These include a critical race feminist analysis of men of color matriculating into a higher education doctoral program (Squire et al., 2018). In this autoethnographic study, five Black men explored their intersecting identities (e.g., race, class, gender, sexuality orientation, and nationality), " (b) the doctoral choice process and (c) why they chose to enroll in the program" (p. 19). The commitment to social justice initiatives at the school, the school's affirmation of various marginalized identities, and the collaborative environment were factors in deciding to attend the school (Squire et al., 2018). Einbinder (2020) interviewed 21 Master of Social Work (MSW) students who graduated from a CRT-centric program. A content analysis identified four themes: (a) CRT resonated with students, (b) CRT concepts were hard to master beyond three specific aspects of the Black/White Binary, oppression and privilege, (c) tying the theory to practice was difficult and frustrating and (d) they wanted more examples of tying CRT to practice and a better clarification of the concept of privilege (p. 322).

In the workplace, CRT framed a study on racial microaggressions (Ackerman-Barger et al., 2020). Participants were nurses of color, from new graduates to those with more than 25 years of experience. They ranged in age from their 20 s to over 70 years old. They told of stories of exclusion including social prejudice, needing to defend one's writing skills, being identified as different, being confronted by racism, and discouraged from pursuing a nursing career. Their stories of inclusion included being recognized for being the best student nurse, being supported by others, having good faculty mentors, being validated for who one is, and being defended by one's peers.

Additionally, CRT may be tailored to specific communities. In addition to race, LatCrit "addresses issues often ignored by critical race theorists such as language, immigration, ethnicity, culture, identity, phenotype, and sexuality" (Solorzano & Bernal, 2001, p. 311). Scholars of Asian Crit note "how White supremacy homogenizes" and "essentializes" Asian Americans (p. 940). Asian Crit recognizes how the intersectionality of historical conditions and positionalities affect Asian American's experiences (e.g., colonialism, gender, sexual orientation, ableism). Like CRT, Asian Crit values "story, theory, and practice" and "advocates against imperialism in scholarly arenas and for centering the voices of Asian Americans in education discourse" (p. 941). Brayboy (2005) focuses on colonization's effect on Tribal communities as well as US policies and educational policies that focus on the assimilation of Native Americans in his discussion of TribalCrit (Brayboy, 2005). Brayboy (2005) states, "U.S. policies toward Indigenous peoples are rooted in imperialism, White supremacy, and a desire for material gain" (p. 429).

Queer Theory

A third marginalized positionality is sexuality. Teresa de Lauretis's (1991) piece titled *Queer Theory: Lesbian and Gay Sexualities* introduced the term queer theory. The main concepts of the work include questioning heterosexual identity formation as the norm and the importance of the term "queer" representing men and women, arguing the term "gay" sets up the dominance of the male experience and makes lesbians invisible. Queer theory questions "obvious categories (man, woman, Latina, new, butch, femme), oppositions (man vs. woman, heterosexual vs homosexual), or equations (gender = sex) upon which conventional notions of sexuality and identity rely" (Hennessey, 1993, p. 964). Queer theory possesses a "postmodern conception of identity as an ensemble of unstable and multiple positions contests traditional formulations of sexuality as a personal issue" (p. 964).

Capobianco (2020) uses queer theory lens and "a multi-level analysis of structural contexts" (p. 12) to investigate the inclusion of Lesbian, Gay, Bisexual, Transgender, Questioning/Queer, Intersex, Asexual, and those who describe themselves on other ways such as pansexual or gender fluid (LGBTQIA +) community in international education research. Queer theory "challenge[s] the paradoxes of essentialism and constructivism" (p. 17). Capobainaco (2020) critiques structural levels at the macro, meso, and micro levels in higher education to further interrogate the literature on LGBTQIA + individuals in the literature. Queer theory can be used to critique each structural level. At the macro-level, public policy environments and higher education environments can foster inclusion. Meso-level environments include institutional characteristics that affect LGBTIQIA + inclusion (Capobainaco, 2020). Colleges can support LGBTQIA + individuals through programs, libraries, and counseling centers (Capobainaco, 2020). Micro-level factors include an individual's power to create initiatives and to have allies. From a practical standpoint, faculty must understand at the macro and meso levels how public policies affect international education for their LGBTQIA + students and work for more inclusive policies. Using a queer theoretical lens can "foreground queer voices" (p. 27). International education leaders need to "invest in their individual champions, at the micro-level, working day-today to carry out sustainable change" (p. 28).

Nelson (2002) discusses why queer theory may be useful in teaching English as a Second Language. Queer theory "questions the need for sexual identities" so it "problematizes all sexual identities" rather than making some more acceptable than others (p. 48). The authors delineate how to create "gay-friendly environments for learning and teaching" (p. 45) which include addressing homophobia at the institutional level, including LGBTQIA + examples in the curriculum and in class discussions, "considering the educational needs of these learners, creating work environments where individuals who are LGBTQ feel safe and gaining support from professional organizations" (Nelson, 2002). ESL students can learn that "sexual identities are not universally accomplished but may be produced or "read" in different ways in different cultural contexts" (p. 47).

LIMITATIONS AND CRITIQUES

The previously-described theories and approaches provide a broad spectrum of possibility for explaining learning, knowing, and resisting from a critical and social justice perspectives. And yet, as with all theory, they each have their limitations and legitimate critiques. Here, we present some of those limitations and critiques so that educators, leaders, and organizers may make better informed choices when planning or engaging in learning.

Social-Emancipatory

There are critiques of the social-emancipatory approach to learning. Weiler (1991) notes the similarities between feminist and Freireian pedagogies including the ideas of "social transformation," "common assumptions concerning oppression, consciousness, and historical change" (p.450). Weiler (1991) takes issue with how Freire sees individuals as either the oppressors or the oppressed. Weiler (1991) troubles this simplistic oppressor/oppressed binary noting that individuals could occupy both roles. Although the teacher can "instigate a dialogue between teacher and student, based on their common ability to know the world and to act as subjects in the world" (p. 454), there is the assumption that the teacher and students have "the same reality, the same oppression and the same liberation" (p. 454). Weiler wonders how individuals work through simultaneously being the oppressed and the oppressor, a challenge to some degree addressed by Allman's (2010) approaches.

Weiler (1991) critiques Freire's simplistic view of the teacher/student dynamics. Women instructors who use feminist pedagogy and claim authority in the classroom model this behavior to women students. Alternatively, classroom practices such as negotiating assignments demonstrate how power can be shared. Weiler notes that there is not a unitary "women's experience" or "oppressed person's" experience. She (1991) concludes, "Freire sets out these goals of liberation and social and political transformation as universal claims, without exploring his own privileged position or existing conflicts among oppressed groups themselves" (p. 469). Weiler (1991) states that feminist theorists are challenging "the use of such universal terms as oppression and liberation without locating these claims in a concrete historical or social context" (p. 469).

Freire (2018) assumes that his Western values translate to Eastern and indigenous culture (Bowers, 1983). His oppressed/oppressor binary, negative view of "banking education" and his "use of metaphors like freedom, liberation, critical reflection, praxis, and the idea that man's historical mission is to create a new society." (p. 937). Bowers continues, "Ironically, it is Freire's insistence that the primary purpose of the education process is to change the culture, and to strengthen the learners' capacity to take control of their own lives, that is the source of cultural invasion" (p. 938).

Psycho-Critical

Critics noted Mezirow's lack of attention to the larger social context (Clark & Wilson, 1991; Collard & Law, 1989) and that the theory was not "a comprehensive theory of social change" (Collard & Law, 1989, p. 104). Additional critiques of Mezirow's theory include its modernist framework that "accepts a unitary conception of power and... leaves unquestioned the disciplinary matrix within which education takes place" (p. 90). Cunningham (1992) alleged Mezirow focused on personal transformation over social transformation. Taylor (1997) reviewed 39 studies by Mezirow and found that "affective learning, nonconscious learning, relationships and the collective unconscious" was downplayed (pp. 51–52). In his later work, Mezirow acknowledged the role of emotions and intuition in the transformative learning process (Mezirow, 2009) and the importance of culture in the transformative learning process (Mezirow, 2012).

Critical Race Theory

Some academics are opposed to the critical study of race (Horowitz, 2006; McWhorter, 2000) while others argue that critical race theory is not a theory but a set of tenets (Zorn, 2018). Perhaps the most constructive critique of the theory is offered by Cabrera (2018) who states that although "Crits frequently refer to system racism/White supremacy as the cause of race-based educational inequality...there is not a 'mental model of racism' embedded in CRT" (p. 214). Cabrera suggests that "incorporating the hegemony of Whiteness into CRT can help address some of the current limitations of this approach to higher education scholarship" (p. 224). Adding this theory to CRT helps operationalize racism and also "frames racism as probabilistic as opposed to deterministic [which] moves CRT away from the pitfall of racial essentialism" (p. 225). Inserting the hegemony of Whiteness into the theory means that it may be more likely People of Color may see their oppression but this cannot be assumed and "White people can also become aware of their complicity of the oppression of People of Color" (p. 226).

Feminism

Reformist feminisms such as liberal feminism and Marxist feminism are critiqued for not emphasizing differences among or with race, class, and sexual orientation (Lober, 2012). Liberal feminism is criticized for seeing too many similarities between men and women and not focusing on the different qualities (Lorber, 2012). Socialist feminism is seen as not focused enough on gender (Lorber, 2012). Transnational feminists focus on labor inequalities among women and girls and "patriarchal family structures and cultural practices harmful to women and girls" (p. 90). This type of feminism has "alienated indigenous feminists with their own programs for change" (p. 90).

Gender-resistant feminisms each have their own critiques. Radical feminism is criticized for its lack of focus on racial and ethnic differences among women as well as alienating child-free women by focusing on the value of motherhood (Lorber, 2012). Lesbian feminism idealizes the lesbian relationship and this can divide heterosexual women and lesbians in a common cause

(Lorber, 2012). Psycho-analytic and cultural feminism ignore different ways of parenting and focus on the "heterosexual nuclear family" (p. 168). Standpoint feminism is criticized for lacking a unified perspective and marginalizing men's perspectives.

Gender rebellion feminisms have their critics. A criticism of social construction feminism is that "changing gendered behavior does not necessarily change gendered organizations" (p. 207). Multiracial/multiethnic feminism is taken to task for not focusing enough of feminist issues (Lorber, 2012). Feminist studies of men need to look more closely at "hegemonic men in all the areas where they still dominate, especially corporations and politics" (p. 253). The critiques of the postmodern and queer theory feminisms note that "gender as a status is subsumed under sexual variance" and that the "postmodern category deconstruction and queering undermine the fight for women's rights" (p. 284). Third-wave feminism is seen as focusing too much on individual identities "rather than political groups" and that their political action is not "long-term and sustained" (p. 304).

Queer Theory

Criticisms of queer theory include the challenge of putting it into practice. It is considered an "elitist" and "ivory tower" theory in contrast to the queer activism in the LGBT community (Watson, 2005). Another critique concerns the "commodification of 'queer' and its role in supporting mass consumerism and capitalism" (p. 76). Queer theory is a "repackaged and revitalized commodity used by universities in their efforts for renewed consumption" (p. 76). Hennessey (1993) criticizes the theory for lack of the investigation of class in queer theory.

Queer theory is critiqued for its exclusion of bisexuality. Erickson-Schroth and Mitchell (2009) "has come to theorize only homosexual identity, mainly at the expense of other sexual possibilities (p. 312). Queer theory has stopped short of addressing the power structures that "underlie our organization of sexuality—something bisexuality speaks to on a daily basis" (p. 313). The authors state with hope that "In the most productive circumstances, theories of bisexuality and queer theory will mutually inflect one another, ultimately forcing a reconceptualization of categories of sexual difference that extend far beyond our current notions of them" (p. 313). Queer theory is also criticized for the erasure of "transgender subjectivity" (Namaste, 1996, p. 194) including those who identify or "live as drag queens, transsexuals, and/or transgenders" (Namaste, 1996, p. 183). Once again, although queer theory provides a critique of the heteronormativity of the performance of gender, more critical examination of the context in which drag queens perform, namely a context defined by gay, male culture, is not closely examined by queer theory (Namaste, 1996). Ethnography and enthnomethodology more closely consider the "social, historical, and cultural background" where drag queens perform and have a more nuanced interpretation than does queer theory.

CONSIDERATIONS FOR PRACTICE AND ORGANIZATIONS

From this exploration of multiple approaches to teaching and learning for resistance and both personal and social change, we recognize that it can be a particular conundrum to consider how such perspectives might be applied in practice. Similarly, navigating the continuum from individual to group to organization to society is an ongoing challenge.

First, adult educators and human resource development professionals need to recognize the social and cultural norms of each educational setting. Educators also must be sensitive to how the intersection of various positionalities within particular social contexts affect their experiences. Teachers and learners should understand that individuals can be simultaneously oppressed, engaged in oppression, and working toward open dialogue on such issues. Instructors or leaders need to consider the power dynamics in the classroom or group and how their own personal and cultural biases that may affect instruction. Allman's (2010) principles and aims for critical education, while perhaps a lot to take in, provide an excellent starting point for one's frame of mind and possible shared objectives.

While more straightforward in connection to individual learning, Freire's (2018) social-emancipatory philosophy and Mezirow's (2000) psycho-critical approach both can inform social justice efforts in groups and organizations. Some well-known organizations use dialogue, problem posing and grassroots organizing principles to promote social change. The Highlander Research and Education Center (HREC) (formerly Highlander Folk School) use "people's experience and knowledge to develop collective analysis and strategies for action for positive social change" (2021a, para. 1). In the 1930s and 1940s, the school organized and trained labor leaders. In the 1950s and 1960s, they taught workshops that helped to end segregation and "laid the groundwork for many of the movement's most important initiatives including the Montgomery bus boycott, the Citizenship Schools, and the founding of the Student Nonviolent Coordinating Committee (SNCC)" (2021b, para. 10). Addressing the struggles of those living in Appalachia has been a focus of the organization since the 1960s. From the 1970s-1990s, HREC supported "anti-strip mining and worker health and safety struggles" (2021b, para. 11) ecological issues, and globalization concerns. Since 2000, HREC's mission includes "leadership development among Latino immigrants and young people" (2021a, para. 12) and programs "to advance multi-racial, inter-generational movement for social and economic justice in our region" (para. 13).

Mezirow's (2000) psycho-critical approach may connect well to service-learning and community-based learning such as described by Coyer et al. (2019). This approach makes sense for situations in which working with or serving others may support increased awareness of privilege or oppression for individuals. Ideally, heightened awareness would in turn lead to ally or advocacy behaviors and attitudes.

Approaches grounded in aspects of identity may function for both individual and group/organizational learning and resistance. Such theories may be useful in exploring aspects of one's own identity, validating the views of oppressed or minoritized populations, uncovering systemic bias or oppression in groups, organization, or societal functions, and organizing appropriate responses. As described in prior examples, learning may be designed and led by a professional educator (as in the university-based CRT examples), or community organizers (Zarestky et al., 2019), or undertaken as an individual endeavor, perhaps combining perhaps multiple approaches, such as transformative learning and CRT. In these learning processes, individual learning contributes to group learning and creates a more cohesive, shared knowledge base and, ideally, shared vision for future actions and goals.

CONCLUSIONS

The previously discussed philosophies and theories form a foundation from which to explore their potential for supporting and explaining learning, knowing, and resisting. These approaches help respond to the questions of "What do we hope to accomplish through adult learning?" and "What can adult learning do for us?" from a critical and social justice perspective within organizations and other spaces of organizing. These theories and frameworks provide a starting point from which learners and leaders can build processes that support individual and team development. Through adult learning, we hope to build the knowledge and skills, in ourselves and others, through which we abolish oppression.

REFERENCES

Ackerman-Barger, K., Boatright, D., Gonzalez-Colaso, R., Orozco, R., & Latimore, D. (2020). Seeking inclusive excellence: Understanding racial microaggressions as experienced by underrepresented medical and nursing students. *Academic Medicine: Journal of the Association of American Medical Colleges, 95*(5), 758–763. https://doi.org/10.1097/ACM.0000000000003077

Allman, P. (2010). *Critical education against global capitalism: Karl Marx and revolutionary critical education.* Sense Publishers.

Bowers, C.A. (1983). Linguistic roots of cultural invasion in Paulo Freire's pedagogy. Reprinted in 1993, in *Critical essays on education, modernity, and the recovery of the ecological imperative* (pp. 34–52). Teachers College Press.

Brayboy, B. M. J. (2005). Toward a tribal critical race theory in education. *The Urban Review, 37*(5), 425–446. https://doi.org/10.1007/s11256-005-0018-y

Cabrera, N. L. (2018). Where is the racial theory in critical race theory? A constructive criticism of the crits. *The Review of Higher Education, 42*(1), 209–233. https://doi.org/10.1353/rhe.2018.0038

Capobianco, S. L. (2020). Examining international education research and practice through a queer theory Lens. *Frontiers: The Interdisciplinary Journal of Study Abroad, 32*(1), 12–32. https://doi.org/10.36366/frontiers.v32i1.432

Clark, M. C. & Wilson, A. L. (1991). Context and rationality in Mezirow's theory of transformative learning. *Adult Education Quarterly, 41*(2), 75–91. https://doi.org/10.1177%2F0001848191041002002

Clover, D. E., Etmanski, C., & Reimer, R. (2017). Gendering collaboration: Adult education in feminist leadership. *New Directions for Adult and Continuing Education, 2017*(156), 21–31.

Collard, S., & Law, M. (1989). The limits of perspective transformation: A critique of Mezirow's theory. *Adult Education Quarterly, 39*(2), 99–107. https://doi.org/10.1177%2F0001848189039002004

Collins, P. H. (2000) *Black feminist thought: Knowledge, consciousness, and the politics of empowerment* (2nd ed.). HarperCollins.

Coyer, C., Gebregiorgis, D., Patton, K., Gheleva, D., & Bikos, L. (2019). Cultivating global learning locally through community-based experiential education. *Journal of Experiential Education, 42*(2), 155–170. https://doi.org/10.1177%2F1053825918824615

Cunningham, P. M. (1992). From Freire to feminism: The North American experience with critical pedagogy. *Adult Education Quarterly, 42*(3), 180–191. https://doi.org/10.1177%2F074171369204200306

de Lauretis, T. (1991). *Queer theory: Lesbian and gay sexualities 3*(2). Indiana University Press.

Delgado, R., & Stefancic, J. (2017). *Critical race theory: An introduction 20.* New York University Press.

Delores Huerta Foundation. (2021). About the Delores Huerta Foundation. https://doloreshuerta.org/about-the-foundation/

Dewey, J. (1938). *Experience and education.* Kappa Delta Pi.

Einbinder, S. D. (2020). Reflections on importing Critical Race Theory into social work: The state of social work literature and students' voices. *Journal of Social Work Education, 56*(2), 327–340. https://doi.org/10.1080/10437797.2019.1656574

Elias, J. L. & Merriam S. B. (2005). *Philosophical foundations of adult education* (3rd ed.). Krieger.

English, L. M. (2020). Re-infusing adult education with a critical feminist framework. In F. Finnegan & B. Grummell (Eds.), *Power and Possibility: Adult education in a diverse and complex world* (pp. 97–106). Sense Publishers.

English, L. M., & Irving, C. J. (2015). *Feminism in community: Adult education for transformation.* Brill Sense.

Erickson-Schroth, L., & Mitchell, J. (2009). Queering queer theory, or why bisexuality matters. *Journal of Bisexuality, 9*(3–4), 297–315. https://doi.org/10.1080/15299710903316596

Follett, M. P. (1941). *Dynamic administration: The collected papers of Mary Parker Follett* (H. C. Metcalf & L. Urwick, Eds.). Harper & Brothers.

Freire, P. (2018). *Pedagogy of the oppressed.* (30th anniversary edition). Bloomsbury Publishing.

Formosa, M. (2012). Critical geragogy: Situating theory in practice. *Journal of Contemporary Educational Studies Sodobna Pedagogika, 63*(5), 36–54. https://www.um.edu.mt/library/oar//handle/123456789/1212

Hennessey, R. (1993). Queer theory: A review of the *differences* special issue and Wittig's 'The Straight Mind', *SIGNS: The Journal of Women In Culture and Society 18*(4), 964–973

Highlander Research and Education Center. (2021a). Mission & Methodologies. https://www.highlandercenter.org/mission/

Highlander Research and Education Center. (2021b). Our History. https://www.highlandercenter.org/our-history-timeline/

Hoggan, C. (2016). A typology of transformation: Reviewing the transformative learning literature. *Studies in the Education of Adults, 48*(1), 63–82. https://doi.org/10.1080/02660830.2016.1155849

Holst, J. D. (2011). Frameworks for understanding the politics of social movements. *Studies in the Education of Adults, 43*(2), 117–127. https://doi.org/10.1080/02660830.2011.11661608

Hooks, b. (1994). *Teaching to transgress: Education as the practice of freedom.* Routledge.

Horowitz, D. (2006). *The professors: The 101 most dangerous academics in America.* Regnery Publishing.

Kolb, D. A. (1984). *Experiential learning: Experience as a source of learning and development.* Prentice Hall.

Kroth, M. & Cranton, P. (2014). *Stories of transformative learning.* Sense.

Larri, L., & Whitehouse, H. (2019). Nannagogy: Social movement learning for older women's activism in the gas fields of Australia. *Australian Journal of Adult Learning, 59*(1), 27–52.

Lee, A. J., Harrell, M., Villarreal, M., & White, D. (2020). The value of teaching Critical Race Theory in prison spaces: Centering students' voices in pedagogy. *Humanities, 9*(2), 41.

Lindeman, E. C. (1926). *The meaning of adult education.* New Republic.

Lorber, J. (2012). *Gender inequality: Feminist theories and politics.* (5th edition). Oxford University Press.

Maslow, A. H. (1970). *Motivation and personality* (2nd ed.). HarperCollins.

McWhorter, J. H. (2000). *Losing the race: Self-sabotage in black America.* Free Press.

Merriam, S. B. & Baumgartner, L. M. (2020). *Learning in adulthood: A comprehensive guide* (4th ed.). Jossey-Bass.

Mezirow, J. (2000). Learning to think like an adult: Core concepts of transformation theory. In J. Mezirow & Associates (Eds.), *Learning as transformation: Critical perspectives on a theory in progress* (pp. 3–33). Jossey-Bass.

Mezirow, J. (2009). Transformative learning theory. In J. Mezirow, E. Taylor & Associates (Eds), *Transformative learning in practice* (pp. 18–31). Jossey-Bass.

Mezirow, J. (2012). Learning to think like an adult. In E. W. Taylor & P. Cranton (Eds.), *The handbook of transformative learning: Theory, research, and practice* (pp. 99–115). Jossey-Bass.

Namaste, K. (1996). Tragic misreadings: Queer theory's erasure of transgender subjectivity. In B. Beemyn & M. Eliason (Eds.), *Queer studies: A lesbian, gay, bisexual and transgender anthology.* New York University.

Nelson, C. D. (2002). Why Queer Theory is useful in teaching: A perspective from English as a second language teaching. *Journal of Gay & Lesbian Social Services, 14*(2), 43–54. https://doi.org/10.1300/J041v14n02_04

Ross-Gordon, J. M., Rose, A. D., & Kasworm, C. E. (2017). *Foundations of adult and continuing education.* Jossey-Bass.

Schön, D. A. (1987). *Educating the reflective practitioner.* Basic Books.

Sedgwick, E. K. (2008). *Epistemology of the closet* (2nd ed.). University of California Press.

Solorzano, D. G., & Bernal, D. D. (2001). Examining transformational resistance through a critical race and LatCrit theory framework: Chicana and Chicano students in an urban context. *Urban Education, 36* (3), 308–342. https://doi.org/10.1177%2F0042085901363002

Souza, D. T., Wals, A. E., & Jacobi, P. R. (2019). Learning-based transformations towards sustainability: A relational approach based on Humberto Maturana and Paulo Freire. *Environmental Education Research, 25*(11), 1605–1619. https://doi.org/10.1080/13504622.2019.1641183

Squire, D. D., Kelly, B. T., Jourian, T. J., Byrd, A. M., Manzano, L. J., & Bumbry, M. (2018). A critical race feminist analysis of men of color matriculating into a higher education doctoral program. *Journal of Diversity in Higher Education, 11*(1), 16. https://psycnet.apa.org/doi/10.1037/dhe0000025

Taylor, E. W. (1997). Building upon the theoretical debate: A critical review of the empirical studies of Mezirow's transformative learning theory. *Adult Education Quarterly, 48*(1), 34–59. https://doi.org/10.1177/074171369704800104

Thurer, S. L. (2005). *The end of gender: A psychological autopsy.* Routledge.

Tong, A. & Botts, T. F. (2018). Feminist thought: A more comprehensive introduction (5th ed.). Westview Press.

United Farm Workers. (2021). Our Vision. https://ufw.org/about-us/our-vision/

Vaccaro, A. (2017). Does my story belong? *An Intersectional Critical Race Feminist Analysis of Student Silence in a Diverse Classroom, NASPA Journal about Women in Higher Education, 10*(1), 27–44. https://doi.org/10.1080/19407882.2016.1268538

Watson, K. (2005). Queer theory. *Group analysis, 38*(1), 67–81. https://doi.org/10.1177%2F0533316405049369

Weiler, K. (1991). Freire and a feminist pedagogy of difference. *Harvard Educational Review, 61*(4), 449–475. https://doi.org/10.17763/haer.61.4.a102265jl68rju84

Wood, B. E., Taylor, R., Atkins, R., & Johnston, M. (2018). Pedagogies for active citizenship: Learning through affective and cognitive domains for deeper democratic engagement. *Teaching and Teacher Education, 75,* 259–267. https://doi.org/10.1016/j.tate.2018.07.007

Zarestky, J., Sisco, S., Alston, G. D., & Collins, J. C. (2019). Adult learning and inclusive feminism: Historical and contemporary perspectives on social justice and political activism. *New Horizons in Adult Education and Human Resource Development, 31*(4), 4–17. https://doi.org/10.1002/nha3.20261

Zorn, J. (2018). Critical race theory in education: Where farce meets tragedy. *Academic Questions, 31*(2), 203–211. https://doi.org/10.1007/s12129-018-9699-z

Reconceptualizing Human Capital Theory: Working and Relating on the Global Stage

Maria Cseh, Oliver S. Crocco, and Jessica Hinshaw

Normative Conceptualization of Human Capital Theory

Human Capital Theory (HCT) is the result of an exploitative mindset in economics with origins in the production and commodification of physical capital that spread to the work and expertise of human beings. According to Merriam-Webster (n.d.), the word "capital" is defined as "a stock of accumulated goods especially at a specific time and in contrast to income received during a specified period; accumulated goods devoted to the production of other goods; [and] accumulated possessions calculated to bring in income." In essence, capital refers to assets used to generate income. According to Blair (2011), the term human capital was likely first used by Pigou (1928), but the explicit notion of improving human capabilities as a means of increasing production goes back to Adam Smith (1776). Later, Becker (1993), winner of the Nobel Prize in Economics—and someone often referenced in human

M. Cseh (✉) · J. Hinshaw
The George Washington University, Washington, D.C, USA
e-mail: cseh@gwu.edu

J. Hinshaw
e-mail: Jessica_hinshaw@gwu.edu

O. S. Crocco
Louisiana State University, BatonRouge, LA, USA
e-mail: olivercrocco@lsu.edu

187

J. C. Collins and J. L. Callahan (eds.), *The Palgrave Handbook of Critical Human Resource Development*, https://doi.org/10.1007/978-3-031-10453-4_11

resource development (HRD) scholarship as an early contributor to HRD theory and research—expounded at length on the concept of human capital and wrote about the "activities that influence future monetary and psychic income by increasing the resources in people. These activities are called investments in human capital. The many forms of such investments include schooling, on-the-job training, medical care..." (p. 11). The idea of human capital has expanded over time and led many social scientists to define it broadly as "the skills, knowledge, and capabilities of the workforce of a firm, or of the population of a country, as well as the organizational arrangements and networks of relationships those people have formed that enable them to be more innovative and productive" (Blair, 2011, p. 49). To what end? The normative narrative embedded within HCT is that investments in these forms of human capital drive "the marginal productivity of labour [and that] marginal productivity drives earnings" (Marginson, 2019, p. 287). Thus, investments of this kind, like other forms of financial investment, are meant ultimately to increase profit. While this narrative has been critiqued in a variety of contexts from a host of perspectives (see Lawson, 2012; Bowles & Gintis, 1975) the core of HCT remains intact and economists prefer honing the theory rather than reconceptualizing it (Marginson, 2019).

The tenets of HCT are closely related and embedded in the discourse around human resource development (HRD). In particular, this relationship can be seen in that "[t]he fundamental principle underpinning [HCT] is the belief that peoples' learning capabilities are of comparable value to other resources involved in the production of goods and services" (Nafukho et al., 2004, pp. 545–546). Despite challenges to this view by HRD scholars (McLean & Kuo, 2014; Storberg, 2002) this understanding of human capital has become the normative approach in HRD and can be found explicitly and implicitly in HRD scholarship (e.g., Dobbs et al., 2008; Gaudet et al., 2017; Nafukho et al., 2010; Zula & Chermack, 2007). A view of HRD infused with borrowings from HCT is laden with underlying values. For HRD researchers and practitioners whose work is informed by this legacy and ongoing influence of HCT, a critical HRD approach is needed to unpack the underlying values driving this conceptualization.

First, human capital is different from other forms of capital in that it can only be temporarily lent to others and cannot be owned or traded on the market apart from human slavery (Picketty, 2014, p. 46). In fact, according to Picketty (2014), "attributing monetary value to the stock of human capital makes sense only in societies where it is possible to own other individuals fully and entirely" (p. 163). This elucidates one of the driving values of HCT as ownership of another person. In the mid-nineteenth century, slaveholders would commonly attribute monetary amounts to the value they saw in each of their slaves depending on their physical traits and track their "depreciation" over time (Rosenthal, 2018, p. 127). While slavery is technically illegal around the world, this conceptualization has informed our understanding of human capital today. As Beckert and Rockman (2016) assert, it was "the eighteenth- and nineteenth-century version of *human capital*—property rights in enslaved human beings—[that] helped facilitate the more salutary sense of human capital as a society's commitment to the education of its population in the name of economic growth" (p. 23). The idea of ownership still propels normative HCT in today's "wage slaves," i.e., people working long hours for minimal pay in an endless cycle of poverty (Kaufman, 2020, p. 62).

A second value undergirding HCT is the idea of return on investment. A firm or country invests in its people with the expectation that they will achieve a certain monetary return on their investment. This value positions those in power in control of when, how, and what types of investments are utilized with the primary motivation to derive value from those investments. Seeking a return on one's investment makes any improvement in human capital the means to an end, i.e., profit. This type of instrumental use of people toward an alternate end is philosophically unethical according to the deontological moral philosophy of Enlightenment thinkers such as Immanuel Kant (Kant, 1785). Kaufman (2020) likens this process of treating others as a means to an end as that of the relationship between horses and their masters. In that relationship, masters "select, train, compensate, form into teams, strategize how to get the most value from, direct with orders and commands, motivate and align with carrot/stick inducements... [and] care about their lives and well-being to the degree it is financially profitable" (p. 62). In this paradigm, those in power invest in and control the individual workers as a means of deriving so-called value, i.e., profit.

The normative conceptualization of HCT is embedded in the "American-based high-performance paradigm" (Kaufman, 2020, p. 51) and thus values linear progression according to a series of so-called best practices that lead to desired outcomes. When the primary desired outcome is financial earnings, then the ultimate goal becomes finding the correct combination of investments to maximize that singular outcome. This conceptualization of HCT has led to increasingly extractive thinking about the role and value of people in the workplace and needs reconceptualization. If HRD scholars and practitioners espouse the well-being of humans in the workplace, we must challenge notions such as HCT that perpetually prioritize organizational outcomes above human welfare.

Reconceptualizing HCT

After unveiling the main underlying exploitative values within HCT, it is incumbent upon us to comparatively introduce the values and philosophies of a reconceptualized HCT (see Table 11.1) which are meant to "optimize human interest, organization advancement, and social impact" (Bierema & Callahan, 2014, p. 436). Reconceptualizing HCT requires converting the normative values into a new set of values embedded within the dimension of "relating" (Bierema & Callahan, 2014, p. 437) and preserving the dignity of all people

Table 11.1
Reconceptualizing
Human Capital Theory

Normative Values	Reconceptualized Values
Ownership	Mutuality
Return on Investment	Human Agency
Profit	Dignity
Singular, Dominant Approach	Multiple Culturally Informed Approaches

within the global ecosystem. The concept of relating recognizes that all HRD is "grounded in relationships" (Bierema & Callahan, 2014, p. 437).

Mutuality

Whereas normative HCT values ownership, reconceptualized HCT values mutuality. Mutuality refers to organizational policies and practices that recognize "the legitimate claims of multiple stakeholders" where "employee needs are taken as a goal rather than as a means to an end" (Walton, 1985, p. 49). Given that mutuality is embedded in relationship with others, it goes beyond mere reciprocity or transaction (Lewis & Olshansky, 2016). Rather, mutuality is based on "mutual authenticity, empathy, and empowerment" (Ghosh et al., 2020, p. 322).

This idea of mutuality has been explored in the context of the gig economy where HRD interventions are used to build relationships with gig workers (Yerby & Tickell, 2020). However, in many cases, power differentials between talent managers and gig workers lacked mutuality and led to "building apparently faux relationship[s] to ensure continuity of service for customers" (Yerby & Tickell, 2020, p. 103). For a relationship to embody relating as understood by Bierema and Callahan (2014), it cannot simply leverage interpersonal interactions as a tool to increase organizational commitment. Relationships must authentically value the life and nature of another human as an end to itself. Even in what many consider an inherently hierarchical relationship like mentoring, Bierema and Hill (2005) writes that mentoring "works best when it evolves naturally and there is chemistry and mutuality in the relationship" (p. 558).

Thus, when mutuality becomes the operative value in a relationship, it opens opportunities for learning from one another. This is particularly salient in the global context where learning across cultures is readily available given increased access to technology. Valuing mutuality in the global context requires that HRD scholars and practitioners come to their work "with a sense of humility about the nature of our knowledge" as well as its limits (Cseh et al., 2019, p. 114).

Human Agency

Whereas normative HCT values return on investment, reconceptualized HCT values human agency. Grounded in philosophy (e.g., Aguilar & Buckareff, 2010; Bishop, 1989), the concept of human agency posits that humans can be aware of the choices available to them, make decisions based on their desires, and take responsibility for their decisions (Kuchinke, 2013). In short, the core principles of human agency based on the work of Bandura (1989, 2006) are "intentionality, forethought, self-reactiveness, and self-reflectiveness" (Yoon, 2019, p. 335). Yoon (2019) introduces an agentic HRD model that aligns these human agency principles with HRD processes in the "human agency-based individual transformation (HABIT) model" that recognizes human agency as occurring within an open system and includes reciprocal influences between humans and their environments (p. 344).

This recognition highlights the connection between human agency and the idea of relating according to Bierema and Callahan (2014). In some ways, human agency within open systems represents a paradox or tension between "autonomy and community" (Elliott & Turnbull, 2003, p. 466). Human agency recognizes the somewhat paradoxical reality that human behavior, mindsets, and knowledge occurs within mutually constituting global systems. This kind of "global systems thinking" is a type of mindset that understands how HRD, even when occurring in "local systems" is interconnected with forces around the world (Cseh et al., 2019, p. 110). Thus, valuing human agency paradoxically recognizes the ability of people to make decisions about their lives and work and shares a sense of humility about the limits of our knowledge and skills and their interconnection with the world as a whole.

Dignity

Whereas normative HCT values profit, reconceptualized HCT values dignity. Dignity recognizes the intrinsic value of life, that there are "moral limits to markets," and that some things, e.g., human life, are not commodifiable goods (Sandel, 2012, p. 16). Harkening back to Kant (1785), "everything has either a price or a dignity. Whatever has a price can be replaced by something else as its equivalent; on the other hand, whatever is above all price, and therefore admits of no equivalent, has a dignity" (p. 435, as cited by Pirson et al., 2014). In the context of a reconceptualized HCT, the focal point of all human activity must be the preservation of dignity. Dignity in work occurs when workers have autonomy, a sense of meaning, respect, and opportunities for learning and growth whereas dignity at work is multidimensional and includes wellness, equal opportunity, the ability to voice concerns, and "just reward" (Bolton, 2010, p. 166).

The lens of dignity is useful in reframing discourse in HRD because it highlights the intrinsic value of human life as well as everything that supports human activity in the workplace, "including animals and the planet itself" (Bal et al., 2020, p. 460; Bal, 2017). This subverts normative HCT that not only values profit over human life, but has put profit over the well-being of the environment (Klein, 2014). A dignity perspective can be applied to HRD-related concepts such as employee relations, mentoring, and resilience, which elevates responsibility for these HRD activities from that of the individual to the community. In the case of resilience, HRD practitioners operating from a paradigm of dignity "become concerned with how communities and resilient people may help and support others to be resilient as well" (Bal et al., 2020, p. 461). Dignity is precisely a concern for HRD scholars and practitioners given the centrality of human relationships in organizations and the moral obligation to respond to injustice (Byrd, 2018).

Multiple Culturally Informed Approaches

Whereas normative HCT values a singular, dominant approach to produce the desired performance outcome, reconceptualized HCT values multiple approaches contextualized in a variety of cultural contexts. These reconceptualized values are aligned with the principles of a moral economy (Bolton et al., 2016; Booth, 1994), which predates the market economy common in which the normative conceptualization of HCT is embedded. In a moral economy, "norms, customs and contentions of kinship and small-scale communities are shaped by peoples' implicit conceptions of the 'good' that governs economic life via notions of mutual reciprocity" (Bolton et al., 2016, p. 584). In the context of mutual reciprocity and serving human needs, work becomes "a source of self-actualization" (Bolton et al., 2016, p. 584). Although in past decades discussions about the foundations of a moral economy appeared in scholarly circles, the COVID-19 pandemic has reasserted the need to shift away from normative notions of human capital to this idea of a moral economy. In fact, it is the very concepts of a reconceptualized HCT that are key to successfully navigate a pandemic, i.e., "attending to human well-being, need, and care of self and others" (Makhulu, n.d., para 5). Our heightened consciousness as a result of the pandemic reminds us of Sayer's (2007) observation that we are "vulnerable beings, physically, psychologically economically and culturally dependent on others throughout our lives" (p. 568). Normative HCT takes advantage of these vulnerabilities whereas these reconceptualized values recognize these shared vulnerabilities and elevate values that do not take advantage of them. The pandemic offers a chance for "reprioritizing" and "restructuring" the economy (Michaelson, 2020, para 17–18) to ensure that workers have a sense of dignity, human agency, and mutuality. As our consciousness is developing and paradigms are evolving related to how we conceptualize work, labor, careers, and human development, we must seek to redefine our understanding of expertise on the global stage.

Furthermore, looking to Indigenous understandings could enhance culturally informed perspectives on working and relating on the global stage. While

Indigenous groups have had vastly different experiences and epistemologies that cannot be collectivized, some key elements of Indigenous ways of knowing and being inform the reconceptualization of HCT. For instance in some Indigenous cultures, knowing is tied to being in relationship with self, the community, the universe, and the natural environment (Cajete, 2005). This connection and embeddedness, especially enhanced through storytelling and art, allows individuals and collectives to emphasize respect and care for each other (Cajete, 2017).

Working and Relating on the Global Stage

This section redefines working and expertise from a global perspective with an emphasis on valuing culturally embedded knowledge and being. The colonial legacy of hegemonic forces has devalued culturally embedded knowledge and being by framing work and expertise in terms of what contributes to the economic engine of growth. The contributions of individuals to workplaces are not merely commodifiable packages of knowledge, skills, mindsets, and dispositions, but rather how their time and energy at work contribute collectively to relationships and collective dignity and thriving in the global ecosystem. As presented and discussed in the 2010 documentary film, "Schooling the World: The White Man's Last Burden," the operative paradigm of Western legitimate knowledge and education did not have the intended economic impact (Black, 2010). Several examples of "schooling" the children in low-income regions of the world by using a Western curriculum that forbid children to use their mother tongue and cultural practices, led to the loss of dignity in addition to an array of negative unintended consequences such as higher poverty rates, displacement, loss of indigenous knowledge, and loss of connection to their communities.

A core concept in our work as HRD researchers and practitioners is the idea of expertise (Grenier & Kehrhahn, 2008). Thus, the process of reconceptualizing HCT necessarily leads to a discussion about our understanding of expertise and its meaning in a global environment. When considering the development of expertise, the market economy approach, exemplified by normative HCT, differs clearly from the moral economy, exemplified through the reconceptualized HCT values. In the market economy, expertise is developed as a means of achieving the greatest quantity of work with the goal of gaining the most profit. In a moral economy, expertise is fostered as a means of achieving the greatest quality of work while preserving dignity. For scholars such as Bolton et al. (2016), "defining quality work is an understanding of meaningful and dignified work as a source for human flourishing and well-being, connecting people to each other and the social values and norms of a given society" (p. 583). Thus, expertise and quality of work are inextricably connected with human flourishing and well-being.

When developing expertise, the market economy prioritizes short-term gains, with little regard for the health and wellness of employees (e.g., burnout) to ensure the highest profit. When developing expertise, the moral economy prioritizes long-term gains with high regard for health and human flourishing that ultimately leads to the preservation of human agency and dignity. In the moral economy, profit is still achieved but only as a means to well-being. The fundamental incongruence between the market and moral economies is the notion that human life is made up of "'priceless' aspects of our humanity—including character, virtue, integrity (moral, physical, psychological), knowledge, wisdom, love, trust, and forgiveness" (Pirson et al., 2016, p. 466).

Much of HRD scholarship remains siloed and is infused with ethnocentrism (Cseh & Crocco, 2020) and HRD professionals are often contracted to perform work in organizations operating from HCT's normative values. Thus it is incumbent on both HRD scholars and practitioners to function as change agents within their work. As Elliott and Turnbull (2003) remind us, as HRD scholars and practitioners, we must always be willing to ask, "for what purpose and to what ends we are engaging in HRD" (p. 469).

CONCLUSIONS

In reconceptualizing HCT, we must be conscious of its historical ties to liberalism/neoliberalism and how this has contributed to dominating and intersecting systems of oppression. Normative HCT is an "ideological device which reifies the role of the individual" in their own job attainment (Holborow, 2012, p.94), concealing that human capital acquisition is actually "a social product, not an individual investment decision" (Tomaskovic-Devey et al., 2005, p.58). For instance, many individuals reside in situations of precarity that neoliberalism has exacerbated or even created. Members of the working class, people of color, people with disabilities, immigrants, and displaced individuals, among others, often face many barriers to individual investment in higher education and employers' facilitating their on-the-job learning and skill development. Furthermore, researchers have found that there are substantial differences in earning potential between white males and people of color based on both "endogenous human capital," or employer-facilitated activities that include training, experience, and tenure, as well as returns on educational investment (Tomaskovic-Devey et al., 2005, p. 82).

These phenomena cannot be understood without thoughtfully employing critical race, gender, disability, and Indigenous learning theories to question the foundation and role of HCT within these discriminatory practices and outcomes. While reconceptualized HCT must holistically engage with these theoretical perspectives, two key practices are especially helpful: *recognizing intersecting systems that distribute power unevenly* and *seeking out and listening to counter-narratives*. First discussed by Crenshaw (1991), intersectionality recognizes how social constructs like race, gender, sexual orientation, disability, location, etc., are interconnected. While current emphasis has been placed on individual intersecting identities, Crenshaw's (1991) original intent was to look at these categorizations from a systems lens to understand and critique how society distributes power and advantage to some and not others, requiring a critical understanding of history and context. Using an intersectional lens demands that reconceptualized HCT practitioners question systematic discrepancies for employees, such as in wages/earning potential, who are favored for training and promotion, and who sits in leadership positions within the company.

Listening for counter-narratives "can challenge the perceived wisdom of those at society's center by providing a context to understand and transform established belief systems" (Solórzano & Yasso, 2002, p.36). Counter-narratives often view resistance as a site for generative learning and development, as it gives people on the margins a way to protect themselves and reclaim their power. By challenging centered belief systems and recognizing resistance as something to be leaned into and learned from instead of overcome, reconceptualized HCT can help researchers and practitioners be more empathetic, responsive, and gain a nuanced picture of employee's experiences, expectations, and desires.

References

Aguilar, J. H., & Buckareff, A. A. (2010). *Causing human actions: New perspectives on the causal theory of action.* Massachusetts Institute of Technology Press.

Aktouf, O. (1992). Management and theories of organizations in the 1990s: Toward a critical radical humanism? *Academy of Management Review, 17*(3), 407–431. https://www.jstor.com/stable/258717

Bal, M. (2017). *Dignity in the workplace: New theoretical perspectives.* Palgrave Macmillan.

Bal, M., Kordowicz, M., & Brookes, A. (2020). A workplace dignity perspective on resilience: Moving beyond individualized instrumentalization to dignified resilience. *Advances in Developing Human Resources, 22*(4), 453–466. https://doi.org/10. 1177/1523422320946115

Bandura, A. (1989). Human agency in social cognitive theory. *American Psychologist, 44*(9), 1175–1184. https://doi.org/10.1037//0003-066x.44.9.1175

Bandura, A. (2006). Toward a psychology of human agency. *Perspectives on Psychological Science, 1*(2), 164–180. https://doi.org/10.1111/j.1745-6916.2006.000 11.x

Becker, G. (1993). *Human capital: A theoretical and empirical analysis with special reference to education* (3rd ed.). University of Chicago Press.

Beckert, S., & Rockman, S. (2016). Introduction: Slavery's capitalism. In. S. Beckert & S. Rockman (Eds.), *Slavery's capitalism: A new history of American economic development.* University of Pennsylvania Press.

Bierema, L. L., & Callahan, J. L. (2014). Transforming HRD: A framework for critical HRD practice. *Advances in Developing Human Resources, 16*(4), 429–444. https:// doi.org/10.1177/1523422314543818

Bierema, L. L., & Hill, J. R. (2005). Virtual mentoring and HRD. *Advances in Developing Human Resources, 7*(4), 556–568. https://doi.org/10.1177/152342 2305279688

Bishop, J. (1989). *Natural agency: An essay on the causal theory of action.* Cambridge University Press.

Black, C. (Director). (2010). *Schooling the world: The white man's last burden* [Film]. Lost People Films.

Blair, M. M. (2011). An economic perspective on the notion of 'Human Capital.' In A. Burton-Jones & J.-C. Spender (Eds.), *The Oxford handbook of human capital* (pp. 49–70). Oxford University Press.

Bolton, S. (2010). Being human: Dignity of labor as the foundation for the spirit-work connection. *Journal of Management, Spirituality and Religion, 7*(2), 157–172. https://doi.org/10.1080/14766081003746422

Bolton, S., Laaser, K., & McGuire, D. (2016). Quality work and the moral economy of European employment policy. *Journal of Common Market Studies, 54*(3), 583–598. https://doi.org/10.1111/jcms.12304

Booth, W. J. (1994). On the idea of the moral economy. *American Political Science Review, 88*(3), 653–667. https://doi.org/10.2307/2944801

Bowie, N. E. (2019). Dignity and meaningful work. In R. Yeoman, C. Bailey, A. Madden, & M. Thompson (Eds.), *The Oxford handbook of meaningful work* (pp. 36–50). Oxford University Press.

Bowles, S., & Gintis, H. (1975). The problem with human capital theory—A Marxian critique. *The American Economic Review, 65*(2), 74–82. https://www.jstor.org/stable/1818836

Byrd, M. Y. (2018). Does HRD have a moral duty to respond to matters of social injustice? *Human Resource Development International, 21*(1), 3–11. https://doi.org/10.1080/13678868.2017.1344419

Cajete, G. (2005). American Indian epistemologies. *New Directions for Student Services, 2005*(109), 69–78. https://doi.org/10.1002/ss.155

Cajete, G. (2017). Children, myth and storytelling: An Indigenous perspective. *Global Studies of Childhood, 7*(2), 113–130. https://doi.org/10.1177/2043610617703832

Capital. (n.d.). In *Merriam-Webster's online dictionary* (11th ed.). https://www.merriam-webster.com/dictionary/capital

Crenshaw, K. (1991). Mapping the margins: Intersectionality, identity politics, and violence against women of color. *Stanford Law Review, 43*(6), 1241–1299. https://doi.org/10.2307/1229039

Cseh, M., & Crocco, O. S. (2020). Globalizing HRD academic practice: Developing a global mindset for teaching and research. *Advances in Developing Human Resources, 22*(1), 51–71. https://doi.org/10.1177/1523422319886288

Cseh, M., Crocco, O. S., & Safarli, C. (2019). Teaching for globalization: Implications for knowledge management in organizations. In M. Fedeli & L Bierema (Eds.), *Connecting adult learning and knowledge management* (pp. 105–118). Springer Nature. http://dx.doi.org/10.1007/978-3-030-29872-2_6

Dobbs, R. L., Sun, J. Y., & Roberts, P. B. (2008). Human capital and screening theories: Implications for human resource development. *Advances in Developing Human Resources, 10*(6), 788–801. https://doi.org/10.1177/1523422308325761

Elliot, C., & Turnbull, S. (2003). Reconciling autonomy and community: The paradoxical role of HRD. *Human Resource Development International, 6*(4), 457–474. https://doi.org/10.1080/13678860210155395

Gaudet, C. H., Brown, H. Q., & Lunsford, D. L. (2017). HRD curriculum meets global human capital challenge. *Advances in Developing Human Resources, 19*(2), 124–137. https://doi.org/10.1177/1523422317695211

Ghosh, R., Hutchens, H. M., Rose, K. J., & Manongsong, A. M. (2020). Exploring the lived experiences of mutuality in diverse formal faculty mentoring partnerships through the lens of mentoring schemas. *Human Resource Development Quarterly, 31*(3), 319–340. https://doi.org/10.1002/hrdq.21386

Gilbert, R. (2020). *Building back better with jobs: Mainstreaming business models for decent work.* Business Fights Poverty. https://businessfightspoverty.org/action-too lkit-building-back-better-with-jobs/

Grenier, R. S., & Kehrhahn, M. (2008). Toward an integrated model of expertise redevelopment and its implications for HRD. *Human Resource Development Review, 7*(2), 198–217. https://doi.org/10.1177/1534484308316653

Hadjisolomou, A., & Simone, S. (2021). Profit over people? Evaluating morality on the front line during the COVID-19 crisis: A front-line service manager's confession and regrets. *Work, Employment and Society, 35*(2), 396–405. https://doi.org/10.1177/0950017020971561

Holborow, M. (2012). Neoliberalism, human capital and the skills agenda in higher education- The Irish case. *Journal for Critical Education Policy Studies, 10*(1), 93–111.

Kant, I. (1785). *Groundwork for the metaphysics of morals.* Koenigsberg.

Kaufman, B. E. (2020). The real problem: The deadly combination of psychologization, scientism, and normative promotionalism takes strategic human resource management down a 30-year dead end. *Human Resource Management Journal, 30*(1), 49–72. https://doi.org/10.1111/1748-8583.12278

Klein, N. (2014). *This changes everything: Capitalism vs. the climate.* Simon & Schuster.

Kuchinke, K. P. (2013). Human agency and HRD: Returning meaning, spirituality, and purpose to HRD theory and practice. *Advances in Developing Human Resources, 15*(4), 370–381. https://doi.org/10.1177/1523422313498563

Lawson, T. (2012). Mathematical modelling and ideology in the economics academy: Competing explanations of the failings of the modern discipline?". *Economic Thought, 1*(1), 3–22.

Lewis, C., & Olshansky, E. (2016). Relational-cultural theory as a framework for mentoring in academia: Toward diversity and growth-fostering collaborative scholarly relationships. *Mentoring & Tutoring: Partnership in Learning, 24*(5), 383–398. https://doi.org/10.1080/13611267.2016.1275390

Makhulu, A-E. (n.d.). The moral economy of COVID-19. Duke University Department of Cultural Anthropology. https://culturalanthropology.duke.edu/moral-eco nomy-covid-19

Marginson, S. (2019). Limitations of human capital theory. *Studies in Higher Education, 44*(2), 287–301. https://doi.org/10.1080/03075079.2017.1359823

McLean, G. N., & Kuo, M.-H.C. (2014). A critique of human capital theory from an HRD perspective. *HRD Journal, 5*(1), 11–21.

Merriam-Webster. (n.d.). Capital. In *Merriam-Webster.com dictionary.* https://www.merriam-webster.com/dictionary/capital

Michaelson, C., (2020, May 26). Clap all you like now, but workers with meaningful jobs deserve to be valued in a post-coronavirus economy too. *The Conversation*. https://theconversation.com/clap-all-you-like-now-but-workers-with-meanin gful-jobs-deserve-to-be-valued-in-a-post-coronavirus-economy-too-136472

Nafukho, F. M., Graham, C. M., & Muyia, H. M. A. (2010). Harnessing and optimal utilization of human capital in virtual workplace environments. *Advances in Developing Human Resources, 12*(6), 648–664. https://doi.org/10.1177/152342231 0394791

Nafukho, F. M., Hairston, N. R., & Brooks, K. (2004). Human capital theory: Implications for human resource development. *Human Resource Development International, 7*(4), 545–551. https://doi.org/10.1080/1367886042000299843

Picketty, T. (2014). *Capital in the twenty-first century*. The Belknap Press of Harvard University Press.

Pigou, A. (1928). *A study in public finance*. Macmillan.

Pirson, M., Goodpaster, K., & Dierksmeier, C. (2014). Human dignity and business. *Business Ethics Quarterly, 26*(4), 465–478. https://doi.org/10.1017/S1052150X 0000628X

Pirson, M., Goodpaster, K., & Dierksmeier, C. (2016). Human dignity and business. *Business Ethics Quarterly, 26*(4), 465–478. https://doi.org/10.1017/beq.2016.47

Pissarides, C., & Thomas, A. (2018). *The future of good work: The foundation of a modern moral economy*. Institute for the Future of Work. https://www.ifow.org/publications/the-future-of-good-work-the-foundation-of-a-modern-moral-economy

Rosenthal, C. (2018). *Accounting for slavery: Masters and management*. Harvard University Press.

Sandel, M. J. (2012). *What money can't buy: The moral limits of markets.*

Sayer, A. (2007). Dignity at work: Broadening the agenda. *Organization, 14*(4), 565–581. https://doi.org/10.1177/1350508407078053

Smith, A. (1776). *An inquiry into the nature and causes of wealth of nations*. W. Strahan and T. Cadell.

Solórzano, D. G., & Yosso, T. J. (2002). Critical race methodology: Counter-storytelling as an analytical framework for education research. *Qualitative Inquiry, 8*(1), 23–44. https://doi.org/10.1177%2F107780040200800103

Storberg, J. (2002). The evolution of capital theory: A critique of a theory of social capital and implications for HRD. *Human Resource Development Review, 1*(4), 468–499. https://doi.org/10.1177/1534484302238437

Tomaskovic-Devey, D., Thomas, M., & Johnson, K. (2005). Race and the accumulation of human capital across the career: A theoretical model and fixed-effects application. *The American Journal of Sociology, 111*(1), 58–89. https://doi.org/10.1086/431779

Walton, R. (1985). Toward a strategy of eliciting employee commitment based on a policy of mutuality. In R. Walton & S. Wood (Eds.), *HRM trends and challenges* (pp. 35–69). Harvard Business School Press.

Yerby, E., & Tickell, R. P. (2020). Talent disrupted: Opportunities and threats for human resource development (HRD) strategy and practice in the gig economy through the critical HRD lens. In M. Loon, J. Stewart, & S. Nachmias (Eds.), *The future of HRD (Vol. 1)* (pp. 93–114). Palgrave Macmillan.

Yoon, H. J. (2019). Toward agentic HRD: A translational model of Albert Bandura's human agency theory. *Advances in Developing Human Resources, 21*(3), 335–351. https://doi.org/10.1177/1523422319851437

Zula, K. J., & Chermack, T. J. (2007). Human capital planning: A review of literature and implications for human resource development. *Human Resource Development Review, 6*(3), 245–262. https://doi.org/10.1177/1534484307303762

Challenging Dominant Ideologies and Expanding the Narrative Habitus in Spaces of Organizing Through Critical Thinking

Robin S. Grenier and Kristi Kaeppel

Understanding the human experience comes in part from the stories we tell. The propensity for storytelling, to take discrete events and information and weave them into coherent stories, is one of the defining features of what makes us human (Gelder, 2005). Narratives shape our values, attitudes, and beliefs and help us to make sense of phenomena across a range of contexts— in our personal lives, in our workplaces, and in our society. Storytelling is found across the globe, begins early in life, and is thought to have conferred an adaptive advantage to humans because of the way stories helped transmit critical information needed for survival and facilitated social cohesion (Bietti et al., 2019). As storytellers, we observe events, identify patterns, and from them, build a coherent narrative (Shermer, 2002). This process assuages us as it protects us from two forces that humans tend to be averse to: uncertainty and randomness (de Berker et al., 2016). As a defining characteristic of humanity, we construct stories and use them for making sense of the world. Moreover, according to Jackson (1998) storytelling "fills an existential need to be more than 'bit players' in our lives" (p. 176) and a story can serve as

R. S. Grenier (✉)
Neag School of Education, University of Connecticut, Storrs, CT, USA
e-mail: robin.grenier@uconn.edu

K. Kaeppel
Brown University, Providence, Rhode Island, USA
e-mail: kristi_kaeppel@brown.edu

© The Author(s), under exclusive license to Springer Nature
Switzerland AG 2023
J. C. Collins and J. L. Callahan (eds.), *The Palgrave Handbook of Critical Human Resource Development*, https://doi.org/10.1007/978-3-031-10453-4_12

201

a "vital human strategy for sustaining agency in the face of disempowering circumstances" (p. 14).

Scholars have described stories as allusive (Polletta & Lee, 2006); as "fact wrapped in an emotion that can compel us to take action" (Dickman, 2003, p. 1); and as orienting inscriptions of past performances and scripts for future performances (Barry & Elmes, 1997). More pragmatically, stories are defined by having themes, characters, and plots that help provide a structure to experiences, establish culture and identity, and shape relationships among individuals. And although many like Czarniawska (1997) describe a story as largely linear, having "a plot comprising causally related episodes that culminate in a solution to a problem" (p. 78), some, like Boje (2001), who studied the use of stories in organizations, claim a story isn't linear. Instead, he says it is more cyclic or spiraling, and is a complex, fragmented, and nonlinear performance of sensemaking. These antenarratives (Boje, 2001) are polyphonic, nonlinear, often collective, and sit "in the middle" and in-between." Because they don't have the attached beginnings and endings necessary for achieving narrative closure, the story is highly dynamic, and evolves from "reterritorialize an epic-labyrinth of other antenarratives" (Boje, 2006, p. 40).

Early works in organizational management recognized the potential of stories, with the likes of Mitroff and Kilmann (1976) and Boje and his colleagues (1982) leading the way with investigations of organizational stories and myths. From there, HRD scholars undertook their own research to expose the power of stories to uncover identity development (Horrocks & Callahan, 2006), assist HRD practitioners in mining for cultural levers (Joyner, 2012), and aid organizations as a crisis management tool (Kopp et al., 2011).

Among many outcomes, stories can optimize learning (Tyler, 2007), reveal how White privilege operates (Hunn, et al., 2006), help people deal with change (Beigi et al., 2019), and build empathy (Sautner & Medina, 2018). Yet, as powerful and as helpful as stories can be in making sense of our worlds and work, they can also lead us away from the nuances and complexities of reality due to the human preference to fit events into the most common, but not necessarily most truthful, narratives (Gelder, 2005). Stories can oversimplify and misrepresent the multilayered complexity of people and their cultures, as novelist Chimamanda Ngozi Adichie (TED, 2009) discussed in her TED Talk on the danger of a single story. These enduring, yet myopic stories, can rob people of their dignity by reducing their character and motives to ones found in a familiar narrative arc. Proliferated stories then become part of what Fleetwood (2016) called the narrative habitus that structures the stories we tell about our lives, fitting them into preexisting molds that, in turn, shape social actions. These stories, when so ingrained in our culture, become part of an unquestioned and hegemonic ideology and become the master narrative (McLean & Syed, 2015) that excludes other realities. Conversely, if we take a critical theoretical approach and employ critical thinking as a way to question ideologies in service of human emancipation (Brookfield, 2005), then stories can be instrumental in confronting and countering the very ideologies they often serve to propagate.

If organizations are storytelling systems (Boje, 1991), then the field of HRD must continue to investigate narratives, stories, and storying and more focus must be given to situating stories as a means of perspective-taking that can interrogate and challenge the status quo and long-held assumptions (Galinsky & Ku, 2004; Todd et al., 2011). We sought to contribute to this aim by embracing a more Critical HRD perspective that sees stories as a means of liberating people from their own biases and rigid beliefs. A critical approach to HRD involves exploring and challenging hegemonic narratives that shape how we approach work (Gedro et al., 2014) and calls on the use of learning tools, such as critical thinking and reflection to aid in these humanistic goals (Bierema & Callahan, 2014). Informed by a critical framing of narrative habitus (Fleetwood, 2016; Frank, 2010) that theorizes connections between stories and social practices, this chapter addresses the potential of how critical thinking about the stories told in organizations can challenge dominant ideologies, expose individuals and organizations to alternative views, experiences, and ultimately different ways of operating.

Narrative Habitus Through a Critical Theory Lens

In this chapter, we use the concept of narrative habitus, coined by Fleetwood (2016), to describe the internalization of narratives that shape individual and social action, and then, we describe how critically interrogating stories and creating counternarratives broaden the narrative habitus. One's narrative habitus is influenced by one's culture, which makes certain stories prevalent and available, while limiting or excluding others. In career fields, narrative habitus is found in an organization's culture through its use of "vocabulary, narrative formats, tropes, discursive formats and subject positions" (Fleetwood, 2016, p. 181). In other words, the narrative habitus structures the organization's storying. This is significant as storying reproduces social structures through repetition (Jackson, 1998) and at the same time "sustains and motivates action" and "structure how stories are received, including notions of truth" (p. 181). In many ways, narrative habitus forms what Bourdieu (1979) calls "practical sense" in that, it is difficult for individuals to go beyond their sense of reality because the narrative habitus is absolute and well-tried. When looked at through a critical theory lens, these internalizations, or embodiments of narratives, can be critiqued for perpetuating dominant ideologies that are, by their nature, exclusionary. Some stories fail to receive consideration or the narrative habitus can limit the individual from creating new narratives that might better serve them. As Lyotard (1986) remarked in every telling of a story a way to marginalize or forget another way of telling the story is provided.

Stories in Spaces of Organizing

Organizations are discursive spaces where the telling of stories in and by organizations makes them narrative entities. Stories are a tool for organizational development (Tyler, 2007), learning (Abma, 2003; Whyte & Classen, 2012), and transformation (Driscoll & McKee, 2007) and can facilitate decision-making in these complex environments (Oliver & Roos, 2005). Storytelling provides a means for enacting and communicating one's knowledge (Fisher, 1987), and expressing emotions, values, and meanings (Gabriel, 2000). It also provides a way to organize experiences and frame the development and exchange of interpretations (Boje, 1991). Beigi et al. (2019) define organizational storytelling as an ongoing process of narrative sensemaking and meaning and knowledge construction that occurs among and between those in an organization in order to understand the past, as well as share the present, and construct the future. It is "a collective system in which the performance of stories is a key part of members' sensemaking and a means to allow them to supplement individual memories with institutional memory" (Boje, 1991, p. 106). So, unlike more linear conceptions of storytelling, in spaces of organizing, it is a process plagued by partial tellings, starts and stops, and assumed agreements that are never quite finished (Boje, 2006). But that is not a problem because, despite a lack of plot or any linear coherence, the listeners are so familiar with the recurring themes they can simply fill in the blanks, thus exemplifying how storying can solidify organizational identity and influence sensemaking.

Brown (2006) states that organizational identity is always evolving, yet some stories that communicate an organization's identity remain constant or persist in updated versions. This is because the stories are "…being systematically re-told to new recruits during processes of socialization…" and "certain themes, major protagonists and watershed events may feature in many versions of an organization's identity for years, but changes in circumstances and personnel mean that very few stories and story fragments survive for decades" even in as a reinterpretation, where they are "to be pared down, revised, and co-opted into other stories" (p. 744). As Czarniawska (1997) puts it, stories "capture organizational life in a way that no compilation of facts ever can," this is "because they are carriers of life itself, not just 'reports' on it" (p. 21). In this way, our identities are created and made coherent through narratives we tell about ourselves and others (McAdams et al., 2001; McLean & Syed, 2015) in organizations. As such, it is important to understand that stories are guided by cultural and societal master narratives—the paradigmatic stories of norms, values, morality, and ethics that are dictated by the dominant political and cultural narratives that favor particular discourses of a society or institution. These majoritarian stories (also referred to as monovocals, master narratives, or standard stories) are stories of privilege—whether it be race, gender, class, or other forms, these stories "carry layers of assumptions" that persons in positions of privilege bring with them (Solórzano & Yosso, 2002, p. 28). Thus, majoritarian stories privilege "Whites, men, the middle and/or upper class, and heterosexuals by naming these social locations as natural or normative points of reference" (p. 28). This means that within spaces of organizing, many are excluded from narratives and their imagined selves are limited by the narrative habitus of the cultures and microcultures they find themselves in.

Trice and Beyer (1993) contend that the true context or substance of an organization's culture resides in its ideologies—which are often communicated through the majoritarian story. Dominant, organizational ideologies are the essence of the beliefs of those in power; the internalized (Hallett, 2003), unquestionable norms and attitudes that people accept to guide their thinking and behaviors (Ogbor, 2001; Rusaw, 2000). Ideology is a powerful mechanism since it drives, tacit mental models that shape perceptions in organizations, fuel intraorganizational bias, and lead to more common, and more subtle forms of discrimination (Auster, 1994; Cortina, 2008; Ely & Padavic, 2007; Roberson et al., 2007). It is no wonder those in positions of power tend to reinforce and retain their power by retaining others who likewise embrace stories that perpetuate the dominant ideology (Auster & Prasad, 2016).

This is the case in the stories Boje (1995) highlights in his work, including those from the Walt Disney Company. At Disney, he notes that it is nearly impossible to find the truth in the narratives of the organization because, after the death of Walt Disney, the company began to transform the organization with stories that modernize their core values. To illustrate this difference Boje describes a contrast within the Walt Disney Company between the official stories authored by the company and stories told by employees. For example, Jack Kinney (1988), an early employee of Disney described not being allowed to sign drawings he made with his own name, which led to a perpetuated story that Disney created all the animation himself. Although Boje (1995) emphasizes the possibility that Disney's official story could be true, the dominant ideology perpetuated by the organization's story put Walt Disney at the center which led not only ignored and marginalized significant contributions from people like Kinney without whom the film studio's success would have been unlikely, it creates a myth that "establishes some nonrealistic standards of efficiency which form a permanent sense of failure among employees, because they present real people as ideal individuals, non-realistic patterns of explanation and expectation" (Boguszewicz-Kreft et al., 2019, p. 43).

Beyond stories as myths that project a particular image or ethos, as was the case at Disney, stories told by and in spaces of organizing can work (both intentionally and unintentionally) to marginalize others. From a critical, social constructionist approach then, storying is a social construction that occurs within a context of power that is perceptual in nature. That means that as a cultural manifestation, power is discursively established in stories that are perceived as authoritative. Scholars like Marilyn Byrd (2009) and Evands and Feagin (2012) have described this phenomenon. Byrd (2009), in her study of the leadership experiences of African American women in predominantly White organizations described one participant working in a utility company and explained how organizational narratives about affirmative action and quota hiring lead to coworkers believing she was not deserving of her position and that she likely hadn't earned her job. Thus, rather than marginalization based on only the visible characteristics of individuals, marginalization may in part be a result of the institutionalized stories that are perpetuated by those in power.

INTERROGATING DOMINANT IDEOLOGIES THROUGH CRITICAL THINKING

A critical approach to interrogating stories in spaces of organizing, requires critical thinking as discussed by educators who viewed critical thinking as involving examining power and privilege and the systems that serve to propagate them (Brookfield, 2005; Ten Dam & Volman, 2004), in contrast to seeing critical thinking as an apolitical tool. Critical adult educator, Brookfield (2005), claimed that one of the primary goals of adult learning is to critique ideologies that we have been socialized into but which may not serve us, or others, fairly. Similarly, in taking a critical approach to HRD, we apply the idea of ideology critique to the stories that are embedded in organizations and come to shape employee behavior and attitudes.

The antidote to the hegemonic effect of dominant narratives like those recalled by Byrd's (2009) participants is to interrogate them and recognize them as one set of stories among others that hold equal weight in describing human experiences. In order to do this, individuals must employ their ability to think critically which involves analyzing and evaluating information, identifying assumptions, and refraining from forming conclusions until one has engaged in a comprehensive exploration of the presented ideas and contentions (AAC&U, 2011; Scriven & Paul, 1987). When done by the individual, it can expand their repository of stories, their narrative habitus, and can serve to resist the illusion of a single cohesive narrative to accurately reflect the complexity and ambiguity of reality. Organizational leaders and all those working in organizational settings should interrogate the prevailing stories in their organizations, to ask what stories are obscured by these more prevalent stories, and to consider what opportunities exist to harness critical storytelling to challenge dominant ideologies.

MITIGATING BIAS IN PREVAILING STORIES

Critical thinking is needed to counter the way dominant narratives bias our thinking and can be applied toward the interrogation of long-held stories that shape organizational values and practices, or those that employees may unwittingly be acting on, despite a lack of conscious awareness. While the word bias carries with it a negative connotation, a cognitive bias is often adaptive in that it allows us to make quick decisions. Biases are features of human reasoning, much of which occurs through noting associations and patterns, and coming to expect these patterns (Johnson-Laird, 2010; Kahneman, 2011). Stories are a prominent way we learn these associations, and they are particularly conducive to retention with each retell, strengthening the related associations and crowding out alternative associations (Pasupathi, as cited in Beck, 2015). As such, a story that is repeated often and early in one's life, comes to be *the* expected story.

This becomes an issue when stories are founded on falsities that get reproduced, such as the overinflated notion of Black criminality (Geiger-Onato & Philips, 2003) that arises from stories of "gangsters" and "thugs." This stereotype is a form of bias that arises from exposure to repeated stories that ingrain associations. Western culture has no shortage of workplace stereotypes that limit our conceptions and stigmatize those who fall outside the expected norms. For instance, as a consequence of growing up in a patriarchal society, individuals implicitly encode an association of being male with being a leader, even as research shows women being rated more highly on a majority of leadership competencies including taking initiative, developing others, and engaging in collaboration and teamwork (Zenger & Folkman, 2019).

For instance, in discussing the stories behind healthcare triumphs, Harman (2020) warns of the dangers of over ascribing progress to single male leaders, saying

> [male-dominated storytelling] increases the space men take up in our narratives and imagination on global health, reproducing the norm of men as leaders and individual visionaries that get things done—the single heroic leader with the necessary vision, dynamism, and obstinacy to address the world's greatest problems. Focusing on the individual or emphasising their stubborn quest for change obscures the collaborative nature on which most breakthroughs and delivery in science and global public health take place. (p. 777)

Likewise, founding and hero stories, like the one from Disney, that are ostensibly meant to instill a sense of pride in employees, but upon further scrutiny, can be largely mythical and obscure the contributions of others to bias employees. Critical reflection of organizational stories, helps, as Brookfield (2016) noted, to challenge "assumptions we embrace as being in our best interests when in fact they are working against us" (p. 3). As such, in interrogating prevailing stories, individuals might find that attributing breakthroughs or inventions to a single person or elite group of people reifies the notion that, for instance, a massive compensation disparity is justified since the contributions of those at lower ranks are not viewed as valuable.

This means that for those working in organizations, a critical approach to storytelling/listening in these spaces involves working to be self-aware of how the human mind constructs narratives to make events cohesive (Van Gelder, 2001), and recognize that the storyteller's background and prior experiences will influence the way they perceive and experience events, and thus the way they consume and create stories. In this way, they will know, as Bordieu (1999) wrote, that the only way to see the whole picture is to present a multiplicity of point of views, including those that sometimes conflict and compete.

This consideration of multiple viewpoints is an inherent part of critical thinking; indeed, it's been said that the mark of a critical thinker is the ability to hold multiple views in one's mind simultaneously (Zare & Othman, 2015). It is also this ability that protects individuals from some of the dangers of stories which include readily accepting appealing, yet not wholly true, stories. This underscores the need for more critical consumption of stories. Stories that provoke strong emotions are more appealing and given more attention; and are transmitted than more mundane ones (Brady et al., 2017), which can make them potent tools for propaganda and internet disinformation campaigns (Vosoughi et al., 2018).

Furthermore, debiasing researchers have started to understand interventions that can mitigate the effect of cognitive biases, and many of these involve deliberately prompting people to consider alternative explanations, viewpoints, and stories. In a study meant to inform policing, O'Brien (2009) found that when participants were told to reconsider their initial hypotheses about who was guilty of committing a crime and come up with an alternative, their confirmation bias was reduced when compared to a control group not given this instruction. In another technique that prompts people to think of alternatives, Blair et al. (2001) asked participants to imagine a counter stereotype such as a strong woman, and found that doing so weakened gender bias on the Implicit Association Test (IAT). These interventions, if not repeated, may be short-lived in their impact, but they hold clues to how debiasing can work within spaces of organizing by presenting people with stories that challenge dominant narratives and facilitating storytelling between diverse individuals in order to broaden perspectives and diminish the danger of a single, pervasive story.

REFRAMING STORIES

A second mechanism for interrogating dominant stories, and for weakening the inherent biases in them, is to reframe traditional narratives. Drawing on the work of Benammar (2012), the reframing of a prevailing story first requires a recognition of the core belief presented in the story then analyzing this core belief by addressing the reasons for why that belief exists and identifying "supporting beliefs" that support the core contention. Next, reframing involves constructing the opposite of each of the supporting beliefs to generate variations on these opposites until you find extreme formulations. Finally, in the suspended disbelief stage, you identify and consider contrary supporting beliefs by asking what would happen if they were all true. Note that this process entails key critical thinking skills such as identifying and evaluating premises and generating alternative explanations. When individuals are able to resist the comfort of their existing mental models and evaluate alternatives, they open themselves up to new beliefs and interpretations that broaden their narrative habitus. For instance, crime is often seen as an unethical, shameful act often attributed to an individual's moral deficiencies, but it could also be reframed to be viewed as the rational outcome of constrained opportunities. Such a reframing does not negate the real human suffering that crime causes; in fact, understanding its driving forces could help prevention efforts. In organizational settings, a parallel is that of the "troublemaker" employee who frequently dissents and is generally not looked upon favorably, despite the fact that dissent can have beneficial outcomes such as improving communication channels in the workplace (Kassing, 2008).

The importance of reframing narratives is in the destigmatization and demarginalization of those who have different stories and traits; by acknowledging and honoring those stories, valuable perspectives are provided. In an organizational setting, calling into question prevailing practices and reframing organizational narratives promotes inclusivity as members are invited to take a critical stance and reframe narratives that are more reflective of their lived experiences and values. This, in turn, can foster more agency and autonomy, which are associated with a range of workplace benefits (Deci et al., 2017).

SEEKING OUT COUNTER-NARRATIVES

Although some organizational narratives are chosen (or enforced) as official, legitimate, or correct and require critical interrogation, Czarniawaska (2017) notes that there are still yet other stories that exist and can act to defy and contradict the master narrative. A third way to challenge dominant stories in spaces of organizing is through counternarratives (Bamberg & Andrews, 2004) or counterstories (Nelson, 1995). These are described as "the stories which people tell and live which offer resistance, either implicitly or explicitly, to dominant cultural narratives" (Andrews, 2004, p. 1). As Frandsen et al. (2016) point out, counternarratives may not be told publicly (although social media use is becoming more common) and instead may only be shared within specific communities. Because counternarratives are situated in the "unmanaged" terrain of an organization (Gabriel, 1995), HRD practitioners may need to engage in role negotiation (Frandsen et al., 2016) and look for clues about the existence of counternarratives in union meetings, break and lunch rooms, and in training environments in order to harness these stories to expand the organization's narrative habitus, and call on such stories to facilitate perspective-taking that promotes empathy.

Counternarratives or stories act as a mode of critical thinking of both individuals and organizations in ways that allow for a more holistic and inclusive view of reality in four ways. First, the counterstory can put a human and face to an experience, while building community among those at the margins of society. For example, communities like those in Philadelphia (Good, 2016), when faced with possible closures of local schools, subverted the dominant narrative of closures espoused by state and local governments by naming their own reality (Ladson-Billings, 2013) through stories that captured the symbolic, emotional, and historical implications of these closures on people, their community, and their sense of place. The counter stories were a response to normative accounts that also helped audiences connect with the struggles faced by those served by the threatened schools. As Syeed (2019) notes, these narratives countered the calls for school closures while also intentionally challenging the dominant logic and reasoning of officials by providing identity-constituting portrayals (Nelson, 1995) of those affected.

Second, counter stories challenge the dominant, perceived wisdom of the majority through a form that encourages understanding and transforming of established belief systems. Bourdieu and Wacquant (1992) describe organizations as places of struggle that are occupied by the dominant who toil to establish hegemony through means including controlling the master narrative. Even so, what is considered the master narrative and what is considered counter are not static and instead are subject to placement shifts (Bamberg & Andrews 2004).

Utoft (2020) offers her own work during the COVID-19 pandemic as one-way contribution to a dominant narrative in academia. While she addresses a common refrain of the relationship between academic productivity and work–life balance, she offers a counter to the more commonly accepted image of women academics during that time—that of those balancing work and motherhood. Her story is, according to her, a "generally overlooked position from which to approach these issues" (p. 779) because although much has been written about women academics who are working mothers, this has become a master narrative that ignores those like herself who are single and live alone. Utoft (2020) asks her reader,

> During the lockdown, scholars who are mothers struggle to get any work done and feel guilty towards their kids when they finally sit down to work (Ahmad, 2020; De Coster, 2020). The question thus becomes: will you accept my struggle as legitimate when it strays from this normative perception of what the struggles of 'women' in their work lives presumably concern? (p. 783)

She highlights how she does not fit into the master narrative while also (and equally important) offers a counternarrative to the perceptions that being a single woman means being a carefree academic, unhampered by familial responsibilities and thus able to write and research prolifically. In this way, Utoft encourages understanding of her experience and works to transform the established belief systems around academic productivity and work–life balance for women academics.

Third, counternarratives can act against isolation experienced by those at the margins of society by emphasizing that they are not alone. For Jason Arday (Arday & Mirza, 2018), his counternarrative *Being Black, Male and Academic* provides a personal account of his exclusion and marginalization and his struggle to find a place in academia. This included the sense of isolation that came from "his 'hidden' inner battle to overcome his hurdles as an autistic learner" that were "very different from his outward facing presence as a 'visible' Black male, which unsettles the normativity of Whiteness within academia" (p. 12). Thus, counter stories like Araday's serve to disrupt the social isolation he experienced at his institution and the stigma he felt as an autistic learner, while at the same time building empathy in others.

Lastly, counter stories are a teaching tool (Delgado, 1989; Lawson, 1995). This was the case in Kenya when counternarratives were used to challenge long-standing master narratives regarding female genital mutilation (Gabriel, 2016). The prevailing story mimicked beliefs that women are naturally promiscuous unless their genitalia is physically altered (Mackie & LeJeune, 2009), that mutilation is a prerequisite for marriage, and as a rite of passage into adulthood (Matanda et al., 2021). The resistance to this dominant narrative was dramatic. Serving as opposition to genital mutilation counter stories slowly educated the public to gradually alter the authoritative text (Hansen & Lundholt, 2019; Kuhn, 2017) and although genital mutilation still occurs, ultimately the persistent counternarratives resulted in bans on female genital practices (Hansen & Lundholt, 2019).

CONCLUSION

Critical thinking and reflection take us beyond our everyday, intuitive modes of thinking and making decisions and prompts us to think more carefully, effortfully, and slowly. Reflection allows us to make meaning of events and connect them to other experiences, which facilitates learning (Kolb, 1984). However, as Brookfield (2016) points out, not all reflection is necessarily critical. He argues that critical reflection requires uncovering power and hegemony and the ways that assumptions can work against individuals' interests. Further, critical reflection can be applied to autobiographical stories that individuals hold about themselves where they are positioned as protagonists in the organizational story, or conversely, as victims of circumstances depending on the degree of agency one thinks they have (McAdams, 2013). Without critical reflection, individuals, especially those in senior positions, who have met their goals may generalize the experiences in their own story to others. The storyteller assumes others in the organization should be able to reach the same goals, yet the individual fails to recognize the external forces that contributed to their success (Pasupathi, as cited in Beck, 2015).

Spaces of organizing serve as a narrative habitus as storying becomes a transition bridge (Ashforth, 2001) spanning identities, roles, and social interactions to bring about a future that would not otherwise exist (Boje, 2001, 2010; Yolles, 2007). Departing from traditional applications of storying, we suggest that stories can serve as a means of interrogating organizational hegemony. As a tool for critical thinking, storying can critique existing ideologies, practices, and narratives, initiate debiasing, and facilitate perspective-taking that promotes empathy.

A critical approach to HRD invokes the spirit of critical theory to emphasize humanity and allow for the self-actualization of all individuals. In practice, this means turning a critical eye on the stories, assumptions, and perspectives that underlie our work. Questioning how stories of the heroic leader or problem solver perpetuates existing power structures and diminishes the power of others, or how stories maintain the status quo and receive a mythical place in the company while other stories are ignored is important. Those working to support employee and organizational development should teach critically reflective practices that encourage individuals to interrogate an organization's narratives.

Although on the surface, engaging in critical reflection might be viewed as destabilizing to the organization, it can benefit the organization. For instance, stories that champion overworking can promote the work habits that lead to burnout which comes at a cost of errors and employee turnover (Abate et al., 2018). Challenging this story, and acknowledging it as one way of working among others, can signal that other narratives are possible—such as the employee who worked within her normal hours, balanced her job responsibilities with being a caretaker, and nevertheless played a vital role in the success of the organization.

The ability to look beyond one's own experiences, or the dominant narratives and show compassion and the possibility of different realities, creates another benefit. Through critical reflective practices that Bell (2010) called 'concealed stories' can be exposed. Concealed stories are those that attempt to challenge the status quo, but these narratives are "constantly overshadowed, pushed back into the margins, and conveniently 'forgotten' or repressed" (p. 43) in organizations. For example, the story of the employee who dutifully worked for the company, without incident, and despite this failed to get promoted or was let go when the job was moved overseas. Such a story clashes with the American notion of meritocracy and the company's promise that through hard work one can live comfortably with all their basic needs met. The myopic, uncritical individual who ponders the story will search for a reason to justify the employee's conditions rather than reconsider the dominant narrative those perceptions are built on. Without a critically reflective approach to the existing narrative habitus means that concealed stories are not only illconsidered, but also are not even considered a possibility.

We have proposed that one way forward is to harness the human proclivity for storytelling; first, by recognizing how stories become embedded in individuals and spaces of organizing as part of a narrative habitus that is capable of both propelling and limiting social action in accordance with how behaviors fit or do not fit archetypal cultural narratives. From there, we have a duty to interrogate these narratives and ask critical questions about whose story it is and whose story *it is not*. Then, we can facilitate democratic learning through the sharing of stories and perspectives between stakeholders, which works to blunt the power of hegemonic narratives and opens up space for a multitude of perspectives and realities.

References

Abate, J., Schaefer, T., & Pavone, T. (2018). Understanding generational identity, job burnout, job satisfaction, job tenure and turnover intention. *Journal of Organizational Culture, Communications and Conflict, 22*(1), 1–12.

Ahmad, A. S. (2020, March 27). *Why you should ignore all that Coronavirus-inspired productivity pressure.* The Chronicle of Higher Education.

Abma, T. A. (2003). Learning by telling: Storytelling workshops as an organizational learning intervention. *Management Learning, 34*(2), 221–240.

Andrews, M. (2004). Opening to the original contributions: Counter-narratives and the power to oppose. In M. Bamberg and M. Andrews (Eds.), *Considering counter-narratives: Narrating resisting making sense* (pp. 1–6). John Benjamins Publishing.

Arday, J., & Mirza, H. S. (Eds.). (2018). *Dismantling race in higher education: Racism, whiteness and decolonising the academy.* Springer.

Ashforth, B. E. (2001). *Role transitions in organizational life: An identity-based perspective.* Lawrence Erlbaum.

Association of American Colleges and Universities (AAC&U). (2011). Critical thinking VALUE rubric. Retrieved from https://www.aacu.org/value/rubrics/critical-thinking

Auster, E. R., & Prasad, A. (2016). Why do women still not make it to the top? Dominant organizational ideologies and biases by promotion committees limit opportunities to destination positions. *Sex Roles, 75*, 177–196. https://doi.org/10.1007/s11199-016-0607-0

Auster, E. (1994). Demystifying the glass ceiling: The organizational and interpersonal dynamics of gender bias. *Business in the Contemporary World, 5*(3), 47–68.

Bamberg, M., & Andrews, M. (Eds.),s (2004). *Considering counter-narratives: Narrating, resisting, making sense* (Vol. 4). John Benjamins Publishing.

Barry, D., & Elmes, M. (1997). Strategy retold: Toward a narrative view of strategic discourse. *Academy of Management Review, 22*(2), 429–452.

Beck, J. (2015). Life's stories. *The Atlantic.* Retrieved from: https://www.theatlantic.com/health/archive/2015/08/life-stories-narrative-psychology-redemption-mental-health/400796/

Beigi, M., Callahan, J., & Michaelson, C. (2019). A critical plot twist: Changing characters and foreshadowing the future of organizational storytelling. *International Journal of Management Reviews, 21*(4), 447–465. https://doi.org/10.1111/ijmr.12203

Bell, L.A. (2010) *Storytelling for social justice. Connecting Narrative and the Arts in Antiracist Teaching.* Routledge.

Benammar, K. (2012). *Reframing: The art of thinking differently.* Boom.

Bierema, L., & Callahan, J. L. (2014). Transforming HRD: A framework for critical HRD practice. *Advances in Developing Human Resources, 16*(4), 429–444.

Bietti, L. M., Tilston, O., & Bangerter, A. (2019). Storytelling as adaptive collective sensemaking. *Topics in Cognitive Science, 11*(4), 710–732.

Blair, I. V., Ma, J. E., & Lenton, A. P. (2001). Imagining stereotypes away: The moderation of implicit stereotypes through mental imagery. *Journal of Personality and Social Psychology, 81*(5), 828.

Boguszewicz-Kreft, M., Kreft, J., & Żurek, P. (2019). Myth and Storytelling: The Case of the Walt Disney Company. In J. Kreft, S. Kuczamer-Kłopotowska, & A.

Kalinowska-Żeleźnik (Eds.), *Myth in Modern Media Management and Marketing* (pp. 22–49). IGI Global.

Boje, D. M. (1991). The Storytelling organization: A study of story performance in an office- supply firm. *Administrative Science Quarterly, 36*, 106–126. https://doi.org/10.2307/2393432

Boje, D. M. (1995). Stories of the storytelling organization: A postmodern analysis of Disney as "Tamara-land." *Academy of Management Journal, 38*, 997–1035. https://doi.org/10.5465/256618

Boje, D. M. (2001). *Narrative methods for organizational and communication research.* Sage.

Boje, D. M. (2006). Breaking out of narrative's prison: Improper story in storytelling organization. *Storytelling, Self, Society, 2*(2), 28–49.

Boje, D. M. (2010). *Storytelling and the future of organizations: An antenarrative handbook.* Routledge.

Boje, D. M., Fedor, D. B., & Rowland, K. M. (1982). Myth making: A qualitative step in OD interventions. *The Journal of Applied Behavioral Science, 18*(1), 17–28. https://doi.org/10.1177/002188638201800104

Bourdieu, P. (1979) La Distinction: Critique sociale du jugement. Paris: E´ditions de Minuit. [Translated by Richard Nice. (2010) Distinction: A Social Critique of the Judgement of Taste. London: Routledge].

Bourdieu, P. (1999). *The space of points of view* (pp. 3–5). Social suffering in contemporary society.

Bourdieu, P., & Wacquant, L. J. (1992). *An invitation to reflexive sociology.* University of Chicago press.

Bowles, M. (1997). The myth of management: Direction and failure in contemporary organizations. *Human Relations, 50*(7), 779–803.

Brady, D. L., Brown, D. J., & Liang, L. H. (2017). Moving beyond assumptions of deviance: The reconceptualization and measurement of workplace gossip. *Journal of Applied Psychology, 102*(1), 1.

Brookfield, S. (2005). *The power of critical theory for adult learning and teaching.* Open University Press.

Brookfield, S. (2016). So what exactly is critical about critical reflection. Researching critical reflection: *Multidisciplinary perspectives,* 11–22.

Brown, A. D. (2006). A narrative approach to collective identities. *Journal of Management Studies, 43*(4), 731–753. https://doi.org/10.1111/j.1467-6486.2006.00609.x

Byrd, M. Y. (2009). Telling our stories of leadership: If we don't tell them they won't be told. *Advances in Developing Human Resources, 11*(5), 582–605.

Cortina, L. M. (2008). Unseen injustice: Incivility as modern discrimination in organizations. *Academy of Management Review, 33*(1), 55–75. https://doi.org/10.5465/AMR.2008.27745097

Czarniawska, B. (1997). *Narrating the organisation: Dramas of institutional identity.* University of Chicago Press.

Czarniawska, B. (2017). *An emergence of narrative approaches in social sciences and in accounting research.* The Routledge Companion to Qualitative Accounting Research Methods. Routledge, 184–199.

de Berker, A. O., Rutledge, R. B., Mathys, C., Marshall, L., Cross, G. F., Dolan, R. J., & Bestmann, S. (2016). Computations of uncertainty mediate acute stress responses in humans. *Nature Communications, 7*, 10996.

Deci, E. L., Olafsen, A. H., & Ryan, R. M. (2017). Self-determination theory in work organizations: The state of a science. *Annual Review of Organizational Psychology and Organizational Behavior, 4,* 19–43.

De Coster, M. (2020). Towards a relational ethics in pandemic times and beyond Limited accountability, collective performativity and new subjectivity. *Gender, Work & Organization,* 1– 6.

Delgado, R. (1989). Storytelling for oppositionists and others: A plea for narrative. *Michigan Law Review, 87*(8), 2411–2441. https://doi.org/10.2307/1289308

Dickman, R. (2003). The four elements of every successful story. *Reflections: The SOTL Journey for Knowledge, Learning, and Change. 4*(3), 51–58.

Driscoll, C., & McKee, M. (2007). Restorying a culture of ethical and spiritual values: A role for leader storytelling. *Journal of Business Ethics, 73*(2), 205–217.

Ely, R., & Padavic, I. (2007). A feminist analysis of organizational research on sex differences. *Academy of Management Review, 32*(4), 1121–1143. https://doi.org/10.5465/AMR.2007.26585842

Evans, L., & Feagin, J. R. (2012). Middle-class African American pilots: The continuing significance of racism. *American Behavioral Scientist, 56*(5), 650–665.

Fisher, W. (1987). *Human communication as narration: Toward a philosophy of reason, value, and action.* University of South Carolina Press.

Fleetwood, J. (2016). Narrative habitus: Thinking through structure/agency in the narratives of offenders. *Crime, Media, Culture, 12*(2), 173–192. https://doi.org/10.1177/1741659016653643

Frandsen, S., Kuhn, T., & Lundholt, M. W. (Eds.). (2016). *Counter-narratives and organization.* Routledge.

Frank, A.W. (2010). *Letting stories breathe: A socio-narratology.* University of Chicago Press.

Gabriel, Y. (2000). *Storytelling in organizations: Facts, fictions and fantasies.* Oxford University Press.

Gabriel, Y. (2016). Narrative ecologies and the role of counter-narratives: The case of nostalgic stories and conspiracy theories. In S. Frandsen, T. Kuhn & M. Wolff Lundholt (Eds.), *Counter-narratives and organization,* (pp. 208–226). Routledge.

Gabriel, Y. (1995). The unmanaged organization: Stories, fantasies and subjectivity. *Organization Studies, 16*(3), 477–501.

Galinsky, A. D., & Ku, G. (2004). The effects of perspective-taking on prejudice: The moderating role of self-evaluation. *Personality and Social Psychology Bulletin, 30*(5), 594–604. https://doi.org/10.1177/0146167203262802

Gedro, J., Collins, J. C., & Rocco, T. S. (2014). The "critical" turn: An important imperative for human resource development. *Advances in Developing Human Resources, 16*(4), 529–535.

Geiger-Oneto, S., & Phillips, S. (2003). Driving while black: The role of race, sex, and social status. *Journal of Ethnicity in Criminal Justice, 1*(2), 1–25.

Gelder, T. V. (2005). Teaching critical thinking: Some lessons from cognitive science. *College Teaching, 53*(1), 41–48. https://doi.org/10.3200/CTCH.53.1.41-48

Good, R. M. (2016). Histories that root us: Neighborhood, place, and the protest of school closures in Philadelphia. *Urban Geography, 1–24,*. https://doi.org/10.1080/02723638.2016.1182286

Hallett, T. (2003). Symbolic power and organizational culture. *Sociological Theory, 21*(2), 128–149. https://doi.org/10.1111/1467-9558.00181

Hansen, P. K., & Lundholt, M. W. (2019). Conflicts between founder and CEO narratives: Counter-narrative, character and identification in organisational changes. *Frontiers of Narrative Studies, 5*(1), 94–111.

Harman, S. (2020). The danger of stories in global health. *The Lancet, 395*(10226), 776–777.

Horrocks, A., & Callahan, J. L. (2006). The role of emotion and narrative in the reciprocal construction of identity. *Human Resource Development International, 9*(1), 69–83. https://doi.org/10.1080/13678860600563382

Hunn, L., Guy, T. C., & Manglitz, E. (2006). Who can speak for whom? Using counter storytelling to challenge racial hegemony. *Proceedings of the annual conference of the Adult Education Research Conference.*

Jackson, S. (1998) Telling stories: Memory, narrative and experience in feminist research and theory. In K. Henwood, C. Griffin, & A. Phoenix A (Eds.), *Standpoints and differences: Essays in the practice of feminist psychology* (pp. 45–64).

Johnson-Laird, P. N. (2010). Mental models and human reasoning. *Proceedings of the National Academy of Sciences, 107*(43), 18243–18250.

Joyner, F. F. (2012). Story mining: Eliciting stories and mining their content for cultural levers. *Human Resource Development International, 15*(5), 627–633. https://doi.org/10.1080/13678868.2012.722843

Kahneman, D. (2011). *Thinking, fast and slow.* Macmillan.

Kassing, J. W. (2008). Dissent in organizations. *The International Encyclopedia of Communication.*

Kinney, J. (1988). *Walt Disney and assorted other characters*: An Unauthorized Account of the Early Years at Disney's. Harmony Books.

Kolb, D. A. (1984). *Experiential Learning: Experience as the Source of Learning and Development.* Prentice-Hall.

Kopp, D. M., Nikolovska, I., Desiderio, K. P., & Guterman, J. T. (2011). "Relaaax, I remember the recession in the early 1980s …": Organizational storytelling as a crisis management tool. *Human Resource Development Quarterly, 22,* 373–385. https://doi.org/10.1002/hrdq.20067

Kuhn, T. (2017). Communicatively constituting organizational unfolding through counternarrative. In S. Frandsen, T. Kuhn & M. Wolff Lundholt (Eds.), *Counternarratives and organization*, (pp. 17–42). Routledge.

Ladson-Billings, G. (2013). Critical race theory—What it is not! In M. Lynn & A. Dixson (Eds.), *The handbook of critical race theory in education* (pp. 34–47). Routledge.

Lawson, R. (1995). Critical race theory as praxis: A view from outside to the outside. *Howard Law Journal, 38*(2), 353–370.

Lyotard, J.-F. (1986). *The postmodern condition: A report on knowledge.* Manchester University Press.

Mackie, G., & J. LeJeune. (2009). "Social Dynamics of Abandonment of Harmful Practices: A New Look at the Theory." Special Series on Social Norms and Harmful Practices, *Innocenti Working Paper 6*: 2009–06.

Matanda, D. J., Kabiru, C. W., Okondo, C., & Shell-Duncan, B. (2021). Plurality of beliefs about female genital mutilation amidst decades of intervention programming in Narok and Kisii Counties, Kenya. *Culture, Health & Sexuality,* 1–32.

McAdams, D. P., Josselson, R. E., & Lieblich, A. E. (2001). *Turns in the road: Narrative studies of lives in transition.* American Psychological Association.

McAdams, D. P., & McLean, K. C. (2013). Narrative identity. *Current Directions in Psychological Science, 22*(3), 233–238.

McLean, K. C., & Syed, M. (2015). Personal, master, and alternative narratives: An integrative framework for understanding identity development in context. *Human Development, 58*(6), 318–349. https://doi.org/10.1159/000445817

Mitroff, I. I., & Kilmann, R. H. (1976). On organizational stories: An approach to the design and analysis of organizations through myths and stories. In R. H. Kilmann, L. R. Pondy, & D. P. Slevin (Eds.), *The management of organization design: Strategies and implementation* (pp. 189–207).

Nelson, H. L. (1995). Resistance and insubordination. *Hypatia, 10*(2), 23–40.

Neuhauser, P. (1993). *Corporate legends and lore: The power of storytelling as a management tool.* McGraw-Hill Companies.

O'Brien, B. (2009). Prime suspect: An examination of factors that aggravate and counteract confirmation bias in criminal investigations. *Psychology, Public Policy, and Law, 15*(4), 315.

Ogbor, J. O. (2001). Critical theory and the hegemony of corporate culture. *Journal of Organizational Change Management, 14*(6), 590–608. https://doi.org/10.1108/09534810110408015

Oliver, D., & Roos, J. (2005). Decision making in high velocity environments: The importance of guiding principles. *Organization Studies, 26*(6), 889–913. https://doi.org/10.1177/0170840605054609

Polletta, F., & Lee, J. (2006). Is telling stories good for democracy? Rhetoric in public deliberation after 9/11. *American Sociological Review, 71*(5), 699–721.

Roberson, L., Galvin, B. M., & Charles, A. C. (2007). When group identities matter: Bias in performance appraisal. *Academy of Management Annals, 1,* 617–650. https://doi.org/10.1080/078559818

Rusaw, A. C. (2000). Uncovering training resistance: A critical theory perspective. *Journal of Organizational Change Management, 13*(3), 249–263. https://doi.org/10.1108/09534810010330896

Scriven, M., & Paul, R. (1987). Critical thinking as defined by the national council for excellence in critical thinking. *8th Annual International Conference on Critical Thinking and Education Reform,* 25–30.

Sautner, K., & Medina, G. (2018). Using storytelling to establish justice: How civic education can change police community relations. *Journal of Museum Education, 43*(2), 114–125. https://doi.org/10.1080/10598650.2018.1454734

Shermer, M. (2002). *Why people believe weird things: Pseudoscience, superstition, and other confusions of our time.* Macmillan.

Solórzano, D. G., & Yosso, T. J. (2002). Critical race methodology: Counter-storytelling as an analytical framework for education research. *Qualitative Inquiry, 8*(1), 23–44. https://doi.org/10.1177/107780040200800103

Syeed, E. (2019). "It just doesn't add up": Disrupting official arguments for urban school closures with counterframes. *Education Policy Analysis Archives, 27,* 110.

TED. (2009, October 7). The danger of a single story: Chimamanda Ngozi Adichie [Video]. YouTube. https://www.youtube.com/watch?v=D9Ihs241zeg

Ten Dam, G., & Volman, M. (2004). Critical thinking as a citizenship competence: Teaching strategies. *Learning and Instruction, 14*(4), 359–379.

Todd, A. R., Bodenhausen, G. V., Richeson, J. A., & Galinsky, A. D. (2011). Perspective taking combats automatic expressions of racial bias. *Journal of Personality and Social Psychology, 100*(6), 1027–1042. https://doi.org/10.1037/a0022308

Trice, H. M., & Beyer, J. M. (1993). *The cultures of work organizations*. Prentice-Hall.

Tyler, J. A. (2007). Incorporating storytelling into practice: How HRD practitioners foster strategic storytelling. *Human Resource Development Quarterly, 18*(4), 559–587. https://doi.org/10.1002/hrdq.1219

Utoft, E. H. (2020). 'All the single ladies' as the ideal academic during times of COVID-19? *Gender, Work & Organization, 27*(5), 778–787.

Van Gelder, T. (2001). How to improve critical thinking using educational technology. In G. Kennedy, M. Keppell, C. McNaught, & T. Petrovic (Eds.), *Meeting at the Crossroads. Proceedings of the 18th Annual Conference of the Australian Society for Computers* In Learning In Tertiary Education (ASCILITE 2001) (pp. 539–548). Biomedical Multimedia Unit, The University of Melbourne.

Vosoughi, S., Roy, D., & Aral, S. (2018). The spread of true and false news online. *Science, 359*(6380), 1146–1151. Chicago.

Whyte, G., & Classen, S. (2012). Using storytelling to elicit tacit knowledge from SMEs. *Journal of Knowledge Management, 16*(6), 950–962. https://doi.org/10.1108/13673271211276218

Yolles, M. (2007). The dynamics of narrative and antenarrative and their relation to story. *Journal of Organizational Change Management, 20*(1), 74–94. https://doi.org/10.1108/09534810710715298

Zare, P., & Othman, M. (2015). Students' perceptions toward using classroom debate to develop critical thinking and oral communication ability. *Asian Social Science, 11*(9), 158.

Zenger, J., & Folkman, J. (2019). *Women score higher than men in most leadership skill*. Harvard Business Review.

CHAPTER 13

Applying Critical (Self) Advocacy and Social Justice Through Employee Resource Groups

Stephanie Sisco

As diversity and inclusion develops into an essential part of organizational planning and strategic practice, employee resource groups (ERGs) have become significantly more popular since they first emerged in the 1960s. Organizations have used ERGs as a strategy to engage their employees, minimize discrimination litigation, create diverse communities of practice, and invest in a more socially conscious workplace. Essentially, ERGs provide organizational leaders with the opportunity to directly address their employees' workplace concerns, recognize diverse perspectives, and collaboratively work to enhance diversity and inclusion. On account of these initiatives, research indicates that employee resource groups positively contribute to performative outcomes (Dutton, 2018; Welbourne & McLaughlin, 2013). Equally important, studies have demonstrated that there are benefits that directly influence the learning and development of marginalized employees (Friedman & Holtom, 2002; Sisco, 2020; Welbourne et al., 2017). ERGs have also become a way for ERG members to increase their visibility and strengthen their voice in organizations (Colgan & McKearney, 2012; Jordon, 2020; McNulty et al., 2018).

In some instances, organizations have provided opportunities for their ERG members to bring attention to oppressive structures and social systems that exist within and outside the workplace (Briscoe & Safford, 2010; Byrd, 2022; Green, 2018; Sisco, 2019). As organizations and their employees become

S. Sisco (✉)
University of Minnesota, Minneapolis, MN, USA
e-mail: pleasant@umn.edu

219

J. C. Collins and J. L. Callahan (eds.), *The Palgrave Handbook of Critical Human Resource Development*, https://doi.org/10.1007/978-3-031-10453-4_13

more openly involved in sociopolitical affairs, additional research is needed to support and justify this shift. Thus, the main objective of this chapter is to describe how ERGs serve as an emancipatory strategy for marginalized, outnumbered, and/or excluded employees to practice advocacy and pursue social justice. In doing so, core principles of critical social theory and self-advocacy are used as a framework to examine the ongoing need for members of oppressed social groups (i.e., LGBTQ, persons with disabilities, women, and racial minorities) to incite social change for themselves and their communities.

THEORETICAL FOUNDATION AND BACKGROUND

Disparate histories and proximity to power and privilege create different experiences for each minority group. Social divisions created by those who have power and privilege have also contributed to how minorities experience the world differently and understand their positionality in relation to others (Sisco, 2020). These differences should be taken into consideration when attempting to support the needs and ambitions of each group. Critical social theory (CST) recognizes the value of understanding the singularity of each social group as a way to appropriately respond to the needs of each group and minimize social disparities (Calhoun, 1995). This idea is grounded in Pierre Bourdieu's social theory to understand how people make sense of their reality. Collins (2019) explained that the critical perspective of social theory brings attention to the social problems, social inequalities, social injustices, and other social barriers that need to be dismantled in order to improve the conditions of society. So, in many ways, CST draws upon participatory and emancipatory processes to raise social consciousness and promote social justice, which leads some critical social theorists to position advocacy as a natural and necessary function of emancipation (Collins, 2019; Freeman & Vasconcelos, 2010). Thus, the aim of CST is to liberate those who are dominated by oppressive structures and social systems. CST suggests individuals constrained by such an environment should seek enlightenment, empowerment, and emancipation.

When describing each outcome of CST, Calhoun (1995) explained that enlightenment should be sought by members of the oppressed social classes, so they are encouraged to acknowledge the extent of their disadvantages and understand how those in power maintain social disparities. Empowerment refers to finding ways to disrupt the oppressive structures and social systems that interfere with opportunities for growth and liberation for marginalized social groups, which requires mobilizing energy and confidence among those who are disadvantaged. Under this belief, these acts of advocacy are intended to lead to emancipation. In the context of this text, CST is used as motivation to pluralistically examine how ERG members of different minority groups practice self-advocacy to overcome oppressive structures and social systems.

Self-Advocacy

Advocacy is widely understood as the support of a particular cause or policy (Merriam-Webster, n.d.), yet, *self-advocacy* is not found in all dictionaries that include "advocacy," and it does not have a universal definition. Nonetheless, self-advocacy has been commonly perceived as both a social movement (Atkinson, 2002; Petri, 2017; Williams & Shoultz, 1982) and as the act or skill of advocating (Sievert et al., 1988; Van Reusen et al., 1994).

Research about self-advocacy is mainly situated in disabilities literature. Common themes concerning self-advocacy in the field of disabilities largely focus on empowerment (Petri, 2017; Stack & McDonald, 2018; Williams & Shoultz, 1982) and self-determination (Field & Hoffman, 1994; Wehmeyer & Palmer, 2003). Test and his colleagues (2005) summarized these components in a conceptual framework based on numerous definitions of self-advocacy. They identified four main facets of self-advocacy: (a) knowledge of self, (b) knowledge of rights, (c) communication, and (d) leadership. When describing each component they explained that knowledge of self is about knowing one's own interests, preferences, strengths, needs, learning style, and other personal attributes. Knowledge of rights included knowing one's rights as a citizen, and more specifically, knowing one's rights as a member of a particular protected class based on antidiscriminatory laws (e.g., race, gender, age, national origin, people with physical and mental disabilities, etc.). Awareness of necessary actions and resources needed to incite political action was also connected to one's knowledge of their rights. The remaining two features of the conceptual framework are less about personal descriptions and more about how to enact self-advocacy.

Drawing from a collection of other important literature in self-advocacy (i.e., Nezu et al., 1991; Wehmeyer & Lawrence, 1995; Wehmeyer & Palmer, 2003), Test and others (2005) argued that communication and leadership were dominant traits of self-advocacy. They described communication as a multifaceted skill that involves subcomponents such as negotiation, persuasion, articulation, listening, and compromise. Subsequently, they explained the last component, leadership, involves learning the roles and dynamics of a group, as well as how to function within a group of individuals who share common experiences. The authors emphasized that leadership is about developing an understanding of one's role within a group, and ultimately finding the courage to stand up for the rights of their group(s) through organized participation and political action. The culmination of each of the above components provides an orientation into self-advocacy, and it also helps verify that self-advocacy is not the same as self-promotion or self-agency.

Understanding the Distinction: Self-Advocacy, Self-Promotion, and Self-Agency

Acknowledging the distinction between self-advocacy, self-promotion, and self-agency is not intended to measure the salience of each term or suggest they are mutually exclusive. Rather, the point of distinction is to understand that they are not interchangeable constructs. Self-advocacy is focused on changing sociopolitical outcomes through self-awareness and collaboration (Petri, 2017; Test et al, 2005). Contrastingly, self-promotion and self-agency have an individualized focus that is not necessarily intertwined with political action or the empowerment of a particular group. However, self-agency does acknowledge the importance of dominance and power. Self-agency, commonly referred to as *agency*, is rooted in the words "agent" and "action," and when combined, agency is defined as "a thing or person that acts to produce a particular result" (Burkitt, 2016, p. 323). When used in the social sciences, agency remains an ambiguous concept that is applied in different ways. "The sociological lens conceptualizes agency as a function of social structures within which individuals are embedded, whereas, psychological traditions conceptualize agency as a self-regulatory capacity of an individual" (Clark, 2016, p. 5). Despite these differences, each definition acknowledged that individuals are a part of a system or structure where their autonomy is conditional. Thus, the underlying focus is the individual. Self-agency does not inherently bring attention to a particular event, cause, or issue like self-advocacy.

The distinction between self-advocacy and self-promotion is more straigthforward than self-agency. Similar to self-advocacy, self-promotion is understood as a tactic to secure sociopolitical gains (Giacalone et al., 1986), but the two terms are different because self-promotion is considered situational and individualistic, whereas self-advocacy is oppositional and communal. However, the individualism of self-promotion alludes to the additional complexity of self-advocacy. Atkinson (2002) explained that self-advocacy can be recognized as an individualized pursuit of "speaking up" for one's self, but "self-advocacy, in practice, often means advocacy in a group, 'speaking up' with and for other people..." (p. 122). On account of this distinction, the remainder of the text will recognize self-advocacy as the collective practice to "speak up" for the interests and causes affiliated with a group.

Self-Advocacy in Practice

As mentioned, self-advocacy is a central theme within disabilities research. Attention to self-advocacy is also a relevant concern in the practice of providing disability services and resources to the disability community (Stack & McDonald, 2018; Wehmeyer & Palmer, 2003). Aside from ensuring, they are provided with the necessities to address their disabilities, Pennell (2001) explained that persons with disabilities must develop a mindset that places them in a position to feel empowered to protect themselves against mistreatment, which can range from being abused to being blatantly ignored. The author further explained the ability to develop this mindset is a socialization process that requires intentionality and guidance.

When considering the determination needed to achieve this level of self-care and independence, self-advocacy can be recognized as an invaluable skill (Van Reusen et al., 1994) that can be taught through training and instruction (Nezu et al., 1991; Sievert et al., 1988). Much of this work takes place within education, mainly within higher and adult education (Field & Hoffman, 1994; Wehmeyer & Palmer, 2003). Pennell (2001) claimed the objective of learning self-advocacy is to "stand up for oneself and to help other people with disabilities stand up for themselves by speaking up, speaking out, and speaking loud" (p. 223). Others have recognized the importance of obtaining these goals, and have developed tools and strategies to help persons with disabilities find their voice and project their voices with self-determination and purpose. When reviewing the effectiveness and range of services offered in an organizational context, Rath and Royer (2002) argued that technological instruments, program modifications, and individualized assistance were among the most effective approaches to enhance the learning experience of persons with disabilities. The authors also found that counseling, therapy, and self-development programs were helpful ways to help persons with disabilities "cope with disabilities within the[ir] environment and by aiding them in making decisions about their future" (p. 370). In each instance, persons with disabilities benefit from the support of others as they develop and refine their self-advocacy skills.

Equal Treatment and Persons with Disabilities. Adult learners with disabilities pursuing adult basic education (i.e., literacy, numeracy, general educational development exam preparation, English as a second language, etc.,) and/or workforce education have traditionally been underserved due to funding availability and access to trained personnel with attention to special needs (Ross-Gordon, 2001). Despite the lack of resources and support for adult learners with disabilities, it is not uncommon for employees with disabilities to manage their challenges without the help of their employer. When referring to the ingenuity and independence of persons with disabilities, Hiemstra (1998) explained that both self-directed learning strategies and self-advocacy are needed to enhance the learning experience and personal empowerment of learners with physical, cognitive, psychological, and other disabilities. Gadbow and Du Bois (1998) expanded on Hiemstra's claims to emphasize that the relationship between self-directed learning and self-advocacy should begin prior to persons with disabilities entering the workforce to prepare for disrespectful bias and negative attitudes that are often directed toward persons with disabilities in the workplace. By developing self-directed learning skills in the classroom, the authors believe that persons with disabilities will be more equipped with the confidence and sensibility to advocate for suitable accommodations and pursue career opportunities. Meeting this objective continues to be an ongoing problem. In 2020, only 17.9% of persons with disabilities who are of working age (18–64) worked full or part-time, compared to 61.8% of the non-disabled population; and although these figures take into consideration the coronavirus, there is a significant gap in percentage points between the two groups (U.S. Bureau of Labor Statistics, 2021). On account of this statistic, other ways to support persons with disabilities in the workplace are needed to address this disparity. In fact, the extent of this issue may be larger than what is reflected in the data, because self-disclosure among individuals who self-identify as a person with disabilities is known to be underrepresented, especially in the workplace.

Equal Rights and the LGBTQ Community. The issue of self-disclosure in the workplace is a problem that is experienced by other minority groups. In particular, members of the lesbian, gay, bisexual, transgender, and queer (LGBTQ) community have been known to struggle with personal and external barriers to sharing their sexual orientation and/or gender identity and expression with their employer and colleagues. In this case, self-advocacy has been promoted as a way to overcome social stigma and advocate for equal rights, protection, and benefits at work (Sadowski, 2020). Self-advocacy can also be described as a dynamic and contextually based strategy that has more than one approach. Daly-Cano and colleagues (2015) explained that the limitations and fear to practice self-expression in intimidating environments lead many individuals to engage in different approaches to self-advocacy, such as *proactive, reactive, and retroactive*. The authors described *proactive self-advocacy* as intentional acts to ensure their basic needs are met, while *reactive self-advocacy* happens when individuals are placed in a position to confront a challenging situation with the aim to maintain their basic needs. People who have experienced *retroactive self-advocacy* "learned from their mistakes and advocated for themselves after reflecting about their failures" (Daly-Cano et al., 2015, p. 221). By recognizing that there are various approaches to self-advocacy, the authors acknowledged that external locus of control may inhibit the ability of individuals to activate their self-advocacy, even when they have a strong willingness to practice self-advocacy.

Despite the growing awareness of LGBTQ concerns and self-advocacy, the practice of advocacy has a greater presence in community-based and other non-profit organizations. LGBTQ advocacy groups have a history of engaging in social and political affairs to defend the LGBTQ community. Youth homelessness, social inclusion, legal protection, and the mental and physical safety of the LGBTQ community are some of the leading concerns that are given attention by advocacy groups (Sadowski, 2020). Within these groups, self-advocacy is used as a strategy to navigate institutions and systems that have historically and presently excluded LGBTQ members from receiving the same resources and opportunities as their non-LGBTQ counterparts. Thus, the fight for equal rights remains central to the civil rights and social movements associated with the various identities and beliefs represented within the LGBTQ community.

Equal Opportunity and Women. Similar to other minorities, the struggle for women to achieve equality is a continued sociopolitical movement, but self-advocacy at the individual level maybe difficult for some women. Issues of domestic violence, gender bias, and harassment often go unreported because many women practice silence (Fitzgerald et al., 1995; Wang & Huh, 2019). This was evident in a study by Cortina and Magley (2003) who researched over 1,100 women working in the public sector and found that silence among victimized women is a learned condition that is reinforced by social norms that inherently place men in positions of power and authority, which can leave some women to feel powerless. They concluded that many women fear work retaliation and social retaliation from both other women and their men colleagues; and consequently, they choose to remain silent victims. Other studies have recognized similar trends (Aiston & Fo, 2021; Wang & Huh, 2019), and women's advocacy organizations and feminist groups like, *Equality Now, TimesUp, Zonta International*, and several others have responded to this phenomena by leading self-advocacy campaigns to encourage women to activate their voice, as well support other women who have experiences of being minimized, objectified, and/or mistreated.

The ability to openly express confidence and work toward the empowerment of women is a privilege that is not afforded to all women. Within many western cultures, women have gradually challenged social and political restraints that limit their personhood. In the United States, for instance, women have joined together to demand the right to vote, enter the workforce, pursue education in science, technology, engineering, and mathematics, join the military, and hold positions of influence and power in local, state, and federal government. Essentially, women have advocated to simply have the same opportunities as men. Other women from different countries, cultures, and political regimes have had a different experience of finding autonomy in their womanhood. In the twenty-first century, there are many women around the world who are still gravely oppressed. Some women have restrictions on how they dress, how they speak to men, what they learn and cannot learn, and some women are told to limit their desires. The latter is particularly true in the case of female genital mutilation (FGM), a form of women circumcision that has no medical benefit but a form of control over women's bodies. According to the World Health Organization (2020), FGM is an ongoing practice that is performed in over thirty countries across Africa, Asia, and the Middle East. In these countries, women are stripped away of the same opportunity to feel the same sensations as men. Unfortunately, FGM and other invasive customs are so ingrained into some cultures, that self-advocacy may be perceived as a threat to an entire culture, as opposed to a form of liberation.

Although women in the United States have made great strides gaining access to opportunities that were formerly exclusive to men, there are still other barriers that disrupt the progress of some women, especially those who identify as Black, Indigenous, or other Persons of color (BIPOC). BIPOC women do not receive the same opportunities as White women. Their experience is compounded by racism, xenophobia, and other discriminatory ideologies. Studies have continually identified that White and non-White women do not obtain the same level of success, which has been explained through multiple frameworks including, *intersectionality* (Crenshaw, 1991), *interlocking oppression* (Kalsem & Williams, 2010), and *race-gender subordination* (Harris & Leonardo, 2018). Such research further solidifies the privilege experienced by both White men and women. So, although women are still in the pursuit of having the same position of power as men, White women seem to be better positioned to obtain the same opportunities as men. White women who fail to acknowledge their White privilege create in-group tension and additional oppressive experiences for racially marginalized women (Kalsem & Williams, 2010). This means that the lack of awareness of some White women has been known to deny the reality that Black women, Indigenous women, and other women of color are subjected to a greater extent of sexism and misogyny on account of racism. Therefore, women who identify as BIPOC and hope to have the same opportunities as White men and women tend to advocate for more than equality.

Equity and Racial Minorities. Knowing the difference between equality and equity is important to understanding why equality is an insufficient way to support certain minority groups. Moreover, it should also be understood that equity has become a more progressive and intentional way to acknowledge the conditions that make our experiences different and unique from one another. When examining equity from a sociological perspective, Cook and Hegtvedt (1983) explained that "All social systems evolve mechanisms for distributing valued resources and for allocating rights, responsibilities, costs, and burdens" (p. 218). Thus, equity is a conditional approach to the process of distribution that recognizes that some groups require more or less, while equality maintains that all should receive the same.

In the case of racial minorities, equality has been problematic for some groups because they carry a history of being exploited, exterminated, and/or excluded, which has implications on their present and future standing. So, although society may have removed the mechanisms (e.g., slavery, racial segregation, colorlines, etc.) that once dehumanized their ancestors, the disruption to the development, learning, and progress of racial minorities presently places them at a disadvantage to those who once benefited from exploiting, exterminating, and/or excluding racial minorities. This idea is further complicated because there is evidence that seems to suggest the same dehumanizing and discriminatory practices still exist in our current social systems. These examples include the disproportionately high incarceration of Black men, the routine killing of Black men by the police, the denial and deprivation of citizenship for non-White immigrants, the disparity in the quality of healthcare experienced by BIPOC women, as well as the lack of pathways and support to careers, professional development, and suitable education for BIPOC youth. Moreover, there are also individuals who continue to deny that racism still exist; thereby, interrupting the progress of racial equity by attempting to remove critical race theory from general education curricula, overturn affirmation action laws, rebuke diversity, equity, and inclusion initiatives, adopt colorblind ideology and/or promote claims of White victimhood. On account of these continued attacks on racial equity, it reinforces the need for racial minorities to obtain more resources and support to offset the potential opportunities, intellectual growth, and social capital that has been deprived by the injustices that characterize their history and arguably their present reality.

Understanding the Need to Practice Self-Advocacy via ERGs

Social issues, like the obstacles described above, have always had implications for the law and order of society, and they also shape the way individuals understand themselves and the world around them. Accordingly, social issues are relevant in many contexts. In regard to social issues in the workplace, there has been a gradual shift from only acknowledging how social issues impact organizational outcomes, to now realizing how social issues influence the well-being of their stakeholders (Colgan & McKearney, 2012; Dutton, 2018; Green, 2018). This shift has created new ways for employers to communicate, support, and learn from their employees. Company social intranets, employee engagement strategies, and new executive positions and departments dedicated to diversity, equity, and inclusion have become trends that signify that employers are aspiring to be more responsive to the needs of their stakeholders and consumer base (Jeske & Calvard, 2020). Employee resource groups have become another way for organizations to develop their employer–employee relationship (McNulty et al., 2018; Welbourne & McLaughlin, 2013), and become more attuned to social issues (Jordan, 2020; Sisco, 2020). To further understand the function of employee resource groups, this section serves as a literature review by exploring how ERGs are used by different minority groups to advocate for their needs in the workplace, and to advance social justice for their respective communities.

The growing trend of ERGs is not an entirely new concept. They share a few similarities with labor unions. Both ERGs and labor unions share the same objective of representing the self-interest of employees, but one of the key differences is how they are affiliated with organizations. Labor unions have traditionally operated as external entities that are comprised of employees seeking protection and representation (Kurtz, 2002), while ERGs are integrated into the organization as a resource for employees seeking support and opportunities to collaborate with their colleagues and their employer (Jordan, 2020; Welbourne et al., 2017). Additionally, both ERGs and labor unions negotiate policies and resources with their employer, but labor unions have been characterized of having an adversarial relationship, while ERGs have been known to work in conjunction with organizational leaders to advance their agendas (Freeman & Rogers, 1999; Kurtz, 2002; Sisco, 2020). Despite these particular differences, the efforts of ERGs and labor unions tend to benefit the members within and outside their group, yet the key distinction between ERGs and labor unions is the proactive approach and commitment put forth by organizations that offer ERGs. Ultimately, organizations use ERGs to help fulfill their social responsibility by offering professional development opportunities to underrepresented employees, providing leadership pathways, and sponsoring community outreach initiatives (Friedman & Holtom, 2002; Jordan, 2020; Sisco, 2019). These objectives are intended to benefit all social groups that are represented by employee resource groups, but it is important to recognize the unique barriers experienced by each ERG. According to the limited research that specifically focuses on employer-sponsored social networks, Table 13.1 presents a brief overview of studies that focus on ERGs from the perspective of a particular social group. Additionally, only sources that addressed *workplace challenges* and *organizational support* were included in the literature review.

Among the 15 studies that were reviewed, only 5 ERGs focused on the experiences of racial minorities, but each of those studies mentioned different aspects of how race has impacted the experience of each group. Workplace visibility, for instance, was an issue that seemed to impact racial minorities in different ways. Baker (2009) found that Hispanic professionals struggled with being placed in low-visibility jobs, and Weng (2019) explained that many Asian American professionals are seen as being from the same culture and background, and they are assumed to have the same expertise and are often placed in the same positions. Contrarily, Sisco (2019) explained that Black professionals deal with negative preconceptions of their Blackness and the Black community that results in limited opportunities and low representation. Other issues relating to workplace visibility include the restriction of cultural symbols and customs that are salient to indigenous groups, as discussed in a study by McPhee et al. (2017), who examined the experiences of Aboriginal ERG members.

Other findings were focused on LGBTQ ERGs. This group had the most sources for a single social group, and a range of workplace challenges was identified, which included issues that were closely related to other groups. Barriers to self-disclosure, for example, were mentioned as a problem for LGBTQ ERG members (Creed & Scully, 2011; Githens & Aragon, 2009), and Vogel (2011) also identified self-disclosure as a workplace challenge for persons with disabilities. Within these studies, the authors described how some ERG members question their employer's commitment to support them. Apprehension to engage in interpersonal relationships was mentioned as well. McNulty et al. (2018) specifically mentioned that LGBTQ members may experience fear of being "outed" by their co-workers. Moreover, Raeburn (2004) described how dominating social norms have created obstacles for some LGBTQ ERG members to acculturate into the workplace and advance their careers. This point was similar to a concern that surfaced among women ERG members. On more than one occasion, it was determined that some women feel pressure to project masculine characteristics and submit to patriarchal norms as a strategy to aid their professional development and career progression (Bierema, 2005; Donnelle & Langowitz, 2009); however, other women in ERGs have taken

Table 13.1 Critical Review of Employee Resource Groups

Employee Resource Group	Workplace Challenges	Organizational Support	Sources
Aboriginal	Maintaining cultural ideals and customs while assimilating into the workplace	Sponsor annual community conference Provide resources for back-to-school and Christmas gifts programs Establish mentorship programs with senior managers	McPhee et al., 2017
Asian American	Learning and navigating American culture as a first/second generation immigrant Being misidentified as a monolithic group that share the same expertise and ambitions	Collaborate with ERGs across different companies to support Asian American community organizations Sponsor events for Pan-Asian fundraisers	Weng, 2019
Black/African American	Struggling to find a sense of belonging due to the lack of social support and career optimism Combating negative and false perceptions of Black professionals that manifest via racial bias, stereotyping, and tokenism	Provide career development opportunities and workforce training for ERG members Offer diversity training to all employees Host roundtable discussions to engage in critical dialogue about social issues impacting the Black/African-American community (i.e., racism, education and employment disparities) with internal and external ERG members Provide financial support to schools and community organizations to help minimize racial disparities	Friedman et al., 1998 Sisco, 2019
Hispanic	Being placed at lower to mid-level pay grades in jobs with low visibility, despite being members of the largest minority racial group	Participate in community-based supplier programs to support Hispanic-owned businesses	Baker, 2009

(continued)

Table 13.1 (continued)

Employee Resource Group	Workplace Challenges	Organizational Support	Sources
LGBT(Q)	Confronting HR about employment benefits and workplace safety. Examples include: -Managing self-disclosure -Requesting restrooms for trans employees -Reporting incidents of harassment Combating gender norms and social stigma established by heteronormativity	Acknowledge request to update and/or create more inclusive and "welcoming" policies for LGBT members Proclaim the organization as an ally to the LGBT community and encourage employees to undergo training and/or self-identify as allies	Colgan & McKearney, 2012 Creed & Scully, 2011 Githens & Aragon, 2009 Raeburn, 2004 McNulty et al., 2018
Persons with Disabilities	Navigating a work environment with mobility barriers and enduring working conditions that trigger invisible disabilities Being reluctant to self-disclose a disability in fear of stigmatization, resulting in repercussions related to job security	Accommodate request to improve working conditions and flexibility for persons with disabilities and caregivers Encourage all employees to engage in volunteerism to support disability awareness Inform all employees about adaptability and inclusivity literature to destigmatize mental illness and accommodate physical limitations	Gould et al., 2020 Vogel, 2011
Women	Being denied access to leadership positions due to the resiliency of patriarchal values embedded in the workplace Being submerged in a male-dominated culture with limited access to influential positions Being subjected to gender-prescribed positions that leave minimal interaction with key organizational leaders	Promote all employees to consider gendered power relations and challenge socially perpetuated gender inequalities Provide programming to support work-life balance, and teach business acumen, negotiation, and leadership skills Connect women leaders with other ambitious women to mentor, support, and increase visibility of women in leadership positions	Bierema, 2005 Donnelle & Langowitz, 2009 O'Neil et al., 2011

a different approach. O'Neil and others (2011) found that some women in ERGs struggle with the stress of limiting their interest to gender-prescribed roles as a way to invest in their job security. In both instances, it was clear that overpowering social norms that reinforce male hegemony minimize the autonomy and ambitions of women to express themselves freely and pursue the same opportunities as their male colleagues.

Critically Examining How Self-Advocacy in ERGs is Enacted Through Organizational Support

Understanding the unique experiences of minorities in the workplace is only one step in a continuous process to disrupt and dismantle oppressive structures and social systems. The actions taken to address the challenges experienced by ERG members varied throughout each of the 15 articles; however, main themes emerged to illustrate how organizations support their ERGs. Firstly, the need for critical dialogue and knowledge sharing was referenced in many ways. The establishment of mentorship programs (McPhee et al., 2017; O'Neil et al., 2011), roundtable discussions (Sisco, 2019); diversity training (Friedman et al., 1998), and the dissemination of materials about how to support oppressed social groups (Vogel, 2011) each emphasized the value of critical dialogue and knowledge sharing. The necessity to create time and space for minorities to share their oppressive experiences can be interpreted as a source of enlightenment. This notion corresponds to the first tenet of critical social theory, in which enlightenment is recognized as the enhanced consciousness of members within oppressed social groups (Calhoun, 1995). The same can be said for the second objective of CST, empowerment. ERGs are more than a forum to exchange opinions and verbal affirmations to enlighten one another. Although progress might vary for different groups, actionable items that reflect social change should guide the objectives of each social group.

Thus, the second theme is the commitment of organizations to implement changes that aim to minimize disparities among social groups that impact their internal and/or external stakeholders. These trends consisted of employers changing their policies to create a more "welcoming" culture (Colgan & McKearney, 2012) and an accommodating environment (Gould et al., 2020). The goal of investing in an accommodating environment was not exclusively mentioned to support persons with disabilities, it also aligned with the efforts described by Donnelle and Langowitz (2009) when they explained that organizations can support women ERG members (and other non-members) by offering work–life balance accommodations, such as childcare coverage, extended maternity leave, and flexible hours. Other forms of support included offering professional development courses to develop skills that may not come naturally to some women, such as practicing business acumen, negotiation, and leadership skills.

Another way organizations supported the empowerment of ERGs was by providing financial assistance to mobilize the cause of ERG members. In the case of the Aboriginal group (McPhee et al., 2017), Asian American group (Weng, 2019), and Black group (Sisco, 2019), research indicated that charitable giving from the organization helped to advance the agenda of each ERG. However, it is worth noting that only race-based ERGs in the current sample included monetary donations from their employers as a major form of support. Presumably, all employer-sponsored social groups receive some form of monetary support, but it may not be a pressing matter for each group. Another presumption is that the other ERGs in Table 13.2 (LGBTQ, persons with disabilities, and women) include members who identify as White, and such groups may have other ways to secure financial capital and/or use their social capital to promote their social causes.

Although resources, needs, and progress vary for different social groups, the collective objective should be to advocate for a fair and just system—not to do better than the other groups (Sisco & Collins, 2018). Based on the assumptions of critical social theory, a shared vision and collective action is needed to grant emancipation to oppressed groups seeking enlightenment and empowerment (Freeman & Vasconcelos, 2010). Therefore, emancipation from oppressive structure and social systems serves as the primary goal, which is arguably the most difficult to achieve for all social groups. However, social groups that have some form of power and privilege seemed to be better positioned to advance their own objectives before other social groups. Unsurprisingly, this was the case for the LGBTQ ERGs in the sample. Among the LGBTQ ERG studies, the authors described the immediate need for organizations to update their standards and policies to reflect social and political changes that ensued from LGBTQ social movements (Githens & Aragon, 2009; McNulty et al., 2018; Raeburn, 2004). Examples included assigning mandatory diversity and inclusion training with a focus on allyship development, and restructuring the organizational language, culture, and environment to be inclusive of trans and non-binary perspectives.

Table 13.2 Critical Themes of Organizational Support

Critical Social Theory Foci	Organizational Support Themes	Referenced ERGs
Enlightenment	Create opportunities for ERG members to engage in critical dialogue and knowledge sharing	Racial minorities, Persons with disabilities, women, LGBTQ
Empowerment	Implement organizational changes that support oppressed social groups	Persons with disabilities, women, LGBTQ
Emancipation	Participate in social movements and political discourse	LGBTQ

Again, the organizational support to engage in sociopolitical affairs was unmatched by other ERGs represented in the sample, yet, similar to the preceding theme, there is reason to believe that individuals with "White privilege" make up the constituency of LGBTQ ERGs. In this case, White men also have membership, which places the LGBTQ social group in a unique position to hold at least some degree of both power and privilege. Additionally, some suspect this group to expand, as more individuals gain support and more confidence to disclose their LGBTQ identity and gender expression. This assumption coincides with the results of a Gallup poll taken in 2012 and 2022, in which Jones (2022) concluded that the number of Americans in the United States who identify as someone other than heterosexual has increased from 3.5 to 7.1% over the course of ten years. In addition to this fact, it is also reasonable to believe that the LGBTQ community will continue to grow substantially, given the recent social movement to empower LGBTQ children and young adults by "operationalizing resilience" and "uplifting the LGBTQ's youth resistance and power" to reconceptualize dominant structures, values, and ideals (Friedman, 2021).

When everything above is considered, it helps explain the continued advancement of LGBTQ social initiatives. The disparity between their success and race-based ERGs suggest that racism is a key factor as well—not just White privilege. This was evident in a study conducted by Sisco (2019), which explored the experience of a member who held dual membership in a Black ERG and veteran ERG. The participant claimed the veteran ERG, which was primarily comprised of White men, was often given praise, accolades, and even awards, while the Black ERG was scrutinized for doing the same work. More specifically, the participant explained that the hiring of veterans was perceived as an honorable gesture, while the hiring of people from the Black community with similar qualifications and experience left some of his White colleagues upset. The participant said that they referred to the Black hires as "diversity hires," a form of charity, or some sort of political statement. This case is one of many examples of how these subtle divisions occasionally go unnoticed, and unfortunately, they persist because they are unchallenged, and it perpetuates the same "separate but equal" false narrative that has historically and presently stalled the progress of racial minorities.

In addition to this particular finding, it is important to acknowledge how top *Fortune 500* companies have responded to recent politically charged events, such as the murder of George Floyd that occurred amid the 2020 pandemic. Many companies, for instance, showed their support and empathy for the injustices experienced by the Black community through social media posts and publicized letters from executive leaders. In fact, when Sternbeck et al. (2021) analyzed the top performing *Fortune 500* companies across 21 sectors (n = 105), they found that roughly 70% of companies made a public message about racial injustice, and "working together" emerged as the leading theme. Yet, in spite of these new developments, research about how organizations work with their Black ERGs to heighten their sensitivity and involvement in advancing racial justice is still significantly unexplored. Consequently, more research is needed to understand and assess how organizations are working with their ERGs to engage in political discourse and avoid repeating the same mistakes of the past. New directions in organizational studies, like organizational behavior, industrial–organizational psychology, and human resource development are well-positioned to help facilitate the changes needed to eliminate oppressive structures and social systems in the workplace, and guide the sociopolitical advocacy of organizations.

IMPLICATIONS FOR HRD RESEARCH AND RECOMMENDATIONS FOR ERGs

When approaching the subject of employee resource groups from an HRD perspective, there are several missed opportunities for research. There are many things HRD researchers and specialists can learn from ERGs, and there are also ways that the field of HRD can further contribute to the development of employee resource groups. In this final section, implications for HRD research and recommendations for ERGs are discussed.

IMPLICATIONS FOR HRD RESEARCH: APPLYING A SOCIAL JUSTICE APPROACH TO RESEARCH IN HRD

The integration of employee resource groups into an organization's structure invites conversation to acknowledge critical issues and consider steps toward social change. These discussions and concerns are increasingly becoming normal in mid-size and large organizations. Companies are beginning to expand their organizational mission to be recognized for being socially responsive to the needs of their internal and external stakeholders. In the past 10 years, corporate social responsibility, employee welling, and business ethics have gained more attention in organizational studies, because it has arguably become more relevant in practice. The rise of social media has also increased the awareness of local and global events that occasionally resulted in the call for everyone, including for-profit and non-profit organizations to take a stance on divisive issues. At the very least, there is growing anticipation for organizational leaders to put forth a comment, tweet, post, or public letter that acknowledges that they are informed of the sociopolitical events and tragedies that shape everyone's reality. This has led to social justice becoming less taboo in corporate conversations. The same should be true for research. If the goal is to understand and guide practice, research about organizations should place social justice at the center of attention. In HRD, social justice discourse is slowly developing and it has mainly been led by two streams of thought, the morality paradigm and diversity and inclusion rationale, both of which occupy space within the context of critical human resource development research.

Morality Paradigm. Traditionally, HRD has been limited to conservative research interests that primarily adhere to the immediate concerns of organizational leaders, and therefore, "HRD focuses little on issues of social justice in the workplace or larger social context" (Bierema & Cseh, 2003, p. 23). Instead, social justice should be valued in the same way economic growth is prioritized (Cunningham, 2004). Fortunately, there have been long-standing advocates for social justice in HRD and they have made significant strides to rally attention toward social justice issues. Byrd (2014a), for instance, has helped create pathways to discuss topics that address the inequalities that exist in human resources. When explaining why this topic is relevant to the work of human resource developers, she has made compelling arguments to demonstrate how work performance, globalization, and the future of work require a humanizing and cross-cultural consciousness to sufficiently meet the demands of organizations and respond to the needs of its members. In turn, these insights have set the groundwork to consider the moral obligations of organizational leaders, and recently, this lens has been useful to explore the relationship between ERGs and "morally inclusive organizations" (Byrd, 2022). Although there is still considerable support needed to advance social justice research in HRD, other critical scholars have incorporated a social justice perspective in their research (Alfred et al, 2020; Bohonos & Sisco, 2021; Collins et al., 2021, 2019; Sisco et al., 2020) to demonstrate how organizations can become more socially responsible.

When discussing how HRD should move forward amidst COVID-19, Bierema (2020) reinforced the need to practice a more humanistic approach when she claimed that "HRD can promote social justice through researching incivility in organizations, discovering how to transform mindsets of privilege and marginalization, and identifying humanitarian leadership behaviours" (p. 355). Similarly, Crocco and Greiner (2021) explained that those who are responsible for directing and facilitating organizational learning during COVID-19 should not be pressed to return to traditional learning strategies. As an alternative, the authors invite individuals to discover new ways of "making meaning" and embrace other ways of learning. In each of these instances, the moral consciousness embodied by organizations help set the foundation to advance social justice initiatives. This suggests that organizational leaders must be willing to acknowledge diverse perspectives, and look beyond the business case.

Diversity and Inclusion Rationale. Instead of being restricted to an organizational lens, social justice has also been researched from an individual and group perspective. More specifically, studies have focused on liberating minorities by exploring how they experience injustice in organizations and throughout society (Chapman & Gedro, 2009; Ghosh, 2016; Hutchinson & Kovach, 2019; Sims et al., 2021; Sisco et al., 2019). This type of research has often been coupled with D&I concepts and principles, and since social justice and D&I often share a common purpose and represent similar sentiments about humanity and ethics, they infer the importance of one another.

This is evident when social justice is discussed in organizational and management studies. Theodorakopoulos and Budhwar (2015) explained that diversity and inclusion language is occasionally used to represent social justice initiatives as a strategy to appeal to the "business case" of investing in the well-being of organizational members and social issues. This particular strategy may be deemed effective, but it can also be perceived as a less radical approach to social change. Some critical theorists, for instance, argue that diversity and inclusion is more about social awareness and localized change, whereas social justice is focused on social change on a large scale that has immediate implications for the redistribution of resources, political ideology, and social welfare (Lerner & Fulambarker, 2018). Consequently, whether or not D&I and social justice are used to reference the same goals or they represent different degrees of social change, they inform one another, and they are both necessary to advocate for the eradication of oppressive structures and social systems.

Recommendations for ERGs: Creating a Balanced Approach to Employee Resource Groups Through an HRD Perspective

Although HRD has been slow to react to employee resource groups, this popular trend presents an opportunity for HRD specialists to help enrich the development of ERG members and strengthen the relationship between organizational leaders and the various social groups that represent ERGs. One goal would be to help create more parity among ERGs by gaining a deeper understanding of the current disparities between the various groups. This approach would require organizational leaders to be more proactive in their support of ERGs. Instead of relying on different groups to educate organizational leaders about the injustices that influence the history, culture, and present circumstance of each ERG, organizational leaders should enter discussions with ERGs with a familiarity of who they are, so they can focus on what each ERG hopes to accomplish. HRD professionals can act as intermediaries between organizational leaders and ERGs by strategically identifying barriers and gaps that influence the development and progress of ERG members, and facilitating negotiations to determine equitable ways the organization can support each group. Many groups may be in need of common resources to create a more leveled playing field, but the themes identified in the above literature review indicate that each group will also need a customized strategic plan that captures the goals, needs, and essence of each ERG. Human resource developers who specialize in training and development and organization development are both suited to facilitate this suggestion because this approach is founded on common tools used in HRD practice, such as knowledge sharing and workplace learning. On account of this recommendation, everyone plays an active role to implement social change through ERGs, and the application of HRD is further fortified by guiding the learning and development of another essential organizational function.

CONCLUSION

More intentional efforts and less reactive measures are needed to shift the values needed for human resource developers to become effective change agents to advance social justice. This shift begins with meaningful dialogue, new ways of understanding and practicing HRD, and the continued exploration of untapped possibilities to invest in the learning and development of organizations and their members. Throughout this text, the different objectives and needs among oppressed social groups have been a central focus to illustrate how employee resource groups enlighten and empower minorities to pursue social justice through self-advocacy. The core principles of critical social theory was also used as a framework to explore how ERGs can develop into an emancipatory strategy in organizations. When considering how HRD can engage in this work, a critical approach is necessary for both research and practice. CHRD can help nurture the ongoing development of ERGs by challenging organizational leadership to think beyond performative goals and broaden their perspective to consider their social impact. However, the success of HRD to fulfill this vision is conditional upon HRD's willingness to reexamine the way educators, researchers, and practitioners conceptualize social justice in organizations, especially within the context of the workplace.

REFERENCES

Aiston, S. J., & Fo, C. K. (2021). The silence/ing of academic women. *Gender and Education, 33*(2), 138–155.

Alfred, M. V., Ray, S. M., & Zarestky, J. (2020). HRD and social justice: Education in support of the UN sustainable development goals. *New Horizons in Adult Education and Human Resource Development, 32*(4), 4–16.

Atkinson, D. (2002). Self-advocacy and research. In B. Gray & R. Jackson (Eds.), *Advocacy & learning disability* (pp. 120–136). Jessica Kingsley.

Baker, J. S. (2009). Buying into the business case: a bona fide group study of dialectical tensions in employee network groups. Doctoral Dissertation, Texas A&M University, College Station.

Bierema, L. L. (2005). Women's networks: A career development intervention or impediment? *Human Resource Development International, 8*(2), 207–224.

Bierema, L. L. (2020). HRD research and practice after 'The Great COVID-19 Pause': The time is now for bold, critical, research. *Human Resource Development International, 23*(4), 347–360.

Bierema, L. L., & Cseh, M. (2003). Evaluating AHRD research using a feminist research framework. *Human Resource Development Quarterly, 14*(1), 5–26.

Bohonos, J. W., & Sisco, S. (2021). Advocating for social justice, equity, and inclusion in the workplace: An agenda for anti-racist learning organizations. *New Directions for Adult and Continuing Education, 2021*(170), 89–98.

Briscoe, F., & Safford, S. (2010). Employee affinity groups: Their evolution from social movement vehicles to employer strategies. *Perspectives on Work, 14*(1), 42–45.

Burkitt, I. (2016). Relational agency: Relational sociology, agency and interaction. *European Journal of Social Theory, 19*(3), 322–339.

Byrd, M. Y. (2014a). Re-Conceptualizing and re-visioning diversity in the workforce: Toward a social Justice paradigm. In M. Y. Byrd & C. L. Scott (Eds.), *Diversity in the workforce: Current issues and emerging trends* (pp. 334–346). Routledge.

Byrd, M. Y. (2014b). Race and diversity in the workforce. In M. Y. Byrd & C. L. Scott (Eds.), *Diversity in the workforce: Current issues and emerging trends* (pp. 334–346). Routledge.

Byrd, M. Y. (2018). Does HRD have a moral duty to respond to matters of social injustice? *Human Resource Development International, 21*(1), 3–11.

Byrd, M. Y. (2022). Employee resource groups: Enabling developmental relationships to support socially just and morally inclusive organizations. In *HRD perspectives on developmental relationships* (pp. 219–237). Palgrave Macmillan.

Calhoun, C. (1995). *Critical social theory: Culture, history, and the challenge of difference.* Wiley-Blackwell.

Chapman, D. D., & Gedro, J. (2009). Queering the HRD curriculum: Preparing students for success in the diverse workforce. *Advances in Developing Human Resources, 11*(1), 95–108.

Clarke, S. N., Howley, I., Resnick, L., & Rosé, C. P. (2016). Student agency to participate in dialogic science discussions. *Learning, Culture and Social Interaction, 10*, 27–39.

Colgan, F., & McKearney, A. (2012). Visibility and voice in organisations: Lesbian, gay, bisexual and transgendered employee networks. *Equality, Diversity and Inclusion: An International Journal, 31*(4), 359–378.

Collins, J. C., Zhang, P., & Sisco, S. (2021). Everyone is invited: Leveraging bystander intervention and ally development to cultivate social justice in the workplace. *Human Resource Development Review, 20*(4), 486–511.

Collins, P. H. (2019). *Intersectionality as critical social theory.* Duke University Press.

Cook, K. S., & Hegtvedt, K. A. (1983). Distributive justice, equity, and equality. *Annual Review of Sociology, 9*(1), 217–241.

Cortina, L. M., & Magley, V. J. (2003). Raising voice, risking retaliation: Events following interpersonal mistreatment in the workplace. *Journal of Occupational Health Psychology, 8*(4), 247.

Creed, W. D., & Scully, M. A. (2011). Songs of ourselves: Employees' deployment of social identity in workplace encounters. *Journal of Management Inquiry, 20*(4), 408–429.

Crenshaw, K. (1991). Mapping the margins: Intersectionality, identity politics, and violence against women of color. *Stanford Law Review, 43*, 1241–1299.

Crocco, O. S., & Grenier, R. S. (2021). Not all those who wander are lost: Critically reflective research for a new HRD landscape. *Advances in Developing Human Resources, 23*(1), 55–65.

Cunningham, P. (2004). Critical Pedagogy and Implications for Human Resource Development. *Advances in Developing Human Resources, 6*(2), 226–240.

Daly-Cano, M., Vaccaro, A., & Newman, B. (2015). College Student Narratives about Learning and Using Self-Advocacy Skills. *Journal of Postsecondary Education and Disability, 28*(2), 213–227.

Donnellon, A., & Langowitz, N. (2009). Leveraging women's networks for strategic value. *Strategy & Leadership, 37*(3), 29–36.

Dutton, K. (2018). Increasing diversity, awareness, and inclusion in corporate culture: Investigating communities of practice and resource groups among employees. *Development and Learning in Organizations, 32*(6), 19–21.

Field, S., & Hoffman, A. (1994). Development of a model for self-determination. *Career Development for Exceptional Individuals, 17*, 159–169.

Freeman, R. B., & Rogers, J. (1999). What do workers want? Voice, representation, and power in the American workplace. In S. Estreicher (Ed.), *Employee representation in the emerging workplace: Alternatives/supplements to collective bargaining* (pp. 3–31). Kluwer Law International.

Freeman, M., & Vasconcelos, E. F. S. (2010). Critical social theory: Core tenets, inherent issues. *New Directions for Evaluation, 2010*(127), 7–19.

Friedman, E. J. (2021). *Safer brave spaces that empower queer and trans students.* Emerald Publishing Limited.

Friedman, R., & Holtom, B. (2002). The effects of network groups on minority employee retention. *Human Resource Management, 41*(4), 405–421.

Friedman, R., Kane, M., & Cornfield, D. B. (1998). Social support and career optimism: Examining the effectiveness of network groups among black managers. *Human Relations, 51*(9), 1155-1177.

Fitzgerald, L. F., Swan, S., & Fischer, K. (1995). Why didn't she just report him?: The psychological and legal implications of women's strategies for responding to sexual harassment. *Journal of Social Issues, 51*, 117–138.

Gadbow, N. F., & Du Bois, D. A. (1998). *Adult learners with special needs: Strategies and resources for postsecondary education and workplace training.* Krieger.

Ghosh, R. (2016). Gender and diversity in India: Contested territories for HRD? *Advances in Developing Human Resources, 18*(1), 3–10.

Giacalone, R. A., & Rosenfeld, P. (1986). Self-presentation and self-promotion in an organizational setting. *The Journal of Social Psychology, 126*(3), 321–326.

Githens, R. P., & Aragon, S. R. (2009). LGBT employee groups: Goals and organizational structures. *Advances in Developing Human Resources, 11*(1), 121–135.

Gould, R., Harris, S. P., Mullin, C., & Jones, R. (2020). Disability, diversity, and corporate social responsibility: Learning from recognized leaders in inclusion. *Journal of Vocational Rehabilitation, 52*(1), 29–42.

Green, W. M. (2018). Employee resource groups as learning communities. *Equality, Diversity and Inclusion: An International Journal, 37*(7), 634–648.

Harris, A., & Leonardo, Z. (2018). Intersectionality, race-gender subordination, and education. *Review of Research in Education, 42*(1), 1–27.

Hiemstra, R. (1998, March). Self-advocacy and self-directed learning: A potential confluence for enhanced personal empowerment. In *SUNY Empire State College Conference.*

Hutchins, H. M., & Kovach, J. V. (2019). ADVANCING women academic faculty in STEM careers: The role of critical HRD in supporting diversity and inclusion. *Advances in Developing Human Resources, 21*(1), 72–91.

Jeske, D., & Calvard, T. (2020). Big data: Lessons for employers and employees. *Employee Relations, 42*(1), 248–261.

Jones, J. (2022, February 17). *LGBTQ identification in U.S. ticks up to 7.1.* Gallup. https://news.gallup.com/poll/389792/lgbt-identification-ticks-up.aspx

Jordan, K. (2020). Tales from the real world: Employee resource groups (ERGs) as advocates in corporate America, In J. A. Bruce & K. E. McKee (Eds.), *Transformative leadership in action: Allyship, advocacy & activism (building leadership bridges)* (pp. 163–170). Emerald Publishing Limited.

Kalsem, K., & Williams, V. L. (2010). Social justice feminism. *UCLA Women's Law Journal, 18,* 131–194.

Kurtz, S. (2002). *Workplace justice: Organizing multi-identity movements.* University of Minnesota Press.

Lerner, J. E., & Fulambarker, A. (2018). Beyond diversity and inclusion: Creating a social justice agenda in the classroom. *Journal of Teaching in Social Work, 38*(1), 43–53.

McNulty, Y., McPhail, R., Inversi, C., Dundon, T., & Nechanska, E. (2018). Employee voice mechanisms for lesbian, gay, bisexual and transgender expatriation: The role of Employee-Resource Groups (ERGs) and allies. *International Journal of Human Resource Management, 29*(5), 829–856.

McPhee, D., Julien, M., Miller, D., & Wright, B. (2017). Smudging, connecting, and dual identities: Case study of an aboriginal ERG. *Personnel Review, 46*(6), 1104–1119.

Merriam-Webster. (n.d.). *Advocacy.* In *Merriam-Webster Dictionary.* https://www.merriam-webster.com/dictionary/advocacy

Nezu, C. M., Nezu, A. M., & Arean, P. (1991). Assertiveness and problem-solving training for mildly mentally retarded persons with dual diagnoses. *Research in Developmental Disabilities, 12*(4), 371–386.

O'Neil, D. A., Hopkins, M. M., & Sullivan, S. E. (2011). Do women's networks help advance women's careers? Differences in perceptions of female workers and top leadership. *Career Development International, 16*(7), 733–754.

Pennell, R. L. (2001). Self determination and self-advocacy: Shifting the power. *Journal of Disability Policy Studies, 11*(4), 223–227.

Petri, G., Beadle-Brown, J., & Bradshaw, J. (2017). "More honoured in the breach than in the bbservance"—Self-Advocacy and human rights. *Laws, 6*(4), 26.

Raeburn, N. C. (2004). *Changing corporate America from onside Out: Lesbian and gay workplace rights, Vol. 20,* University of Minnesota Press.

Rath, K. A., & Royer, J. M. (2002). The nature and effectiveness of learning disability services for college students. *Educational Psychology Review, 14*(4), 353–381.

Ross-Gordon, J. M. (2001). Understanding and planning for adult learners with disabilities. *Adult Learning, 12*(2), 2–4.

Sadowski, M. (2020). *Safe is not enough: Better schools for LGBTQ students.* Harvard Education Press.

Sievert, A. L., Cuvo, A. J., & Davis, P. K. (1988). Training Self-Advocacy Skills to adults with mild handicaps. *Journal of Applied Behavior Analysis, 21*(3), 299–309.

Sims, C. M., Carter, A. D., Sparkman, T. E., Morris, L. R., Jr., & Durojaiye, A. (2021). On Black male leadership: A study of leadership efficacy, servant leadership, and engagement mediated by microaggressions. *Advances in Developing Human Resources, 23*(4), 354–383.

Sisco, S. (2020). Race-conscious career development: Exploring self-preservation and coping strategies of black professionals in corporate America. *Advances in Developing Human Resources, 22*(4), 419–436.

Sisco, S. (2019). A hermeneutic phenomenological study of black professionals in employee networks: Critically exploring social interests and participatory learning at work. Retrieved from the University of Minnesota Digital Conservancy, https://hdl.handle.net/11299/202432

Sisco, S., & Collins, J. C. (2018). Employee resource groups: Separate but equal? *New Horizons in Adult Education and Human Resource Development, 30*(3), 60–63.

Stack, E. E., & McDonald, K. (2018). We are "both in charge, the academics and self-advocates": Empowerment in Community-Based Participatory Research. *Journal of Policy and Practice in Intellectual Disabilities, 15*(1), 80–89.

Sterbenk, Y. M., Ward, J., Luttrell, R., & Shelton, S. (2021). Silence has no place: A framing analysis of corporate statements about racial inequity, immigration policy and LGBTQ rights. *Corporate Communications: An International Journal, 27*(2), 404–421.

Theodorakopoulos, N., & Budhwar, P. (2015). Guest editors' introduction: Diversity and inclusion in different work settings: Emerging patterns, challenges, and research agenda. *Human Resource Management, 54*(2), 177–197.

Test, D. W., Fowler, C. H., Wood, W. M., Brewer, D. M., & Eddy, S. (2005). A conceptual framework of self-advocacy for students with disabilities. *Remedial and Special Education, 26*(1), 43–54.

U.S. Bureau of Labor Statistics. (2021, February 24). *Persons with a disability: Labor Force Characteristics–2020*. https://www.bls.gov/news.release/pdf/disabl.pdf

Van Reusen, A. K., Bos, C. S., Schumaker, J. B., & Deshler, D. D. (1994). The self-advocacy strategy for education and transition planning. Lawrence, KS: Edge Enterprises.

Vogel, N. (2011). Disability employee resource groups. *Profiles in Diversity Journal, 13*(4), 86–86.

Yi-Ren, W., & Huh, Y. (2019). Empower the powerless: Practical implications for breaking silence. *Industrial and Organizational Psychology, 12*(3), 350–354.

Wang, Y. R., & Huh, Y. (2019). Empower the powerless: Practical implications for breaking silence. *Industrial and Organizational Psychology, 12*(3), 350-354.

Wehmeyer, M., & Lawrence, M. (1995). Whose future is it anyway? Promoting student involvement in transition planning. *Career Development for Exceptional Individuals, 18*, 69–83.

Wehmeyer, M., & Palmer, S. (2003). Adult outcomes for students with cognitive disabilities three-years after high school: The impact of self-determination. *Education and Training in Developmental Disabilities, 38*, 131–144.

Welbourne, T. M., & McLaughlin, L. L. (2013). Making the business case for employee resource groups. *Employment Relations Today, 40*(2), 35–44.

Welbourne, T. M., Rolf, S., & Schlachter, S. (2017). The case for employee resource groups: A review and social identity theory-based research agenda. *Personnel Review, 46*, 1816–1834.

Weng, S. S. (2019). Formation of an Asian American nonprofit organization through the partnership between corporate employee resource groups and community organizations. *Human Service Organizations: Management, Leadership & Governance, 43*(3), 153–170.

Williams, P., & Shoultz, B. (1982). *We can speak for ourselves*. Souvenir Press.

World Health Organization. (2020, February 3). *Female genital mutilation*. https://www.who.int/news-room/fact-sheets/detail/female-genital-mutilation

CHAPTER 14

Reflecting on Leadership, Leading, and Leaders

Carole J. Elliott

REFLECTING ON LEADERSHIP, LEADING, AND LEADERS

What we understand leadership to be, what a leader looks like, and the places and spaces in which leadership takes place are important issues for HRD scholars and professionals to question and reflect upon. As critical HRD scholars, we accept a responsibility to problematize what is accepted as the leadership norm, and to propose alternatives to leadership practice when individuals or groups with little formal power are not treated equitably. This sometimes requires us to speak truth to power, which can be emotionally taxing and render us politically vulnerable. In such instances, it is helpful to have access to frameworks, or thinking tools, that ground in theory how we challenge leadership norms that privilege the few at the expense of the many.

In this chapter, I will propose a thinking tool that CHRD scholars can adopt and adapt when researching leadership, developing leadership capacity within an organizational context, or acting as a citizen seeking the sustainability of a resilient democracy. To do so, I will examine historical perspectives of/for leadership, leading and leaders, and the consequences and challenges of these perspectives for the theory and practice of Critical HRD (CHRD). The chapter begins by discussing the contribution of the field of critical leadership studies (CLS) and suggests how CHRD can engage with CLS to position HRD in a more socially conscious space. The chapter's brief overview of CLS will draw

C. J. Elliott (✉)
University of Sheffield, Sheffield, UK
e-mail: carole.elliott@sheffield.ac.uk

J. C. Collins and J. L. Callahan (eds.), *The Palgrave Handbook of Critical Human Resource Development*, https://doi.org/10.1007/978-3-031-10453-4_14

attention to the reasons for its emergence and reflect on the overlaps between CHRD and CLS both epistemologically and methodologically. For example, CLS has in part emerged as a response to the dominance of positivist methods that decontextualize understandings of leadership. A stimulus for CHRD's development is the dominance of a masculinist performative paradigm which risked placing HRD in a position wherein it was unable to perform its pivotal role of "humanistically facilitating development and change" (Bierema, 2009, p. 69). As Robinson and Kerr (2018, p. 664) observe, "leadership studies as an academic field conforms to the self-consciously 'scientific' paradigm that dominates the social sciences and political sciences in the United States (Abbott, 1998; Ross, 1992; Steinmetz, 2011), exhibiting a neglect of issues of power and a suspicion of the intrusion of values (as being 'ideological') into research (Collinson, 2014; Ross, 1992; Tourish, 2011)." The purpose of this chapter is, therefore, to examine the consequences of leadership studies' negligence of the sociohistorical conditions in which understandings of leadership and its practice have emerged. The chapter will also suggest ways in which CHRD scholars and professionals can contribute to a restructuring of leadership in theory and practice.

The chapter is structured to provide insight into the consequences of leadership studies' methodological and theoretical limitations. In doing so my intention is to discuss the consequences of leadership studies' negligence of the sociohistorical conditions in which understandings of leadership and its practice have emerged. The resilience of leadership as a White, masculinist, heteronormative activity is in part connected to dominant epistemologies and associated methodologies that marginalize individuals who identify as LGBTQIA, women, people of color, and individuals who are neurologically diverse. Through the framework of *People, Place, and Process*, the chapter will present critical lenses helpful to the interrogation of the who, where, and how of leadership, and the practice of leaders. Leadership studies, and by extension CHRD, require closer engagement with theory that has the analytic capacity to offer critically conscious alternatives oriented around justice, community, and shared responsibility in spaces of organizing. The chapter will conclude with reflections on, and visions for, more socially responsible leadership learning and development practices.

CRITICAL LEADERSHIP STUDIES

Critical theory provides scholars of leadership and HRD with alternative lenses to examine and reevaluate the theory that has traditionally been applied to understand leadership, and to the development of leaders and leadership. If you are reading this book, you will most likely already be dissatisfied with the "answers" that traditional leadership theories provide. A reliance on the dominant archetype of the great corporate leader (Sinclair, 2005), for example, reflects deeply held assumptions about "the necessity of a heroic, heterosexual masculine performance" (Sinclair, 2005, p. ix) reinforced by theories reporting the white male experience. If we proceed to apply theories that describe leadership as a masculinist activity that is only performed by a small percentage of the world's population to inform a leadership development program, we impose an understanding of leadership as an individualistic activity. This reinforces perceptions of how leadership is undertaken, where leadership takes place, and which individuals are regarded as legitimate leaders.

Critical leadership studies attempt to disrupt constructions of leadership that reproduce leadership as an ethical and moral practice (Liu & Baker, 2016). From a CLS perspective, it is important to question the "emerging genre" (Liu & Baker, 2016, p. 422) of leadership theories, such as authentic (Gardner et al, 2005), and servant leadership (Greenleaf, 1977) theory, that celebrate leaders who purportedly demonstrate altruistic behaviors. The fixation of leadership theory with the morality, or otherwise, of individual leaders reinforces a romantic view of leadership that regards it as "all inclusive and all good" (Alvesson & Blom, 2014). While recently the field of critical leadership studies has faced valid criticism about its lack of reflexivity with respect to its use of the terms leadership, leader, and follower (Learmonth & Morrell, 2017, p.259), critical leadership studies growth is linked to the more established critical management studies (CMS).

Critical studies place their object of study in a broader cultural, political, and economic context and consider how the phenomenon of study relates to "sources of broader asymmetrical relations in society" (Alvesson & Deetz, 2000, p 1). A critical study of leadership's examination of the lack of CEO positions occupied by people of color, therefore, would not place its analytic focus on why *individual* people of color are unlikely to occupy positions of power in the corporate world. A critical analysis by contrast would begin the analytic process by posing different questions to challenge, rather than to confirm, what is socially and politically established as the reason for this inequity and traditional approaches to "solve" the problem. From a Critical Theory standpoint, therefore, "generalized observations and prescriptions on social structures and behaviour" should be regarded as "interested" rather than neutral "to uncover what has been made obscure and to question what others insist should be obvious" (Reynolds, 1998, p. 187).

The following sections will focus on the who (people), where (place), and how (process) of leadership theorizing and practice to provide insights on how leadership theory reinforces unequal power relationships. Deepening the understanding of who leadership research has traditionally focussed upon, and where and how leadership research is undertaken, sensitizes us to the possibility of reconceptualizing leadership in our research and practice. In taking this approach, the aim is to deepen understanding of the constraints imposed by normative theories of leadership when attempting to theorize and practice leadership development in a more socially conscious way.

PEOPLE

Conceptions of leadership largely draw on the leadership stories and expe-riences of a limited population and so do not represent the conditions in which most people experience their lives. Studies of leadership and leaders in the Anglo-American literature particularly have predominantly taken a White, western form of masculinity (Calas & Smircich, 1996; Sinclair & Evans, 2015) as the norm. Most leadership literature has been developed by men, and so it is not surprising that this focus on male leaders' experiences promotes White male values as the behavioral managerial norm (Elliott & Stead, 2008; Lamsa & Sintonen, 2001). To understand and develop leadership as a more socially conscious and inclusive practice, this section discusses literature that recognizes social categories, including race, gender, and age as inherent to processes of organizing.

Jackson and Parry (2011) report that one of the most popular questions in relation to leadership focuses on whether there is a difference between men and women leaders. This ostensible recognition of the potential for diverse leadership experiences simultaneously reveals the limitations of individualistic approaches to theorizing. Studies that focus on the difference between men and women leaders are rooted in sex role stereotypes (Schein, 1973), which either confirm or disconfirm whether men or women possess the character-istics, temperament, or attitudes for leadership normally attributed to men. While there has been a more recent focus on how women achieve leadership positions, many studies continue to be preoccupied with identifying which *female* characteristics align with leadership theories that claim to be guided by ethical and moral principles. Representations of women's leadership in leader-ship theory, and celebrations of women's leadership success in the media, share a tendency to position women leaders against purportedly neutral leadership norms or behaviors. For example, during the Global Financial Crisis (GFC), women were positioned as an ethical alternative to the styles of masculinist leadership that led to the financial crisis (Elliott & Stead, 2018). Nevertheless, qualitative inquiry designed to understand the sociocultural assumptions that sustain a gender binary that associates women with the feminine and men with the masculine, draws attention to the resilience of gendered stereotypes. In the case of the GFC, we note how in the context of a financial services sector, where women had been largely absent, women then become positioned by politicians and commentators as an antidote to toxic and hubristic leadership (Elliott & Stead, 2018). Women's way of leading became the "antidote" due to women's apparent aversion to risk and their embodiment as an antidote to the "young men in black suits" (Elliott & Stead, 2018, p. 21). While this presents as a societal shift, it restricts women's agency by reproducing tropes of women as "carers" and "nurturers."

In analyzing what promises to be the beginning of a move away from masculine domination of leadership, we observe how traditional understand-ings of gender and leadership sustain gender inequality at senior organizational levels through the resilience of gendered asymmetries of power. Despite the long-term consequences of the GFC on many sections of society, there have been minimal improvements in the number of women occupying CEO or board-level positions. Catalyst (2020) reports that, while women employed by S&P 500 companies comprise 44.7% of employees, only 5.8% of CEOs are women, and 21.2% of Board Seats are occupied by women. Of the women who do occupy CEO positions, the majority of these women are White. From entry-level positions to the most senior positions of authority, women of color remain poorly represented. In 2020, women of color represented 18% of entry-level positions and few advanced to leadership roles. Women of color represent 12% of managers, 9% of senior managers/directors, 6% of VPs, 5% of SVPs, and 3% of C-suite positions.

When the leadership literature talks about women and leadership, it is predominantly the experience of White women. When crosscultural leadership researchers have examined organizations outside white settings, they have generally "imposed theory developed from this milieu onto people of color or women" (Gambrell, 2016, p. 294). However, a body of research has emerged over recent years that draws attention to the racialized nature of leadership research (Ospina & Foldy, 2009; Ospina & Su, 2009; Parker, 2002). Similar to studies that identify how discourses of gender and leadership influence identities and institutions, race also influences how we view, experience, and are acted upon in society and across organized settings. Parker's (2002) study of African American women's leadership illustrates how leadership knowledge can be enhanced when whiteness is decentered (Liu & Baker, 2016), and when research pays attention to how "power intersects with race and gender to structure conflict in dominant culture organizations" (Parker, 2002, p. 264).

Studies that have drawn attention to the role of race in the social construction of leadership are essential to develop leadership theory and leadership development practices that are more inclusive. However, it is not only people of color who have race (Baker & Liu, 2016; Sinclair, 2005). Several scholars argue that by paying attention to the racialization of White leaders, we can unhinge whiteness "from its location as transparent, dominant and ordinary" (Nayak, 2003, p. 173) and emphasize that associating whiteness with leadership is not a morally or ethically neural activity. CHRD scholars and professionals can challenge the resilience of the racialized and gendered symbolic order (Smith & Nkomo, 2003) that perceives women leaders of color to be inferior to white women leaders. Racism manifests in different ways and if we fail to acknowledge and interrogate how it reproduces inequity, we risk failing to make a change (Bhopal, 2018).

PLACE

The question of where leadership and leaders have been studied is important to address if we are to understand more deeply the resilience of normative understandings about leadership. Leadership theories have maintained a dominant

North American bias (Den Hartog & Dickson, 2004), and the locations in which studies of leadership have taken place contain several biases. Large business organizations in the Global North have tended to provide the majority of leadership studies' empirical sites. Political and military contexts have also been a traditional source for the development of leadership theory (e.g. Grint, 2000, 2005). Auto/biographies of business, military, and political leaders remain a source of fascination in the media and popular culture. These predispositions perpetrate the systemic underrepresentation of minorities (Gambrell, 2016; Yelamarthi & Mawasha, 2008) in leadership positions.

Conjoined with the question about the "where" of leadership research is the "how" of leadership research, which will be addressed in more detail in the "Process" section. The question of "how" is linked to the question of "where" as an evaluation of the empirical sites of leadership research requires a critical questioning of embedded norms in studies of leadership and power. To develop an extended and deeper consciousness of how power relations shape leadership and organizing processes, it is helpful to look beyond the usual sites used to undertake leadership research. Gambrell's (2016) study of Lakota women leaders, for example, highlights how management policies based on western paradigms perpetuate the systemic underrepresentation of indigenous peoples in the United States. The sites in which we choose to study leadership can provoke us to reconceptualize leadership, particularly when focusing on leadership's intersection with social categories such as race, gender, and class. Ospina and Su (2009) recount the social changes in the small town of Port Gibson, Mississippi that followed the Cornerstone Theater Company's interracial production of Romeo and Juliet that cast a local Black student as Romeo and a local White student as Juliet. Ospina and Su (2009) articulate the possibility for social change leadership when, as in the Port Gibson example, the relationship between race and leadership is illuminated. Elliott and Stead's (2008) study of six leading women draws attention to the significance of the environment in which leadership practice takes place. They cite the experience of a Northern Irish community activist, May Blood, who worked at the grassroots level in the Northern Ireland Peace Process, and who in 1996 helped establish the Northern Ireland Women's Coalition. Spending her adult years in a tense political environment in a society where women and children had little status, she developed a strategic ability to find ways to transcend sectarian boundaries. In a setting in which a wall, referred to as a peace line, existed to separate Protestant and Catholic communities, Blood was able to cross the peace line due to the perceived lesser status of women: "I wasn't considered orange (Protestant) or green (Roman Catholic)—I was only a woman" (Elliott & Stead, 2008, p. 172). The experience of May Blood illustrates how the intersection of gender and place shapes how leadership is practiced, and who is perceived to have leadership legitimacy.

Recognizing the significance of the spaces in-between formal organizations for local community development in the studies of Gambrell (2016), Ospina and Su (2009), and Elliott and Stead (2008), draws attention to how leadership practice cannot be separated from the setting in which it takes place. The collective visionary leadership established by Ella Baker during the civil rights movement (Jackson, 2021; Ransby, 2003) similarly recognizes the power and knowledge of people without institutional authority possess in order to prioritize "transformative accountability" (Jackson, 2021, p. 8). In Baker's view, "authentic" leadership could not be imposed from above or outside, "rather, the people who were most oppressed had to take direct action to change their circumstances" (Ransby, 2003. P. 170). Baker's form of inclusive leadership is one element of the sociohistorical legacy of the Black Lives Matter (BLM) movement, which is "part of a broader and longer effort for Black liberation that includes collectives not just in the present, but in the past and future" (Jackson, 2021, p. 9). BLM leadership, according to one of its cofounders, "is collective and community-based, not singular or charismatic; that accountability is central to this communal ethic" (ibid).

Leadership research that moves beyond western institutions and organizational forms offer several challenges to dominant white masculinist norms. These masculinist norms in turn are intimately intertwined with leadership studies' reification of individual leaders. That is, in researching leadership, we predominantly focus on the experiences of individual leaders in a narrow range of contexts. Familiarizing ourselves with how leadership is done differently outside corporate structures, or in communities that do not privilege any one individual, provide examples we can use as reflective touchpoints to challenge understandings of where leadership happens, and what leadership looks like in the research projects we pursue, or the changes we wish to make to organizational practice.

Process

How leadership and the practice of leaders are studied, including the language in which leadership is studied (Schedlitzki et al., 2017), has consequences for how we understand what leadership is, how it can take a more socially conscious form, and who is afforded leadership legitimacy. Leadership is predominantly studied from within the positivist paradigm. The editors of *Leadership Quarterly*, the dominant journal in the leadership studies field, consider the study of leadership (LQ) as "a 'mature science': 'leadership and leader performance are not a matter of opinion but rather a matter of fact… leadership research is a scientific discipline" (Atwater et al., 2014 [cited in Robinson & Kerr, 2018, p. 664]). *LQ* thus favors articles that apply experimental psychology methods rather than studies more attuned to examining processes of power and privilege.

However, if leadership research intends to be more critical and not solely offer alternatives that "partly break with and reinforce the domination of leadership" (Alvesson & Kärreman, 2016, p. 142) then a break from "alternative" (ibid) views of leadership is needed. Alvesson and Kärreman (2016) suggest that alternatives to leadership include peer relations, coworkership, professionalism, and organizing processes. Reflecting on the damage inflicted on society by the economic crisis initiated by the Global Financial Crisis (GFC), Mintzberg (2009) argues that there is a greater crisis in companies. He identifies the "depreciation of community," itself as a consequence of short-term management tactics, an inflation of the importance of CEOs and the reduction of employees to "fungible commodities" in the form of human resources. These calls suggest a need not only to look beyond the usual sites for leadership theory development, but also encourage more anthropological or ethnographic approaches to examine these sites.

Recent interest in decentralized protest movements, "made possible by technology" (Fotaki & Foroughi, 2022, p. 2), point to the possibility of leaderless organizations in their eschewal of non-hierarchical structures. Adopting an activist research perspective, Fotaki and Foroughi's (2022) study incorporated ethnographic methods to inform their exploratory-inductive (Bansal & Corley, 2012) study of the XR (Extinction Rebellion) movement. In addition to the use of research methods not commonly included in the "fact"-based quantitative research designs favored by Atwater et al (2014), Fotaki and Foroughi's (2022) use of Lacanian psychoanalysis to interpret their findings provides insight into the "notion of fantasy as a necessary condition for imagining different modes of organizing" (p. 15).

Drawing inspiration from other disciplines, such as the arts and humanities, can be fruitful when seeking alternative and creative methods for leadership research. Gatto and Callahan (2021) propose the application of critical discourse analysis (CDA) to dystopian fiction as a means to disrupt hegemonic masculinity. Dystopian fiction often features stories of gendered marginalization where leadership is concentrated in the hands of a self-selected elite. By applying CDA to dystopian fiction, Gatto and Callahan (2021) propose an analytic tool that helps to peel "back layers of gendered power discourse in organisations" (p. 183). Novels such as *The Handmaid's Tale* (Atwood, 1985) or *1984* (Orwell, 1949), act as cultural references to totalitarian forms of leadership dominated by "hyper-masculine and ideological societal rule" (Gatto & Callahan, 2021. p. 186) and can act as a "boundary object" (Carlile, 2002) to address and transform problematic knowledge. Gatto and Callahan's (2021) method could therefore be adapted to leadership development interventions, particularly when challenging dominant ideologies of the kind discussed by Grenier and Kaeppel in Chapter 11 of this book.

As CHRD scholars and professionals who are concerned to reconceptualize leadership as a more equitable practice, we have a responsibility to examine the biases and stereotypes we hold, consciously or otherwise, about who can be a leader, and the sites of possibility for leadership practice. Callahan and Elliott (2020) adopt an autoethnographic approach to undertake a reflexive analysis of an attempt to employ a distributed leadership process to stimulate policy change in a professional organization. By applying systems psychodynamic theorizing to their experience, they were able to identify the power of their and others' fantasy spaces in guiding decision making in an organized space. Fantasy spaces "serve as unconscious primers to ways of knowing, feeling, and being within a group" (p. 507). They can be positive in helping groups navigate complex political environments, but they can prevent groups from learning new ways of moving forward. Challenging their actions and reflections through a theoretically informed reflexive analysis helped to understand the how and why of leadership failure.

For CHRD professionals committed to practices of equity and inclusion in the workplace, Callahan and Elliott (2020) were presented with a salutary reminder that it is not necessarily sufficient to move away from hierarchical organization structures to instil more inclusive practices. While organizational leaders might attach themselves to a range of "fantasies," for example, regarding how an organizational redesign might further "engage" employees, ignoring issues of power will hinder aspirations to inclusivity. If you are reading this book, you are interested in alternative ways to practice and to understand how individuals and organizations can learn and develop in a more socially and environmentally conscious way. HRD professionals can play a significant role in recogniszing how issues of power are a constant organizing force in the workplace.

CONCLUSION

An aim of this chapter was to draw attention to ways in which the choices we make when designing leadership research can have entwined political and practical consequences that extend beyond the theoretical contribution we aspire to in our published work. This chapter has discussed traditional approaches to leadership research, and it has presented critical and creative ways to research and understand leadership.

Embracing reflexivity in HRD research and practice (Bierema, 2015) is one way in which HRD professionals can develop practices that are less harmful to all employees. In this chapter, I have used the framework of People, Place, and Process as a heuristic device that can also be used as a prompt to ask questions, such as: "whose interests does this decision favour?" "what are the origins of this decision and where will it be implemented?" and "how was this decision arrived at and how will it be implemented?" By highlighting leadership research that moves beyond western institutions and organizational forms, this chapter provides examples that offer several challenges to dominant White masculinist norms.

Fortunately, HRD has a range of tools and learning practices that can help us to reflect on assumptions and beliefs about leadership. These tools range from challenging the discourse about leadership to working with colleagues to develop our everyday practices and interactions to reflect the more socially inclusive organization in which we aspire to work. To challenge heteronormative leadership discourses that exclude individuals with less privilege,we can begin by challenging our word choices. HRD is brought into being by discourse (Lawless et al, 2011), and discourse is not neutral. Formal and informal theories are social constructions in that they reflect shared interpretations of how we perceive, experience, and make sense of the world (Bierema, 2015).

Recognizing how our implicit leadership theories (Schyns & Riggio, 2016) reflect the informal, everyday theories that we consciously or unconsciously hold about the ideal leader, or leaders in general, could be one way to begin a process of collective reflection about the "fantasy" (Callahan & Elliott, 2020) of leadership your organization shares. Communication processes such as action learning conversations (Yorks et al., 1999), or reflective structured dialogue (Gower et al., 2007), could be incorporated into a range of learning and development interventions to share and understand assumptions held by individuals at all levels of the organization. Engaging in communication processes designed to promote greater understanding of how individuals assign legitimacy (Stead et al., 2021) to certain individuals as leaders, and not to others, could provide a foundation for CHRD to create organizations with more inclusive leadership practices. But it also requires HRD professionals to recognize wider structural issues.

If organizations are microcosms of society, then to deepen analyses of leadership practice requires us to grapple with how social constructions of leadership more widely influence social constructions of leadership in the workplace. We need to engage in cycles of critical reflexivity in development interventions, and at the Boardroom level, to deconstruct our assumptions and to develop strategies to create alternative (Stead & Elliott, 2012) leadership practices for inclusive leadership.

REFERENCES

Abbott, A. (1998). The causal devolution. *Sociological Methods Research, 27*(2), 148–181.

Alvesson, M., & Blom. M. (2014). *All-inclusive and all good: The hegemonic ambiguity of leadership.* European Group for Organization Studies.

Alvesson, M., & Deetz, S. (2000). *Doing critical management research.* Sage.

Alvesson, M., & Kärreman, D. (2016). Intellectual failure and ideological success in organization studies. *Journal of Management Inquiry, 25*(2), 139–152. https://doi.org/10.1177/1056492615589974

Atwater, L. E., Mumford, M. D., Schriesheim, C. A, & Yammarino, F. J. (2014). Retraction of leadership articles: Causes and prevention. *The Leadership Quarterly, 25*(6), 1174–1180.

Bansal, P., & Corley, K. (2012). Publishing in AMJ – Part 7: What's different about qualitative research? *Academy of Management Journal, 55,* 509–513.

Bhopal, K. (2018). *White privilege: The myth of a post-racial society.* Policy Press.

Bierema, L. L. (2009). Critiquing human resource development's dominant masculine rationality and evaluating its impact. *Human Resource Development Review, 8,* 68–96.

Bierema, L. L. (2015). Critical human resource development to enhance reflexivity, change discourse and adopt a call-to-action. *Human Resource Development Review, 14,* 119–124.

Calas, M. B., & Smircich, L. (1996). The woman's point of view: Feminist approaches to organisation studies. In S. R. Clegg, C. Hardy, & W. R. Nord (Eds.), *Handbook of organization studies* (pp. 218–257). SAGE.

Callahan, J. L., & Elliott, C. (2020). Fantasy spaces and emotional derailment: Reflections on failure in academic activism. *Organization, 27*(3), 506–514. https://doi.org/10.1177/1350508419831925

Carlile, P. R. (2002). A pragmatic view of knowledge and boundaries: Boundary objects in new product development. *Organization Science., 13*(4), 355–457.

Catalyst. (2020). *Women CEOs of the S&P500.* https://www.catalyst.org/research/women-in-sp-500-companies/ (retrieved on 8th April, 2021)

Collinson, D. (2014). Dichotomies, dialectics and dilemmas: New directions for critical leadership studies? *Leadership, 10,* 36.

Den Hartog, D. N., & Dickson, W. (2004). Leadership and culture. In J. Antonakis, A. T. Cianciolo, & R. J. Sternberg (Eds.), *The nature of leadership* (pp. 249–278). Sage.

Elliott, C., & Stead, V. (2008). Learning from leading women's experience: Towards a sociological understanding. *Leadership, 4,* 159–180.

Elliott, C., & Stead, V. (2018). Constructing women's leadership in the UK press during a time of financial crisis: Gender capitals and dialectical tensions. *Organization Studies., 39,* 19–45.

Fotaki, M., & Foroughi, H. (2022). Extinction Rebellion: Green activism and the fantasy of leaderlessness in a decentralized movement. *Leadership, 18*(2), 224–246. https://doi.org/10.1177/17427150211005578

Gambrell, K. M. (2016). Lakota women leaders: Getting things done quietly. *Leadership, 12,* 293–307.

Gardner, W. L., Avolio, B. J., Luthans, F., et al. (2005). 'Can you see the real me?' A self-based model of authentic leader and follower development. *The Leadership Quarterly, 16*(3), 343–372.

Gatto, M., & Callahan, J. L. (2021) Exposing interpellation with dystopian fiction: A critical discourse analysis technique to disrupt hegemonic masculinity, In V. Stead, C. Elliott & S. Mavin (Eds.), *Handbook of Research Methods on Gender and Management.* Edward Elgar Publishing.

Gower, K., Cornelius, L., Rawls, R., & Walker, B. R. (2007). Reflective structured dialogue: A qualitative thematic analysis. *Conflict Resolution Quarterly, 37,* 207–222.

Greenleaf, R. K. (1977). *Servant leader: A journey into the nature of legitimate power and greatness.* Paulist Press.

Grint, K. (2000). *The arts of leadership.* Oxford University Press.

Grint, K. (2005). Problems, problems, problems: The social construction of leadership. *Human Relations, 58,* 1467–1494.

Jackson, B., & Parry, K. (2011). *A very short, fairly interesting and reasonably cheap book about studying leadership.* Sage.

Jackson, S. J. (2021). Black lives matter and the revitalization of collective visionary leadership. *Leadership, 17,* 8–17.

Lamsa, A.-M., & Sintonen, T. (2001). A discursive approach to understanding women leaders in working life. *Journal of Business Ethics, 34,* 255–267.

Lawless, A., Sambrook, S. A., Garavan, T., & Valentin, C. (2011). A discourse approach to theorising HRD: Opening a discursive space. *Journal of European Industrial Training, 35*, 264–275.

Learmonth, M., & Morrell, K. (2017). Is critical leadership studies 'critical'? *Leadership, 13*, 257–271.

Liu, H., & Baker, C. (2016). White knights: Leadership as the heroicisation of whiteness. *Leadership, 12*, 420–448.

Mintzberg, H. (2009). Rebuilding Companies as Communities. *Harvard Business Review.* July–August. https://hbr.org/2009/07/rebuilding-companies-as-communities (accessed on 12 April, 2021).

Nayak, A. (2003). *Race, place and globalization: Youth cultures in a changing world.* Berg.

Ospina, S., & Foldy, E. (2009). A critical review of race and ethnicity in the leadership literature: Surfacing context, power and the collective dimensions of leadership. *The Leadership Quarterly, 20*(6), 876–896.

Ospina, S., & Su, C. (2009). Weaving color lines: Race, ethnicity, and the work of leadership in social change organizations. *Leadership, 5*(2), 131–170.

Parker, P. S. (2002). Negotiating identity in raced and gendered workplace interactions: The use of strategic communication by African American women senior executives within dominant culture organizations. *Communication Quarterly, 50*(3&4), 251–268.

Ransby, B. (2003). *Ella Baker and the Black Freedom Movement. A radical democratic vision.* University of North Carolina Press.

Reynolds, M. (1998). Reflection and critical reflection in management learning. *Management Learning, 29*, 183–200.

Robinson, S., & Kerr, R. (2018). Women leaders in the political field in Scotland: A socio-historical approach to the emergence of leaders. *Leadership, 4*, 662–686.

Ross, D. (1992). *The origins of American social science.* CUP.

Schedlitzki, D., Case, P., & Knights, D. (2017). Ways of leading in non-Anglophone contexts: Representing, expressing and enacting authority beyond the English-speaking world. *Leadership, 13*, 127–132.

Schein, V. E. (1973). The relationship between sex role stereotypes and requisite management characteristics. *Journal of Applied Psychology, 57*(2), 95–100.

Schyns, B., & Riggio, R. E. (2016). Implicit leadership theories. In A. Farazmand (Eds.), *Global encyclopedia of public administration, public policy, and governance.* Springer. https://doi.org/10.1007/978-3-319-31816-5_2186-1

Sinclair, A. (2005). *Doing leadership differently: Gender, power and sexuality in a changing business culture.* Melbourne University Press.

Sinclair, A., & Evans, M. (2015). Difference and leadership. In B.Carroll, J. Ford & S. Taylor (Eds.), *Leadership: Contemporary critical perspectives.* Sage.

Smith, E. L. B., & Nkomo, S. M. (2003). *Our separate ways: Black and white women and the struggle for professional identity.* Harvard Business Press.

Stead, V., & Elliott, C. (2012). Women's leadership learning: A reflexive review of representations and leadership teaching. *Management Learning, 44*, 373–394.

Stead, V., Elliott, C., & Gardiner, R. A. (2021). Leadership legitimacy and the mobilization of capital(s): Disrupting politics and reproducing heteronormativity. *Leadership, 17*(6), 693–714. https://doi.org/10.1177/17427150211018314

Steinmetz, G. (2011). Bourdieu, historicity, and historical sociology. *Cultural Sociology, 5*(1), 45–66.

Tourish, D. (2011). Leading questions: Journal rankings, academic freedom and performativity: What is, or should be, the future of Leadership? *Leadership, 7,* 367–381.

Yelamarth, K., & Mawasha, P. R. (2008). A pre-engineering program for the under-represented, low income and/or first generation college students to pursue higher education. *Journal of STEM Education, 9,* 5–15.

Yorks, L., Marsick, V. J., & O'Neil, J. (1999). Lessons for implementing action learning. *Advances in Developing Human Resources, 1,* 96–113.

CHAPTER 15

Applying Critical, Feminist Perspectives to Developmental Relationships in HRD

Laura L. Bierema, Weixin He, and Eunbi Sim

Developmental relationships (DRs) are mutual bonds between two or more individuals focused on learning and growth that incorporate mentoring, coaching, networking, sponsorship, and other capacity-building activities that potentially advance careers (Bierema, 2022). Technology has enabled DRs across geographical and cultural boundaries, making their access and outcomes more probable and equitable (Bierema, 2017a; Bierema & Hill, 2005; Bierema & Merriam, 2002). The purpose of this chapter is to provide a critical framework for developmental relationships as a mechanism for change in spaces of organizing and provide strategies for making DRs a sphere for promoting diversity, equity, justice, and inclusion. We introduce critical feminist developmental relationships—CFDRs—as a term and process.

Most DR discourses are laden with assumptions that such relationships are good, helpful, and crucial to advancement—notions that have received little challenge (Lea, 2012; Semenjuk & Worrall, 2000). We trouble that assumption by wondering if DRs are largely good, resulting in more just, inclusive,

L. L. Bierema (✉) · W. He · E. Sim
University of Georgia, Athens, GA, USA
e-mail: bierema@uga.edu

W. He
e-mail: Weixin.He@uga.edu

E. Sim
e-mail: esim@uga.edu

J. C. Collins and J. L. Callahan (eds.), *The Palgrave Handbook of Critical Human Resource Development*, https://doi.org/10.1007/978-3-031-10453-4_15

diversified, and equitable organizations? Activities including mentoring and sponsorship have been critiqued for reproducing prevailing power relations and reinforcing patriarchy and exclusion in organizations (Alston & Hansman, 2020; Johnson-Bailey & Cervero, 2004; Mott, 2002). Coaching has been criticized for being disconnected with sociocultural context (Du Toit & Sim, 2010; Passmore & Law, 2009; Shoukry, 2016; Western, 2012, 2017), lack of critical perspectives (Schultz, 2010), or consideration for using coaching to address wider social issues (Shoukry, 2016; Shoukry & Cox, 2018). Shoukry and Cox (2018) asserted that neoliberal values of improving performance and effectiveness pepper the discourse of coaching and challenged that coaching lacks acknowledgment as a social process. What they mean is alternatively viewing DRs as "both a product and a contributor to the reshaping of its social context" (p. 414). According to Alston and Hansman (2020):

> We assert it would be very ignorant, careless, and somewhat an act of mentoring malpractice to assume that mentoring relationships are not affected by the present sociopolitical environment that is grounded in the historically motivated ideals to further perpetuate the protection of dominant cultures' privilege and power (cultural categories such as white, cisgender male, heterosexual, Christian, upper-class, able-bodied, and of the like). (p. 85)

DR malpractice may occur whenever mentors, coaches, and other helping affiliations overlook or ignore the fraught context of work and how to effectively help their colleagues navigate oppression and injustice. Oppressive environments target individuals and groups based on race, ethnicity, gender, sexuality, age, socioeconomic status, and other positionalities that often intersect and interlock to create structural inequality. Oppression also has damaging effects on humans where they are taught to accept and advance mindsets that protect the dominant group (hegemony) which causes feelings of alienation and estrangement, and often prevents people from engaging in needed critical reflection and challenging the status quo (Shoukry, 2016). How might DRs disrupt the binary structures that reproduce dominant power structures in organizations and society? The literature offers scant exploration or explanation of how DRs might be more emancipatory (Alston & Hansman, 2020).

We explore CFDRs in this chapter by describing developmental relationships (DRs) in HRD, offering a critique of traditional developmental relationships, critiquing DRs from an intersectional feminist viewpoint, decolonizing DRs from a transnational feminist viewpoint, and reimagining DRs that actively and mindfully advance gender equity, social justice, and solidarity.

Developmental Relationships (DRs) in Human Resource Development (HRD)

Human Resource Development (HRD) is about relations between the organization and employees. In building a healthy relationship between employer and employee, it is critical for HRD as a framework to help employees develop their skills, knowledge, and capacities, which in turn improves an organization's effectiveness, performance, and outcomes. Bierema and Callahan (2014) defined critical HRD as "the process of engaging human and organizational systems that relate, learn, change, and organize in ways that optimize human interest, organization advancement, and social impact" (p. 8). Specific measures by HRD include employee career development in the forms of formal and informal training and mentorship, in which developmental relationships are formed.

Developmental relationships have been heavily researched, but not specifically focused on HRD. Gibson (2008) observed,

> The concept of multiple developmental relationships is relatively new to the HRD field...Although developmental relationships are increasingly seen as important for human resource development (HRD), their exploration with respect to the specific domains of career development and leader development has been largely independent. (p. 652)

McDonald and Hite (2005) identified different types of mentoring, such as peer mentoring and mentor networks, and suggested the diversity and complexity of this emerging construct may have potential application to the field of HRD.

We contend it is time to apply critical perspectives to developmental relationships in HRD as an additional process for promoting diversity, justice, equity, and inclusion in organizations and society. To understand the process of and how to build DRs in HRD, it is of paramount importance to understand various types of developmental relationships, particularly, their definitions and functions.

Defining Traditional Developmental Relationships (TDRs)

Literature has provided various definitions of the traditional mentoring relationship, which is commonly acknowledged by scholars and practitioners as based on one-on-one, face-to-face interactions between the mentor and mentee. In general and broadly, developmental relationships are defined as either formal or informal relationships which involve an individual interested in mentoring the development of another (Rock & Garavan, 2006). Douglas and McCauley (1999) defined formal developmental relationships as "formal management development initiatives that pair up employees with peers, senior managers, or outside consultants for the purposes of learning and development" (p. 207).

The most influential and classic mentoring definition is by Kram (1985), who described the affiliation as a type of developmental relationship in which a senior, usually more experienced, mentor provides career and psychosocial support to a junior and less experienced protégé. Typically, TDRs rely primarily on face-to-face in-person communication (Bierema, 2022), and phenomenological boundaries from traditional mentoring relationships perspective are organizational, hierarchical, single dyadic, that focus on protégé learning at dyad level (Higgins & Kram, 2001).

In this traditional type of developmental relationships, the power differential is clear-cut with mentor power over protégé. In mentor/mentee TDRs, because the mentor usually is a senior and more experienced, the mentee is often in a less powerful position and therefore might be more vulnerable in the relationship. Ragins (1997) showed that the mentor's positional relationship or "power" versus the mentee may affect the quality of the developmental relationships that form in TDRs. But according to Barstow (2008), the power differential may have value in helping relationships if used wisely and appropriately. "[A power differential can] create a safe, well-boundaried, professional context for growth" and "offers clients confidence in their caregiver's knowledge, training and expertise, direction and support" (Barstow, 2008, p. 58).

However, Bierema and Merriam (2002) found that the definitions and functions of mentors vary widely, and they established that "there are many definitions and roles of mentors, and demonstrated that mentoring success has traditionally been assessed with regard to mutual commitment and frequent contact between the mentor and protégé" (p. 214). Higgins and Kram (2001) also suggested that "the operational definition of a mentoring relationship has varied considerably in the past couple of decades" (p. 266).

Most critiques with regard to formal DRs have been about traditional one-on-one mentoring programs. For example, criticism of the mentoring program goals is often cited as in conflict with the organizational culture. In response to these criticisms and other problems associated with formal developmental relationships, literature suggests that organizations have begun to focus on alternative types of DRs developmental relationships (Douglas & McCauley, 1999).

DEFINING NONTRADITIONAL DEVELOPMENTAL RELATIONSHIPS (NDRs)

Researchers have been aware of the TDRs limitations and agree that there exist different types of developmental relationships rather than solely TDRs. Bierema and Hill (2005) defined, compared, and contrasted traditional mentoring and virtual mentoring, and argued that "traditional, face-to-face mentoring relationships are not always practical in a knowledge society where communication is instantaneous, computer mediated, and global" (p. 557). Hence, the rise of virtual mentoring or e-mentoring.

e-Mentoring is not the only DR innovation. For example, McDonald and Hite (2005) identified alternative forms of mentoring relationships, which include peer and mentor networks. Chesler and Chesler (2002) proposed alternative models to describe nontraditional developmental relationships which include age, peer, community, etc. Their alternative NDRs models are: multiple mentoring, peer mentoring, and collective mentoring. "Multiple mentoring encourages the protégé to construct a mentoring community based on a diverse set of helpers instead of relying on a single mentor" (pp. 51–52). Peer mentoring is a strategy that "simultaneously builds community and de-emphasizes seniority and hierarchy" (p. 52). Collective mentoring is "an evolution of the multiple mentor/single mentee model whereby senior colleagues and the department take responsibility for constructing and maintaining a mentoring team. Thus, mentoring becomes neither an individual one-on-one activity, nor one solicited and designed solely by the protégé" (p. 52).

Ragins (1997) also made a strong case against reliance on the traditional single mentor model in TDRs, arguing that "It is important for organizations to avoid sending the implicit message that once a protégé has an assigned (formal) mentor, this mentor is sufficient and that they should not attempt to gain an informal mentor" (p. 17). Higgins and Kram (2001) proposed the concept of developmental network and define an individual's developmental network as "the set of people a protégé names as taking an active interest in and action to advance the protege's career by providing developmental assistance" (p. 268).

In their framework, Higgins and Kram (2001) illustrated the multiple factors that shape the emergence of developmental network types, which integrate social network theory and methods with research on mentoring. Specifically, there are two main dimensions: the diversity of individuals' developmental networks and the strength of the developmental relationships that make up these networks. They reviewed the literature on traditional forms of mentoring and on the changes in the current career environment, which "suggest particular shifts in the sources and nature of mentoring relationships today" (p. 267). According to their descriptions, NDRs are not relationships between only two persons—a mentor and protégé, rather, they are relationships among people in a developmental network. They depicted the phenomenological boundaries from developmental network perspective that is intra- and extra-organizational (e.g., profession, community, family), multilevel, multiple dyadic/networked relationships, mutual and reciprocal, career/person related and at both network level and dyad level (p. 268).

An interesting example of NDRs with younger/older mentoring dyad against traditional older/younger concept can be drawn from Merriweather and Morgan (2013), in which the mentor is a junior assistant professor while the mentee is a senior who's the mentor's mother's age. While TDRs mostly focus on a traditional intergenerational mentorship (older mentor and younger mentee), this story is a rather nontraditional instance in a nontraditional developmental relationship. In a traditional mentorship, the balance and nature of power are clear. The mentor who is older, more experienced, and more knowledgeable holds the most power over the mentee. What about the age factor in which mentor/mentee relationship is formed between a young AP mentor and an older and more experienced mentee? What kind of DR is this? It is obviously not the case as in the TDRs. In the scenario described in Merriweather and Morgan (2013), unlike a traditional mentorship, the mentor and mentee both had legitimate power. Dr. Lisa's (the mentor) power came from her position as assistant professor, while Miss Berta's (the mentee) power was from her lived experience as a senior. Because of this "age" difference that is very nontraditional in a mentoring relationship in which power is found, power differential is not the same as in TDRs. Age actually acted as a cultural factor that hid expectations about the power inherent in the relationship: Miss Berta expected the power to be in Dr. Lisa's hands since she was a professor and the mentor, while Dr. Lisa unconsciously conferred referent power to Miss Berta who came to the relationship with generational power because she was of the same generation as Dr. Lisa's mother. So, in this kind of NDR, actually, there is a lack of power differential, or, the power differential is blurred. It also reveals that approaches for TDRs might not be as effective as for NDRs where mentees were senior to their mentors, and there's potential to erode some of the traditional power dynamics that tend to structure TDRs (Bierema & Merriam, 2002).

Introducing the Concept of Virtual Developmental Relationships (VDRs)

The digital revolution has evolved the dynamics of different developmental relationships in HRD. And the "virtual medium provides a context and exchange that may not be possible to replicate in face-to-face mentoring relationships" (Bierema & Merriam, 2002, p. 219). In conceptualizing e-mentoring relationship, Bierema and Merriam (2002) have proposed "a definition and conceptual framework from which to understand e-mentoring," and defined e-mentoring as "a computer-mediated, mutually beneficial relationship between a mentor and a protégé which provides learning, advising, encouraging, promoting, and modeling, that is often boundaryless, egalitarian, and qualitatively different than traditional face-to-face mentoring" (p. 214). This definition "has two elements that distinguish e-mentoring from traditional mentoring: the boundaryless configuration of e-mentoring and the egalitarian quality of the exchange" (p. 219).

e-Mentoring is virtual mentoring. Bierema and Hill (2005) asserted that virtual mentoring can be quite different from, more flexible and easier to manage, less costly and more attractive than traditional face-to-face mentoring programs. Especially,

It has the potential to make mentoring available to individuals such as women and people of color who might otherwise have difficulty finding a mentor...E-mentoring crosses boundaries of race, class, and gender by targeting marginalized groups in society such as minorities, low-income students, and young girls and women. (p. 559)

The virtual context of e-mentoring requires different communication skills and interactions and allows more flexibility for creating and sustaining developmental relationships than face-to-face mentoring (Bierema & Hill, 2005; Bierema & Merriam, 2002).

Then, most recently, Bierema (2022) coined the term "Virtual Developmental Relationships" (VDRs) in her chapter published in *HRD Perspectives on Developmental Relationships* (Ghosh & Hutchins, 2022). Bierema (2022) termed "these mutual, technology-enabled partnerships focused on learning and growth as virtual developmental relationships or VDRs, in contrast to traditional developmental relationships (TDRs), which rely on primarily in-person communication" (p. 2).

According to Bierema (2022), virtual developmental relationships may happen between the dyads "through digital platforms such as teleconference, videoconference, social media, instant messaging, meeting platforms, email, websites, texting, or a blend of these digital communication modalities" (p. 10). She delved into the technical and human factors in VDRs and suggested that such affiliations "offer increased access, affordability, equity, and inclusion for individuals seeking career support" (p. 29). The human dynamics in VDRs, she asserted, "involve building sensitivity and capacity to address JEDI (justice, equity, diversity, and inclusion) issues and navigating diverse dyads where misunderstanding and distrust may challenge mutuality in the mentoring or coaching dyad" (p. 1). She further asserted, from a critical HRD (CHRD) perspective, that "JEDI sensitivity is particularly important since technology makes VDRs more accessible regardless of geography, organization, or positionality" (p. 25).

The concept of VDRs include virtual collaboration, virtual communications skills different than that in face-to-face communications. According to Bierema (2017a),

We are living in a global age of multinational corporations and individuals who are working, learning, and communicating from home across time and space. So, without doubt, this type of e-mentoring VDRs "makes it easier to work around family demands, work schedules, and time zones to engage in developmental relationships.... also widens potential mentoring relationships to the global community, increasing the pool of potential mentors and protégés. (p. 485)

Because mentoring forms developmental relationships, and e-mentoring is engagement in a developmental relationship between a mentor and a protégé that is mediated by a computer in a virtual environment, therefore, virtual developmental relationships (VDRs) are formed. In VDRs, geographical and cultural barriers that might have limited corporate mentoring programs and prevented individual and group mentoring dyads that are separated geographically from working together.

It is worth noting that traditional developmental relationships in mentoring usually describe the scenario where a senior mentors younger (e.g., Kram's [1985] classic definition of mentoring describes it as a didactic relationship where career and psychosocial support are provided to a junior employee by a more senior, experienced colleague in the organization), while in Bierema and Merriam's (2002) conceptual framework of e-mentoring, it is not necessarily based on a wise elder dispensing advice and instruction to a protégé. Rather, it is a mutually beneficial relationship that is highly versatile and can be adapted to work in a variety of settings (p. 219). As Bierema and Merriam pointed out, e-mentoring:

> Has the potential to cross barriers of race, gender, geography, age, and hierarchy that are rarely crossed in traditional mentoring relationships. By offering a "safe" context for establishing relationships between diverse parties, e-mentoring holds the potential to erode some of the traditional power dynamics that tend to structure mentoring relationships. (p. 220)

HRD in organizations has an important role in fostering developmental relationships, especially the virtual developmental relationships (VDRs). Because "the evolving context for developmental relationships—most notably virtual relationships—merits further exploration as this may serve to increase access considerably, especially for women and people of color" (Gibson, 2008, p. 667).

CRITIQUING TDRs FROM FEMINIST PERSPECTIVES

Feminists have asked provocative questions to interrogate traditional organizations, which were performance-oriented, masculine-dominated, and White-centered. Joan Acker's (1990) theory of gendered organizations stemmed from a critical inquiry: is organizational structure gender-neutral? Pointing out that focusing its analysis exclusively on gender is incomplete in understanding the complex interweaving of inequality in the workplace, Acker (2012) maintained that the gendering process could be understood from an intersectional lens. This means that the gendering process of TDRs needs to be expanded to other oppressive processes (e.g., racializing, class creating) and take note of the overarching hegemony, and ideology reproduced under the interlocking inequity of organizational systems.

The intersectional viewpoint may contribute to unpacking the dynamic and structural marginalization and oppression of women employees with different social categories and contexts (e.g., race, class, nation, sexuality) during the formation, process, and result of TDRs. For example, old boy networks or mentoring for women in the organization may be interrogated considering the interlocking system of inequality. Through integrative literature review, Manongsong and Ghosh (2021) found that diversified mentoring relationships, such as matching mentor and mentee from different backgrounds with different power structures due to the lack of minoritized group members in the workplace, are likely to aggravate oppression of minoritized women leaders without great care. Harris (2022) said current mentoring programs for women that encourage competition and personal achievement in the organization have become a new form of performing neoliberal praxis, far from transforming the workplace into a more just, equitable context. These results demonstrating the problems of TDRs show that TDRs in the workplace should be scrutinized from the standpoint of feminism and ways they may erode, rather than elevate equity. In this vein, this section focuses on intersectional and transnational feminism that may have implications for deconstructing TDRs.

Questioning DRs from an Intersectional Feminist Viewpoint

Reproducing gendered organizations that buttress a normative structure in the workplace, created by white heterosexual, cisgender elite men, will accelerate the marginalization of other workers and decrease diversity in the organization. Intersectional feminists have questioned traditional organizational theories and practices that disregarded how asymmetrical power structure impacts workers' experiences with intersectional identities, especially from historically excluded groups (e.g., women of color). The perspective of intersectional feminists is based on intersectionality, coined by Kimberlé Crenshaw (1989), which is a way of understanding the influence of intersecting power relations and interrelated social categories on social relations and individual experiences (Hill Collins & Bilge, 2020). For example, intersectionality illuminates how privilege and marginalization are intersecting, how multiple social categories (e.g., gender, race, ethnicity, nationality, sexuality, etc.) are interrelated, and how the power differentials have an impact on the lives of people and society. The intersectional feminist perspective enables unpacking the power dynamic ignored in TRD theories and practices.

Several studies revealed that TDRs failed to capture the intersection of gender and race/ethnicity, which didn't help women of color advance in the organization, especially in science, technology, engineering, and mathematics (STEM) academia (e.g., Corneille et al., 2019; Valdivia, 2021). Given that studies introduced DRs as a good intervention to support women of color by developing social capital and network (Liu et al., 2019; Sanchez-Hucles & Davis, 2010) and women of color had higher needs for career-related, psychosocial, and role-model mentoring than that of counterparts (Payne et al., 2011), the results demonstrating that DRs are not effective for women of color is of concern.

Given these findings, it is imperative to offer meaningful DRs with women leaders from historically marginalized groups. Many studies that analyzed the leadership experiences of women of color with an intersectional feminist lens (e.g., Byrd, 2009; Ngunjiri & Hernández, 2017) showed how they were disempowered and excluded while being pressured to improve their abilities and existence in the workplace. This means that women of color often face difficulty despite their high positions. Mentors, coaches, and others in DRs should stop disregarding the impact of whiteness on DRs and foregrounding the femininity of elite white women leaders to build a network (Liu, 2021). Colorblindness and white supremacy in TDRs are still prevalent due to asymmetrical power relations embedded in oppressive organizational structures and embodied implicit bias. Alternative DRs should consider the influence of the intersection of multiple identities on the purpose, principles, and processes of DRs.

DECOLONIZING DRs
FROM A TRANSNATIONAL FEMINIST VIEWPOINT

The contexts of organizational theories and practices, including DRs, are centered on Western, educated, industrialized, rich, and democratic (WEIRD) countries. It is likely that existing theories and practices in TDRs are not applicable or suitable for workplaces located in non-WEIRD countries. Thus, TDRs need to be decolonized from a transnational feminist perspective. From an intersectional perspective, transnational feminism focuses on the experiences and situations of women in non-WEIRD countries, and interrogates uneven global power structure stemming from global neoliberalism, colonialism, and imperialism (Collins et al., 2019; Hundle et al., 2019). Although both global feminism and transnational feminism explore experiences of women beyond the nation, global feminism typically focuses on comparisons between countries whereas transnational feminism not only focuses on similarities and differences but also finds "scattered hegemonies" (Grewal & Kaplan, 1994, p. 18) across the nations, such as global economic structures and patriarchal nationalisms (Hundle et al., 2019). Moreover, transnational feminism refuses global inequality and the idea of global sisterhood while considering power differentials between nations (Mason, 2017; Mohanty, 1991).

Transnational feminists have pointed out that previous studies neglected the experiences of non-Western, Third World, or Global South women while centering on the experiences of privileged women (e.g., White, middle-class, heterosexual, cisgender women). The Eurocentric approach under capitalism and neoliberalism has produced research results tailored to the U.S and Western European contexts while ignoring asymmetrical geopolitical powers across the world. Thus, from a transnational feminist viewpoint, it is likely that the results of previous studies about DRs do not apply to global contexts, especially non-Western, Third World, or Global South. In order to end reproducing developmental relationship studies only for privileged women located in dominant worlds, the perspective of transnational feminists aiming to reveal how globalization and capitalization affected the lives of women across the globe would be helpful.

Transnational in "transnational feminism" means transcending a nation (Mason, 2017). "Transnational spaces are composed of tangible geographic spaces that exist across multiple nation-states *and* virtual spaces" (Purkayastha, 2012, p. 56). People in the transnational spaces might experience oppression or marginalization much less than in the in person U.S. national space by cultivating more salient relationships with people in diverse locations (Purkayastha, 2012). Not only attentive to the intersections of marginalization in the mentoring practices, but transnational feminists seeking solidarity under the coloniality of mainstream society are also attentive to creating collaborative relationships of trust and building mutual respect and alliance throughout the mentoring process (Mullings & Mukherjee, 2018).

REIMAGINING DEVELOPMENTAL RELATIONSHIPS TOWARD GENDER EQUITY, SOCIAL JUSTICE, AND SOLIDARITY

Recognizing power differentials and focusing on both structural change and relationships between mentor and mentee focused on equity and justice would be the core promise of alternative DRs (Harris, 2022). Alternative DRs need to create the collective "we": "who-are-not-one-and-the-same-but-are-this-together" (Braidotti, 2022, p. 8) to transform and redeem the workplace buried in neoliberalism. This solidarity is based on "affirmative relational ethics" (p. 9) that creates horizontal relationships (Braidotti, 2022). We would like to reimagine alternative DRs, which advocate promoting gender equity and social justice in the workplace.

Alston and Hansman (2020) lamented the lack of literature examining the possibility of emancipatory mentoring. What makes DRs transformative engagements that impact diversity, equity, and inclusion, and disrupt the prevailing power relations? Alston and Hansman noted that such engagements should incorporate a process of adult learning and development that builds capacity to critically analyze hegemonic structures that impinge equity in organizations, explaining,

> Ontologically and epistemologically, some mentoring experiences can be troublesome for folx [spelling is intentional to demonstrate cultural respectfulness] who are members of underrepresented, minoritized, and disenfranchised groups as they continue to grapple with their positionalities in the space of leadership development. (p. 89)

Their approach integrated Freire et al.'s (1987) notion of "democratic substance" and ethical democracy in mentoring relationships in which mentees self-construct mentoring goals and objectives and function as co-creators of dialogic exploration and learning through the mentoring relationship.

Alston and Hansman explained, when mentoring provides the opportunity for reflection on hegemonic and systemic organization and social structures that oppress, mentees have the opportunity to build knowledge, understanding, and capacity for action.

Alston and Hansman (2020) introduced a model for leadership development mentoring, emphasizing "cultural respectfulness" as the most crucial component of mentoring and incorporating *cultural awareness*—seeing oneself as a cultural being and recognizing others' cultural diversity; *cultural sensitivity*—accepting cultural diversity without judgment; and *cultural humility*—embracing cultural diversity as a lifelong learning duty based in self-evaluation and critique and a commitment to rebalancing power relations. Their "T.A.K.E. G.O.O.D. C.A.R.E. Model for Inclusive Mentoring" (Alston & Hansman, 2020, p. 88) introduced 12 components for inclusive mentoring including: trust, accountability, kinship, emancipation, grace, objectives, openness, rejecting traditional conceptualizations of mentoring, courage, affirmation, reflection, and engagement. We build on their model and other concepts presented in this chapter to introduce a new model of critical feminist developmental relationships.

A Model of Critical Feminist Developmental Relationships—CDFRs

The Alston–Hansman's (2020) model offered a useful roadmap for both the mentor and mentee, information helpful for a range of developmental relationships. What the "T.A.K.E. G.O.O.D. C.A.R.E. Model for Inclusive Mentoring" did not provide is a process to help the mentoring dyad make sense of power relations, gender hegemony, injustice, and exclusion through a more holistic, systemic lens, as their unit of analysis is the individual mentoring relationship. Shouskry and Cox's (2018) critique of coaching could be applied to DRs non-systemic focus in general:

> The growth of coaching is, in part, a reflection of a wider social phenomenon – a Western-led global move towards more focus on the individual as an independent social unit, and the set of personal competences that are claimed to be behind success....[where it] takes place within a discourse of competition, return on investment, goal attainment and self-actualisation and that, from a critical perspective, there is a danger that coaching becomes merely a tool for organisational and social conformity, where individuals get professional help to become more integrated into a pervasive ideology and where power dynamics may be at play (p. 414)

We contend that for developmental relationships to dismantle systemic oppression, they must not only hone effective developmental relational and learning skills among the dyad, but also build capacity to navigate cultural and organizational systems that function to preserve the status quo and take actions to disrupt hegemonic organizations and systems.

We propose a model of critical feminist developmental relationships— CFDRs that spells out the characteristics and goals of these relationships, as well as strategies to promote CFDRs, and implications for research and practice. Drawing on Shoukry and Cox's (2018) adaptation of Bennett (1993a, 1993b) model of intercultural sensitivity within social context (Fig. 15.1), we explore different levels of criticality and feminism in DRs. Bennett (2004) created the "Developmental Model of Intercultural Sensitivity— DMIS" (1986, 1993a, 1993b; Bennett & Bennett, 2004) centering in the developmental shift from *ethnocentrism*—experiencing one's culture as primary and central to reality to *ethnorelativism*—the opposite of ethnocentrism in which one experiences their culture as one reality among many cultures.

Bennett's (1993a, 1993b) model is based on two intersecting axes, (1) *Understanding of cultural diversity*, which echoes the work of Alston and Hansman (2020), and (2) *Adherence to social order*, which integrates a focus on social and political context. Understanding of cultural diversity (the horizontal axis) ranges from *absolutism*—an ideal set of cultural values exists; to *relativism*—all cultural values are equally important, there are no ideals. The vertical axis, adherence to social order, ranges from *conformism*—adhering to accepted values and norms of the social context; to *criticality*—challenging limitations and changing accepted values and norms to achieve desired outcomes. DRs along these continua (Absolutism—Relativism and Conformism—Criticality) create four distinctive stances toward social contexts in developmental relationships according to Bennett:

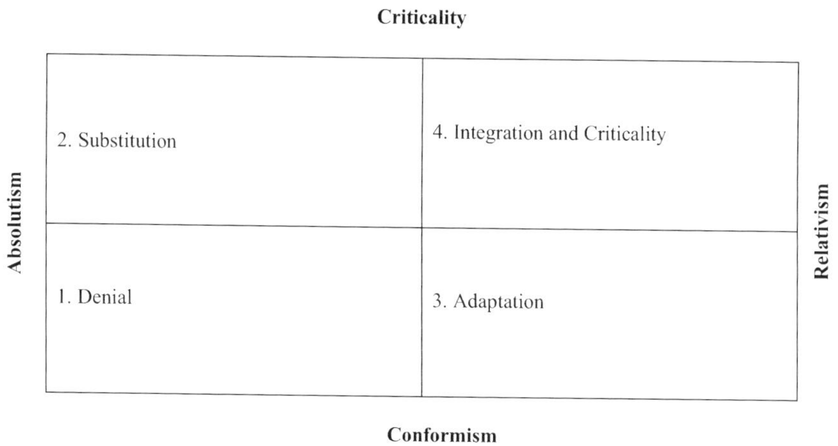

Criticality

Absolutism	2. Substitution	4. Integration and Criticality	Relativism
	1. Denial	3. Adaptation	

Conformism

Fig. 15.1 Bennett's model of intercultural sensitivity within social context

1. Denial (absolutism and conformism): Ignoring the social context and focusing on the individual;
2. Substitution (abolitionism and criticality): Proposing other cultural and social views as being superior;
3. Adaptation (relativism and conformism): Aligning DRs with the existing social context; and
4. Integration and Criticality (relativism and criticality): Respecting the context and working with it, as well as helping the dyad to critically understand and act on the context.

Shoukry and Cox (2018) posited that each of the four roles has important implications for developmental relationships (p. 419). We developed a Critical Feminist Developmental Relationships—CFDRs—model that elaborates the fourth aspect of the Bennett Model of Intercultural Sensitivity within Social Context, "integration and criticality." We think valuing diverse cultures and approaching social context critically are pivotal to building DRs that challenge the status quo and create justice and inclusion in organizations and society.

CFDR Goals and Characteristics

In order to promote justice, equity, diversity, and inclusion in society and organizations, CFDRs aim to achieve the following three goals. First, dismantle hegemonic structures. Second, replace hegemonic structures with more equitable and just systems. Third, address organization and wider social inequities and injustices. Figure 15.2 outlines the seven characteristics of CFDRs in elaboration of Bennett's "integration and criticality" quadrant of the model. Each is discussed in this section in terms of definitions, examples, and practical strategies to apply CFDRs.

Values Emancipatory DRs

The first characteristic of the critical feminist developmental relationships (CFDRs) model is valuing emancipation. Increasingly, DRs help leaders more effectively attend to issues of organization diversity, equity, and inclusion (Whitmer & Hopkins, 2018). Emancipatory work involves participatory and empowering learning, understanding and utilizing power dynamics embedded in society, sharing lived experiences of participants, and reflecting and thinking critically about lived experience and aiming for social transformation (Freire, 1970; Shoukry, 2016). Given the participative nature of DRs, they are natural sites for promoting mutuality and equality in the dyad. Thus, CFDRs reject solely focusing DRs' processes on personal and internal change and places equal or more value on creating structural and social change. Shoukry (2016) asked important questions and related to coaching for emancipation: "How does oppression affect individuals? And how can they liberate themselves from its implications?" (p. 413).

Criticality

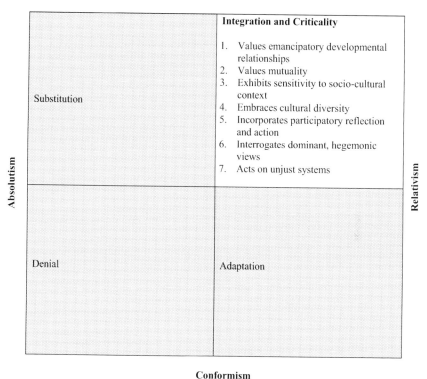

Conformism

Fig. 15.2 Model of critical feminist developmental relationships in social context

According to Shoukry's (2016) research with 22 coaches who used an emancipatory approach, coaching for emancipation is enabled through understanding the dynamics of emancipation, development, and empowerment through three activities: (1) Encouraging the *retelling of narratives* using consciousness-raising and naming the lived experience of oppression to create a narrative of such; (2) *Renewing beliefs* with process of self-reflection to understand structural contributors to oppression, as well as surface individual mindsets and assumptions; and (3) Creating ways of *fighting back* against oppression through learning new mindsets and behaviors of resistance and change. Although CFDRs likely occur within organizational settings, their ultimate purpose is to transform the social system of inequality continuously oppressing marginalized groups due to asymmetrical power differentials and unchallenged power relations.

Values Mutuality

The second characteristic of the CFDRs model is concerned with mutuality. Mentoring has historically been associated with the character Mentor in Homer's *Odyssey*, yet the poetic work is often drawn on uncritically and accounts of the romanticized, violent, masculinized process usually go uncritiqued (Garvey, 2017). Francois Fenelon (1854), Archbishop of Cambrai and tutor of Louix XIV's grandson is credited with the first literary use of mentor in *Les Adventures de Telemaque* (1699) where he described mentoring as a caring, supportive, and challenging educational relationship. We embrace Fenelon's viewpoint in creating CFDRs.

CFDRs privilege mutuality; avoiding one-way direction in the process that privileges the mentor, instead advocating bidirectional movement in relationships. Mutuality in DRs means there are reciprocal and shared developments, growth, expectations, and understanding between all participants, including mentors and mentees, coaches and coaches, and between organizations and individuals. Friendship, nurturance, open-mindedness, and trustworthiness are required to build up mutuality in DRs (Beyene et al., 2002).

Exhibits Sensitivity to Sociocultural Context

Third, in the CFDRs model is tuning into the contextual dynamics. Shoukry and Cox (2018) introduced complexities that the integration and criticality position should take into account: The complex effect of social context on the coaching process and relationships, especially in interculturally sensitive contexts. CFDR assumes dependent mechanisms between the DR process and oppressive socioculture context that different laws, politics, and acknowledges power structures have different influences on mentor and mentee. Thus, CFDR requires participants to understand and be sensitive to the sociocultural context. Participants in DRs can reflect on social context by considering their own positionalities (e.g., gender, race, socioeconomic status, gender identity, sexuality, religion, physical ability, and other personal attributes), how they intersect, and ways they engage with the contexts of work and society. Shoukry (2016) recommended key activities of emancipatory coaching as including empowering dialogue, consciousness-raising, cross-role analysis, critical reflection, discovering new worlds, engaging in a narrative of liberation, and reflective action as key strategies for evolving personal and system transformation through DRs.

Embraces Cultural Diversity

The fourth element of the CFDRs model is to value diversity. Cultural diversity is defined as "the representation, in one social system, of people with distinctly different group affiliations of cultural significance" (Cox, 1993, p. 6).

A multicultural workplace with cultural diversity not only values human diversity but also welcomes diverse talents and perspectives without discrimination and prejudice (Byrd & Scott, 2018; Cox, 1993). Partners engaged in DRs can assess their level of Diversity Intelligence (Hughes, 2016) and use meetings to explore new perspectives and ways of providing mutual support for learning and being in contested environments. Banerjee-Batist et al.'s (2019) integrative literature review of mentoring recognized the areas of gender, ethnicity, culture, and age as key sociocultural factors in DRs, concluding gendered barriers proved most challenging at the initiation of the developmental relationship due to the lack of women mentors and the need for cross-gender mentoring. The ethnicity-based barriers were based in preferences for same ethnicity mentors, yet confounded by their paucity, meaning most dyads were cross-ethnic, creating problems when mentors were ill-prepared to understand and learn about racism. CFDR fully accepts cultural diversity by recognizing different opinions, needs, backgrounds, and power differentials in the process of DRs. CFDRs request all participants to begin with constructive, sensitive, and considerate dialogue.

Incorporates Participatory Reflection and Action

Fifth in the CFDRs model is engaging in critical reflexivity and action. Bierema (2003, 2005, 2017a, 2017b) proposed a conceptual framework of gender consciousness, incorporating the two axes of awareness and action. CFDRs may raise the "consciousness advocates" who engage in critical activism and take risks to challenge asymmetrical power relations in the organization as well as have a sophisticated understanding of gendered power structure (Bierema, 2003, 2005, 2017b). CFDRs need to be designed to integrate their awareness and behavior and develop participants who are willing to transform gendered workplaces.

Interrogates Dominant, Hegemonic Views

Sixth in the CFDRs model is contesting hegemony. Under the White supremacist capitalist heteropatriarchal society, workplaces have been dominated by gendered, racialized, and neoliberal hegemonies. Participants in CFDRs are encouraged to question the hegemonic viewpoint since CFDRs ultimately aim for social transformation and are not limited to personal development. Further, CFDRs recognize how hegemonic views have oppressed non-Western, Global South, and Third World, and try to decolonize TDRs by questioning imperialistic and colonialist practices embedded in TDRs. To decolonize TDRs, they may utilize reflective structured dialogue that challenges their own assumptions and create a shared understanding (Bierema & Rawls, 2022). By interrogating dominant and hegemonic views embedded in workplaces, CFDRs may contribute to promoting social justice.

Bierema (2022) underscored if the DR dyad is to be mutually supportive and effective in mixed pairings based on race, gender, sexuality, ability, or other aspects of positionality, capacity to learn about racism, sexism, and other isms dominating society is crucial. The ability to dialogue about issues of injustice and inequity in ways that build trust and help mutually problem solve are also essential relational skills in DRs. Carroll and Barnes (2015) asserted that effective cross-race mentoring and coaching depends on mentors' and coaches' cognizance of privilege and bias and how they affect their developmental relationships. They outlined five broaching styles of avoidant, isolating, incongruent, congruent, and infusing, for addressing these issues, along with the level of cultural competence. Bierema (2022) reimagined their recommendations and related them to potential conversations about race in developmental relationships.

Acts on Unjust Systems

Finally, the CFDRs model is acting to change unjust systems. It is our hope that CFDRs provide structure and impetus to help individuals and organizations involved in DRs to follow Shoukry and Cox's (2018) suggestion that integration and criticality tilt the balance in these affiliations to:

> Promote capability in handling the complexity inherent in many social settings, especially where oppression and inequality have been institutionalized and internalised and have become part of everyday practices. The position of integration and criticality upholds the same view of relativism as in the position of adaptation, in terms of acknowledging and respecting the cultural context, but balances it with a process of criticality that involves an examination of the assumptions, norms, expectations and limitations of the cultural system and how they affect the individual being coached. (p. 422)

CFDRs are intended to examine how oppression and inequality are part of organization acculturation processes and how they can be resisted through meaning making and taking small and grand actions to contest them.

Anti-oppressive practices are aimed at changing social patterns that create divisions based on race gender, disability, sexual orientation, age, and other positionalities (Burke & Harrison, 2004). Burke and Harrison (2004) advocated that anti-oppression work is driven by challenging inequalities. Such practice demands reflexivity, sensitivity to historical and geographical context, and viewing the personal as political.

IMPLICATIONS FOR RESEARCH AND PRACTICE

We view this chapter as an important step in reimagining how developmental relationships can play a more substantial role in enhancing justice, equity, diversity, and inclusion in organizations and society. We recommend that a systematic study of our critical feminist developmental relationships model be conducted. How are the seven characteristics of integration and criticality bolstered or blocked in DRs? What are proven strategies for effective DRs that prevail in changing the social order? How can participants in DR view the engagement as larger than individual development? What are the best pedagogies and strategies for learning and teaching about CFDRs? We also think it is worth considering the following questions: How can DRs more strategically impact social isms? How can DRs be more cross-and intercultural? How might DRs develop critical consciousness and transformation? How should DRs benefit individual, organization, and community health? How can we apply critical frameworks to DR research and practice?

We call for empirical studies supporting the value of CFDRs. For example, future research may conduct a case study on these affiliations and find organizational characteristics and leadership strategies that drive CFDRs and demonstrate specific principles and processes of using these relationships to contest inequality and injustice. Quantitative studies to test the positive impacts of CFDRs on employees and organizations may contribute to developing CFDRs.

Implications for practice include developing more critically oriented development of people involved in developmental relationship dyads, including resources for dyads to use as they engage in their relationships. Serving partners engaged in DRs virtually is also valuable as VDRs hold great promise for making DRs more accessible and equitable without organizational or geographical borders.

Conclusion

This chapter introduced a critical feminist framework for developmental relationships—CFDRs—as a mechanism for change in spaces of organizing and to provide strategies for making DRs a sphere for promoting diversity, equity, and inclusion. We considered DRs in HRD and reimagined how they might foster more gender equity, social justice, and solidarity in organizations and society. We close with the wisdom of Paulo Freire who based his liberatory pedagogy on conviction that by understanding hegemonic structures, humans can change them.

> [T]o be a good liberating educator; you need above all to have faith in human beings. You need to love. You must be convinced that the fundamental I of education is to help with the liberation of people, never their domestication. You must be convinced that when people reflect on their domination they begin a first step in changing their relationship to the world. (Freire, 1971, p. 62)

References

Acker, J. (1990). Hierarchies, jobs, bodies: A theory of gendered organizations. *Gender & Society, 4*(2), 139–158. https://doi.org/10.1177/089124390004 002002

Acker, J. (2012). Gendered organizations and intersectionality: Problems and possibilities. *Equality, Diversity, and Inclusion: An International Journal, 31*(3), 214–224. https://doi.org/10.1108/02610151211209072

Alston, G. D., & Hansman, C. A. (2020). Embracing diversity and inclusive mentoring practices for leadership development. *New Directions for Adult & Continuing Education, 2020*(167/168), 83–94. https://doi.org/10.1002/ace.20400

Banerjee-Batist, R., Reio, T. G., Jr., & Rocco, T. S. (2019). Mentoring functions and outcomes: An integrative literature review of sociocultural factors and individual differences. *Human Resource Development Review, 18*(1), 114–162. https://doi.org/10.1177/1534484318810267

Barstow, C. (2008). The power differential and the power paradox. In *Hakomi Forum* (Vol. 19, pp. 20–21).

Bennett , M. J. (1993a). Towards ethnorelativism: A developmental model of intercultural sensitivity. In R. M Paige (Ed.), *Education for the intercultural experience* (pp. 21–71). Intercultural Press.

Bennett, J. M. (1993b). Cultural marginality: Identity issues in intercultural training. In R. M. Paige (Ed.), *Education for the intercultural experience* (2nd ed., pp. 109–135). Intercultural Press.

Bennett, M. J. (1986). A developmental approach to training for intercultural sensitivity. *International Journal of Intercultural Relations, 10*(2), 179–196. https://doi.org/10.1016/0147-1767(86)90005-2

Bennett, M. J. (2004). Becoming interculturally competent. In J. S. Wurzel (Ed.) *Toward multiculturalism: A reader in multicultural education*. Intercultural Resource Corporation.

Bennett, J. M., & Bennett, M. J. (2004). Developing intercultural sensitivity: An integrative approach to global and domestic diversity. In D. Landis, J. Bennett, & M. Bennett (Eds.), *Handbook of intercultural training* (3rd ed, pp. 147–165). Sage.

Beyene, T., Anglin, M., Sanchez, W., & Ballou, M. (2002). Mentoring and relational mutuality: Proteges' perspectives. *The Journal of Humanistic Counseling, Education and Development, 41*(1), 87–102. https://doi.org/10.1002/j.2164-490X.2002.tb00132.x

Bierema, L. L. (2003). The role of gender consciousness in challenging patriarchy. *International Journal of Lifelong Education, 22*(1), 3–12. https://doi.org/10.1080/02601370304825

Bierema, L. L. (2005). Women's networks: A career development intervention or impediment? *Human Resource Development International, 8*(2), 207–224. https://doi.org/10.1080/13678860500100517

Bierema, L. (2017a). eMentoring: Computer mediated career development for the future. In *The Sage handbook of mentoring* (pp. 482–498). Sage.

Bierema, L. L. (2017b). No woman left behind: Critical leadership development to build gender consciousness and transform organizations. In S. R. Madse (Ed.), *Handbook of research on gender and leadership* (pp. 145–162). https://doi.org/10.4337/9781785363863

Bierema, L. L. (2022). "Can you hear me now?" Technical and human factors in virtual developmental relationships. In R. Ghosh & H. M. Hutchins (Eds.), *HRD perspectives on developmental relationships* (pp. 241–272). Palgrave Macmillan.

Bierema, L., & Callahan, J. L. (2014). Transforming HRD: A framework for critical HRD practice. *Advances in Developing Human Resources, 16*(4), 429–444. https://doi.org/10.1177/1523422314543818

Bierema, L. L., & Hill, J. R. (2005). Virtual mentoring and HRD. *Advances in Developing Human Resources, 7*(4), 556–568. https://doi.org/10.1177/152342 2305279688

Bierema, L. L., & Merriam, S. B. (2002). E-mentoring: Using computer mediated communication to enhance the mentoring process. *Innovative Higher Education, 26*(3), 211–227. https://doi.org/10.1023/A:1017921023103

Bierema, L. L., & Rawls, R. (2022). Using reflective structured dialogue (RSD) to discuss racism: A professional development workshop. In *2022 Academy of Human Resource Development Conference* (Virtual).

Braidotti, R. (2022). *Posthuman feminism.* Polity Press.

Burke, B., & Harrison, P. (2004). Anti-oppressive practice. In M. Robb (Ed.), *Communication, relationships and care* (pp. 141–148). Routledge.

Byrd, M. Y. (2009). Telling our stories of leadership: If we don't tell them they won't be told. *Advances in Developing Human Resources, 11*(5), 582–605. https://doi.org/10.1177/1523422309351514

Byrd, M. Y., & Scott, C. L. (Eds.). (2018). *Diversity in the workforce: Current issues and emerging trends.* Routledge.

Carroll, M. A., & Barnes, E. F. (2015). Strategies for enhancing diverse mentoring relationships in STEM fields. *International Journal of Evidence Based Coaching and Mentoring, 13*(1), 58–69. https://search.informit.org/doi/10.3316/informit.899 386072831002

Chesler, N. C., & Chesler, M. A. (2002). Gender-informed mentoring strategies for women engineering scholars: On establishing a caring community. *Journal of Engineering Education, 91*(1), 49–55.

Collins, L. H., Machizawa, S., & Rice, J. K. (2019). Transnational psychology of women. In L. H. Collins, S. Machizawa, & J. K. Rice (Eds.), *Transnational psychology of women: Expanding international and intersectional approaches* (pp. 15–42). American Psychological Association.

Corneille, M., Lee, A., Allen, S., Cannady, J., & Guess, A. (2019). Barriers to the advancement of women of color faculty in STEM: The need for promoting equity using an intersectional framework. *Equality, Diversity and Inclusion, 38*(3), 328–348. https://doi.org/10.1108/EDI-09-2017-0199

Cox, T. H. (1993). *Cultural diversity in organizations: Theory research and practice.* Berrett-Koehler.

Crenshaw, K. (1989). Demarginalizing the intersection of race and sex: Black feminist critique of antidiscrimination doctrine, feminist theory and antiracist politics. *University of Chicago Legal Forum, 1989,* 139–168.

Douglas, C. A., & McCauley, C. D. (1999). Formal developmental relationships: A survey of organizational practices. *Human Resource Development Quarterly, 10*(3), 203–220. https://doi.org/10.1002/hrdq.3920100302

Du Toit, A., & Sim, S. (2010). *Rethinking coaching: Critical theory and the economic crisis.* Palgrave Macmillan.

Fenelon, F. (1854). *Les aventures de télémaque, fils d'Ulysee.* Leavitt and Allen.

Freire, P. (1970). *Pedagogy of the oppressed*. The Continuum International Publishing Group Ltd.

Freire, P. (1971). To the coordinator of a cultural circle. *Convergence, 4*(1), 61–62. https://www.proquest.com/scholarly-journals/coordinator-cultural-circle/docview/1437904521/se-2?accountid=14537

Freire, P., Fraser, J. W., Macedo, D., McKinnon, T., & Stokes, W. T. (1987). *Mentoring the mentor: A critical dialogue*. Peter Lang Publishing.

Garvey, B. (2017). Philosophical origins of mentoring: The critical narrative analysis. In D. A. Clutterbuck, F. K. Kochan, L. G. Lunsford, N. Dominguez, & J. Haddock-Millar (Eds.), *The Sage handbook of mentoring* (pp. 15–33). Sage.

Ghosh, R., & Hutchins, H. M. (2022). *HRD perspectives on developmental relationships*. Springer.

Gibson, S. K. (2008). The developmental relationships of women leaders in career transition: Implications for leader development. *Advances in Developing Human Resources, 10*(5), 651–670. https://doi.org/10.1177/1523422308323935

Grewal, I., & Kaplan, C. (1994). Introduction: Transnational feminist practices and questions of postmodernity. In I. Grewal & C. Kaplan (Eds.), *Scattered hegemonies: Postmodernity and transnational feminist practices* (pp. 1–36). University of Minnesota Press.

Harris, D. A. (2022). Women, work, and opportunities: From neoliberal to feminist mentoring. *Sociology Compass, 16*(3). https://doi.org/10.1111/soc4.12966

Higgins, M. C., & Kram, K. E. (2001). Reconceptualizing mentoring at work: A developmental network perspective. *Academy of Management Review, 26*(2), 264–288. https://doi.org/10.5465/amr.2001.4378023

Hill Collins, P., & Bilge, S. (2020). *Intersectionality* (2nd ed.). Polity.

Hughes, C. (2016). *Diversity intelligence: Integrating diversity intelligence alongside intellectual, emotional, and cultural intelligence for leadership and career development*. Palgrave Macmillan.

Hundle, A. K., Szeman, I., & Hoare, J. P. (2019). What is the transnational in transnational feminist research? *Feminist Review, 121*, 3–8. https://doi.org/10.1177/0141778918817

Johnson-Bailey, J., & Cervero, R. (2004). Mentoring in black and white: The intricacies of cross-cultural mentoring. *Mentoring & Tutoring: Partnership in Learning, 12*(1), 7–21. https://doi.org/10.1080/1361126042000183075

Kram, K. E. (1985). Improving the mentoring process. *Training & Development Journal, 39*(4), 40–43.

Lea, Y. (2012). The praxis of mentoring: Power, organizing and emancipation. *Journal of Teacher Education for Sustainability, 14*(1), 39.

Liu, H. (2021). *Redeeming leadership: An anti-racist feminist intervention*. Policy Press.

Liu, S. N. C., Brown, S. E., & Sabat, I. E. (2019). Patching the "leaky pipeline": Interventions for women of color faculty in STEM academia. *Archives of Scientific Psychology, 7*(1), 32. https://doi.org/10.1037/arc0000062

Manongsong, A. M., & Ghosh, R. (2021). Developing the positive identity of minoritized women leaders in higher education: How can multiple and diverse developers help with overcoming the impostor phenomenon? *Human Resource Development Review, 20*(4), 436–485. https://doi.org/10.1177/15344843211040732

Mason, C. L. (2017). Transnational feminism. In N. Mandell & J. L. Johnson (Eds.), *Feminist issues: Race, class and sexuality* (pp. 62–89). Pearson.

McDonald, K. S., & Hite, L. M. (2005). Reviving the relevance of career development in human resource development. *Human Resource Development Review, 4*(4), 418–439. https://doi.org/10.1177/1534484305281006

Merriweather, L. R., & Morgan, A. J. (2013). Two cultures collide: Bridging the generation gap in a non-traditional mentorship. *Qualitative Report, 18,* 12.

Mohanty, C. T. (1991). Under western eyes: Feminist scholarship and colonial discourses. In C. T. Mohanty, A. Russo, & L. Lourdes Torres (Eds.), *Third world women and the politics of feminism* (pp. 51–78). Indiana University Press.

Mott, V. W. (2002). Emerging perspectives on mentoring: Fostering adult learning and development. In C. Hansman (Ed.), Critical perspectives on mentoring: Trends and issues (ED99CO0013) (pp. 5–14). ERIC. https://eric.ed.gov/?q=ED465045

Mullings, B., & Mukherjee, S. (2018). Reflections on mentoring as decolonial, transnational, feminist praxis. *Gender, Place, & Culture, 25*(10), 1405–1422. https://doi.org/10.1080/0966369X.2018.1556614

Ngunjiri, F. W., & Hernández, K. A. C. (2017). Problematizing authentic leadership: A collaborative autoethnography of immigrant women of color leaders in higher education. *Advances in Developing Human Resources, 19*(4), 393–406. https://doi.org/10.1177/1523422317728735

Passmore, J., & Law, H. (2009). Cross-cultural and diversity coaching. In *Diversity in coaching: Working with gender, culture, race and age* (pp. 4–16).

Payne, S. C., Thompson, R. J., & Pesonen, A. (2011, April). *Mentoring in academia: Who needs it?* Paper presented at the 26th Annual SIOP Conference, Chicago, IL.

Purkaystha, D. (2012). Intersectionality in a transnational world. *Gender & Society, 26*(1), 55–66. https://doi.org/10.1177/0891243211426725

Ragins, B. R. (1997). Diversified mentoring relationships in organizations: A power perspective. *Academy of Management Review, 22*(2), 482–521. https://doi.org/10.5465/amr.1997.9707154067

Rock, A. D., & Garavan, T. N. (2006). Reconceptualizing developmental relationships. *Human Resource Development Review, 5*(3), 330–354. https://doi.org/10.1177/1534484306290227

Sanchez-Hucles, J. V., & Davis, D. D. (2010). Women and women of color in leadership: Complexity, identity, and intersectionality. *American Psychologist, 65*(3), 171–181. https://doi.org/10.1037/a0017459

Schultz, F. (2010). *The politics of work coaching—Between impairing vision and creating visions.* Retrieved from University of Surrey website: http://epubs.surrey.ac.uk/2445/1/politics_SCHULZ.pdf

Semeniuk, A., & Worrall, A. (2000). Rereading the dominant narrative of mentoring. *Curriculum Inquiry, 30*(4), 405–428. https://doi.org/10.1111/0362-6784.00172

Shoukry, H. (2016). Coaching for emancipation: A framework for coaching in oppressive environments. *International Journal of Evidence Based Coaching and Mentoring, 14*(2), 15–30. https://search.informit.org/doi/10.3316/informit.554478402927112

Shoukry, H., & Cox, E. (2018). Coaching as a social process. *Management Learning, 49*(4), 413–428. https://doi.org/10.1177/1350507618762600

Valdivia, A. N. (2021). Intersectionality and mentoring as organic praxis: When feminist killjoys are too hot to be mentors. *Communication, Culture and Critique, 14*(4), 692–695. https://doi.org/10.1093/ccc/tcab055

Western, S. (2012). *Coaching and mentoring: A critical ext.* Sage.

Western, S. (2017). The key discourses of coaching. In T. Bachkirova, G. Spence, & D. Drake (Eds.), *The Sage handbook of coaching* (pp. 42–61). Sage.

Wittmer, J. L. S., & Hopkins, M. M. (2018). Exploring the relationship between diversity intelligence, emotional intelligence, and executive coaching to enhance leader development practices. *Advances in Developing Human Resources, 20*(3), 285–298. https://doi.org/10.1177/1523422318778004

PART IV

Reconnecting

CHAPTER 16

Identity, Privilege, and Power in Critical HRD

Tonette S. Rocco, Robert C. Mizzi, and Greg Procknow

Hamlin and Stewart (2011) wrote "HRD is, in essence, any process or activity that helps or enables individuals, groups, organisations or host systems to learn, develop and change behaviour for the purpose of improving or enhancing their competence, effectiveness, performance and growth" (p. 213). This definition of HRD provides a basic understanding of what HRD practitioners do and what scholars investigate and is the result of an analysis of definitions of HRD over fifty years which focused on performance improvement, competency, and knowledge. The definitions assume neutrality and uniformity among everyone involved in HRD, and do not consider the effect of identity, power, and privilege on these processes (Rocco et al., 2018). This absence provokes the following questions: Do HRD processes and activities affect all individuals, groups, and organizations equally? Are *unity*, *respect*, and *diversity* goals achieved through these processes? Or, are these concepts not even considered? Do HRD practitioners and scholars critically examine

T. S. Rocco (✉)
Florida International University, Miami, FL, USA
e-mail: roccot@fiu.edu

R. C. Mizzi
University of Manitoba, Winnipeg, MB, Canada
e-mail: Robert.Mizzi@umanitoba.ca

G. Procknow
York University, Toronto, ON, Canada
e-mail: gregprocknow@live.com

© The Author(s), under exclusive license to Springer Nature Switzerland AG 2023
J. C. Collins and J. L. Callahan (eds.), *The Palgrave Handbook of Critical Human Resource Development*, https://doi.org/10.1007/978-3-031-10453-4_16

the ways in which they marginalize individuals, disrespect ways of knowing not sanctioned by the organization or system being served, and/or create and sustain divisive workspaces? These questions are critical, illustrating the institutionalization of oppression and marginalization and challenging systems of privilege and power. It may seem unusual to examine exclusion tendencies within a field that is so centered on "development," but if HRD is to progress across groups, people, and organizations, we need to take seriously the positive *and* negative effects of our engagements. Ironically, critical theory was developed by white men, and yet has become the foundation of inquiries introducing identity into management and organizational studies and fields such as HRD (Rocco et al., 2014).

Critical HRD (or CHRD) troubles the commodification of work products created through an individual's knowledge, skills, and education in service of economic gain of an organization. CHRD is concerned with the value of this work product being enhanced or diminished because of the individual's identity (Fenwick, 2004). Through a cursory look at salary differences, we share an example of how identity and the value of work are intertwined. In the United States, white women earn 80 cents to a dollar earned by white men on average. Black women earn 62 cents, Latinas earn 54 cents, Asians earn 90 cents, and Native Americans earn 57 cents to a dollar earned by a white man (Bleiweis, 2020). There is also a racial wage gap for men (Miller, 2020), while not as large a gap as that between women and men, the gap demonstrates that gender and race determine the value of a work product/service. This inequity illustrates that identity matters, certain identities are systemically and socially privileged over others, and those in power sustain and strengthen the systems that create societal and workplace inequities. HRD, as a crucial component of organizational systems, is not absolved from creating and sustaining this inequity. Inequity in the workplace stems from the long history of patriarchy, colonialism, and white supremacy in the United States and elsewhere. Social transformation in workplaces begins, in part, with learning the various emancipatory and critical theories that help us understand work and learning experiences. Therefore, the purpose of this chapter is to expand HRD's narrow definitions and introduce and overview the theoretical bases which inform a critical understanding of the ways in which identity, privilege, and power are central to individual learning, (dis)empowerment, and experience.

IDENTITY

Identity is "a shared set of meanings that define individuals in particular *roles* in society…, as members of specific *groups* in society…, and as *persons* having specific characteristics that make them unique from others… (original italics)" (Stets & Serpe, 2013, p. 31). While this definition serves as a starting point to discuss identity, McInnes et al. (2017) argued that identity is generally unexamined in organizational processes. This lack of attention may be because theorizing and addressing identity concerns in any social situation can be a complex endeavor, and often connected to notions of power and privilege.

Everyone identifies with various occupations, roles, communities, relationships, and networks across their lifespan. For instance, someone may start their career as a prison guard in a city and transition later to become a teacher in a small town. Their relationships with colleagues will undoubtedly change and so will their communities and networks as a result of this transition. Culture (i.e., the behaviors, knowledge, laws, beliefs, or characteristics underpinning a society) influences these identifications. For example, a cultural influence can be an unquestioned expectation to be employed in a specific profession and at a certain pay scale. When there lacks congruency with cultural norms, workers may feel like a failure or outsider to their families and peers. Usher and Solomon (1999) explained that

> 'culture' is seen as structuring the way subjects think, make decisions and act and as the source of norms, attitudes, and values. Culture constitutes the patterns of meaning, beliefs and values through which subjects understand their experience and forge their sense of identity. (p. 158)

Keeping culture in mind as an overarching influence on identity and identifications, social interactions and social contexts also impact identity. There are two related theoretical positions most utilized in educational and organizational research when it comes to identity and their social influences: *social identity theory* and *social learning theory*. We explain both in turn.

SOCIAL IDENTITY THEORY

Social identity theory focuses on "understanding how individuals make sense of themselves and other people in the social environment" (Korte, 2007, p. 168). Korte explained interactions and memberships facilitate identity-formation through focal groups (in-groups) or other groups (out-groups). Through interactions and memberships, individuals then develop and categorize their social identity. Korte further suggested, "the resulting identity, in effect, depends on the situation and the relative strengths of internal and external categorizations at the time. The emphasis on process recognizes the relational, dynamic, contextual, and constructed nature of social identity" (p. 169). The processes that construct identity are undoubtedly complex (Tajfel, 2010). The complexity is a result of how identity functions as cultural expression, is perceived by others, is fluid, and is (re)constructed over time (Brown, 2019; Schmidt, 2016). Identity is in constant flux and evolves with social, economic, political, and technological changes that surround us (Brown, 2019). Tajfel (2010) wrote of the origins and development of individual identity in relation to their social and physical worlds, stating that memberships to certain groups can influence identity-formation. Some group memberships can be more impactful than others, depending on the situation.

There can be temporary moments where people interpret their identity as 'stable' so that they can put it to work, whether through interpretation, expression, or analysis. This does not mean that identity is fixed. Jørgensen and Keller (2008) wrote "The term *identity* involves an interest in the identification processes of individuals within social networks. When individuals participate in negotiations of meaning, they also negotiate their identities. It is these identification processes that make negotiation processes meaningful to them [original italics]" (p. 528). Negotiation processes are ongoing throughout the lifespan.

Oftentimes there can be multiple identifications (e.g., identifying as being a part of the Black and queer communities), which can be considered as intersectionality (Syed & Metcalfe, 2017). As Patricia Hill Collins (2019) explained, the concept of intersectionality originated by and for Black women in hopes of understanding their oppressive and interconnecting racialized and gendered experiences. There are four guiding principles to intersectionality: (1) race, class, gender, sexuality, and other systems of power are interdependent and shape one another; (2) intersecting power relations lead to complex interdependent social inequalities; (3) the social location of individuals within intersecting power relations shapes their experiences; and (4) solving problems, such as forming epistemic resistance to hegemony, require intersectional analysis. Intersectionality maps the relational framework of overlapping inequalities and power relations among people (Crenshaw, 1991). People can hold membership with multiple communities and be fluid and performative in expressions of their memberships, depending largely on the social context. A common denominator in social identity theory is that people search for a sense of self, inclusive of experiences with and expressions of emotion, and, through doing so, begin to construct their identities (Horrocks & Callahan, 2006). Horrocks and Callahan wrote that communication and reciprocity promote feelings of comfort, confidence, and safety among groups, while maintaining a sense of productivity and purpose.

Within a Western context, identity has been traditionally expressed as fixed and monolithic, whereby individuals identify within neat and tidy boxes based on their race, gender, ability, sexuality, geography, religion, and so forth. This systemic approach of assigning subject positions is problematic as it structures and makes permanent relations between people. Each position interacts with each other in tandem, constantly negotiating context and growth (Rutherford, 1990). Further, a Western interpretation of identity is individualistic in tone by focusing on goal achievement and accountability to be considered 'successful' (Mizzi & Rocco, 2013; Wang et al., 2005). A part of this success means that people also identify with professional groups, such as being a soldier, teacher, engineer, or a physician, and to an amount that their identity is closely connected to their profession (Schmidt, 2016). Work validates individual identity, especially for white-collar employees. Work then becomes a centralized and important space to create meaning and develop personal identity (Githens, 2009).

Expressions of certain identities can be muted as a form of self or social regulation, and sometimes they can be 'out and proud' as means to conform to a status quo or generate discussion and change. Alongside these personal and professional identity groups come various forms of power. The more similarities within the group, the increased likelihood the social identity is considered more salient than the personal identity (McInnes et al., 2017), and that people will stereotype themselves toward an archetype (Korte, 2007). Yet, as Korte explained, this tendency to stereotype also means a dehumanization of others who do not fit the 'mold.' While those within the stereotype benefit by way of increased self-esteem and favouritism, discrimination and conflict trigger those outside the stereotype. For example, someone who is given legislative authority to be a leader means they can make decisions based on their way of knowing the world and navigating systems that secure advantage to some individuals over others (Collins, 2012). Denial of knowledge is a denial of identity and practice. This suppression and exclusion cause marginalization of identity, which results in limiting opportunities for problem-solving and creativity and proliferating tension and conflict (Jørgensen & Keller, 2008; Preston & Arthur, 1997).

Within an Eastern (or non-Western) context, identity is formed and expressed through a collectivist orientation. Theorizing a social identity means that relationships, status, belonging, and practices are more pronounced, and the declaration of a fixed identity is counter-cultural and possibly even viewed as a Western, hegemonic, political practice. For example, Dutch Anthropologist Gloria Wekker (2006), in her conversations with Indigenous women who have intimate relationships with women in Suriname, asked if the women identified as "lesbian." The women questioned what they could gain by having an actual "identity" toward achieving happiness. Relationships, belonging, and social status define people and give them value in a non-Western context. When there is exclusion from certain relationships and a loss of status, then that can equate to losing oneself in a Western sense. For that purpose, communication patterns may be less overt, confrontational, or declarative than in Western countries, as people do not want to be rejected by their communities or be viewed as privileged (Mizzi & Rocco, 2013).

Social Learning Theory

Bandura's (1977) Social Learning Theory is useful in terms of understanding the necessary credibility, empowerment, role modeling, and reinforcement elements needed for teaching and learning to be influential in the classroom. Modeling becomes an essential component in educational scenarios (Bandura, 1977). To act as effective role models, according to a theory of social learning, educators would need to observe, practice, adopt, and model contextualized behaviors and attitudes to engage in meaningful work with their students (Bandura, 1977). Social learning theory suggests that identity development is a process of interaction between community and people (Jørgensen & Keller,

2008). Through this interaction, new frameworks emerge that benefit both the individual and the organization.

Non-participation in learning spaces also shapes identity (Jørgensen & Keller, 2008). If people are unwelcomed or refuse to participate in the educational experience, then they miss out on opportunities for group and personal identity-development. As Jørgensen and Keller explained, identity is *lived* through participation and roles, is *negotiated* through work and life, is *social* due to membership in multiple communities, is *learning* through taking into account past and present understandings, and is a *nexus* where multiple memberships and experiences shape identity. A way of producing harmony and cohesion among identities is for organizations to enhance communication, from the very top, that diversity, or an appreciation and support for diverse identities in the workplace, forms a core value of the organization (De Souza et al., 2017). HRD practitioners are in a useful position to lead an inclusion effort where everyone is welcomed, their voices are heard, pedagogy and content are meaningful, and privilege is questioned.

PRIVILEGE

Privilege is "any unearned asset or benefit received by virtue of being born with a particular characteristic or into a particular class" (Rocco & West, 1998, p. 173). This unearned asset forms the foundation for the individual's knowledge of self (Rocco & West, 1998) providing benefits which the individual with privilege remains oblivious (McIntosh, 1989). Privilege allows individuals to view themselves and members of their privileged group as morally neutral/superior, the norm, and their lives and aspirations as ideal. One way to look at privilege is as a special advantage which is granted and not earned, an entitlement which benefits the recipient as the recipient remains unaware of this state (Black & Stone, 2005). According to Black and Stone, privilege is "any entitlement, sanction, power, and advantage or right granted to a person or group solely by birthright membership in a prescribed group or groups" (p. 245). For example, unearned privilege could be how people are born into a wealthy family, and therefore do not have concerns for their daily needs. Earned privilege "are attained through exerting effort to achieve an end product" (Rocco & West, 1998, p. 173).

On one hand, educational attainment is often considered an *earned* privilege, which, in turn, influences career progression and success, depending on the educational institutions' ranking and reputation. On the other hand, access to education is often determined by *unearned* privilege such as someone's race, class, or gender, for instance. If hard work was all that was necessary for measuring career progression and success, we would not need to keep track of how many corporate leaders are women, black, and/or LGBTQ.

Rocco and West (1998) described the manifestations of privilege as power, access, status, credibility, and normality. The determinants of privilege are personal attributes which include ability, gender, religion, ethnicity, race, sexual orientation, age, and class. While Black and Stone (2005) discussed seven domains of privilege which are race/ethnicity, gender, sexual orientation, socioeconomic status, age, ableness, and religious affiliation, these personal attributes (in)form identity. Certain identities such as white, straight, cisgender men are seen as the norm forming the basis for developmental models and learning theories that stress individualism, linear thinking, and self-sufficiency (Flannery, 1994). White, straight, cisgender male traits are viewed as preferred traits, desirable because their work practices represent the norm, thus inheriting privilege by way of being cast as the model of how workers should perform and achieve. Rewards, such as promotion or salary increases, are therefore granted to anyone who sustains the norm. Since white men are the standard, most of the work done on privilege and oppression is around gender and race, ignoring the other determinants that shape access to meaningful work and overall job satisfaction, such as sexuality, ability, or class. These determinants or categories are socially constructed "to simplify the complexities of multiple identities and multiple realities" (Reynolds & Pope, 1991, p. 175).

Privilege exists as a triarchy of interlocking psychosocial, reciprocal, and structural realms interacting simultaneously to privilege some and oppress others (Rocco & West, 1998). The psychosocial realm is the "internalized uncritical acceptance of assumptions gained through socialization" (Rocco & West, 1998, p. 176). The socialization includes indoctrinating privileged groups with feelings of adequacy and superiority. Accepting and not questioning the roots of these feelings becomes tacit knowledge.

The reciprocal realm involves interactions with others which reveal assumptions about social roles and rights, for instance, a man driving a car instead of the woman who owns the car when they are together. These "identity privileges...legitimize problematic assumptions about identity and entitlement" (Carbado, 2005, p. 199). Supporting the belief that those that have power, earned their power and the privilege that accompanies it and oppressed groups "earned their exclusion" by virtue of some deficiency of character (Black & Stone, 2005, p. 243). These interactions manifest in microaggressions which are intentional or unintentional verbal, nonverbal, and environmental words, or actions "that communicate hostile, derogatory, or negative messages" (Sue, 2010, p. 3). For example, white men who make decisions at a morning coffee club, and then have subsequent tokenistic meetings to invite 'input' from diverse peoples can be an example of a microaggression that excludes social difference and secures white privilege.

The structural realm maintains and sanctions the privileged status through consistent use of norms, policies, and language (Rocco & West, 1998). Macroaggressions sustain the structural realm through systems of oppression at the community and societal levels. Macroaggressions are actions that mean to exclude groups directly or by omission. Macroaggressions are composed of microassaults which occur in public spaces and are supported by "nuanced behaviors that exist in a particular or specific context" (Osanloo et al.,

2016, p. 6). Microassaults are "a verbal or nonverbal attack meant to hurt the intended victim through name-calling, avoidant behavior, or purposeful discriminatory actions" (Sue et al., 2007, p. 274). Macroaggressions are intentional and calculated to produce long-term and sustained consequences. Publicly characterizing a racialized group as lazy, worthless, or a drain on society is a clear example of violent, macroaggressive behavior.

Workplaces are sites where various forms of privilege operate hegemonically to subjugate workers with difference, or force workers to appropriate white straight male privilege. For instance, workers in diverging states of mind are without mental health privileges (Wolframe, 2013). 'Sane privilege' can best be described as "when mentally hale and hearty citizens have never been mistaken or stigmatized as mentally ill and have access to privileges that people with mental illness do not" (Procknow, 2019a, p. 15). One example of this privilege is the fact that people in sane states of mind are scarcely asked to speak for other sane people (Wolframe, 2013). Normates are not sensibly aware that they possess such a positive, mental health privilege (Procknow, 2019b). This form of privilege shapes the makeup of organizations, disallowing some states of mind while effusively welcoming conformist ones. This is especially evident in the way one receives career advice (Wolframe, 2013), or is counseled not to establish career goals that seem unrealistic for those struggling with health concerns (Procknow, 2019b). Another example of this privilege is that sane employees can exhibit overt happiness without being prejudged as manic or delirious, whereas mad employees who evince signs of elation or joy have their behaviors questioned as symptomatic of their mental illness (Wolframe, 2013). It is clear through these examples that privilege reinforces an institutionalized binary within the workplace of acceptable/unacceptable identities, practices, expressions, and values.

POWER

This section touches on the dialectical development of the phenomena of power from classical, traditional, and radical perspectives. Weber (1978) conceived of power as "the probability that one actor within a social relationship will be in a position to carry out his own will despite resistance, regardless of the basis on which this probability rests" (p. 53). Weber's definition reflects the notion that an increase in one party's power leads to a commensurate decrement of another party's power (Heiskala, 2001). Thus, the definition of power relations is the relationship in which one party exerts power over another, compelling their compliance in subtle ways to get them to do as they say (Basden, n.d.).

Power has been classically viewed as being primarily vested in property of persons or collectives (Knights, 2009). In this sense, power is entreated as a social resource that can be transferred or redistributed (Jo & Park, 2016). Power is seen as an attribute of wealth and capital ownership, thus power is the means of production which rests within the remit of the bourgeoisie (e.g., the wealthy class) (Wolff, 2017). Marx links power to oppressive capitalist states and implicates its relation to class domination. Consequently, workers suffer the indignities of being in the lower ranks of class inequality and domination (Jessop, 2012). Workers, estranged symbolically and materially from the products of their labor, undergo 'alienation.' Power remains exploitative and routinizes coercive force that deprives individuals of their *savoir faire* to realize their human potential (Knights, 2009). Engels famously coined 'false consciousness' to account for the internalized force within the working masses that prevents them from rejecting their exploitation (Jessop, 2012). Emancipation from labor exploitation is actualized when the bourgeoisie concedes ownership over the means of production to the working class (Fenwick, 2014).

The politics of power in Gramsci's analysis resides in ideology. The ruling class cannot dominate and control by force and coercion alone. Gramsci extended Marx and Engels thoughts on powerlessness, economic exploitation, and false consciousness with the notion of 'hegemony' (Brookfield, 2004). Hegemony refers to the manufacture of consent (Bajpai & Sahni, 2008). Hegemony is twofold: firstly, win over the consent of the subordinated classes and bring them under the ideological sway of the bourgeoisie. Rather than flexing their political muscle the powerful deploy ideological tactics and cozy up to monolithic cultural institutions, such as media, higher education, and religious institutions to form the basis of consent (Daldal, 2014). Secondly, hegemony concerns the ideological ascendency of the power elite's values and norms, taken together as 'common sense,' over subjugated swathes of society which accept such values and norms as natural and thus maintain the 'status quo' (Carnoy, 1986). The subordinated classes are lulled into a culture of consensus and persuaded to view the world in a manner that favors the supremacy of the hegemonic class/order (Bajpai & Sahni, 2008). The powerless in turn confuse and conflate their own interests with the interests of the powerful. They tacitly have a hand in sustaining the status quo rather than refuting its taken-for-granted commonsensical norms. Power relations are configured through counter-hegemonic struggles; that is unseating the dominant ideas of what comprises normal and what knowledge is accepted as legitimate.

Foucauldian Notions of Power

Foucault's framing of power represents a rupture from juridical analyses of power relations that straightforwardly envisage the mechanisms of power as prohibitive and repressive, suggesting instead that power can be positive and productive (Foucault, 2000). The basis of Foucault's inquiry on power articulates 'the how of power' not in the sense of how it manifests itself, but the manner or method in which is it exercised, and what happens when individuals assert power over others (Foucault, 1982). That is, disclosing power relations, their location(s), and point(s) of application; namely, suppressed bodies bearing some degree of marginality (Daldal, 2014). Power is omnipresent and evidenced when exercised (Välikangas & Seeck, 2011). Power is analogous to social relations, in all places that cannot easily be dismissed in Foucault's analyses (Knights, 2009). Power is neither confined to a singular institution or structure, nor is it something that sentient beings are endowed with. Yet, one is never shorn of power (Knights, 2009).

Foucault (2000) was most concerned with "the formation of subjectivity," notably "not power, but the subject" (p. 327), and the consequences of power and the production of subject identity. One cannot study the constituting of subject identity without studying the orthodoxical power relations responsible (Välikangas & Seeck, 2011). In '*The Subject and Power*,' Foucault theorized three 'modes of objectification' specific to the way human beings are recast as subjects through power relations. Firstly, individuals are objectified through medical and social scientific paradigms (Daldal, 2014). Foucault employed the term 'power/knowledge' "to signify that power is constituted through accepted forms of knowledge, scientific understanding, and 'truth'" (Stephen, 2019, n. p.). Every society has its 'regimes of truth'; that is "the types of discourse[s] which it accepts and makes function as true" (Foucault, 1980, p. 131). The relationship between 'knowledge' and 'power' reveals how some knowledge claims are suppressed while other knowledge claims are legitimated through power (Jo & Park, 2016). The singling out from where a certain discourse originates "indicates those with authority, the power to define the knowable and permissible" (Jo & Park, 2016, p. 395). Authorities enact a discourse to induce specific ways of thinking about and acting upon human beings in ways desired by the dominant class. *Technologies of power* objectivize subjects by shaping and regulating their conduct and guide them toward certain ends that replicate (or imitate) the best (or worst) features of the regime in power (Foucault, 1997). Secondly, the technologies of power produce subject identity along 'dividing practices,' such as the mad/sane, sick/healthy, the convicted/innocent. These dichotomies serve to exclude the former. For instance, psychiatrists, doctors, and judges classify individuals as mad, ill, and criminal and lay claim to their conduct, i.e., cure, reform, incarcerate, respectively (Knights, 2009). This power over subjugated bodies and minds molds them into a replicant of the wider population Foucault termed 'Biopower' (Knights, 2009). In other words, professional bodies of knowledge author hegemonic scripts setting out what conduct is tolerable, normative, and deviant. These technologies of power (or scripts) minimize marginality (Foucault, 1991). Those not meeting the normal profile are scrupulously surveilled. Surveillance then is "coded as discourse" (Mambrol, 2016). This discourse sets out who is allowed to say what, when, and how (Caldwell, 2007). Power is obtained and diffused "through lines of conformity" (Deetz, 2003, p. 29). Conformers that live up to this norm are rewarded with privilege or prestige, thus in this context power is productive. Non-conformists are disciplined, and their differences are reduced to unintelligibility within the given social context. They only obtain intelligibility insofar as their bodies and behaviors cohere well with the norms of the ruling establishment (Sørensen, 2014). This results in the making of a normalized body.

Lastly, the third mode of objectification is self-subjectivizing: the process by which humans turn themselves into subjects (Foucault, 1982). Subject and subjectivity are solely formed through power. Power mends the subject to their identity (Sørensen, 2014) and "imposes a law of truth on [them] which [they] must recognize and which others have recognized in [them]" (Foucault, 1982, p. 781). They learn to call themselves the subject of some declared collective (e.g., racialized or disabled). This exemplifies how power relations run through the inscription of non-normative identity. Differently, pressures to conform also lead to self-subjectivizing (Sørensen, 2014) whereby subjects discipline themselves by catering their behaviors to the ruling elites' prescribed conduct codes (Knights, 2009). The power imperative cajoles subjects to speak on behalf of, and in the name of, power and uncritically embrace its norms (Sørensen, 2014).

Foucault recognized that the subject is "both the target and the vehicle of power" (Sørensen, 2014, para. 6). Specifically, subjectivity is a site of becoming where the oppressed can bring about 'the strategic reversibility' of power relations: "the ways in which the terms of governmental practice can be turned around into focuses of resistance" (Gordon, 1991, p. 5). Foucault proffered some points of resistance to enable subjects to wrest themselves from the tentacles of the technologies of power and resist the prevailing configurations of power from which these technologies operate (Välikangas & Seeck, 2011). Power is positive in that it is necessary "to mobilize the power of others" (Knights, 2009, p. 155). Wherever exercises of power lay exactly resistance will be found. Power is everywhere and, in equal measure, resistance to it. Resisting power results in a change to its form (Knights, 2009). Subjects can reinscribe discourses into sites of power and resistance with the goal to subvert the machinations of power, its rituals of truths, and codes of conformity (Gaventa, 2003). Challenging them renders them fragile and susceptible to thwart (Foucault, 1998). Foucault introduced the term *technologies of self* to refer to reflective individuals possessing an array of techniques at their disposal to invoke resistance (Välikangas & Seeck, 2011). This includes revisiting, revising, and conducting "a certain number of operations on their own bodies and souls," to create new modes of being and behavior (Foucault, 1988, p. 18) dissimilar from those imposed on them by the workings of power regimes (Raffnsoe et al., 2017).

Steven Lukes and the Three-Dimensions of Power

In 1974, Lukes published '*Power: A Radical View,*' conceptualizing power through a three-dimensional model. Each dimension signals conflict and decisions. The first one-dimensional approach posits a discrete scenario where party A has power over party B to get them to do something they are overtly resistant to (Donovan, 2015) and would not otherwise do (Jo & Park, 2016).

Yet, one-dimensional power is restrictive in accounting for occasions in "which visible conflict has been deflected" (Knights, 2009, p. 147). Lukes remedies this shortcoming by turning to Bacharach and Baratz (1970) to inform his second dimension. This dimension concerns non-decision making. The power structure chooses who partakes in the conversation and what they converse about (Donovan, 2015). Power is hidden and conflict is covert. Lukes conceived of a third dimension that focuses on how shaping decisions prolongs power domination (Kirby et al., 2000). This is accomplished by influencing and reshaping individuals' consciousness, perceptions, and cognitions through the process of socialization and control of information to prevent people from airing their grievances (Lukes, 1974). Conflict here is latent. This dimension has a behavioral focus unlike the first two that entails getting subordinates to interiorize norms and comply even when it is contrary to their best interests to do so (Knights, 2009). They accept their role in the existing field of power relations because they can neither see nor imagine an alternative to the hegemonic order, or they trust that it is natural (organic) (Lukes, 1974), or they are relatively unaware that party A is exercising power over them (Donovan, 2015).

To summarize, Foucault's framing of power was a departure from Marx insomuch that he viewed the mechanisms of power not as a reflection of oppressive economic structures in need of eradication, but as positive and productive (Foucault, 2000). Gramsci saw power restricted to the authority of a central bloc or aligned superstructure which wields power as an implement of coercion. Gramsci and Foucault both viewed "power as a relation of force that only exists in action" (Daldal, 2014, p. 149), however they differed on the point of application where power is exercised. Gramsci expressed power as being localized in hegemonic orders. Foucault theorized that power is everywhere and, in equal measure, resistance to it. To both, power rules by consent. Lukes (2005) rejected Foucault's 'power is everywhere' explication "as leaving no escape from domination" and that "there is no freedom from it or reasoning independent of it" (p. 12).

IDENTITY, PRIVILEGE, AND POWER IN HRD

Social identification is often affiliated with employee and management experiences and relations, yet what is necessary to understand is how social identification shapes HRD policies and practices (McInnes et al., 2017). What has been understood about identity in the literature is often stated through power dynamics and experiences of marginalization and privilege. Metcalfe (2008), for example, explained the impact on gendered structured and gendered cultural practices in the workplace, and implications for an HRD identity. Metcalfe wrote, being seen to be engaged in an equality-intervention initiative positioned women's networks as potentially powerless. This 'silencing' of gender development strategies by women themselves reaffirms the ambivalent process of managing identity work, and highlights the ways in which gendered power relations are intertwined with everyday social and organizational practices. (p. 452)

Metcalfe's point demonstrated power shapes and structures organizational and employee identities. In another example, Bohonos (2019) argued for more inquiry into HRD using Critical White Studies, which involved the analysis of White identity by challenging White experience as the neutral norm, a privileged position. Bohonos wrote, "White identity is difficult to define in the contemporary context because Whites often conceptualize themselves as raceless" (p. 320). Both case examples demonstrate that HRD should not be exclusive in terms of personal identity (Collins, 2012). Gender or race based interventions designed to rectify inequities as the exclusive province of women or ethnic or racial minorities should be designed to include men and white men particularly. This approach might encourage discussion and stimulate solutions that have not been considered. More importantly, creating interventions that involve only marginalized employees to solve equity issues has the potential to further oppress those the intervention was meant to support. Further, these interventions add more work onto marginalized employees to solve organizational problems that they did not create, which Clarke and Matthew (2021) referred to as a 'minority tax.'

It is clear that claiming space and identity for marginalized people is an important step to advance equality, civility, fairness, and justice in the workplace. Although problematic given the fluid nature of identity, the practice of self-identifying for HR purposes to determine the kind and amount of diversity can be useful for hiring and promotion purposes as well as anti-discrimination policy and programs. Within an LGBTQ context, De Souza et al. (2017) explained that,

> when organizations that do not address discrimination based on sexual orientation or gender identity, LGBT employees may feel excluded and perceive their organizations are sending implicit messages encouraging them to hide their sexual orientation or gender identity at work; when LGBT employees spend energy hiding their true identity, their productivity is less than optimal. (p. 127)

Yet, claiming and articulating identity as a framework to advance rights can cause what those in dominant positions refer to as "identity politics" in the workplace. Identity politics explores common experiences of oppression from the perspective of certain groups (Heyes, 2002). One controversy around identity politics is whether groups accept their identities as fixed, and therefore create change in their organizations, or whether they reject defining identity because not all subscribe to identity-categories, but still rightfully deserve freedom and acceptance in the workplace (Gamson in Githens,

2009). Another controversy is that someone who holds a marginalized identity status may experience multiple struggles, both against those with in dominant positions and other marginalized people who think about and frame their marginality differently. For example, those who identify as 'sexual minorities' and reject 'LGBT' labels, are often not consulted with or have their sexualities discussed in the workplace (Mizzi & Walton, 2014). Any form of identity-exclusion leads to a loss of opportunity for learning and development. As Collins (2012) wrote, "conversations about leadership that primarily consider dominant identity groups (e.g., White people, heterosexuals, men, the able-bodied, etc.) may be less productive than those who think about leadership from the perspective of diverse groups of people who make up our workforces" (p. 350). We agree with Collins, but also extend his argument to include those leaders who lead through Western frameworks also screen out opportunities for further development and dialogue.

Given the increasingly transnational and global nature of organizations, recent HRD research, such as Wang et al. (2005), Mizzi and Rocco (2013), and Syed and Metcalfe (2017), argued that a Western dominance of research into identity and HRD exists, and that this perspective screens out the possibility of considering contributions from non-Western identities in the workplace, and their experiences with power and privilege. As globalization continues to become widespread, HRD professionals may experience greater tensions between individualistic and collectivist notions of identity in the workplace. HRD professionals will need to create learning spaces to educate around the various influences on and interpretations of identities (Mizzi & Rocco, 2013) rather than simply privileging Western ideologies. Non-Western individuals, especially those who are women, may be viewed as subservient and powerless by the West, yet Syed and Metcalfe (2017) signaled the contrary, questioning the homogeneity of the non-Western female identity by the West. Forming dialogue around different conceptualizations of identity may alleviate some of the tension in multi-national workplaces. For example, Wang et al. (2005) explained that Confucian cultural heritage contains five aspects of self: (a) hierarchy and harmony, (b) group orientation, (c) networks/relationships, (d) maintaining face or showing respect, and (e) time orientation. These values shape organization and management practices through interpersonal relationships (respect for hierarchy in the workplace), decision-making processes (taking personal responsibility for tasks and maintaining harmony), ruling by man (decisions are unquestionable; problems are resolved through interaction and not through regulation), and HR practices (feelings more important than competence; loyalty is rewarded; seniority is preferred over performance and training; social harmony is prioritized). Awareness into these cultures, and how they form identity, is becoming paramount in organizations. What may emerge over time is a hybridity of individualistic and collectivist forms of identity in the transnational workplace, and that HRD will be one of these sites for dialogue and development. Above all, *unity*, *respect*, and *diversity* should be the primary goals when it comes to considerations of HRD and identity, privilege, and power.

Troubled in Terms of Learning and (Dis)Empowerment, and Work

Individuals in the learning process "are in a key position to question, challenge, and critique the principles and assumptions underpinning learning" (McGuire & Jørgensen, 2011, p. 74). Procknow (2019b) explored the normative taken-for-granted bodily and gestural performances of instructors in graduate human resource development and adult education programs. Their prose, faciality of instruction, and delivery of subject matter formed the core of 'sane performativity,' i.e., they performed in ways taken-for-granted as sane and normal. Their performances of sanity were routine. However, for a learner with a diagnosed mental illness they had to dilute their instructors' sane performances into self-directed lessons from which to learn. The curriculum was twofold: discursive and performative. Once learned, they adopted these gestures, gaits, and movements and collapsed them into their identity to blend into wider organizational or societal identities. Not only is the power of saneness often unspoken and seen as an accepted fact, it coerces neurodivergent learners to repeat the sanity on view (Procknow, 2019a). By impersonating his instructors' sane behaviors, he reproduces hegemonic saneness and entrenches sane normativity in learning spaces supposedly supportive of equity. Consequently, sound states of mind are entreated as superior while unsound ones are rendered inferior. CHRD practitioners need to critically reflect upon their identities, privilege, and power relations they maintain with students, surrender said power, and make themselves vulnerable to questioning (Sambrook, 2008).

Lawless et al. (2012) found that when students enrolled in a traditional curriculum of HRD and were introduced to CHRD it enabled them to become more questioning and critical toward previous unquestionable acceptance of the time-honored HRD scholarship. Their comments reflected CHRD discourse and lead them to call HRD's take as read assumptions framing the field into question. More importantly, all students claimed to have transferred this praxis of interrogating norms and speaking truth to power to their work organizations (Lawless et al., 2012).

Power relations have a direct impact "on organizational processes of learning and change" (Elliot & Turnbull, 2005, p. 30). Organizations are sites where power is socially reproduced (Knights, 2009). HRD professionals who employ critical approaches to emancipate employees from hegemonic power structures transform learning into a means of challenging widely held beliefs about learning and hegemony over the lower ranks (Avci, 2016). HRD professionals can devise sensitivity training programs to endorse cohesion across employees embodying the norm and those running contrary to it by building an 'organization-specific identity' from the bottom up (Kulkarni, 2012).

Organizational training can produce power as much as it can erode it. There are severe consequences to power loss. Training can "address issues of power and control" and minimize the loss of control felt by trainees in learning contexts (Callahan, 2005, p. 1064). For some female cadets enrolled in the U.S. Air Force Academy (USAFA), personal power and control stripping training practices resulted in the development of maladaptive eating disorders to retrieve "control over their own bodies" (Callahan, 2005, p. 1064). In this case, training of otherwise 'normal' women produced in them a disability (Procknow & Rocco, 2016). By restyling their health in non-conforming ways, they invoked 'eating disorder' in the interests of resistance.

HRD practitioners can carry critical theory into practice by becoming 'tempered radicals' (Nackoney & Rocco, 2008). These 'radicals' walk the interstitial lines between conformity and rebellion (Nackoney & Rocco, 2008). Their power is sourced from not being entirely integrated into the dominant culture. They are outsiders looking in, "quietly engag[ing] with organizational power and politics, and [using] it strategically to bring about both individual and organizational change" (Nackoney & Rocco, 2008, p. 5).

Additionally, instructors can redress the marginality of learners by increasing their representation in training design and programming by editing their subjugated knowledge(s) into the curriculum (Castrodale, 2017), deferring to the disadvantaged for their experiential claims, and permitting them to counter prevailing hegemonic scripts (Castrodale, 2017). For instance, instructors can 'madden' their curriculum by inviting learners with diagnosed mental disorders to share their lived experiences and needs with a class or organization (Procknow, 2017).

CHRD is based on the principle that by giving voice to the oppressed, power is taken away from the oppressor (Sambrook, 2008). This involves using the HRD role as intermediaries in power relations to stymy the elite's attempts at divesting workers' voice (Donovan, 2015). For example, when employees with marginal identities have no voice, their knowledge is subjugated. They struggle to get their ways of knowing, behaving, and being in the world accepted as truth (Procknow, 2017). Their truths are denied the same equitable playing field as so-called normal employee groups and their knowledge is censored and sneered at by those seeking to sustain the status quo (Procknow, 2017). When they are denied dialogic equivalency within normative structures this constitutes epistemic violence (Liegghio, 2013). This violence is directed at shushing the Other's spoken narratives in workplaces and learning spaces (Procknow, 2019b). Not only does this violence efface their sense of identity and selfhood by discrediting them as illegitimate knowers, it also "invalidates the epistemic value of their subjectivities (their truths)" (Procknow, 2019b, p. 514). Epistemic violence prevents Othered workers from speaking out against the powerful, that which Lukes (1974) deemed the silencing of grievances. Not only does epistemic violence masticate away at their knowledge, worldviews, and their ways of being, they are stripped of their ability to script their own narratives in hegemonic institutions that concern their own betterment. The norm, then, becomes the Othered unable to volition-ally engage in dialogic exchanges themselves (Procknow, 2017). HRD can create anti-oppressive avenues to allow the powerless to share their subju-gated knowledge, to contest regimes of truth, and restore some semblance of power back to those that seemingly forfeited it upon entering the organization (Procknow, 2017).

IMPLICATIONS

HRD needs to a priori assess the meaning of identity, privilege, and power critically before mapping and rolling out specified training interventions to improve performance and inspire breakthroughs in organizational develop-ment (Jo & Park, 2016). We offer some ways below that can help HRD researchers and practitioners to reassess the meaning of identity, privilege, and power critically.

Communities of practice (Jørgensen & Keller, 2008) and employee resource groups (Githens, 2009) are two ways to negotiate, construct, and articulate identity in the workplace. People learn more about themselves and their capabilities through these kinds of groups. People construct and sustain various identities as a result of their social interactions in the workplace, but the strength of certain identities is based on the individual, group, and context (Korte, 2007; Schmidt, 2016). Due to this heightened emphasis on contex-tuality, and that individuals generally move around to multiple professional and personal contexts throughout their lifespan, the number of identities a person can have can be boundless (Schmidt, 2016). Communities of practice and employee resource groups can be important spaces that promote dialogue around identity, work, and learning.

Privilege holds deep connections to identity. HRD practitioners must work to destabilize political centers that privilege certain workers and shut out 'others.' This destabilization is not without controversy, as diversity training programs have been resisted by those in the majority who did not want to change or lose their privilege (Ma Rhea, 2007). HRD practitioners need to recognize and deconstruct their own privilege and closely examine practices and systems that sustain privilege in the workplace. Consider how privilege filters into conversations around revenue, experience, production, and hier-archy, rather than focusing on the human diversity that shape workplaces, and then confront that privilege with the aim to creating equitable change (Collins, 2012). Power is not divorced from conversations around privilege, as power can exclude or embrace identities that 'fit' the workplace and bestow and withdraw privilege.

CHRD practitioners may take up matters of power as what Franco Basaglia coined "negative workers," described as "technician[s] of practical knowl-edge" (i.e., educators, trainers) (Scheper-Hughes, 1993, p. 541). These 'technicians' "collude with the powerless to identify their needs against the interests of the bourgeois institution" (e.g., psy-complex, universities, work)

(Scheper-Hughes, 1993, p. 541). CHRD supports the critical analysis of asymmetrical power relations within work organizations; especially the organization's taken-for-granteds (Fenwick, 2014). For example, in the HRD literature the assumed norm has been that people with disabilities are the ones managed not the ones leading (Procknow et al., 2017). Procknow et al. (2017) theorized the prototypicality of the disabled ascending to positions of authentic leadership. Their work supposes that power imbalances can begin from the bottom up. For example, when 'normal' workers refuse to accept a disabled leader the same way they would an able-bodied leader. Their true selves are not reflected in those whom they lead. Upon being accepted as someone with power they need the identity markers necessary to convey they are like them. When authenticity is applied to non-visible difference and abilities, questions arise whether those with dissimilar characteristics can find resonance with any uniform 'they,' regardless of how their difference sets them apart. They call the legitimacy attached to their acquisition of power into question not just to lead them, but to lead generally. Also, power imbalances rest in configurations of power from the top down. For instance, nondisabled, white, male, straight, leaders may resist sharing power with someone they label 'not able' or 'capable' and perceived as an employment equity hire. In either scenario, delegitimization blunts the disabled leaders' ability to be recognized as 'authentic' in a leadership modality that demands they present their true selves. The authors suggest that HRD can deconstruct and reconstruct leadership development programs to be inclusive of disability difference and other social differences and successfully facilitate power changing hands in the organization from the nondisabled to the disabled, or at the very least help break that power impasse (Procknow et al., 2017). Above all, HRD needs to interrogate the meaning of identity, privilege, and power critically during the conceptualization, development, and implementation stage of any interventions to improve performance, change culture, enhance employability, and develop the organization (Jo & Park, 2016).

REFERENCES

Avci, O. (2016). Critical theory and what it has to offer to human resource development. *Uluslararası Ekonomik Araştırmalar Dergisi, 2*(1), 33–41.

Bajpai, K., & Sahni, V. (2008). Hegemony and strategic choice. In C. Chari's (Ed.), *War, peace and hegemony in a globalized world: The changing balance of power in the twenty first-century* (pp. 103–108). Routledge.

Bandura, A. (1977). *Social learning theory.* General Learning Press.

Basden, A. (N.D.). *Reflections on power and power relations.* http://kgsvr.net/dooy/power.html

Black, L. L., & Stone, D. (2005). Expanding the definition of privilege: The concept of social privilege. *Journal of Multicultural Counseling and Development, 33*(4), 243–255.

Bleiweis, R. (March 24, 2020). Quick facts about the gender wage gap. *Center for American Progress*. https://www.americanprogress.org/issues/women/reports/2020/03/24/482141/quick-facts-gender-wage-gap/

Bohonos, J. (2019). Including critical whiteness studies in the critical human resource development family: A proposed theoretical framework. *Adult Education Quarterly*, 69(4), 315–337. https://doi.org/10.1177/0741713619858131

Brookfield, S. D. (2004). *The power of critical theory: Liberating adult learning and teaching*. Jossey-Bass.

Brown, N. (2019). Identity boxes: Using materials and metaphors to elicit experiences. *International Journal of Social Research Methodology*, 22(5), 487–501. https://doi.org/10.1080/13645579.2019.1590894

Caldwell, R. (2007). Agency and change: Re-evaluating Foucault's legacy. *Organization*, 14(6), 769–792.

Callahan, J. (2005). Power, control, and gender: Training as catalyst for dysfunctional behavior at the United States Air Force Academy. In M. Morris, F. M. Nafukho, & C. M. Graham (Eds.), *Academy of human resource development conference proceedings* (pp. 1064–1070). Academy of Human Resource Development.

Carbado, D. W. (2005). Privilege. In E. P. Johnson & M. G. Henderson (Eds.), *Black queer studies* (pp. 190–212). Duke University Press. https://doi.org/10.1515/9780822387220-011

Carnoy, M. (1986). *The state and political theory*. Cambridge University Press.

Castrodale, M. (2017). Critical disability studies and mad studies: Enabling new pedagogies in practice. *The Canadian Journal for the Study of Adult Education*, 29(1), 49–66.

Clarke, C., & Matthews, J. (2021). Advancement and leadership development. In D. Telem & C. Martin (Eds.), *Diversity, equity and inclusion* (pp. 11–21). Springer.

Collins, J. C. (2012). Identity matters: A critical exploration of lesbian, gay, and bisexual identity and leadership in HRD. *Human Resource Development Review*, 11(3), 349–379. https://doi.org/10.1177/1534484312446810

Crenshaw, K. (1991). Mapping the margins: Intersectionality, identity politics, and violence against women of color. *Stanford Law Review*, 43, 1241–1299.

Daldal, A. (2014). Power and ideology in Michel Foucault and Antonio Gramsci: A comparative analysis. *Review of History and Political Science*, 2(2), 149–167.

De Souza, E. R., Ispas, D., & Wesselmann, E. D. (2017). Workplace discrimination against sexual minorities: Subtle and not-so-subtle. *Canadian Journal of Administrative Sciences*, 34(2017), 121–132. https://doi.org/10.1002/CJAS.1438

Deetz, S. (2003). Disciplinary power, conflict suppression and human resources management. In M. Alvesson & H. Willmott (Eds.), *Studying management critically* (pp. 23–45). Sage.

Donovan, P. (2015). Practicing power: Undiscussables, power and HRD. In J. L. Callahan, J. Stewart, C. Rigg, S. Sambrook, & K. Trehan (Eds.), *Realising critical HRD: Stories of reflecting, voicing and enacting critical practice* (pp. 176–198). Cambridge Scholars Publishing.

Elliot, C., & Turnbull, S. (2005). *Critical thinking in human resource development*. Routledge.

Fenwick, T. (2014). Conceptualizing critical human resource development (CHRD): Tensions, dilemmas, and possibilities. In R. Poell, T. Rocco, & G. Roth (Eds.), *Routledge companion to human resource development* (pp. 113–123). Routledge.

Fenwick, T. J. (2004). Toward a critical HRD in theory and practice. *Adult Education Quarterly, 54*(3), 193–209.

Flannery, D. D. (1994). Changing dominant understandings of adults as learners. *Confronting Racism and Sexism. New Directions for Adult and Continuing Education, 61,* 47–57.

Foucault, M. (1980). *Power/knowledge.* Pantheon Books.

Foucault, M. (1982). The subject and power. *Critical Inquiry, 8*(4), 777–795.

Foucault, M. (1988). "Technologies of the self:" Lectures at University of Vermont, Oct. 1982. *Technologies of the self,* 16–49. University of Massachusetts Press.

Foucault, M. (1991). *Discipline and punish: The birth of a prison.* Penguin.

Foucault, M. (1997). Technologies of the self. In P. Rabinow's (Ed.), *Michel Foucault: Ethics, subjectivity and truth* (pp. 223–252). Penguin.

Foucault, M. (1998). *The history of sexuality: The will to knowledge.* Penguin.

Foucault, M. (2000). *Power.* New Press.

Gaventa, J. (2003). *Power after Lukes: A review of the literature.* Institute of Development Studies.

Githens, R. (2009). Capitalism, identity politics, and queerness converge: LGBT employee resource groups. *New Horizons in Adult Education and Human Resource Development, 23*(3), 18–31. https://doi.org/10.1002/nha3.10347

Gordon, C. (1991). Governmental rationality: An introduction. In G. Burchell, C. Gordon, & P. Miller (Eds.), *The Foucault effect: Studies in governmentality* (pp. 1–51). The University of Chicago Press.

Hamlin, B., & Stewart, J. (2011). What is HRD? A definitional review and synthesis of the HRD domain. *Journal of European Industrial Training, 35*(3), 199–220.

Heiskala, R. (2001). Theorizing power: Weber, Parsons, Foucault and neostructuralism. *Social Science Information, 40*(2), 241–264.

Heyes, C. (2002). Identity politics. In E. Zalta (Ed.), *The Stanford encyclopedia of philosophy.* https://plato.stanford.edu/entries/identity-politics/

Hill Collins, P. (2019). Intersectionality's definitional dilemmas. *Annual Review of Sociology, 41,* 1–20. https://doi.org/10.1146/annurev-soc-073014-112142

Horrocks, A., & Callahan, J. L. (2006). The role of emotion and narrative in the reciprocal construction of identity. *Human Resource Development International, 9*(1), 69–83. https://doi.org/10.1080/13678860600563382

Jessop, B. (2012). Marxist approaches to power. In E. Amenta, K. Nash, & A. Scott (Eds.), *The Wiley-Blackwell companion to political sociology* (pp. 3–14). Wiley.

Jo, S. J., & Park, S. (2016). Critical review on power in organization: Empowerment in human resource development. *European Journal of Training and Development, 40*(6), 390–406. https://doi.org/10.1108/EJTD-01-2016-0005

Jørgensen, K. M., & Keller, H. D. (2008). The contributions of communities of practice to human resource development: Learning as negotiating identity. *Advances in Developing Human Resources, 10*(4), 525–540. https://doi.org/10.1177/152342208320374

Kirby, M., Kidd, W., Koubel, F., Barter, J., Hope, T., Kirton, A., Madry, N., Manning, P., & Triggs, K. (2000). *Sociology in perspective.* Heinemann.

Knights, D. (2009). Power at work in organizations. In M. Alvesson, T. Bridgman, & H. Willmott (Eds.), *The Oxford handbook of critical management studies* (pp. 144–165). Oxford University Press.

Korte, R. F. (2007). A review of social identity theory with implications for training and development. *Journal of European Industrial Training, 31*(3), 166–190. https://doi.org/10.108/0309059071073950

Kulkarni, M. (2012). Social networks and career advancement of people with disabilities. *Human Resource Development Review, 11*(2), 138–155.

Lawless, A., Sambrook, S., & Stewart, J. (2012). Critical human resource development enabling alternative subject positions within a master of arts in human resource development educational programme. *Human Resource Development International, 15*(3), 321–336. https://doi.org/10.1080/13678868.2012.689214

Liegghio, M. (2013). A denial of being: Psychiatrization as epistemic violence. In B. A. LeFrançois, R. Menzies, & G. Reaume (Eds.), *Mad matters: A critical reader in Canadian mad studies* (pp. 122–129). Canadian Scholars Press.

Lukes, S. (1974). *Power: A radical view.* Macmillan.

Lukes, S. (2005). *Power: A radical view* (2nd ed.). Palgrave Macmillan.

Ma Rhea, Z. (2007). Where the global meets the local: Workforce diversity education. In L. Farrell & T. Fenwick (Eds.), *Educating the global workforce: Knowledge, knowledge work and knowledge workers* (pp. 127–140). Routledge.

Mambrol, N. (2016). *Foucault's concept of power.* https://literariness.org/2016/04/05/foucaults-concept-of-power/

McGuire, D., & Jørgensen, K. M. (2011). *Human resource development: Theory and practice.* Sage.

McInnes, P., Corlett, S., Coupland, C., Hallier, J., & Summers, J. (2017). Exploring traditions of identity theory for human resource development (HRD). In K. Black, R. Warhurst, & S. Corlett (Eds.), *Identity as a foundation for human resource development* (pp. 21–38). Routledge.

McIntosh, P. (1989). White privilege: Unpacking the invisible knapsack. *Peace and Freedom, 49*(4), 10–12.

Metcalfe, B. D. (2008). A feminist poststructuralist analysis of HRD: Why bodies, power and reflexivity matter. *Human Resource Development International, 11*(5), 447–463. https://doi.org/10.1080/13678860802417569

Miller, S. (June 11, 2020). Black workers still earn less than their white counterparts. *Society for Human Resource Management.* https://www.shrm.org/resourcesandtools/hr-topics/compensation/pages/racial-wage-gaps-persistence-poses-challenge.aspx

Mizzi, R. C., & Rocco, T. (2013). Deconstructing dominance: Towards a reconceptualization of the relationship between collective and individual identities, globalization and learning at work. *Human Resource Development Review, 12*(3), 364–382. https://doi.org/10.1177/1534484313477410

Mizzi, R. C., & Walton, G. (2014). Catchalls and conundrums: Theorizing 'sexual minority' in social, cultural and political contexts. *Philosophical Inquiry into Education, 22*(1), 81–90.

Nackoney, C. K., & Rocco, T. S. (2008). Critically strategic HRD: Possibility or pipe dream? *Proceedings for the 48th Adult Education Research Conference* (pp. 282–287). St. Louis, MO. https://newprairiepress.org/aerc/2008/papers/49/

Osanloo, A. F., Boske, C., & Newcomb, W. S. (2016). Deconstructing macroaggressions, microaggressions, and structural racism in education: Developing a conceptual model for the intersection of social justice practice and intercultural education. *International Journal of Organizational Theory and Development, 4*(1), 1–18.

Preston, R., & Arthur, L. (1997). Knowledge societies and planetary cultures: The changing nature of the consultancy in human development. *International Journal of Educational Development, 17*(1), 3–12.

Procknow, G. (2017). Silence or sanism: A review of the dearth of discussions on mental illness in adult education. *New Horizons in Adult Education and Human Resource Development, 29*(2), 4–24.

Procknow, G. (2019a). The pedagogy of saneness: Sane-centricity in popular culture as pedagogy. *New Horizons in Adult Education & Human Resource Development, 31*(1), 4–21.

Procknow, G. (2019b). The pedagogy of saneness: A schizoaffective storying of resisting sane pedagogy. *International Journal of Qualitative Studies, 32*(5), 510–528.

Procknow, G., & Rocco, T. S. (2016). The unheard, unseen, and often forgotten: An examination of disability in the human resource development literature. *Human Resource Development Review, 15*(4), 379–403.

Procknow, G., Rocco, T. S., & Munn, S. L. (2017). (Dis) ableing notions of authentic leadership through the lens of critical disability theory. *Advances in Developing Human Resources, 19*(4), 362–377.

Raffnsoe, S., Mennicken, A., & Miller, P. (2017). The Foucault effect in organizational studies. *Organizational Studies, 40*(2), 155–182.

Reynolds, A. L., & Pope, R. L. (1991). The complexities of diversity: Exploring multiple oppressions. *Journal of Counseling & Development, 70*, 174–180.

Rocco, T. S., Bernier, J., & Bowman, L. (2014). Critical race theory and HRD: Moving race front and center. *Advances in Developing Human Resources, 16*(4), 457–470.

Rocco, T. S., Munn, S. L., & Collins, J. C. (2018). The critical turn in human resources development. In M. Milana, J. Holford, S. Webb, P. Jarvis, & R. Waller (Eds.), *The Palgrave international handbook on adult and lifelong education and learning* (pp. 227–244). Palgrave Macmillan.

Rocco, T. S., & West, G. W. (1998). Deconstructing privilege: An examination of privilege in adult education. *Adult Education Quarterly, 48*(3), 171–184.

Rutherford, J. (1990). A place called home: Identity and the cultural politics of difference. In J. Rutherford (Ed.), *Identity: Community, culture and difference* (pp. 9–27). Lawrence & Wishart Ltd.

Sambrook, S. (2008). Critical HRD: A concept analysis. *Personnel Review, 38*(1), 61–73.

Scheper-Hughes, N. (1993). *Death without weeping: The violence of everyday life in Brazil*. University of California Press.

Schmidt, S. (2016). An honor to train: The professional identity of army trainers. In I. R. M. Association (Ed.), *Professional development and workplace learning: Concepts, methodologies, tools, and applications* (pp. 1692–1707). IGI Global.

Sørensen, M. K. (2014, September). *Foucault on power relations*. http://www.irenees.net/bdf_fiche-notions-242_es.html

Stephen, A. (2019). *Philosophy for busy people*. Michael O'Mara Books.

Stets, J. E., & Serpe, R. T. (2013). Identity theory. In J. DeLamater & A. Ward (Eds.), *Handbooks of sociology and social research* (pp. 31–60). Springer.

Sue, D. W. (2010). Microaggressions, marginality, and oppression. In D. W. Sue (Ed.), *Microaggressions and marginality, manifestation, dynamics, and impact* (pp. 3–24). Wiley & Sons.

Sue, D. W., Capodilupo, C., Torino, G., Bucceri, J., Holder, A., Nadal, K., & Esquilin, M. (2007). Racial microaggressions in everyday life: Implications for clinical practice. *American Psychologist, 62*(4), 271–286.

Syed, J., & Metcalfe, B. D. (2017). Under western eyes: A transnational and postcolonial perspective of gender and HRD. *Human Resource Development International, 20*(5), 403–414. https://doi.org/10.1080/13678868.2017.1329367

Tajfel, H. (2010). *Social identity and intergroup relations.* Cambridge University Press.

Usher, R., & Solomon, N. (1999). Experiential learning and the shaping of subjectivity in the workplace. *Studies in the Education of Adults, 31*(2), 155–163.

Välikangas, A., & Seeck, H. (2011). Exploring the Foucauldian interpretation of power and subject in organizations. *Journal of Management and Organization, 17*(6), 812–827.

Wang, J., Wang, G., Ruona, W. E. A., & Rojewski, J. W. (2005). Confucian values and the implications for international HRD. *Human Resource Development International, 8*(3), 311–326. https://doi.org/10.1080/13678860500143285

Weber, M. (1978). *Economy and society* (G. Roth & C. Wittich, Trans). University of California Press.

Wekker, G. (2006). *The politics of passion: Women's sexual culture in the Afro-Surinamese diaspora.* Columbia University Press.

Wolff, J. (Winter 2017 Edition). Karl Marx. In E. N. Zalta (Ed.), *The Stanford encyclopedia of philosophy.* https://plato.stanford.edu/archives/win2017/entries/marx/.

Wolframe, P. M. (2013). The madwoman in the academy, or, revealing the invisible straightjacket: Theorizing and teaching saneism and sane privilege. *Disability Studies Quarterly, 33*(1). http://dsq-sds.org/article/view/3425

CHAPTER 17

Community, Intersectionality, and Social Justice in Critical HRD

Catherine H. Monaghan and E. Paulette Isaac-Savage

The purpose of this chapter is to expand the current dialogue concerning the ways an individual's privileged and/or marginalized identities and communal affiliations impact the experience and (re) production of relationships—positive, negative, and neutral—in organizational spaces. The premise of this chapter is that a humanistic view of social justice within organizations that defines any space as neutral maintains the status quo.

In examining the literature on intersectionality, community, and social justice, a critical race theory (CRT) and a critical human resource development (CHRD) framework along with Black Feminist Thought (BFT) supports our argument. The use of Black Feminism is especially useful in unpacking the intersectionality of employees. We argue that to bring about genuine change within organizations, relationships must shift to a level that is outside the current system of white privilege to allow those who are currently invisible or in the margins to have legitimate power and a substantial seat at the strategic planning table.

In the section on community, we address the myriad of communities that are part of the relating space within organizations. Here we juxtapose Bierema and Callahan's (2014) relating framework with CRT, CHRD, and BFT. We

C. H. Monaghan (✉)
Cleveland State University, Cleveland, OH, USA

E. P. Isaac-Savage
University of Missouri-St. Louis, St. Louis, MO, USA

© The Author(s), under exclusive license to Springer Nature Switzerland AG 2023

J. C. Collins and J. L. Callahan (eds.), *The Palgrave Handbook of Critical Human Resource Development*, https://doi.org/10.1007/978-3-031-10453-4_17

307

also consider ways practitioners of CHRD can use antiracist policies and practice to address the needs of historically marginalized groups through the production of positive relationships in spaces of organizing. In the conclusion, we situate social justice initiatives within recommendations for CHRD practitioners.

There are two traditional views of Human Resource Development (HRD), hard and soft. Hard HRD means that the organization should only employ the minimum resources required to hire, train, and retain employees (Botero et al., 2004). Here HRD embodies transactional interactions between the employee and management or organization as opposed to relationships. Soft HRD focuses on the human side and presupposes that everyone can "win" when all are involved and nurtured (Peach-Martins & Wood, 2010). However, while seeming to help individuals develop in their career, it is our belief that it does so by maintaining the dominant power structures that are antithetical to social justice. In the process, individuals of historically marginalized groups do not enjoy the full benefits of development and promotion; these are still open predominantly to white males. Next, we define the lenses of CRT, CHRD, and Black Feminism that will be used to examine the literature of intersectionality, community, and social justice within organizations.

CRITICAL RACE THEORY

Formulated in the 1970s, CRT "sought to stage a simultaneous encounter with the exhausted vision of reformist civil rights scholarship" with the "emergent critique of left legal scholarship" (Crenshaw et al., 1995, p. xix). Rollock and Gillborn (2011) identified five major principles of CRT: centrality of racism, white supremacy, voices of people of color, interest convergence, and intersectionality. CRT made its entry "to the field of adult education by Elizabeth Peterson" (Isaac et al., 2010, p. 361). It is now a convergence of elements from various race-based theories such as Afrocentrism, BFT, and multiculturalism and offers "a unique lens with which to view practice and work toward social justice" (Isaac et al., 2010, p. 361). CRT uses an analysis of various policies and processes that recreate racism and injustice. According to Bowman et al. (2009), "a key theme of CRT is that racism is ordinary and pervasive" (p. 233). Another, perhaps more accurate analysis is that CRT is about whiteness and the privilege that accrues with the color of your skin. "Racism and White Supremacy have a long history in the United States. Rooted in religion, White supremacy arrived with the Puritans and is promoted by present day intellectuals" (Baumgartner, 2010, p. 106).

The current scholarship on historically marginalized groups is situated in the concept of antiracism. Juxtaposed with stress, "forms of power-loss anxiety", and fear, antiracism is a prejudicial function (Hall, 2015, p. 319). Antiracists support antiracist policy through their actions or antiracist ideas (Kendi, 2019). Feminist scholarship, while not described as antiracist, largely excludes the experiences of Black women.

Black Feminist Thought

BFT is a "critical social theory aimed to empower African American women within the context of social justice sustained by intersection oppressions" (Collins, 2000, p. 22). Starting in the 1970s, The Combahee River Collective challenged white feminists to examine their privileged position in society (Flannery & Hayes, 2001). The Collective contested the movement's dismissal of race and racism as equally essential to social justice (Roumell & James-Gallaway, 2021). Further, bell hooks (1994) emphasized that when addressing issues of diversity "feminist scholars must change [their] ways of seeing, talking and thinking" (p. 112). This is essential in the CHRD space, if practitioners are to engage with employees and leaders who possess various modes of intersectionality. Ironically, it has been suggested that HRD lacks critical analysis incorporating BFT that accounts "for intersectionality" and contests the "domination, oppression, alienation, and struggle of marginalized groups or that consider strategies that emancipate oppressed groups and transform organizations" (Bierema, 2020, p. 353).

BFT plays a crucial role in our understanding of the dynamics and practices within organizations. This is important when considering the multiple positions that employees occupy in an organizational space creating different experiences based on an individual's intersectionality.

Intersectionality

Intersectionality finds its roots in Black feminism. Often credited to Crenshaw (1991), intersectionality "references the critical insight that race, class, gender, sexuality, ethnicity, nation, ability, and age operate not as unitary, mutually exclusive entities, but as reciprocally constructing phenomena that in turn shape complex social inequalities" (Collins, 2015, p. 2). It explicitly analyzes power in social structures and organizations at multiple levels (Walker et al., 2019). Rosette et al. (2018) argue the positions women often occupy are the lack of sufficient organizational support and the penalty for being a mother, among other things. At the intersection of gender is race. Lean In (2020) reported women's experiences are worse than men's, and for Black women, in particular, their experiences are even worse. They do not interact with their senior leaders often, and "face more day-to-day discrimination" (Lean In, 2020, p. 13), and can be penalized for their ambition. One of the major factors for Black women's underrepresentation in management positions is the "broken rung" (p. 6). They cannot climb up the ladder, because the first rung is broken. Furthermore, they often lack support and access, even if they are invited to sit at the table. These and other challenges call for the HRD field to look at itself more critically.

CRITICAL HRD

Since the end of the twentieth century, there has been a push to move HRD in a more critical direction. In moving in this direction, critical theory (Brookfield, 2014), critical management studies (CMS) (Alvesson & Willmott, 2003), and critical pedagogy (Freire, 1970, 2000) have been used to enrich the discussion. One of the results of this interrogation and integration is a new discipline within HRD known as Critical Human Resource Development (CHRD) (Sambrook, 2008). CMS is the precursor to CHRD and has been defined as "a branch of management theory that critiques our intellectual and social practices, questions the 'natural order' of institutional arrangements, and engages in actions that support challenges to prevailing systems of domination" (Cunliffe et al., 2002, p. 489).

CHRD is defined by Bierema and Callahan (2014) as "the process of engaging human and organizational systems that relate, learn, change, and organize in ways that optimize human interest, organization advancement, and social impact" (p. 436). Fenwick (2005) further postulates that the purpose of using a critical framework in the arena of HRD is to question and contest the status quo that generally guides our HRD practice. Within CHRD, relating involves looking at concerns of various stakeholders, focusing on incivility and resistance along with the intersectionality of the actors that create the liminal spaces (Bierema & Callahan, 2014).

SOCIAL JUSTICE

Social justice can be defined as "the conditions in society in which all members have the same basic rights, security, opportunities, obligations, social benefits and the way in which human rights are manifested in everyday lives of people at every level of society" (Ingram & Walters, 2007, p. 27). The opposite is social injustice. Acts of social injustice have been shown to "interfere with work relationships, decrease job satisfaction, and performance, create stressful conditions, and prevent an overall sense of well-being" (Byrd, 2018, p. 3).

Social justice is usually viewed as belonging primarily to the sphere of some non-profit organizations. For instance, the YWCA's mission is to eliminate racism and empower women (YWCA, 2021). Here we explore the wider implications for social justice within all organizations and the way community and intersectionality can either contribute or deter the occurrence of social justice for privileged or marginalized identities. Social justice in the organizational space requires "a critical lens to confront and expose the manifestations of continued acts of bias, prejudice, and other societal forms of injustice against historically marginalized groups" (Bohonos et al., 2019, p. 19).

COMMUNITY

In this section, the various types of communities that are commonly found within organizations are discussed. This includes both formal and informal communities or networks that are created among peers in the workplace. We focus on networks in general, then mentoring, Employee Resource Groups (ERG), and affinity groups. We explore the broader question of how they might impact the experiences of the members and the interaction and structure of these relationships within organizations.

Community was usually thought of as something that occurs in the personal or civic realm of one's life. However, over the last half century, managerial and HRD discourse has appropriated the term and practice into organizational life through the human relations movement (Elliott & Turnbull, 2003). At the heart of community is the basic assumption of trust among the members. Organizational relationships may fail to meet this fundamental assumption due to the short-term nature of organizational relationships, especially in the current climate of multiple careers with multiple organizations. There are also shifting power dynamics that can cause instability and the blurring of boundaries. Have employees given organizations too much power to define what communities they should belong to within an organization? Do individuals' affiliations with a particular intra-organizational community serve to increase their social capital? Hellerstein and Neumark (2020) define "social capital as networks of relationships among people who are connected by where they live or work. Thus, social capital, in contrast to human capital, resides in the connections among people rather than in their individual characteristics" (p. 127). The creation of social capital is an important component of communities within organizations.

Many organizations are behemoths. According to Statista (2020), Walmart is the world's largest corporation based on the number of employees, as of 2019, 2.2 million. Since increasing its workforce by 500,000 workers in, 2020, Amazon employs 1.3 million people (Sopher, 2021). Further down the list of the top 50 organizations is Target. Target employs even less than Amazon does at 368,000 employees (Statista, 2020). Even if all these employees were centered in one location it would still be necessary to create communities within the organizations.

Networks

Networks are the backbone of communities within organizations. Individuals may be hired based on their connection through their network and by extension because of their social capital. Networks also help individuals find powerful allies or mentors that can significantly advance their careers. Networks can position individuals to be placed on high-profile and significant projects, which in turn position the individual for quick advancement. "There is now a wealth of evidence linking the nature and quality of inter-personal networks within organizations to various indicators of individual attainment" (Srivastava, 2015, p. 427).

Networks usually benefit men over women and whites over employees who are members of historically marginalized groups. Srivastava (2015) cited Campbell's (1988) study, who "found differences in the networks of employed men and women, with the former having networks with greater occupational range and socioeconomic diversity than the latter" (p. 431). In an effort to overcome the limitations of inter-personal networks, which rely on who an individual is able to connect with, as well as how their network connections are configured, HRD has developed mechanisms that are more formal. These are designed to help create a more level playing field, especially for women and individuals who are members of historically marginalized groups. Informal and formal types of communities are discussed next.

Mentoring

While mentoring usually takes the shape of a dyad, it has the potential to bring the mentee into the community of the organization in a more visible way and with a stronger connection than an employee without a mentor would experience. Mentors are "experienced and knowledgeable individuals who are committed to providing career and psychosocial support to one or more protégés" (Srivastava, 2015, p. 430). Most mentor/mentee relationships happen on an informal basis. Perhaps an employee starts working at an organization and someone sees some potential in this new employee and decides that they, as a mentor, have something to contribute to enhancing the mentee's career. Having a protégé implies that the successes of the protégé will naturally accrue in some way to the mentor. Therefore, while the mentee gains in terms of knowledge, especially about the political workings of an organization, the mentor also stands to gain through the association. Most mentors would not use their valuable time to help someone unless they thought that the mentee would enhance the mentor's standing in the organization as well. Srivastava (2015) states, informal mentoring...develops spontaneously and often lasts a long time, "whereas formal mentoring...relationships...arise from organizational interventions - typically in the form of voluntary assignment or matching of protégés - and often exist for a shorter duration" (p. 430).

Mentor/mentee relationships are a more formal and high-powered method of networking. Using a CRT, CMS, and Black Feminist lens, it is important to explore the power dynamics present in every dyad of this type. Due to the nature of the relationship, there is a strong power dynamic at work. The mentor has the knowledge, experience, and connections that are valuable to the mentee. This power dynamic can be somewhat balanced as in peer-to-peer mentoring or very unbalanced based on a number of factors. The first factor is that the more prestigious the mentor, the more chance there is for the power to reside almost exclusively with the mentor. Another factor is gender differences, especially if the mentee is a woman. Finally, it is important to consider any racial/cultural differences that might exist between the dyad. "The unacknowledged and not resisted power of hegemony thwarts the effectiveness of the many well-intentioned mentors who work with [mentees] from non-dominate cultural groups, in particular" (Merriweather, 2012, p. 103). From the Black Feminist lens, this relationship calls for an understanding of intersectionality in the power dynamic. Even the use of the terms protégé and mentor used to define mentoring implies an underlying power imbalance.

Employee Resource Groups and Affinity Groups

Employee Resource Groups (ERG) is another type of community. They provide "networking, an opportunity to showcase skills and learn new ones, and the chance to impact your community" (Burjek, 2019, para. 1). ERG create communities with individuals at a particular organization and strives to impact the community where they are located (Green, 2018). ERG are also known as Business Resource Groups, and, according to Catalyst (2020), "are voluntary, employee-led groups that foster a diverse, inclusive workplace aligned with organizational mission, values, goals, and business practices, and objectives. Other benefits include the development of future leaders, increased employee engagement and expanded marketplace reach" (p. 1).

Another term used for formal communities within organizations is affinity groups. Affinity groups "are based on common interests that bring employees together to share their concerns and address common problems as well as encourage camaraderie and fellowship" (Glassman & Glassman, 2017, (p. 104). Not surprisingly, these groups are very popular. Hall (2015) found that "over 90% of Fortune 500 firms have some type of affinity, networking, or resource group".

In critiquing these communities from a CRT, CHRD, and a BFT perspective, we find that these communities within organizations primarily serve to maintain the status quo while appearing to be acts that further the social justice mission of the organization. By their very nature, they create segregated groups of employees centered on a social/cultural construct that restricts the expression of the intersectionality of the workforce of an organization. As an example, many organizations have ERG for Black, Indigenous and People of Color (BIPOC), Women, LGBTQ+ community, and employees with Disabilities. However, the concept of intersectionality would question this arbitrary divide. For instance, should a Black woman join both the ERG for BIPOC and the one for Women? Moreover, would she be welcomed at the Women ERG based on an assumption that the ERG which best defines her is the BIPOC?

It is notable that organizations do not feel the need to create an ERG for their white cis-gender male employees. This is because the organizational norms, policies, and practices are designed so that they are automatically provided with networking, leadership/career development, and other opportunities to help them succeed. Corporations, especially now, see these communities as indispensable to their business model to fulfill their mission as organizations of diversity and inclusion or to be part of the greater societal movements such as Black Lives Matter.

All of our lenses ask HRD practitioners to question the effectiveness of these groups. Do they really create more opportunities for career success for the community members or do they just continue the illusion of social justice and equality? What additional work-related tasks are created for group members that are not required of those who do not belong to ERG or affinity groups? This might include group meeting time, intra-group mentoring, community, or client outreach. Is involvement in these groups valued by the organization with assignment to highly visible career enhancing projects or additional compensation? Alternatively, does the organization view it as a "perk" for members? How do individuals view their participation? Bierema (2005) found that women viewed belonging to a women's network as detrimental rather than supporting their career within the organization. Sixty years after Affirmative Action, what is the result of waiting for these "qualified" candidates to move through the pipeline and up the career ladder? According to a 2020 article in *Fortune Magazine*, in 1988 there were two women CEOs running Fortune 500 companies in the United States. In, 2020, there were 37 women CEOs, "an all-time record" (Hinchliffe, 2020, para 1). However, not one of these women was Black or Latinx, although there were three "women of color". Also, these female CEOs tend to be in charge of organizations whose asset size puts them near the bottom of the Fortune 500 list; only seven women run Fortune 100 Companies (Hinchliffe, 2020, para 11). In addition, "despite years of diversity programs and pious pledges by Corporate America, the ranks of African-American chief executives running Fortune 500 companies remain maddeningly slim. There were only five Black CEOs on the 2020 list" (Wahba, 2020, para 1). While they may provide a supportive environment that can decrease the sense of isolation experienced by employees who belong to historically marginalized groups, the dynamic of white privilege and patriarchy is still the dominant culture within organizations.

RELATIONSHIPS IN SPACES OF ORGANIZING

In this section, we discuss how various relationships within organizations are impacted by communities, networking, and intersectionality. Using the frameworks discussed above, we examine the issues of positive, neutral, and negative relationships within organizations.

"Relating forms the context for learning, changing, and organizing and has tremendous leverage in our ability to facilitate effective HRD when relationships between people are nurtured and developed in a positive direction" (Bierema & Callahan, 2014, p. 437). Using Bierema and Callahan's (2014) framework of CHRD actions associated with relating, we will expand on their work using the critical frameworks of CRT, CMS, and Black Feminism presented. Their framework has four main CHRD actions: context, stakeholders, process, and method.

Context

When discussing context, Bierema and Callahan (2014) suggest that relating from a CHRD perspective is situated in three areas, (a) acknowledging asymmetrical power relation", (b) "forms the context for learning, changing and organizing", and (c) "values cultural diversity" (p. 437). We suggest that this level of superficial positive relating maintains the status quo at the expense of social justice and actually leads to negative relationships.

In 2020, CRT, BFT, and CMS would maintain that organizations in the United States need to understand that it is illegal to discriminate and that the definition of discrimination cannot depend on a vague concept of whether it was intentional or not. CHRD practitioners need to strive for going beyond acknowledging the existence of asymmetrical power relations to mitigating the abuses that have and can occur when those types of power relations are not challenged when they lead to harm. For example, instances of sexual harassment need to be dealt with swiftly, seriously, and with accountability and transparency.

As Bierema and Callahan (2014) point out, HRD frames the context for learning, changing, and organizing. This also includes framing recruitment practices within organizations. HRD needs to do more to create positive relationships in organizations. We define a positive relationship as one where everyone has the same opportunities and experiences a culture and climate that provides a place of safety and space to thrive in one's career and is inclusive of everyone, not just those who can meet the norms of the dominant, patriarchal culture that currently exists.

One place to start would be within the HRD arena of the organization. First, it would be paramount to intentionally hire employees who are from historically marginalized groups. One way to achieve this would be to develop a policy that sets a target of raising the number of employees who are hired that are part of a marginalized group. This might occur because a policy states that the hiring search cannot be closed until there is at least a 50% representation of marginalized groups in the hiring pool. However, because of intersectionality, the intent is not to label candidates into neat boxes related to the various ERG. For instance, possible candidates for determining a representative pool might be a Black woman, a Hispanic lesbian, or perhaps even a white male with autism. In this example, some characteristics may be observable but many may be invisible. Second, with this in mind an organization might ask itself how many of its current employees, who belong to an invisible marginalized group, feel very safe to share this aspect of themselves with management and co-workers. Third, they need to open up and promote training and development, mentoring, and leadership opportunities to all employees in a manner that is equitable for all and not dependent on who you know or if you happen to be at the right table at the right time. Again, transparency and accountability are important.

Finally, in building positive relationships, HRD needs to be intentional about creating a culture where microaggressions are replaced with micro-affirmations. "Microaggressions are the brief and commonplace daily verbal, behavioral, and environmental indignities, whether intentional or unintentional, that communicate hostile, derogatory, or negative racial, gender, sexual-orientation, and religious slights and insults to the target person or group" (Sue, 2010, p. 21). This requires education about these practices and their effects on individuals and the corporate culture. This includes the perspective from those who are experiencing these practices and a culture that does not placate those who engage, either intentionally or unintentionally, in microaggressions. In other words, those who are engaging in negative relationship activity need to experience the consequences of not being part of the team and corporate culture.

Of course, the leadership of an organization actually develops the culture and they need to be driving the initiative for an organization who acts as though social justice is as important as the bottom line. In actuality, social justice can be a major contributor to the bottom line. Research has shown that "organizations with at least 30% women in leadership roles outperform their competitors by an increased profit margin of six percent" (Gordon, 2017, para 4). The Boston Consulting Group found that "companies that have more diverse management teams over and above gender diversity have 19% higher revenue due to innovation" (Powers, 2018, para 2). Given these facts, one has to wonder why CEOs and Board of Directors are leaving so much profit on the table. While the HRD arena might be a place to start, CHRD practitioners must then move their agenda throughout the entire organization.

Stakeholders

Stakeholders are the next piece in the relating framework. The "organization, community and environment [must be taken] into account" and "distinguish between stakeholders and shareholders" (Bierema & Callahan, 2014, p. 437). Bohonos (2019) accurately expands on this framework by suggesting that a CHRD practitioner "recognizes interlocking privileges, recognizes intersecting oppressions [and] recognizes personal agency and ability to subvert privileges and/or overcome oppressions" (p. 329).

We suggest that employees and managers, particularly executives, need to understand clearly how the system of privilege operates within their organizations. What is the composition of the Board of Directors, Executive team, and management? With the help of their HRD departments, they need to examine or audit the current policies that maintain privileges of the dominant group members. They need to examine critically their policies of hiring, development, and retention. A common practice, especially among large organizations, is to recruit and hire individuals who have graduated from the top 50 MBA programs as determined by such rankings from *US News & World Report* or *Forbes*, for example (Curtin & Gasman, 2003). Due to arbitrary factors used in these rankings, most Historically Black Colleges and Universities (HBCUs) with top-notch graduates never see a recruiter from a prestigious organization. Therefore, the quality of candidates is not the issue; the recruiters are just doing what they have always done and not expanding their recruiting efforts to include institutions that have served historically marginalized groups (Curtin & Gasman, 2003). This hampers organizations in their efforts to recruit the best talent when someone chooses to attend an HBCU or a Tribal University rather than a predominantly white institution (PWI). It continues the status quo while ignoring the diversity of the organizational communities, the intersectionalities represented in their employees, and breeds injustice and inequity rather than social justice. It also hampers organizations in their efforts to recruit and retain the best talent if the only place they are recruiting from is a PWI.

In terms of retention, a relational question needs to be asked. Are those diverse candidates we hire developing and remaining with the organization or are they leaving? The answer to this question should lead executives and HRD professionals to ask why. Asking why, instead of just collecting statistics, will enable organizations to determine what they are doing well and where they need to improve. However, given the stakes that are involved from the employee side, it is important that these questions be asked by an outside third party who is committed to protecting the employees' privacy and sharing the information with the organization in a truthful way. In addition, the third party needs to include members of the diverse groups that are being surveyed.

If the organization is developing and promoting diverse talent, then it might be easy to assume that they are good at developing positive relationships. One would hope this is true. But our experiences in various organizations bears out the premise that even if those that are classified as a member of a marginalized group are succeeding, it may be in spite of negative relationships rather than because the corporate culture has created a positive environment for all employees. In this case, the organization is usually deploying double standards while asking employees who are members of historically marginalized groups to "go along and not make waves;" they should not bring up the microaggressions that they encounter or make dominant group members uncomfortable in any way. The cultural message from the organization is that employees who are members of marginalized groups just need to engage in collegial relationships with employees in the dominant group who are working from stereotypical behaviors and assumptions when interacting with diverse co-workers. The fact that this creates negative encounters within the space of the organization is too often ignored, or the employee who identifies as a member of a marginalized group is blamed for the negativity. In any event, the responsibility for creating a positive relationship with work colleagues is placed on the shoulders of the marginalized employee. It takes an emotional and physical toll on employees who are being targeted, no matter what the intentionality. According to Winters (2020),

A 2018 report by Catalyst, an organization that researches workplace experiences for women, titled *Day-to-Day Experience of Emotional Tax among Women and Men of Color in the Workplace*, found that as a result of, or in anticipation of, unfair treatment, professionals of color report a high number of instances of being 'on guard' to protect themselves against racial and gender bias, causing what they describe as an emotional tax. (p. 123)

This is just one example of the intersectionality of race and gender that is part of the Black Feminist canon. It is the responsibility of the organizational leaders, from the C-suite on down, to constantly strive to create a culture where positive relationships are fostered across the various organizational spaces and intersectionalities in order to first imagine and forge an organization whose core mission is rooted in social justice.

Process

Process is the third aspect of the relating framework. Bierema and Callahan (2014) suggest that the best process to create the foundation of "relating" is one that "embraces values of humanism…addresses dynamics of resistance and incivility…problematizes human capital approaches…[and] explores implications of emotions within organizations" (p. 437). Bohonos (2019) delineated their suggestions even further. He proposes that processes encourage "individuals to endeavor to undercut their own privilege…listen to the voices of the historically marginalized…[and] is receptive to bottom-up change initiatives" (p. 329).

Human capital is considered a resource of the organization much like physical assets. Although human capital is a less tangible asset, it assumes that all skills and knowledge of the individual employees can be increased and monetized (Adams & Sydie, 2001). Humanism assumes that all individuals are inherently good and learning is about individual development, therefore employees should be allowed to choose what they want to know and learn. On the other hand, CRT, Black Feminism, and CHRD would question whether social justice can be achieved if employees maintain the status quo by refusing to participate actively in development opportunities that would require them to examine and change their worldviews. Therefore, if CHRD embraces the values of humanism, it clashes with a social justice orientation. "Social justice requires a critical lens to confront and expose the manifestation of continued acts of biases, prejudice, and other societal forms of injustice against historically marginalized groups" (Bohonos et al., 2019, p. 19). Social justice would be a given, not an aspiration, if all individuals were inherently good. In general, social justice and diversity education within an organization must be mandated. It also needs to be hardy enough to cause individuals to be uncomfortable as they examine their own biases and prejudices and how it affects their behavior toward historically marginalized individuals both within the organization and outside of its walls. CHRD practitioners can begin by using Cannon's (1990) ground rules for discussions. One pertinent rule is "agree not to blame ourselves or others for the misinformation we have learned in the past, but accept responsibility for not repeating misinformation after we have learned otherwise" (para. 19). In addition, we need to educate our learners that we can only grow and develop by moving out of our comfort zones.

We would like to expound on the suggestions by both Bierema and Callahan (2014) and Bohonos (2019). We think that an organization with a social justice mandate would be a place where all stakeholders actively engage in their own education about the full history of this country. This includes learning about the place that white privilege has played in ensuring that some are able to move up the various rungs of the corporate ladder, while others are held back in more entry-level positions. As discussed earlier, hiring, development, and promotions should intentionally seek individuals from the most diverse talent pool possible. In fact, an excellent practice would be to keep positions opened until a very diverse pool of the best possible talent has been assembled. In the beginning, this might appear to slow the process down. However, by committing to recruiting from HBCUs and Tribal Universities, as well as PWIs, we believe organizations will learn that they are able to find the best possible hires for their open positions in a reasonable timeframe. Other ways to increase the type of diversity to fulfill a social justice mandate would be to ask those who are part of the organization's diversity membership to recommend and network to bring more candidates to the table.

As part of this educational endeavor, it is important to, as Bohonos (2019) points out, listen to the voices of the marginalized while those who are privilege resist the temptation to explain their view as only a misunderstanding. This might include a woman talking about a gender issue or a member of a historically underrepresented group talking about their experience of racial or intersectional microaggressions or anyone else on the intersectionality spectrum. We must accept their experiences as genuine and use positive relational dialogues to ensure that the organization has the tools to continue to develop aspects of their social justice mission.

Method

In Bierema and Callahan's (2014) framework, the last piece is the method of developing individuals within an organization. Their methods incorporate "participative and collaborative processes" (p. 437). In our view, this incorporation must place the voices of historically marginalized individuals and groups as the standard to begin developing these processes. Bohonos (2019) goes a step further in his focus of relating methods to outcomes of learning by "increasing awareness of unconscious bias and encouraging ally development" (p. 329).

It is important to define the word ally. "Ally is not an identity, it is a practice" (Kivel, 2016, p. 207). This means, first, to increase our awareness of the privileges of dominant group employees and the obstacles this creates for historically marginalized groups. Those who are working from the perspective of CHRD need to work from the assumptions that racism and white privilege are always contesting antiracism for control of the way the organization engages in constructing their corporate culture and community in the midst of intersectionality and social justice. We need to go beyond focusing on individual behavior and development and look at the patterns and practices that create the culture of the organization (Kivel, 2016). "At the organizational level those engaged in HRD must be role models" (Monaghan, 2010, p. 61). This requires members of the organization to model antiracist relationships. This is an important method to change negative relating and create genuine spaces of positive relating.

Another important aspect of learning within organizations committed to social justice is the need to enact "critical consciousness and cultural competencies [that] then become the foundations of developing a practice of culturally responsive [learning]" (Merriweather, 2012, p. 107). These would take place across the organization in all forms of relating as employees engage in positive relationships.

DISCUSSION/CONCLUSION

As the previous discussion suggests, a humanistic social justice view defining spaces as neutral maintains the status quo. Those who insist on standing on neutral ground only serve to undermine the execution of change within organizations. There are several issues that organizations and individuals need to address to become more critical and intentional in their practices.

> HRD professionals need to be aware that assuming that the dominant culture [or even a portion of it] is neutral within an organization creates implicit double standards and the color-blind posturing prevents many Whites from acknowledging how policies and group norms [especially in relational spaces] disproportionately benefit majority group members. (Bohonos, 2019, p. 323)

If HRD and organizations are striving for social justice, they must not fall into the trap that there can be neutral relationships anywhere within the organization. The danger of neutrality is that it perpetuates the status quo at the expense of those who are not members of the dominant group. Neutrality allows discrimination to continue because it reinforces the precedent that if unequivocal discriminatory intent cannot be established then discrimination did not occur. This mindset can be used to silence the negative impacts that are occurring in relationships within the organization. Relationships can be positive and create real equity or they can be negative and maintain the status quo. There is no neutral ground when striving for social justice.

References

Adams, B. N., & Sydie, R. A. (2001). *Sociological theory*. Pine Forge Press.

Alvesson, M., & Willmott, H. (Eds.). (2003). *Studying management critically*. Sage.

Baumgartner, L. M. (2010). White whispers: Talking about race in adult education. In V. Sheared, J. Johnson-Bailey, S. A. J. Colin, E. Peterson, & S. Brookfield (Eds.), *Handbook of race and adult education* (pp. 105–118). Jossey-Bass.

Bierema, L. L. (2005). Women's networks: A career development intervention or impediment? *Human Resource Development International, 8*(2), 207–224.

Bierema, L. L. (2020). HRD research and practice after 'The great COVID-19 pause': The time is now for bold, critical, research. *Human Resource Development International, 23*(4), 347–360. https://doi.org/10.1080/13678868.2020.17799

Bierema, L. L., & Callahan, J. L. (2014). Transforming HRD: A framework for critical HRD practice. *Advances in Developing Human Resources, 16*, 429–444.

Bohonos, J. W. (2019). Including critical whiteness studies in the critical human resource development family: A proposed theoretical framework. *Adult Education Quarterly, 69*(4), 315–337. https://doi.org/10.1177/0741713619858131

Bohonos, J. W., Otchere, K. D., & Pak, Y. K. (2019). Teaching and learning social justice in human resource development graduate programs: Preparation for research and practice. *New Horizons in Adult Education & Human Resource Development, 37*(4), 18–35. https://doi.org/10.1002/nha3.20262

Botero, J., Djankov, S., La Porta, R., Lopez-De-Silanes, S., & Shleifer, A. (2004). The regulation of labour. *Quarterly Journal of Economics, 119*, 1339–1382.

Bowman, L., Rocco, T., & Peterson, E. (2009). The exclusion of race from mandated continuing legal education requirements: A critical race theory analysis. *Seattle Journal for Social Justice, 8*(1), 229–250.

Brookfield, S. D. (2014). Foundations of critical theory. *Advances in Developing Human Resources, 16*, 417–428.

Burjek, A. (2019, August 12). *Interview with Jomo Castro*. Chief Learning Officer (online). https://www.chieflearningofficer.com/2019/08/12/ergs-are-beneficial-for-employees-and-their-communities/

Byrd, M. Y. (2018). Does HRD have a moral duty to respond to matters of social injustice? *Human Resource Development International, 21*(1), 3–11.

Campbell, K. E. (1988). Gender differences in job-related networks. *Work and Occupations, 15*, 179–200.

Cannon, L. W. (1990). Fostering positive race, class, and gender dynamics in the classroom. *Women's Studies Quarterly, 18*, 126–134.

Catalyst. (2020). *Employee Resource Groups*. https://www.catalyst.org/topics/ergs/#:~:text=Employee%20Resource%20Groups%20(ERGs)%20are,engagement%2C%20and%20expanded%20marketplace%20reach

Collins, P. H. (2000). *Black feminist thought: Knowledge, consciousness and the politics of empowerment* (2nd ed.). Routledge.

Collins, P. H. (2015). Intersectionality's definitional dilemmas. *Annual Review of Sociology, 41*, 1–20. https://doi.org/10.1146/annurev-soc-073014-112142

Crenshaw, K. (1991). Mapping the margins: Intersectionality, identity politics, and violence against women of color. *Stanford Law Review, 43*(6), 1241–1299. https://doi.org/10.2307/1229039

Crenshaw, K. Gotanda, N., Peller, G., & Thomas, K. (Eds.). (1995). *Critical race theory: The key writings that formed the movement*. The New Press.

Cunliffe, A., Forray, J. M., & Knights, D. (2002). Considering management education: Insights from critical management studies. *Journal of Management Education, 26*(5), 489–495. https://doi.org.proxy.ulib.csuohio.edu/10.1177/105 256202236722

Curtin, M. A., & Gasman, M. (2003). Historically Black college MBA programs: Prestige, rankings, and the meaning of success. *Journal of Education for Business, 79*(2), 79–84. https://proxy.ulib.csuohio.edu:2096/10.1080/08832320309599093

Elliott, C., & Turnbull, S. (2003). Reconciling autonomy and community: The paradoxical role of HRD. *Human Resource Development International, 6,* 457–474.

Fenwick, T. (2005). Conceptions of critical HRD: Dilemmas for theory and practice. *Human Resource Development International, 8*(2), 225–238.

Flannery, D. D., & Hayes, E. (2001). Challenging adult learning: A feminist perspective. In V. Sheared & P. A. Sissel (Eds.), *Making space: Merging theory and practice in adult education* (pp. 42–56). Bergin & Garvey.

Freire, P. (1970/2000). *Pedagogy of the oppressed* (30th Anniversary, Trans. M. B. Ramos). Continuum.

Glassman, A. M., & Glassman, M. (2017). The use of affinity groups by fortune 100 firms. *Journal of Business Diversity, 17*(2), 104–114.

Gordon, S. (September 26, 2017). Female leaders boost the bottom line. *Financial Times* digital version. https://www.ft.com/content/f88a7c58-96ff-11e7-8c5c-c8d 8fa6961bb

Green, W. M. (2018). Employee resource groups as learning communities. *Equality, Diversity and Inclusion: An International Journal, 37*(7), 634–648.

Hall, R. (2015). Anti-Racist racism as a judicial decree: Racism in the twenty-first century. *Journal of African American Studies, 19*(3), 319–328. http://www.jstor.org/stable/43525597

Hellerstein, J. K., & Neumark, D. (2020). Social capital, networks, and economic well-being. *Future of Children, 30*(1), 127–152. https://proxy.ulib.csuohio.edu:2096/10.1353/foc.2020.0002

hooks, b. (1994). *Teaching to transgress*. Routledge.

Hinchliffe, E. (2020). The number of female CEOs in the Fortune 500 hits an all-time record. Fortune. https://fortune.com/2020/05/18/women-ceos-fortune-500-2020/

Ingram, I. L., & Walters, T. S. (2007). A critical reflection model to teach diversity and social justice. *Journal of Praxis in Multicultural Education, 2*(1), 23–41.

Isaac, E. P., Merriweather, L. R., & Rogers, E. E. (2010). Chasing the American dream: Race and adult and continuing education. In C. E. Kasworm, A. D. Rose, & J. M. Ross Gordon (Eds.), *Handbook of adult and continuing education: 2010 Edition* (pp. 359–368). Sage.

Kendi, I. X. (2019). *How to be an antiracist*. One World.

Kivel, P. (2016). How white people can serve as allies to people of color in the struggle to end racism. In P. A. Rothenberg (Ed.), *White privilege: Essential readings on the other side of racism* (5th ed., pp. 207–213). Macmillan.

Lean In. (2020). *The state of Black women in corporate America*. Lean In. https://media.sgff.io/sgff_r1eHetbDYb/2020-08-13/1597343917539/Lean_In_-_State_of_Black_Women_in_Corporate_America_Report_1.pdf

Merriweather, L. R. (2012). A need for culturally responsive mentoring in graduate education. *All About Mentoring, 42*(Winter), 103–108.

Monaghan, C. H. (2010). Working against the grain: White privilege in human resource development. *New Directions for Adult and Continuing Education, 125*, 53–64. https://doi.org/10.1002/ace.362

Peach-Martins, L., & Wood, G. (2010). HRM in manufacturing. In I. Roper, R. Prouska, & U. Chatrakul Na Ayudhya (Eds.), *Critical issues in human resource management* (pp. 293–308). Chartered Institute of Personnel and Development, CIPD House.

Powers, A. (2018, June 27). A study finds that diverse companies produce 19% more revenue. *Forbes*, digital version. https://www.forbes.com/sites/annapowers/2018/06/27/a-study-finds-that-diverse-companies-produce-19-more-revenue/#5729f9f2506f

Rollock, N., & Gillborn, D. (2011). *Critical race theory (CRT)*. British Educational Research Association. http://www.bera.ac.uk/files/2011/10/Critical-Race-Theory.pdf

Rosette, A. S., Ponce de Leon, R., Koval, C. Z., & Harrison, D. A. (2018). Intersectionality: Connecting experiences of gender with race at work. *Research in Organizational Behavior, 38*, 1–22.

Roumell, E. A., & James-Gallaway, A. D. (2021). Social movements, community education, and the fight for racial justice: Black women and social transformation. *New Directions for Adult and Continuing Education, 2021*, 21–31. https://doi.org/10.1002/ace.20422

Sambrook, S. (2008). Critical HRD: A concept analysis. *Personnel Review, 38*(1), 61–73. https://doi.org/10.1108/00483480910920714

Sopher, T. (2021, February 2). *Amazon now employs nearly 1.3 million people worldwide after adding 500,000 workers in 2020*. Geekwire. https://www.geekwire.com/2021/amazon-now-employs-nearly-1-3-million-people-worldwide-adding-500000-workers-2020/

Srivastava, S. B. (2015). Network intervention: Assessing the effects of formal mentoring on workplace networks. *Social Forces, 94*(1), 427–452.

Statista. (2020). *Top 50 companies based on number of employees*. https://www.statista.com/statistics/264671/top-50-companies-based-on-number-of-employees/

Sue, D. W. (2010). *Microaggressions in everyday life: Race, gender and sexual orientation*. John Wiley & Sons Inc.

Wahba, P. (2020, June 1). The numbers of Black CEOs in the Fortune 500 remains very low. *Fortune Magazine* digital version: https://fortune.com/2020/06/01/black-ceos-fortune-500-2020-african-american-business-leaders/

Walker, H. M., Culham, A., Fletcher, A. J., & Reed, M. G. (2019). Social dimensions of climate hazards in rural communities of the global North: An intersectionality framework. *Journal of Rural Studies, 72*, 1–10. https://doi.org/10.1016/j.jrurstud.2019.09.012

Winters, M. F. (2020) *Black fatigue: How racism erodes the mind, body and spirit*. Berrett-Koehler Publishers, Inc.

YWCA. (2021). *About*. YWCA. https://www.ywca.org/about/

Understanding and Reducing Negative Interpersonal Behaviors: A Critical HRD Approach to Improve Workplace Inclusion

Tomika W. Greer and April L. Peters

Over the past 60 years, workplaces have slowly become increasingly more diverse with respect to race, ethnicity, sex, and other individual differences. Early efforts to diversify the workplace were implemented to offer more opportunities to a wider range of people, regardless of their perceived differences. However, as diverse groups of people entered the workplace, they were met with resistance from the organization's structure, norms, and policies in addition to individual employees' attitudes and beliefs about diversity. This truth complicated the experiences of diverse people in the workplace and resulted in them being excluded from the organizational in-group and subject to inequitable treatment within the organization. Furthermore, the lived experiences of diverse people in organizational settings have been silenced by the diversity rhetoric (Byrd, 2018), perpetuating the narrative that diversity has been achieved and there is little more work to do to achieve a harmonious productive diverse workforce.

T. W. Greer (✉)
Department of Human Development and Consumer Sciences, College of Technology, University of Houston, Houston, TX, USA
e-mail: twgreer@uh.edu

A. L. Peters
Department of Educational Leadership and Policy Studies, College of Education, University of Houston, Houston, TX, USA
e-mail: apeters-hawkins@uh.edu

325

J. C. Collins and J. L. Callahan (eds.), *The Palgrave Handbook of Critical Human Resource Development*, https://doi.org/10.1007/978-3-031-10453-4_18

Despite increased diversity among newly hired employees, there remain issues in the workplace related to how diverse individuals are treated once they join organizations. For example, throughout the 1990s, it was obvious that women and racial/ethnic minorities were severely underrepresented in leadership positions. Even though they held jobs that previously were unavailable to them, they still were not being given opportunities to assume the leadership roles that continued to be occupied by white men. This phenomenon has been called the "glass ceiling" and represents just one example of why diversity alone is not an ultimate goal. Instead, *inclusion* emerged as a new target to help organizations achieve social justice and provide equitable opportunities to a diverse workforce.

As more employees are demanding inclusion, organizations must realize the importance of moving past diversity. Fostering inclusion in the workplace requires a culture of positive reciprocal relationships among the people in the organization. Yet, workplace relationships are easily eroded by acts of injustice against the diverse members of the organization. The purpose of this chapter is to explore microaggressions, discrimination, incivility and bullying as four types of negative interpersonal behaviors that threaten inclusion in the workplace. These acts of social *in*justice can "interfere with work relationships, decrease job satisfaction and performance, create stressful conditions, and prevent an overall sense of well-being" (Byrd, 2018, p. 3).

Relationships and Relating in the Workplace

Relationships between people in the workplace are foundational to the practice and study of Human Resource Development (HRD) as people work interdependently to enable organizing and achieve the goals of the organization (Bierema & Callahan, 2014). Sias (2012) noted, "interpersonal relationships are ongoing entities characterized by, and constituted in, regular patterned interaction" (p. 106). In the workplace, these relationships can be generally categorized as positive or negative. Positive workplace relationships involve respectful interactions resulting in synergy, effective teamwork and perhaps, genuine friendship. Alternately, negative relationships can contribute to employees feeling excluded in the workplace, which is the opposite of inclusion (Sias, 2012).

The ways in which people interact and relate with each other in the workplace affects their job experiences, attitudes, and performance. Specifically, positive workplace relationships have been linked to higher organizational commitment, involvement, and knowledge sharing (Greer & Egan, 2019; Madsen et al., 2005). Conversely, negative workplace relationships are associated with lower job satisfaction, lower organizational commitment, and higher intentions to leave the organization (Morrison, 2008). Furthermore, negative workplace relationships that become hostile can impact psychological and physical health of employees (da Silva João & Saldanha Portelada, 2019). Positive workplace relationships and negative workplace relationships are defined by the interactions between people in the relationship. Essentially, the ways people interact—their interpersonal behaviors—differentiate the nature of workplace relationships.

In this chapter, we use a Critical HRD lens (see Fenwick, 2005) to interrogate microaggressions, discrimination, incivility, and bullying as interpersonal behaviors that prevent and erode positive relationships in the workplace. Our perspective is that these negative interpersonal behaviors usually occur in the context of perceived power differences between the perpetrator and the target/victim whereby the perpetrator is perceived to have more influence and power in the workplace than the target. Power differences in the workplace often mirror the historic power differences in the wider society, making the young, female, LGBTQ, and People of Color vulnerable to these negative interpersonal behaviors. As a result, these groups of people suffer the consequences of being excluded through negative workplace relationships (Sias, 2012). Further, we recognize these behaviors do not occur in a vacuum. Instead, they extend beyond dyadic interactions and are affected by previous interactions while shaping future interactions in a contextual climate that either condones these behaviors or punishes them (Jones et al., 2017).

We begin the chapter by identifying the contributors and consequences of each of these four types of interpersonal behaviors. We highlight both personal and organizational factors that contribute to and result from these behaviors. Next, we offer vignettes as examples of how negative interpersonal behaviors show up in spaces of organizing. Finally, we offer solutions for how to reduce workplace microaggressions, discrimination, incivility, and bullying; including references and suggested readings for educating leaders and facilitating conversations about these behaviors in the workplace.

Understanding Negative Interpersonal Behaviors

Interpersonal behaviors that threaten workplace inclusion can be categorized by the *approach* used by the perpetrator and the *level of occurrence*. Approaches can be viewed on a spectrum from passive behaviors to aggressive behaviors. Occurrence can range from sporadic episodes to continuous habits. Taken together, these characteristics form a taxonomy used to understand and characterize threatening behaviors that impede workplace inclusion. It is important to emphasize that occurrence and approach are continuums along which instances of negative interpersonal behaviors may be characterized (Jones et al., 2017). Though approach and occurrence may appear to be correlated in some instances, they are distinct factors that help to define negative interpersonal behaviors. In Fig. 18.1, we present a taxonomy of negative interpersonal behaviors based on the approach and the occurrence.

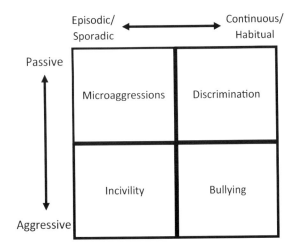

Fig. 18.1 A taxonomy of negative interpersonal behaviors

PASSIVE AND EPISODIC/SPORADIC BEHAVIORS

Negative interpersonal behaviors that are passive and episodic are known as microaggressions. "Microaggression refers to prejudicial behaviors that are demeaning, humiliating, unethical, disrespectful, and unjust and target socially disadvantaged and socially stigmatized groups" (Byrd, 2014, pp. 337–338). Microaggressions can be intentional or unintentional and appear in brief, commonplace interactions that communicate racial slights and insults toward the target of these behaviors (Sue, et al., 2007, p. 271). The prejudicial behaviors are "demeaning, humiliating, unethical, disrespectful, and unjust and target socially disadvantaged and socially stigmatized groups" (Byrd, 2014, pp. 337–338). Microaggressions can occur unconsciously and sporadically as snubs, dismissive looks, gestures, and/or tones; and are often dismissed as being harmless (Sue et al., 2007). They can be viewed as passive behaviors because they are not often flagged or resisted. Furthermore, they are episodic because they usually occur between the perpetrator(s) and the target(s) in the moments when they are interacting directly.

Racism in America has undergone a shift from overt acts to subtle and implicit expressions (Sue et al., 2008a) that are potentially more harmful than the overt acts (Jones et al., 2017). These subtle implicit forms of racism have manifested into what is known today as modern racism, symbolic/implicit racism, and aversive racism (Sue et al., 2007, 2008b). These three forms of modern racism share the concept of being disguised, concealed, and more difficult to identify and acknowledge (Sue et al., 2007). Racial microaggressions, created by Pierce in 1970, is a modern form of racism (Sue et al., 2007). They are insults, indignities, and marginalizing messages sent toward people unaware or aware of the hidden messages (Sue et al., 2007). Microaggressions reflect the unconscious worldview of White supremacy and are seen in three forms: microassualt, microinsult, and microinvalidation (Sue et al., 2007, 2008b).

Microassault is a verbal or nonverbal attack intended to hurt a person through name calling or discriminatory actions (Sue et al., 2007). This form of microaggression is committed on an individual level and would be referenced as "old fashioned" racism, i.e., using racial epithets or being biased against interracial interactions (Sue et al., 2007). Microinsults are subtle snubs that clearly communicate insulting and insensitive thoughts toward a person's racial heritage or identity; for example, telling a person "you are so articulate" (Sue et al., 2007, 2008a). Microinvalidation negates psychological thoughts, feelings, or experiences of a Person of Color; for example, asking a person "Where were you born?" (Sue et al., 2007, 2008a). Overall, microassaults are conscious and deliberate, while microinsults and microinvalidation are unconscious and subtle (DeCuir-Gunby et al., 2020). Given the invisible nature of microinsults and microinvalidations, they have the power to oppress People of Color because of their ambiguous nature (Sue et al., 2008a).

Research has shown microaggressions are associated with poor mental health by attacking the integrity and imposing false realities on People of Color, and physical health outcomes due to negative coping strategies (Donovan et al., 2013; Sue et al., 2008b; Williams, 2020). On an individual level, when a person experiences a microaggression, it elicits both a psychological and physiological stress response (Williams, 2020). Reactions following an experience with microaggressions vary with feelings of depression, low self-esteem, confusion, anxiety, anger, hopelessness, paranoia, and fear (Sue et al., 2008b; Williams, 2020). Since microaggressions occur daily, it has been conceptualized as a chronic stressor that may result in negative coping strategies (i.e., denial and/or substance abuse), which in turn may lead to negative physical health problems such as hypertension and/or a dysfunctional immune response (Williams, 2020).

Microaggressions experienced within the work setting can impair performance in the workplace (Sue et al., 2007). The term microinequities is used within the work setting to describe being overlooked, under respected, and devalued because of one's race or gender and creates inequities further contributing to the glass ceiling effect among People of Color (Sue et al., 2007, 2008a). These outcomes affect People of Color psychologically and spiritually in the workplace (Sue et al., 2008b). Beyond the individual impacts, microaggressions can infiltrate interracial interactions, institutional practices, and social policies (Sue et al., 2008a).

Passive and Continual/Habitual Behaviors

Discrimination is an example of a passive behavior that is continual and habitual, meaning it occurs perpetually and is woven into the structure, policies, procedures, and practices of the organization. Workplace discrimination denies an individual or group of people equal treatment by the actions of an employer, supervisor, or co-worker (Einarsen et al., 2020). It includes "unfair terms and conditions that systematically impair the ability of members of certain groups to work, often motivated by beliefs of superiority over a disadvantaged outgroup when compared to a dominant group" (Creighton, 2017, p. 1).

Discrimination can be blatant or subtle and can be due to age, gender, sexual orientation, and/or race (Sellers & Shelton, 2003; Xu & Chopik, 2020). Three forms of discrimination are recognized: individual, institutional, and structural (Pincus, 1994). Individual discrimination occurs between two people who differ in gender, race, sexual orientation, and/or age. Institutional discrimination occurs using policies implemented by majority groups to intentionally harm minority groups. Structural discrimination occurs through seemingly race-neutral policies which have differentially harmful effects on marginalized groups, keeping them in a subordinate position within the organization.

Much research has focused on gender and sexuality work discrimination (Marks et al., 2020). However, few studies focus on other aspects of diversity and work discrimination. Research has shown that African Americans experience higher levels of mistreatment, everyday discrimination, subtle racism, and additional stress on the job compared to their Caucasian counterparts (Brown et al., 2016; Deitch et al., 2003). Immigrant professionals experience verbal discrimination, including sarcasm, stereotypes, and skepticism stemming from their ethnicity (Shenoy-Packer, 2015). Asian Americans science students experience discrimination in the form of high expectations imposed in the workplace, which causes undue stress for them (McGee et al., 2017).

Similar to microaggressions, discrimination in the workplace may be difficult to combat due to the ambiguous nature to identify (Deitch et al., 2003). Perpetrators of discrimination may not be aware they are engaging in discriminatory behavior (Deitch et al., 2003; Xu & Chopik, 2020). Furthermore, employees who are exposed to workplace discrimination may be less likely to report these incidents for fear of possible retaliation (Offermann et al., 2014).

Aggressive and Episodic/Sporadic Behaviors

Episodic aggressive behaviors are known as acts of incivility. The notion of civility is rooted in moral implications of treating people with dignity and respect (Andersson & Pearson, 1999). "Workplace incivility is low-intensity deviant behavior with ambiguous intent to harm the target, in violation of workplace norms for mutual respect. Uncivil behaviors are characteristically rude and discourteous, displaying a lack of regard for others" (Andersson & Pearson, 1999, p. 457). Therefore, workplace incivility is disrespectful and signals indifference toward the person on the receiving end. Given the aggressive nature of incivility, it is impossible to achieve the ideals of relating in the workplace when incivility is present.

Left unaddressed, workplace incivility can spiral other types of mistreatment in the workplace, inciting aggression, violence, deviant behavior, and antisocial behavior that eventually harms the organization and/or its members (Andersson & Pearson, 1999). This escalation can be triggered when the disrespected employee perceives that her/his social identity has been damaged, when that employee becomes angry about the disrespectful behavior, or when that person seeks revenge for the disrespectful treatment. In all cases, these social interactions are unhealthy for workplace relationships and persist to undermine inclusion in the workplace.

Incivility can take on several forms—including furtive, face-to-face, and online. "Furtive behaviors [include] eye rolling, gossip, the muttering of derogatory comments, and social exclusion. Face-to-face behaviors [include] public ridicule, personal attacks, blatant interruptions and overtalking, yelling, and cutting short conversations or phone calls, as well as more physically aggressive actions like throwing objects. [Uncivil] online behaviors [include] nonresponse to e-mails, rude e-mails, passive–aggressive e-mails, and disparaging posts on social media platforms" (Pattani et al., 2018, p. 1571). Incivility can be intentional or unintentional. Incivility can also include seemingly small acts as well as more overt disrespectful behavior. The damaging effects follow, regardless of the initial intentions of the perpetrator. Likewise, no matter the perceived magnitude of the uncivil behavior, the incivility does not go unnoticed by the person who experiences this treatment whether the perpetrator was intentionally disrespectful or not.

Employees who have been the target of uncivil behavior in the workplace reduce their commitment to the organization and disengage from extra-role tasks and activities outside of their job responsibilities (Pearson et al., 2000). They are likely to contemplate changing jobs, many will quit, and others will sabotage relationships and equipment in the workplace (Pearson & Porath, 2005). Incivility can evoke adverse cognitive reactions as targets recognize the uncivil treatment, as well as adverse affective reactions that include confusion and fear of what may happen next, including retaliation (Hutton, 2006; Pearson et al., 2000).

Aggressive and Continual/Habitual Behaviors

Bullying is a deliberate, continual, and intense form of aggression that severely interferes with relating in the workplace. Workplace bullying is a form of violence (Namie, 2003) and can be defined as "repeated unwelcomed negative act or acts (physical, verbal, or psychological intimidation), that can involve criticism and humiliation, intended to cause fear, distress, or harm to the target from one or more individuals in any source of power with the target of the bullying having difficulties defending himself or herself" (Bartlett & Bartlett, 2011, p. 71). Trauma to the target of bullying occurs because of the intensity of the behaviors in addition to the repeated, ongoing nature of bullying.

Though workplace bullying typically involves sub-lethal and non-physical violence, on a 10-point scale of levels of organizational disruption, "incivilities range from 1 to 3, while bullying covers mild to severe interference with the accomplishment of legitimate business interests, reflecting scores of 4–9. The highest score is reserved for battery and homicide which grind work completely to a halt" (Namie, 2003, p. 1). In addition to damaging workplace relationships and organizational interests, bullying can severely traumatize the target of the bullying by damaging their psychological health, increasing the prevalence of anxiety, depression, post-traumatic stress disorder, and identity crisis (Fox & Cowan, 2015; Saunders et al., 2007). Employees who are bullied are likely to engage in counterproductive work behaviors resulting in reduced productivity, decreased performance, and organizational withdrawal behaviors, such as absenteeism, turnover, and early retirement (Cortina et al., 2001; Fox & Cowan, 2015).

High work pressures and resultant tension among employees can kindle workplace bullying (Pauksztat & Salin, 2020). Bullying is a manifestation of evident power differentials in spaces of organizing such as the workplace. Acts of workplace bullying can be categorized as work-related, personal, or physical/threatening (Bartlett & Bartlett, 2011). Direct acts of bullying include verbal attacks, persistent criticism, intimidation, and manipulation. Work-related bullying also can include overloading the target with work, delegating menial tasks to the target, setting unrealistic goals for the target to meet, withholding pertinent job-related information from the target, and blocking the target from receiving a promotion. Personal acts of workplace bullying can be indirect, such as isolating, ignoring, and excluding the target or spreading gossip, lies, and false accusations (Saunders et al., 2007).

Perpetrators of bullying are motivated by the need to control their targets (Namie, 2003). These offenders are often narcissistic, angry, vengeful, and anxious (Herschcovis et al., 2015). They are more likely to have previously been bullied themselves (Hauge et al., 2009). The cyclical nature of bullies who become bullies increases the urgency to reduce and annihilate bullying to protect relationships in the workplace.

VIGNETTES OF NEGATIVE INTERPERSONAL BEHAVIORS

Left unaddressed, microaggressions, discrimination, incivility, and bullying can take root in an organization as the status quo, which would disproportionately damage employees with less power while advantaging employees with more power. From our perspective, the negative interpersonal behaviors are more damaging when they are subtle enough to go undetected or unchecked, allowing them to seep into the culture of the organization. Alternately, we implore employees, managers, and leaders to become keenly aware of what these behaviors look like in practice. For demonstration, below we offer four scenarios that illustrate microaggression, discrimination, incivility, and bullying. Further, we offer a brief analysis of each scenario to deepen the reader's understanding of the behaviors exhibited in the scenario.

MICROAGGRESSION SCENARIO

Enrico is a Hispanic man in his mid-20s. He is in graduate school and has earned a competitive graduate fellowship award along with four other students. All the other students are white. During weekly meetings with their faculty sponsor, Enrico has experienced several microaggressions. The faculty sponsor initially assumed he was not an American citizen, stating "if you're here illegally, I'm not sure you'll want to participate in this fellowship." His fellow peers have made comments about how well he speaks English and joked about "taco Tuesdays" and Cinco de Mayo around the office. One peer asked him where he is from upon learning that Enrico is Spanish speaking. Although the faculty sponsor and Enrico's peers generally display benign behaviors toward him, they still engage in microinsults, invalidation, and other microaggressive behavior. Enrico is afraid to speak up on his own behalf or report the microaggressive behavior out of fear that he will lose the fellowship.

Microaggressions are often cloaked acts of racism or sexism (Byrd, 2014; Sue, 2008a, b). These behaviors create an unwelcoming environment for those who experience them. They are often ongoing and repetitive. Enrico is experiencing a challenging work culture because of the constant barrage of racist insults. At times, the statements may be "well-meaning," such as the comment about his English fluency. However, these comments are racist and caustic. This is an example where additional training and development on professional culture and implicit bias would be educative for building a healthy, diverse, and inclusive workplace.

DISCRIMINATION SCENARIO

Mary is an accomplished 40-year-old Asian American woman and a new employee at ACME Inc. Most of her co-workers have been employed at ACME for over 10 years. All her co-workers within her unit are men. Mary has been experiencing a variety of gender discriminatory behaviors from co-workers that make her uncomfortable. For instance, her boss asks her to have his coffee made and to fetch coffee for his colleagues during department meetings. During department meetings she is the only one asked to take notes (although before she joined the department, everyone took turns as note takers). She is not invited out to happy hours with colleagues. When she asked about this, she was told that it is because they know she has "wife and mother duties" at home after work. During staff meetings, often when she attempts to provide input, she is interrupted, or a male colleague engages in "mansplaining" her responses by providing a condescending explanation. When an opportunity arose for a promotion to a leadership position within the unit, Mary applied. She did not get the promotion. When she inquired why, since she is the most qualified person in the unit, she was told that leadership was "man's work." In short, Mary feels that her supervisor and co-workers treat her like a "little woman" rather than a respected, valuable member of the team.

In this scenario, Mary is experiencing gender discrimination. She is the only woman working with a team of men and they participate in gender-oppressive expectations (e.g., making coffee, taking notes, being excluded from after-work events with colleagues) concerning her interactions with male colleagues. While her co-workers may think these behaviors are harmless, as a woman in this environment, Mary is experiencing discrimination that prevents her from advancing within the organization. For many women, gender discrimination is amplified by their intersecting identities (such as race) (McGee et al., 2017).

INCIVILITY SCENARIO

Janet, an African American woman in her mid-30s, was driving to work and preparing to park her car. Her senior colleague, Betsey (a white woman in her mid-40s), was also trying to park. The parking lot was nearly full. Janet spotted a person pulling out of a parking spot and waited with her blinker on for the spot. Betsey saw Janet waiting for the spot but pulled into the spot before Janet could and parked. Janet circled the lot several times before finally locating a parking spot. She parked and went inside to her office on the third floor. She passed Betsey's office where Betsey was inside at her desk. Janet's office was next door to Betsey. Betsey said "Good morning, Janet. Sorry I took your spot" in a disingenuously pleasant voice. Betsey is a senior employee of the company, Janet is not. Janet felt disrespected and without recourse. However, their co-worker, Barry, witnessed the entire episode—in the parking lot and later in the office. Barry is a white man in his mid-50s with similar organizational status as Betsey and slightly longer organizational tenure. He walked into Betsey's office and called Janet in to hear what he had to say to Betsey. He told Betsey that her behavior was unacceptable and was less than polite in the words that he chose. He threatened Betsey with disciplinary action if he saw her treating Janet like that again in the future.

The incivility in this scenario is multi-faceted as both Betsey and Barry were uncivil. The first act of incivility occurred when Betsey disrespected Janet who had less organizational power. Betsey's actions were disrespectful and she acknowledged this in her off-handed apology. Janet was left to wonder if this was motivated by race or the fact that Betsey is a senior colleague, or some combination of the two. When Barry stepped into the scenario to leverage his organizational power and correct the incivility he witnessed, he also committed an uncivil act in the way he spoke to Betsey. However, he felt justified in responding to an uncivil act with his own display of incivility. If his interaction with Betsey brings about social justice, then his actions are an example of "justified incivility" (Applebaum, 2020). Justified incivility disrupts the hegemonic civility that oppresses marginalized people by lulling bystanders and observers of uncivil behaviors to remain civil in these circumstances. Though Barry's acts may be justified, the risk in this scenario is that Betsey will persist in her incivility as a form of resistance against Barry's threats and Janet will continue to be a target, undermining relationships between all three co-workers.

BULLYING SCENARIO

Ashley, a 25-year-old white woman, is a first-year graduate research assistant working for Dr. Powers. Dr. Powers, a middle-aged white man, has a reputation for patronizing junior faculty and research assistants. Dr. Powers assigned Ashley a data analysis task to complete but did not specify a deadline. Ashley was already working on a literature review for the project. In the past Dr. Powers yelled at her about how she prioritized her work tasks for him, so she decided to avoid a confrontation with him, she should complete the literature review first. She completed the literature review and turned it in. Dr. Powers sent an email demanding a meeting with her. When she arrived, he asked her why the data analysis was incomplete. Ashley answered that she prioritized the literature review since Dr. Powers did not indicate a due date for the data analysis. Dr. Powers told her she might need to consider another assistantship if she could not get his work done—a threat he constantly used with his graduate assistants. He also mentioned that he was the reason she was accepted into the academic program and the reason she got an assistantship. His feedback on her deliverables was often unnecessarily negative or nonexistent, a major reason his graduate assistants are fearful of working with him. He does not provide constructive feedback or mentoring, but rather, is condescending and sarcastic or downright rude in his comments. Ashley is afraid that if she requests a different assistantship, Dr. Powers will blackball her, given his power in the department and across the university.

Workplace bullying is psychologically violent as well as traumatizing (Namie, 2003). It often occurs where there is a power differential. In this scenario, Dr. Powers, a faculty member, implicitly threatens Ashley's assistantship. Other graduate assistants are afraid to work with him because he has created a culture of fear and intimidation. This environment is difficult because of the ongoing and aggressive nature of bullying. In a scenario like this, it would be helpful if a senior faculty or administrator could mediate or intervene. Left unaddressed, this issue could affect student experiences and program/department reputation.

Within all four of these scenarios, negative interpersonal behaviors amplify power differences and exclude the targets from respectful treatment in the workplace. We urge managers and organizational leaders to interpret similar negative interpersonal behaviors in the context of historical inequities to identify even the most subtle instances of microaggressions, discrimination, incivility, and bullying. In doing so, marginalized workers will feel safer and perpetrators can be educated and appropriately disciplined, thereby creating a more inclusive work environment for all employees (Marshburn et al., 2017). With no intervention by the organizations (and society-at-large), these types of interactions are unlikely to change course (Jones et al., 2017; Mara et al., 2021). Recognizing the need to change and replace these behaviors, we describe ways to reduce negative interpersonal behaviors in the next section.

REDUCING NEGATIVE INTERPERSONAL BEHAVIORS

Categorizing negative interpersonal behaviors based on the commonalities related to *approach* and *occurrence* allows for unifying these behaviors for the purpose of identifying and combatting these harmful behaviors (Jones et al., 2017). By understanding the characteristics of microaggressions, discrimination, incivility, and bullying; employees and organizational leadership can more effectively reduce these behaviors that threaten workplace inclusion. The range of approach and occurrence that characterize these behaviors requires an assortment of solutions to reduce these behaviors. Our approach to reducing microaggressions, discrimination, incivility, and bullying is based on the assumption that these behaviors are targeted at people in the workplace who are underrepresented, marginalized, and generally have less status and organizational power (Pearson et al., 2000)—including racial and ethnic minorities, women, and those who are lesbian, gay, transgender, and/or queer. The strategies that we discuss should be viewed in this light.

In general, the passive behaviors must be brought to the forefront of the consciousness of the organization by raising awareness of their prevalence in the organization. These behaviors persist because they are often subtle, existing in seemingly minor comments and unexamined organizational structures, practices, and policies. Accordingly, to reduce these behaviors, intentional action should be taken to expose them and educate the organizational members on why they are unacceptable. On the other hand, aggressive behaviors are usually damaging, overt behaviors. Perpetrators of aggressive behaviors may require disciplinary action to reduce the behaviors. This discipline could include involuntary separation from the organization or legal action.

Behaviors that are episodic and sporadic may be reduced when the targets of these behaviors are empowered to resist the perpetrators. Organizational leaders and supervisors can empower the target of these behaviors by offering a method for reporting the behaviors, or responding directly to the offensive episode, without fear of retribution. Perhaps, this strategy would require new policies and vocal support from senior leadership. Moreover, the presence of continual and habitual behaviors suggests a culture or sub-culture within the workplace that supports the existence of these negative behaviors, allowing them to persist on a continual basis. As a result, a culture change is needed to reduce these behaviors. Using a variety of interventions, this culture change

Table 18.1 Strategies for reducing negative interpersonal behaviors in the workplace

Behaviors	Approach	Occurrence	Reduction strategies
Microaggressions	Passive	Episodic/ Sporadic	Bring to organizational consciousness and empower the targets to resist
Discrimination	Passive	Continual/ Habitual	Bring to organizational consciousness and initiate culture change
Incivility	Aggressive	Episodic/ Sporadic	Administer disciplinary action and empower the targets to resist
Bullying	Aggressive	Continual/ Habitual	Administer disciplinary action and initiate culture change

would destroy the current status quo to rebuild the values and beliefs that govern behaviors within the organization.

In Table 18.1, we summarize how each of the strategies described herein can be used to specifically attack microaggressions, discrimination, incivility, and workplace bullying.

Raise Awareness

Raising awareness of the prevalence and consequences of negative interpersonal behaviors is an initial step toward creating more inclusive environments. As noted by Marshburn et al. (2017), managers and organizational leaders should be able to identify the behaviors, address the behaviors, and monitor the behaviors to reduce the prevalence and consequences. To fully understand the prevalence of negative interpersonal behaviors, organizational leaders can use data collection methods to solicit anonymous experiences from employees at all levels of the organization (Pearson & Porath, 2005). These leaders must know how to interpret these experiences and identify negative interpersonal behaviors through a critical perspective of historic inequities with a goal of achieving social justice for marginalized employees.

Training interventions based in a Critical HRD paradigm can raise the awareness needed to spark change in the workplace. Accordingly, effective training will equip participants with knowledge of historic inequities and how they manifest in the workplace; describe and demonstrate negative interpersonal behaviors; instill a social justice perspective that empowers participants to disrupt negative interpersonal behaviors; and suggest actions to spread awareness and promote an inclusive environment. Ultimately, this training should help managers and organizational leaders acknowledge negative interpersonal behaviors as a threat to inclusion that undermines individual and organizational outcomes.

However, raising awareness, in itself, is not enough to reduce negative interpersonal behaviors because "being aware seldom translates into application and prevention of diversity concerns of protected class employees within many workplaces" (Hughes, 2018, p. 260). As noted in Table 18.1, raising awareness should be coupled with empowering the targets and affecting organizational culture change to combat microaggressions and discrimination.

Empower Diverse Voices

Due to the power differences between the perpetrators and the targets of negative interpersonal behaviors, the targets will often feel unable to voice their experiences and the consequences of the maltreatment in the workplace. Essentially, their voices become muted in the organization, particularly for groups that are marginalized in the wider society (Kissack, 2010). Their silenced voices lead to exclusion and, eventually, turnover. As a result, the negative interpersonal behaviors remain unreported, unnoticed, and unaddressed. As noted by Sims (2009), Critical HRD can be used as a tool for giving voice to the silenced in organizations. For targets of negative interpersonal behavior, a critical approach begins with dialogue focused on examining power differences, leading to providing voice to the marginalized to reveal the misuse of power in the relationships (Sims, 2009).

Furthermore, leadership styles within the organization can profoundly impact whether employees feel empowered to use their voice or not (Robinson & Shuck, 2019). Therefore, management training can reduce the likelihood of negative interpersonal behaviors as managers learn to be fair and supportive of employees while empowering them to use their voices and report these behaviors (Hershcovis et al., 2015). To win the confidence of the targets of negative interpersonal behaviors, organizational leaders and managers should consistently follow through on investigations and efforts to correct the problems after every reporting (Pearson & Porath, 2005). Leaders and managers must also concern themselves with monitoring the aftermath of reporting, to avoid retaliation and other unwanted outcomes of reporting negative interpersonal behaviors exhibited by perpetrators who hold more organizational power than the targets of the behaviors (Bergman et al., 2002; Marshburn et al., 2017).

Exit interviews may also present an opportunity to hear diverse voices even as they leave the organization. Employees who may have never felt empowered to report their true experiences within the organization may be more willing to report negative interpersonal experiences upon their separation from the organization, especially after they have secured a new job with a different organization (Pearson & Porath, 2005). These interviews should remain confidential but can be used to identify potential problems in the organization and the subsequent effects on employees and organizational turnover.

Dispense Corrective and Disciplinary Actions for Offenses

Our third suggestion for reducing negative interpersonal behaviors involves consistent consequences for perpetrators of these behaviors. When employees are aware of policies and procedures regarding disciplinary action and potential termination for inappropriate behaviors, those behaviors are effectively deterred (Johnson & Indvik, 2001). As shown, in Table 18.1, we encourage disciplinary actions for perpetrators of aggressive actions, including incivility and bullying.

Organizational leaders and managers should strive to intervene upon the first known negative interpersonal behaviors between employees to instill confidence in the targets and avoid proliferation of these behaviors (Pearson & Porath, 2005). An initial offense may warrant corrective action to include conversations with the perpetrator, written documentations of the offenses, and training on how to recognize the behavior and avoid it in the future. Perpetrators should receive explicit instructions for how to correct their behavior and an expectation for no more offenses. If their behavior does not improve, additional sanctions can include demotion (for managers/supervisors), suspension, or termination of employment (Johnson & Indvik, 2001).

Finally, applying Critical HRD to corrective and disciplinary action requires that the associated processes and procedures are equitably applied to all members of the organization, regardless of their status, social group, or relative societal/organizational power. Therefore, managers and organizational leaders should be held accountable for their own contributions to negative interpersonal behaviors, examining their own motives and actions while also correcting their organizational peers and subordinates (Andersson & Pearson, 1999; Pearson & Porath, 2005).

Build Inclusive Organizational Cultures

Left unaddressed, negative interpersonal behaviors can become cyclical as former targets become perpetrators of these behaviors, contributing to organizational cultures that diminish inclusivity (Jones et al., 2017). Instead, specific attention toward building inclusive organizational cultures can help to reduce negative interpersonal behaviors and break the cyclical nature of negative interpersonal behaviors.

In Table 18.1, we noted organizational culture change as a strategy for reducing negative interpersonal behaviors that are continual and habitual, including discrimination and bullying. We advocate for organizational culture change because one aspect of organizational culture is the implicit understanding of how people relate to each other in the organization. This standard for relating is a manifestation of the status quo that Critical HRD seeks to dismantle. Therefore, we encourage organization members to reflect on the impact and unintended exclusionary consequences of existing structures, processes, policies, and other elements within the culture of the organization. Sims (2009) argued that diverse groups of employees should also be specifically invited to participate in examining the impacts of existing organizational structures.

Creating the necessary culture change requires establishing, communicating, and reinforcing unambiguous policies and standards for acceptable behavior across the organization (Hershcovis et al., 2015). Culture change can require a critical look at recruitment as a foundational organizational practice that can alter employee relationships by hiring and developing people who will engage in positive interpersonal behaviors (Pearson & Porath 2005). Andersson and Pearson (1999) suggested "practical means of achieving this outcome include: (1) conducting multiple interviews of applicants by a wide representation of future associates and then listening to and acting on the feedback from those interviewers; (2) building internship programs during which prospective permanent hires can gain realistic job/culture previews while the potential employer and co-workers gain a more accurate sense of prospects' fit; and (3) scrupulously following through on reference checks, including contacts from applicants' more distant past, from which there are no immediate pressures on referents to "help" the employee move on" (p. 468). Hiring people who contribute to a positive inclusive culture can effectively disrupt the status quo as appropriate interpersonal behaviors become the normal way to interact with other members of the organization.

Another area of interest for Critical HRD is the pervasive culture of overwork in many organizations. As artifacts of the organizational culture, demanding workloads, role ambiguity, lack of job control, and a stressful work environment can contribute to negative interpersonal behaviors (Hershcovis et al., 2015; Parchment & Andrews, 2019). In these cases, positive changes to the organizational culture will require an examination and communication of role expectations. One role expectation for every job in the organization should be to exhibit positive interpersonal behaviors when interacting with other employees, regardless of perceived workplace stressors and power differences. This expectation should be tied to performance management and career advancement (Pearson & Porath, 2005). To support a positive organizational culture, performance assessments for all role expectations will need to be reasonable and potential rewards should be appropriate for reasonable performance, to avoid burnout and toxic competition that can lead to negative interpersonal behaviors.

Training can also equip employees with coping skills to combat stress, manage conflict, and regulate their emotions in the workplace, which will result in more positive interpersonal behaviors (Hershcovis et al., 2015; Johnson & Indvik, 2001; Pearson & Porath, 2005). Organizational leaders and managers should additionally learn to serve as role models for how to treat people respectfully even when stress and emotions are high (Pattani et al., 2018). Their adherence to positive interpersonal behaviors will infiltrate the organizational policies, processes, and structures that support the prevalence of negative interpersonal behaviors. When the leaders and managers exhibit appropriate behavior consistently, the culture of the organization will change accordingly.

Conclusion

The overarching purpose of this chapter was to describe the characteristics of negative interpersonal behaviors that threaten the formation and development of inclusive workplaces that honor and celebrate diversity while minimizing experiences of marginalization in the workplace. We offered a taxonomy based on two defining characteristics of these behaviors: *approach used by the perpetrator* and *level of occurrence*. Microaggressions, discrimination, incivility, and bullying were described in terms of these characteristics. We advocate for zero-tolerance expectations for these behaviors in all organizations (Pearson & Parath, 2005).

In this chapter, we explained a variety of strategies that may be employed to reduce each of these injustices, based on the approach and occurrence. Our suggestions offer a tailored strategy for reducing each type of negative interpersonal behavior. One suggested Critical HRD intervention involves using training programs to educate organizational members on the manifestations of negative interpersonal behaviors, empower the targets of negative interpersonal behavior, and redirect perpetrators of negative interpersonal behaviors. At the time of this writing, several reputable online workshops and training programs exist to accomplish these objectives. Some examples include:

- Racial Microaggressions: https://coralearning.org/product/racial-microaggressions/
- Bullying and Harassment: https://worktowellness.com/workshop/bullying-harassment/
- Workplace Bullying: https://www.govtraining.com/course/2-hr-workplace-bullying-workshop/

Using a Critical HRD perspective, we contend that negative interpersonal behaviors should be interpreted through a lens of historic power differentials and social disadvantages that unfairly limit women, ethnic and racial minorities, and sexual minorities (Marshburn et al., 2017). This contextualization allows organizational leaders to identify microaggressions, discrimination, incivility, and bullying to respond appropriately. The appropriate response requires that leaders acknowledge marginalized identities involved in these interactions and address the issue with sensitivity around historic inequities. We, therefore, offer a few additional resources for organizational leaders and managers. These books will provide context and additional strategies to support what we have provided in this chapter.

- Jakes, T. D. (2005). *The ten commandments of working in a hostile environment: Your power is your purpose.* Berkeley Publishing Group, NY.
- Jana, T., & Baran, M. (2020). *Subtle acts of exclusion: How to understand, identify, and stop microaggressions.* Berrett-Koehler Publishers, Incorporated.

- Levchak, C. C. (2018). *Microaggressions and modern racism: Endurance and evolution.* Springer.
- Maravelas, A. (2020). *Creating a drama-free workplace: The insider's guide to managing conflict, incivility, and mistrust.* Red Wheel/Weiser.
- Sutton, R. I. (2007). *The no asshole rule: Building a civilized workplace and surviving one that isn't.* Business Plus.

Ultimately, the vital work of supporting diversity in an organization is accomplished through inclusion in the workplace. Negative interpersonal behaviors erode relationships and create exclusion in the workplace (Sias, 2012). As organizational leaders and managers seek to improve workplace relationships and advance inclusion, a Critical HRD approach can be leveraged to meet these objectives.

References

Andersson, L. M., & Pearson, C. M. (1999). Tit for tat? The spiraling effect of incivility in the workplace. *Academy of Management Review, 24*(3), 452–471.

Applebaum, B. (2020). When incivility is a form of civility: Challenging the comfort of willful ignorance. *Educational Theory, 70*(6), 717–730.

Bartlett, J. E., & Bartlett, M. E. (2011). Workplace bullying: An integrative literature review. *Advances in Developing Human Resources, 13*(1), 69–84.

Bergman, M. E., Langhout, R. D., Palmieri, P. A., Cortina, L. M., & Fitzgerald, L. F. (2002). The (un) reasonableness of reporting: Antecedents and consequences of reporting sexual harassment. *Journal of Applied Psychology, 87*(2), 230–242.

Bierema, L. L. & Callahan, J. L. (2014). A framework for critical HRD practice: Transforming HRD. *Advances in Developing Human Resources, 16*(4), 429–444.

Brown, B. A., Henderson, J. B., Grazy, S., Donovan, B., Sullivan, S., Patterson, A., & Waggstaff, E. (2016). From description to explanation: An empirical exploration of the African-American pipeline problem in STEM. *Journal of Research in Science Teaching, 53*(1), 146–177.

Byrd, M. Y. (2014). Re-conceptualizing and re-visioning diversity in the workforce: Toward a social justice paradigm. *Diversity in the workforce: Current issues and emerging trends*, 334–346.

Byrd, M. Y. (2018). Does HRD have a moral duty to respond to matters of social injustice? *Human Resource Development International, 21*(1), 3–11.

Cortina, L. M., Magley, V. J., Williams, J. H., & Langhout, R. D. (2001). Incivility in the workplace: Incidence and impact. *Journal of Occupational Health Psychology, 6*, 64–80.

Creighton, S. (2017). *Reducing risks From workplace discrimination* (ProQuest Dissertations Publishing). http://search.proquest.com/docview/1972093783/

da Silva João, A. L., & Saldanha Portelada, A. F. (2019). Mobbing and its impact on interpersonal relationships at the workplace. *Journal of Interpersonal Violence, 34*(13), 2797–2812.

DeCuir-Gunby, J. T., Johnson, O. T., Womble, C., McCoy, W. N., & White, A. M. (2020). African American professionals in higher education: Experiencing and coping with racial microaggressions. *Race Ethnicity and Education, 23*(4), 492–508.

Deitch, E. A., Barsky, A., Butz, R. M., Chan, S., Brief, A. P., & Bradley, J. C. (2003). Subtle yet significant: The existence and impact of everyday racial discrimination in the workplace. *Human Relations, 56*(11), 1299–1324.

Donovan, R. A., Galban, D. J., Grace, R. K., Bennett, J. K., & S. Z. Felici´e. (2013). Impact of racial macro- and microaggressions in black women's lives: A preliminary analysis. *Journal of Black Psychology, 39*(2), 185–196.

Einarsen, S. V., Hoel, H., Zapf, D., & Cooper, C. L. (Eds.). (2020). *Bullying and harassment in the workplace: Theory.* CRC Press.

Fenwick, T. (2005). Conceptions of critical HRD: Dilemmas for theory and practice. *Human Resource Development International, 8*(2), 225–238.

Fox, S., & Cowan, R. L. (2015). Revision of the workplace bullying checklist: The importance of human resource management's role in defining and addressing workplace bullying. *Human Resource Management Journal, 25*(1), 116–130.

Greer, T. W., & Egan, T. M. (2019). Knowledge management for organizational success: Valuing diversity and inclusion across stakeholders, structures and sectors. In M. Fedeli & L. L. Bierema (Eds.), *Connecting adult learning and knowledge management* (pp. 119–136). Springer.

Hauge et al. (2009). Individual and situational predictors of workplace bullying: Why do perpetrators engage in the bullying of others? *Work and Stress, 23*(4), 349–358.

Hershcovis, M. S., Reich, T. C., & Niven, K. (2015). Workplace bullying: Causes, consequences, and intervention strategies. *SIOP White Paper Series*, Society for Industrial and Organizational Psychology, UK, London. http://eprints.lse.ac.uk/66031/

Hughes, C. (2018). The role of HRD in using diversity intelligence to enhance leadership skill development and talent management strategy. *Advances in Developing Human Resources, 20*(3), 259–262.

Hutton, S. A. (2006). Workplace Incivility. *The Journal of Nursing Administration, 36*(1), 22–28.

Johnson, P. R., & Indvik, J. (2001). Slings and arrows of rudeness: Incivility in the workplace. *Journal of Management Development, 20*(8), 705–714.

Jones, K. P., Arena, D. F., Nittrouer, C. L., Alonso, N. M., & Lindsey, A. P. (2017). Subtle discrimination in the workplace: A vicious cycle. *Industrial and Organizational Psychology, 10*(1), 51–76.

Kissack, H. (2010). Muted voices: A critical look at e-male in organizations. *Journal of European Industrial Training, 34*(6), 539–551.

Madsen, S. R., Miller, D., & John, C. R. (2005). Readiness for organizational change: Do organizational commitment and social relationships in the workplace make a difference? *Human Resource Development Quarterly, 16*(2), 213–234.

Mara, L., Ginieis, M., & Brunet-Icart, I. (2021). Strategies for coping with LGBT discrimination at work: A systematic literature review. *Sexuality Research and Social Policy, 18,* 339–354.

Marks, L. R., Yeoward, J., Fickling, M., & Tate, K. (2020). The role of racial microaggressions and bicultural self-efficacy on work volition in racially diverse adults. *Journal of Career Development.* https://doi.org/10.1177/0894845320949706

Marshburn, C. K., Harrington, N. T., & Ruggs, E. N. (2017). Taking the ambiguity out of subtle and interpersonal workplace discrimination. *Industrial and Organizational Psychology, 10*(1), 87–93.

McGee, E., Thakore, B., & LaBlance, S. (2017). The burden of being "model": Racialized experiences of Asian STEM college students. *Journal of Diversity in Higher Education, 10*(3), 253–270.

Morrison, R. L. (2008). Negative relationships in the workplace: Associations with organisational commitment, cohesion, job satisfaction and intention to turnover. *Journal of Management & Organization, 14*(4), 330–344.

Namie, G. (2003). Workplace bullying: Escalated incivility. *Ivey Business Journal, 68*(2), 1–6.

Offermann, L. R., Basford, T. E., Graebner, R., Jaffer, S., De Graaf, S. B., & Kaminsky, S. E. (2014). See no evil: Color blindness and perceptions of subtle racial discrimination in the workplace. *Cultural Diversity and Ethnic Minority Psychology, 20*(4), 499–507.

Parchment, J., & Andrews, D. (2019). The incidence of workplace bullying and related environmental factors among nurse managers. *JONA: The Journal of Nursing Administration, 49*(3), 132–137.

Pattani, R., Ginsburg, S., Johnson, A. M., Moore, J. E., Jassemi, S., & Straus, S. E. (2018). Organizational factors contributing to incivility at an academic medical center and systems-based solutions: A qualitative study. *Academic Medicine, 93*(10), 1569–1575.

Pauksztat, B., & Salin, D. (2020). Targets' social relationships as antecedents and consequences of workplace bullying: A social network perspective. *Frontiers in Psychology, 10*, 3077.

Pearson, C. M., Andersson, L. M., & Porath, C. L. (2000). Assessing and attacking workplace incivility. *Organizational Dynamics, 29*, 123–137.

Pearson, C. M., & Porath, C. L. (2005). On the nature, consequences and remedies of workplace incivility: No time for "nice"? Think again. *Academy of Management Perspectives, 19*, 7–18.

Pincus, F. L. (1994). From individual to structural discrimination. In F. L. Pincus & H. J. Ehrlich (Eds.), *Race and ethnic conflict: Contending views on prejudice, discrimination and ethnoviolence* (pp. 82–87). Westview Press.

Robinson, R., & Shuck, B. (2019). A penny for your thoughts: Exploring experiences of engagement, voice, and silence. *Journal of Organizational Psychology, 19*(4), 121–135.

Saunders, P., Huynh, A., & Goodman-Delahunty, J. (2007). Defining workplace bullying behaviour professional lay definitions of workplace bullying. *International journal of law and psychiatry, 30*(4–5), 340–354.

Sellers, R. M., & Shelton, J. N. (2003). The role of racial identity in perceived racial discrimination. *Journal of Personality and Social Psychology, 84*(5), 1079–1092.

Shenoy-Packer, S. (2015). Immigrant professionals, microaggressions, and critical sensemaking in the U.S. workplace. *Management Communication Quarterly, 29*(2), 257–275.

Sias, P. M. (2012). Exclusive or exclusory: Workplace relationships, ostracism, and isolation. In B. L. Omdahl & J. H. Fritz (Eds.), *Problematic Relationships in the Workplace* (Vol. 2, pp. 103–119). Peter Lang.

Sims, C. (2009). The impact of African American skin tone bias in the workplace: Implications for critical human resource development. *Online Journal for Workforce Education and Development, 3*(4), 1–17.

Sue, D. W., Capodilupo, C. M., Torino, G. C., Bucceri, J. M., Holder, A., Nadal, K. L., & Esquilin, M. (2007). Racial microaggressions in everyday life: Implications for clinical practice. *American Psychologist, 62*, 271–286.

Sue, D. W., Capodilupo, C. M., & Holder, A. (2008a). Racial microaggressions in the life experience of Black Americans. *Professional Psychology: Research and Practice, 39*(3), 329–336.

Sue, D. W., Nadal, K. L., Capodilupo, C. M., Lin, A. I., Torino, G. C., & Rivera, D. P. (2008b). Racial microaggressions against Black Americans: Implications for counseling. *Journal of Counseling & Development, 86*(3), 330–338.

Williams, M. T. (2020). Microaggressions: Clarification, evidence, and impact. *Perspectives on Psychological Science, 15*(1), 3–26.

Xu, Y. E., & Chopik, W. J. (2020). Identifying moderators in the link between workplace discrimination and health/well-being. *Frontiers in Psychology, 11*, 458.

CHAPTER 19

Theorizing the Role of Ally Attitudes and Behaviors in Shaping Inclusive Spaces of Organizing: The Institutional Allyship Model

Ciarán McFadden

Introduction

The purpose of this chapter is to explore how an organization can act as an ally, by protecting, defending and standing up for underrepresented and marginalized individuals and groups, and to highlight how the HRD function may also utilize their own resources, networks and scope to encourage and exemplify allyship.

Although research on allyship is limited within the business, management and organizational studies literatures (Sabat et al., 2013), there is mounting interest in this concept and practice, and a growing recognition in its importance in fostering inclusion in the workplace. However, much of the literature focuses on the individual level (Erskine & Bilimoria, 2019), showing how individuals become allies, and the antecedents and consequences involved. This chapter instead looks at how the organization itself can become an ally, and offers a model to draw together and simplify the main elements of allyship at the institutional level.

The first part of this chapter explores what allyship is—definitions, key practices, antecedents and outcomes. The role of the HRD function is then explored in the form of the 'Institutional Allyship Model', a process made up of key critical HRD practices, identified by Bierema and Callahan (2014), which simplifies allyship and highlights key areas where the HRD function can

C. McFadden (✉)
Edinburgh Napier University, Edinburgh, Scotland
e-mail: C.McFadden@napier.ac.uk

347

J. C. Collins and J. L. Callahan (eds.), *The Palgrave Handbook of Critical Human Resource Development*, https://doi.org/10.1007/978-3-031-10453-4_19

act as an agent for change to promote institutional allyship. Lastly, recommendations for practitioners and future researchers interested in institutional allyship are provided.

DEFINING (AND REDEFINING) ALLYSHIP

Discussion concerning allyship often centers on the individual person as an ally; as Broido's (2000, p. 3) definition puts it, allies are "members of dominant social groups". Allyship is therefore often conceptualized as occuring on the level of the individual (Russell & Bohan, 2016), with much of the scholarship focused on this level—for example, in discussing the development of an individual's ally identity (Broido, 2000); the antecedents of becoming an ally (Duhigg et al., 2010), how individuals can be encouraged to become allies (Perrin et al., 2014); or how allies can help reduce workplace discrimination efforts (Sabat et al., 2013). Collins (2015), however, broadened the discussion to encapsulate how the HRD field can become better allies to the LGB community, following Bishops's (2002) framework for social justice ally development and offering insight into how a group of individuals can work toward allyship status. While a small number of authors (e.g., Broido & Reason, 2005; Russell & Bohan, 2016) have discussed how allyship could operate at an institutional level—*institutional allyship*—there is little discussion on how we may conceptualize and practice allyship on a broader level than the individual.

The events of the past few years, including the reinvigorated support and mass media/social media coverage of the Black Lives Matter and #MeToo movements, have prompted a discussion on how institutionally and structurally engrained discrimination can lead to inequality for marginalized groups, and how simply 'not engaging in discrimination' is not enough; one must actively work to confront and dismantle discriminatory practices and structures. However, an individual or group of individuals can at many times be relatively powerless, because of a lack of resources, networks, or platforms, to effectively address systemic discrimination. With that in mind, we must fight fire with fire, and radically reconfigure both our conceptualizations of allyship and of the role of the HRD function, in other words, to take the present concept of 'ally' and place it at the institutional level.

As Cheng et al. (2019, p. 45) highlight, "as a nascent research area, the theoretical definitions and boundaries surrounding allyship are not fully developed". However, some common themes arise in the various definitions of allyship. Broido (2000, p. 3) defines allies as "members of dominant social groups (e.g., men, Whites, heterosexuals) who are working to end the system of oppression that gives them greater privilege and power based upon their social group membership", while Washington and Evans (1991, p. 195) define an ally as "a person who is a member of the 'dominant' or 'majority' group who works to end oppression in his or her personal and professional life through his or her support of, and as an advocate with and for, the oppressed population". Cheng et al. (2019), Ji (2007), Madsen et al.

(2020) and Sabat et al. (2013) highlight that allyship can take the form of both supportive behaviors and advocacy behaviors—the former centering on providing psychological comfort and solidarity for those experiencing discrimination and stigma, and the latter centering on active outward engagement in efforts to change or overthrow societal norms, practices and systems (Sabat et al., 2013).

Three key aspects of allyship thus emerge from these studies: the ally is a member of traditionally dominant social group; they are working to end oppression and systems of oppression; and they are doing so through both support and advocacy behaviors. One may note that, although much of the scholarship on allyship focuses on the individual level, these key aspects of allyship do not preclude the existence of an organization acting as an ally—indeed, what an individual can do in this regard could be performed at a greater scale and lead to greater impact if an organization were to engage in allyship. A cognitive reframing is needed, to move ourselves away from only considering an inclusive organization as one that *contains* a lot of individual allies, to also considering an inclusive organization as one that *is* an ally in and of itself. With access to greater resources and networks, and the ability to write or inform policy and practice, the institution-as-ally can inspire unprecedented, extensive transformations of not only itself, but of customers, suppliers, competitors and others within its ecosystem. They can utilize the organizational brand and identity to engage in advocacy and support, just as the individual does so.

We have seen smatterings of institutional allyship within the corporate landscape in recent years—Nike, Ben and Jerry, and Starbucks, despite occasional stumbles, have all been particularly outspoken (compared to other brands) in their vocal and financial support and advocacy in relation to, e.g., Black Lives Matter (Aratani, 2020), same-sex marriage (Smith, 2013), and the rights and safety of refugees (Parker et al., 2020). For example, in 2020 Nike pledged $40 million (Nike, 2020) to support the Black community; controversially pledged support of Colin Kaepernick after he kneeled during the national anthem in protest of racial injustice; donated to the US marriage equality campaign (Zeigler, 2013); and most recently tied its executives' compensation to progress on new diversity and inclusion targets by 2025 (Thomas, 2021). However, in many cases active allyship within a politically charged debate may constitute a risk, and thus only large, financially secure companies like Nike may afford to take so public a stance; smaller and/or less stable organizations may find it more difficult to engage in allyship like this. The campaigns are also huge in terms of scale and the amount of investment needed. It is presumptuous to assume that every organization could reconfigure to become an effective ally at this scale, even disregarding the threat of backlash. Thus, more research is needed to examine what steps organizations can take to engage in allyship in a prudent-yet-effective manner, without jumping to the magnitude exemplified by those companies above. In conceiving allyship at the organizational level, we can begin to envisage a realistic process through which institutions can become more welcoming for all employees, and in helping to promote a more equitable society.

THE HRD FUNCTION AS ALLY

HRD practitioners can utilize their role-specific resources and connections to encourage allyship at the institutional level. While they may not necessarily have more organizational power and influence than another employee, they are in some ways the gatekeepers to knowledge and learning within the organization, and thus can serve an important role in promoting institutional allyship. While it will differ from organization to organization and from industry to industry, making the conceptual and practical move from individual-as-allies to the organization-as-ally puts greater onus upon the HRD function to respond. With the latter, fundamental overhauls of the mission and purpose of the HRD function are needed: moving away from the instrumentalist learning approach and masculine rationalities so common within HRD practice (Bierema, 2009) and utilizing the resources and networks available to them as development experts. Much as Bierema and Callahan (2014) prompt us to consider the 'human' within human resource development, the institution-as-ally process would involve a reimagining and expansion of the term 'development'; development can still relate to traditional learning, in the 'upskilling' sense, but can also now include interventions like consciousness-raising, anti-discrimination training, and advocacy workshops.

How does a HRD practitioner encourage a complex, multifaceted organization to engage in the complex, multifaceted practice of allyship? To answer this, one may turn to the Bierema and Callahan's (2014) original CHRD framework that serves as inspiration for the structure of this entire handbook. They identify four key practices—Relating, Learning, Changing and Organizing, that "optimize human interest, organization advancement, and social impact" (Bierema & Callahan, 2014, p. 436). As in Collins et al. (2015), these four practices can be used to show that CHRD practitioners can advocate, or act as allies, for all marginalized groups within the workplace: "relating, learning, changing, and organizing on behalf of others" (Collins et al., 2015, p. 218). CHRD takes into account the asymmetric power relations that exist within organizations (Gedro et al., 2014), and challenges the masculine rationality (Bierema, 2009), commodification of workers (Brookfield, 2014), and over-deference to shareholders and profits to the detriment of other stakeholders (Bierema & Callahan, 2014; Fenwick, 2004). It is within these contexts that Bierema and Callahan (2014) situate their key practices. In exploring each practice in turn, one may begin to theorize how a CHRD practitioner can create a more inclusive organization.

Although the key practices are depicted as standalone (yet clearly interlinked) concepts within the original article (Bierema & Callahan, 2014), in adapting them for use within advocating and allyship, they have been brought together in this chapter in a model (see Fig. 19.1), inspired by Collins and

Chlup (2014) who highlight the ongoing and interlinked nature of an individual's development as an ally (following Bishop, 2002) and the role that HRD may play in this. The model presented in Fig. 19.1—the Institutional Allyship Model—highlights how the HRD department may encourage institutional allyship. In constructing the key CHRD practices as a model when engaging in allyship within organizations, we move our attention from disparate, standalone issues that may occupy one or two practices, to following a particular focus (be that a marginalized group, a movement, a specific inclusion issue) through a form of reciprocal ongoing process—a simplified course of continuous action that can help break down the complexities and nuances of allyship.

The model arranges the four key CHRD practices that Bierema and Callahan (2014) identified into positive-feedback loops, and also includes the resulting combinations of these practices. For example, institutions hoping to engage in meaningful allyship must Learn how to organize effectively, and part of that Organizing effort may include the organizing of practices, policies and procedures that encourage Learning.

The model's structure highlights the interlinked and ongoing nature of the practices, reflecting the ever-evolving context of diversity and inclusion,

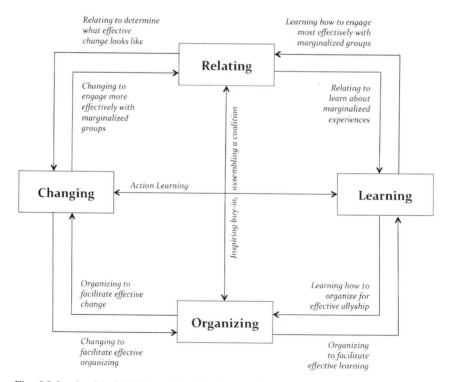

Fig. 19.1 A critical HRD model of institutional allyship

and the differing and developing challenges of each marginalized group. As can be seen in Fig. 19.1, the model is action-oriented: there is no particular beginning or end to it, just as allyship itself is characterized as an ongoing action (Williams & Sharif, 2021). The Change practice—wherein permanent advancements are made to improve the lives of marginalized group members— may reflect a form of consequence of engaging in allyship, but should not be seen as an end, but merely the beginning of more advanced allyship.

One can follow this institutional allyship process while considering a particular marginalized group and the specific problems they face, or use it to address inclusion goals at a larger organizational level, without focusing on any one group in particular. The choice between a narrow or broad approach is potentially affected by resources such as time and money; the former represents a 'deep-dive' into a particular group's challenges and the tailoring of solutions and change to their specific needs and context, and would constitute a best-fit approach. The latter can explore common issues affecting a number of groups (e.g., marginalization, lack of representation) and so can more efficiently address concerns, while still basing their efforts within their specific organizational context (i.e., more general in nature, but not simply buying in a potentially ineffective 'best-practice' solution).

Below, each practice within the model is discussed; firstly, Bierema and Callahan's (2014) original explanation of the key CHRD practice is described; then, how this practice can be used to engage in better allyship is explored; lastly, the role of the practice within the entire model is established.

Relating

The key practice of Relating is in direct opposition to masculine rationality and commodification being uncritically seen as 'natural' within organizations (Bierema & Callahan, 2014). Relating is a practice that characterizes 'human resources' first and foremost as 'humans', acknowledging and responding to the inherent emotional, psychological and social issues that abound within the employment relationship, collegial relationships, and the relationship between the employee and their own career.

The active part of the Relating practice centers around addressing issues that may arise as a result of these personal aspects of organizational life, such as how resistance and incivility, perhaps stemming from an overtly masculine, commodifying culture, can manifest. Relating promotes fruitful collaborations, participation and employee voice, and aims to involve all stakeholders, including those that may be traditionally sidelined or excluded, in changes and developments within the organization.

Relating in an allyship sense may first involve breaking down the barrier that demarcates the organization and the 'outside world', which often determines what is seen as relevant, acceptable or even 'professional' within the business environment, and what belongs to (and should remain in) one's private life. However, recent events have perhaps spurred the beginning of the erosion of that 'professional wall': for example, in the past few years the Black Lives Matter and MeToo movements became too big for organizations to ignore (Davies, 2020; Norton & Saldanha, 2022), as they might have with issues seen as 'political', 'sensitive' or 'controversial' in the past (Hsu, 2020). The general public expected a response from organizations and often received it in the form of social media posts or other brief statements. The personal is political, and is now professional; issues like systemic discrimination, sexual harassment and institutional racism, which may have been sidelined in past decades, are now seen as de rigueur within diversity and inclusion discourse, at least in some organizations. However, that does not mean that individuals will be willing to open up about personal, identity-related issues that were, for many years, seen as beyond the scope of everyday business. In this sense, Relating as a practice within the Institutional Allyship Model may not only involve engaging with employees at an emotional, psychological and social level (which is surely a prerequisite of allyship), but also rebranding the HRD function within one's organization to an extent—being seen not simply as the mechanistic, demanding taskmasters of old equipped with mandatory health and safety trainings, but as a co-creator of an inclusive and accepting organizational environment, with the achievement of social justice (and not only profit) as a key goal. As part of this rebranding (and perhaps reorganization), the HRD function should attempt to become a trusted ally with whom those from marginalized groups can discuss issues that affect their lives, both in and outside of the workplace. However, the marginalized groups must actually be represented within the organization in the first place to allow conversations in the workplace to happen; otherwise, HRD practitioners may have to go outside of their organization to find inspiration for the next step.

Standpoint theorists argue that those who are traditionally marginalized have an automatic epistemic privilege concerning inclusion, exclusion, discrimination (Harding, 1991), and what is required within effective allyship—particularly within the specific organizational, industry or societal context. The stories, anecdotes and experiences that these employees share can form a basis of understanding for CHRD practitioners to begin to formulate tailored plans that can make the organization a more inclusive place to work. As part of the Institutional Allyship Model, therefore, Relating helps one to open up and participate in conversations with those from marginalized groups and listen to their perspectives and the challenges or issues that they may face, both within and outside of the organization. This may involve engaging on an individual basis or utilizing other voice mechanisms. A range of employee voice mechanisms, such as union groups, employee resource networks or anonymous suggestion schemes, can allow employees from marginalized groups to engage with the Relating practice and influence the design of allyship initiatives, while still retaining control over the scope and depth of the discussion (Marchington & Wilkinson, 2008; McFadden & Crowley-Henry, 2018). Having a variety of voice mechanisms in place as part of the Relating practice may be particularly important where one's marginalized identity is concealed, or where there is mistrust or a fear of repercussions on the part of the employee (Bell et al., 2011; McFadden & Crowley-Henry, 2018).

The topics discussed as part of the Relating practice could range from interpersonal discrimination (Drury & Kaiser, 2014) to structural discrimination, everyday experiences or lifelong career and identity-related issues, but the range of topics discussed should be chosen by those within the marginalized group, not by the would-be ally. The automatic epistemic privilege that marginalized group members have should prompt those engaging in institutional allyship to remember their role within the process—as facilitators and enablers of allyship, and ideally part of a coalition, but not necessarily the leaders or agenda-setters. This may be a hard pill to swallow for those used to positional power, but at its heart, the Relating practice within the Institutional Allyship Model is about acknowledging one's ignorance about issues such as marginalization, discrimination and exclusion affecting a certain group, and engaging in the Allyship process from an open and receptive place, unclouded by preexisting conceptions about what it means to be a member of this group.

The structure of the Institutional Allyship Model highlights the Relating practice's connections with the other practices—Learning, Changing and Organizing. Listening to and directly Relating with those from marginalized groups allows CHRD practitioners to Learn about the former's experiences—the more effective the Relating is, the more comprehensive the Learning will be. Importantly, Relating is situated within the specific organizational context—local issues and challenges can be learned about, as well as more general problems and experiences. Relating helps the would-be ally to determine what effective Change looks like, from those whom the changes will affect most. Change goals that are ineffective, or worse, purely performative (see *Performative Allyship* below) can be improved or abandoned, with the insight from the Relating stage providing clarity and direction. Relating leads to better Organizing—the building of a coalition that will bring about Change requires buy-in from those with power and resources, mutual understanding across all parties, a commonality of goals, and a shared strategy into which everyone can have input.

LEARNING

As Bierema and Callahan (2014) argue, although learning is traditionally a key distinguishing feature of HRD, the approach to learning often espoused within Western organizations is based on an instrumentalist logic—learning as a tool to address deficiencies, in this context is a lack of knowledge or mastery—and learning is thus a way of correcting it. The deficiency may lie at the organizational level (i.e., a competitor has moved ahead or innovated in some way and the organization must keep up) but will inevitably trickle down and become characterized as an individual talent or development issue that must be addressed. HRD's traditional role, of course, is to keep abreast of this process for the sake of the profit motive. In this way learning and knowledge become a commodity (Bierema, 2009; Bierema & Callahan, 2014) that can be bought and sold. Characterizing a personal development process in this way can lead us to view learning like other commodities (e.g., gold, real estate, plant): devoid of emotion, feeling, aspiration, or motivation. Another consequence of commodifying learning is that learning which is not associated with directly plugging a hole in the organization's knowledge may be viewed as unconstructive, irrelevant or even wasteful; if a very direct line can't be drawn from this intervention to the profit motive, why should an organization sponsor it, or an individual employee (who must strive for efficiency at all times) engage in it (Brookfield, 2014)?

In Bierema and Callahan's (2014) original article, the key practice of Learning was related more to how one learned rather than what one learned—as well as questioning the traditionally mechanistic approach to learning, this practice seeks to look at the learning process within organizations: the extended learning environment that lies both inside and outside of the organization, the needs and goals of the learners, engaging in critical thinking and actions, and considering how different viewpoints and beliefs can enhance one's learning. Importantly, this step also considers what constitutes knowledge, who is 'allowed' to learn it, and the asymmetric power relations inherent in both questions.

In bringing the key practice of Learning into the realm of allyship, we can distinguish between *learning as an individual* and *learning as a group*. The Learning step builds on the foundation provided by the Relating step; having begun to engage in meaningful conversations about the experiences of employees from marginalized groups and the challenges and issues they face, the HRD practitioner can separately begin to 'do their own homework' on these issues, rather than depending on the employee to lead the charge—in other words, *Learning as an individual*. In this way, the marginalized employee themselves can avoid the 'minority tax'—the disparate time and effort that individuals from marginalized groups often have to expend in engaging with diversity and inclusion initiatives in organizations (Rodríguez et al., 2015). An important part of the Learning process may be the *unlearning* of entrenched and taken-for-granted assumptions and norms, in order to better facilitate the Relating, Organizing and Changing practices (Nixon, 2019).

Having educated themselves on these issues more, to the point where they are comfortable and knowledgeable enough to start to develop interventions for the organization, the HRD practitioner may then start *Learning as a group* (Wilson et al., 2007). This could involve workshops led by the practitioner, seminars involving paid speakers from within or outside of the organization, book clubs or employee network-led events that explore the issues raised in the Relating step in more detail. Because the practitioner is presumably not an expert in the subject matter, the approach of these inventions should be exploratory rather than prescriptive—a social constructivist approach (Vygotsky, 1978) akin to feminist consciousness-raising groups

(Kravetz, 1978), rather than a traditional, classroom-like approach. The purpose of these interventions can not only be about giving information to employees but can also play a part in the Relating practice—the practitioner may get a greater sense of what members of traditionally dominant groups (e.g., white employees, heterosexual employees, non-disabled employees) feel and think about diversity and inclusion issues, what they struggle to or do not understand, and what requires further explanation and discussion.

In designing interventions in such a way, Learning may extend beyond the subject matter that the HRD practitioner initially engaged with, and become an ongoing conversation between employees that can add to everyone's understanding; becoming more than a relaying of facts or statistics, but helping in "expanding and building...worldviews in an effort to create new perspectives" (Collins & Chlup, 2014, p. 487). As participants and learners within the intervention, dominant group members may be less likely to engage in the opposition, resistance and backlash encountered as part of many diversity efforts (Mobley & Payne, 1992).

Organizing

The Organizing practice within the Institutional Allyship Model relates to "critical organizational development" (Bierema & Callahan, 2014, p. 440), and works to build coalitions, structures, policies, practices and procedures that can facilitate, support and encourage the Changing, Learning and Relating practices.

Callahan (2013, p. 300) defines 'organization' as "a [relatively] voluntary collective of actors committed to interacting toward a mutually constructed and interpreted endeavor or set of endeavors". Coalitions are a key part of the success of any change initiative (Kotter, 1996). Bierema and Callahan (2014) highlight how the key CHRD practice of Organizing involves highlighting the role of storytelling and sensemaking in organizing, taking into account not just organizational actors but other stakeholders (rather than shareholders), the community and the outer environment. They highlight the importance in locating organizing in relation to change, and thus this part of the Institutional Allyship Model is important in order to bring about the foundations of the Changing practice; to obtain buy-in, engagement and ownership from stakeholders; and to put in place structures and policies that will support the long-term success of change initiatives related to allyship.

As well as Changing, Organizing can facilitate better Learning and better Relating. As mentioned above, Organizing can help to identify and exploit opportunities for development at the individual and institutional level, for example through workshops, mentoring and reverse mentoring, and other collaborative learning interventions. By virtue of bringing people together, Organizing facilitates better Relating, through the sharing of ideas and experiences, which in turn can help achieve buy-in from a wide range of people, including the organization's leadership, who can direct resources and be a champion of the allyship process.

Various scholars (e.g., Kotter, 1996; Stouten et al., 2018; ten Have et al., 2016) argue that trust is an important part of coalition-building, with trust in coalition members in each other and from management a key consideration. One might also add trust *in* management to those requirements; because most contemporary organizations put profit or surplus at the top of their priorities, the organization may have to be wary of their Organizing being seen by the employees solely as an exercise to aid the profit motive (à la performative allyship, explored below), rather than for reasons related to achieving social justice— indeed, that could be an issue experienced within the entire Institutional Allyship Model. This may potentially alienate those who could be of help within the process, who could avoid taking part because they may mistrust the process or the practitioner, or may feel that getting involved could put them at odds with management and/or their profit-driven agenda. Practically speaking, however, one may have to deploy the profit motive to secure buy-in from those assigning resources; a common challenge to EDI practitioners, whose work must often straddle the social justice case and the business case (Tomlinson & Schwabenland, 2010). A delicate balancing act is thus required.

Changing

Change, in this context, is with a capital C. It refers to conscious and meaningful change directed specifically at making a more inclusive workplace and society for those from marginalized groups. Although Learning, Relating and Organizing are all in themselves types of change (at the individual, group and organizational level), the Change referred to here relates to the concrete consequences of bringing together these other practices and taking action to fundamentally improve the experiences of marginalized groups. The Change involved in this step may be a major one, like, for example the integration of inclusion goals within the organization's performance management and talent management strategies. It may also be a minor change—a necessary update, rather than drastic overhaul, of an existing inclusion policy, reflecting the continuously evolving nature and differing focuses of social justice.

The types of effective Change that could be introduced into the organization depend, naturally, on the context of the organization and the needs of the particular marginalized group(s) involved. The existence of seemingly infinite variations of potential Change could cause inaction through doubt and indecision, yet we can utilize the much more established field of change leadership to consider how to plan a successful Change strategy, to foresee what challenges may arise, and plan how to overcome them (Kotter, 1996; Lewin, 1951). Common reasons for resistance to a change initiative may include uncertainty about the unknown, a fear of failing, disruptions to one's routine, too few resources to enact change, the rigidity and size of the organization, a lack of trust between managers and employees and a lack of management support

(Rosenberg & Mosca, 2011). Various scholars (Kotter, 1996; Lewin, 1951) have proposed methods and processes of tackling resistance to Change, which may be of use here, but we can also readily see how the other CHRD practices within the Institutional Allyship Model can address these common reasons for resistance. Learning can increase one's knowledge and self-efficacy related to allyship, diversity and inclusion and in doing so help address and disperse fears of the unknown, of potential failure and of disruptions. Relating can help to build trust between management and employees, and to secure management buy-in (and thus resources, in many cases). Effective Organizing can help allow would-be resisters to become part of the process, and to bring in policies, practices and procedures that can counter any rigidity within organizational structures.

The Change practice interacts with the other practices, as highlighted in the Institutional Allyship Model in Fig. 19.1. Change and Learning are common partners that have been previously studied in the form of action learning (e.g., Kolb, 1984), wherein change in one's behavior and approach can stimulate reflection, learning and further modifications. Change can inform and improve the Relating practice; positive changes or additions to employee voice mechanisms, for example, would represent an improvement in the work experiences of marginalized (if not all) employees, and improve the Relating stage in ongoing institutional allyship. Similarly, Change in Organizing practices may allow a greater facilitation for organizing coalitions, conversations, engagement and the improvement/addition of policies and procedures in ongoing institutional allyship endeavors.

At this point in the process, after bringing in positive changes that will improve the workplace and career experiences of marginalized employees, it may be tempting to rest on one's laurels and declare one's work finished. However, as mentioned above, and as argued by Collins and Chlup (2014), the development of allies is an ongoing process; issues regarding equality, diversity and inclusion are constantly changing and evolving, thus it would be remiss of a true institutional ally to end the process here. Instead, the benefits of all the experience gained during this process can be drawn upon to engage in more advanced and far-reaching allyship.

RECOMMENDATIONS

Complexities in the Definition and Focus of Allyship

As discussed above, a number of authors highlight how allyship can take different forms—as both supportive or advocacy behaviors (Cheng et al., 2019; Ji, 2007; Madsen et al., 2020; Sabat et al., 2013). In addition, as Forbes and Ueno (2019) find, allyship can be characterized in some respects as a 'moving target' within a particular group, because there may be differing views across individuals as to what constitutes allyship—in their study, some queer participants saw allyship as akin to close friendship wherein the salience of their sexuality was lowered; while some included political activism and the recognition and celebration of difference in their definition of allyship; and others wanted straight allies to recognize and use their privilege to help queer people when needed, but focused more on the interpersonal (rather than political) level, bridging both of the former definitions.

The effective practice of allyship becomes more complicated when one considers intersectionality (Crenshaw, 1989), and the "multidimensionality" (p. 139) that those who face oppression based on multiple marginalized identities experience, yet considering intersectionality is an important part of allyship (Bishop, 2002; Collins, 2015). As Crenshaw (1989) argues, a single-axis analysis distorts the true picture of discrimination because it often focuses on those who, while belonging to one marginalized group, are otherwise privileged. In taking cues from social justice movements, organizations must not replicate the mistakes that many of these movements have been accused of making, such as the centering of cisgender, white, gay men in Pride and queer events/discourse (Johnson, 2019), or of middle-class white women from the Global North in the #MeToo movement (De Benedictis et al., 2019; Ghadery, 2019; Page & Arcy, 2020). As well as engaging in active allyship with regard to group-wide issues, organizations and the HR function should also consider issues that those with intersectional identities may face, and not unconsciously center otherwise-privileged group members and their interests in their allyship efforts.

The term 'ally' has its roots within the LGBTQ movement, where it was used since the 1990s in its modern social justice sense to describe heterosexual people who were supportive of and/or took part in LGBTQ campaigns and protests (McElya, 2019). The term has also been used in relation to characterize men supporting women and feminism in popular discourse (e.g., Hess, 2014; Johnson & Smith, 2018) and academia (e.g., Drury & Kaiser, 2014). The Black Lives Matter movement, particularly toward the end of the 2010s, used 'ally' to describe supporters and contributors within the movement who were white, and it is here that the popularity of *ally* took off. Google Trends shows that the number of searches of 'Allyship', 'Allyship Definition' and 'Performative Allyship' all peak in June 2020—coinciding with world-wide rallies protesting systemic racism and police brutality in the weeks following the murder of George Floyd. Books related to racism, anti-racism and white allyship, including 'How to be an Antiracist' (Kendi, 2019), 'Me and White Supremacy' (Saad, 2020) and 'Why I'm No Longer Talking to White People about Race' (Eddo-Lodge, 2017), reached and stayed on the top of best-seller lists in June 2020 (McEvoy, 2020). One can argue, then, that the popular conceptualization of allyship is related to LGBT rights and women's rights, but especially with the anti-racism movement. However, this raises the question regarding what allyship looks like for other marginalized groups. Are there core principles and practices inherent in all allyship, no matter what the focus is, or should a ground-up, best-fit approach always be taken, because of the unique nuances, needs and characteristics of each group?

By looking at individual allyship to anchor this discussion on the organizational allyship, we can benefit from years of scholarship to help us in understanding the meaning and process of allyship. However, as this more recent research has shown, the exact targets, processes and tasks within individual allyship may be more complex than first envisaged, which may cause a lack of focus and effectiveness within the practice of institutional allyship. To act as an effective ally, organizations must consider and prepare for the complexity inherent within effective allyship, and can utilize the practices outlined above, particularly Relating, to gain insight into what effective allyship actually consists of in their particular context.

Performative Allyship: A Cautionary Tale

Sumerau et al. (2021) highlight how participants in their study, who self-identified as allies, constructed allyship as a form of apolitical, passive friendship with an individualized or personal focus (being kind and understanding and emphasizing care and concern to marginalized group members), rather than an active, political act targeting structural inequalities. The authors evoke Goffman's (1959) work on impression management to highlight how impressions can often carry as much social weight as concrete actions; this is at the heart of *performative allyship*—wherein the actual primary goal of allyship (or at least, of adopting the 'ally' label) is to benefit the social standing of the individual, rather than the ostensible goal of helping to end the oppression faced by marginalized group members (van Leeuwen & Taüber, 2010; Radke et al., 2020).

As noted above, performative allyship became well known to a wide audience after the murder of George Floyd by police officer Derek Chauvin, and it is within this context that a cautionary tale regarding performative allyship may be found. June 2, 2020 became 'Blackout Tuesday', when millions of users across the world posted a black square on their Instagram feeds. Blackout Tuesday was originally started by music executives Jamila Thomas and Brianna Agyemang, who used the hashtag #theshowmustbepaused and asked for those in the industry to suspend their usual social media postings for one day, "in observance of the long-standing racism and inequality that exists from the boardroom to the boulevard" (Sinanan, 2020). However, the movement grew globally, and so too did the criticisms and issues associated with it. Millions of individuals began posting black squares and using #BlackLivesMatter as the caption, unaware of the campaign's original intention. The hashtag, which for many activists was a way of organizing, protesting and educating in relation to anti-racism, was flooded with black squares to the point where useful information about Black Lives Matter, protests and racial injustice was obscured (Wellman, 2022; Willingham, 2020). Many companies also engaged with Blackout Tuesday and posted their own black squares, with white text denouncing racism—including Citigroup, Google and Amazon, who were subsequently alleged to have donated hundreds of thousands of dollars to members of the US Congress who are rated "F" by civil rights organization NAACP (Legum, 2020).

The questionable authenticity of both organizations and individuals engaging in Blackout Tuesday has been commonly characterized as a form of performative allyship (Blair, 2021; Wellman, 2022) and as *clicktivism, slacktism* or *hashtag activism*—a low effort, noncommital way of digitally engaging with social justice movements (George & Leidner, 2019; Wellman, 2022). Because it is easy for many to do, yet does not require actual work or commitment, performative allyship may distort the true strength and reach of a social justice movement, making effective organizing more difficult (Wellman, 2022). Performative allyship, especially that which is thought to arise primarily from a corporate profit motive (Du et al., 2010; Weber, 2008), may also lead to distrust in the leadership and integrity of organizations from both customers and employees from marginalized groups (Yuan, 2020), which may make engaging marginalized individuals in the design and execution of *genuine* allyship initiatives in the future more difficult. We must therefore move beyond performative allyship at the institutional level and at the individual level, to help build an effective and trusting coalition between social justice groups, organizations and individuals. The Institutional Allyship Model offers a simplified process with which organizations can begin to engage in meaningful, ongoing and genuine allyship.

Recommendations for Future Research

Focus of Research

Comparatively more has been written about the role and strategies of allies in reference to the allyship of female employees (e.g., Drury & Kaiser, 2014; Madsen et al., 2020), LGBTQ employees (e.g., Brooks & Edwards, 2009; Collins et al., 2015; Russell & Bohan, 2016), and ethnic and racial minority employees (e.g., Broido, 2000; Johnson & Pietri, 2020; Williams & Sharif, 2021), yet this is a low bar—research on allyship in the organizational context is itself quite scant (Sabat et al., 2013).

Therefore, more research on allyship in general is needed, in part to help theorize further on the boundaries and complexities of allyship, what it means to be an ally, and what conflicts, experiences and consequences may arise from engaging in allyship. It would also be useful to break the concept down further to examine how allyship differs within different contexts—not only in differing industry contexts, where one might assume natural adaptions and variations, but also in how allyship looks different, for example, when it's centered on Black employees (Erskine & Bilimoria, 2019) compared to when it's centered on LGBTQ employees (Forbes & Ueno, 2019) and so on; how allyship looks when directed toward those who have intersectional identities (Collins, 2015), and those groups that have not been the focus of much research in the business, management and organizational studies literatures, for example, those with different forms of disabilities (Abes & Zahneis, 2020) and those who face discrimination on the basis of social class (Bettencourt, 2020). The Institutional Allyship Model presented in this chapter is by design equally useful as a basic tool for engaging in allyship efforts regardless of the marginalized group in question. However, it too requires further study and of course modification and adaptation to suit the specific needs of each particular group; perhaps there are a few universal components of effective allyship, but allyship will look different depending on whom it is directed toward, the context in which allyship is being enacted, and which individual, group or organization is enacting it.

CONCLUSION

This chapter discussed how the HRD department and allies within the organization can help to contribute to the creation of an inclusive environment for those from marginalized groups. A simplified process, the Institutional Allyship Model, is one of the first to encapsulate at the theoretical level how HRD practitioners may use key CHRD practices (Bierema & Callahan, 2014) to deconstruct and simplify the complex concept and practice of allyship, and show how the organization can act as an ally in and of itself. In doing so, it is hoped that more and more organizations can start to utilize their resources, social capital, status, and reach to help improve the lives of marginalized people everywhere.

REFERENCES

Abes, E. S., & M. E., Zahneis. (2020). A Duoethnographic Exploration of Disability Ally Development. *Disability Studies Quarterly, 40*(3).

Aratani, L. (2020, June 12). Starbucks reverses stance and allows staff to wear Black Lives Matter clothing. *The Guardian*. https://www.theguardian.com/business/2020/jun/12/starbucks-black-lives-matter-clothing

Bell, M. P., Özbilgin, M. F., Beauregard, T. A., & Sürgevil, O. (2011). Voice, silence, and diversity in 21st century organizations: Strategies for inclusion of gay, lesbian, bisexual, and transgender employees. *Human Resource Management, 50*(1), 131–146.

Bettencourt, G. M. (2020). "You can't be a class ally if you're an upper-class person because you don't understand": Working-class students' definitions and perceptions of social class allyship. *The Review of Higher Education, 44*(2), 265–291.

Bierema, L. L. (2009). Critiquing human resource development's dominant masculine rationality and evaluating its impact. *Human Resource Development Review, 8*, 68–96.

Bierema, L. L., & Callahan, J. L. (2014). Tranforming HRD: A framework for critical HRD practice. *Advances in Developing Human Resources, 16*(4), 429–444.

Bishop, A. (2002). *Becoming an Ally: Breaking the cycle of oppression in people* (2nd Ed.). Halifax: Fernwood Publishing.

Blair, K. (2021). Empty gestures: Performative utterances and allyship. *Journal of Dramatic Theory & Criticism, 35*(2), 53–73.

Broido, E. M. (2000). The development of social justice allies during college: A phenomenological investigation. *Journal of College Student Development, 41,* 3–18.

Broido, E. M., & Reason, R. D. (2005). The development of social justice attitudes and actions: An overview of current understandings. *New Directions for Student Services, 110,* 17–28.

Brookfield, S. D. (2014). Foundations of critical theory. *Advances in Developing Human Resources, 16*(4), 417–428.

Brooks, A. K., & Edwards, K. (2009). Allies in the workplace: Including LGBT in HRD. *Advances in Developing Human Resources, 11*(1), 136–149.

Callahan, J. L. (2013). 'Space, the final frontier'? Social movements as organizing spaces for applying HRD. *Human Resource Development International, 16*(3), 298–312.

Cheng, S. K., Ng, L. C., Traylor, A. M., & King, E. B. (2019). Helping or hurting? Understanding women's perceptions of male Allies. *Personnel Assessment and Decisions, 5*(2), 6.

Collins, J. C. (2015). Identity matters: A critical exploration of lesbian, gay, and bisexual identity and leadership in HRD. *Human Resource Development Review, 11*(3), 349–379.

Collins, J. C., & Chlup, D. T. (2014). Criticality in practice: The cyclical development process of social justice allies at work. *Advances in Developing Human Resources, 16*(4), 481–498.

Collins, J. C., McFadden, C., Rocco, T. S., & Mathis, M. K. (2015). The problem of transgender marginalization and exclusion: Critical actions for human resource development. *Human Resource Development Review, 14*(2), 205–226.

Crenshaw, K. (1989). Demarginalizing the intersection of race and sex: A Black feminist critique of anti-discrimination doctrine, feminist theory and anti-racist politics. *University of Chicago Legal Forum, 1989*(1), 139–167.

Davies, R. (2020, June 20). *Firms are waking up to race issues, but critics say hashtags aren't enough.* The Observer.

De Benedictis, S., Orgad, S., & Rottenberg, C. (2019). #MeToo, popular feminism and the news: A content analysis of UK newspaper coverage. *European Journal of Cultural Studies, 22*(5–6), 718–738.

Drury, B. J., & Kaiser, C. R. (2014). Allies against sexism: The role of men in confronting sexism. *Journal of Social Issues, 70*(4), 637–652.

Du, S., Bhattacharya, C. B., & Sen, S. (2010). Maximizing business returns to Corporate Social Responsibility (CSR): The role of CSR communication. *International Journal of Management Reviews, 12*(1), 8–19.

Duhigg, J. M., Rostosky, S. S., Gray, B. E., & Wimsatt, M. K. (2010). Development of heterosexuals into sexual-minority allies: A qualitative exploration. *Sexuality Research and Social Policy, 7,* 2–14.

Eddo-Lodge, R. (2017). *Why I'm no longer talking to white people about race.* Bloomsbury.

Erskine, S. E., & Bilimoria, D. (2019). White allyship of afro-diasporic women in the workplace: A transformative strategy for organizational change. *Journal of Leadership and Organizational Studies, 26*(3), 319–338.

Fenwick, T. (2004). Towards a critical HRD in theory and practice. *Adult Education Quarterly: A Journal of Research and Theory, 54*(3), 193–209.

Forbes, T. D., & Ueno, K. (2019). Post-gay, political, and pieced together: Queer expectations of straight allies. *Sociological Perspectives, 63*(1), 159–176.

Gedro, J., Collins, J. C., & Rocco, T. S. (2014). The "critical turn": An important imperative for human resource development. *Advances in Developing Human Resources, 16*(4), 529–535.

George, J. J., & Leidner, D. E. (2019). From clicktivism to hacktivism: Understanding digital activism. *Information and Organization, 29,* 100249.

Ghadery, F. (2019). #Metoo—has the 'sisterhood' finally become global or just another product of neoliberal feminism? *Transnational Legal Theory, 10*(2), 252–274.

Goffman, E. (1959). *The presentation of self in everyday life.* Penguin.

Harding, S. (1991). *Whose science? whose knowledge?: Thinking from women's lives.* Cornell University Press.

Hess, A. (2014, October 15). *Male allies are important, except when they're the worst.* Slate.

Hsu, T. (2020, May 31). Corporate voices get behind 'black lives matter' cause. *The New York Times.*

Ji, P. (2007). Being a heterosexual Ally to the lesbian, gay, bisexual, and transgendered community: Reflections and development. *Journal of Gay & Lesbian Psychotherapy, 11*(3–4), 173–185.

Johnson, G. (2019, June 30). *White gay privilege exists all year, but it is particularly hurtful during Pride.* NBC Think.

Johnson, I. R., & Pietri, E. S. (2020). An ally you say? Endorsing White women as allies to encourage perceptions of allyship and organizational identity-safety among Black women. *Group Processes & Intergroup Relations,* Dec. 2020.

Johnson, W. B., & Smith, D. G. (2018, October 12). How men can become better allies to women. *Harvard Business Review.*

Kendi, I. X. (2019). *How to be an Antiracist.* Bodley Head.

Kolb, D. A. (1984). *Experiential learning: Experience as the source of learning and development.* Prentice Hall.

Kotter, J. P. (1996). *Leading change.* Harvard Business Press.

Kravetz, D. (1978). Consciousness-raising groups in the 1970's. *Psychology of Women Quarterly, 3*(2), 168–186.

Lewin, K. (1951). *Field theory in social science.* Harper & Brothers.

Legum, J. (2020, June 2). Corporations tweet support for Black Lives Matter. Their FEC filings tell a different story. *Popular Information.* https://popular.info/p/corporations-tweet-support-for-black?s=r

Madsen, S. R., Townsend, A., & Scribner, R. T. (2020). Strategies that male allies use to advance women in the workplace. *Journal of Men's Studies, 28*(3), 239–259.

Marchington, M., & Wilkinson, A. (2008). *HRM at work: People management and development* (4th ed.) Chartered Institute of Personnel & Development.

McElya, M. (2019). Who Is an Ally? Boston Review. https://bostonreview.net/articles/micki-mcelya-history-social-justice-ally/

McEvoy, J. (2020, June 11). Books about racism dominate best-seller lists amid protests. *Forbes.*

McFadden, C., & Crowley-Henry, M. (2018). 'My People': The potential of LGBT employee networks in reducing stigmatization and providing voice. *The International Journal of Human Resource Management, 29*(5), 1056–1081. https://doi.org/10.1080/09585192.2017.1335339

Mobley, M., & Payne, T. (1992). Backlash! The challenge to diversity training. *Training & Development, 46*(12), 45–52.

Parker, G., Evans, J., & Thomas, D. (2020, August 12). Ben & Jerry's clashes with UK home secretary over migrants. *Financial Times*. https://www.ft.com/content/bd848384-52b7-4973-b495-7075dbfe3f07

Nike (2020). *NIKE, Inc. Statement on commitment to the black community*. https://news.nike.com/news/nike-commitment-to-black-community

Nixon, S. (2019). The coin model of privilege and critical allyship: Implications for health. *BMC Public Health, 19*, 1637.

Norton, L. & Saldanha, R. (2022, March 2). How metoo forced companies to see the business risks of sexual misconduct. *Morningstar*.

Page, A., & Arcy, J. (2020). #MeToo and the politics of collective healing: Emotional connection as contestation. *Communication, Culture and Critique, 13*(3), 333–348.

Perrin, P. B., Bhattacharyya,S., Snipes, D. J. Calton, J. M., & Heesacker, M. (2014). Creating lesbian, gay, bisexual, and transgender Allies: Testing a model of privilege investment. *Journal of Counseling Development, 92*(2), 241–251.

Radke, H. R., Kutlaca, M., Siem, B., Wright, S. C., & Becker, J. C. (2020). Beyond Allyship: Motivations for advantaged group members to engage in action for disadvantaged groups. *Personality and Social Psychology Review, 24*(4), 291–315. https://doi.org/10.1177/1088868320918698

Rodríguez, J. E., Campbell, K., M., & Pololi, L. H. (2015). Addressing disparities in academic medicine: What of the minority tax? *BMC Medical Education, 15*(6).

Rosenberg, S., & Mosca, J. (2011). Breaking down the barriers to organizational change. *International Journal of Management & Information Systems, 15*(3), 139–146.

Russell, G. M., & Bohan, J. S. (2016). Institutional allyship for LGBT equality: Underlying processes and potentials for change. *Journal of Social Issues, 72*(2), 335–354.

Saad, L. (2020). *Me and white supremacy: How to recognise your privilege, combat racism and change the world*. Quercus.

Sabat, I. E., Martinez, L. R., & Wessel, J. L. (2013). Neo-activism: engaging allies in modern workplace discrimination reduction. *Industrial and Organizational Psychology, 6*(4), 480–485.

Sinanan, J. (2020, June 4). Blackout tuesday: The black square is a symbol of online activism for non-activists. *The Conversation*. https://theconversation.com/blackout-tuesday-the-black-square-is-a-symbol-of-online-activism-for-non-activists-139982

Smith, A. (2013, March 28). Starbucks CEO holds his ground on gay marriage. *CNN*. https://money.cnn.com/2013/03/26/news/companies/starbucks-gay-marriage/

Stouten, J., Rousseau, D. M., & De Cremer, D. (2018). Successful organizational change: Integrating the management practice and scholarly literatures. *Academy of Management Annals, 12*(2), 752–788.

Sumerau, J. E., Forbes, T. D., Grollman, A., & Mathers, L. A. B. (2021). Constructing allyship and the persistence of inequality. *Social Problems, 68*(2), 358–373.

ten Have, S., ten Have, W., Huijsmans, A. B., & Otto, M. (2016). *Reconsidering change management: Applying evidence-based insights in change management practice* (Vol. 16). Routledge.

Thomas, L. (2021, March 11). Nike sets fresh diversity targets for 2025, and ties executive compensation to hitting them. *CNBC*. https://www.cnbc.com/2021/03/11/nike-sets-diversity-goals-for-2025-ties-executive-comp-back-to-them.html

Tomlinson, F., & Schwabenland, C. (2010). Reconciling competing discourses of diversity? The UK non-profit sector between social justice and the business case. *Organization, 17*(1), 101–121. https://doi.org/10.1177/1350508409350237

van Leeuwen, E., & Täuber, S. (2010). The strategic side of out-group helping. In S. Stürmer & M. Snyder (Eds.), *The psychology of prosocial behavior: Group processes, intergroup relations, and helping* (pp. 81–99). Wiley-Blackwell.

Washington, J., & Evans, N. J. (1991). Becoming an Ally. In N. J. Evans & V. A. Wall (Eds.), *Beyond tolerance: Gays, lesbians and bisexuals on campus*. Washington, D.C.: American College Personnel Association.

Weber, M. (2008). The business case for corporate social responsibility: A company-level measurement approach for CSR. *European Management Journal, 26*(4), 247–261.

Wellman, M. L. (2022). Black squares for black lives? Performative allyship as credibility maintenance for social media influencers on Instagram. *Social Media & Society, 8*(1).

Williams, M., & Sharif, N. (2021). Racial allyship: Novel measurement and new insights. *New Ideas in Psychology, 62*(2021).

Willingham, A. J. (2020, June 2). Why posting a black image with the 'Black Lives Matter' hashtag could be doing more harm than good. *CNN*. https://edition.cnn.com/2020/06/02/us/blackout-tuesday-black-lives-matter-instagram-trnd/index.html

Wilson, J. M., Goodman, P. S., & Cronin, M. A. (2007). Group learning. *Academy of Management Review, 32*(4).

Vygotsky, L. S. (1978). *Mind in society: The development of higher psychological processes*. Cambridge, Mass: Harvard University Press.

Zeigler, C. (2013, November 20). Nike fully endorses same-sex marriage, commits nearly $300k to their Equality PAC. *Outsports*. https://www.outsports.com/2013/11/20/5126576/nike-gay-marriage-oregon-pac

Understanding Emotion to Enhance Learning for Individuals, Communities, and Organizations

Deborah N. Brewis and Rose Opengart

INTRODUCTION

Emotions have always been a part of the way we relate to other people—in each of our everyday interactions we navigate the way we feel, how others feel about themselves, and the way they feel about us. These feelings represent a nexus of the way we see ourselves and our place in the world, our relationships to others, the ways in which we are 'successful' or valued. Each of those interactions is shaped by the hopes, fears, and uncertainties that we bring to it, affecting not only what happens in that moment but also how patterns of interactions are likely to develop over time. Our skills in navigating, processing, and transforming emotions are core capabilities on which the accomplishment of social life relies. It may seem strange, then, that the emotional lives of organizational actors have been a rather neglected area of management and organization theory, even more surprising perhaps for the area of human resource development. Although the body of work on emotions can be considered comparatively small, it is vibrant, insightful, compelling, and has gripped our imaginations in research, teaching, and practice over many years.

D. N. Brewis
University of Bath, Bath, Somerset, UK
e-mail: d.brewis@bath.ac.uk

R. Opengart (✉)
Texas A&M University, College Station, TX, USA
e-mail: Opengart@tamu.edu

J. C. Collins and J. L. Callahan (eds.), *The Palgrave Handbook of Critical Human Resource Development*, https://doi.org/10.1007/978-3-031-10453-4_20

367

In the following chapter, we introduce the case for close attention to emotions as part of the process of learning. We do this by providing an overview of some of the major domains of scholarly thought that have developed as an entryway to these areas. First, we recount some of the explanations that have been offered for why emotions have only played a supporting, or background, role in management and organization studies through its history of development, before moving on to a discussion of why the absence of full engagement with the topic poses a problem for human resource development. We lay out some of the psychological and sociological approaches to theorizing emotions in HRD, considering these issues at the level of individual, community, and organizational learning—as they are interlinked—and consider specific impacts in the area of equality, diversity, and inclusion. We attempt to anatomize the key issues that have been raised through the use of these theoretical tools, along with some of the ethical implications of the practices developing around emotion management.

These topics are, of course, not exhaustive, but the following text will provide you with a window into the field, and an excellent 'jumping off point' to deep dive into any issues you wish to explore further.

WHY EMOTIONS ARE INTEGRAL TO HUMAN RESOURCE DEVELOPMENT

Why Have Emotions Been Missing from HRD?

The display of emotions in one's job has historically been viewed as irrational, non-controlled, and something which needed to be managed (Domagalski, 1999). Researchers seem to agree that this inclination to separate emotion and cognition has resulted in 'marginalizing emotions and elevating rationality to a supreme position' (Dirkx, 2001, p. 67). Dirkx (2008) stated that emotions have 'for many years been regarded as separate from both our cognitive and bodily processes, and an anathema to reason and knowing' (p. 14). Eynde and Turner (2006) agreed that, 'still far too often, the head (cognitions) and the heart (emotions) are perceived as two distinct entities when learning is concerned' (p. 373). But why has this been the case? In part we can trace this to a philosophical perspective that views the separation of heart and mind as *possible* in the legacy of the much-cited 'Cartesian mind–body dualism' (Thanem, 2016), although this notion may not have been produced in the writings of Descartes himself (see Butler & Dunne, 2012). Another facet of the explanation may lie in how the separation of emotionality from working life has become *desirable*. If we examine the fashions of approach to management that have gained a stronghold in different eras of history, we get some sense as to how this has occurred.

As part of her work examining the status of the worker in contemporary management through tracking technologies, Moore (2017) develops a useful 'six wave' timeline for understanding the way in which the human body—and its material and emotional needs—has been viewed in different eras of management development—shifting back and forth between being seen as something integral or separate to the interests of management. Starting from 1870 to 1900, Moore describes the first wave as 'Industrial Betterment.' In this era, the normative management approaches that had been dominant prior to the US Civil War had largely ignored issues of employee welfare. Figures such as James Montgomery (Scottish poet and editor) and Robert Owen (Welsh social reformer and key investor in the development of cooperativism, trade unionism, and the New Lanark textile mills) had been making recommendations for a form of 'welfare capitalism' that considered the wellbeing of workers as an important part of organizing and employer responsibility. These calls had largely gone unheeded until this time when a handful of clergymen and intellectuals began to have some influence and 'industrial partnerships' began to gain ground as a concept for work (Barley & Kunda, 1992). The industrial betterment model included initiatives such as social clubs, education for workers' children, and other benefits. However, this era was followed up by a sharp turn into Scientific Management (1900–1923): influenced by the work of F.W. Taylor and the Gilbreths, this approach to management drew a stark distinction between the mind and body in relation to work, with the former seen to be the domain of skilled management and the latter located in the 'unskilled' workforce. Workers' bodies were subject to scrutiny through fine-grained measurement: heart rate, fatigue levels, time taken to complete each element of the production process. Employees were regarded much as machines that could be subject to scientific study and optimized for maximal output (Fleischmann & Ozbilgin, 2009 for an intersectional re-reading of Scientific Management). Remaining influential for over a quarter of a century, and interpreting Moore's analysis of it, we can see how this way of thinking about work and working life may have led to the casting out of emotion almost entirely beyond the frame for management interest and research.

Later, Moore recounts waves of 'Human Relations' and 'Organizational Culture and Quality' that sought to return to a recognition of workers as thinking, feeling beings and brought sociology, psychology, and anthropology to bear on generating understandings of organizational life. After some further diversions back and forth to approaches that resisted and reposition the field away from an emphasis on the 'human side' of management (Moore, 2017), the question of how work becomes meaningful for people gained an increasingly central place in management research from the 1980s onward as the labor market transformed in ways that placed greater emphasis on generating knowledge and symbolic capital, engaging workers, improving the employment relationship, and as a fundamental human need (for more, see Bailey et al., 2019; Yeoman, 2014). There have been important critiques of the way in which organizations have implemented the cultivation of strong workplace cultures and the dynamics of power that this can entail both (Alvesson & Willmott, 2002), but work in this broad area remains a key area of interest for human resource development today. Within this stream of work, there remain concerns about who becomes included, and seen as belonging in organizations, and this research gives us further clues as to why emotions become backgrounded as an area of priority or even attention in practice. The concept of the 'ideal worker' describes the fantasy employee around which many workplace policies are modelled: a worker who can work for long hours, for uninterrupted periods of time, who is ever-flexible, and is even able to move geographically if required, a notion connected with the 'gendered organization' (Acker, 2006).

EMOTIONS AND WORKPLACE INEQUALITIES

Such a model as the 'ideal worker' leaves little room for the accommodation of emotional life. Although there is some increased recognition today in theory that many, if not all, working lives fail to live up to this ideal, in practice we still have a long way to come in re-modeling our organizational policies, programs, and employee support to account for the diverse ways in which our lives, social roles, and bodies are not accounted for by 'standard templates.' The influence of masculine rationality on the field—the organization's identification with masculine characteristics such as being strong, mechanical, assertive, objective, and controlled (Bierema, 2009), has inevitably resulted in a field that might not value emotions. In addition, emotions have been traditionally associated with women and women's work (Becht et al., 2001; Fischer & LaFrance, 2015). Women, at least in the cultures of the Global North-West[1] that have come to dominate the propagation of HRD theory and practice, have occupied a socially subordinate position and thus women's work, often involving emotion work of some kind, has also become devalued (Levanon et al., 2009; Magnusson, 2009).

Yet, there has also been contestation of this, asserting that emotions are an integral part of learning in the workplace as well as an essential component of critical thought (Callahan, 2004). Bierema and Callahan (2014) have argued that masculine rationality undermines the field's humanistic values and philosophy of facilitating development and change. The authors further contend that humanistic goals seek improved systems, both human and organizational, and rather than prioritizing profit and commodifying employees, HRD's humanistic goals have long been considered as both valued and critical to the field of HRD. Metcalfe and Rees (2010) proposed the departure from humanism as a result of what Acker (2006) called the 'gendered organization,' a concept that recognizes how gendered relations—both social and economic—are built into the structure of work organizations. This structure produces norms, policies,

---

[1] We recognize that distinctions such as 'Global North/South' or 'West/East' grossly oversimplify the complex dynamics of power, wealth distribution, colonization and whiteliness throughout history, and contemporary issues resulting from historical inequalities such as vulnerability to climate change; and therefore employ this concept here as a way of highlighting the specificity of the knowledge and practices propagated from countries such as the United States, United Kingdom, Europe, Australia, and Canada.

and practices that result in gender inequality in the workplace (Fox-Kirk et al., 2020).

The gendering of emotions in work and working life has serious negative implications for women in the workplace, both affecting the value placed on their labor and associated career prospects (Becht et al., 2001). The exclusion of emotions from work, and their association with women, also has negative implications for men, meaning that the recognition of emotional experiences, and emotional display are considered anathema to masculinity and (masculine) professionalism (Fischer et al., 2013). Concerns have been raised regarding such forms of masculinity as an antecedent to poor mental wellbeing (Bradstreet & Parent, 2017; Gerdes & Levant, 2018; Hammond, 2012;) and contributor to the reinforcement of gender inequalities and the gender binary (viewing gender as strictly male/female) that lead to poor outcomes across the gender spectrum (Fischer et al., 2004).

Work that involves emotional capabilities has itself been shown as gendered. Assumptions about the role of women in society, beliefs around the 'natural' attributes of women, and gendered division of labor has meant that women have often been overrepresented and undervalued in care work, service work, primary teaching, and other roles associated with forms of 'women's work', e.g. in digital spheres, (Arcy, 2016) that involve the skillful management of emotions (Akin et al., 2014; Husso & Hirvonen, 2012; Sachs & Blackmore, 1998). Such work often bears costs and risks to those undertaking it that have also been overlooked and recognized as such (Akin et al., 2014; Colley, 2006). Furthermore, women are often held to higher expectations in the emotional aspects of work, bearing greater emotional demands, and more stringent monitoring (Grugulis, 1997), potentially trapping them in a cycle of prescription and reiteration of a gendered performance: the 'natural' female emotional adeptness.

At a global level, the dominance of management theory emanating from, and prioritizing, North America, the United Kingdom, Australia, and Europe, has meant that the 'ideal worker' envisaged within the structure of the gendered organization is not only gendered and ableized but racially marked (Boussebaa, 2020; Boussebaa & Brown, 2017; Dar et al., 2020, Nkomo, 1992). We see how this invisible ideal at the center of our organizing, quietly but powerfully marginalizes those who require, for example, flexible working patterns and employment stability, or recognition of inequalities in standards for recruitment, evaluation; or of unpaid labor being undertaken; to be able to work on a level playing field with their colleagues (Alberti et al., 2018; Chung et al., 2021; Liu & Baker, 2016; Liu et al., 2015; Rofcanin et al., 2017). Shared parental leave, baby loss leave, menstrual flexibility, racial stress policies, and adaptations for chronic pain sufferers are just some of the areas that are being advanced in response to recognizing the importance of worker embodiment today (Boncori & Brewis, 2021; Dy, 2020; Owen, 2018).

In short, the field of theory and practice in HRD has often failed to contest the notion of the ideal worker with the straight, white, middle-class male (along with dimensions of social positionality such as being able-bodied and upper-caste), and emotionality and embodiment primarily with women and women's work that have been socially devalued or undervalued. Critical HRD approaches are well-positioned to offer an antidote to many of these challenges, starting with the re-integration of emotion into our understandings of work, workers, learning, and change.

Humanism in HRD

A humanistic approach to HRD is one strand of critical thought that has been proposed by the field to address some of the concerns so far laid out in this chapter. The humanistic foundation in HRD is derived from the field of humanistic psychology and the work of Carl Rogers, and is grounded in principles asserting that employees are the primary basis for added value in an organization (McGuire et al., 2005). As an employee-centered form of management, Humanism offers the return of employee performance and commitment as a result of recognition, acknowledgment of value, care, and commitment shown to employees (Mcguire et al., 2005). The idea behind the application of humanism to the modern workplace is to treat employees not like cogs in a machine, but to create a workplace culture where employees feel valued, happy, and secure—where they feel treated like people and there are partnerships, mentorships, and teams, rather than ranks and hierarchies. The theory suggests that employees want to contribute, work hard, and stay with a company that cares for them.

The literature has supported the argument that employee-centered management approaches have many benefits. Aktouf (1992) suggested that humanistic approaches can transform the passive and obedient Taylorist employee into an active and cooperative one, and argued that workers should have control over their own environments and working conditions. Schuster (1998) found that employee-centered management practices make significant contributions to organizational performance. In addition, researchers in human resources have established a relationship between HRM and HRD practices with organizational performance (Alagaraja, 2013). Saks (2006) found that perceived organizational support predicts both job and organization engagement and subsequently, in 2019, concluded that both job characteristics and perceived organizational support are significant predictors of work engagement. Thus, Humanistic and employee-focused HRD and HRD practices seem logical as a foundation for HRD.

Yet, there have been significant challenges to its implementation. HRD has become strongly influenced by a dominant rationality in which masculine characteristics of assertiveness, objectivity, control, and performance are privileged. In other words, HRD has drifted away from the vision that humanism originally set in motion (Bierema & Callahan, 2014). Furthermore, Mcguire et al. (2005) argued that humanistic approaches to HRD, with developmental ideals focused on employee self-actualization, do not coincide with organizational actions, goals, budgetary constraints, and a market-driven economic philosophy. The authors suggest that a performance paradigm in HRD is incompatible with and unrealistic alongside the humanistic approach.

Since two seemingly incompatible streams of thought have emerged, it is clear that the path forward for HRD must involve a change. Firstly, performative theories cannot dominate the field if we are to avoid drifting away from human values toward efficiency and performance and money. Secondly, in order to favor the original humanistic values, we will need to critically consider practices that champion the maximization of human capital and increasing efficiency, to the detriment of wellbeing and equality. Such care in critical thinking about the implementation of HRD would allow for the existence of diverse values, including the expression of emotion, and consequently, people of all genders would be able to bring their whole selves to work.

EMOTIONS AS PART OF LEARNING

The psychological and sociological theories of emotion that have developed as part of wider organization studies are particularly relevant to the field of HRD since its interests and practices are primarily concerned with training and development, that is—learning. Emotions have a longer history of recognition as part of the learning process more generally and so this is a rich area of theory that we can turn to for understanding of how emotions form part of the way an organization can foster learning among its members.

As research gradually began to recognize that emotions are not the antithesis of rationality, as had been so traditionally valued (Putnam et al., 1993), but instead a key part of *how we reason* and therefore relate to one another socially. Taking this logic further, we can even argue that emotions are part of the very way that we think in general; the way we process information (Nussbaum, 2003). The growth of interest in these areas is a reflection of increasing acceptance that everyday emotions are a part of organizational life. The foundation for many of the lines of research that connect emotions and learning is the notion that learning is ultimately a process of meaning-making. Dirkx (2006) has noted that 'relatively few scholars and practitioners in adult and higher education regard emotion as integral to the meaning-making process' (p. 16). Conversely, Gabriel and Griffiths argue that 'far from being emotional deserts, organizations are full of emotions and passion' (2002, p. 214). A growing body of publications indicates that emotions and cognition are both interrelated and interdependent (Domagalski, 1999, p. 1).

Sensemaking theories are grounded in a social constructionist perspective and view the change that occurs through processes of learning to be chiefly a product of (re)constituting the way in which we understand the world, including our identities (who we are, and who we are in relation to others), the nature of the world, and what is legitimate or moral (Brown et al., 2009; Colville et al., 2016; Weick et al., 2005). If organizations are the continual

achievement of—or striving for—a collective understanding of goals and practices, then they can be said to be a product of sensemaking (Weick et al.,
2005). At the level of the individual, Maitlis et al. (2013) show in their work
how emotions provide the stimulus to begin periods of sensemaking, and the
energy to fuel it. They discuss how emotions can influence whether this process
remains solitary, or becomes interpersonal; and whether it is generative or integrative. The process of 'making sense' is highly political and the outcome of
whose logics and values become dominant, accepted, or taken for granted is
influenced by both positive emotions such as pride, joy, and gratitude; as well
as negative ones such as fear and guilt (Mikkelsen & Wahlin, 2020).

Dirkx (2008) has shown that teachers are aware of the extent that emotions
come into play when teaching. The author found that across multiple settings,
adult teaching was acknowledged as being rooted in the relationships developed between teachers and students, and is therefore, inherently emotional.
Brookfield (2013) also noted the importance of emotions in learning due to
power dynamics within the adult classroom. The author further contends that
teachers who teach about power, racism, or any challenge to the dominant
rationality, experience an even greater intensity of emotion in the classroom,
in line with extensive research by Derald Wing Sue (2013). Furthermore,
teachers may process their own emotional response to the interactions of
the classroom, where these emotions inform reflections on the perception
and self-evaluation of their teaching skills. This may result in them gaining
confidence in their roles, or conversely perceiving the emotional character of
certain interactions as indicative of failure. According to Brookfield, failures
in the classroom are experienced more emotionally than successes (2013).
The studies of Crossman (2007) and Demetriou et al (2009) both examined teachers and the interplay of emotions and relationships in learning.
Crossman (2007) also suggested the importance of context, discussing how
teaching and learning occur within a particular context, between people who
interact, have relationships, and experience feelings about those relationships.
Individual learning involves not only the mind, but the body and emotions
and are embedded in social and physical contexts. Emotions affect communication and engagement between people and serve as a catalyst for learning
(Demetriou et al, 2009). Such studies indicate that skills are required in the
workplace at an individual as well as interpersonal level.

Clarke (2006a, 2006b) suggested that the development of emotional abilities is influenced by the specific workplace context and by performing the job
itself. Through observing workplace learning in UK hospice workers, Clarke
concluded that emotional abilities are best developed on-the-job, and therefore understood when considered within the specific work context in which
they are performed. The authors suggest that this may be the most effective manner in which to develop emotional abilities, rather than through
traditional, decontextualized training interventions. Emotions may also impact
trainers, trainees, and the effectiveness of training designs. Short and Yorks
(2002) shared examples of how emotions can play a critical role, including

potential situations such as: influencing attitudes toward learning needs and attending training, response to course material, process, and context, as well as social interactions. Emotions could also potentially act to obstruct the performance and effectiveness of both trainers and trainees.

In a comprehensive review of the role that emotional and aesthetic labor plays in HRD, Grugulis (2007) develops an argument surrounding the growth in importance of and emphasis on the 'soft skills' in organizing: 'the way workers feel and the feelings they produce in others have become, for many, the main aim of work' (2007, p. 29). As an accompaniment to this, the centrality of emotional acuity poses to recruitment and selection as attributes that can be highly subjective to evaluate thus rendering the process at increased mercy of dominant power relations relating to gender and race. The review considers the extensive degree to which contemporary professionals are required to demonstrate certain kinds of commitment and engagement to their jobs through dressing and even 'feeling' in particular ways. Emotions therefore represent both ways of making sense of interactions, but also ways in which organizational members seek to shape the ways in which others make sense of them. As such, Grugulis describes emotions as an integral part of the modern employment contract, integrated with the constellation of control mechanisms through which management exercises subtle, or 'soft' (Aromaa et al., 2020) forms of control through identity work (see also Knights & Willmott, 1999; Stavrakakis, 2008; Sturdy et al., 2006), factors that necessarily inform how we consider the developmental practices of HRD.

PSYCHOLOGICAL APPROACHES TO EMOTIONS IN HRD

In this section, we take a slightly 'deeper dive' into two primary contributors to the theorization of emotions in organizations that take a psychological perspective. Starting with psychodynamics, an approach that considers how the unconscious mind may influence and be influenced by emotions as we seek to organize ourselves with others; and subsequently emotional intelligence, as it pertains to the ability to process information about one's own emotions and those of others, as well as the ability to use this information to guide thoughts and behavior.

Psychodynamics

Psychodynamic theories are a perspective that takes a 'depth' psychology approach to understanding the workings of the mind (Gabriel, 1999). It considers how both mind and body are intertwined in experiencing the world. Psychodynamics has been a fruitful area of management research in helping us to understand strong emotional responses or what may appear to be irrational behaviors, by examining them as products of the unconscious processes of the mind. Psychodynamics refers broadly to theories developed from the psychoanalytic perspective and often confers particular attention to the early stages as being critical in the development of the adult subject. This perspective relies on the assumption of psychic causality, which says that our feelings and behaviors come from somewhere in our minds, even if that location is not consciously known to us. As with many 'grand theories' it would be difficult to fully explore the contributions and complexity of the approach, and the debates that surround it (see for example Kenny, 2009). However, in the following section, we will introduce some of the key ideas from this theoretical framework as a starting point to showing what it can offer in terms of understanding emotions and learning.

In *The Interpretation of Dreams* (1900), Freud introduced what is known as the topographical model of the mind. This maps three main levels of the mind: the conscious, the preconscious, and the unconscious. The first encompasses the material (thoughts, feelings, memories) that are known to us, the second contains material that we are aware of but which we are not paying attention to at a given moment, and the third contains material that are *not* known to us, that have been repressed. The unconscious holds certain thoughts, feelings, desires, and fantasies outside of the conscious mind as a form of protection so that we become unaware of them. This repressed material is constituted of that which would conflict, be deemed unacceptable or reprehensible within the moral social frameworks in which we live, and according to psychodynamic theory, we all experience drives, impulses, and desires of this nature. In the topology of the mind, the three levels are characterized as the ego, the id, and the superego. Starting with the id, this area of the psyche seeks instant gratification and operates according to the 'pleasure principle' seeking immediate fulfillment of desires. The ego on the contrary, is the decision-making area of the mind, operating according to the 'reality principle' of what is realistic, feasible, and appropriate. Supporting this function is the superego which is the conscience of the psyche providing guidance on moral frameworks, prohibitions, and positive aspirational frameworks. This develops later in childhood, learnt from caregivers through rewards, punishments, and traditions. According to this theory, when we contravene the standards set out by the superego we feel anxiety, guilt, and a desire to atone or make amends. Such 'senses' contribute to our embodied experience of work, but may not be recognized under the umbrella of 'emotions.' This framework has been used to understand the way in which people experience organizational life, see for example analysis of female executives in accounting and finance in Baker and Brewis (2020a, 2020b) and Baker and Kelan (2019).

A more common approach to psychodynamics that may be found in the management and organizational studies literature draws from the writings of Jacques Lacan. Lacan's writings are dense and difficult to follow (it is argued, deliberately) and, consequently, are difficult to summarize concisely. For the purposes of this short introduction, however, we can say that Lacan takes an approach that places a greater emphasis on language in early childhood development. More precisely, it is the construction of the symbolic order of our social fabric that Lacan sees as fundamental to the way in which we begin to understand ourselves as subjects and to develop a sense of agency. The sense of self that we build relies upon a 'system of signifiers that constitutes the source of all social meanings and identities' (Nadesan & Trethewey, 2000, p. 225). Some of these signifiers play a more dominant role than others, for example relating to gender, race, sexuality, and class. This symbolic order allows us to articulate ourselves in relation to others (as different to or similar to others) in combination with fantasies to which we become deeply attached (Glynos, 2008; Kenny et al., 2020). Our reality and experience can, however, never fully 'be grasped and represented in language' and this causes us anxiety, we are always continuously 'becoming' in organizations (Harding, 2007). At times, we sense antagonism between the symbolic coherence that we search for, but which can never fully be achieved, and the unconscious part of the psyche helps us to cope with this (Driver, 2009).

These perspectives can aid us in gaining an understanding of the role that emotions play in processes of learning, and thus development, as it helps us to appreciate: a) why individuals may engage in behaviors that may initially seem to us illogical or counter-productive, and b) the role of early childhood development in the way we encounter new situations and ideas as adults. It offers an alternative way of conceptualizing emotion, positioning deep-seated anxiety as a central player in determining our responses in organizational life. Psychoanalytic work in management and organization studies has helped us to advance our understanding of learning significantly: Antonacoupolou and Gabriel (2001) anatomize the ways in which emotions are products of learning, and facilitate or inhibit learning in various, subtle ways; Vince and Saleem (2004) show how the psychic processes that lead to blame represent a barrier to learning in the public sector; Clancy et al. (2012) explore the emotion of disappointment as being more than simply a threat to organizational effectiveness, and instead characterize it as an 'integrative emotion' that could provide grounds for organizational learning; and Jarret and Vince argue that 'psychoanalytic theories offer a framework for the study of emotions in organizations and for the paradoxical tensions arising from emotions' (2017, p. 48). These are just a few examples of the types of insight that have developed from this rich stream of thought. In sum, psychodynamics leads us to recognize that organizations are emotional terrains where any attempt to manage them is rife with potential problems and unexpected consequences (Gabriel & Griffiths 200), and ultimately, that there are areas of organizational life that are simply—and fundamentally—*un*manageable (Gabriel, 1995).

Emotional Intelligence

Emotional intelligence has become a key concept within the field of organizational behavior at large. Although the concept of emotional intelligence (EI) was initially popularized by Goleman (1995), there has been interest in the concept since Salovey and Mayer first published on the topic (Salovey & Mayer, 1990). Since then, research on emotional intelligence has continued, resulting in a range of competing models which describe emotional intelligence as ability-based, personality-based, as well as mixed models. Much of the EI research has suggested the importance of emotional intelligence to success in the workplace. Understanding what emotional intelligence is and its importance in the workplace is critical in today's increasingly competitive world. HRD can help set standards of behavior and support learning, leadership development, and performance improvement alongside the development of EI.

Salovey and Mayer's original emotional intelligence definition conceptualizes emotional intelligence as the ability to process information about your own emotions as well as those of others. It is also the ability to use this information to guide your own thoughts and behavior (Salovey & Mayer, 1990). The Salovey and Mayer (1990) definition of emotional intelligence is preferable because it focuses on emotional abilities that link cognition and emotion, while Goleman's (1995) definition includes social competencies that some consider to be personality traits and attitudes. In the following discussion, we offer a summary of the principal areas of research within EI to support the understanding of how EI can influence learning. Areas of research covered include EI and individuals, EI and organizations, EI and gender, and EI and culture.

EI can be considered a core concept in HRD because without a foundation of emotional competencies and emotional intelligence, learning cannot proceed successfully (Singh, 2007), as learning is enabled and enhanced through emotional abilities. In his work, Clarke (2010) sought to increase recognition of the role that emotion plays in impacting learning processes and outcomes. He examined the notion that emotional competence will affect learning by influencing the processes of critical reflection and engagement in the learning process. The author suggested that individuals use critical reflection and dialogue in order to challenge previously held beliefs and create new meaning; in other words, learn. In other studies examining a connection between emotional abilities and learning, Offermann et al (2004) found some support for a positive correlation between exam grades within teams and emotional intelligence and Hjerto (2010) concluded that high emotional intelligence is beneficial for learning outcomes in work groups. The traditional cognitive approach to individual learning has obscured the importance of emotion. These studies on EI can further enhance our understanding of the role that emotions play for individuals in the process of learning.

Emotional intelligence may also serve as a critical foundation and necessity for organizational learning to occur. Jordan (2005) examined the emotional skills required for organizational learning and suggested that each facet of EI as identified by Mayer and Salovey (1997), including: (a) emotional awareness, (b) emotional facilitation, (c) emotional knowledge, and (d) emotional regulation, are linked to the five disciplines associated with organizational learning as identified by Senge (1992). These included:

Personal mastery: Personal mastery will be enhanced from high emotional awareness and the ability to regulate their emotions.

Mental models: Challenging personal assumptions will be easier for those who have high emotional awareness.

Systems thinking: The main emotional intelligence ability that contributes to systems thinking is high emotional understanding.

Team learning: Improved team learning will occur if there is high emotional awareness and the ability to regulate emotions.

Building a shared vision: High emotional facilitation abilities, or the ability to generate emotions in others and affect the climate are essential for leaders to disseminate a shared vision and to ensure that employees take ownership of that shared vision.

In sum, Jordan (2005) concluded that organizations and programs that apply and utilize emotional intelligence can more effectively help employees learn and cope with change. Several empirical studies have examined the connection and impact of emotional intelligence on organizational learning. Dissanayaka et al (2010) studied bank employees in Sri Lanka and found EI to be positively and significantly related to organizational learning. Singh (2007) found support for a positive and significant role of emotional intelligence in organizational learning. The author argued that job behaviors required for organizational learning are the result of the interplay of both cognitive and emotional abilities and that in order to understand the organizational learning process, one must study both the cognitive and the emotional abilities of employees. Pradhan et al (2017) investigated the moderating role of emotional intelligence in the organizational learning of executives in manufacturing organizations and found that the relationship between organizational learning and performance was more significant among those executives who had higher EI levels.

In a comprehensive review of published research on emotional intelligence specifically within the HRD field, Faria and Nafukho (2015) identified themes, including: conceptual connections, aspects of EI training and development, EI measurement tools, EI career profiles of individuals, the influence of context in EI interpretation, the role of EI in interpersonal interactions, and the impact of EI on leadership development and performance. The scope of articles on training and development address the potential for strengthening one's EI. Some authors concluded that training resulted in little or no improvement (Beigi & Shirmohammadi, 2010; Clarke, 2006a, 2010; Muyia & Kacirek, 2009) and others identified potential improvements in EI from team-based training interventions (Clarke, 2006b, 2010; Moriarty & Buckley, 2003). One author suggested that educating participants on the inner biological workings of the mind would increase EI (Kunnanatt, 2012). Research indicates that some jobs might lead to more development of EI skills than others, as a result of increased challenges and experiences (Dimitriades, 2007; Yildirim, 2007). Along this line of thinking, Yildirim found that, except for the EI aspect of self-management, IT and sales employees were significantly different from each other in all aspects of the Emotional Competence Inventory. Research connecting EI and interpersonal relationships addresses the role that EI might play in enhancing interpersonal relationships. The literature addresses how EI can affect relationships between leaders and followers (Graham, 2009), between professors and students (Beigi & Shirmohammadi, 2010), and can improve collaborative problem-solving skills (Jordan &Troth, 2002). EI and Leadership have been studied with contradictory findings. Objectivity and rationality in the workplace were challenged with Goleman's (1995, 1998, 2001) publications on the role of emotions in leader effectiveness. He suggested the notion that emotions had an important place in leadership excellence. Yet the HRD literature shows contradictory findings in this regard with some stating that the association between EI and leadership effectiveness is exaggerated and lacks scholarly support (Antonakis, 2003; Fambrough & Hart, 2008; Weinberger, 2009), while others strongly support it (Ashkanasy & Tse, 2000; Ayiro, 2009; George, 2000; Shuck & Herd, 2012). As for EI measurement, HRD researchers examined different conceptual frameworks and approaches to measurement. Muyia (2009) reviewed the models and the well-known instruments while McEnrue and Groves (2006) conducted a thorough review of various measurement tools. Alternatively, using tests to measure EI was challenged by Lincoln (2009), as he warned against potentially harmful consequences.

The role of context in the interpretation of EI has been studied as a critical aspect of understanding the expression and use of emotions. The context in which emotions are expressed may need to consider a person's emotional intelligence skills as well as the necessary emotion work for the workplace. The context is a crucial element that brings meaning to the expressed emotions, as it is difficult to understand the reasoning behind a particular emotion without contextual knowledge (Opengart, 2005). Opengart demonstrated the importance of integrating EI and emotion work, because both contextual and social factors set the stage for organizationally appropriate expressions of emotions. The author argued that emotionally intelligent behaviors require an individual to be contextually aware—of what emotions are expected, acceptable and unacceptable in a given environment.

An allied area of research examines EI and gender, but is one that has yielded inconclusive results regarding the relationship between them. Early research in this area mainly measured all four facets of EI together (referring to the ability model, as defined by Salovey & Mayer, 1990). For example, Ciarrochi et al. (2001), using the MEIS, found that women out-performed men in overall EI as well as in emotion perception. Day and Carroll (2004) concluded that women scored significantly higher than men overall on the MSCEIT. Van Rooy et al (2005) examined EI scores of 275 participants and found that female participants scored slightly higher than male ones. Joseph and Newman (2010) found that differences in sex-based groups depended on which type of measure was used to assess EI, with no average gender-based differences when a self-report measure was used, but significant differences favoring women for performance-based EI tests. Thus the authors concluded that women have higher EI scores than do men.

While many studies have found that women outperform men in at least some aspects of EI, in some cases there were no clear differences in EI between men and women. Gunkel et al. (2014) found that female participants had lower scores in the areas of self-emotional appraisal and regulation of emotion, yet they scored higher than men in the emotional appraisal of others and in the use of emotion. Meshkat and Nejati (2017) administered the mixed measure EQI to 455 undergraduate university students in Iran and found that there was no significant difference in their total EI score, but women scored higher in emotional self-awareness, interpersonal relationship, self-regard, and empathy. In a study carried out in the United Kingdom, Arteche et al. (2008), using a sample of employees, did not find a significant relationship between gender and overall EI. However, some of the disparities in results may be a consequence of the type of measure. Brackett et al. (2006) found that performance and self-rated measures of EI were not strongly related, suggesting that self-perception of one's EI may not be accurate, thereby making results from those kinds of measures irrelevant.

The case has also been made for a cultural dimension to emotional intelligence. Utilizing a sample of over 2000 people in nine countries, Gunkel et al. examined the influence of Hofstede's cultural dimensions and found that collectivism, uncertainty avoidance, and long-term orientation have a positive effect on emotional intelligence. In fact, Pathak and Mulidharan (2020) suggest a culture-specific EI (CSEI). The authors argue that since emotions and their experience, expression, and management are driven by cultural values, that EI is culturally embedded and culturally specific. Similarly, Ragins and Winkel (2011) stated that expectations of emotional displays may vary for American women with different cultural backgrounds including African-American, Asian-American, and European-American women. Although Hofstede's cultural dimensions model continues to be influential, it is worth keeping in mind that it has also received criticism for overgeneralizing both the national cultures it seeks to capture, and its impact on the organizational contexts to which they are applied.

We may also draw together here discussions about culture and gender. Fisher and La France (2015) argued that the fact that women are considered to be more emotional than men is more indicative of cultural stereotypes and values than about actual gender differences. Shields (2002) studied the relationship between gender and emotion and argued that each constructs the other, and the way we learn and practice emotion is in itself a gendered process, with displays of emotion characterized as 'good' or 'bad' depending on whether they are congruent with masculine or feminine norms. Thus, it is important for us to consider how EI is socially constructed, because perceptions and judgment of men's and women's emotional skills and displays are derived in relation to the dominant symbolic representations of feminine and masculine within the context (Thory, 2012). This poses a problem for organizational and individual learning; pointing to the need to question how we can challenge and resist socially constructed mandates for gender through our learning practices.

SOCIOLOGICAL APPROACHES TO EMOTIONS IN HRD

In this section, we delve into some of the approaches that help us to think through the way in which emotions inform our organizational environments, which have emerged from theory with roots in sociology and allied disciplines. We first draw attention to a discussion on the importance of context and culture in the workplace, exploring how emotions form a crucial element of any change process that is occurring in that environment. This section rounds out with a breakdown of three key concepts that are used in the field: emotion work, emotional labor, and emotion management; outlining and delineating between them.

Context, Culture, and Change

Learning about emotion is shaped by a particular context (Bierema, 2008) as is the individual experience of emotion (Opengart, 2005) and its regulation (Von Scheve, 2012). The context in which EI is applied also plays an important role in the perception and development of emotionally intelligent behaviors and is thus shaped by social factors. Context is a critical element that allows a person to bring meaning to the application of EI and to interpret how and why to express a particular emotion (Opengart, 2005). Singh (2007) addressed the importance of context by describing individual learning as affecting organizational learning because of shared mental models. The author suggested that individual learning is connected to organizational learning through such factors as positive learning climate. This supports earlier work by Short and Yorks (2002), who examined the emotionality of training and suggested that training context influences appropriate emotional responses. They argue that the emotions of trainers and their reactions to trainees are dictated by rules and public management of their emotions. They suggest that emotion can inhibit learning for training participants and advocate facilitating the training process by developing the right climate and environment for discussing emotions and establishing a safe context for dialogue.

Argyris and Schön strongly developed and illustrated the connection between individual and organizational learning. The authors (1974) suggested that people have mental maps about how to act in situations, involving how they plan, implement, and review their actions. It is these maps that guide people's actions rather than the theories they explicitly espouse—yet few people are aware of the maps or theories they use (Argyris, 1982). In other words, there is a divide between theory and behavior/action. The authors described '*theories-in-use*,' which we use to represent our actions to others and which direct our actual behavior. The words we use to convey what we would like others to think we do, he called '*espoused theory*.' Argyris (1982) argues that effectiveness results from a match between theory-in-use and espoused theory, and if they are not congruent, and a mismatch occurs between intention and outcome, this creates an opportunity for reflection, dialogue, and learning. In this case Argyris and Schön state that two responses occur, and these are referred to as single and double-loop learning, where learning involves the detection and correction of error. When something goes wrong, often people will look for another strategy that works within the governing variables. According to Argyris and Schön (1974), this is *single-loop learning*. Alternatively, one can question and scrutinize the actual governing variables. This is what they call *double-loop learning*. This learning may then lead to a change in the governing variables and in how strategies and consequences are framed.

Thus, they came to explore the nature of organizational learning. Specifically, the authors describe the importance of exploring behaviors and patterns of beliefs if organizations are to learn and develop. An organization demonstrates *single-loop* learning when the organization continues with its present policies and objectives after errors are detected and corrected. On the contrary, *double-loop* learning occurs when after error is detected, correction occurs in ways that involve changes in an organization's underlying norms, policies, and objectives. The argument is that double-loop learning is critical, particularly in rapidly changing and often uncertain contexts (Argyris, 1982, 1990; Argyris & Schon, 1974).

It has become a common refrain that today's organizations have no choice but to engage in continual change through organizational learning and be a 'learning organization' (Senge, 1992; Watkins & Marsick, 1993). There has been a boom in attention to managing change with regard to organizational behavior: an organization's ability to deal with change through learning has been championed as providing a competitive advantage (Singh, 2007; Skinner et al., 2002) or even a 'competitive weapon' (Singh, 2007, p. 50). One of the most influential theorists on organizational change, Senge (1992) proposed that successful change can be realized using the framework of the learning organization. Through the concept of the learning organization, Senge (1992) elaborated on the need for organizations and employees to learn and continuously improve their skills and abilities. This body of theory posits that organizations must move beyond expressing ideas of the past and must continuously engage and transform. Learning is also key simply to survival. Singh (2007) suggests that 'for an organization to survive and grow, it has to let all its members from the lowest rung to the top-most level to learn as one entity rather than the other way round' (p. 56).

Argote and Miron-Spektor (2011) have provided a theoretical framework for analyzing organizational learning which takes context into consideration. The authors suggest that the environmental context includes outside factors and can vary along many dimensions. This environmental context affects the organizational experience, which then interacts with the context in order to create knowledge—thereby creating an interactive effect where organizational learning occurs in a context that includes the organization and the environment in which the organization is embedded. Organizational learning is viewed as an ongoing cycle, affecting future experiences, and creating continuous organizational learning.

Emotion Work, Emotional Labor, and Emotion Management

The three concepts of 'emotion work,' 'emotional labor,' and 'emotion management' have become useful concepts in social analyses of work and are important to distinguish. This can, however, be a tricky task as they have been used loosely and sometimes interchangeably in published research. To delineate them for our purposes, we refer to 'emotion work' as a practice that workers engage in and that has benefit 'in use' but which is not remunerated, and 'emotional labor' as having a more direct link to exchange of labor for pay. Callahan and McCollum (2002) use this delineation to argue that the term emotion work should be used only in situations where workers are managing emotions for their own benefit and are not compensated for it. On the other hand, the term emotional labor is appropriate when the management of emotions is compensated in some manner. 'Emotion management,' we use to refer to the regulation of one's emotions in response to social rules that govern behavior. We also examine how this term can refer to a worker's response to the particular rules that emanate from managerial control.

Emotion work was first defined by Hochschild (1979) as the effort to control or change emotions in oneself or in others in order to meet social guidelines. These culturally embedded guidelines, or latent 'feeling rules,' govern how a person should feel: 'Feeling rules are seen as the side of ideology that deals with emotion and feeling. Emotion management is the type of work it takes to cope with feeling rules' (p. 511), 'Essentially, emotion work demands that employees feel particular emotions themselves in order to produce specific and desirable reactions in others' (Grugulis, 2007, p. 95). Opengart has integrated the concepts of EI and emotion work in order to illustrate the contextual and social factors that dictate organizationally appropriate emotional expression. She argued that emotionally intelligent actions and decisions require an individual to be aware of context—of what emotions are expected, acceptable and unacceptable within a given culture. EI is constructed within the norms of the *organizational* culture and context (Opengart, 2005) as well as an individual's society (Bierema, 2008).

The process of 'working on one's emotions' might not necessarily involve suppression or pretense; an individual may also conjure up feelings within themselves, for example to 'psych oneself up' for an encounter. Hochschild names three 'deep' techniques of emotion work: *cognitive* (changing images or ideas through modifying emotions associated with them), *bodily* (changing the somatic or physical symptoms of emotions), and *expressive* (changing the gestures or other performances of emotions). Each technique attempts to transform the experience of emotion, and are often combined and interlinked (p. 562). Hochschild goes on to discuss what we refer to as emotional labor: 'When deep gestures of exchange enter the market sector and are bought and sold as an aspect of labor power, feelings are commoditized.' (p. 569), drawing out how the types of jobs that demand this form of labor were shaped by social class, being—at the time of writing—to a greater extent associated with middle-class roles and therefore middle-class parenting. Taking a contemporary global view, and looking at an example such as call center work, we see complexity in the association between class or other social status and emotional labor depending on the context and analytical perspective (see Korczynski, 2003; Nath, 2011; Narli & Akdemir, 2019). Through this work, we have also learnt more about strategies employed to cope with the strain of this form of labor at individual and community levels, as Grugulis notes: 'emotional labour involves workers in simulating emotions they do not always feel and subordinating their needs to those of customers and clients. This may, as shown above, bring pleasure, but it also brings pain' (p. 108). In other recent work, von Scheve C. (2012) stated that emotional labor does not primarily pursue individual goals, but is regarded as an instrumental strategy to increase economic success of an organization.

Many of the theoretical insights, organizational dynamics, and opportunities for practice that have been introduced in this chapter give rise to questions about the desirability or possibility of finding ways to manage emotions either as individuals or as a community. Further than this, however, we might also consider the ethical dimension of what emotional management entails. Referring to work by Goffman on the way we 'present' ourselves to others, Grugulis notes that 'everyone is involved in the conscious and unconscious management of impressions […] understood in this way emotion management is a natural process. […] Yet what Goffman fails to take account of are the power relations that exist in the workplace. Expressive and performative elements may be a normal part of any life but when they are used in the workplace under the direction of management they become commodities' (2007, pp. 102–103).

Looking at the management of emotions as response to the exercise of power, we have recognized that attempts to influence the 'inner' lives of organizational actors represent the mobilization of control on the part of managers. Alvesson and Willmott (2002) discuss how organizations that manage through 'culture' seek to shape the identities of employees through a form of 'soft' regulation that operates often imperceptibly and, depending on whose interests one looks at the issue, insidiously. Rahmouni et al. (2019) show how this can lead to resistance. Brewis develops a similar argument in relation to inclusion training, complicating an often taken-for-granted 'good' (2019); and warns that emotions can be co-opted into an organizational strategy to the detriment of advancing equality (2017). Going further, Moore (2017) investigates contemporary self-tracking technologies and the way in which they too produce covert regulatory effects at the affective and embodied level.

As management and management technologies continue to innovate, critical reflection on how it is implemented, for whose interests, and at what cost will be crucial. Grugulis (2007) notes that: 'work is not redesigned to accommodate employees' emotions: rather employees are redesigned to fit what is deemed as necessary at work' (p. 94).

Stepping away from the direct hand of management, work has begun to explore how emotions are *social*. Deploying the concept of 'affect' to describe this Ahmed (2018) shows how emotions are a key part of sociability wherein we register the emotions of others and this creates bonds, even at the scale of a nation (2014b). For an overview of key writers on 'affect' see Hunter and Kivinen (2022). This line of work has made way for the development of understanding into why social structures that most consider unjust and unwanted continue to exist. Trying to understand the phenomenon of racism as a feature of society, Ahmed (2004) highlights how emotions that become felt in relation to groups of people are informed by the past and by what is felt as the 'collective.' She argues that negative affect seems to 'stick' to certain groups of people, powerfully influencing how they are positioned in the socio-symbolic hierarchy and contributing to the durability of racism (2014a). In parallel, she argues that 'happiness' as a socially acceptable emotion has impeded the progress of feminism as the discourses that privilege it mean that the movement is experienced negatively as causing unhappiness, and that the persistent recognition of societal inequality is a 'killjoy' who must be stopped (2010).

Management scholars have begun to explore what this means for the processes of sensemaking and learning in organizations (Vitry et al., 2020). Research into how racism is taught and discussed in organizations, including higher education, has revealed the complex emotional dynamics in operation. Derald Wing Sue (2013) anatomizes the emotional fallout in situations where (white) people experience what we might refer to as 'racial stress'—a form of distress where lack of practice engaging with 'race talk' (about race, racism, white privilege, and whiteness) causes feelings that may include anxiety and guilt. Common defense reactions to this stress include crying, physical or emotional withdrawal, pointing to exceptions, denying the experience, derailing and focusing on intentions rather than effects (DiAngelo, 2018; Sue, 2013, 2016). In order to confront and break down these barriers to learning conversations around race, alongside becoming what Sue conceptualizes as more racially 'literate' to engage in these dialogues, we may also see the necessity of greater emotional reflexivity and regulation as recognized in the ground-rules developed by anti-racist activist communities. There is much more to understand about how emotions operate at the level of the community and how these dynamics shape opportunity and oppression in working lives. We might also consider the question of ethics, and glimpse potential future avenues of research and practice by viewing the management of emotions as part of social justice praxis in advancing equality.

CONCLUSION AND IMPLICATIONS

We hope that this chapter has shown how emotions are a fundamental part of how we organize and therefore how they need to be a core component of work in human resource development. We have introduced some of the key concepts that will help you orient your own further learning as well and integrate this awareness into HRD practice. By charting the way in which emotions have been sidelined in the history of management theory and practice, we have delved into some of the false dichotomies that the neglect of this topic presents in the organizational space. First, a prescriptive and damaging binary of feminine/masculine in relation to emotional experience, expression, and labor: the dominance of masculine rationality—an association between a 'masculine' reason positioned in contrast to 'feminine' emotionality—still has an enduring effect in our working lives and material implication for the labor market. The gendered ascription of emotion means that people of all genders face difficulties in bringing their whole selves to work.

Implications for practice suggest the importance of a critical approach to HRD, as CHRD is well-positioned to contest accepted beliefs of workers, will challenge the gendering of emotion, alongside the gender binary itself, and can resist and facilitate the transformation toward healthier workplaces. Second, we have shown how other axes of power such as class and race shape how emotions circulate and often serve to retrench inequalities and argue that there are opportunities and responsibilities in the future development of HRD to explore how practice can resist this. Overall, we have produced a map of the ways in which emotion is a fundamental part of learning. By looking at a constellation of concepts using the heuristic tool of delineating sociological and psychological perspectives, we see how emotions strongly influence the way we organize, as they are experienced and expressed at the level of the individual, group, and community. As for research implications, HRD also needs to critically assess and integrate concepts and theory, and ultimately prioritize emotion in our work within HRD. This will allow us to increase our capacity to transform organizations into spaces that are more effective as well as inclusive, that promote wellbeing, and which reflect our nature and needs as *human*.

REFERENCES

Acker, J. (2006). Inequality regimes: Gender, class, and race in organizations. *Gender & Society, 20*(4), 441–464.

Ahmed, S. (2004). Collective feelings: Or, the impressions left by others. *Theory, Culture & Society, 21*(2), 25–42.

Ahmed, S. (2018). Sociable happiness. Chapter 3 In D. Spencer, K. Walby & A. Hunt (Eds.), *Emotions matter* (pp. 40–62). University of Toronto Press.

Akın, U., Aydın, İ, Erdoğan, Ç., & Demirkasımoğlu, N. (2014). Emotional labor and burnout among Turkish primary school teachers. *The Australian Educational Researcher, 41*(2), 155–169.

Aktouf, O. (1992). Management theories of organizations in the 1990's: Towards a critical radical humanism? *Academy of Management Review, 17*(3), 407–417.

Alagaraja, M. (2013). HRD and HRM perspectives on organizational performance: A review of literature. *Human Resource Development Review, 12*(2), 117–143.

Alberti, G., Bessa, I., Hardy, K., Trappmann, V., & Umney, C. (2018). In, against and beyond precarity: Work in insecure times. *Work, Employment and Society, 32*(3), 447–457.

Alvesson, M., & Willmott, H. (2002). Identity regulation as organizational control: Producing the appropriate individual. *Journal of Management Studies, 39*(5), 619–644.

Antonacopoulou, E. P., & Gabriel, Y. (2001). Emotion, learning and organizational change: Towards an integration of psychoanalytic and other perspectives. *Journal of Organizational Change Management, 14*(5), 435–451. https://doi.org/10.1108/EUM0000000005874

Antonakis, J. (2003). Why "emotional intelligence" does not predict leadership effectiveness: A comment on Prati, Douglas, Ferris, Ammeter, and Buckley (2003). *The International Journal of Organizational Analysis, 11*(4), 355–361. https://doi.org/10.1108/eb028980

Arcy, J. (2016). Emotion work: Considering gender in digital labor. *Feminist Media Studies, 16*(2), 365–368.

Argote, L., & Miron-Spektor, E. (2011). Organizational learning: From experience to knowledge. *Organization Science, 22*(5), 1123–1137.

Argyris, C., & Schon, D. A. (1974). *Theory in practice: Increasing professional effectiveness.* Jossey-Bass.

Argyris, C. (1982). The executive mind and double-loop learning. *Organizational Dynamics, 11*(2), 5–22.

Argyris, C. (1990). *Overcoming organizational defenses: Facilitating organizational learning.* Allyn & Bacon.

Aromaa, E., Eriksson, P., & Montonen, T. (2020). Show it with feeling: Performed emotions in critical sensemaking. *International Journal of Entrepreneurship and Innovation Management, 24*(4–5), 266–280.

Arteche, A., Chamorro-Premuzic, T., Furnham, A., & Crump, J. (2008). The relationship of trait EI with personality, IQ and sex in a UK sample of employees. *International Journal of Selection and Assessment, 16*, 421–426.

Ashkanasy, N. M., & Tse, B. (2000). *Transformational leadership as management of emotion: A conceptual review.*

Ayiro, L. P. (2009). An analysis of emotional intelligence and the performance of principals in selected schools in Kenya. *Advances in Developing Human Resources, 11*(6), 719–746.

Bailey, C., Lips-Wiersma, M., Madden, A., Yeoman, R., Thompson, M., & Chalofsky, N. (2019). The five paradoxes of meaningful work: Introduction to the special issue 'meaningful work: Prospects for the 21st century.' *Journal of Management Studies, 56*(3), 481–499.

Baker, D. T., & Brewis, D. N. (2020a). The melancholic subject: A study of self-blame as a gendered *Society, 82*, 101093.

Baker, D. T., & Kelan, E. K. (2019). Splitting and blaming: The psychic life of neoliberal executive women. *Human Relations, 72*(1), 69–97.

Baker, D. T., & Brewis, D. N. (2020b). The melancholic subject: A study of self-blame as a gendered and neoliberal psychic response to loss of the 'perfect worker.' *Accounting, Organizations and Society, 82,* 101093.

Barley, S. R., & Kunda, G. (1992, September 1). Design and devotion: Surges of rational and normative ideologies of control in managerial discourse. *Administrative Science Quarterly, 37*(3), 363–399.

Becht, M. C., Poortinga, Y. H., & Vingerhoets, A. J. J. M. (2001). Crying across countries. In A. J. J. M. Vingerhoets, & R. R. Cornelius (Eds.), *Adult crying: A biopsychosocial approach* (pp. 135–159). Brunner Routledge.

Beigi, M., & Shirmohammadi, M. (2010). Training employees of a public Iranian bank on emotional intelligence competencies. *Journal of European Industrial Training, 34*(3), 211–225. https://doi.org/10.1108/03090591011031728

Bierema, L. L. (2008). Adult learning in the workplace: Emotion work or emotion learning? *New Directions for Adult and Continuing Education, 2008*(120), 55–64.

Bierema, L. L. (2009). Critiquing human resource development's dominant masculine rationality and evaluating its impact. *Human Resource Development Review, 8*(1), 68–96.

Bierema, L., & Callahan, J. L. (2014). Transforming HRD: A framework for critical HRD practice. *Advances in Developing Human Resources, 16*(4), 429–444.

Boncori, I., & Brewis, D. N. (2021). *The body of work* series, funded by the Wellcome Trust, https://bodyofworkseminar.wordpress.com/

Boussebaa, M. (2020). Identity regulation and globalization. In A. D. Brown (Ed.), *The oxford handbook of identities in organizations.* Oxford University Press.

Boussebaa, M., & Brown, A. D. (2017). Englishization, identity regulation and imperialism. *Organization Studies, 38*(1), 7–29.

Brackett, M. A., Rivers, S. E., Shiffman, S., Lerner, N., & Salovey, P. (2006). Relating emotional abilities to social functioning: A comparison of self-report and performance measures of emotional intelligence. *Journal of personality and social psychology, 91*(4), 780–795.

Bradstreet, T. C., & Parent, M. C. (2017). To be (healthy) or not to be: Moderated mediation of the relationships between masculine norms, future orientation, family income, and college men's healthful behaviors. *Psychology of Men & Masculinity, 19,* 500–511. https://doi.org/10.1037/men0000129

Brewis, D. N. (2017). Social justice 'lite'? Using emotion for moral reasoning in diversity practice. *Gender, Work & Organization, 24*(5), 519–532.

Brewis, D. N. (2019). Duality and fallibility in practices of the self: The 'inclusive subject' in diversity training. *Organization Studies, 40*(1), 93–114.

Brookfield, S. D. (2013). *Powerful techniques for teaching adults.* ProQuest Ebook Central https://ebookcentral.proquest.com

Brown, A. D., Gabriel, Y., & Gherardi, S. (2009). Storytelling and change: An unfolding story. *Organization, 16*(3), 323–333.

Butler, N., & Dunne, S. (2012). Duelling with dualisms: Descartes, Foucault and the history of organizational limits. *Management & Organizational History, 7*(1), 31–44.

Callahan, J. L. (2004). Breaking the cult of rationality: Mindful awareness of emotion in the critical theory classroom. *New Directions for Adult and Continuing Education, 102,* 75–83.

Callahan, J. L., & McCollum, E. E. (2002). Obscured variability: The distinction between emotion work and emotional labor. *Managing Emotions in the Workplace*, 219–231.

Chung, H., Birkett, H., Forbes, S., & Seo, H. (2021). Covid-19, Flexible Working, and Implications for Gender Equality in the United Kingdom. *Gender & Society*, 08912432211001304.

Ciarrochi, J., Chan, A. Y., & Bajgar, J. (2001). Measuring emotional intelligence in adolescents. *Personality and individual differences, 31*(7), 1105–1119.

Clarke, N. (2006a). Emotional intelligence training: A case of caveat emptor. *Human Resource Development Review, 5*(4), 422–441.

Clarke, N. (2006b). Developing emotional intelligence through workplace learning: Findings from a case study in healthcare. *Human Resource Development International, 9*(4), 447–465.

Clarke, N. (2010). Developing emotional intelligence abilities through team-based learning. *Human Resource Development Quarterly, 21*(2), 119–138.

Clancy, A., Vince, R., & Gabriel, Y. (2012). That unwanted feeling: A psychodynamic study of disappointment in organizations. *British Journal of Management, 23*(4), 518–531.

Colley, H. (2006). Learning to labor with feeling: Class, gender and emotion in childcare education and training. *Contemporary Issues in Early Childhood, 7*(1), 15–29.

Colville, I., Pye, A., & Brown, A. D. (2016). Sensemaking processes and Weickarious learning. *Management Learning, 47*(1), 3–13.

Crossman, J. (2007). The role of relationships and emotions in student perceptions of learning and assessment. *Higher Education Research & Development, 26*(3), 313–327.

Dar, S., Liu, H., Martinez Dy, A., & Brewis, D. N. (2020). The business school is racist: Act up! *Organization*, 1350508420928521.

Day, A., & Carroll, S. (2004). Using ability-based measure of emotional intelligence to predict individual performance and group citizenship behaviors. *Personality and Individual Differences, 36*(6), 1443–1458.

Demetriou, H., Wilson, E., & Winterbottom, M. (2009). The role of emotion in teaching: Are there differences between male and female newly qualified teachers' approaches to teaching? *Educational Studies, 35*(4), 449–473.

DiAngelo, R. (2018). *White fragility: Why it's so hard for white people to talk about racism*. Beacon Press.

Dirkx, J. M. (2001). The power of feelings: Emotion, imagination, and the construction of meaning in adult learning. *New Directions for Adult and Continuing Education, 2001*(89), 63.

Dirkx, J. (2006). Engaging emotions in adult learning: A Jungian perspective on emotion and transformative learning. New Directions for Adult and Continuing Education, 109, 15–26. Jossey-Bass *Adult and continuing education, 2008*(120), 7–18.

Dirkx, J. M. (2008). The meaning and role of emotions in adult learning. *New Directions for Adult and Continuing Education, 2008*(120), 7–18.

Dimitriades, Z. S. (2007). Managing emotionally intelligent service workers: Personal and positional effects in the Greek context. *Journal of European Industrial Training, 31*(3), 223–240.

Dissanayaka, D. R., Janadari, M. P. N., & Chathurani, R. A. I. (2010). *Role of emotional intelligence in organizational learning: An empirical study based on the banking sector in Sri Lanka."*. University of Kelaniya, Srilanka.

Domagalski, T. A. (1999). Emotion in organizations: Main currents. *Human Relations, 52*(6), 833–853.

Driver, M. (2009). Struggling with lack: A Lacanian perspective on organizational identity. *Organization Studies, 30*(1), 55–72.

Dy, A. M. (2020). *Racial stress leave initiative*, University of Loughborough. See https://www.lboro.ac.uk/news-events/news/2020/october/bame-support/

Eynde, P., & Turner, J. E. (2006). Focusing on the complexity of emotion issues in academic learning: A dynamical component systems approach. *Educational Psychology Review, 18*(4), 361–376.

Fambrough, M. J., & Kaye Hart, R. (2008). Emotions in leadership development: A critique of emotional intelligence. *Advances in Developing Human Resources, 10*(5), 740–758.

Farnia, F., & Nafukho, F. M. (2016, February). Emotional intelligence research within human resource development scholarship. *European Journal of Training and Development, 40*(2), 90–110. https://doi.org/10.1108/EJTD-11-2014-0073

Fischer, A. H., Eagly, A. H., & Oosterwijk, S. (2013). The meaning of tears: Which sex seems emotional depends on the social context. *European Journal of Social Psychology, 43*, 505–515. https://doi.org/10.1002/ejsp.1974

Fischer, A., & LaFrance, M. (2015). What drives the smile and the tear: Why women are more emotionally expressive than men. *Emotion Review, 7*(1), 22–29.

Fischer, A. H., Rodriguez Mosquera, P. M., Van Vianen, A. E., & Manstead, A. S. (2004). Gender and culture differences in emotion. *Emotion, 4*(1), 87.

Fleischmann, A., & Ozbilgin, M. F. (2009). Queering the principles: A Queer/intersectional reading of Frederick W. Taylor's 'The Principles of Scientific Management'. *Equality, diversity and inclusion at work: Theory and scholarship*, 159–170.

Fox-Kirk, W., Gardiner, R. A., Finn, H., & Chisholm, J. (2020). Genderwashing: The myth of equality. *Human Resource Development International, 23*(5), 586–597. https://doi.org/10.1080/13678868.2020.1801065

Gabriel, Y. (1995). The unmanaged organization: Stories, fantasies and subjectivity. *Organization Studies, 16*(3), 477–501.

Gabriel, Y. (1999). *Organizations in depth: The psychoanalysis of organizations*. Sage.

Gabriel, Y., & Griffiths, D. S. (2002). Emotion, learning and organizing. *The learning organization*.

George, J. M. (2000). Emotions and leadership: The role of emotional intelligence. *Human Relations, 53*(8), 1027–1055.

Gerdes, Z. T., & Levant, R. F. (2018). Complex relationships among masculine norms and health/well-being outcomes: Correlation patterns of the conformity to masculine norms inventory subscales. *American Journal of Men's Health, 12*, 229–240. https://doi.org/10.1177/1557988317745910

Glynos, J. (2008). Ideological fantasy at work. *Journal of political Ideologies, 13*(3), 275–296.

Goleman, D. (1995). *Emotional intelligence: Why it can matter more than IQ*, Bantam.

Goleman, D. (1998). *Working with emotional intelligence*. Bantam.

Goleman, D. (2001). Emotional intelligence: Issues in paradigm building. In C. Cherniss & D. Goleman (Eds.), *Emotional intelligence workplace: How to select for, measure, and improve emotional intelligence in individuals, groups, and organizations* (pp. 13–26). Jossey-Bass.

Graham, C. M. (2009). Communications technology, emotional intelligence, and impact on performance: A conceptual exploration of connections. *Advances in Developing Human Resources, 11*(6), 773–783.

Grugulis, I. (1997). The consequences of competence: A critical assessment of the Management NVQ. *Personnel Review.*

Grugulis, I. (2007). *Skills, training, and human resource development.* Palgrave. Chapter 6, pp. 92–114.

Gunkel, M., Schlägel, C., & Engle, R. L. (2014). Culture's influence on emotional intelligence: An empirical study of nine countries. *Journal of International Management, 20*(2), 256–274.

Hammond, W. P. (2012). Taking it like a man: Masculine role norms as moderators of the racial discrimination—Depressive symptoms association among African American men. *American Journal of Public Health, 102*(Suppl. 2), S232–S241. https://doi.org/10.2105/AJPH.2011.300485

Harding, N. (2007). On Lacan and the 'becoming-ness' of organizations/selves. *Organization Studies, 28*(11), 1761–1773.

Hjertø, K. B. (2010). *The relationship between emotional intelligence and learning outcomes, and the mediating role of emotional conflict.*

Hochschild, A. (1979). Emotion work, feeling rule, and social structure. *American Journal of Sociology, 85,* 551–575.

Hunter, C., & Kivinen, N. (Eds.). (2022). *Affect in organization and management.* Routledge.

Husso, M., & Hirvonen, H. (2012). Gendered agency and emotions in the field of care work. *Gender, Work & Organization, 19*(1), 29–51.

Jarrett, M., & Vince, R. (2017). Psychoanalytic theory, emotion and organizational paradox. In M. W. Lewis, W. K. Smith, P. Jarzabkowski, & A. Langley (Eds.), *The handbook of organizational paradox: Approaches to plurality* (pp. 48–65). Oxford University Press.

Jordan, P. J. & Troth, A. C. (2002). Emotional intelligence and conflict resolution: Implications for human resource development. *Advances in Developing Human Resources,* Special Edition Perspectives of Emotion and Organizational Change, *4*(1), 62–79.

Jordan, P. (2005). Dealing with organizational change: Can emotional intelligence enhance organizational learning. *International Journal of Organizational Behavior, 8*(1), 456–471.

Joseph, D. L., & Newman, D. A. (2010). Emotional intelligence: An integrative meta-analysis and cascading model. *Journal of Applied Psychology, 95*(1), 54–78.

Kenny, K. (2009). Heeding the stains: Lacan and organizational change. *Journal of Organizational Change Management.*

Kenny, K., Haugh, H., & Fotaki, M. (2020). Organizational form and pro-social fantasy in social enterprise creation. *Human Relations, 73*(1), 94–123.

Knights, D., & Willmott, H. (1999). *Management lives: Power and identity in work organizations.* Sage.

Korczynski, M. (2003). Communities of coping: Collective emotional labour in service work. *Organization, 10*(1), 55–79.

Kunnanatt, J. T. (2012). Emotional intelligence–neurobiological insights for HRD/training professionals. *Economics, Management, and Financial Markets, 3,* 53–69.

Levanon, A., England, P., & Allison, P. (2009). *Social Forces (university of North Carolina Press), 88*(2), 865–891. https://doi.org/10.1353/sof.0.0264

Lincoln, Y. S. (2009). Rethinking emotional intelligence: An alternative proposal. *Advances in Developing Human Resources, 11*(6), 784–791.

Liu, H., & Baker, C. (2016). White Knights: Leadership as the heroicisation of whiteness. *Leadership, 12*(4), 420–448.

Liu, H., Cutcher, L., & Grant, D. (2015). Doing authenticity: The gendered construction of authentic leadership. *Gender, Work & Organization, 22*(3), 237–255.

Magnusson, C. (2009). *European Sociological Review,* 25(1), 87–101, 15. 4 Charts, 1 Graph. https://doi.org/10.1093/esr/jcn035

Maitlis, S., Vogus, T. J., & Lawrence, T. B. (2013). Sensemaking and emotion in organizations. *Organizational Psychology Review, 3*(3), 222–247.

Mayer, J. D., & Salovey, P. (1997). What is emotional intelligence? In P. Salovey & D. J. Sluyter (Eds.), *Emotional development and emotional intelligence* (pp. 3–34). Basic Books.

McEnrue, M. P., & Groves, K. (2006). Choosing among tests of emotional intelligence: What is the evidence? *Human Resource Development Quarterly, 17*(1), 9–42.

McGuire, D., Cross, C., & O'Donnell, D. (2005). Why humanistic approaches in HRD won't work. *Human Resource Development Quarterly, 16*(1), 131–137.

Meshkat, M., & Nejati, R. (2017). Does emotional intelligence depend on gender? A study on undergraduate English majors of three Iranian universities. *SAGE Open, 7*(3), 2158244017725796.

Metcalfe, B. D., & Rees, C. J. (2010). Gender, globalization and organization: Exploring power, relations and intersections. *Equality, Diversity and Inclusion: an International Journal, 9*(1), 5–22. https://doi.org/10.1108/02610151011019183

Mikkelsen, E. N., & Wåhlin, R. (2020). Dominant, hidden and forbidden sensemaking: The politics of ideology and emotions in diversity management. *Organization, 27*(4), 557–577.

Moore, P. V. (2017). *The quantified self in precarity: Work, technology and what counts.* Routledge.

Moriarty, P., & Buckley, F. (2003). Increasing team emotional intelligence through process. *Journal of European Industrial Training, 27* (2/3/4), 98–110.

Muyia, H. M. (2009). Approaches to and instruments for measuring emotional intelligence: A review of selected literature. *Advances in Developing Human Resources, 11*(6), 690–702.

Muyia, H. M., & Kacirek, K. (2009). An empirical study of a leadership development training program and its impact on emotional intelligence quotient (EQ) scores. *Advances in Developing Human Resources, 11*(6), 703–718.

Nadesan, M. H., & Trethewey, A. (2000). Performing the enterprising subject: Gendered strategies for success (?). *Text and Performance Quarterly, 20*(3), 223–250.

Narlı, N., & Akdemir, A. (2019). Female emotional labour in Turkish call centres: Smiling voices despite low job satisfaction. *Sociological Research Online, 24*(3), 278–296.

Nath, V. (2011). Aesthetic and emotional labour through stigma: National identity management and racial abuse in offshored Indian call centres. *Work, Employment and Society, 25*(4), 709–725.

Nkomo, S. M. (1992). The emperor has no clothes: Rewriting "race in organizations." *Academy of Management Review, 17*(3), 487–513.

Nussbaum, M. C. (2003). *Upheavals of thought: The intelligence of emotions.* Cambridge University Press.

Offermann, L. R., Bailey, J. R., Vasilopoulos, N. L., Seal, C., & Sass, M. (2004). The relative contribution of emotional competence and cognitive ability to individual and team performance. *Human Performance, 17*, 219–243.

Opengart, R. (2005). Emotional intelligence and emotion work: Examining constructs from an interdisciplinary framework. *Human Resource Development Review, 1*, 49–62.

Owen, L. (2018). Menstruation and humanistic management at work. *Guest Editors: Christina Schwabenland and Paul Harrison.*

Pathak, S., & Muralidharan, E. (2020). Implications of culturally implicit perspective of emotional intelligence. *Cross-cultural research, 54*(5), 502–533.

Pradhan, R. K., Jena, L. K., & Singh, S. K. (2017, April). Examining the role of emotional intelligence between organizational learning and adaptive performance in Indian manufacturing industries. *Journal of Workplace Learning, 29*(3), 235–247. https://doi.org/10.1108/JWL-05-2016-0046

Putnam, L. L., Mumby, D. K., & Fineman, S. (1993). *Organizations, emotion and the myth of rationality.*

Rahmouni Elidrissi, Y., & Courpasson, D. (2019). Body breakdowns as politics: Identity regulation in a high-commitment activist organization. *Organization Studies,* 0170840619867729 & Winkel, D. E. (2011). Gender, emotion and power in work relationships. *Human Resource Management Review, 21*(4), 377–393.

Ragins, B. R., & Winkel, D. E. (2011). Gender, emotion and power in work relationships. *Human Resource Management Review, 21*(4), 377–393.

Rofcanin, Y., Las Heras, M., & Bakker, A. B. (2017). Family supportive supervisor behaviors and organizational culture: Effects on work engagement and performance. *Journal of Occupational Health Psychology, 22*(2), 207.

Saks, A. M. (2006). Antecedents and consequences of employee engagement. *Journal of Managerial Psychology, 21*(7), 600.

Sachs, J., & Blackmore, J. (1998). You never show you can't cope: Women in school leadership roles managing their emotions. *Gender and Education, 10*(3), 265–279.

Salovey, P., & Mayer, J. (1990). Emotional intelligence. *Imagination, Cognition and Personality, 9*, 185–211.

Schuster, F. E. (1998). *Employee-Centered Management: A Strategy for High Commitment and Involvement.* Quorum Books.

Senge, P. (1992). *The Fifth Discipline.* Random House.

Shields, S. A. (2002). *Speaking from the heart: Gender and the social meaning of emotion.* Cambridge University Press.

Short, D. C., & Yorks, L. (2002). Analyzing training from an emotions perspective. *Advances in Developing Human Resources, 4*(1), 80–96.

Shuck, B., & Herd, A. M. (2012). Employee engagement and leadership: Exploring the convergence of two frameworks and implications for leadership development in HRD. *Human Resource Development Review, 11*(2), 156–181.

Singh, S. K. (2007). Role of emotional intelligence in organizational learning: An empirical study. *Singapore Management Review, 29*(2), 55–74.

Skinner, D., Saunders, M. N. K., & Thornhill, A. (2002). Human resource management in a changing world. *Strategic Change, 11*(7), 341–345.

Stavrakakis, Y. (2008). Peripheral vision: Subjectivity and the organised other: Between symbolic authority and fantasmatic enjoyment. *Organization Studies, 29*(7), 1037–1059.

Sturdy, A., Brocklehurst, M., Winstanley, D., & Littlejohns, M. (2006). Management as a (self) confidence trick: Management ideas, education and identity work. *Organization, 13*(6), 841–860.

Sue, D. W. (2013). Race talk: The psychology of racial dialogues. *American Psychologist, 68*(8), 663.

Sue, D. W. (2016). *Race talk and the conspiracy of silence: Understanding and facilitating difficult dialogues on race.* John Wiley & Sons.

Thanem, T. (2016). The Body. Chapter 20 in R. Mir, H. Willmott, M. Greenwood (Eds.) *The Routledge companion to philosophy in organization studies* (pp. 276–284). Routledge.

Thory, K. (2012). A gendered analysis of emotional intelligence in the workplace issues and concerns for human resource development. *Human Resource Development Review, 12*(2), 221–244.

Van Rooy, D. L., Alonso, A., & Viswesvaran, C. (2005). Group differences in emotional intelligence scores: Theoretical and practical implications. *Personality and Individual Differences, 38*(3), 689–700.

Vince, R., & Saleem, T. (2004). The impact of caution and blame on organizational learning. *Management Learning, 35*(2), 133–154.

Vitry, C., Sage, D., & Dainty, A. (2020). Affective atmospheres of sensemaking and learning: Workplace meetings as aesthetic and anaesthetic. *Management Learning, 51*(3), 274–292.

von Scheve, C. (2012). Emotion regulation and emotion work: Two sides of the same coin? *Frontiers in Psychology, 3*, 496. https://doi.org/10.3389/fpsyg.2012.00496

Watkins, K. E., & Marsick, V. J. (1993). *Sculpting the learning organization: Lessons in the art and science of systemic change.* Jossey-Bass Inc., 350 Sansome Street, San Francisco, CA 94104–1310.

Weick, K. E., Sutcliffe, K. M., & Obstfeld, D. (2005). Organizing and the process of sensemaking. *Organization Science, 16*(4), 409–421.

Weinberger, L. A. (2009). Emotional intelligence, leadership style, and perceived leadership effectiveness. *Advances in Developing Human Resources, 11*(6), 747–772.

Yeoman, R. (2014). Conceptualizing meaningful work as a fundamental human need. *Journal of Business Ethics, 125*(2), 235–251.

Yildirim, O. (2007). Discriminating emotional intelligence-based competencies of IT employees and salespeople. *Journal of European Industrial Training, 31*(4), 274–282.

CHAPTER 21

New, Emerging, and Alternative Forms of Learning and Knowing: Perspectives to Inform a More Critical HRD

Chelesea Lewellen, *Esther Pippins, and Jeremy Bohonos*

REFLECTING ON NEW, EMERGING, AND ALTERNATIVE FORMS OF LEARNING AND KNOWING

The purpose of this chapter is to reflect upon forms of learning and knowing which have historically received less attention, but which nonetheless offer meaningful tools for describing, promoting, and understanding knowledge in spaces of organizing as well as address how various forms of learning and knowing interact with social justice action. This chapter will explore the "different types of learning, different places of learning, different philosophies of learning, [and] different purposes of learning" which inform, influence, and shape development and performance in spaces of organizing (Bierema & Callahan, 2014, p. 438). Within critical HRD, learning and knowing should be conceived of as dynamically linked to action for social justice; thus, forming

C. Lewellen (✉)
Educational Administration and Higher Education, School of Education, Southern Illinois University Carbondale, Carbondale, IL, USA
e-mail: chelesea.lewellen@siu.edu

E. Pippins · J. Bohonos
Department of Counseling Leadership, Adult Education & School Psychology, Texas State University, San Marcos, TX, USA
e-mail: esp33@txstate.edu

J. Bohonos
e-mail: jbohonos@txstate.edu

J. C. Collins and J. L. Callahan (eds.), *The Palgrave Handbook of Critical Human Resource Development*, https://doi.org/10.1007/978-3-031-10453-4_21

the basis for praxis in our field. When viewed this way, we can recognize how engagement with social justice struggle is a form of embodied knowing that facilitates further learning, while learning should be an activity of fierce resistance to oppression. In the following sections, we will explore the importance of developing our capacity to feel and love, building empathy, bearing witness, affirming the need for change, and taking critically engaged action as crucial components of learning and knowing in critical HRD. This chapter organizes a discussion of critical ways of learning and knowing around a civil rights protest song in recognition that scholarly production around social justice starts with social movement and other actions for social justice and that scholars lose direction and vitality when they are not guided by social movements (Roediger, 2017).

Affirming the Need for Change: *The Answer Better Be (Yeah, Yeah)*—Nina Simone, 1967

LEARNING, KNOWING, AND ACTING

With overt racism, nativism, and xenophobia retaking center stage in American politics (Zarestky & Collins, 2019) and in the global political arena, we are once again entering a period of time where it is impossible for people of good conscious to deny the need for major social justice-oriented changes at all levels of human organization (Segal & Wagaman, 2017). While these issues are never far from the spotlight and while it never should have been necessary to make a "business case" for diversity or otherwise convince learners that critical perspectives were important, the crisis point in American race relations brought about by decades of apathy from mainstream American politics requires HRD to affirm its moral responsibility to combat injustice (Byrd, 2018). When moral beings face the legacy of Donald J. Trump, the bigoted and shady real estate entrepreneur, turned reality star, subsequently turned president, they encounter continued support for an injustice system that increasingly functions as an oppressive force in African and Native American communities (Alexander, 2010; Garza, 2014). These moral beings must affirm the need for deeper learning and knowledge related to social justice, a reckoning with the social injustices that caused the condition and must lead to action for social justice (Byrd & Scott, 2010). We will argue that this learning, knowing, and acting process needs to be routed in love and empathy, centered in people from marginalized communities' counter-narratives, and dedicated to pursuing a range of tactics, strategies, and always a plan toward action.

THE CoVID CONNECTION

The need for change originates with a dissatisfaction in the current state and structure of organizational culture (Khan & Khan, 2019). Working remotely during the CoVID pandemic, contrary to popular belief, did not infuse an abundance of free time into our lives, rather the shift to working from home created a degree of flexibility (Mauer, 2020). The shift in venue afforded time for deep reflexivity for some to examine how we spend our time and stimulated shifts in our perspective to reevaluate personal and professional priorities. Additionally, an awareness of social injustices and inequality in the world, and a call to action emerged as we turned our attention to the increased news coverage of racial violence and systemic racism (Farkas & Romaniuk, 2020). Interestingly, distance from in-office micro and macro aggressions, discrimination, and other mental health aggregators highlighted the ongoing dissatisfaction of career choices. Minoritized persons reported an increase in peace and focus on self-care (Tulshyan, 2021).

Each year, scholars and practitioner scholars come together in annual conferences to share innovations and advances in scholarship. The CoVID pandemic has changed the way we gather, frequently prompting us to move to virtual spaces to continue sharing our work (Bierema, 2020; Pleyers, 2020). As we negotiate this new way of interacting, there should be a call to demand that permanent tracks that explore race and racism be built into our conferences and journals. At the conclusion of our annual conferences, we should task ourselves to return to our respective campuses and organizations with a fiery determination to put this practice into action. To BE an antiracist, one must take action in advocating for antiracism and against all forms of discrimination as a viable and meaningful part of an organizational identity.

CIVIL RIGHTS AND EQUALITY

The Civil Rights movement produced innumerable freedom singers (Rose, 2007), who thrust themselves into civil rights activism. Some came into advocacy spaces gradually while others were galvanized by incomprehensible domestic terrorist events (Feldstein, 2005). Acts of racial terror had indelible effects on the community, activists, and the nation. Artists and entertainers, once thought to avoid trauma and bring levity and joy to their audiences, felt compelled to use their talents to promote freedom and equality for African American people (Loudermilk, 2013; Rose, 2007).

Nina Simone, prolifically gifted singer, songwriter, and pianist enjoyed an eclectic and critically acclaimed run as a multitalented entertainer, was drawn to social justice work after the bombing of the Sixteenth Street Baptist Church in Birmingham, Alabama in 1963 (Feldstein, 2005; Kernodle, 2008). In addition to the property damage, psychological impact, and trauma, the domestic terrorist event claimed an irreplaceable treasure that day. Four young girls, Addie Mae Collins, Carol Denise McNair, Carole Robertson, and Cynthia Wesley, aged 11–14 years old, died in the church bombing. Simone was infuriated by the racist domestic terrorism event and subsequently wrote the tome "Mississippi Goddamn" (Kernodle, 2008; Loudermilk, 2013) an unapologetically confrontational song that laid bare the savage and brutal reality of racism. It quickly became a political anthem and a call to action for Black activists and allies alike. The song's lyrics conveyed Simone's anguish and fury asking for basic human rights yet receiving only lies and misleading information. A verse describes a sense of resolve in accusing the aggressors and the country of lying and ultimately losing Simone's trust. Throughout the chorus, she demands equality for herself and her family while rejecting the notion of residing in the same neighborhood as those who failed her possibly a jab at the concept of separate but equal.

The ballad was largely banned in the Southern states, an area which disproportionately represented the bulk of racial violence incidents, which only increased its overall popularity (Feldstein, 2005). Five years prior to the debut of "Mississippi Goddamn", jazz singer Billie Holiday released "Strange Fruit" a tune that laid bare the savage brutal reality of racism. The lyrics examined the symbolism of the horrifying living legacy of lynched black bodies as ornamental adornments or "fruit" hanging from trees (Margolick, 1999). Holiday faced significant criticism and legal actions to prohibit her performance and promotion of the song. Ongoing harassment and subjection to legal and societal pressures ultimately exacerbated her battle with addiction. Both songs, achingly beautiful, melodically hypnotic, yet clear in their message that racism and its talons of oppression that frequently result in the death of minoritized people, are monstrous and malevolent. Over a half century has passed since Simone's "Mississippi Goddamn" and Holiday's "Strange Fruit" yet the visceral outrage embodied in both songs are still very much relevant today. These songs are applicable to contemporary events such as the murder of David McAtee, George Perry Floyd, Dreasjon "Sean" Reed, Breonna Taylor, Elijah Ellis, Botham Shem Jean, Sandra Bland, and the list unbelievably goes on. Police shootings of unarmed Black and African Americans are modern-day lynchings, that result in little to no accountability for officers (Brown et al., 2021) and further traumatize Black people (Richardson, 2021). The calls to action have not ceased as contemporary artists including Jill Scott, Kendrick Lamar, Low Key, and Ruby Ibarra continue to educate listeners about racial violence and demand that HRD scholars and practitioners decenter our own comfort and acquiescence in order to engage a formidable enemy (Bohonos et al., 2019).

Love, Eros, and Ecstasy: *Do I Move You, Are You Willing?* —Nina Simone, 1967

LOVE IS A VERB

When activated, love is a fully engaged, immersive experience that touches something deep within us creating an emotional and physical memory of familiarity. This internal transformation can have meaningful real-life consequences that can subsequently inspire and affect those around us (Hull, 2002; West, 2017). Love elevates and can create an impression of actual or perceived similarity and connection in another entity: a connection that seems authentic and innate (Gibran, 1924; Kasl & Yorks, 2016). Essentially, the lover sees some aspect of themselves in the object of their desire or seeks to connect in some way to the object of their affection. Demonstrative actions closely follow and the love affair begins. In this same sense, our relationships with teaching and knowing for social justice are like a love affair (hooks, 1994).

It is imperative that we recognize learning as a multifaceted physical and emotional activity (Delgado & Stefanic, 2019; Kasl & Yorks, 2016) and that all of the learning, discussion, and exchange of ideas are carried out by embodied beings. Learning is a complex and multidimensional undertaking that involves transfer of information but also transfer of feeling, heightened sensitivity to information, and comprehensive acknowledgment of feelings including sympathy and empathy (Bierly et al., 2000; Hull, 2002; Riess, 2017; Watts & Dumbreck, 2013). Recent increases in the visibility of the ongoing injustices experienced by minorities, particularly Black men and women have moved the traditional distance objective regard to racism to one that is more intimate (Jones-Eversley et al., 2017; Pleyers, 2020). This wealth of access to information and news stories has sparked a move toward understanding.

Empathy: *When I Touch You, Do You Quiver?*—Nina Simone, 1967

What Is Empathy

What makes seeing one's humanity so difficult? On a Sunday afternoon, as Ahmaud Arbery jogged in a residential area in Brunswick, Georgia as he so often did being an avid jogger, three men gave chase, caged him like an animal, and eventually killed him. To the men, Ahmaud represented otherness, something foreign. Lost in this example of modern-day vigilantism was the humanity in their decisions that fateful day and Ahmaud's as he fought nobly until his last breath? More importantly, why was empathy missing, and could it have changed this circumstance if these three men saw themselves in Ahmaud Arbery's shoes?

Empathy, as it is defined and practiced, encapsulates the notion of the extended mind. In its earliest meaning, empathy encouraged us to extend the mind outside of the self. The coining of the term empathy began in 1908 as a translation for the German art historical term, Einfühlung, which literally means, in-feeling (Lanzoni, 2018). Einfühlung referred to capturing the aesthetic act of transferring one's feeling into the forms and shapes of objects. Since the Einfühlung response of in-feeling of objects, empathy has morphed into a more nuanced meaning relative to placing oneself in another's position or within their frame of reference. Thus, empathy's contemporary usage is to "feel with" rather than "feel for" (Jerrett et al., 2021). Deemed as a trained skill, talent, or inborn ability and bestowed as psychological and moral nature, empathy refers to our capacity to grasp and understand the mental and emotional lives of others (Lanzoni, 2018). Simply put, the practice of empathy allows people to walk a mile in another's shoes.

Genuine empathy requires the following three skills: "the ability to share another person's feelings; the cognitive ability to perceive what another person is feeling; and a socially beneficial intention to respond compassionately to that person's distress" (Steed, 2019, Introduction, para. 2). The first skill denotes emotional empathy, sometimes called affective or primitive empathy, which is the empathy we have inherently. According to Steed (2019), emotional empathy is connected to emotional contagion, which is mimicking emotions or behaviors in another person's emotions or behaviors. For example, a person begins to smile upon seeing another person smiling or feeling concerned after seeing someone cry. Because emotional empathy is so closely tied to people within our inner circles, it can be the empathy most practiced with a variety of people within various circumstances.

The second skill denotes cognitive empathy or perspective-taking. "Cognitive empathy (is) accurate knowledge about the contents of another person's mind, including how the person feels" (Hodges & Myers, 2007, p. 297). Cognitive empathy occurs when people actively seek perspective to understand what others may be thinking in response to specific situations. However, cognitive empathy is not without challenges. It is easy to empathize with people we identify with or have challenges empathizing with people we encounter who we perceive as being unlike us. Hodges and Myers (2007) suggest that it is difficult to empathize with those we do not identify with because there is no baseline of perspective; therefore, we may perceive them as foreign or a possible threat. Thus, a potential risk or perceived threat may evoke acts to defend instead of acts of empathy.

The last skill denotes empathic concern, an emotional reaction characterized by compassion, tenderness, softheartedness, and sympathy. Moreover, empathic concern is other-oriented emotion evoked by perceiving someone in need (Steed, 2019). For example, empathic concern can be illustrated through the act of someone running to the aid of another who is severely injured and in desperate need of assistance. Whether that individual helps the person directly or calls for assistance from other parties, their empathy is demonstrated through an act of compassion. Similar to an outward mindset, empathic concern focuses on others, particularly their well-being, without tangible benefit to the empathizer.

EMPATHY AND WAYS OF KNOWING

Empathy is not just a way to extend our moral compass; an empathic presence introduces us to various ways of knowing. These ways of knowing can be embodied in feelings, memories, imaginings, and or bodily enactments brought forth by one's encounter with another (Rosan, 2012). Rogers (1964) argues that empathy could be conceptualized in a trifold. First, a subjective way of knowing wherein empathy is turned inward to the knower. In subjective knowing, an individual formulates an inner assumption and validates it through external cues or stimuli. This process involves the individual attempting to understand implicit meanings of their experience (Clark, 2004; Clark & Butler, 2020). Although subjective knowing is a rudimentary way of knowing, subjective responses are fundamental to everyday life.

Second, Rogers (1964) suggested an objective way of knowing in which an individual's empathic understanding could be directed toward groups who have external frames of reference. In this process, assumptions are "analyzed through external observations, and empathic inferences are made regarding the reactions of trusted groups, usually consisting of one's colleagues" (p. 113). A consensus of judgments assists in formulating the basis for understanding the experiences of members of the reference group. Reference groups comprised of members from diverse backgrounds foster a more accurate objective way of knowing (Clark, 2004; Clark & Butler, 2020). Objectively derived data from reference groups, particularly colleagues, represent primary sources of reputable knowledge and empathic understanding of the reference groups' experiences.

Third, an interpersonal way of knowing is where the direction of empathy is toward another individual. An interpersonal way of knowing acknowledges the phenomenological experience of an individual through nonverbal and verbal communication (Clark & Butler, 2020). For example, this process may involve listening perceptively to another individual as completely as possible to convey a sense of the individual's inner feelings and meanings. A relational approach emphasizes grasping the phenomenological perspectives of an individual in an interpersonal context (Clark, 2004). The focus is on the other person, and direct interaction with that individual constitutes the primary way of knowing about their private world of meanings.

EMPATHY IN PRACTICE

People sometimes fear the unknown or unfamiliar. Often, they flock to perceived safe spaces and surround themselves with people who look like them or have similar interests and lifestyles. The result is an empathy deficit caused by social circles that have become too homogeneous and because humans naturally hold biases (Miller, n.d.). Empathy is something that human beings ordinarily engage in, and most human beings possess the capacity to enact empathy (Warren, 2018). Whether an individual's conception of empathy in the personal or professional context aligns with their general understanding of the concept, there are benefits in using empathy as a mechanism for moving beyond their worldviews to understand those held by other people.

Empathy has a pivotal interpersonal and societal role in challenging long-held assumptions regarding social justice. Empathy is the conduit in which social transformation flows by sharing experiences, needs, and desires. According to Zembylas (2018), critical theories, particularly Freirean theory and critical pedagogy, empathy is essential in achieving social justice and dismantling oppressive behaviors. Empathy is central to efforts that instigate the affective transformation of individuals and processes of social transformations that acknowledge and question oppressive hierarchies of power (Zembylas, 2018). Moreover, social justice is not just action but an ideology that embraces a just society, and empathy, which is at the heart of social justice, is where social transformation begins.

Because empathy is the basis for understanding, one can conclude that there is no effective intervention without empathy and all effective interventions have to be empathic (Clark & Butler, 2020). Adopting an empathic practice is more than a tolerance exercise; it requires reinforcing everyone's individual expertise and humanity. Empathy offers an avenue for individuals to question themselves while constructing an understanding of the interdependence of self and others (Hasio, 2016). By examining self and seeking other perspectives, particularly marginalized groups, an empathic process is how we navigate the complexities of social justice, teach social justice, and implement programs that foster fairness and equality. For HRD, empathy can be the foundation upon which a central cohesive source of support and stability is fostered throughout an organization, particularly in promoting fairness and equity. By integrating the concept of empathy within their framework for developing personal and organizational skills, HRD can create and nurture workplace climates that make it possible to work cooperatively with people who have very different experiences, preferences, styles, and opinions.

Bearing Witness Through Testimony: *Do I Groove You? Tell the Truth Now*—**Nina Simone, 1967**

TALKING AND TESTIFYING

Mamie Till, mother to Emmitt who was brutally lynched in 1955 when he was only 14 years old, understood the power in the old adage that a picture tells a thousand words. When Till insisted her son's coffin remain open, she wanted the world to see what they did to her baby. As photographs of her son Emmitt's mutilated corpse circulated across the country, she bore witness to the unbearable pain of losing her child to the hateful violence of white supremacy while speaking to the horrors, heartbreak, and realities of racism. The images bore witness in ways that words alone could not, galvanizing a generation of activists to resist lynching and other forms of racism (Tyson, 2017). Her testimony, in images, represented every Black mother's fear and bore witness to the disparities of justice for Blacks in the United States and was an example of the multiple deaths experienced by African Americans when you are repeatedly confronted with images of murdered and mutilated Black bodies (Marriott, 2000; Wright, 1945).

Perhaps one of the most powerful ways to clear one's soul is to share our experiences with others. When practiced in psychology, bearing witness is a particular space for sharing traumatic experiences. Pikiewicz (2013) advises that "bearing witness is a valuable way to process an experience wherein an individual can obtain empathy and support to lighten their emotional load by sharing their experiences with a witness to obtain catharsis" (para. 2). Merriam Webster (n.d.) defines bearing witness informally as a method for showing something exists or is true and more formally as a way to make a statement saying that one saw or knows something. For the marginalized, bearing witness can be more than talking and testifying about one's experience being continuously treated as insignificant and peripheral members within our society (Salcedo, 2022). Toliver (2020) posits that bearing witness is a "means to reaffirm the humanity of the storyteller because they share their lives and experience with those willing to listen" (p. 507). More than just basic commentary, bearing witness or giving testimony can be seen as bearing one's soul in narrative, weaving together the rich untold stories that define lives and existence.

To bear witness requires a search for evidence of the ontological match between world, self, and human meaning (Popescu, 2018). In this context, Popescu calls attention to what potentially resides in all of us, which is a dissenters' expression and a natural multiplicity of the human experience. According to Ariss (2021), witness is "a powerful and evocative word that has extraordinary moral and cultural forces because of its connections with concepts of suffering, justice, and truth" (p. 115). Witnessing involves at least two parties, someone who testifies and others who listen and acknowledge what they have heard. Within this context, witnessing can be effectively used as a form of survivor testimony, particularly in retelling human rights violations and requesting audiences to become morally accountable for events (Ariss, 2021). Whatever form of witnessing or testimony takes place, it is centered on the idea of giving the othered, the marginalized, and the voiceless a platform to articulate their suffering of discursive injustice. With justice being understood as granting another person what they are due, what is owed or deserved in some sense (Bateza, 2021), bearing witness through testimony becomes the vehicle pushing past the silence and ignorance of social inequity and injustice. Thus, the oppressed voice and allies engage in critical questioning and explicit discussion on the discomforts of daily life and what makes a more just society.

BEARING WITNESS AS A PRACTICE

Myers (2020) reminds us of the two roles that fear plays in hearing testimony. First, "fear leads us to be wary of otherness and to silence difference", and second, "fear forces conformity to preestablished norms and metrics of understanding" (p. 403). The practice of bearing witness and testimony must not be impelled by fear but somewhat disruptive to address the lack of parity and other social problems in organizations. Jordan (2021) points out that "the rise of misinformation, conspiracy theories, and coded rhetoric have epistemic defects, including the resistance to revising false beliefs in light of better information and the difficulty of thinking beyond one's social location" (para. 2). To achieve scalable, sustainable, and necessary change, bearing witness and testimony must have its voice within organizations to filter in the multitude of narratives that promote humility among persons who have not lived under the specter of racism, marginalization, or oppression.

Bearing witness and testimonies is meant to provoke thought, empower voice, and prompt change. Change within organizations requires work and commitment. Each employee has a different role in assisting in change. Leaders in organizations may exercise courage in taking risks weighing the big picture to ascertain ways for supporting change; however, witnesses who share their testimony add the credibility of their experiences and narratives to empower others to act.

Testimonio

McIntosh and Churcher (2020) refer to testimonio as "a genre told in first person by a narrator who is also the real protagonist or witness of the events he or she recounts" (p. 20). Testimonios are used to articulate an urgent voice drawn from an experiential, self-conscious, narrative giving the narrator the power of agency and centrality of subject (Salcedo, 2022). Rich in oral and written traditions, testimonio takes on various forms such as memoirs, oral histories, qualitative vignettes, prose, song lyrics, or spoken word (Reyes & Curry-Rodriguez, 2012). Testimonio text is steeped and constructed in the discourse of solidarity. Testimonio offers oppressed and silenced groups opportunities to speak from the margins and raise their voices about their circumstances. Women of underrepresented groups notably employ testimonio because of its unique characteristic of intentional, political, and conscientized reflection (McIntosh & Churcher, 2020; Reyes & Curry-Rodriguez, 2012). While testimonio is a vehicle for demanding recognition, soliciting attention, and urging action, the audience has a significant role in recording, translating, and editing the delivered testimonies to ensure that these voices are heard. Testimonio is not to be hidden and kept secret; it requires active participatory readers and listeners who act on behalf of the speaker intending to arrive at justice and redemption (Reyes & Curry-Rodriguez, 2012). Although testimonios bolter both individual and organizational awareness, organizations, in particular, can resource initiatives that support changes to structures or behaviors that overlook the experiences and narratives defined through testimonio and its objective to call for action.

Counternarratives

Bell (1995) refers to the counternarrative as a form of critical race theoretical writing using first-person storytelling through creative expression. This methodological tool highlighting the experiential knowledge of people of color has a rich history that continues to span racialized and ethnic group experiences in the United States (James-Gallaway & Baber, 2021). The counternarrative formulated from direct descriptive accounts disrupts dominant discourses by amplifying and uplifting the voices of historically marginalized people of color in a system of racism that privileges the voices of white people to disenfranchise people of color (Dixson & Rousseau Anderson, 2018; James-Gallaway & Baber, 2021). The counternarrative is connected to CRT's central tenet of the unique voice, which argues that because of their different histories and experiences with oppression, people of color may be able to communicate with their white counterparts about matters that Whites are unlikely to know (Blaisdell, 2021). Counternarrative as storytelling has been utilized across communities of people of color as a survival tactic (Delgado, 1989), particularly in a U.S. society where racism is endemic and plagued with the evolving nature of racism (James-Gallaway & Baber, 2021). The counternarrative is often used to debunk majoritarian stories which re-inscribe myths, meritocracy, and colorblindness. Counternarrative may also challenge and contradict pervasive stereotypes; however, one of its most important uses is building community and coalitions among people of color who experience similar and differing racial realities (Blaisdell, 2021). This coalition-building aspect is crucial to organizations seeking to foster a sense of community around social justice issues and freedom from oppressive conditions.

Sisco et al. (2019) suggest that when supporting social movements, organizations demonstrate a genuine interest in social movement causes and not merely use their support as opportunities to build social capital for their organizations. Given its role in creating a more holistic understanding of learning and development within and outside the workplace, HRD particularly has a role in supporting social justice initiatives and advancing the social movement learning that is richly and uniquely informed by voices that bear witness to firsthand knowledge of disparities (Bohonos & Sisco, 2021). Bearing witness should not be treated merely as a device for bearing one's soul. For HRD practitioners, acts of sharing one's testimony should be recognized as unique opportunities to learn.

Considering Tactics and Strategies: *Are You Ready for This Action?*—**Nina Simone, 1967**

We Are in This Together

Translating intention into a plan of action requires trust in knowledge, inspired leadership, and a kinship/relationship with the movement (hooks, 1994; Khan & Khan, 2019). The absence of knowledge can inspire well-intentioned but poorly executed action and a lack of kinship/ownership of the initiative can result in dispassionate, short-lived enthusiasm for the cause and misguided attempts to address organizational injustice (Alexander, 2010; Bohonos & James-Gallaway, 2022). The results of non-knowing can be counterproductive at best and catastrophic at worst. Proceeding with well-informed measured risks outweighs wanton disregard that is focused solely in the interest of moving forward. How to proceed with marching orders? How do words/intention inspire one to action? How does understanding affect the level of action? These questions become a critical part of self-assessment in the initial stages of social justice initiatives that demand that we move and are stirred to intelligent action. Moral agency, moral urgency, and a keen knowledge base are essential to taking critically engaged action.

Simply put, empathy is the act of putting yourself in someone else's story to build an understanding from their point of reference (Godcharles et al., 2019). In matters of social justice, there is no effective intervention without empathy and empathic practices. For HRD practitioners, empathy is a critical component for building and sustaining positive workplace relationships, fostering diversity and inclusion, and encouraging cooperation and collaboration. Empathy is at the heart of what a dynamic and grow-oriented HRD does in valuing inclusivity. Bearing witness is to show that something exists or is true. Sharing testimony gives agency to voices not often heard. Bearing witness and testimony is more than talking and testifying about one's experience, bearing witness represents unique opportunities for HRD practitioners to adopt and adapt learning initiatives that are informed by marginalized voices with firsthand knowledge of disparities.

Empathy conjures a near euphoric shared experience that positions absence as merely the sense of distance between the observer and the observed (Cain-Miller, n.d.). A virtual connection emerges when empathy is fully engaged, one that mirrors the emotions and the consequences, real or imagined, lived or perceived, of the recipient and this can have a profound impact and consequently move one to social justice action (Cartabuke et al., 2019; Godchares, 2019). The ally/observer sees themselves in the social injustice narrative, superimposing their existence in the experience as an active participant, rather than a bystander. It is an experience similar to a phantom muscle memory when one listens to music that evokes a deep sadness or jubilant memory as a hand or heart moves in unison with the tempo. Through learning and active awareness, one is ultimately moved to action as an advocate for social justice.

Empathetic Social Justice Learning

The level of social justice learning one may achieve is linked to the degree a participant can "see themselves in the struggle" of the oppressed. Thus, social justice coalition building requires members of various social groups to recognize their shared humanity with other groups. Deepening senses of empathy should be recognized as important components of learning in Critical Human Resource Development (CHRD) (Byrd, 2018; Byrd & Scott, 2010; Kasl & Yorks, 2016). Without empathy, well-intentioned actions do not always translate into sound execution. Empathy for topics and causes that bear a personal interest or strike one's moral compass can elicit a different level of sympathy/empathy when the cause is dissimilar or unfamiliar or controversial. There is a motivation behind learning that is closely linked with familiarity (Hein, et al., 2016). The ability to see oneself in and identify with social justice causes that encompass value for the participant is thought to heighten deep learning. Deep learning, surface learning, and non-learning are terms used in educational research to distinguish between the impact and quality of learning (Hay, 2007).

There is a seeming shared trauma among marginalized and minoritized people, those who are victims of systemic discrimination and racism, to some degree, all labor under divisive circumstances which are frequently cloaked in xenophobia, anti-gay sentiment, sexism, racism, and other discriminatory practices. Though this shared experience exists, a lack of sympathy and empathy distances us physically, emotionally, and spiritually from another's trauma and pain. We can subdivide and prioritize our pain over someone else's which can lead cyclical process of mistrust and injury. We, too often, labor under the burdens of discrimination alone or in small factions, when sustainable changes can only be attained on a systemic level when coalitions are formed around empathy and love.

The phrase "Faith without works is dead" intends to communicate that "works", activities and actions are a necessary and consequential byproduct of ethical conviction. In antiracism work, well-intentioned efforts without action are meaningless wherein inaction facilitates and supports social injustice (Kendi, 2019). Action is a critical component that must be executed in order to tangibly disrupt, disarm, and dismantle systemic oppression.

Racism is not solely a BIPOC's (Black Indigenous Person of Color's) problem or responsibility, ableism is not a disabled person's problem or responsibility, and transphobia is not a transperson's problem or responsibility because minoritized people did not create systemic oppression nor are they primarily responsible for its maintenance or benefit from its existence. Oppression and discrimination are issues that seek to isolate and divide individuals. These oppressive tactics thrive by making victims of discrimination feel isolated and alone, hopeless and unloved. Discrimination is crafted to freeze us into inaction by not defending ourselves or others who may need help. Addressing these inequities is a human rights issue that requires compassion and a sense of community and comradery. It is imperative that comprehensive efforts that task allies and stakeholders to work together to dismantle systems of oppression are intentional and ongoing. Privileged individuals in leadership positions who are decision makers, colleagues, and scholars all bear an increased responsibility to speak up and speak out against racism, sexism, ableism, homophobia, transphobia, and discrimination of all kinds for a more diverse, inclusive, engaging, and equitable environment. Performative allyship that individuals who self-identify as well-intentioned allies, should frequently revisit their methods of engagement and commit to the challenge of ongoing education, collaborative learning, and actionable efforts to promote antiracism with equal enthusiasm when it is most as well as least convenient.

Conclusions

Systemic racism and discrimination are monumental issues, a clear and present danger, to all of us; however, racism, frequently assigned to minoritized persons as their responsibility to resolve, solve, and absolve, is not a black problem nor a minoritized person's problem, for minoritized people did not create, implement, nor do they sustain racism or systemic oppression or benefit from it (Sullivan, 2014). Racism is a humanity issue and although we should all work together to dismantle it, it is imperative that those who created, sustain, and benefit from racism lead the charge rather than actively or passively indulge when it is convenient or politically correct to do so (Bohonos, 2019; Kivel, 2017; Sullivan, 2014). The time for change is now. Recent events such as the murder of Mr. George Floyd, though enzymatic in its initial reaction, require sustained ongoing efforts to meaningfully impact systemic issues of institutionalized discrimination.

A critical component of antiracism work is action (Kendi, 2019). The list of viable actions that one can take particularly those in positions of power such as HRD professionals, to advance inclusivity is significant such as using one's privilege to create hostile environments for racism, creating circumstances wherein racism is unable to take root nor thrive, challenging peers and colleagues who are known to be problematic, in real time as offenses occur, and publicly advocating for underserved communities and colleagues (Kendi, 2019; Trepagnier, 2017). Though groups legislate, create, and implement policies that ultimately govern our organizations and institutions, HRD in organizations and academia plays a vital role through practitioner engagement and scholarly contributions (Bierema, 2020). HRD colleagues and scholars bear a disproportionate responsibility to speak up and speak out against discrimination and workplace hostility and advocate for a more diverse, inclusive, engaging, and equitable culture (Bierema, 2020; Byrd, 2018). The need for change becomes evident and essential revealing a goal to create environments where discrimination is unacceptable and unaccepted.

Using privilege to create hostile environments for racism assists in disrupting and dismantling long-held beliefs that have taken root. Challenge peers and colleagues who are covertly and/or overtly problematic in real time as these offenses occur. Each of us is responsible for antiracism work. The goal is to create environments where racism is unaccepted and unacceptable.

There are numerous alternative ways of learning and knowing that facilitate deep meaningful connections and promote understanding. This chapter explored the emotional and connective methods for learning teaching and knowing drawing upon the legacy of Nina Simone's music and lyrics. Affirming the need for change by specifically identifying areas that requires assistance as well as a desire to actively participate sparks a journey into learning. Ongoing societal inequities coupled with the brutality of racism is ever-present and contemporary freedom fighters are still in demand.

The approach to social justice proposed in this chapter utilizes love, eros, and ecstasy as a vehicle to engage both victims of discrimination and allies in social justice movements by promoting empathy. Empathy is a shared experience that places both subject and observer, victim and person of privilege, in a similar space to bear witness to the pain and consequences of injustice and be moved to do something about it.

Although learning and knowing is covered extensively in research, there is ample opportunity to expand the literature by exploring this unique approach to social justice. Love and empathy are not new, however creating organizational awareness and dynamic cultural changes toward inclusion utilizing a love and empathetic approach is unusual and, we propose, effective. The HRD industry can be mechanized and sterile, with a focus on adhering to policy and increasing productivity without a meaningful and concerted effort toward promoting supporting and engaging with social justice. Scholars who explore organizational culture do not consistently include pointed discussions about underrepresentation in leadership as a result of systemic discrimination. Exploration of systemic oppression practices is relegated to special tracks in conferences and episodic one-offs in organizations rather than a malevolent condition that requires a permanent and consistent place. We lack an industry and global acknowledgment that systemic oppression affects everyone and it is built into the very organizations and spaces we frequent. The authors recommend continued research that explores how love, eros, and empathy can promote individual and organizational engagement in social justice and confront inequities.

References

Alexander, M. (2010). *The new Jim Crow: Mass incarceration in the age of colorblindness*. New Press.

Ariss, R. (2021). Bearing witness: Creating the conditions of justice for First Nations children. *Canadian Journal of Law and Society/La Revue Canadienne Droit et Société, 36*(1), 113–133.

Bateza, A. M. (2021). Bearing witness against unbearable whiteness: Lessons from Luther for confronting racism today. *Dialog, 60*(2), 198–205. https://doi.org/10.1111/dial.12664

Bell, D. A. (1995). Who's afraid of critical race theory? *University of Illinois Law Review, 1995*(4), 893–910.

Bierema, L. L. (2020). HRD research and practice after 'The great COVID-19 pause': The time is now for bold, critical, research. *Human Resource Development International, 23*(4), 347–360. https://doi.org/10.1080/13678868.2020.1779912

Bierema, L., & Callahan, J. L. (2014). Transforming HRD: A framework for critical HRD practice. *Advances in Developing Human Resources, 16*(4), 429–444.

Bierly, P. E., Kessler, E. H., & Christensen, E. W. (2000). Organizational learning, knowledge and wisdom. *Journal of Organizational Change Management, 13*(6), 595–618. https://doi.org/10.1108/09534810010378605

Blaisdell, B. (2021). Counternarrative as strategy: Embedding critical race theory to develop an antiracist school identity. *International Journal of Qualitative Studies in Education (QSE)*, 1–21. https://doi.org/10.1080/09518398.2021.1942299

Bohonos, J. W., & James-Gallaway, A. (2022). Enslavement and the foundations of human resource development: Covert learning, consciousness raising, and resisting antiblack organizational goals. *Human Resource Development Review*, 15344843221076292.

Bohonos, J. W. (2019). Including critical whiteness studies in the critical human resource development family: A proposed theoretical framework. *Adult Education Quarterly, 69*(4), 315–337.

Bohonos, J. W., Otchere, K. D., & Pak, Y. K. (2019). Teaching and learning social justice in human resource development graduate programs: Preparation for research and practice. *New Horizons in Adult Education and Human Resource Development, 31*(4), 18–35. https://doi.org/10.1002/nha3.20262

Bohonos, J. W., & Sisco, S. (2021). Advocating for social justice, equity, and inclusion in the workplace: An agenda for anti-racist learning organizations. *New Directions for Adult and Continuing Education, 2021*(170), 89–98.

Brown, H. L., Ponton, D., III., Howard, C., Sanchez, P., & Blake, C. (2021). Black lives and the police. *Journal of the National Medical Association, 113*(4), 392–395.

Byrd, M. Y., & Scott, C. L. (2010). Integrating dialogue on forms of racism within human resource development workforce diversity courses and workplace settings: Implications for HRD. In C. Graham (Ed.), *Proceedings of the academy of human resource development 2010 international research conference in the Americas.*

Byrd, M. Y. (2018). Does HRD have a moral duty to respond to matters of social injustice? *Human Resource Development International, 21*, 3–11. https://doi.org/10.1080/13678868.2017.1344419

Cain-Miller, C. (n.d.). *How to be more empathetic.* A year of living better guides - *The New York Times.* https://www.nytimes.com/guides/year-of-living-better/how-to-be-more-empathetic

Cartabuke, M., Westerman, J. W., Bergman, J. Z., Whitaker, B. G., Westerman, J., & Beekun, R. I. (2019). Empathy as an antecedent of social justice attitudes and perceptions. *Journal of Business Ethics, 157*(3), 605–615. https://doi.org/10.1007/s10551-017-3677-1

Clark, A. J. (2004). Empathy: Implications of three ways of knowing in counseling. *Journal of Humanistic Counseling, Education and Development, 43*(2), 141. https://doi.org/10.1002/j.2164-490X.2004.tb00014.x

Clark, A. J., & Butler, C. M. (2020). Empathy: An integral model in clinical social work. *Social Work, 65*(2), 169–177. https://doi.org/10.1093/sw/swaa009

Delgado, R. (1989). Storytelling for oppositionists and others: A plea for narrative. *Michigan Law Review, 87*(8), 2411–2441. https://doi.org/10.2307/1289308

Delgado, R., & Stefanic, J. (2019). *Understanding words that wound.* Routledge.

Dixson, A. D., & Rousseau Anderson, C. (2018). Where are we? Critical race theory in education 20 years later. *Peabody Journal of Education, 93*(1), 121–131. https://doi.org/10.1080/0161956x.2017.1403194

Farkas, K. J., & Romaniuk, J. R. (2020). Social work, ethics and vulnerable groups in the time of coronavirus and Covid-19. *Society Register, 4*(2), 67–82.

Feldstein, R. (2005). "I don't trust you anymore": Nina Simone, culture, and Black activism in the 1960s. *The Journal of American History, 91*(4), 1349–1379. https://doi.org/10.2307/3660176

Garza, A. (2014, October 7). *A herstory of the #BlackLivesmMatter movement by Alicia Garza*. The Feminist Wire. https://thefeministwire.com/2014/10/blacklivesmatte r-2/

Gibran, K. (1924). *The prophet*. Oneworld Publications

Godcharles, B. D., Rad, J. D., Heide, K. M., Cochran, J. K., & Solomon, E. P. (2019). Can empathy close the racial divide and gender gap in death penalty support? *Behavioral Sciences & the Law, 37*(1), 16–37. https://doi.org/10.1002/bsl.2391

Hasio, C. (2016). Are you listening? How empathy and caring can lead to connected knowing. *Art Education, 69*(1), 25–30. https://doi.org/10.1080/000 43125.2016.1106852

Hay, D. B. (2007). Using concept maps to measure deep, surface and non-learning outcomes. *Studies in Higher Education, 32*(1), 39–57. https://doi.org/10.1080/ 03075070601099432

Hein, G., Engelmann, J. B., Vollberg, M. C., & Tobler, P. N. (2016). How learning shapes the empathic brain. *Proceedings of the National Academy of Sciences, 113*(1), 80–85. https://doi.org/10.1073/pnas.1514539112

Hodges, S. D., & Myers, M. W. (2007) "Empathy," In R. F. Baumeister & K. D. Vohs (Eds.), *Encyclopedia of Social Psychology*, Sage, pp. 296–298. https://sk.sag epub.com/reference/socialpsychology/n179.xml

hooks, b. (1994). *Teaching to transgress: Education as the practice of freedom*. Routledge.

Hull, K. (2002). Eros and education: The role of desire in teaching and learning. *Thought & Action, 18*, 19–32.

James-Gallaway, C., & Baber, L. (2021). Utilities of counterstorytelling in exposing racism within higher education. In M. Lynn, & A. D. Dixson (Eds.), *Handbook of critical race theory in education* (2nd ed., pp. 221–235). Routledge.

Jerrett, A., Howell, P., & Dansey, N. (2021). Developing an empathy spectrum for games. *Games and Culture: A Journal of Interactive Media, 16*(6), 635–659. https://doi.org/10.1177/1555412020954019

Jones-Eversley, S., Adedoyin, A. C., Robinson, M. A., & Moore, S. E. (2017). Protesting Black inequality: A commentary on the civil rights movement and Black lives matter. *Journal of Community Practice, 25*(3–4), 309–324. https://doi.org/ 10.1080/10705422.2017.1367343

Jordan, C. (2021, January 21). *Bearing witness to testimonies of antiblackness*. SSRC The immanent frame. Retrieved November 20, 2021, from https://tif.ssrc.org/ 2021/01/21/bearing-witness-to-testimonies-of-antiblackness/

Kasl, E., & Yorks, L. (2016). Do I really know you? Do you really know me? Empathy amid diversity in differing learning contexts. *Adult Education Quarterly, 66*(1), 3–20. https://doi.org/10.177%2F0741713615606965

Kendi, I. X. (2019). *How to be an antiracist*. One world.

Kernodle, T. L. (2008). "I wish I knew how it would feel to be free": Nina Simone and the redefining of the freedom song of the 1960s. *Journal of the Society for American Music, 2*(3), 295–317. https://doi.org/10.1017/S1752196308080097

Khan, N. A., & Khan, A. N. (2019). What followers are saying about transformational leaders fostering employee innovation via organisational learning, knowledge sharing and social media use in public organisations?. *Government Information Quarterly, 36*(4). https://doi.org/10.1016/j.giq.2019.07.003

Kivel, P. (2017). *Uprooting racism-: How white people can work for racial justice*. New Society Publishers.

Lanzoni, S. (2018). *Empathy: A history*. Yale University Press. https://doi.org/10.2307/j.ctv5cgb7s

Loudermilk, A. (2013). Nina Simone & the civil rights movement: Protest at her piano, audience at her feet. *Journal of International Women's Studies, 14*(3), 121–136.

Margolick, D. (1999). Performance as a force for change: The case of billie holiday and "strange fruit." *Law & Literature, 11*(1), 91–109. https://doi.org/10.1080/1535685X.1999.11015589

Marriott, D. (2000). *On black men*. Edinburgh University Press. https://doi.org/10.1515/9781474470704

Mauer, R. (2020, December 16). *Remote employees are working longer than before*. SHRM. https://www.shrm.org/hr-today/news/hr-news/pages/remote-employees-are-working-longer-than-before.aspx

McIntosh, H., & Churcher, K. (2020). Navigating Alma's gang culture: Exploring testimonio, identity, and violence through an interactive documentary. *Journal of Film and Video, 72*(3–4), 16–31. https://doi.org/10.5406/jfilmvideo.72.3-4.0016

Myers, J. D. (2020). Bearing witness to God: Ricoeur and the practice of religious testimony. *Literature and Theology, 34*(4), 391–407. https://doi.org/10.1093/litthe/fraa018

Pikiewicz, K. (2013, December 3). *The power and strength of bearing witness*. Psychology Today. https://www.psychologytoday.com/intl/blog/meaningful-you/201312/the-power-and-strength-bearing-witness

Pleyers, G. (2020). The pandemic is a battlefield. Social movements in the COVID-19 lockdown. *Journal of Civil Society, 16*(4), 295–312. https://doi.org/10.1080/17448689.2020.1794398

Popescu, D. (2018). The Importance of bearing witness. *East European Politics and Societies, 32*(2), 315–319. https://doi.org/10.1177/0888325417745129

Reyes, K. B., & Curry-Rodríguez, J. E. (2012). Testimonio: Origins, terms, and resources. *Equity & Excellence in Education, 45*(3), 525–538. https://doi.org/10.1080/10665684.2012.698571

Richardson, A. V. (2021). Black bodies at risk: Exploring the corporeal iconography of the anti-police brutality movement. *Journalism*, 14648849211064072.

Riess, H. (2017). The science of empathy. *Journal of Patient Experience, 4*(2), 74–77. https://doi.org/10.1177/2374373517699267

Roediger, D. R. (2017). The wages of whiteness: Race and the making of the American working class. *Class: The Anthology*, 41–55.

Rogers, C. R. (1964). Toward a science of the person. In T, W. Wann (Ed.), *Behaviorism and phenomenology: Contrasting bases for modern psychology* (pp, 109–140). University of Chicago Press. https://doi.org/10.177%2F002216786300300208

Rosan, P. J. (2012). The poetics of intersubjective life: Empathy and the other. *The Humanistic Psychologist, 40*(2), 115–135. https://doi.org/10.1080/08873267.2012.643685

Rose, L. P. (2007). The freedom singers of the civil rights movement: Music functioning for freedom. *Update: Applications of Research in Music Education, 25*(2), 59–68. https://doi.org/10.1177%2F87551233070250020107

Salcedo, A., Williams, P., Elias, S., Valencia, M., & Perez, J. (2022). Future direction in HRD: The potential of testimonio as an approach to perturb the dominant practices in the workplace. *European Journal of Training and Development*.

Segal, E. A., & Wagaman, M. A. (2017). Social empathy as a framework for teaching social justice. *Journal of Social Work Education, 53*(2), 201–211. https://doi.org/10.1080/10437797.2016.1266980

Sisco, S., Valesano, M., & Collins, J. C. (2019). Social movement learning and human resource development: An agenda for a radical future. *Advances in Developing Human Resources, 21*(2), 175–192. https://doi.org/10.1177/1523422319827917

Steed, S. (2019). *Empathy at work* (1st ed.). O'Reilly Media, Inc.

Sullivan, S. (2014). *Good white people: The problem with middle-class white anti-racism.* SUNY Press.

Toliver, S. R. (2020). Can I get a witness? Speculative fiction as testimony and counterstory. *Journal of Literacy Research, 52*(4), 507–529.

Trepagnier, B. (2017). *Silent racism: How well-meaning white people perpetuate the racial divide* (2nd ed). Taylor & Francis. https://doi.org/10.4324/9781315284453

Tulshyan, R. (2021, July 23). Return to office? Some women of color aren't ready. *The New York Times.* https://www.nytimes.com/2021/06/23/us/return-to-office-anxiety.html

Tyson, T. B. (2017). *The blood of emmett till.* Simon and Schuster.

Warren, C. A. (2018). Empathy, teacher dispositions, and preparation for culturally responsive pedagogy. *Journal of Teacher Education, 69*(2), 169–183. https://doi.org/10.1177%2F0022487117712487

Watts, F., & Dumbreck, G. (Eds.). (2013). *Head and heart: Perspectives from religion and psychology.* Templeton Foundation Press.

West, C. (2017). *Race matters, 25th anniversary: With a new introduction.* Beacon Press.

Wright, R. (1945). *Black boy.* Harper and Brothers Publishers.

Zarestky, J., & Collins, J. C. (2019). Social justice in the era of a racist president: A critical call to action. *New Horizons in Adult Education and Human Resource Development, 31*(4), 1–3. https://doi.org/10.1002/nha3.20260

Zembylas, M. (2018). Reinventing critical pedagogy as decolonizing pedagogy: The education of empathy. *Review of Education, Pedagogy, and Cultural Studies, 40*(5), 404–421. https://doi.org/10.1080/10714413.2019.1570794

A Collective Autoethnographic Journey Toward Academic Repair: Unfolding Restorative Micro-Repair Practices

The Kintsugi Collective

The Kintsugi Collective is a collective of people working in business schools in the UK, France, and Denmark. Participating in this chapter were (in random order): Maribel Blasco, Copenhagen Business School, Denmark; Sarah Robinson, Rennes School of Business, France; Jamie Callahan, Durham University Business School, UK; Tony Wall, Liverpool Business School, UK; Carole Elliott, University of Sheffield Management School, UK; Tali Padan, Copenhagen Business School, Denmark; and Annemette Kjærgaard, Copenhagen Business School, Denmark. As a collective, we want to embrace the spirit of kintsugi in work—"ultimately to guide shadows to beauty's ends".

Email addresses for each of the above are: Maribel Blasco: mbl.msc@cbs.dk Sarah; Robinson: sarah.robinson@rennes-sb.com; Jamie Callahan: jamie.callahan@durham.ac.uk; Tony Wall: t.wall@ljmu.ac.uk; Carole Elliott: carole.elliott@sheffield.ac.uk; Tali Padan: tp.msc@cbs.dk; Annemette Kjaergaard: amk.msc@cbs.dk.

The Kintsugi Collective (✉)
Copenhagen Business School, Frederiksberg, Denmark

Durham University Business School, Durham, UK

Liverpool Business School, Liverpool, UK

Rennes School of Business, Rennes, France

University of Sheffield Management School, Sheffield, UK

417

J. C. Collins and J. L. Callahan (eds.), *The Palgrave Handbook of Critical Human Resource Development*, https://doi.org/10.1007/978-3-031-10453-4_22

Academia is in a state of disrepair. The neoliberal university, with its unrelenting performativity, metrics obsession (Butler & Spoelstra, 2014; Jones et al., 2020), and increasing individualization has produced isolating, dehumanizing (Ratle et al., 2020), and stressful workplaces (Morrish, 2019; Smith & Ulus, 2020) that call into question whether academia constitutes a viable arena for a life's devotion (Harley, 2019: 286; Sandhu et al., 2019). The current system rewards individual careerism and narrow single mindedness at the expense of more eclectic and collective endeavors (Clarke & Knights, 2015). Not surprisingly, many have fiercely condemned the current academic system (see Harley, 2019), with some scholars even proposing that academics should leave the system altogether (Ahmed, 2016; Perel, 2018), or aim to transform it entirely (Parker, Martin, 2018). Yet for most academics, who both love their vocation and rely on it to make ends meet, these are not viable paths (Alvesson & Gabriel, 2016). It is from this ambivalent space that the concepts we present here emerge.

To find meaningful ways to resolve our work and reconnect with one another within neoliberal institutions, we seek to imagine practices that enable spaces of difference within workplaces. Drawing from some of our collective writings (e.g., The Kintsugi Collective, 2019, 2021), we rethink how practicing human resource development professionals can realistically bring about constructive changes in and through their everyday working lives by engaging in micro-practices that enable restorative repair. We see repair as "not outside of dominant governing regimes and practices, but shaped by them" (Graziano & Trogal, 2019: 203–204). Thus, rather than throwing out a broken object or system, repair involves creating practices that enable the imagining and careful nurturing of different scenarios and relations.

The imaginative possibilities of such restorative micro-repair practices are anchored in our sense of place embodied by our collective, which we have named the 'Kintsugi Collective', inspired by the Japanese practice of repairing broken crockery using golden glue, making the repaired piece more beautiful than the original by virtue of, and not despite, its cracks.

Our agenda is to share our experiences and experiments as a scholarly collective to inspire others wishing to 'repair' their own workspaces. Our exemplar is grounded within academia, but the dimensions of our journey have resonance in any workspace. In this chapter, we use autoethnographic inspiration to describe the spontaneous unfolding of the relational process that is our collective, which we believe is enabling us to cultivate such practices of modest repair which facilitate humane workspaces.

To this end, our contribution is to offer restorative micro-repair as a means to forge reconnections within CHRD practice. Through reflecting on the unfolding of our journey we have identified some cornerstones for this type of alternative practice. These include the development of loose *structures* that enable divergent thinking and practices, an attention to group *processes* and an emphasis on *communality* through a relational, community-based approach. In telling the formation story of our own restorative micro-repair space, we set the stage to reflect upon how these cornerstones can serve to help others engage in micro-repair practices to reconnect to one another.

Collaborative Autoethnography—Writing Our Story to Illuminate Repair

In recounting our experiences as a means to illuminate how others may practice repair, we engage in a collective form of autoethnography (Grenier, 2015; Tienari & Taylor, 2019). Our reflections on our own processes of repair serve to reinforce the identity we have created in this space we call the Kintsugi Collective. The collective is comprised of eight scholars at different stages of our careers (from PhD student to Professor) and hailing from multiple international backgrounds (American, Danish, English, and Israeli). Our common search for repair provided the contextualization for our reflections that enabled us to interpret our collective personal experiences (Chang, 2013) of micro-repair within neoliberal spaces.

Our interpretation and analyses took place through a series of dialogic processes (Padilla, 1993 as cited in Murakami-Ramalho et al., 2008). Over the period of two years, we had five, two- to three-day retreats to develop and reflect upon our collective identity and purpose. The first was when we met at an 'unconference' in St Andrews, Scotland. We held two meetings in Copenhagen, Denmark and a meeting in Chester, England. Our fifth meeting was in Glasgow, Scotland. A sixth meeting was planned for Durham, England, when the global Covid-19 pandemic derailed our in-person meetings. At these meetings, we had individual and small group reflections and the full group came together to dialogue, capture our reflections in collectively written 'field notes', and derive meaning and themes from the reflections.

In this chapter, we share the story of how we set out to repair ourselves, and how we discovered the ways in which our own micro-repair practices can serve as both catalyst and model for others to change the way they conceptualize work in a neoliberal context. We incorporate two styles of autoethnographic writing (Chang, 2013). We use a descriptive-realist style, telling collectively crafted stories of our experiences, to provide the foundation for an analytic-interpretive approach to discuss the meaning of those experiences.

The Unfolding

We gathered in a historic building at St Andrews University on a sunny summer's day in 2018 to attend an 'unconference'. Most of us were not sure what to expect, but we had submitted ideas of papers we were working on with the hopes of progressing those works to further our own publication agendas. The unconference presented a visage of playing by the rules of the game, while simultaneously violating them. It created a space for open-ended, divergent thinking and experimentation, collective and relation-driven innovation, and an emphasis on process rather than outputs. In doing so, the unconference moved us away from reflecting on our own performative publication projects and toward a reflection upon our practices that facilitate 'repairing' broken workplaces.

Unconferences present a free space for thinking about, and discussing, broad issues together with no obligation to end up with a 'product'. These broad discussions make it easier to connect with colleagues in a more collaborative and less instrumental or performative way. This broad focus, and permissiveness of meandering dialogue, is radical as it subverts systemic pressure toward focused and effective 'product development'. The discussion-based format also subverts conventional conference structure in several ways: it enables in-depth, lengthy discussion and free elaboration of ideas that are still embryonic; it alters the whole nature of 'feedback' at a conference; and it does not foreground individuals' contributions. The lack of keynote speakers or sub-group leaders lends itself to a lack of hierarchy, giving each participant an equal voice at the outset. This de-hierarchization embedded within the unconference facilitated our lack of awareness of the structural inequalities of our own group, which made it that much easier for us to simply value the expertise and insight we each brought to the table without looking for a positional authority (Horton et al., 1997). However, as a participant-driven conference, the dynamics differ from year to year, depending on the space and how participants interact in it.

At the unconference, we found ourselves in a large group discussing academic activism. Due to the ethos of our setting, we wanted to continue the conversation, to see how it could be translated into practice beyond the unconference, but we did not yet know how. In hindsight, the 'how' developed organically through email and video conference exchanges between meetings; a commitment by all members to at least three face-to-face meetings per year rotating across our respective countries; and maintaining the ethos in our meeting formats. With this in mind, our cornerstones of practice—*structure*, *process*, and *communality*—emerged.

STRUCTURE

As scholars of learning, we know that the context in which learning is situated (Lave & Wenger, 1991) is significant for the development of a creative and collaborative learning environment. We did not articulate the spatial constraints that frustrated our, and others' learning, during our first conversations at the unconference. But the attention we have paid to our use of space and place are inherent to our collective practice.

Metaphors of space infuse performance management structures that constrain us. The loose structures that shape our discussions were formed during our first meeting and continue to characterize how we work together. We were drawn together because we were intrigued by the idea of how we might repair academia from within. Our teaching and research is 'ranked' against hierarchies of judgment which individualize learning and research activities to fragment (Alakavuklar, 2017) the potential for collective inquiry. Our practice is designed to work toward meaningful engagement in the moment, in a way that is inclusive, collaborative, and creative. We take joy in working together, but recognize that when eight people are immersed in a creative process we need a loose structure to act as a container (Vince, 2002) for our thinking.

Individually and collectively we have occasionally reflected on how the pressure to perform academia as a series of measurable outputs infiltrates our thoughts when we are together. During our third meeting we discussed our progress in working toward our goals. Our long-term agenda is not marked by a series of dates against which 'X' task needs to be completed, yet some of us felt a little uneasy about our progress in creating the artifacts of our practice. This has caused us to reflect on how we can become conditioned to measure the value of our work against a timetable defined by others.

Part of our commitment to restorative repair involves continually experimenting with the way we spend time together. Some of our first moments as a group were spent unsettling the established boundaries of the conference by sitting on the grass talking, and walking together to buy coffee and ice cream. These informal spaces have influenced our learning, and their informality is a way to work from within and protect us from the glare of public performance before we were ready to present.

When we did begin to present our work, our repair practices took the form of unsettling conference rituals in order to create structures that enabled divergent thinking. Academic conferences are ritualized ceremonies that socialize members into the academic community (Egri, 1992) and thus serve to reproduce the neoliberal culture of academe (Nicolson, 2017). Academic conferences tend to organize with strict agendas, predetermined content, fixed streams, and planned PowerPoint presentations. Thus, although organization and management conferences—particularly critical or alternative ones—purport to problematize and question existing ways of organizing and to foster alternatives, this conventional, ritualistic way of organizing persists. Our forays into participation as a Collective disrupted such assumptions of conference structure with a view to 'repairing' them in the sense of prompting people to stop up and reflect critically on the often dehumanizing conference ritual itself.

For example, in one interactive session at a conference, we simulated the relentless pressure of pursuing grant opportunities by having a Collective member 'accept' a phone call from a prospective funder in the middle of a presentation; the other two presenters continued with the workshop as if this were 'normal'. At the end of the presentation, we asked participants to place themselves on one side of the room if they agreed these were 'acts of activism' and on the other side if they disagreed. The facilitated groups then discussed the characteristics, aims, and methods of academic activism.

That violation produced resistance, with some participants questioning the legitimacy of the way in which we unsettled the conventional paper-presentation format. On the one hand, this shows that such micro-repair practices risk being seen as irrelevant 'noise'. On the other hand, it is precisely by relating to what is already there instead of dissociating oneself from it that enables micro-repair acts to succeed in facilitating change.

PROCESS

Organizing in ways that promote loose structures and collective focus can seemingly contribute to disrupting the salience of outputs such as articles or challenging the means by which they are typically measured (e.g., ranked at '2 stars' or above). Here, our interactions have been characterized by a collective curiosity about being together in a longer-term compassionate process rather than by tightly specified goals accompanied by a highly specified plan of action for delivering outputs which would be recognized and rewarded in our respective contexts. As such, this apparent acceptance of ambiguity and indeterminacy regarding tangible deliverables contradicts typical academic practices often associated with tenure and promotion (MacIntosh et al., 2017).

Initial indications of such dynamics repeatedly appeared during the unconference. On one occasion, early into the unconference, we noticed how a small group of our original formation had splintered and had mapped out the chapters for a new book. We shared our curiosity around the intentionality and tactics of this smaller group, which seemed to function as a way of us sharing—or even asserting—our values around inclusion and inclusive practice. Similarly, on another occasion toward the end of the unconference, one of the facilitators indicated it was 'time to start thinking about your variables'. Despite this attempt to move participants toward more precise action and planning for new research studies, we were still sharing our stories of what connected us (or not). We were not ready to finalize our thinking; we were busy creating our sense of place by enjoying, exploring, and learning 'who we are' together. We have held strongly to this 'time lingering' approach as an antidote to the "punishing intensification of work" (Gill, 2016: 46) as it enables us to 'dwell' in intellectual processes rather than be slaves to outcomes (The Kintsugi Collective, forthcoming).

Instead, as a collective, we seek to 'change time' by experimenting with alternative ways of thinking about, and practicing, time in our work. Although potentially risky given the target driven metrics we are evaluated by, we believe that, done consciously, it can be a powerful way to prioritize and reclaim relationships and offer a sense of pleasure, meaningfulness, and purpose in our work. To that end, we unsettle the short-term, goal-oriented nature of our work by resisting the urge to formulate and work toward specific goals. We allow ourselves to be steered by curiosity about what might emerge if we accompany one another, without haste, in a longer-term intellectual process. We spend time at each meeting engaged in social and collegial dialogue, sharing personal updates and inspiring readings and experiences. Our scholarly products are consistently a consequence of our time lingering, intellectual dwelling with one another, not a conscious goal. This acceptance of ambiguity and indeterminacy regarding tangible deliverables runs counter to typical contemporary practices in academe (MacIntosh et al., 2017) and elsewhere.

This unsettling of traditional practice extends to our process of writing. Academic writing is usually a solitary process, even when collaboratively authored. Our collective writing approach similarly reflects the value placed on process rather than the delivery of highly efficient and effective written outputs. The approach involves a person typing into a document projected onto a large screen so others can request revisions or make suggestions to enhance the text. Revisions are made until we all agree with the text or until we can accommodate what has been produced within the time together (some polishing may happen outside of our time together). The approach is analogous to co-crafting a piece of art that simultaneously has all of us within it (we have all contributed to its creation), but also none of us (as discernible individuals).

We continue to return to a line of inquiry raised at one of our first meetings—our identity and purpose—as we felt it important in guiding the form of our work together moving forward. The statement we wrote together reflected a processual orientation of being. Not only was this co-created, once again accepting ambiguity and indeterminacy, it was also agreed as being a loose container for our work which was subject to change at some future, unknown point. It embodied and celebrated 'the processual' in contrast to the demands of contemporary academic life to be clear cut, and efficiently and effectively managed for ultimate productivity. It codified the heterotopic space that forms our collective sense of place regardless of our locale.

COMMUNALITY

With our loose structure and processual focus guiding the intent of our work, we take time to begin every meeting with an open conversation about what is on our minds, on our desks, and in our lives to re-create the shape of our working space as constructive and connected. We actively seek practices that develop our ability and willingness to share and embrace vulnerability. At our meetings together, we have supported one another with celebration for a birthday, a promotion, a birth, and with sadness for a death. These often invisible and unacknowledged moments of sharing have enabled us to tap into emotions that bond us.

We recognized early that food is a "recipe for friendship" (Woolley & Fishbach, 2017: 1), and this recognition emerged as we resisted conference structures and expectations to work at certain places and times. We risked ire from the unconference facilitators for returning late to a session because we opted to go for coffee and ice cream at a local hotspot. Sharing food with one another is "the very stuff of sociality [that is] in danger of disappearing"

(Mennell, Murcott & van Otterloo, 1992 as cited in Fischler, 2011: 529). The danger, Fischler (2011) concludes, is due to the individualization of work processes that are the very focus of our restorative repair practices.

Our academic context conspires against our ability to generate ways of caring and human contact (Alvesson & Gabriel, 2016). In response, we take both a collective and individual restorative micro-repair approach to prefigure the kind of workplace we hope to experience. First, we seek to work collectively and in flexible constellations within our group. Second, we build caring into our electronic communications by the way we close our emails.

In our collective and flexible micro-repair work practices, we celebrate the golden threads that join our passions and create a sense of place together. The security of such a place gives us freedom within space; the "quality of place is that it has the power to order and to focus human intentions, experiences and actions spatially" (Seamon & Sowers, 2008: 44). The Kintsugi Collective has become our sense of place, regardless of the space in which we find ourselves; and we privilege that place in the way we engage in our micro-repair practices. In one of our most significant repair micro-acts, we write with collective authorship, randomly listing names of contributing members in the acknowledgments. This rejection of individualization of academic performance and performativity takes courage, and indeed has resulted in skepticism from some editors.

As individuals, we have adopted a more mindful approach to closing our emails that generates caring and compassion in ourselves and, we hope, our readers. As we have noted previously (The Kintsugi Collective, 2021), email can be depersonalizing, in particular within a context of bureaucratic expectations and time pressures. Both writing and receiving emails is increasingly fraught with anxiety within academe (Kiriakos & Tienari, 2018). The micro-repair practices we enact here are intended to intervene in the anxiety by finding ways to close our emails with caring, compassion, and, indeed, love, at the forefront of our minds. We do this by consciously and manually typing 'love', 'warm regards', 'with kindness', and so forth. This intentional act is a form of resistance against the 'emptiness' and impersonal character of automated signature blocks and their symbolic resonance to the masculinized hyper-efficiency of the contemporary workplace.

Summary

We began our journey inspired by the loose structure of the unconference. Our process emerged as we attempted to create a collective sense of place within the spaces defined by the unconference meeting structure. The resulting relational and community-based way of being and working infuses each of our changing meeting spaces with a sense of place (Gurian, 2001) that enables us to celebrate the golden threads that join us. We believe that these three cornerstones of our restorative micro-repair practice—namely an emphasis on *structure*, *process*, and *communality*—are the transferable threads that others can use to keep the spirit of such unconferences alive.

Moving Forward: Elements of Restorative Micro-Repair...and Risk

In this relatively traditional piece of academic communication, we have presented what we believe constitutes the cornerstone of our own search for an alternative vision of academic practice: (a) loose structures, (b) a process orientation, and (c) a relational, community-based approach. Our intention is not to offer a one-size-fits-all model for 'fixing' academia or to pave the way for a return to some kind of nostalgic academe—or any other type of institution. Rather, our aim has been to share our collective experiences and experiments with displacing ourselves from the instrumentalized, individualized, and output-oriented structures that currently pervade academic life. Like in the Japanese art of *kintsugi*, this is about treating the breakage of our workplaces as an opportunity to modestly create something even lovelier than the original. From the enactment of different dimensions emerges a space that enables divergent rather than convergent thinking and within which we collaborate rather than compete. We argue that even though this space is process-focused rather than output-focused, one happy consequence is that it results in a range of conventional (for us, academic) outputs.

This is important since we are not searching for a quiet, safe space where we can be left alone with self-centered academic navel-gazing. We *do* wish to disperse our research so that it can make an impact on society; and we do find that academia has something to offer that makes it worth repairing. However, if academic work is to be relevant to beyond satisfying neoliberal performance management systems, we need to continually test the boundaries established by such systems by being simultaneously disobedient and reflexive. As we have suggested, this is not (necessarily) a matter of refusing to play by the rules of the game. Rather, it is, as we noted earlier, about contesting the rules of the game while playing it. It is this contestation that promises reward, while embodying risk. Unsurprisingly, these risks are inherent within the neoliberal system that we seek to disrupt. The three greatest limitations we see to the restorative micro-repair approach we propose include performativity, invisibility, and prudence.

In many ways, the micro-repair practices we engage in undermine us within the current context of a performative academia; we are challenged by individual performance measures and increasing work intensification constrains our time. We risk being ensnared into performing in a conventional way to preserve our careers and our dedication to micro-repair practices involves a conscious sacrifice for each of us.

We also risk invisibility. Our alternative form of organizing as a collective resists and obscures the prized neoliberal individualism (Keshtiban et al., 2021). We face the critique that privileging the collective is irresponsible for our early career scholars who feel compelled to 'make a name' for themselves as individuals; that their contribution becomes invisible when it is embedded in the collective. We also risk that gatekeeping structures and power brokers will refuse to acknowledge or recognize us as a collective subject, rendering us invisible.

Finally, our need to be prudent fiscally and physically became more apparent during the global Covid-19 pandemic. Originally, our concerns were that limited funding would constrain our ability to meet as desired (3–4 times per year), attend conferences to disseminate our work, and hold and attend workshops that enrich our learning and engagement. This concern remains. But the physical risks of such travel and collegial gatherings were heightened as a result of the pandemic. As travel restrictions began to be lifted, we planned to meet in person in Durham, England, but those plans were dashed when another surge of the virus demanded prudence in traveling. While we held virtual meetings, we found that these short bursts of a few random hours failed to produce the dimensions of structure, process, and communality that made our in-person retreats so meaningful.

CONCLUSION

In this chapter, we described the unfolding of a scholarly collective triggered by an unconference and its ideas about organic and participant-driven organization. In the early process of becoming a collective searching for alternative spaces within academia, our work has predominantly focused on challenging the working conditions within academia. However, this has fuelled a more general collective interest in the concept of restorative micro-repair that might find relevance also in settings outside academia.

Those beyond academe will find resonance for relating restorative micro-repair practices to wellbeing in the workplace (The Kintsugi Collective, 2021). Our practice of disrupting the efficient, yet cold, standardized signature block by adding a manually typed message of warmth and compassion to our recipient is relevant for anyone. Socializing with colleagues over lunch is being re-discovered as an important factor in improving employee wellbeing and productivity (Corvo et al., 2020). Our struggle with recreating the meaningfulness of structure, process, and communality in virtual meetings is something that all organizations now face; as the pandemic has normalized virtual meetings and working from home, organizations must grapple with the implications and trade-offs of virtual working. Finally, encouraging the collective over the rugged individual in practice and policy is something organizations can explore: what networks are available to employees, how are employees assessed, and what spaces are available for encouraging collaboration while maintaining spaces for privacy?

Moving our collective forward, we will use our experiences with modest micro-repair practices within our own work in academia as stepping stones for exploring the concept of micro-repair in contexts outside academia in order to contribute to furthering the understanding and creation of spaces for repair. With this agenda, we hope to inspire others toward 'doing' their work differently. For academics like us and many of those reading this chapter, we aspire to let academia and academic knowledge 'act' differently and create valuable impact in the broadest sense.

References

Ahmed, S. (2016). *Resignation.* https://feministkilljoys.com/2016/05/30/resign ation/ (accessed 14 June 2022).

Alakavuklar, O. (2017). Labour of becoming a (critical) management scholar: Ambivalences, tensions and possibilities. *Ephemera: Theory and Politics in Organization,* 17.

Alvesson, M., & Gabriel, Y. (2016). Grandiosity in contemporary management and education. *Management Learning, 47*(4), 464–473. https://doi.org/10.1177/135 0507615618321

Butler, N., & Spoelstra, S. (2014). The regime of excellence and the erosion of ethos in critical management studies. *British Journal of Management, 25*(3), 538–550. https://doi.org/10.1111/1467-8551.12053

Chang, H. (2013). Individual and collaborative autoethnography as method. In S. H. Holmes, T. E. Adams, & C. Ellis (Eds.), *Handbook of autoethnography,*(pp. 107–122), Left Coast Press Inc.

Clarke, C. A., & Knights, D. (2015). Careering through academia: Securing identities or engaging ethical subjectivities? *Human Relations, 68*(12), 1865–1888. https://doi.org/10.1177/0018726715570978

Corvo, P., Fontefrancesco, M. F., & Matacena, R. (2020). Eating at work: The role of the lunch-break and canteens for wellbeing at work in Europe. *Social Indicators Research, 150*(3), 1043–1076. https://doi.org/10.1007/s11205-020-02353-4

Egri, C. P. (1992). Academic conferences as ceremonials: Opportunities for organizational integration and socialization. *Journal of Management Education, 16*(1), 90–115. https://doi.org/10.1177/105256299201600107

Fischler, C. (2011). Commensality, society and culture. *Social Science Information, 50*(3–4), 528–548. https://doi.org/10.1177/0539018411413963

Gill, R. (2016). Breaking the silence: The hidden injuries of neo-liberal academia. *Feministische Studien, 34*(1), 39–55. https://doi.org/10.1515/fs-2016-0105

Graziano, V., & Trogal, K. (2019). *Repair matters.*

Grenier, R. S. (2015). Autoethnography as a legitimate approach to HRD research: A methodological conversation at 30,000 feet. *Human Resource Development Review, 14*(13), 332–350. https://doi.org/10.1177/1534484315595507

Gurian, E. H. (2001). Function follows form: How mixed-used spaces in museums build community. *Curator: The Museum Journal, 44*(1), 97–113. https://doi.org/10.1111/j.2151-6952.2001.tb00032.x

Harley, B. (2019). Confronting the crisis of confidence in management studies: Why senior scholars need to stop setting a bad example. *Academy of Management Learning & Education, 18*(2), 286–297. https://doi.org/10.5465/amle.2018.0107

Horton, M., Kohl, J., & Kohl, H. (1997). *The long haul: An autobiography.* Illustrated edition. Teachers College Press.

Jones, D. R., Visser, M., & Stokes, P., et al. (2020). The performative university: 'Targets', 'terror' and 'taking back freedom' in academia. *Management Learning*, 51(4), 363–377. https://doi.org/10.1177/1350507620927554

Keshtiban, A. E., Callahan, J. L., & Harris, M. (2021). Leaderlessness in social movements: Advancing space, symbols, and spectacle as modes of "leadership". *Human Resource Development Quarterly*, n/a(n/a): 1–25. https://doi.org/10.1002/hrdq.21460

Kiriakos, C. M., & Tienari, J. (2018). Academic writing as love. *Management Learning*, 49(3), 263–277. https://doi.org/10.1177/1350507617753560

Lave, J., & Wenger, E. (1991). *Situated learning, legitimate peripheral participation*. Cambridge University Press.

MacIntosh, R., Beech, N., Bartunek, J., et al. (2017). Impact and management research: Exploring relationships between temporality, dialogue, reflexivity and praxis. *British Journal of Management*, 28(1), 3–13. https://doi.org/10.1111/1467-8551.12207

Morrish, L. (2019). *Pressure vessels: The epidemic of poor mental health among higher education staff*. Higher Education Policy Institute. https://www.hepi.ac.uk/2019/05/23/pressure-vessels-the-epidemic-of-poor-mental-health-among-higher-education-staff/ (accessed 14 June 2022).

Murakami-Ramalho, E., Piert, J., & Militello, M. (2008). The wanderer, the chameleon, and the warrior: Experiences of doctoral students of color developing a research identity in educational administration. *Qualitative Inquiry*, 14(5), 806–834.

Nicolson, D. J. (2017). *Academic conferences as neoliberal commodities*. Palgrave Macmillan.

Parker, M. (2018). *Shut down the business school*. Pluto Press. http://www.plutobooks.com/9781786802408/shut-down-the-business-school (accessed 6 March 2022).

Perel, G. (2018). *What happens when academics quit? Good things, it turns out*. https://www.timeshighereducation.com/blog/what-happens-when-academics-quit-good-things-it-turns-out (accessed 14 June 2022).

Ratle, O., Robinson, S., & Bristow, A., et al. (2020). Mechanisms of micro-terror? Early career CMS academics experiences of 'targets and terror' in contemporary business schools. *Management Learning*, 51(4), 452–471. https://doi.org/10.1177/1350507620913050

Sandhu, S., Perera, S., & Sardeshmukh, S. R. (2019). Charted courses and meandering trails: Crafting success and impact as business school academics. *Academy of Management Learning & Education*, 18(2), 153–185. https://doi.org/10.5465/amle.2017.0385

Seamon, D., & Sowers, J. (2008). Place and placelessness (1976): Edward Relph. In *Key texts in human geography*, (pp. 43–52). https://doi.org/10.4135/9781446213742.n6

Smith, C., & Ulus, E. (2020). Who cares for academics? We need to talk about emotional well-being including what we avoid and intellectualise through macro-discourses. *Organization*, 27(6), 840–857. https://doi.org/10.1177/1350508419867201

The Kintsugi Collective. (2019). The plurality of academic activism: Heterogeneous expression for opening up alternative futures. Paper presented at the *Critical Management Studies Conference* the Open University, Milton Keynes, UK.

The Kintsugi Collective. (2021). Micro-activism and wellbeing: 1,000s of snowflakes and the potential avalanche. In T. Wall, C. L. Cooper, & P. Brough (Eds.), *The SAGE handbook of organizational wellbeing*, (pp. 542–557).

Tienari, J., & Taylor, S. (2019). Feminism and men: Ambivalent space for acting up. *Organization*, 26(6), 948–960. https://doi.org/10.1177/1350508418805287

Vince, R. (2002). The impact of emotion on organizational learning. *Human Resource Development International*, 5(1), 73–85. https://doi.org/10.1080/13678860110016904

Woolley, K., & Fishbach, A. (2017). A recipe for friendship: Similar food consumption promotes trust and cooperation. *Journal of Consumer Psychology*, 27(1), 1–10. https://doi.org/10.1016/j.jcps.2016.06.003

INDEX

J. C. Collins and J. L. Callahan (eds.), *The Palgrave Handbook of Critical
Human Resource Development*, https://doi.org/10.1007/978-3-031-10453-4

Printed in the United States
by Baker & Taylor Publisher Services